Plymouth Argyle
A Complete Record 1903-1989

Plymouth Argyle
A Complete Record 1903-1989

Brian Knight

Breedon Books Sport

First published in Great Britain by
The Breedon Books Publishing Company Limited
45 Friar Gate, Derby DE1 1DA
1989

ISBN 0 907969 40 2

Printed by Butler and Tanner Limited, Frome.
Jacket designed by Graham Hales and printed by Arkle Print, Northampton.

CONTENTS

Introduction

WHILE I have made every attempt to ensure that the facts and figures presented in this book are accurate, I am unable to claim that they are infallible. Indeed, since my primary sources — contemporary newspapers — are not always in agreement on such basic facts as scorers and line-ups, I am led to question whether an absolutely definitive work is possible. Generally speaking, the further back one goes, the more difficult the problem. This is not so much a reflection on the availability of material as to the style in which it was presented. In the period before World War One, the reader of Argyle football reports was usually confronted with solid slabs of small type, relieved by the minimum of paragraphs or sub-headings. All events during a match — corner-kicks, shots, goals — received the same reporting treatment and the researcher has to sift carefully among the small print to discover even such basic information as the name of the Argyle scorer. There was even one report of several inches length which managed to omit the name of the latter altogether.

These reports became more readable after Argyle entered the Football League but even then were not always reliable and, where line-ups were included, they did not always account for late changes of personnel. One *Football Herald* notice in the 1920s apologized to readers for having wrongly identified the Argyle scorer in the previous week's game on the grounds that there had been a last-minute team change and the Argyle management 'had not thought fit' to inform the press-box. One wonders what the modern generation of reporters think of this predecessor, who apparently had not mastered the first requirement of his craft, recognition of the players.

As stated, I have gone back to the original Press reports in order to compile this work, but I have also compared my findings with previous information published at both national and local Plymouth levels. As a result, I have identified three Smiths (not two) in the 1920s, two forwards named Simpson in the early 1930s and two Wrights later in that decade. Conversely, in the 1950s, there was only one Bell and only one Mitchell, whereas *Rothmans Football League Players Records* lists two of each. For season 1926-7, I spent a long time looking for a J.Carter, who is listed in a number of publications as having played one game for the club. My match-by-match team checks and rechecks having failed to discover him, I was about to conclude that I had overlooked some vital detail when I came across a contemporary issue of the *Western Independant* which listed League appearances for that season. No Carter appeared there either, so I am now inclined to take the view that he did not make an appearance after all.

In more modern times, the introduction of the substitute rule has created new problems for the statistician and there is no common agreement on how they should be recorded. The options are to ignore substitute appearances altogether, to add them to the total of full appearances or to try to distinguish between the two. Heavily influenced by the views of the editor of this series, I have chosen the last. I have also attempted, wherever feasible, to identify the player who was replaced by the substitute but this has not always been possible, particularly in the seasons immediately following the introduction of the rule when, in match reports, substitutes were either ignored completely or faithfully recorded without any indication of whether or not they were called into action.

It will be obvious from the introductory note to that section that, in producing the total career records in terms of appearances and scorers of Argyle players, I have taken into account only peacetime Football League, League Cup and FA Cup matches. (Wartime details and Argyle's period from 1903 to 1920 are recorded in the book but have not been used in that section). Most previously published literature has used only League figures primarily, I suspect, because these were most readily available. Readers will therefore find that I hold the legendary Sammy Black to have made 491 appearances for Argyle whereas *Rothmans Football Yearbook* has for years been listing the 470 League appearances only, and this figure is the one most commonly quoted in debates about how many games the little Scot played for the club.

Finally, to return to the issue of accuracy, I would suggest that, even where full match details exist, there can be legitimate grounds for differences between individual statisticians. Much depends on the criteria adopted. For example, the case of Tommy Tynan may serve to illustrate that totalling the number of goals a player has scored may be a little more complex than it seems. On the one hand, I have accepted that there is video evidence that it was he — not John Clayton — who scored Argyle's third goal against Blackpool in April 1986. However, I have also been impressed by the testimony of the Hull City goalkeeper in September 1988 that it was his own colleague Peter Skipper — not Tynan — who scored Argyle's second goal that day, although I note that the club has apparently credited the latter with the goal. Incidentally, I have not been unaware of the fact that the goalkeeper might have had a vested interest in the matter, it being presumably less blameworthy of him to have been beaten by a teammate than by an opponent.

I noted in a recent publication of one of the 'exile' Argyle Supporters clubs that a stalwart follower of the club, until another supporter mentioned the name to him, had never heard of Marcus Murphy (1946-7). I trust that this book will serve to all readers as an introduction, or reminder, of the lesser-known players who have worn the Argyle shirt — Murphy, along with Roy Nail and Jimmy Gee, to take two more names at random — as well as the more famous like Sammy Black, Jack Leslie, Jack Chisholm and the others, who merit inclusion in the *Argyle Stars* section. Many of us well remember the lesser fry and they too played their part, however small, in creating the history of Plymouth Argyle.

Brian Knight
Cheltenham
June 1989

Photographic Acknowledgements

Photographs supplied by Colorsport, Illustrated London News Picture Library, Popperfoto, Dave Rowntree Photography, *Western Evening Herald.*

Argyle's great goalscorer Tommy Tynan in action against Rotherham United during the 1985-6 promotion season.

THE ARGYLE STORY

IT MUST be admitted that the story of Plymouth Argyle is somewhat lacking in real footballing drama. This is no account of a club which has enjoyed long periods of success, such as Liverpool or the pre-war Arsenal. Neither is it a tale of a climb from rags to riches, such as would befit Wimbledon or Oxford United. It is not even an account of the decline of a great club into the lower reaches of the League, like Burnley or Wolverhampton Wanderers.

Despite changes of manager, not to mention variations in the playing staff, Argyle's successes are very much at a modest level. The events which have, literally, brought Plymothians on to the streets to hail their footballing heroes have been promotions from the Third Division, nothing remotely like a League championship or a Cup win. Indeed, Argyle's record over nearly 70 years of League football has really been remarkably predictable. In a typical Argyle season, the team would have been either doing well in the Third Division, or not so well in the Second, and have made an early exit from any Cup competition. There have, of course, been exceptions to this general pattern, but those have stood out very clearly in relief against the norm.

It has already been pointed out that, with Hull, Plymouth is the largest city in the country never to have had a First Division side. It has become commonplace for newly-appointed managers to enthuse over the potential they have inherited, yet none to date has been able to produce a side which would truly be the pride of Devon and Cornwall.

The reason for this lack of success remains a mystery. The superstitious who attribute it to Argyle's playing in green shirts forget that such colours have done no harm to Glasgow Celtic's pursuit of honours. There is more substance in the contention that Plymouth's relatively remote location makes it consistently difficult to attract many quality players to the area. Yet experience shows that while a number of players (or their wives) fail to settle in the area, there are others, from distant parts of the country, who ask for nothing more than to stay in or near Plymouth, even when their playing days are over.

There are two accounts of the origins of Plymouth Argyle and their unusual name, which might not be mutually exclusive. One is that the club was formed in 1886 by a group of former pupils of colleges and public schools in the area, who took the name of Argyle because they admired the footballing skill displayed by the Argyll and Sutherland Highlanders, then stationed in the area. The other, better known version dates the beginning of Argyle back to 1888 and claims that the founders of Argyle Athletic Club, as it was originally known, selected that distinctive title simply because they had met at a house in Argyle Terrace, Mutley. Whatever the true facts of the beginnings, there is little doubt that by the turn of the century, Argyle Athletic Club was a well-known establishment in the town, comprising soccer, rugby, cricket and athletic sections. At the time, rugby was the leading winter sport in the area, but soccer was beginning to become established, thanks mainly to the lead given by Service soccer teams, and it was the soccer element of the Athletic Club which came to predominate.

Leading members of the club at that time were the Spooner brothers, Clarence, Guy, John and Stanley, who were also prominent in the business life of the town and they were among the band of enthusiasts who stimulated interest in the professional game by inviting some of the leading League clubs in the land to play

Southern League football at Home Park in October 1904. Plymouth Argyle won this match 1-0, beating Southampton with a goal from McLuckie.

exhibition matches against the Argyle amateurs. Aston Villa's visit attracted a crowd of over 15,000 and a crowd of over 16,000 gathered at Home Park in April 1903 to watch an exhibition match between the First Division clubs, Sheffield Wednesday and Notts County.

By that time, the decision had been taken to set up a professional club in Plymouth. Directors were elected and Frank Brettell was engaged as the side's first manager. Thanks to Brettell's persuasiveness and the availability of Home Park, Argyle were elected to the Southern League. It should be noted that, at the time, the Football League consisted of only two divisions and the Southern League had been formed to provide an outlet for the many professional sides in the south of England who were unable to get into the Football League. The standard was high. Tottenham Hotspur won the FA Cup in 1901 as a Southern League team and Southampton reached the Final in 1900 and 1902, also as a Southern League member. Furthermore, when the newly-formed Chelsea applied for admission to the Southern League in 1905, their application was rejected.

Such was the Southern League of those early years of the century. Argyle also gained admittance to the Western League, composed of some of the same Southern League clubs but playing mainly in midweek. Although it was mostly the same Argyle team which played both Southern and Western League fixtures, the latter was generally regarded as the inferior competition. Players' abilities were often tested first in the Western League before they were given a taste of Southern League football.

The original Argyle amateur players were hardly likely to survive at these new League levels, so Frank Brettell was obliged to shop around for a playing staff and the newcomers arrived at Home Park from places as far apart as Edinburgh, Manchester, London and Southampton. Robert Jack, later to become the longest serving Argyle manager, and Jack Robinson, who had won the last of his international caps as England's goalkeeper two years before, were among those early arrivals.

The first-ever professional match played by Argyle was a Western League fixture at West Ham on 1 September 1903 and the newly-formed side won 1-0. Four days later, they began their Southern League membership with another victory, this time at home, over Northampton Town. Even more impressive was a 5-3 home win over Southampton in October — Southampton had been Cup finalists only a couple of years earlier. When it is also recalled that Argyle in their first FA Cup competition held Sheffield Wednesday to a draw, and that Wednesday were that season's League Champions, it can be seen that there was much satisfaction in Plymouth about the way in which matters had developed.

The team's Southern League record was also impressive, considering that Argyle were newcomers to that League. After finishing ninth in the first season, the team was fourth in 1904-05 and fifth in 1905-06. Jack Robinson spent only the first season in guarding the Argyle goal but he was soon succeeded by two giant goalkeepers, the local player 'Tich' Horne and John Willie Sutcliffe, an England international at both rugby and soccer. Charlie Clark, formerly with Everton, dominated the centre of the defence and the side looked to Jack Picken to come up with the goals.

Despite the good progress on the field, however, those early years were a difficult period for Argyle. Robert Jack had been appointed player-manager in 1905 but was lured away from the club by a more attractive offer from Southend United and Bill Fullerton took his place in 1906. Meanwhile, despite the playing successes, attendances were falling at Home Park and the crowds were being drawn to the rugby grounds of Devonport Albion and Plymouth RFC.

From 1907 to 1910, the club functioned without a manager, an experiment that was not without success on the playing field because in 1907-8 the team finished second in the Southern League, and R.Morris became the first Argyle player to receive international honours while playing for the club, when he was selected for Wales in 1908. Nevertheless, the financial position of Argyle was not at all sound and it was again the dedication of the Spooner brothers which saved the club when it was faced with liquidation. Stanley Spooner it was who, in 1913, formed a new company to take over the running of Plymouth Argyle FC.

In the meantime, Robert Jack had returned to the club in 1910 and so resumed a position as manager which he was to hold for nearly 20 more years. With Jack's return and a more secure financial basis for the club, Argyle began to prosper and

Argyle clear a Millwall attack at North Greenwich in January 1906. The Lions won this FA Cup first-round match 2-0, however.

Argyle players from a set of cigarette cards issued in the early 1920s.

achieved their best Southern League performance by winning the championship in 1912-13 with Fred Burch and Bert Bowler scoring 29 and 18 League goals respectively. The war clouds were soon to gather over Europe and a year later Britain was at war with Germany.

Professional football continued in the 1914-15 season but in Plymouth, at least, there was strong criticism that a sport should be engaging the attention of players and spectators at a time when the newspapers were full of lists of wartime casualties. It was a point which had great force in a garrison town such as Plymouth and the amount of coverage given by the local Press to Argyle's performances that season was extremely erratic.

Argyle finished 17th in the table that season but the whole programme was denied any real significance by the war which stripped Argyle, and many other sides, of key players who enlisted in the Services.

The Southern League resumed business in August 1919 but it was the last season in which that group was to function outside the Football League, because in 1920-21 the Southern League had been added to the two Divisions of the Football League and renamed the Third Division. Argyle continued as members of the Southern League, but it then became the competition for reserve sides of Football League clubs.

The omens were good, however, for Argyle's venture into the Football League. They finished fifth in their last season (1919-20) of Southern League football and had a relatively good run in the FA Cup, beating Second Division Barnsley

4-1 before losing 3-1 to Huddersfield Town, who were themselves Cup Finalists that season and promotion winners from Division Two. The star of that Cup sequence was the manager's son, David Jack, who scored five goals in the three rounds and emerged as a player of great potential. The defence also looked in good condition, with relative newcomers in goalkeeper Fred Craig and Moses Russell joining the more established defenders such as Sep Atterbury and Harry Wilcox.

It was therefore not surprising that Plymouth Argyle should soon become recognized as one of the leading sides in the new Third Division South. In the first season of the new division they finished 11th, but then came a remarkable sequence of seasons which gained the club a place in the football record books. For eight seasons, until finally winning promotion in 1929-30, they were on the edge of breaking out of the Third Division. For six consecutive seasons they finished second, so that cynics were heard to mutter that the team did not want promotion, and the annual meetings of the club usually involved an assurance by the chairman that Second Division football was genuinely desired by all involved with Plymouth Argyle.

It was easy to see where the problem lay in that first season of League football. The defence, with Jack Hill emerging as a centre-half with a future, conceded only 34 goals that season. But the forwards scored only one more, and Harry Raymond finished as leading goalscorer with a grand total of seven goals.

Argyle first discovered how difficult would be the gateway into the Second Division in 1921-2 when Southampton, who had been runners-up in the Third Division the previous season, just beat them into first place on goal-average. Argyle's average was 2.62, Southampton's 3.24. Argyle could have settled the issue, however, on the last day of the season, when a point from their away match with Queen's Park Rangers would have given them the title. The home side got a single-goal victory while Southampton jumped above their rivals with a resounding 5-0 win at home to Newport County. There was thus no tangible reward for an Argyle side which had been unbeaten at home throughout the season and had conceded only four goals, the best home record in the whole of the Football League. While Fred Craig, Billy Forbes, Moses Russell and Jack Hill were putting up the shutters at one end, an Argyle discovery, Frank Richardson, was commanding the headlines with his scoring feats. Signed from Barking in company with teammates Alf Rowe and Jack Leslie, Richardson scored a hat-trick in his first game for the club and ended the season with 31 goals, almost as many as the whole Argyle team had scored in the previous season when finishing 11th.

Argyle again finished as runners-up in 1922-3, this time to Bristol City, but the gap between the two top clubs was much wider on this occasion — six points, to be precise. Once more, the team's home record was almost impeccable — no defeats and only six goals conceded — but things were not so easy away from Home Park and Argyle scored only 14 goals on opponents' grounds all season. Richardson's scoring ability was not so prominent that season, but Welshman Jack Fowler burst on to the scene in the latter part of the season with 14 goals in the last 14 games, which brought Argyle 21 points out of a possible 28 and restored them to a place among the leaders after a spell of only one win in eight games in the New Year had apparently ruined any prospects of promotion that season.

The 1923-4 campaign was another season of frustration as Portsmouth took the title. Again, Argyle dropped valuable points in the mid-winter period but the team's form at the end of the season, with ten wins from the last 15 games, was true promotion quality. Jack Hill was a notable absentee from the side that season, the big centre-half having gone on to Burnley and subsequent international honours with England. But Argyle had made two forward discoveries in centre-forward Percy Cherrett from Portsmouth (27 goals in 40 games) and the earlier signing from Barking,

Jack Leslie, who was beginning to attract attention by his displays at inside-left in the latter part of the season.

Second was again to be Argyle's final position in 1924-5 when the team finished its programme of matches at the head of the table, only to be overtaken by Swansea Town who had a match to play. Despite the presence in the stands of the Argyle manager and captain willing on Swansea's opponents, Exeter City, the Welsh club achieved a narrow 2-1 victory to take the title. Swansea also frustrated Argyle in the Cup that season, beating them soundly by 3-0, and it was another Welsh club, Newport County, who inflicted Argyle's only home defeat of the season, winning 2-0 and thus depriving the home team of two points which would have been invaluable in the closing stages of the season. If Percy Cherrett (nine goals) had been able to repeat his scoring form of the previous season, matters might have been different, but it was left to the new left-wing pairing of Jack Leslie and Sammy Black to provide the scoring power that season.

One point was again to be the margin by which Argyle failed to head the table in 1925-6, with Reading, who had ended the previous season in 15th place, taking the championship. There was a new scoring hero wearing the green and black shirt — Jack Cock — who had arrived from Everton late in the previous season and had given notice of his potential with seven goals from ten games. With a full season in which to express himself, Cock scored 31 League goals. That season Argyle supporters could not complain of any goal starvation. Black and Leslie also reached double figures and the whole team went over the century mark with 107 goals. There were two 7-2 victories, over Aberdare and Bournemouth at Home Park, while on the same ground, Southend and Crystal Palace were both beaten 6-2, Norwich by 6-3 and Brighton 5-3. Argyle's total of 71 goals at home that season was the

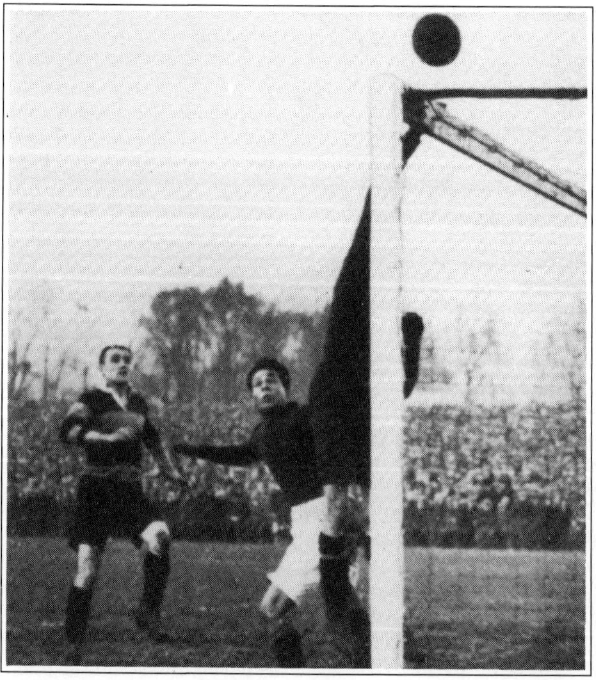

Jack Leslie challenges the Bradford goalkeeper during an FA Cup fourth-round tie at Home Park in January 1929. The Park Avenue club won 1-0.

best in the division and bettered by only one club, Sheffield United, in the whole Football League. Away, their form was less explosive, although there was one remarkable game at the end of November when Argyle played a 5-5 draw with Crystal Palace on a snow-covered pitch.

The 1926-7 season was the last of the six in which Argyle finished as runners-up. Bristol City, who had been relegated after only one season in Division Two, were once more able to take the title. Argyle had an unbeaten home record and their away performance was virtually identical to that of the previous season. Their total of 60 points would have been more than enough to have won the championship of the division at the end of the previous season. Argyle were good that 1926-7 season, but Bristol City were better.

By the standards of the previous six seasons, 1927-8 marked an Argyle decline. Not only did the team finish third, but they were also 12 points behind Millwall, the champions, so that there was little room for any talk of near-misses. Yet there was not really any period during the season when any sustained loss of form by the team could be identified. Ironically, Jack Cock was still getting goals but that season Millwall, Argyle's rivals, were the beneficiaries.

On paper, Argyle seemed to have declined further in finishing fourth in 1928-9, but the situation was more complex than that. At the end of the season, only two points separated the top six clubs in the division and goal-average had to be used to place them in order of merit. At the top on 54 points, Charlton Athletic had the advantage over Crystal Palace by 0.23 of a goal. Below them were four clubs with 52 points and the following goal-averages: Northampton 1.68, Argyle 1.62, Fulham 1.42 and Queen's Park Rangers 1.34. At one point in the season, Argyle looked to have some prospect of serious progress in the FA Cup. Second Division Blackpool were soundly beaten at Home Park in the third round, with Sammy Black getting a hat-trick, but Bradford, also from the Second Division, won by the only goal of the game when Argyle were again drawn at home in the next round.

Knowledgeable football folk were beginning to note that Robert Jack's side was amounting to a very good combination, especially the forwards. The Leslie-Black left-wing combination scored 30 League goals that season and the line was led with considerable skill by the young man from Looe, Raymond Bowden, who scored 21 League goals in his first full season in the first team.

Finally Argyle achieved their ambition. When the League tables were drawn up at the end of the 1929-30 season, Argyle were eight points ahead of their nearest rivals. They finished the season unbeaten at home and won 30 of their 42 games, 18 at home and 12 away. In fact, the side knew defeat on only four occasions that season. Sammy Black headed the scorers with 21 goals and all of the other forwards reached double figures with the exception, strangely enough, of Jack Leslie, but the coloured inside-left more than compensated for that by the general quality of his play . The oldest group of Argyle supporters will well remember the team which first brought Second Division football to Home Park: Craig (Cann later in the season), Bland, Titmuss, Mackay, McKenzie (or Pullen), Hardie, Grozier, Bowden, Vidler, Leslie, Black (with Sloan fitting into the side as the occasion required).

Argyle were undefeated until Christmas Day, when they lost 1-0 at Coventry, and were confirmed champions by Easter when they took full points from the three games. Perhaps it was a collective relaxation after that effort which caused them to lose 3-0 to Crystal Palace in the very next fixture.

It was, therefore, a very confident Argyle side which entered the Second Division in 1930-31, but one which found the opposition a much more difficult proposition. Although there were some notable victories that season, particularly the 'double' over promotion-winning West Bromwich, there were also long periods without a win and the eight defeats which the team suffered at Home Park constituted the worst home record in the club's history at that point. The last match of 1930 brought Argyle's heaviest defeat to date, 9-1 at Everton, the eventual champions. As the bare result implies that the Argyle side was completely outclassed, it should be pointed out that there were extenuating circumstances that afternoon. On Boxing Day, Argyle had beaten Cardiff City 5-1 at Home Park.

The team then boarded the night train at Plymouth for a ten-hour journey in order to play Everton the following day. The home side, on the other hand, had a relatively short journey to Bury on Christmas Day and no fixture on Boxing Day. They were naturally fresher than their visitors who had the added misfortune of losing the toss and being set to face the wind and rain on a heavy pitch. This explanation is not intended to offer excuses for the defeat but simply to point out that the result does not contain the whole story. There was a great deal of resilience in those Argyle pioneers of the Second Division. Within five days of being crushed by Everton, they defeated Barnsley 4-0 at Home Park; they lost 6-3 to Bury in the next match; and three matches later demolished West Bromwich 5-1.

Virtually the same team then went on to reach fourth position the following season. The only newcomers were left-half George Reed from Leeds United, and Bill Harper who came from Arsenal at Christmas to take over in goal. Overall, the Argyle side was in much more consistent form and, just one season after suffering a record defeat, achieved a record victory when they beat Millwall 8-1 in January. Other big wins at Home Park that season — 5-1 against Nottingham Forest, 5-1 against Bury, 5-0 against Oldham and an astonishing 6-0 victory at Southampton — came in very useful at the end of the season when goal-averages were necessary to separate three clubs on 49 points. Argyle, with exactly 100 goals, clearly took the lead over Bury and Bradford.

The club's performance in the FA Cup was also memorable. Manchester United, then a Second Division team, were beaten 4-1 at Plymouth in the third round and the draw for the next round took Argyle to Arsenal, the reigning League Champions and eventually Cup Finalists that season. There were over 65,000 at Highbury that afternoon to see Argyle take the lead, then fall 3-1 behind. Argyle pulled the score back to 3-2, only for Harry Roberts to settle the game for Arsenal when he put through his own-goal while under pressure from the Arsenal forwards.

The 1932-3 season started impressively enough with seven wins from the first 11 games which included decisive victories over Grimsby, Preston and Charlton. However, a more barren period of only three wins in the next 15 matches dragged Argyle down the table from the third place they had earlier occupied. There was a further blow for supporters when Ray Bowden was transferred to Arsenal in March. It would be tempting to trace the team's fall to a final 14th position to the loss of Bowden, but the decline had been evident before his departure.

Nine new players were tried in the side during the following season. Most of them had only a handful of games, but two men who were drafted in to the forward line established their places, George Briggs from Birmingham and Jimmy Cookson from West Bromwich. Cookson had started as a full-back with Chesterfield but had developed into a renowned scorer with West Brom, scoring six goals in one match against Blackpool in 1927. With 27 goals from 29 games, Cookson showed that he had lost none of his scoring flair but the defence looked less secure and conceded five goals on three occasions and four in four other games. Nevertheless, a final position of tenth in 1933-4 was a move in the right direction.

The next three seasons were to see a slow but steady improvement with the team attaining eighth, seventh and fifth position in consecutive seasons. It must be pointed out here that there has been no other period in the club's history when so consistent a Second Division performance has been achieved. The 1934-5 season was one of contrasts, with Argyle performances switching from relegation to promotion standard and back again. Only one of the first ten games was won but, coinciding with the arrival of a new centre-half, Johnny McNeil from junior Scottish football, the side hit top form and won ten and drew three of the next 15 matches. Then came

Read, the Grimsby Town goalkeeper, pushes a shot around the post at Home Park as Argyle winger Briggs leaps over him. Grimsby won this game 2-0 in February 1934, on their way to the Second Division championship.

a spell of four defeats in a row, yielding only one goal, then a final spell of 13 games, of which eight were won.

In 1935-6, Argyle finished one position higher, at seventh, with two more points than in the previous season. Losses and defeats were spread more evenly through the club's progress that season, which saw changes in the forward line, only Jack Vidler and Sammy Black of the old guard still being regular choices.

The 1936-7 season was to mark the end of that successful spell, with Argyle pushed into fifth place on goal-average by Newcastle United. There was another new man in the number-nine shirt, Johnny Connor from Airdrieonians, and the centre-forward contributed 17 goals towards the team total of 71, exactly the same number that they had scored in the previous season.

But the team was of necessity beginning to change, and the following season, 1937-8, saw the end of an era when Sammy Black played his last game for Argyle after a club career spanning 14 years and nearly 500 senior games. It was not a sudden break for Black or his supporters, as injury had restricted his appearances for a couple of seasons, but it was a piquant moment as he was the last link with the team which had gained Second Division football for Plymouth.

Towards the end of the 1930s, the more pessimistic of Argyle followers were beginning to wonder whether that status might be lost after all. In the last two full pre-war seasons, Argyle finished 13th and 15th respectively and an analysis of the results reveals that scoring power had become one of the weaknesses. At one point, the remedy seemed to have been found in centre-forward Bill Hullett, who came from Everton in 1937-8 and scored ten goals in 11 games. He continued in this vein at the start of 1938-9 with ten more goals in 18 games before Argyle yielded to an offer for his services from Manchester United. By the end of that latter season, Argyle seemed to have settled on Dave Thomas as his replacement.

But Jack Tresadern, who had been appointed manager in the previous season, persuaded Welsh international Pat Glover to leave Grimsby Town and lead the Argyle attack. Whether he would have been the answer to Argyle's scoring problems will never be known because only three games of the 1939-40 season had been played when war was declared and the League programme was abandoned.

A continuation of football as normal was clearly impracticable with players being called to the Forces, an evacuation programme in progress and the threat of German air-raids, but after a period of uncertainty, the Football League arranged a programme of fixtures dividing its members on a geographical basis. Thus it was that Argyle found themselves grouped with the Western clubs, Torquay United, Exeter City, Bristol Rovers, Bristol City, Swindon Town and the three Welsh teams — Cardiff City, Swansea Town and Newport County — in a South-Western League. Each club played the others four times, twice at home and twice away, and, as befitted the senior side (Newport had only just been promoted to Division Two), Argyle won the championship.

Successes at Home Park being so relatively rare, it is a pity that the achievement cannot be added to Argyle's honours list, but it was not always easy to take seriously a competition in which Argyle could, for example, beat Bristol City 10-3 one week and play a goalless draw with Cardiff City the following Saturday. By the end of the season, which stretched into June, there was not a great deal of enthusiasm left for this temporary League. Argyle were left with two away games at Newport and both clubs agreed to play one game for four points, simply to conclude the season. The League, however, continued to apply strict regulations and insisted that both matches should be played. Argyle, therefore, travelled up to Newport, lost 6-3 to the home side on the Friday evening and were back on the same pitch on the Saturday afternoon to lose 5-2 — and they still won the championship. These matches effectively marked the end of professional football in Plymouth until it was clear that the war was drawing to an end and the club could apply its mind to returning to normal business.

The German bombing raids on Plymouth during World War Two left their mark on Home Park, the grandstand having been left in ruins while the pitch, more as a result of neglect than anything else, resembled a jungle. It therefore took a great deal of faith to contemplate a return to normal conditions when the war ended, but Jack Tresadern and the directors resolved to respond when the Football League decided to inaugurate an interim season in 1945-6 in preparation for a return to normality in the summer of 1946.

Plymouth Argyle hammered Bristol City 10-3 in a Regional League (South-West Division) match at Home Park on 3 February 1940. It was the only League game played in England that day and attracted a crowd of 896. This picture shows Watts, the visiting goalkeeper, punching clear.

As a warm-up for that interim season, Argyle entered a team mostly composed of young local players in a 'League West Cup' competition in the spring of 1945. Old favourites such as George Silk, Jimmy Rae and Archie Gorman helped to strengthen the team which faced unfamiliar opposition such as Aberaman, Bath City and Lovells Athletic in addition to more established clubs like Swansea Town and Bristol City. Four wins and a draw in nine games was the Argyle record that season, but it was not sufficient to take them to the Cup Final in which Bath City beat Bristol City on aggregate in a two-match fixture by 5-3.

In order to reduce travelling time and expense, the Football League decided that for the 1945-6 season they would add together the First and Second Division members of the League, then divide them on a geographical basis, North and South, with Derby County as the most northerly of the temporary Football League (South). Thus it was that famous First Division sides such as Arsenal, Aston Villa, Chelsea, Charlton Athletic and Wolverhampton Wanderers all arrived at Home Park that season and brought with them their nationally known stars. Players such as Tommy Lawton, Bert Williams, Billy Wright, Cliff Bastin, Laurie Scott, Ronnie Rooke, Raich Carter and Peter Doherty were among the main attractions which brought the crowds, so long starved of soccer action, back to Home Park.

It was certainly not the standard of the Argyle performances which drew them there. Jack Tresadern had a constant headache in cobbling together each week 11 players to operate under the name of Plymouth Argyle. In many cases, his side was not settled until the last minute and its members were often strangers to each other. In all, Tresadern called on 72 players that season, a figure which can be broken down into 24 members of the playing staff, past and present, 27 'guest' players — individuals released by their clubs to play for Argyle on odd occasions — and 21 young local players. Among the guests were one current international, Horace Cumner of Wales and Arsenal, and two inside-forwards who were later to be honoured by their countries, Ernie Taylor of Newcastle United (England) and Jimmy Logie of Arsenal (Scotland). Many of the permanent staff were still in the Services or on war work and had to travel great distances to arrive in Plymouth for home matches. Alec Dyer, then in the Army, came from Aberdeen, and goalkeeper Matt Middleton, working in the mines, travelled from Durham.

In the circumstances, it was hardly surprising that the club's playing record was the worst in its history. Only three games out of the 42-match programme were won, all in the second half of the season, although some consolation could be found in the fact that two of the victories were against leading clubs in the division, Birmingham, the ultimate champions, and Wolves, who finished sixth. Some further consolation was that Argyle did not have the worst defensive record. That belonged to Newport County, who finished one place above them and conceded 125 goals to Argyle's 120.

The experience of 1945-6 had confirmed to Jack Tresadern that team strengthening was required simply for Argyle to retain their Second Division status when the League programme resumed in earnest the following season. Some of the pre-war staff such as Dave Thomas, George Silk, Bob Royston and Alec Dyer would still be of value. Others such as Archie Gorman and Jimmy Rae, who had both begun their careers in the early 1930s, could hardly be expected to last the demands of a full League programme.

He therefore started team building for the future, despite the long run of defeats which marked that transitional season. Bill Shortt, originally a 'guest' from Chester, was added to the permanent playing staff and other arrivals were Bob Thomas, brother of Dave, and also a forward from Brentford and defenders George Poyser (Brentford) and Reg Gibson (Manchester United).

By the summer of 1946, most of the younger members of the pre-war staff who had decided to continue their football careers had returned to Home Park. To the players secured from other clubs, Tresadern added wingers Sid Rawlings (Everton) and Bill Strauss (Aberdeen). The new mixture was then tried out in a pre-season friendly match at home, against Bristol City. The result, a 6-3 defeat for Argyle against Third Division opponents, was a clear indication that 1946-7 would be a very testing time for the club.

In the meantime, the Reserves playing at Bristol had come away with a 3-1 victory and therefore the selectors (selection was not then the manager's sole prerogative) brought five members of the latter side into the first team for the opening match of the new season. The action turned out to be inspired. The team, a combination of mainly pre-war defenders and mainly post-war forwards, delighted a crowd approaching 26,000 with a 3-1 victory over West Ham United, and then went on to register eight victories and five draws in the 18 matches leading up to Christmas. The Christmas period itself was a barren one for Argyle, although there were extenuating circumstances. The 6-1 defeat at Birmingham was at least partly attributable to the fact that goalkeeper George Wright had to leave the field injured; the double defeat by Manchester City was against the eventual division champions; and the 1-0 defeat at Chesterfield on New Year's Day should be placed in the context of injuries forcing Argyle to field a complete reserve defence.

However, all the explanations in the world could not compensate for the fact that no points were won, and when, early in the New Year, Argyle were defeated at Third Division Chester in the third round of the FA Cup, it was evident that the side had begun to lose its way. Eleven defeats in the last 12 matches of the season ensured that Argyle finished the season perilously near the relegation zone. The one victory in that final period of the season stands out because it was so untypical, a 5-2 win at West Bromwich, after an experimental forward line had been tried out.

The bare statistics pointed to the main problem. The attack scored 79 goals with Bob and Dave Thomas heading a list in which four players achieved double figures. The defence, however, conceded 96, a total exceeded only by relegated Newport County.

If Jack Tresadern thought that he simply had to strengthen the defence to achieve the right combination, he was faced with additional team problems during the summer. War-scarred Plymouth was a remote and unattractive location for players separated from their families. Bob Thomas sought and obtained a transfer back to his native London, with Fulham, and full-backs Royston and Dyer both decided to retire from the professional game.

As full-back replacements, Tresadern put his faith in the local player Pat Jones, who had come into the team in the last three matches of the season, and in Paddy Ratcliffe, a signing from Wolverhampton who had not been eligible to play in those last games. But to strengthen the centre of the defence, he surprised the football world by inviting John Oakes, 42 years old and on a free-transfer from Charlton Athletic, to come down to Plymouth and captain the side. Charlton also provided a new centre-forward in Maurice Tadman, for a fee of £4,000, and Tresadern planned that Tadman should be assisted by two inside-forwards whom the manager knew from his Tottenham days, Albert Hall of that club and Arnold Knight, then with Leeds United.

It was perhaps unfortunate that the first test of the new combination as it entered the 1947-8 season should be at Newcastle. The home side had set their sights on the First Division and left the field that August afternoon with a 6-1 victory over Argyle to see them on their way. Argyle's misfortunes were not confined to the result; Tadman broke a wrist in the match and was out of the side until the end of September. In the meantime, the team's record had been abysmal with only five points from a possible 18, and Jack Tresadern lost his job.

Jimmy Rae, already the assistant manager, was appointed in his place but the playing record continued to be mediocre. Neither of the two new inside-forwards had impressed, so at the end of October, Argyle suddenly plunged into the transfer market at a level which was exceptional by the club's standards. Two new inside-forwards, Frank Squires of Swansea and George Dews of Middlesbrough, arrived at Home Park and the latter club also provided a full-back with plenty of experience, Bobby Stuart, who had lost his First Division place at Middlesbrough to the younger George Hardwick and Dick Robinson. The new men certainly strengthened the side and with Oakes giving performances which belied his years, and new youngsters such as Len Boyd, Ernie Edds and Gordon Astall showing great promise for the future, the Argyle record from October onwards was on average a point per game, hardly exhilirating but sufficient to hold off relegation. The final statistics are again revealing with Argyle's total of 20 draws during the season demonstrating that the right balance in the side had still not been found.

Oakes and Stuart had brought a temporary defensive respite to Argyle, but neither could be viewed as long-term investments and in the close season Argyle were again searching for a new centre-half. The choice fell on Ray Goddard of Chelsea and he was joined at Home Park that summer by a Chelsea clubmate, Alec Machin, who had a reputation as a skilful forward or wing-half, and by George Taylor who had played at Aberdeen in the same side as Bill Strauss. The end result, however, continued to be discouraging. Argyle finished in 20th position, one place lower than in the previous season, and supporters' hopes that the club was ambitious received a blow when Len Boyd, who had developed into a fine wing-half, was transferred to Birmingham City early in the New Year. That Machin, who had not been an impressive forward, proved a more than useful replacement for Boyd until he broke a leg against Coventry in April was a small consolation for supporters. Jimmy Rae found silver linings in the dark clouds and discovered that at one point during the season, Argyle took more points in an 18-match spell than 19 of their competitors. Whatever that statistic signified, it certainly was of little account in an overall assessment of Argyle's performance. Late in the season, Argyle paid a five-figure fee to Birmingham City for their Scottish international inside-forward Neil Dougall, but the newcomer played in only three games before injury forced him to miss the rest of the season.

In three successive seasons, Argyle had finished 19th, 17th and 20th respectively. It was therefore hardly a surprise that 1949-50 should see them drop into the 21st and relegation position. Ironically, it was a season in which the side played some of its best football, but scoring goals proved to be a major problem. Only 44 were scored during the season and the side failed to find the net in 17 matches. The arrival in mid-season of two new centre-forwards, Eric Bryant from Yeovil Town and Harold Dobbie of Middlesbrough, made no difference at all. Dobbie did not score one goal for the club and Bryant managed two, one in each of the last two games of the season. It was this failing in the attack which accounts most of all for the fact that Argyle's total number of wins that season was just eight, the lowest in the division.

Defensively, the situation improved with the arrival of the centre-half whom the club had been seeking for so long. Jack Chisholm came from Sheffield United for a fee of £14,000 and, almost simultaneously, Ray Goddard moved out, signing for Exeter City for £5,000. With Ernie Edds also leaving Home Park for Blackburn Rovers at the same time, Argyle's net expenditure on Chisholm barely reached four figures. The new centre-half, immediately appointed captain, made an instant impression. In his first game, against Chesterfield at home, he suffered a cut head and left the field with blood streaming from the wound but returned, his head swathed in bandages, to resume the battle to the delight of the crowd. Chisholm certainly put all his energy into trying to save the club from the final drop, but goalscoring, the department in which the side was so obviously deficient, was not part of the Chisholm repertoire.

The descent into the Third Division South did not lead to any panic measures by the Argyle management. The only notable departures from the scene that summer were those of Frank Squires to Grimsby and Stan Williams back to Aberdeen, both moves being at the players' request. (Squires had the misfortune to achieve an unwanted 'hat-trick' — each of the three clubs he served, Swansea, Argyle and Grimsby, were relegated to the Third Division). With only one major signing, Peter Rattray from Dundee, the implication was clear. The club was confident that the side which lost Second Division football was competent enough to regain it.

That confidence appeared to have been misplaced during the opening weeks of the new season. Only two of the first ten games were won and a rapid return to the Second Division seemed a far more difficult prospect than had been imagined. The tide turned on the last day of September at Bournemouth, when a reshuffled side brought off a 2-0 win. The most significant change had been the return of Neil Dougall to the forwards. In the previous season, he had been tried at right-half and won high praise from Press and supporters alike for the quality of his performances. The Bournemouth match showed that he had the skill to transform the attack and the win marked the start of a successful spell for Argyle during

Bill Shortt clutches the ball to his midriff in order to deny an opportunity to Frank Scrine of Swansea Town during a League match at Vetch Field in December 1952. Jack Chisholm (left) and Paddy Ratcliffe appear to be completely relaxed and confident in Shortt's ability to cope with the situation. Scrine was an Argyle 'guest' player in the 1945-6 season.

which, up to Christmas, they achieved nine victories in 12 League games, including a 5-1 win over Aldershot, 7-1 against Colchester United and 6-0 at Brighton. It was a particularly happy period for Maurice Tadman, who twice scored four goals in a game. It was not such a memorable time for Argyle's former goalkeeper George Wright, who was at the receiving end of that 7-1 scoreline as Colchester's goalkeeper. The BBC added to the misery of George's homecoming that afternoon by choosing the match for its second-half radio commentary.

The improvement continued after Christmas and by the end of the season Argyle had attained fourth place in the division, not quite the place they had hoped for, but sufficient to suggest that the club's policy had been vindicated to some degree.

As the following season was to prove, the men who lost Second Division status for Argyle were just as capable of regaining it. Peter Rattray was the only newcomer in the squad which collected Third Division championship medals that season and, although the Scottish forward's 19 goals played a significant part in the team's success, the difference between the sides of 1950 and 1952 could not be explained in terms of Rattray's introduction alone. Rather it was to be found in the confidence which Third Division opposition had engendered in the side and the understanding which grew out of playing together over long periods. Team selection that season was an almost automatic process and only the inclusion of Tony McShane as wing-half deputy for either Neil Dougall or Johnny Porteous brought any significant variation to the line-up.

Although the opening match at Leyton Orient was lost, Argyle hit top form in their first home game, a 5-0 victory over Crystal Palace which began a run of seven victories in eight matches. A disputed penalty in the home match against Bristol Rovers led to Argyle's sole home defeat of the season, but there were no lasting effects from that set-back and Argyle went on to take 18 points from the next 13 games, many of their successes being achieved in style — a 5-0 home win over Millwall, a 5-2 win at Walsall and a 6-1 win when Shrewsbury were the visitors. Curiously, that Millwall victory was followed the next Saturday by a defeat at the hands of the same club in the first round of the FA Cup in London.

That early exit from the competition freed Argyle to concentrate on the first priority, promotion, which began to look a real possibility when the side registered eight successive wins in the period after Christmas. Only four games were lost in the latter part of the season and by the end of April promotion had been assured. The season finished in something of an anti-climax as Argyle struggled to hold Torquay to a 2-2 draw at home, and then went down 3-0 at Norwich in the last game of the season, but by that time such reverses were merely of academic interest. Second Division football was returning to Home Park.

With Rattray leaving Plymouth for Norwich in the summer, because of personal reasons, two experienced inside-forwards were added to the staff in preparation for life in the higher level. With George Dews as usual finishing off the cricket season with Worcestershire, Sam McCrory, Ipswich's Irishman, and Arthur Smith from West Bromwich came west and both were included in the side for the opening games. And so successful was the start to the season that Dews could not regain his place until October. By Christmas, with 26 points from 22 games, the side was near the top of the table and the possibility of bounding straight into the First Division did not seem wholly impossible.

Furthermore, the prospect of making some real progress in the FA Cup was also on the cards in the New Year. Fortune favoured Argyle in the third and fourth rounds by giving them home advantage, and when the fifth-round draw paired them again at home against Gateshead of the Third Division North, a passage to the quarter-finals seemed to have been reserved. Gateshead, however, pulled off one of the day's big surprises with a second-half goal to give themselves a 1-0 victory.

George Robertson (5) tussles for the ball with Luton's Kelly (9) at Kenilworth Road in October 1954, when Argyle lost 3-1. Rex Tilley (left) is an anxious Argyle onlooker.

In later years, Jack Chisholm maintained that the shock of the defeat by Gateshead caused the side to lose confidence and miss the chance of promotion to the First Division. The record, however, does not really support the contention that the Gateshead match was such a turning point in the team's fortunes. In the 28 League games played until that point, Argyle took 32 points; in the 14 which followed, 17 more were added, virtually the same proportion of points to games. At the final reckoning, fourth place was far better than most associated with the club could have hoped for at the start of the season.

The 1953-4 season therefore seemed to offer Argyle the chance to build on that success and, perhaps with some judicious team-strengthening, aim for that higher spot. What happened in fact suggested that the club had chosen a more negative path. First came the news in the close season that Alex Govan was leaving, on his way to Birmingham City, and within a few weeks of the start of the new campaign, Gordon Astall followed him. Neither of these two talented wingers were adequately replaced and, what was more to the point, they were not only talented but young. As the season unfolded, Jimmy Rae was forced to realize that many of his old brigade were beginning to show their ages and many points were lost in the dying minutes of the matches. It was clearly the time to give younger players their opportunity and none made more of an impact than the local centre-forward Neil Langman, who came into the side late in the season and scored nine goals in as many games. Langman's two in his first game, at Everton, helped to ease the shock of an 8-4 defeat. But the final position that season of 19th was uncomfortably reminiscent of that period before relegation in the late 1940s.

The parallels became even more ominous at the end of 1954-5, when the side ended the season 20th, one position lower still. Two-thirds of the way through that season, however, with the team having gained only five wins in 29 matches, the board decided that a change of manager was needed. Jimmy Rae left Home Park and the vacancy was offered to a national-known figure. Jack Rowley was ending his career at Manchester United, having been capped for England and having won League championship and FA Cup medals with one of the most successful club sides of the period.

Rowley was expected to be a player-manager and to put his considerable reputation as a goalscorer at Argyle's service. His effect on the side was instantaneous. In his first game, Argyle achieved their first away win of the season, 3-2 at Fulham, immediately followed it with another away success at Hull and then made it three wins in a row when Luton came to Home Park. Although that pace could not be maintained, there were four victories in the last ten games of the season, a far better proportion than had been achieved before Rowley's arrival. There were also other hopeful signs such as the emergence of another local striker, Eric Davis, whose eight goals in 15 matches made him joint top scorer that season with Peter Anderson, another young home-grown player who was beginning to fill the gap left by Govan, and Johnny Porteous enjoying a new lease of life as a forward. Jack Chisholm had been forced to retire from the game through injury, but Neil Langman's brother, Peter, had showed both strength and composure when given his chance in the number-five shirt, thus releasing George Robertson to play elsewhere in the defence.

There was therefore reasonable cause for optimism that 1955-6 could witness an Argyle resurgence. In the event, it proved to be one of Argyle's worst seasons and, with 28 points, they finished in 21st place. One curious feature of their performance that season was that the victories won, scattered as they were throughout the campaign, were often decisive. Middlesbrough and Liverpool were both beaten 4-0 and Bristol City 5-0. That last result, on Boxing Day, was oddest of all in that when the same teams met at Bristol for the return game on 27 December, City turned the tables on Argyle with a 6-0 victory. Rowley rang the team changes but could not hit

Bill Shortt (left) and Peter Langman get a ground-level view of one of the three goals which West Ham's Ken Tucker scored against Argyle in a 4-0 defeat at Upton Park in October 1955. This was just one of the defeats that season which cost Argyle their Second Division place.

on a consistently successful combination. In all, 32 players were tried that season but it was the old stagers, such as Bill Shortt, Pat Jones and Neil Dougall, who proved to be the most reliable. There was, however, some hope for the future in the performances of three young local players, Johnny Williams, Reg Wyatt and Charlie Twissell. Williams and Wyatt were to make their marks with the side in later seasons but Twissell, discovered in Navy football and one of the fastest wingers the club has ever had, did not quite fulfil the promise of those early days.

In 1950, relegated Argyle gave notice that the team would continue much as before. Not so in 1956 when the decks were cleared and a number of favourite players left Home Park. Bill Shortt, Les Major, Johnny Porteous, Paddy Ratcliffe and George Willis all took their leave, either because of retirement or transfer.

Any hopes that the club would quickly return to the Second Division received a jolt before the new campaign was only weeks old. The first five games were all lost and after 11 matches Argyle had only one victory to their credit. Even worse, in the second home game of the season they had been drubbed 6-0 by Reading. At least part of the explanation for that disappointing start was a weakness in goal. Argyle had hoped to fill the gap left by Shortt and Major, with the 19-year-old Devonport lad, Peter Dyer, but Dyer's inexperience and, more pertinently, his lack of height, were cruelly exposed during those early games. Jimmy Gee, another local player and an amateur, was no more successful when he was given his chance, so Rowley went into the transfer market and brought the experienced Harry Brown to Plymouth from Queen's Park Rangers who were preferring the future England international, Ron Springett, as their last line of defence. Brown's arrival at Home Park brought more solidity to the defence but it was not until the end of November

Harold Dobbie had more scoring success after leaving Home Park for Torquay United. On this occasion, however, Argyle's visit to Plainmoor in March 1957, there was no opportunity for him to embarrass his former teammates. Goalkeeper Harry Brown comes out to collect the ball and Pat Jones (3) stands ready.

that the side began to recover from those early traumas and a final position in the Third Division South of 18th showed that there was still a great deal of work to be done.

With a completely new board of directors (headed by the wealthy Ron Blindell) behind him, Jack Rowley entered the second season of Third Division football with a strengthened side. In the close season came forward Wilf Carter and goalkeeper Geoff Barnsley, both from West Bromwich and players with some First Division experience; from Portsmouth, winger Harry Penk; and from Old Trafford, two young players who had not achieved places in the United team, full-back Bryce Fulton and wing-half Tommy Barrett. Of these, Carter was the most obviously successful and he proved to be the goalscorer the team had lacked for so long. In the first half of the season he was paired with Neil Langman, but Langman was transferred to Colchester in the November and in the following month, Jimmy Gauld, another crowd-pleaser, arrived from Everton and Rowley tried the tactical move of linking both Carter and Gauld with George Baker, a young Welshman who had been developed by Argyle as a deep-lying centre-forward. The strengthened side finished the season in third position, a much more satisfactory result and one which relieved some of the pressure on Rowley to produce results.

The season was also notable for the final appearance of Pat Jones, after 12 years and over 400 first-team appearances for the club. Jones' story also illustrates one of the less admirable facets of Argyle boards — their parsimony. During Jack Chisholm's spell at Home Park, he had twice threatened a rebellion by the players in order to wring bonuses from the directors; the 1950 FA Cup match with Wolves and the 1954 tour of the United States were the occasions. Each time, Chisholm won his point. But Pat Jones suffered a more personal affront when he injured his groin at Crystal Palace in October 1957. The injury was to keep him out of the side until the following April and the board's initial reaction was to offer him reserve-team wages, completely ignoring the long years of consistent service which Jones had given to the club. Only a personal appeal by the player caused the directors to reverse their decision.

That Rowley had truly discovered a winning combination was confirmed the following season, when Argyle became champions of the newly-formed Third Division (the previous North and South sections having been abandoned). Carter and Gauld set up an irresistible scoring partnership and the defence, with Reg Wyatt established in the middle, also played its part. Argyle's form was championship quality from the start. The record up to the end of 1958 was 14 wins, seven draws and only three defeats. There was a certain faltering in the team's progression in the New Year and at one point two consecutive home defeats were experienced, but an astonishing 8-3 win over Mansfield Town at Home Park restored the side's confidence and Argyle finally pipped Hull City by one point to take the title. Coincidentally, both Argyle and Hull had been relegated together from the Second Division in 1955-6, had gone their separate ways in the divided Third Division and had now returned together to the Second Division.

Rowley also demonstrated, during the course of that season, a welcome tendency to build up the team's strength in depth. New defenders in the form of Gordon Fincham (Leicester City), Len Casey and Wally Bellett (Chelsea) and a new forward, Barrie Meyer of Bristol Rovers, all played their parts in ensuring promotion. Bellett took over at left-back from the versatile Dougall and Fincham's value was shown when injury forced Reg Wyatt out of the side in the critical last few weeks of the season.

'Too good for the Third Division but not good enough for the Second.' The paradox which had marked Argyle's post-war performances was again apparent as the team struggled in the first season back in the Second Division. Two heavy defeats in September, 5-0 at Derby and 6-2 at Middlesbrough, and another 4-1 reversal at Liverpool showed that life was not going to be easy. Manager Jack Rowley was the most notable casualty of the club's difficulties and two of his signings of the previous season, Casey and Bellett, lost their first-team places. The board's attempt to solve the managerial problem was novel; Neil Dougall and George Taylor were jointly elevated from the training staff to positions as joint managers. More orthodox measures were taken to deal with team problems and, in a sudden rush into the transfer market in the January, Argyle emerged with three new but experienced players, George Kirby and Jimmy McAnearney from Sheffield Wednesday and Johnny Newman from Leicester City. All three proved to be good purchases, although Kirby attracted some unfavourable reaction at first when he failed to score for his new club until his 14th game in new colours. A final position of 18th was disappointing for all concerned with the side, although optimists took some encouragement from the fact that the team put on its best display in the last game of the season, beating the champions, Aston Villa, 3-0.

Kirby got among the goals in the following season (1960-61), and his 19, coupled with Wilf Carter's 24 helped to bring Argyle up to a respectable 11th position. There were a number of highlights that season. Wilf Carter scored five goals against Charlton during the Christmas holidays, there were four other occasions when the team scored five goals in a match and the new Football League Cup competition proved to be a big attraction to Plymothians. The Taylor/Dougall partnership as joint managers, however, proved to be unworkable, and after Vic Buckingham had first accepted and then declined the offer of the manager's post, Neil Dougall was given sole charge of affairs.

One of Dougall's managerial moves was to bring Ellis Stuttard back to Argyle as assistant trainer. It was Stuttard who found himself in the manager's chair in November 1961, after three consecutive defeats, in which the opposition scored five times, had seen Argyle slide down the table and in serious danger of losing their Second Division status once again. In a very short time, the slide had not only been halted but the team began to develop a more cohesive look and the final position of fifth was close to being one of the best achievements in Argyle's history. During the course of that revival, Argyle also registered a convincing 3-0 victory over West Ham United in the third round of the FA Cup, but then had the misfortune to be paired in the next round with the eventual Cup winners, Tottenham Hotspur. Spurs' emphatic 5-1 win showed that there was a wide gap between even a rejuvenated Argyle and the country's leading teams.

The period from mid-November to the end of March, 21 games resulting in 12 wins and four draws, marked the high point of Argyle's achievement that season. Those who were not so readily impressed noted with foreboding that the last six games of the season yielded only one point and included a 5-0 defeat at Swansea. Nevertheless, 1962-3 proved to be a reasonably successful season, and there were few grumbles about a final position of 12th. Two new forwards arrived on the scene: Micky Lill, a winger from Everton, and, later in the season, a player with a national reputation, Peter McParland, who had made his name in the 1950s with Aston Villa and Northern Ireland as a left winger. With 11 goals from 18 games, McParland looked to be just the sort of player to take some of the scoring burden off Wilf Carter's shoulders. With 14 goals, the latter had registered his lowest seasonal total since joining Argyle.

Having been formed in 1903, Argyle prepared to celebrate the diamond jubilee at the start of 1963-4. As subsequent events were to show, they only just missed marking the anniversary by losing their Second Division place. The season opened ominously with a 5-0 defeat at Middlesbrough and although such a heavy defeat proved to be the exception, the side had great difficulty in collecting points; by the turn of the year Argyle were at the foot of the table with only three wins to their credit. By this time another change of manager had taken place and Argyle had engaged Andy Beattie, who had made it clear that he was not interested in a permanent post but would try to save the club from what appeared to be inevitable relegation. To strengthen the defence, Beattie went back to one of his former clubs, Nottingham Forest, for Doug Baird and Billy Cobb, and to try to bring some bite into the attack, he went to the Fourth Division for Frank Lord, a centre-forward with a scoring reputation.

Mike Bickle, a local discovery who proved that he could score goals.

Andy Beattie promised no miracles, although Argyle's escape from relegation that season by goal-average was hailed in that year's handbook as 'almost a miracle' and that brief contribution to Argyle caused Beattie to be bracketed with Robert Jack as the most illustrious of Argyle's managers.

Last-minute escapes from relegation might have been dramatic but they were hardly the conclusion to a season which Argyle's well-wishers had hoped for at the beginning of the campaign. Andy Beattie had made it clear from the start that he would act only as a stop-gap manager and there was an unusual handover between him and his successor, Malcolm Allison, unusual for football when so often the previous manager has long vanished from the scene before the new man arrives.

Conscious of the need for team strengthening, Allison brought with him from his former club, Bath City, full-back Tony Book and a midfield player, Keith Sanderson. Book was soon a favourite with the crowd but reactions to Sanderson were mixed, although his manager was roundly to declare that he was the best retriever of the ball on the playing staff, the sort of talent which is not always apparent from the terraces. Allison and the directors soon gave notice that they had ambitions for the club when agreeing to pay Swansea Town a record transfer fee of £45,000 for their Welsh international winger Barrie Jones, and the public appetite was whetted by a very successful run in the League Cup which brought Argyle to the semi-final. Up to Christmas, their League form was also very promising, with 11 wins and three draws from 24 games, but the end of 1964 was depressing with only one point coming from five games and, thereafter, only five of the remaining 18 games were won.

In January, goalkeeper Dave MacLaren was transferred to Wolves and to replace him Allison signed the Republic of Ireland international Noel Dwyer from Swansea. Later in the season, Dwyer was to become the centre of a controversy which led to Allison's departure before he had completed a full season with the club. His team selections had frequently been bold and controversial but it was his persistence with and backing for Dwyer, when some directors held the goalkeeper responsible for the loss of points, which brought matters to a head. At the directors' insistence, Dwyer was dropped from the side on Easter Monday and replaced by the reserve John Leiper. Allison was not the type of manager to react placidly when his professional judgement was questioned and, after an emergency meeting of the board, it was announced that he would be leaving the club.

Derek Ufton, the assistant manager, took over for the remaining games of the season and Argyle's final position of 15th, while clear of the relegation zone, was hardly the outcome which had been hoped for when Allison was appointed. It was, however, three positions better than that achieved the following season when the side finished just four points clear of relegation. That season had witnessed the welcome discovery of a player who could consistently score goals, the burly local player Mike Bickle, but this gain was offset by the transfer of Mike Trebilcock to Everton on New Year's Eve for £20,000. By the end of the season, while his former colleagues struggled, Trebilcock had become the hero of Merseyside with two of the Cup Final goals which defeated Sheffield Wednesday. Trebilcock had scored 11 goals for Argyle that season before his transfer and it was significant that the season ended with him still Argyle's leading scorer. The club's 54 goals in 42 games that season pointed to a weakness in the attack.

The improvement the following season of 1966-7 was only marginal and, although scoring five more goals than in the previous season, Argyle ended with the same number of points and one position lower in the table. There were also a large number of new faces — two new goalkeepers in Peter Shearing and Pat Dunne, new defenders in John Sillett and Mike Everitt and new forwards in Alan Banks, John Mitten and Jimmy Bloomfield. With local players such as Steve Davey, Keith Etheridge and John Tedesco also getting their chance, the playing staff was beginning to look somewhat unfamiliar. Furthermore, Derek Ufton had decided that neither Nicky Jennings nor Barrie Jones figured in his plans and the two wingers, whom many thought were the best that Argyle had fielded since the heyday of Astall and Govan, were transferred to Portsmouth and Cardiff City respectively. Even more regrettable was the departure of Johnny Williams to Bristol Rovers, where he played out the remainder of his career. Such clearances would have been justified if the net result had been an improvement in the team's performance but, very obviously, it was not.

The 1967-8 season proved to be even more disappointing and by the turn of the year, Argyle had won only four games. An early-season plunge into the transfer market did nothing to arrest the slide, despite the arrival of three new forwards in Alan Peacock (Leeds United), Alan Sealey (West Ham United) and Mike Harrison (Blackburn Rovers). Ufton was particularly unfortunate with this group, signed for a total outlay of £36,500 but ultimately making only 30 League appearances between them. In February, Ufton was sacked. His dealings in the transfer market were reckoned to have shown a financial profit: sales £124,250, buys £76,500, profit £47,750. But of what value was that profit when by the end of the season the side was firmly rooted to the bottom of the table with 27 points, the lowest total in the club's League history? It was therefore hardly surprising that the attendance for Argyle's last game of the season at Home Park was the lowest that the club had ever experienced during its League history — 4,678.

The new manager, Billy Bingham, arrived in Plymouth from a similar post with Southport and it was to Merseyside that he looked for players to bolster the side. The result was the arrival at Home Park of centre-half Fred Molyneux from Southport and winger Aiden Maher from Everton (where he had, incidentally, been a close friend of Mike Trebilcock). David Burnside and Bobby Saxton, two other signings late in the previous season, were also on hand to aid Argyle's efforts to climb back into the Second Division. In the light of that ambition, the 1968-9 season was encouraging. The side finished fifth in the table with a goal record of almost parity (53-49). As all Argyle followers knew, the lesson of history was that the team did not immediately bounce back to the Second Division but took a season or two to consolidate before making the final leap. Unfortunately, the pattern of subsequent seasons did not follow the model prescribed. In 1969-70, Argyle finished 17th in the table, in 1970-71 they were 15th, but in 1971-2 they had risen to eighth, more satisfactory but still a long way from the target. By that time, Argyle had dispensed with the services of both Billy Bingham and Ellis Stuttard, who had been recalled to replace him after a poor start to the 1972-3 season when Argyle scored only two victories in their first 12 matches.

The results under new manager Tony Waiters were not an overnight improvement — indeed, a 7-1 defeat at Oldham can be numbered among them — but the club's performance did improve later in the season. At or near the bottom from late September to mid-February, Argyle finally achieved respectability with a spell of ten wins in the last eight games and ended eighth in the division.

Waiters was a manager-coach in the Allison style and, like his predecessor, was to lead Argyle to success in the League Cup. All eyes in Plymouth during 1973-4 were focussed on an amazing sequence of victories on First Division grounds — at Burnley, Queen's Park Rangers and Birmingham City — which brought Argyle to the semi-final of the League Cup and the best chance that the club had ever had of playing at Wembley (the 1965 Final was not a Wembley occasion). As the records show, Argyle fell in the semi-final to Manchester City, going down 2-0 in the replay at Maine Road. Meanwhile the club's League performance was only moderate at best. A brief stay at tenth place in October was the highest

Derek Rickard might not have been particularly tall but no defence could afford to ignore the threat which he represented. In this incident at Leyton in March 1970, Rickard and Orient skipper Terry Mancini appear to be engaging in a 'Spot the Ball' competition. Steve Davey lurks in the background (left).

position attained all season, and the final position of 17th was hardly commensurate with the status of a team seeking a Wembley date.

The season was notable, however, for the emergence of a young forward, Paul Mariner, whose abilities in his first League season provided a ray of hope for the future. Towards the end of the season, Waiters added the Blackpool striker Billy Rafferty, who had been out of favour with the Lancashire club, to the staff. The following season, Rafferty and Mariner set up a scoring partnership which was instrumental in regaining a place in the Second Division for Argyle. From a mid-table position in November, Argyle began a steady climb and remained in the top three positions from Christmas onwards, losing the championship to Blackburn Rovers by only one point. Between them, Rafferty and Mariner scored over half of Argyle's goals that season, Rafferty getting 23 and Mariner 20. Although these attackers took the headlines, the contribution of the defence must not be overlooked. Jim Furnell played in goal in all the League matches and in the two Cup competitions and he had good support from Mike Green and Bobby Saxton in front of him.

Rafferty and Mariner were again in scoring form for Argyle's first season back in the Second Division, but their individual and collective contribution diminished when faced with Second Division defences. Mariner scored 15 and Rafferty 12. An attempt to strengthen the side by the signing of a midfield player, Mick

Argyle pictured in 1974. Back row (left to right): Provan, Hore, Hardcastle, Johnson, Sutton, Griffiths, Pearson, Delve, H.Burrows, Saxton. Second row, standing: Randall, Nickeas, Mariner, Green, Furnell, Aleksic, Rafferty, Rogers, Darke, P.Burrows, Davey. Seated: W.Shearer, B.Ford, K.Blunt, Machin, Tony Waiters (manager), P.Skinnard, E.Stuttard (chief scout), I.Greaves. On ground: Foster, Macey, Harrison, Bayliff, Hurn.

Horswill from Manchester City, proved to be insufficient in itself and the club spent the whole of the season virtually in the last quarter of the table. That particular side also had the unenviable record of not winning a single away game, the only such occasion in Argyle's history.

There were new faces in the side which lined up for the start of the new season in August 1976. Neil Ramsbottom from Sheffield Wednesday was in goal and there were two new men up front, Doug Collins from Burnley, and Brian Hall, a former member of the successful Liverpool squad. Hall appeared by courtesy of the Supporters Club who raised £35,000 for his transfer. Just as it seemed that the club was serious about at least retaining the place in the Second Division, if not exactly setting its sights on the First, Argyle achieved one of those acts of self-destruction which appear from time to time in its history. Their most valuable playing asset was turned into cash. In October, with a quarter of the League programme completed and the club lying in tenth position, Paul Mariner was transferred to Ipswich Town in a transaction valued at £220,000. It was the biggest deal in which both clubs had ever been involved but only some £175,000 was paid in cash, the balance being made up by the transfer of two Ipswich players to Argyle — Terry Austin, who directly succeeded Mariner in the number-nine shirt, and a central defender, John Peddelty.

How successful a season Argyle would have had with Mariner in the team must remain an open question. What is certain is that without him, there was little in the way of an attacking threat as the season's total of 46 goals demonstrates. Argyle cannot be said to have been well served by the players' component of the deal. Austin was no subsitute for Mariner and Peddelty was forced to retire from the game because of a head injury after playing only 30 games for his new club. Some of the money in the Mariner deal was spent on bringing Bruce Bannister from Bristol Rovers to support Austin, and John Craven from Coventry City to help bolster the defence. As the season moved into its final quarter, it was clear that Argyle would be hard put to stay in the Second Division but a mediocre spell from April onwards, during which they lost six of the final nine games, ensured that they dropped beyond the safety level and Second Division status was lost again after only two seasons.

Tony Waiters could foresee that his own future at Plymouth was in doubt, and in April it was reported that he had circularized 'selected' clubs offering the services of himself and the entire coaching and scouting staff because of the 'difficulties at Plymouth.' It was a farsighted move because a month later, Waiters and his assistant, Keith Blunt, were dismissed and deputy manager Mike Kelly was given the unenviable task of monitoring Argyle's fall into the Third Division.

Kelly was well aware that he was expected to restore Second Division football to Home Park but events were to show that he would be faced with a more urgent priority, trying to stop the team sliding right out of the Third Division and into the Fourth. On 14 February, with Argyle holding 21st position and having won only six games during the season, Kelly resigned, Lenny Lawrence, the Reserve team manager, taking over until a new manager could be found. The latter's identity was revealed a month later when Malcolm Allison returned to the Home Park, after 13 years, with the post of 'consultant manager' until the end of the season. Those who maintained that Allison's previous departure was the club's loss could feel some satisfaction with the team's response. The first game under his control was at Portsmouth, where the home side had troubles of their own and occupied the bottom position in the division. Relying mainly on the staff which Kelly and Lawrence had bequeathed to him, Allison's first selection came away with an impressive 5-1 win and although they waited until the last match of the season (when Bradford City, also struggling, were defeated 6-0) to produce anything comparable, the side pulled clear of the relegation zone and Argyle were spared the indignity of a drop into the Fourth.

The managers' records were:

Kelly:	won 6	drew 10	lost 13
Lawrence:	won 1	drew 3	lost 2
Allison:	won 4	drew 4	lost 3

There was obviously much work to be done but a number of younger players, developed by the club's youth policy, made their debuts that season and looked promising material for the future. Martin Hodge, John Uzzell, Gary Megson and Mike Trusson were the players around whom Allison would be expected to build his side. Kevin Hodges joined the others in the team for 1978-9 but, although the side spent much of the season in the upper half of the table, they never really threatened to become serious contenders for promotion, although Fred Binney's scoring record in the number-nine shirt was surpassed by only one other Third Division player, Ross Jenkins of Watford. Binney, however, could not produce the necessary goal spark at Worcester in the first round of the FA Cup and, in front of a packed ground, Argyle were despatched from the season's competition, 2-0.

This proved to be less of a shock than the news at the beginning of January that Malcolm Allison had accepted an offer to return to Manchester City to take complete charge of coaching. Argyle received £35,000 in compensation from City and quickly replaced Allison with their former player Bobby Saxton, who had been managing Exeter City. What difference did the change at the top make? Argyle's record under the respective managers was:

Allison:	won 7	drew 8	lost 7
Saxton:	won 8	drew 6	lost 10

In other words, there was little difference between the two phases and the side finished just below the half-way mark in the table.

It was not a disaster but it was still less than Argyle were hoping for. It was therefore frustrating when the following season produced exactly the same result: points 44, position 15th. A new scorer had arrived on the scene in the person of Dave Kemp from Carlisle United but the transfers to Everton of Martin Hodge in the close season and Gary Megson in December were further confirmation of the fact that Argyle were regarded — and had accepted the assessment — as a side which would not be achieving much themselves. Fees of £135,000 for Hodge and £250,000 for Megson represented good business for Argyle, who had paid nothing for either player but there was little sign that the club was willing to spend comparable sums to build up the side.

The 1980-81 season revealed a more settled side with Kemp again proving a reliable scorer. This time, he registered 28 goals in League and Cup matches, way ahead of the other scorers, none of whom reached double figures that season, and his personal contribution must be reckoned as one of the major factors in Argyle's attainment of seventh position. Once more, however, managerial changes were in the air and in the early summer, Bobby Saxton was attracted by an offer to take over at Blackburn Rovers. A month later, Bobby Moncur was appointed in his place at Home Park.

Moncur's first season saw the side finish tenth and then slightly improve on that record in 1982-3 by finishing eighth. Although such results were obviously not poor, promotion to the Second Division still seemed a remote prospect and alarm set in at the beginning of 1983-4, when the side registered only one win from their first six games. A notable newcomer that summer was centre-forward Tommy Tynan from Newport County, but Tynan had scored only one goal when Moncur and the directors were in conflict over team strengthening and at the end of September, Moncur left the club.

Later in the season, with the appointment of John Hore, attention was diverted to that most unusual Argyle development, a good run in the FA Cup. The story of that sequence is recorded elswhere in this book. Here, it might be pertinent to point out that the team's Leage record at the time came nowhere near their Cup form. From the third round of the Cup to the semi-final, Argyle won only three of 15 League games and among the defeats was a 5-0 drubbing at Oxford, which was an exhilarating experience for the home side, the eventual Second Division champions, but did little for the morale of the Plymouth men. An appearance at Villa Park in the FA Cup semi-final that season was a truly historic occasion for Argyle but it did not really mark the advance in Argyle's fortunes for which many hoped.

When the dreams of Cup glory had faded, Argyle were again faced with the challenge of breaking out of the Third Division, but the early indications as 1984-5 unfolded were that the team would first have to concentrate on staying out of the Fourth Division. On 19 October 1984, Argyle, with only one win from 11 League games, sacked Hore. By December, when Dave Smith was appointed in his place, the team had sunk to 21st position and had relinquished any hopes of a repeat performance in the FA Cup by losing to Hereford United in the second round. A definite improvement from February onwards, when the side lost only six of 22 games, took the relegation worries away. Tynan revealed scoring form for which he had been bought by getting 31 League goals and Argyle finished the season in 15th position.

When Tynan sought a move to Yorkshire, for domestic reasons, in the close season and was transferred to Rotherham United, the prospects of any significant improvement in Plymouth Argyle's fortunes seemed remote, especially when only one win was recorded in the first five games. But a transformation took place from

Argyle's Kevin Hodges (centre) fails to prevent Watford's John Barnes (left) getting in a shot in the FA Cup semi-final game at Villa Park in April 1984.

mid-September to mid-December — 16 matches in which ten victories and four draws saw Argyle climb the table from 20th place to second. The team faltered a little over Christmas after a match at Reading in which Argyle, leading 3-0 with only 25 minutes remaining, were beaten 4-3 by the home side. However, Argyle were not to be easily deflected from the task in hand and the form which they produced in the latter part of the season was promotion quality without a doubt. From February to May, Argyle won 14 of their 18 games, promotion being assured when they defeated Bristol City in late April. Spice was added to the performance by the return of Tynan — on loan — from Rotherham and the centre-forward contributed nine goals in as many games.

For a team which had struggled for so long to regain their Second Division place, the Argyle side of 1986-7 seemed to find their new surroundings far from daunting. Tynan had returned to the club on a permanent transfer and the side continued with the form of the previous season, so that by December they occupied third place in the table and were seriously being considered for promotion. The effort of retaining such an exalted position, however, proved too much and the team slipped a little after Christmas but not diastrously so, finishing seventh. Three more points that season would have taken them into promotion play-offs and the possibility of a First Division place.

Those with long memories (or access to the club's overall record), however, would be aware that it is not in the Argyle tradition to contest for too long at the top of the Second Division and 1987-88 conformed to pattern. After four matches, Argyle headed the Second Division and had registered a notable 6-1 win over Huddersfield Town. Another six goals were recorded against Leeds in October but by that time all the indications were that Argyle would have to settle for a mid-table position. There was, therefore, no surprise when the team finished in 15th position.

The 1988-9 season proved to be another disappointment with Argyle dropping three positions to finish 18th in Division Two. Relief that Second Division status had been preserved was, for most supporters, tempered by the fact that the First Division seemed as far away as ever and the waning of interest in the Plymouth area was reflected in the statistic that the attendance for the last match of the season at Home Park was just under 5,000, whereas earlier in the season the average was nearer the 8,000 mark.

At no time did Argyle ever look to be genuine promotion material and it was fortunate that the side built up a useful stock of points early in the season because there were only four wins in the last 20 games. That sort of form throughout the season would surely have led to relegation.

At least part of that later decline could reasonably be attributed to the loss of two key players in Leigh Cooper and Kevin Summerfield, both of whom suffered broken legs. Neither was adequately replaced and, since both were among the more creative members of the team, the rhythm of the side was inevitably disrupted.

Indeed, it was hard to see how consistency could be easily achieved when Argyle fielded 14 new players during 1988-9, more new faces than they had ever used before in a single season since they joined the Football League.

Ken Brown ended the season with the opportunity to assess his playing assets and it would have been surprising if he had not concluded that, before the 1989-90 campaign dawned, team strengthening was essential. His first priority must surely have been an experienced goalkeeper. Cherry's determination to leave Plymouth early in the 1988-9 season left the club with a major problem which was only temporarily solved by Arsenal's loan of two goalkeepers. Argyle have employed goalkeepers on loan for brief periods in the past, but never before have they played two-thirds of a season without a member of their own staff between the posts.

The central defenders were among the most consistent members of the side, but the Burrows-Smith partnership looked destined to be broken by the decision of the latter to seek a transfer nearer his Yorkshire roots, a recurrence of the old problem that some players are strongly attracted to the Plymouth area and others find it too remote.

Another need was for a creative player to operate in the midfield. It was, of course, hoped that Kevin Summerfield would make a complete recovery from his injury but, even then, some reinforcement in this vital area was necessary.

Finally, there was a forward problem. Pleasure that Tommy Tynan again scored over 20 goals for the club was tempered by the fact that no other player reached double figures and that Tynan, on the wrong side of 30, could not carry the scoring burden alone for ever. In this connection it is a sobering thought that Argyle failed to score in 17 League games. That figure can be put in perspective by comparing it with comparable barren seasons: 1920-21 — (first season in Football League) 20 games without scoring; 1949-50 (relegated) — 17; 1967-68 (relegated) — 18.

It would not, however, be appropriate to end this account of Argyle's playing history on a note of despair or pessimism. Argyle supporters are nothing if not resilient and can always take comfort from the old cliché that things can only get better. There is, at least, the prospect of a talented group of younger players waiting in the wings at Home Park. Gary Penhaligon, Andy Morrison, Owen Pickard, Jason Rowbotham, Peter Whiston, Darren Garner and Martin Barlow could well be the names which will excite the club's historian of the future.

The Home Park Story

Present capacity: 26,000 • Record attendance: 43,596 — 10 October 1936
• Pitch measurements: 112 x 75 yards •

FOOTBALL followers, more accustomed to the typical League grounds of the North and Midlands are often pleasantly surprised to arrive in Plymouth and find that the Argyle ground is located at the edge of the city's largest public park, has an open aspect in all directions and has its own capacious car park. Whatever the variations in the quality of players and officials as the years go by, the ground remains as the club's most enduring asset.

The original Argyle, the amateur club, had a ground in the east side of the city, long since built over, and Home Park was originally built for a rugby team, the now defunct Devonport Albion. After that team had a dispute with the owners, the ground remained unoccupied for three years. In 1901, the ambitious Argyle Athletic Club obtained a long lease on the ground and staged their first event there, an athletics meeting, on Whit Monday 1901.

It was the possession of such a fine ground which helped to support the Argyle case for admission to the Southern League when the club's first football manager, Frank Brettell, began to canvass for support in 1903. By that time, a number of the leading professional clubs in the country — Sheffield Wednesday, Notts County, and Aston Villa among them — had staged exhibition matches on the ground and it had been demonstrated both that there was sufficient interest in the professional game in Plymouth and that the Argyle club had the facilities to support it.

By modern standards, the Home Park of that era was lacking in basic amenities and would certainly not be approved in this safety-conscious age. There was a small wooden grandstand about 40 yards long, but most spectators stood around the pitch on rudimentary slag heap banking, lacking cover, terracing, crush barriers and toilet facilities. Similarly, the approaches to the ground were far removed from the wide metalled roads of today, being mostly along unmade pathways with the main route a narrow lane from Pennycomequick interrupted by a stile.

Even in relatively modern times, the Home Park setting has remained essentially rural. As recently as the 1930s a practice match on the ground could be interrupted as the players abandoned the game in order to try to intercept a wild rabbit which was attempting to sprint from one end of the ground to the other.

Home Park in 1905, pictured during a Southern League game.

Argyle's (and the Southern League's) absorption into the Football League in 1920 was accompanied by necessary improvements to the ground in order to cater for the increase in attendances and when the team finally gained promotion to the Second Division in 1930, big changes were put into effect. The wooden grandstand was demolished and replaced by a more modern construction costing over £11,000. The new edifice, approximately 100 yards long, ran virtually the complete length of the pitch on the Pennycomequick side of the ground. At the same time, the standing spectator was not overlooked. Concrete terracing and crush barriers were built mainly from funds raised by the Supporters Club and the same organization financed the roofing of the terraces at the Devonport end of the ground and the construction of the main entrance on the same side of the ground.

The new grandstand also incorporated players' dressing-rooms and offices which were embellished by the laying of oak flooring on the concrete base. Neither were the little touches forgotten, as when manager Robert Jack introduced an idea which he had noted at another League ground and had the boards behind each goal painted yellow to act as sight screens for his forwards. Unfortunately, of course, they were just as useful to opponents.

In 1936 the improvements allowed Argyle to cram a record crowd of nearly 44,000 into the ground for the visit of Aston Villa while in the 1950s and 60s crowds of 40,000 were recorded for the FA Cup visits of Notts County, Wolverhampton Wanderers and Tottenham Hotspur. By those later dates, however, the ground had experienced some traumatic changes.

The importance of Plymouth as a naval and military centre during the Second World War made it an important target for the *Luftwaffe* in 1941 and Home Park was soon showing the scars of war. The pitch was cratered but, most costly of all, the grandstand was virtually destroyed.

Restoring the ground to something approaching normality in preparation for the resumption of League football in 1945 was a task requiring much expenditure and not a little ingenuity and improvisation. Former Army huts were converted into dressing rooms, redundant trams and buses were brought in to serve as offices and disused railway sleepers were used as replacement terracing on the site of the former grandstand.

Although it could never be asserted that the ground was at its most attractive in those years immediately following the war, the paying public did not seem to have been deterred and it is a cause for reflection that the present ground capacity of 26,000 was quite commonly exceeded by attendances for League games in the forties and fifties.

It was not until 1952, seven years after the ground had been reopened, that a new grandstand was erected on the site of the one destroyed in the war. Floodlights were installed in the mid-fifties, and in 1964-5 the terracing was covered on the Lyndhurst side of the ground, immediately opposite the main stand. There was a period in the late seventies when the covering at the Devonport or Milehouse end had to be removed for safety reasons but it was replaced in 1984 so that three sides of the ground are now covered.

However attractive the ground and its facilities, Plymouth's relatively remote location means that Home Park is not frequently chosen to stage some of the more important national games but in September 1966 the Football League decided to choose the ground for the match between the Football League and the Irish League. It was a particularly significant match in that seven of the Football League side had, a few weeks earlier, been members of England's victorious World Cup team. A crowd of 35,458 paid £8,800 for the privilege of watching the world champions beat the Irish team 12-0. As it was such an historic occasion, the names of the Football League team deserve to be recorded: Bonetti; Cohen, Wilson, Peters,

J. Charlton, Moore, Paine, Byrne, Hurst, Eastham, Connelly. Substitute: Johnny Newman. On two occasions (April 1970 against Bulgaria and October 1973 against Portugal) England under-23 sides played at Home Park, and the ground was also used for a Youth international in which England beat Wales 6-0 in February 1952. Plymouth's remoteness proved to be an advantage in October 1977 when, after crowd disturbances at Old Trafford, Manchester United were ordered to play their European Cup-winners' Cup tie against St Etienne at Home Park. Over 31,000 were in the ground on that unusual occasion but the game which must have brought back memories to the older generation of Plymothians occurred in October 1951 when — just for one day — Home Park was converted back to a rugby ground in order to accommodate the large crowd expected for the rugby fixture between the South-West Counties and the touring South African side. Who knows how many ghosts of the Devonport Albion side of the turn of the century were present on that occasion?

Home Park and surrounding area photographed in September 1971.

OFFICIAL
PROGRAMME
The Pilgrims
P.A.F.C
PLYMOUTH ARGYLE
PRICE 9D
INCLUDING FOOTBALL LEAGUE REVIEW

• The Argyle Managers •

EVEN after a century of League football in this country, the art of club management largely remains a mystery, apparently owing as much to favourable circumstances as to any personal attributes of the managers concerned. The consistently successful managers — Busby, Clough, Shankly, Paisley — are a rare breed and greatly outnumbered by those who either attain little or whose successes are forgotten when their club's fortunes take the downward turn. These patterns can be traced repeatedly in the careers of the men who have managed Plymouth Argyle.

Neither the club's directors nor the paying public have ever made excessive demands on Argyle managers. A respectable position in the Second Division has normally been their realistic expectation and the words of Jimmy Rae, written in 1949, would hardly seem out of place 40 years later. Reviewing the previous season, he pointed out that just five more points would have changed the team's final League position from 20th to ninth and commented: "With such a position, everybody connected with the club would have been happy." It was because of their failure to meet those fairly modest expectations that most of the men reviewed here lost their jobs.

Any assessment of the men who have managed Argyle from 1903 to 1988 cannot fail to take account of the disparity between the number of managers who served the club before and after World War Two. From 1903 to 1947, Argyle had five managers; from 1947 to date they have had 16 managers and 18 managerial changes, the latter figure taking into account the two spells each of Ellis Stuttard and Malcolm Allison. Those figures increase to 17 and 19 respectively if Vic Buckingham's brief spell in the early 1960s can be counted as valid.

Judgement on particular individuals must largely depend on whether they were successful and the criterion for success, in turn, must be determined by whether they brought promotion or an impressive Cup performance to the club. So far as promotion is concerned, Robert Jack, Jimmy Rae, Jack Rowley, Tony Waiters and Dave Smith belong to a select band. Even here, however, closer inspection often reveals flaws in the individual's record. Rae and Rowley had earlier been in charge of sides relegated from the Second Division while Waiters took his team up, only to see it return to the Third two seasons later. Only Robert Jack and Dave Smith have unblemished records in this respect. Smith has another and unique claim to fame. No other Argyle manager has gained promotion for the club so soon after taking up his appointment.

The managers who brought Cup fame to Argyle — success is too strong a word — paradoxically produced teams whose current League form was only moderate (Allison in 1965 and Waiters in 1974) or, in the case of John Hore (1984), was to decline to an alarming degree.

Those who argue that Argyle should follow the Liverpool model and appoint managers from within the club should reflect that this has been done on a number of occasions but rarely with success. Robert Jack, Jimmy Rae, Neil Dougall, Ellis Stuttard, George Taylor, Bobby Saxton and John Hore were all former players elevated to the manager's seat; Derek Ufton and Mike Kelly were already on the staff when the opportunity was offered them. It is worth noting that a high proportion of the men selected for the Argyle manager's job had no previous experience of the demands of managing a League club. William Fullerton, Jimmy Rae, Jack Rowley, Neil Dougall, George Taylor, Ellis Stuttard, Malcolm Allison, Derek Ufton, Tony Waiters, Mike Kelly and John Hore all received their League management baptism with Argyle.

Inexperience was not a charge which could be levelled at the first Argyle manager. The Irishman FRANK BRETTELL had had 28 years' experience in football administration when he arrived at Home Park in 1903. Formerly the secretary of Everton and Bolton Wanderers, he was later to develop into something of a specialist in setting up professional football teams. To the Southern League (which was later to become the Third Division South of the Football League) he introduced Tottenham Hotspur in 1896 and Portsmouth in 1898. Brettell's task was a supporters' dream — to create an Argyle side from scratch, having first persuaded the Southern League secretary that the Home Park set-up could support professional football. In creating his squad, Brettell could draw on his many contacts in the football world but the clubs which he contacted were naturally unwilling to release their best players. Thus, the group which he finally assembled were, to put it kindly, mostly mature footballers. Some contemporaries were not so respectful and one national newspaper, noting Argyle's first-ever game at West Ham, disparagingly referred to the visitors as 'scrap iron'. Rejects they might have been, but the team which Frank Brettell built soon proved that they could hold their own in Southern League football. When Brettell retired in 1906 he could be satisfied that he had successfully launched another club into the world of professional football.

His successor was the first player he had signed as a professional, ROBERT JACK, who combined the duties of manager with those of a player. Jack spent only one season with the club in this capacity, however, before accepting an offer from Southend United. Into his place came WILLIAM FULLERTON, formerly a half-back with Sunderland. Unfortunately for the newcomer, his arrival coincided with a period of financial difficulties for Argyle and, after one season, the club decided to economize and dispense with a manager, leaving the functions to be carried out by a management committee.

ROBERT JACK

This manœuvre was not a success, however, and by 1910 there were fears that Argyle's financial position could lead to the club becoming defunct. Their future was ensured due mainly to the efforts of local businessmen, the brothers Spooner. One of their inspired moves was to invite ROBERT JACK back to Home Park and so began an association between the manager and the club which was to endure for another 28 years.

Bob Jack was originally destined for a legal career but the pull of professional football caused him to abandon his studies. An outside-left, he began his career with Alloa Athletic at the age of 15, was transferred to Bolton Wanderers two years later and stayed with the Lancashire club for six seasons. Before joining Argyle in 1903, he had also played for Preston North End and Burslem Port Vale. Although he did not win international honours at football, he played for England at bowls in his later life. Two of his three sons, David and Rollo, were also on the Argyle playing staff. David played for England when he was with Bolton and Arsenal and then followed his father into the managerial profession. A third son, Donald, played for Bolton.

Under Robert Jack, the team's progress was steady if not spectacular and, at one point agonizingly slow, but it was always progress. In 1912-13, Argyle won the Southern League championship and in 1920-21 they were admitted to the newly-formed Third Division South of the Football League. It was this period that marked Argyle as apparently too good for the Third Division but not good enough for the Second. In their first ten years in the League they were second in the table for six consecutive seasons, and close to the top in the other seasons before promotion was finally won in 1930. At that time only the champions of each regional Third Division went up and there were no play-offs to increase the chances, but it is tempting to think what the Argyle side of that period might have achieved had they been able to enter the higher class of football when they were at the peak of their form.

At one time there were dark mutterings in the city that Argyle did not want promotion, but those more closely connected with the club knew that this was untrue. Promotion, once gained, was not surrendered up to the time of Bob Jack's retirement in 1938. He returned to Southend where he died in 1943 in his late 60s. His ashes were brought to Home Park and scattered over the ground — now devastated by enemy action — with which he had been so closely associated.

Behind all the great playing names of the 1920s and 1930s — Hill, Bowden, Black, Leslie, David Jack — stands the figure of Robert Jack. He hardly ever spent large sums of money on players and a whole host of Argyle stalwarts of that period were obtained for the statutory signing-on fee. Was it his luck or his ability which brought so much talent to Plymouth at the same time? There seems little doubt concerning the answer; Argyle were the team that Jack built.

JACK TRESADERN

Succeeding so dominant a figure was obviously not going to be an easy task and it fell to JACK TRESADERN, who had resigned as Tottenham manager amidst growing unrest at White Hart Lane where it was felt that Tresadern was unlikely to restore Spurs to Division One. A former Burnley and West Ham United player, Tresadern had played for the Hammers in the first Wembley FA Cup Final of 1923 (when David Jack scored the first goal in a Wembley Final) and won two England caps. He started his managerial career with Northampton Town before moving to Tottenham.

Tresadern, who arrived at Home Park in 1938, was in charge for only one full season before the League programme was suspended upon the outbreak of war. Tresadern was called into the Army, emerging in 1945 with the rank of captain to face probably the most difficult task to have confronted any Argyle manager — that of restoring a team to a city and ground bearing the deep scars of war.

Fortunately, the Football League had decided that there should be one transitional season before the resumption of League football. It gave Tresadern time to gather the threads and he was under no illusions about the task in hand. His prediction to the directors at the start of the 1945-6 season: "We shall win no matches but we will have a very good financial season," proved inaccurate in only one detail: Argyle managed to win three games. Compared with that record, a position of

JIMMY RAE...
looking up
and forward...

19th in the first post-war Division Two was quite commendable but the directors were looking for improvements. The 1947-8 season was only a few weeks old when the news broke that Tresadern was leaving. Reading between the lines of the terse official statement at the time points inescapably to the conclusion that Jack Tresadern had been sacked. Certainly, his signings in the 1947 close season had largely proved disappointing although the most controversial of all, the 42-year-old John Oakes from Charlton, could not have been personally criticized, either then or for the rest of the season.

Whatever qualities the board were looking for, they believed that they had found them in Tresadern's assistant, JIMMY RAE. The genial Scotsman was to spend eight years in the manager's position at Home Park, longer than anyone else after Robert Jack. Rae will be chiefly remembered as the man who guided Argyle out of the Third Division South in 1952 but, apart from that and the first season in Division Two when Argyle were at one stage serious challengers for promotion, his period in office was chiefly concerned with fighting relegation. His most inspired move was probably the signing, in late 1949, of Jack Chisholm who took much of the on-field burdens from his manager's shoulders. Perhaps it was no coincidence that the team's decline and the descending of Jimmy Rae's star came when the injuries which had plagued Chisholm throughout his professional career conspired to remove him from the Home Park scene. Whatever the connection between these factors, relegation beckoned and Jimmy Rae's name was added to the list of ex-managers. He left Plymouth soon afterwards and took a public house at Solihull but retained a keen interest in the progress of the Argyle side, "my boys", as he used to call them. As Rae had noted, the team which had at one time promised to storm into Division One had begun to age and their lack of stamina had become evident.

JACK ROWLEY

In choosing JACK ROWLEY to succeed Jimmy Rae, the directors signed a player as well as a manager. A Manchester United player since 1937, Rowley had gained national fame and six England caps as a renowned goalscorer but he chose not to turn out for Argyle in his normal centre-forward position, preferring to take the inside-left role where he could have greater control on the course of the game. His impact on the side was immediate and dramatic. His League debut for Argyle in February 1955 saw them win their first away match of the season; seven days later they won away again and Rowley scored his first goal for the club. By the end of the season Argyle had picked up enough points to avoid relegation, edging just clear of Derby and Ipswich.

Argyle supporters hoped for better things in 1955-6 but they were to be bitterly disappointed. This time there was no reprieve and the club plunged into the Third Division South. There were even more difficult times to follow. Instead of a quick return to Division Two, Argyle found themselves embroiled in a desperate fight to avoid having to apply for re-election. In similar circumstances many clubs would have sacrificed their manager, but patience prevailed at Home Park and Rowley was given the time and the opportunity to rebuild the side. With the help of the goalscoring skills of his signings, Wilf Carter and Jimmy Gauld, Argyle regained their Second Division status in 1959. Within a short while, however, the triumphs were overlooked, the congratulations forgotten. The Second Division was once more to provide Argyle with a demanding test, there were boardroom disputes and suddenly Rowley was packing his bags and leaving Plymouth.

NEIL DOUGALL

A period of managerial confusion then followed. The directors first decided that two former Argyle players, Neil Dougall and George Taylor, should share the responsibility for playing matters while a newcomer, Jess Lowe, was brought in to take care of the administrative side of the manager's job. Dougall and Taylor bore the titles of chief coach and chief trainer respectively. The arrangement, which bore all the marks of an improvisation, was effected after the former Spurs full-back, Vic Buckingham, had agreed to become the new Argyle boss, then changed his mind a few weeks later when Sheffield Wednesday offered him the manager's position at Hillsborough. The dual control proved difficult to implement and although responsibilities became clearer when NEIL DOUGALL was given the title of team manager, the club's playing fortunes did not improve.

In November 1961, another reshuffle of the backroom cards brought assistant trainer ELLIS STUTTARD to the manager's position with Taylor remaining as chief trainer and Dougall being given the titles of chief coach and chief scout. Again, the arrival of a new manager brought a change in playing fortunes. Ellis Stuttard seemed to possess a golden touch and, by Easter 1962, Argyle looked to have a real chance of gaining First Division football after a spell of 13 victories in 18 games had lifted them into third place. Unfortunately, the impetus could not be sustained and with only one win in their last six matches, Argyle had to be content with fifth place. After three years of managerial musical chairs at Home Park, the least fancied of the three former Argyle players involved had finally proved his worth. Although this was Stuttard's first full management job, he had enjoyed some experience as an assistant at Swindon after playing for Argyle and Torquay United.

ANDY BEATTIE

Hopes that Stuttard would further improve Argyle's playing fortunes were not realized. In 1962-3 they had to be content with a mid-table place and worse was to follow. The 1963-4 season opened disastrously and by the end of October, with 16 games played, Argyle had recorded only one victory and the relegation signs were there for all to see. Stuttard stepped down but remained as assistant manager while the main responsibilities were handed to a man who probably had the greatest experience of any post-war Argyle manager. ANDY BEATTIE, the former Preston

North End full-back, won seven caps for Scotland between 1937 and 1939. More important, he had managed Barrow, Stockport County, Huddersfield Town, Carlisle United and Nottingham Forest. Beattie came with a limited objective. He would try to save the club from relegation but did not want a permanent job, preferring to act as a caretaker until Argyle found someone with long-term aims. Within these bounds, Beattie was a success. Argyle avoided relegation — albeit by the slenderest of margins, a goal-average 0.05 superior to that of the 21st-placed club, Grimsby Town.

Beattie's intention of taking the job on a short-term basis had at least allowed

MALCOLM ALLISON

Argyle plenty of time to give serious thought to his replacement. Eventually they went outside the Football League for a much younger man, MALCOLM ALLISON, who had gained some prominence with Romford and Bath City. Formerly a centre-half with Charlton Athletic and West Ham United, Allison's playing career had been brought to a premature end by tuberculosis which resulted in him having a lung removed. Yet, despite being finished as a player in his 30th year, Allison was in no doubt about how he could continue in football. In the 1950s he had been one of a group of West Ham players who discussed and dissected the game at every opportunity. A number of them were later to make their marks in football management and the names of John Bond, Ken Brown, Noel Cantwell and Dave Sexton are familiar to most followers of English football. Argyle's physiotherapist, Malcolm Musgrove, was a member of that same squad.

Allison was flamboyant, extrovert and not at all averse to publicity. He also had strong views about tactics and was probably the first Argyle manager to break with the 1-2-3-5 team formation which had been typical of British football for many years. Tony Book, who had been at Bath when Allison was manager of that Southern League club, joined him at Plymouth to begin his Football League career at the age of 28. If Allison was prepared to gamble on a 'veteran' like Book, he was not afraid to give younger players their opportunity as well. Nicky Jennings had already established himself in the side before Allison's arrival but he was soon joined by other youngsters such as Richard Reynolds, Mike Trebilcock and Norman Piper. Where home-grown talent was not available, Allison, backed by the board, was prepared to spend and he paid a then record Argyle fee of £40,000 for Swansea Town winger Barrie Jones. Allison's team selection was not to everyone's liking, however. Stalwart supporter Sid Tonkin objected to the fact that 'apprentices' were being given extended runs in the team in preference to more mature players and to the general cult of youth which Allison (with the exception of Book) appeared to be encouraging. Under Allison, the team's League form was patchy, a promising first half of the season being overshadowed by an indifferent second period. But the public's imagination was captured by Argyle's performance in the League Cup in which Argyle reached the semi-final. The competition was then in its infancy and lacked the lustre of a Wembley Final but, in the context of Argyle's poor overall record in Cup matches, it represented a landmark.

DEREK UFTON

Whatever plans Malcolm Allison might have had for Argyle, however, were not to be fulfilled because before the season had ended he was at loggerheads with the directors, chiefly over the question of team selection, and Argyle were again faced with the problem of finding a manager.

Perhaps it was in the hope that he could continue the more favoured aspects of Allison's approach that the directors offered the job to DEREK UFTON who had been brought to the club as chief coach by Allison. Ufton and Allison had been playing contemporaries. In fact, it was Ufton's form at centre-half for Charlton which led Allison to West Ham in search of first-team football. Ufton had won an England cap with Charlton and had also proved himself as a first-class cricketer with Kent where he often deputized behind the wicket for the great Godfrey Evans. Moreover, Ufton was both liked and respected during his relatively brief spell at Plymouth. So it was with a fair degree of optimism that club and supporters sat back to watch the next drama unfold. Derek Ufton soon demonstrated that he had his own ideas about which players could bring First Division football to Plymouth and, against mounting criticism, he set about transforming the team. His strategy was to sell the players who could command the largest fees and replace them with those bought for more modest prices. The plan paid off financially. Ufton's dealings in the transfer market resulted in a net profit of nearly £50,000, but from a playing point of view it achieved little. After two seasons in which the side finished in the lower half of the Second Division, Ufton's policy was finally torn to shreds in 1967-8. By February 1968, Argyle looked to be doomed to Third Division football. The side had made early exits from both the FA and League Cups, while the League record was appalling with only three victories in 25 games. Furthermore, public support was beginning to dwindle. Derek Ufton was sacked and never again ventured into club management.

Relegation was assured before Ufton's successor took over and the only debate centred around how long it would take the new manager to get Argyle out of the Third Division. If a man's playing record is any guide to his effectiveness as a manager, then the club's directors made one of the best possible choices when they appointed BILLY BINGHAM. Bingham's playing career had begun with Glentoran and spanned 400 League games as an outside-right with Sunderland, Luton Town, Everton and Port Vale. He had been capped 56 times for Northern Ireland and was their team manager (a position he still held in 1989) when he took over at Home Park. His start was not at all discouraging and in his first season, Argyle finished fifth. It was not all that had been hoped for, of course, but experience had shown that a relegated Argyle often needed a season or two to recover before regaining their Second Division place. When the next two seasons saw Argyle finish in the lower half of the table, however, supporters began to voice discontent with the club's progress under Bingham. Having a national team manager in charge at Home Park carried a certain kudos, but if it meant that his attention could not be given solely to the club, then it was a luxury which should be dispensed with. So began the disputes which were to lead to Billy Bingham's association with Plymouth Argyle being severed. Unlike Ufton, Bingham continued in club management, both in this country with Everton and Mansfield Town, and in Greece.

BILLY BINGHAM

As a temporary measure, Argyle re-appointed ELLIS STUTTARD who had been relieved of the same post ten years earlier. Stuttard had been brought back to Home Park as chief scout by Bingham and he was therefore on the spot and available when the manager's post became vacant. There were no dramatic developments on the field during Stuttard's second spell. Argyle had two seasons in the top half of the table but promotion looked as distant as ever. The board decided that new blood was needed and in October 1972, Stuttard again cleared his desk and moved out of the manager's office, reverting to chief scout. He was to remain with the club in one capacity or another until declared redundant as an economy measure in 1982. He died in 1984.

ELLIS STUTTARD

TONY WAITERS

MIKE KELLY

The new manager, TONY WAITERS, the former Blackpool and Burnley goalkeeper who was capped seven times by England, was yet another entering League management for the first time, although he had acquired a favourable reputation when in charge of the England Youth team. At last, Argyle seemed to be progressing. Under Waiters, they created something of a national sensation by beating a succession of First Division opponents to reach the semi-finals of the League Cup in 1974 and the following season crowned that achievement by regaining their Second Division place. Once more, however, retaining that place seemed to be beyond them. After only two seasons, relegation again beckoned for Argyle and they dropped back into Division Three in 1977. Tony Waiters left and reserve-team manager MIKE KELLY was appointed in his place. Like Waiters, Kelly had been a goalkeeper, although his international honours were confined to an amateur cap before he turned professional with Wimbledon, Queen's Park Rangers and Birmingham City. Far from leading the side back into the Second Division, however, Kelly saw his team slide towards the Fourth and he resigned in February 1978, reserve-team manager LENNIE LAWRENCE taking over temporarily.

A month later, Argyle surprised many people by announcing that MALCOLM ALLISON, the man who had abruptly left Home Park 13 years earlier, was their new manager. In that intervening period, Allison had established a national reputation, mainly because of his partnership with Joe Mercer at Maine Road where the pair had brought fresh glories to Manchester City. A spell managing Crystal Palace had not proved particularly successful and Allison went to coach abroad. His return to Plymouth seemed to be just the tonic the team needed. Not only was relegation avoided, but the side lost only three of the remaining 12 games and finished the season with a flourish, winning 5-1 at Portsmouth and beating Bradford City 6-0 at Home Park in the last match of the season.

Whether or not Allison could have inspired a true resurgence for Argyle must remain a matter of conjecture. In January 1979, with two years of his contract still to run, he accepted an offer from Manchester City to return to the scene of his greatest achievements, this time to work in company with another general manager, the same Tony Book he originally brought to Plymouth as a player. Allison's decision to leave may well have been influenced by the fact that, after a heartening start to the season which took them to fourth place by the end of September, Argyle had slipped to a mid-table position and had been knocked out of the first round of the FA Cup by non-League side Worcester City.

Almost immediately, Argyle announced the name of Allison's successor. He was their former half-back and captain BOBBY SAXTON. Saxton had guided Exeter City out of Division Four in 1977 and the combination seemed ideal — a man with an Argyle background who had already demonstrated his managerial qualities. Whatever the potential, however, it was not to be realized. At the end of 1980-81, Saxton, who had taken Argyle to seventh place in the Third Division, was approached by Blackburn Rovers, seeking a replacement for Howard Kendall who had taken the job at Everton. Saxton accepted the challenge to build on Kendall's achievement at Ewood Park and attempt to lift Blackburn out of the Second Division into the First.

The next managerial change at Home Park brought BOBBY MONCUR to Plymouth. Moncur had impressive credentials. Formerly a half-back with Newcastle United and Sunderland, he had won 16 caps for Scotland and captained the Newcastle side which won the UEFA Cup in 1969. More pertinently, he managed the Heart of Midlothian side which won the Scottish League Championship in 1980. Unfortunately, even such a pedigree was no guarantee of success for Moncur or for Argyle. Matters came to a head early in the 1983-4 season when 'differences of opinion regarding club policy', as the official statement put it, led to Moncur's dismissal. The decision was taken at a point when Argyle had won only one of their opening six League matches. Ironically, it was announced on the night that the team scored an impressive 4-0 win over Scunthorpe United. The differences of opinion between the board and manager reportedly concerned buying new players and it has been said that Moncur had particularly resisted the directors' pressure to buy John Aldridge from Newport County. If so, then the directors had shown

BOBBY SAXTON

BOBBY MONCUR

JOHN HORE

DAVE SMITH

themselves to be the better judges of a player, as Aldridge's subsequent scoring record for Oxford United and Liverpool has demonstrated.

Within a few days the board reverted to the 'former player' network and announced the appointment of JOHN HORE. After finishing his playing career with Argyle and Exeter City, Hore took Bideford Town to the Western League championship for two successive seasons. In view of his inexperience, he was not immediately awarded a contract but after steering Argyle to their first-ever appearance in an FA Cup semi-final, he was given a two-year contract to run from 1 July 1984. Four months later, John Hore was out of a job, the victim of Argyle's poor start to the season which, at that point, had yielded only one victory in ten games and sent them to 21st place in the table.

Hore's replacement was DAVE SMITH who took up his appointment in December 1984 and within 18 months had succeeded where so many of his predecessors had failed, by restoring Second Division football to Plymouth. A Scotsman, Smith played at full-back for Burnley, Brighton and Bristol City and, after a variety of coaching and assistant manager jobs with Sheffield Wednesday, Newcastle United and Arsenal took charge of Mansfield Town and Southend United, leading both clubs out of the Fourth Division. He was actually out of football and working in insurance when Argyle offered him a contract.

Under Dave Smith, the team's playing style focused on the long ball and the quick break, facets of the game which teams such as Watford and Wimbledon had shown could prove successful. Results that season speak for themselves and Argyle not only won promotion but also, in their first season back in the Second Division, at one point made a fair bid for that elusive First Division place. That they did not succeed was to most supporters, less of a failure than a sign that the prospect of reaching the top flight was within Argyle's reach.

KEN BROWN

In the summer of 1988, however, Smith received an attractive offer to manage Dundee United and returned to his home town. At one point the choice of successor appeared to have fallen on Trevor Francis as player-manager before Argyle turned to KEN BROWN, the former West Ham player who won several majors honours with the Hammers before ending his career with Torquay. Brown had a spell as Bournemouth's trainer-coach before joining Norwich City, first as assistant manager and, from 1980, as manager. He twice took Norwich to Division One and to a League Cup Final victory before falling a victim of boardroom politics. He joined Plymouth after flirting briefly with the vacant job of Shrewsbury Town manager.

Brown decided that the Western League did not give Argyle's youngsters the sort of experience that they need in order to step up into the Football League and this is probably one of the chief reasons why he preferred to recruit seasoned professionals from other clubs in his first season at Home Park.

Discounting on-loan goalkeepers, he had brought six newcomers to Argyle by the end of that disappointing season. Of these, only Mark Stuart could be said to have been an unqualified success. Kenny Brown, David Byrne and Sean McCarthy were not far behind him in value, but Calvin Plummer and Greg Campbell were disappointing. With John Matthews and Mark Smith almost certain to have played their last games for Argyle, the side with which we hope Ken Brown takes the club into the 1990s will very probably contain many new faces.

Argyle Stars

PETER ANDERSON

Peter Anderson played in the same Plymouth Schoolboys side as Reg Wyatt and joined the Argyle two years after Wyatt, from the local side Astor Institute. In those days he was mainly a left winger but also had the ability to switch to the other flank. He soon made his mark with the Reserve team but, if his promise was enough to influence Argyle to transfer Alex Govan to Birmingham City, he was by no means thrust into League football. Indeed, Anderson had to wait a full season to win the place vacated by Govan. Although a broken leg in the 1955-6 season threatened his career, he re-established his place in the following season. He was probably at his best in Argyle's promotion season of 1959-60, when he and his opposite wingman, Harry Penk, frequently switched positions during games in order to confuse opponents. In that same season, he scored a hat-trick in Argyle's sensational 6-4 win at Doncaster. In contrast to Govan — his predecessor on the left wing — Peter Anderson was genuinely two-footed and, whereas Govan preferred the quick, incisive thrust at defences, Anderson tended to weave his way along the touch-line, mixing changes of pace and direction before floating over his centres. Like Wyatt, he moved on to Torquay United when his career with Argyle was over and he was a regular choice for United from 1962 to 1964, during which time he made 77 appearances and scored 18 goals.

	LEAGUE		*FA CUP*		*FL CUP*		*TOTAL*	
	App	*Gls*	*App*	*Gls*	*App*	*Gls*	*App*	*Gls*
1952-53	4	2	0	0	0	0	4	2
1953-54	4	0	0	0	0	0	4	0
1954-55	32	8	1	0	0	0	33	8
1955-56	6	4	0	0	0	0	6	4
1956-57	23	3	0	0	0	0	23	3
1957-58	36	5	3	1	0	0	39	6
1958-59	30	7	3	1	0	0	33	8
1959-60	27	3	1	1	0	0	28	4
1960-61	37	4	0	0	6	1	43	5
1961-62	37	3	2	1	1	0	40	4
1962-63	5	2	0	0	1	0	6	2
	241	41	10	4	8	1	259	46

Peter Anderson appeared for Argyle in the last four games of the 1952-3 season. He scored on his second appearance, a 1-1 draw at Doncaster, and also netted in his third game, when Argyle beat Swansea 3-2 at Home Park.

GORDON ASTALL

'Flash' and 'Cannonball', the names of contemporary comic book heroes and applied to Gordon Astall by supporters during his spell at Home Park, immediately convey the style adopted by this right winger, a style based on pace and power. Astall, who had an extremely strong physique, would storm past defences and either deliver a hard cross at head height to his attacking colleagues, or crash in the type of shot which made his nickname so appropriate. He had another weapon in his attacking armoury: he would take any throw-in awarded to Argyle near the opposition goal-line and those strong arms could hurl the ball from the touch-line, right into the middle of the goalmouth and throw many a defence into confusion. Service with the Royal Marines brought Astall to Plymouth and to Argyle's attention in the late 1940s. He made his Second Division debut on the Argyle right wing in February 1948, two months after signing professional forms for the club. After a bright start, his career seemed to falter for a while and there were times when he looked raw and inexperienced. But Argyle's descent to the Third Division in 1950 saw, among other developments, the rejuvenation of Gordon Astall and it was as a Third Division player that he was selected for the England 'B' side in 1952, the first England honours to come the way of an Argyle player since Herbert Batten played against Australia on the FA's 1925 tour. It was not until he left Home Park, however, that Astall was able to add to those honours. Birmingham City, having already signed Alex Govan in the summer of 1953, moved for the other Argyle winger a few months later. While with the Midlands club, for whom he made over 200 League appearances, Astall won two full England caps, was chosen for the Football League representative side and played in the 1956 FA Cup Final 1956. Like Govan, he returned to the West Country to end his career, although in Astall's case he ended his career with Torquay United, then settled in the Torbay area.

	LEAGUE		*FA CUP*		*TOTAL*	
	App	*Gls*	*App*	*Gls*	*App*	*Gls*
1947-48	14	1	0	0	14	1
1948-49	36	5	1	0	37	5
1949-50	11	0	0	0	11	0
1950-51	30	7	1	0	31	7
1951-52	45	18	1	0	46	18
1952-53	39	10	3	1	42	11
1953-54	13	1	0	0	13	1
	188	42	6	1	194	43

Gordon Astall marked his final appearance for Plymouth with a goal in the 4-0 win over Everton at Home Park in October 1953.

SEPTIMUS ATTERBURY

Septimus Atterbury arrived in Plymouth from Swindon Town in 1907 as a 17-year-old to begin an association with the Home Park club which was to last some 30 years, first as a player, then on the training staff. The greater part of his Argyle days were spent in the Southern League and he was renowned as one of the best full-backs in that competition. Tall and strong, he was to form partnerships with Jack Butler and, later, Moses Russell which ensured that the Argyle management had few worries over that department of the defence. By the time that Argyle had entered the Football League, Sep Atterbury's playing days were nearing an end and he had only one season of Third Division football with the club before joining the training staff and combining those duties with appearances for the Reserves. Even then, he was still considered good enough to be selected for the Southern League representative side. The circumstances of his benefit match in 1921 seem odd to the modern follower of the game. He was awarded the full proceeds of the Reserves' game against Swindon Town in November of that year. Since 7,000 people turned up at Home Park for that game, and contemporary reports seemed to find nothing odd in this, it is to be presumed that the arrangement was completely satisfactory to all parties concerned.

	LEAGUE		*FA CUP*		*TOTAL*	
	App	*Gls*	*App*	*Gls*	*App*	*Gls*
1907-08	35	0	2	0	37	0
1908-09	37	1	3	0	40	1
1909-10	34	5	2	0	36	5
1910-11	34	0	1	0	35	0
1911-12	32	0	1	0	33	0
1912-13	33	0	2	0	35	0
1913-14	31	0	2	0	33	0
1914-15	25	0	1	0	26	0
1919-20	33	0	3	0	36	0
1920-21	30	0	2	0	32	0
	324	6	19	0	343	6

Argyle's 1907-08 Southern League line-up. Back row (left to right): Mr W.G.Cleminson, G.Rowlands (trainer), J.C.Pethick, F.W.Black, J.E.Sutcliffe, C.Clark, W.Horne, J.McCormick, J.Cudlipp, C.Vivian (assistant trainer). Middle row: Mr L.H.Crabb, J.Meager, J.Simmons, A.Beard, S.Atterbury, J.Butler, W.Wake, A.J.Wheaton, T.Haynes, Mr F.Deacon. Front row: R.Stirling, A.Leonard, E.Nugent, W.Ingham, R.Morris, F.Burch, A.Holden.

MICHAEL J. BICKLE

As a milkman with the Co-operative Society, Mike Bickle built up a scoring reputation at two levels — on Wednesday afternoons with Co-op Welfare in the Devon Wednesday League and on Saturdays with St Austell in the South-Western League. Eight goals in six games for Argyle Reserves at the end of 1965 were enough to convince manager Derek Ufton that the centre-forward had something to offer the club. Bickle signed professional in December 1965, was given a first-team chance and ended the season with nine League goals in 17 games, a record on which he could well have improved had injury not prevented his appearance for a few games. The initial promise was to be confirmed and he went on to become the club's leading scorer for the next four seasons. He was not tall but was strongly built and able to withstand the heavier challenges of defenders. Twice he scored four goals in a match for Argyle, against Cardiff in October 1966 and against Torquay on Boxing Day 1969. His period with the club was not one of the most successful in Argyle's history; one can only surmise that, as part of a more successful team, his record would have been even better. He had just over a season with Gillingham after leaving Home Park before an injury forced his retirement from the game.

	LEAGUE		*FA CUP*		*FL CUP*		*TOTAL*	
	App	*Gls*	*App*	*Gls*	*App*	*Gls*	*App*	*Gls*
1965-66	17	9	2	3	0	0	19	12
1966-67	33	13	1	0	1	0	35	13
1967-68	25	10	1	0	0	0	26	10
1968-69	30/3	12	1	0	2	0	33/3	12
1969-70	36/3	18	2/1	0	1/1	0	39/5	18
1970-71	24/3	6	0	0	1	0	25/3	6
1971-72	6/1	3	0	0	1	0	7/1	3
	171/10	71	7/1	3	6/1	0	184/12	74

Mike Bickle managed only three goals for Plymouth Argyle in the FA Cup and they all came on his debut in the competition. Bickle's hat-trick against Southern League club, Corby Town, in the third-round tie at Home Park in January 1965, helped Argyle towards a 6-0 victory. Bickle made another six Cup appearances but never scored again. Nor did he manage a goal in six League Cup games.

The legendary England winger, Sir Stanley Matthews, played at Home Park for Stoke City at the beginning and the end of his illustrious career, a period spanning 30 years. He had just passed his 18th birthday when he came to Plymouth in 1933 and was 48 when Stoke came in 1963. In between, he played on the ground for Blackpool in a friendly match in 1954.

SAMMY BLACK

How, one wonders, would some modern coaches assess Sammy Black? He would probably get low marks for his work-rate, his support to the defence and his heading ability (on occasions he had been known to dodge the high ball). At the other end of the scale, he must deserve top marks for his ball-control and match-winning capabilities. There was not much of him — 5ft 6½ins, 11st and size-4 boots — but he certainly lived up to the nickname of the 'Mighty Atom' which was sometimes bestowed on him. Bob Jack discovered him playing for Scottish junior side, Kirkintilloch Rob Roy, on the other side of Glasgow from his Motherwell birthplace. He arrived at Home Park in the summer of 1924, stepped into the League side soon after the start of the new season and was a permanent fixture in the team until he left the club in 1938 — virtually at the end of his career — to join Queen's Park Rangers. As he played but a handful of games for QPR before the outbreak of the war and then returned to Plymouth to work at the Dockyard, it can be reasonably claimed that only his Argyle career matters. It was the partnership which he formed on the Argyle left wing with Jack Leslie which older followers of the game remember. There might be legitimate differences of opinion about whether, as individuals, Leslie and Black have been the best in their positions during Argyle's history. There is little argument that they have never been bettered as a pairing. Argyle used Black mainly on the left wing but he also played a number of games in the inside position and on the opposite flank. It did not matter a great deal where he played because his control was so good and he was such a beautiful striker of the ball with either foot. Time and again, Sammy Black would find the back of the net with a shot from an angle which other players would have considered impossible. So precisely and so often did he place his shots just inside a post, that the story went around that he aimed for the stanchion supporting the net. Only Black could say how much deliberation went into that shooting. It is more likely that he had a natural gift, amounting almost to genius, for doing the correct goalscoring thing. Naturally, he was the idol of the Home Park crowd and a rumour in the 1920s that he might be transferred to another club led to public meetings and a 'Sammy Must Not Go' campaign. Sammy did not go and his aggregate totals of goals and appearances still stand as an Argyle record. There was just one other fault in Sammy which might earn him a black mark in the coach's book. He hated taking a cold shower following a hot one after a match.

	LEAGUE		*FA CUP*		*TOTAL*	
	App	*Gls*	*App*	*Gls*	*App*	*Gls*
1924-25	38	13	1	0	39	13
1925-26	38	19	1	0	39	19
1926-27	36	10	1	0	37	10
1927-28	29	16	1	0	30	16
1928-29	41	10	4	3	45	13
1929-30	37	21	4	4	41	25
1930-31	42	20	1	0	43	20
1931-32	35	15	2	0	37	15
1932-33	41	13	1	0	42	13
1933-34	41	12	1	0	42	12
1934-35	34	7	2	1	36	8
1935-36	37	15	2	1	39	16
1936-37	11	5	0	0	11	5
1937-38	10	0	0	0	10	0
	470	176	21	9	491	185

TONY BOOK

In the summer of 1964 many eyebrows were raised in the football world when it was announced that Argyle's new manager, Malcolm Allison, had signed a player from the club which he had just ceased to manage, Bath City. The doubts concerned not so much the ability of Tony Book, but his years. He was 28 and that seemed too advanced an age to begin a career in the Football League, especially for a player who had spent the best of his playing days combining bricklaying with appearances for his home-town club in the Southern League. The doubters were soon to be silenced. Book adapted quickly to the Second Division and began to turn in displays which marked him as the most complete full-back to wear the club's colours since World War Two. He had all the attributes required for the position: clean tackling, quick recovery, coolness under pressure and an eye for attacking possibilities. But even better things were in store for Book. By the summer of 1966, Allison had joined Joe Mercer at Manchester City and he persuaded the Maine Road club that, even at the age of 30, Tony Book still had something to offer the First Division. His move to Manchester City coincided with the most successful period in that club's post-war history and before his career closed, Book had won League Championship, FA Cup, League Cup and European Cup-winners' Cup medals and in 1969 had been joint Footballer of the Year (with Derby's Dave Mackay). Not a bad record for a player who had spent years in the Southern League. It is tempting to speculate on what other honours might have come Tony Book's way had he begun his League career earlier. An England cap is not at all beyond the realms of possibility and he might well have challenged George Cohen closely for a place in that World Cup England team of 1966. Both with Argyle and with Manchester City, Malcolm Allison had the imagination to see the potential in Tony Book and the courage to act upon his judgement.

	LEAGUE		*FA CUP*		*FL CUP*		*TOTAL*	
	App	*Gls*	*App*	*Gls*	*App*	*Gls*	*App*	*Gls*
1964-65	40	2	2	0	7	0	49	2
1965-66	41	1	2	0	1	0	44	1
	81	3	4	0	8	0	93	3

The transfer of Ray Bowden to Arsenal in 1933 was obviously an unpopular move with supporters. It was conceded that the player was ambitious and it would have been wrong to stand in his way but manager Robert Jack put the matter in a different perspective when addressing the shareholders' meeting that year: "Circumstances demanded the transfer at this moment. It does not do any good to the directors to hide the fact that we were just at the end of our tether as far as finances go. I did not know anybody else to go in order to get money. Our bank overdraft had to be reduced and it was reduced by the transfer of Bowden which we agreed to because we had lost our chance of going up."

RAY BOWDEN

Ray Bowden was 17 and playing for Looe when he came to Argyle's attention. After all, a player who scores over 100 goals in a season for his club, even in junior football, can hardly be overlooked. There was no questioning his talent but there was some doubt in the mind of Robert Jack as to whether Bowden's rather frail physique would stand the rigours of League football. So his introduction to the Third Division was a gradual one. One game in the spring of 1927 — when the critics shook their heads and agreed that the doubts about his strength were probably justified — was followed by two more a year later, games which produced four goals for Bowden and led those critics to wonder whether there was something about the frail young Cornishman after all. By the following season, there was no doubt at all. Ray Bowden was in the Argyle team on merit and, although he never repeated that ratio of two goals per game, as in 1928, his scoring record over the seasons was enough to satisfy most managers. It was certainly enough to attract the attention of Arsenal. Officials of the London club made three trips to Plymouth before they could persuade Ray Bowden to forsake the Argyle forward line which included Jack Leslie and Sammy Black. In fact, Bowden was out of the Argyle side, nursing an injury, when he finally signed for Arsenal in March 1933, for £5,000, then a record for the Gunners and obviously a record incoming fee for Plymouth. He had toured Canada with an FA team in 1931, while an Argyle player. Just over a year after leaving Argyle, he won the first of the six England caps he was awarded with Arsenal. He subsequently played for Newcastle United and returned to Plymouth when his playing days were over to open a sports outfitters' shop.

	LEAGUE		*FA CUP*		*TOTAL*	
	App	*Gls*	*App*	*Gls*	*App*	*Gls*
1926-27	1	0	0	0	1	0
1927-28	2	4	0	0	2	4
1928-29	29	21	3	2	32	23
1929-30	28	18	1	2	29	20
1930-31	33	11	1	0	34	11
1931-32	29	20	2	0	31	20
1932-33	23	9	1	0	24	9
	145	83	8	4	153	87

LEN BOYD

	LEAGUE		FA CUP		TOTAL	
	App	Gls	App	Gls	App	Gls
1946-47	16	4	0	0	16	4
1947-48	37	0	1	0	38	0
1948-49	25	1	1	0	26	1
	78	5	2	0	80	5

Len Boyd has a special place in Plymouth Argyle's history as the first player to be transferred out of Home Park for a five-figure fee, when Birmingham City paid £17,500 for his services in January 1949. It was a measure of the rapid advance made by the young player who, only 18 months earlier, had been regarded as a promising inside-forward but not ready to hold down a place in Argyle's first team. This view of his abilities changed at the start of the 1947-8 season when team reshuffling cast him in the role of a right-half. From that point Boyd's confidence and performance improved rapidly and the big clubs were soon beginning to take notice. Birmingham City were impressed by his display in a match at St Andrew's at the beginning of 1948 but waited another year before making their offer to Argyle in negotiations which were kept secret from the Press and the public until the transfer had been completed. As if to underline Argyle's folly in releasing Boyd, Argyle lost their very next match, 6-1 at Fulham. Birmingham, meanwhile, were to prosper. Boyd was eventually appointed captain and led the Blues to the Second Division championship in 1955 and an FA Cup Final at Wembley the following year. While with Birmingham, Boyd won an England 'B' cap although he never graduated to full international honours. A Londoner, born at Plaistow on 11 November 1923, Boyd had played in the same West Ham Schools team as Ken Green, later to be a teammate at Birmingham, but the outbreak of war seemed to have ended his dreams of becoming a professional. Then an Argyle supporter spotted him playing in Naval football in Malta towards the end of the war and recommended him to the Home Park club. A tall, well-built player with a long stride, Boyd liked nothing better than bringing the ball out of defence into attack, driving the forwards before him with one of those imperious waves which were to become his trademark. Defensive duties sometimes had to take second place when Boyd was on one of those forays but he was always a player who sought to impose himself on a game rather than simply be carried along by the flow of a match.

Len Boyd made his League debut for Argyle in a 4-1 defeat at Filbert Street, Leicester, in October 1946. He made his final appearance for the club in a 2-2 draw at Blundell Park, Grimsby, on New Year's Day, 1949.

DAVID BURNSIDE

	LEAGUE		FA CUP		FL CUP		TOTAL	
	App	Gls	App	Gls	App	Gls	App	Gls
1967-68	12	0	0	0	0	0	12	0
1968-69	42	9	0	0	3	0	45	9
1969-70	15	1	2	1	1	1	18	3
1970-71	36	5	1	0	1	0	38	5
	105	15	3	1	5	1	113	17

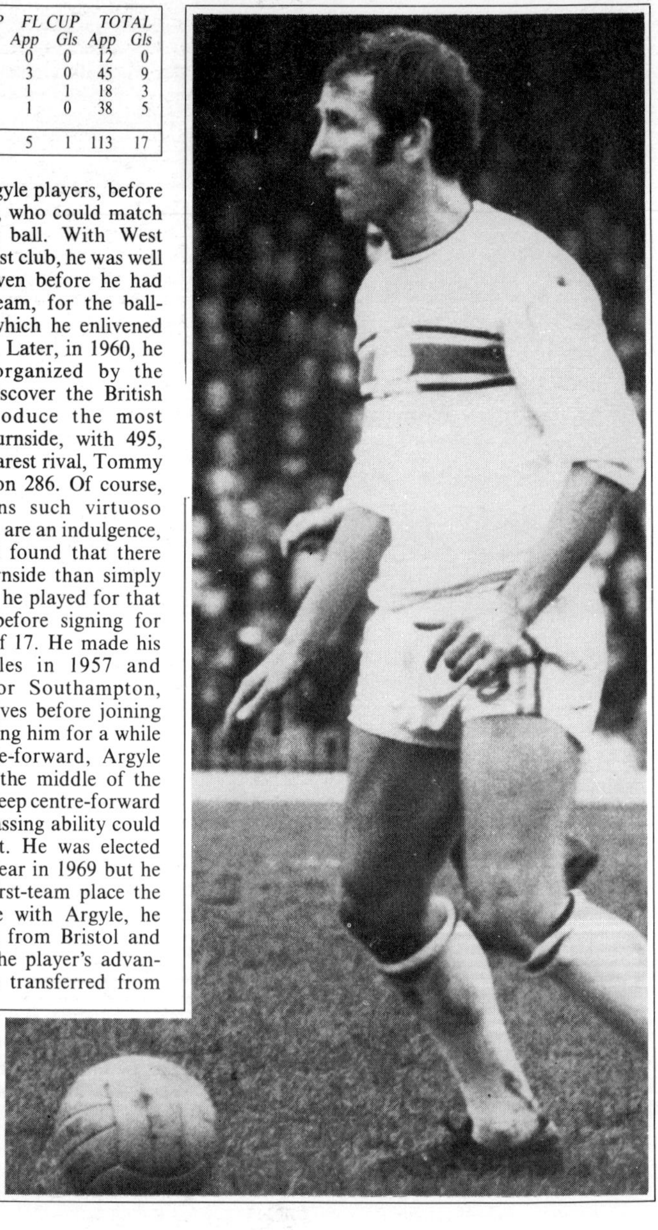

There have been few Argyle players, before or after David Burnside, who could match him for skill with the ball. With West Bromwich Albion, his first club, he was well known to the crowd, even before he had appeared in the first team, for the ball-juggling displays with which he enlivened the intervals at matches. Later, in 1960, he won a competition, organized by the *Sunday Despatch* to discover the British player who could produce the most consecutive headers. Burnside, with 495, was way ahead of his nearest rival, Tommy Harmer of Tottenham on 286. Of course, under match conditions such virtuoso displays, even if possible, are an indulgence, but the clubs he served found that there was more to David Burnside than simply ball-tricks. Bristol-born, he played for that city's schoolboys side before signing for West Brom at the age of 17. He made his debut for the Throstles in 1957 and subsequently played for Southampton, Crystal Palace and Wolves before joining Argyle in 1968. After using him for a while as a conventional inside-forward, Argyle switched Burnside into the middle of the attack, playing him as a deep centre-forward where his control and passing ability could be put to good account. He was elected Argyle's Player of the Year in 1969 but he lost both form and a first-team place the following season. While with Argyle, he commuted to Plymouth from Bristol and it therefore seemed to the player's advantage that he should be transferred from Home Park to Bristol City. However, he remained at Ashton Gate for only three months before moving again, to Colchester United where he spent one season and ended his League career.

WILF CARTER

Every so often (not often enough in the view of most Plymouth supporters) a player will reach the peak of his personal form while playing for Argyle. This category very definitely includes Wilf Carter, who had never been a regular member of the West Bromwich Albion side when he decided to accept Jack Rowley's offer and go to the West Country in 1957. The move was a tonic for both the player and the club. In his first season at Home Park, Carter scored 32 goals and went on to head the list of goalscorers for five seasons. During his Argyle career, he registered six hat-tricks in addition to the five goals he scored against Charlton Athletic at Christmas 1960, a feat which has never been equalled by any other Argyle player in a League match to date. Despite his scoring record, he was not the most technically accomplished player to wear an Argyle shirt. But he had the priceless asset of being able and willing to shoot at every opportunity and from all angles, and the hours of practice he put in during training paid handsome dividends. Of medium height, slim and lithe, he had quick reflexes and could spot the chance which presents itself for only a split second. Born in Wednesbury, Carter joined West Bromwich in 1951 and was playing in the first team by the time he was 18, but he never established an undisputed place in the side. He was therefore not at all reluctant to try his luck with a new club when Rowley made his approach. Carter's least successful season with Argyle was his last when, in a struggling side, it seemed that the old scoring touch had deserted him and he even had a nine-match spell at left-back. He left Argyle the following summer and had two unremarkable seasons with Exeter City before dropping out of League football and joining Bath City in the Southern League.

	LEAGUE		*FA CUP*		*FL CUP*		*TOTAL*	
	App	*Gls*	*App*	*Gls*	*App*	*Gls*	*App*	*Gls*
1957-58	44	26	3	6	0	0	47	32
1958-59	45	22	3	3	0	0	48	25
1959-60	36	22	1	0	0	0	37	22
1960-61	33	24	1	0	7	4	41	28
1961-62	34	19	2	1	1	0	37	20
1962-63	31	14	0	0	0	0	31	14
1963-64	30	7	1	0	2	0	33	7
	253	134	11	10	10	4	274	148

JACK CHISHOLM

If football teams had no place for big, central defenders, it is difficult to see how Jack Chisholm could ever have made a living as a professional footballer. He was not agile enough for a goalkeeper, not fast enough to be a full-back or winger, he lacked the stamina for a midfield player and his ball control was certainly not good enough for a forward. In fact, from a medical point of view, he ought not to have been playing at all. Cartilages had been removed from both his legs, which buckled under the weight of his powerful torso. If, as has been often asserted, all the best players are bow-legged, Jack Chisholm must have been among the greatest of all time. When he lumbered on to the field — and the verb is chosen advisedly — it was easy to see why he had attracted the name 'Jumbo'. As a footballer, Chisholm had many limitations but he wisely played within them, rarely venturing outside the penalty-area and using his height to head away crosses and his bulk to frustrate any opponent foolhardy enough to bear down on the Argyle goal. Small, quick-moving or tall, strong opponents sometimes got the better of Jack Chisholm but not many could claim to have made a habit of so doing. Furthermore, he was the sort of team captain who insisted on having his way and woe betide the colleague who was not giving of his best in Jumbo's eyes. He first signed for Tottenham Hotspur at the age of 17 but the war years took him away from football to be a Guardsman and when it was over he was unable to get a regular place in the Spurs side. In December 1947, he was transferred to Brentford, moved to Sheffield United in March 1949 and in December of the same year went to Argyle for £14,000. The Pilgrims were relegated to the Third Division that year but they were back in the Second within a couple of seasons, Chisholm's drive as captain having had much to do with their success. The injuries which had dogged him throughout his career got the better of him by 1954 and he was forced to retire from the game. Only a professional medical opinion could determine how much his retirement was hastened by the consumption of alcohol but Chisholm never concealed his fondness for liquor. Unfortunately, he was not a success as a publican after his retirement. Jumbo was too prone to proclaim drinks on the house and to neglect his accounts. Even in his playing days, Chisholm was always a personality as well as a player and was well known in the city outside the circle of Argyle followers. Now, following his death and the decision to put an oil painting of him in the sponsors' lounge at Home Park, he has entered the realms of legend. Former England captain Billy Wright, whose Wolverhampton side played against Argyle three times in the FA Cup in the early 1950s, has been quoted as saying that the Wolves likened Jumbo to a bearded pirate captain urging on his Argyle crew during those games. It is a piece of imagery quite consistent with the impression which many of us retain of Jack Chisholm. Unfortunately, it is not altogether accurate. That neatly-trimmed beard which many people associate with Jumbo was a relatively late adornment to the Chisholm visage and not grown until over a year after Argyle's last encounter with Wolves. Like all legends, that of Jack Chisholm promises to get bigger and better.

	LEAGUE		*FA CUP*		*TOTAL*	
	App	*Gls*	*App*	*Gls*	*App*	*Gls*
1949-50	21	0	2	0	23	0
1950-51	39	0	4	0	43	0
1951-52	46	1	1	0	47	1
1952-53	36	1	3	0	39	1
1953-54	33	0	2	0	35	0
	175	2	12	0	187	2

JACK COCK

A Hayle birthplace makes Jack Cock, beyond any doubt, a Cornishman and his selection for England in 1920 made him the first Cornishman to play for his country at soccer. Yet there is more than a suspicion that his association with the Duchy was a purely technical one and there is no evidence that he had any soccer links with the West Country until his arrival at Home Park in 1925. Before World War One, Jack Cock was an amateur with Brentford but had signed professional forms for Huddersfield Town before joining the Army. He won the Military Medal while serving in France and, being posted to London in 1917, resumed his contacts with Brentford as a guest player. At one stage during the war he was reported killed in action but emerged to rejoin Huddersfield after the conflict had ended and within months was selected for his first England game, scoring on his international debut, against Ireland. Chelsea paid Huddersfield what was then a huge sum of £2,500 for him soon afterwards and he won the second of his two caps while with the London club. Again he scored, this time helping England recover from 4-2 down to beat Scotland 5-4 at Hillsborough in April 1920. Everton was his next stopping place in 1923 but after scoring 31 goals in 72 League and FA Cup games for the Merseyside club, he was on his travels again, this time nearer his birthplace as Bob Jack made the double signing from Everton of Jack Cock and Freddie Forbes. The Plymouth manager had seen Cock as the very man to aid Argyle's attempts to reach the Second Division and the centre-forward did not disappoint him, averaging nearly a goal per game during his spell with the Home Park club. Cock, however, was to gain his Third Division championship medal, not with Argyle, but with Millwall whom he joined in 1927, and with whom he continued his scoring exploits. His total of 77 goals for the Lions was to remain a record until Derek Possee overtook it in 1973. Cock later managed Millwall. A fitness fanatic, Jack Cock frequently had to be forced to stop training and his superb physical condition made him a menace to all defences. With the ball, Cock wasted little time in getting into scoring positions; without it, he challenged and harried the opposition. When his playing days were over, his smart appearance and fine tenor voice led him into a brief career on the stage. Indeed, in 1930 he was signed up to appear in a film.

	LEAGUE		*FA CUP*		*TOTAL*	
	App	*Gls*	*App*	*Gls*	*App*	*Gls*
1924-25	10	7	0	0	10	7
1925-26	35	31	1	1	36	32
1926-27	39	32	1	1	40	33
1927-28	6	2	0	0	6	2
	90	72	2	2	92	74

Southend United must have been heartily sick of the sight of Jack Cock in 1925. In the last game of the season he scored a goal in Argyle's 6-0 win over Southend at Home Park. And in the first game of the following season, against the same opposition on the same ground, he netted a hat-trick as Plymouth won 6-2. Corcoran, Black and Leslie also scored in both games.

LEIGH COOPER

Everyone with the best interests of Argyle at heart must hope that the broken leg which Leigh Cooper suffered at Portsmouth in the autumn of 1988 will mean only a temporary set-back to a League career which began ten years ago. At the age of 28, Cooper might reasonably be expected to be at the peak of his ability. He is one of a number of fine products of the Argyle youth policy of the 1970s — Kevin Hodges, Martin Hodge, John Uzzell and Gary Megson were others — and he still looks very much like the teenager who made his League debut in December 1979. In his early seasons with the club he was regarded mainly as a midfield player and the conversion to full-back, where he has been playing more recently, did not come until 1985-6. Not all supporters are convinced that this is Cooper's best position, some arguing that his tackling is not decisive enough for a full-back. Whatever the justice of that view, there can be no dispute that his style of full-back play eschews the merely destructive aspects of defensive work and from his position he is constantly seeking to distribute the ball to good effect. This is not to imply that he is seriously lacking in true defensive qualities. He is fast enough to match the pace of most opponents and he is a persistent tackler with good powers of recovery. His contribution to Argyle's fortunes over the past decade has been noteworthy. But for that incident at Fratton Park, Cooper would surely have been very close to completing 400 first-team games for Argyle by the end of the 1988-9 season. As it is, he can already look back to a Third Division promotion campaign in 1985-6 and to captaining Argyle to the FA Cup semi-finals in 1983-4.

	LEAGUE		*FA CUP*		*FL CUP*		*TOTAL*	
	App	*Gls*	*App*	*Gls*	*App*	*Gls*	*App*	*Gls*
1979-80	14	0	2	0	0	0	16	0
1980-81	28	3	3	0	0	0	31	3
1981-82	43	5	2	0	3	0	48	5
1982-83	45	4	4	0	2	0	51	4
1983-84	43	2	9	0	3	0	55	2
1984-85	19/2	0	2	0	2	0	23/2	0
1985-86	39/1	1	4	2	2	0	45/1	3
1986-87	35	0	2	0	2	0	39	0
1987-88	33/4	0	3	0	2	0	38/4	0
1988-89	15	0	0	0	4	0	19	0
	314/7	15	31	2	20	0	365/7	17

FREDERICK G. CRAIG

	S LEAGUE		F LEAGUE		FA CUP		TOTAL	
	App	Gls	App	Gls	App	Gls	App	Gls
1912-13	4	0	-	-	0	0	4	0
1913-14	10	0	-	-	0	0	10	0
1914-15	24	0	-	-	2	0	26	0
1919-20	40	0	-	-	3	0	43	0
1920-21	-	-	42	0	5	0	47	0
1921-22	-	-	36	0	2	0	38	0
1922-23	-	-	41	0	4	0	45	0
1923-24	-	-	42	0	1	0	43	0
1924-25	-	-	42	0	1	0	43	0
1925-26	-	-	42	0	1	0	43	0
1926-27	-	-	34	3	1	0	35	3
1927-28	-	-	12	1	0	0	12	1
1928-29	-	-	40	0	4	0	44	0
1929-30	-	-	30	1	4	0	34	1
	78	0	361	5	28	0	467	5

For fairly obvious reasons, teams do not normally look to their goalkeeper to take penalty-kicks. There have been exceptions to this rule. Between the wars, Charlton's Sam Bartram was one; Argyle's Fred Craig was another and the entries under 'Goals' in his playing record can be accounted for by his exploits from the penalty-spot. Naturally, the risks involved in such exploits require that the goalkeeper should have an unblemished record from the spot. Fred occasionally missed and, however good the contingency plan executed by the rest of the defence, there was an inevitable period of anxiety as he sprinted back to his goal and the opposition sought to punish him for his effrontery in trying to act out of goalkeeping character. But the occasional dalliances at the other end of the pitch should not be allowed to obscure the fact that Fred Craig was in the Argyle side to stop goals and the tall Scot proved very capable at doing just that. He went to Argyle in 1912, from the Lancashire junior club Larkhill Thistle, when the Argyle goalkeepers were 'Tich' Horne and John Willie Sutcliffe, figures who seem to belong to a very distant past. Craig made his debut for Argyle before World War One, became the regular choice when the war was over, went into the Football League with the club in 1920 and won a Third Division championship medal with Argyle in 1929-30. For much of that season he was also the team captain. He did not go into the Second Division with the team, having been transferred to Barrow before that season opened. A Scottish international cap never came his way but he was selected for an Anglo-Scots XI in 1917. For at least a dozen years, an Argyle side without Fred Craig was an unusual sight and it was perhaps because he knew that his place in the team was safe that Fred used to break the club rules and slip away to the toilet for a half-time smoke.

Fred Craig scored his first penalty goal for Argyle during the 1926-7 season, against Newport County in Plymouth's 4-1 victory at Home Park. The same season he scored in consecutive matches, against Brentford (2-1) and Charlton Athletic (3-1) both at home. His other penalty goals were in the 2-0 win at Crystal Palace in the last game of 1927-8 and at Torquay in 1929-30, when Argyle won 4-3. That final goal came at the beginning of a season when Craig at last won a major honour from the game and he played in the first 30 matches to win a Third Division South championship medal.

GEOFF CRUDGINGTON

Born in Wolverhampton, Geoff Crudgington played for England Schools before joining Aston Villa as a 17-year-old in 1969. But fame with that grand old club eluded him and it was not until he moved to Crewe Alexandra in 1972 that he established himself in the Football League, albeit in one of its lower divisions. Swansea City saw Crudgington as the goalkeeper they needed in their attempt to break out of the Third Division and he played in every match of the 1978-9 season which saw the City promoted to the Second Division. It was, of course, an experience which Crudgington was to repeat with Argyle because when he lost his Swansea place soon after the start of the new season in the Second Division, Argyle — who had sold Martin Hodge — viewed Crudgington as the experienced goalkeeper they needed to replace Hodge. Geoff Crudgington did not let them down. For seven seasons he was the undisputed last line of defence in the Argyle side and it was only the inescapable fact that even goalkeepers cannot go on for ever, that persuaded Argyle to buy Steve Cherry. Now, as Youth Team Manager, he still serves the club, nurturing the new generation of home-grown players.

	LEAGUE		*FA CUP*		*FL CUP*		*TOTAL*	
	App	*Gls*	*App*	*Gls*	*App*	*Gls*	*App*	*Gls*
1979-80	37	0	2	0	0	0	39	0
1980-81	46	0	3	0	2	0	51	0
1981-82	46	0	2	0	4	0	52	0
1982-83	44	0	4	0	2	0	50	0
1983-84	46	0	10	0	4	0	60	0
1984-85	33	0	3	0	2	0	38	0
1985-86	46	0	2	0	2	0	50	0
1986-87	21	0	2	0	2	0	25	0
1987-88	7	0	0	0	2	0	9	0
	326	0	28	0	20	0	374	0

STEVE R. DAVEY

A Plymothian, Steve Davey graduated to first-team football at Home Park via Plymouth Schoolboys and the Argyle apprentice scheme. He signed professional forms for the club in July 1966 and made his first-team debut at the age of 18 the following year, when he also won an England Youth cap. For several seasons he was regarded by the club as a forward but demonstrated his versatility with a successful switch to full-back in 1970, then reverted to a forward position a couple of seasons later. The 1973-4 season marked his most successful spell as a striker. He was second-highest scorer in League games with 12 goals and led the marksmen in the League Cup with seven from six games. How much his absence contributed to Argyle's defeat in the replayed semi-final of that competition can only be a matter for speculation. After leaving Home Park in 1975, for Portsmouth, he had seven more years in League football with Pompey and Hereford United before returning to the West Country to play for Bideford and Liskeard.

	LEAGUE		*FA CUP*		*FL CUP*		*TOTAL*	
	App	*Gls*	*App*	*Gls*	*App*	*Gls*	*App*	*Gls*
1966-67	9/1	3	0	0	0	0	9/1	3
1967-68	20/2	3	0	0	1	0	21/2	3
1968-69	37/1	11	0	0	3	0	40/1	11
1969-70	29/1	5	3	1	1	0	33/1	6
1970-71	29/1	3	1	0	0	0	30/1	3
1971-72	25/1	1	1	0	2	0	28/1	1
1972-73	16/1	9	0	0	1	0	17/1	9
1973-74	42/1	12	3	0	6	7	51/1	19
1974-75	6/2	0	0	0	2	0	8/2	0
	213/11	47	8	1	16	7	237/11	55

GEORGE DEWS

	LEAGUE		FA CUP		TOTAL	
	App	Gls	App	Gls	App	Gls
1947-48	24	2	1	1	25	3
1948-49	39	5	1	0	40	5
1949-50	36	9	2	0	38	9
1950-51	40	17	4	3	44	20
1951-52	44	25	1	0	45	25
1952-53	29	5	3	1	32	6
1953-54	25	8	2	0	27	8
1954-55	20	5	0	0	20	5
	257	76	14	5	271	81

An equable temperament and a capacity for hard work made George Dews a firm favourite with Argyle supporters in the decade following the resumption of League football after World War Two and the club's decision to finally transfer him brought a storm of protest. But the year was 1955, Dews was 34 years old and Argyle had just experienced relegation. It was no time for sentiment and so a loyal servant left Argyle to spend one season with Walsall before disappearing from the League scene. A Yorkshireman, from Ossett, Dews signed for Middlesbrough during the war years and was a fairly regular member of their First Division side in 1946-7. It was, therefore, something of a surprise that both player and club were willing to listen to an approach from Argyle in the autumn of 1947. But, for a joint fee of £11,000, Dews and his veteran full-back teammate, Bobby Stuart, made the long journey south-west. Stuart was already nearing the end of his League career and left Home Park after only one season but Dews went on to make over 270 League and FA Cup appearances for Argyle, scoring over 80 goals. His most successful season was the 1951-2 promotion campaign when he contributed 25 League goals. As an athlete, Dews was quite definitely in the marathon rather than the 100 metres class. He was slightly round-shouldered and moved around the field as though he were carrying an enormous burden. Perhaps that was really so, for Plymouth Argyle certainly had cause to be grateful on many occasions, for the way he made himself available to pick up a clearance, set up an attack and then move into the opposing goalmouth ready for a scoring chance. In later years, Jack Chisholm was jocularly to maintain that the supporters' description of Dews as 'Gentleman George' was thoroughly undeserved, that George was pushing away with the best of them in the middle of the field. That may have been so; certainly Chisholm was nearer the action than those on the terrace or in the stand. But Chisholm never saw Dews commit a vicious or malicious act, although he was often greatly provoked. He just kept plodding on. Dews never completed a full season with Argyle because, at the beginning and end of each campaign, the club released him to play first-class cricket for Worcestershire. Many Argyle supporters followed the fortunes of the Midlands county for no other reason than George Dews, a hard-hitting middle-order batsman and a fine fielder in the deep, played for them.

NEIL DOUGALL

When Argyle paid Birmingham City £13,000 for Neil Dougall in the spring of 1949, they believed that they were recruiting a specialist inside-forward. As later events were to show, however, they were in fact adding to their staff one of the most versatile footballers ever to pull on an Argyle shirt. He wore them all, except for numbers one and 11, and in the days when numbers mattered, he could soon adapt to the role that each demanded. For ten years, it was Dougall to whom Argyle turned when they had a problem position to fill. Injuries and the indifferent form of the team meant that Dougall failed to shine in the early months of his career at Home Park but in the winter of 1950 he hit top form after being switched to right-half, following an injury to George Taylor, and there was even talk of him adding another Scottish cap to the one he had won with Birmingham. Another switch, back into the attack, followed as Argyle faltered in their first season back in the Third Division South but he was at right-half again in the following promotion season, although injuries meant that he had to share the position with Tony McShane. Wing-half was to remain the position in which Dougall showed his best form but before his career at Home Park had ended he was to give the club service for lengthy spells in such diverse positions as left-back and outside-right. Fast on the ground and possessing the intelligence to spot an opening, adept at the short pass or the long, probing ball, he had all the skills. He also had one of the fiercest shots of any player on the books, although his scoring tally was not particularly impressive. Dougall, who was born in Falkirk on 7 November 1921, came from a famous Scottish footballing family and both his father and an uncle were professionals. He continued to serve Argyle in a number of posts — manager, coach and trainer — after his playing career ended.

	LEAGUE		*FA CUP*		*TOTAL*	
	App	*Gls*	*App*	*Gls*	*App*	*Gls*
1948-49	3	0	0	0	3	0
1949-50	30	0	2	0	32	0
1950-51	42	6	3	0	45	6
1951-52	26	3	1	0	27	3
1952-53	41	4	1	0	42	4
1953-54	27	0	0	0	27	0
1954-55	17	1	1	0	18	1
1955-56	29	2	1	0	30	2
1956-57	26	9	1	0	27	9
1957-58	13	0	2	0	15	0
1958-59	20	1	3	0	23	1
	274	26	15	0	289	26

PAT DUNNE

Argyle supporters quickly made up their minds that they approved of Pat Dunne, voting him Player of the Year in his first full season with the club. Dublin-born Dunne, whose full-back brother, Tony, had a distinguished career with Manchester United, failed to break into English football with Everton as a 17-year-old and so returned to his native Ireland. It was Manchester United who persuaded him to re-cross the Irish Sea in 1964 and secured his transfer from Shamrock Rovers. He was United's first-choice goalkeeper in 1964-5 but then lost his place to Harry Gregg and, with United having signed Alex Stepney at the beginning of the 1966-7 season, he could see little prospect of first-team football at Old Trafford. While with United, even when he was in the Reserves, he won five caps for the Republic of Ireland. He arrived at Home Park in February 1967 for £5,000 and was almost immediately plunged into Argyle's fight to stave off relegation, a struggle which culminated in the club's drop to the Third Division in 1967-8. Nevertheless, Pat Dunne's personal efforts in the attempt to stay in the Second Division were recognized by supporters who voted him their choice for the Player of the Year trophy. Cynics might suggest that the Argyle goalkeeper that season had a greater number of opportunities to shine than most of his colleagues, but that was not the way the supporters viewed the matter. He continued as first-choice goalkeeper for two more seasons but carelessness then began to creep into his performances and Jim Furnell was signed from Rotherham to replace him. Dunne had maintained his connections with Irish football and returned to the Republic to play for Shamrock Rovers.

	LEAGUE		*FA CUP*		*FL CUP*		*TOTAL*	
	App	*Gls*	*App*	*Gls*	*App*	*Gls*	*App*	*Gls*
1966-67	11	0	0	0	0	0	11	0
1967-68	41	0	1	0	1	0	43	0
1968-69	46	0	1	0	3	0	50	0
1969-70	38	0	2	0	2	0	42	0
1970-71	16	0	1	0	1	0	18	0
	152	0	5	0	7	0	164	0

Pat Dunne made his League debut for Plymouth Argyle against Huddersfield Town in February 1966 and was on the wrong end of a 3-2 scoreline. Indeed, he had to wait until his eighth League appearance for the club before being on the winning side. That came in a 4-0 victory over Blackburn at Home Park on 15 April. The following season, as Argyle dropped into the Third Division, Dunne missed only one game and he was ever-present in the side that finished fifth in 1968-9.

In his earlier career with Manchester United, Dunne made 66 first-team appearances, 13 of them in European football. His most memorable European campaign for United came in 1964-5 when he was an ever-present as the Old Trafford club reached the Inter-Cities Fairs Cup semi-final before losing a play-off to Ferencváros.

GEORGE W. FOSTER

George Foster, a Plymothian, signed for Argyle in July 1972 and, after graduating through the Football Combination side and playing intermittently for the first team for four seasons as a teenager, finally established himself as a regular choice centre-back in 1977-8. He held that position for four seasons until 1981-2 when, with Argyle preferring a combination of Chris Harrison and Forbes Phillipson-Masters, he tried his luck with other Devon clubs, first to Torquay and then to Exeter City on loan. He played his first game for Exeter against Argyle in December 1981. Transfers then took him to the East Midlands, first to Derby County and then to Mansfield Town, for whom he has already made over 200 League appearances, during which he captained the successful Freight/Rover Trophy team at Wembley in 1986-7. Standing under 6 feet and weighing 12 stones, Foster is slightly on the small side for a central defender but he is a vigorous footballer, crowding opposing strikers and rarely permitting them room in which to move. In 1989 he became player-manager at Mansfield.

	LEAGUE		*FA CUP*		*FL CUP*		*TOTAL*	
	App	*Gls*	*App*	*Gls*	*App*	*Gls*	*App*	*Gls*
1973-74	2/3	0	0	0	0	0	2/3	0
1974-75	0	0	0	0	0	0	0	0
1975-76	9/7	1	0	0	1	0	10/7	1
1976-77	14/1	2	0	0	0	0	14/1	2
1977-78	46	3	4	0	3	0	53	3
1978-79	28	0	1	0	4	0	33	0
1979-80	46	0	2	0	6	0	54	0
1980-81	46	0	3	0	2	0	51	0
1981-82	10	0	0	0	3	0	13	0
	201/11	6	10	0	19	0	230/11	6

JIM FURNELL

Jim Furnell was already approaching the veteran stage and there were flecks of grey in his hair when Ellis Stuttard signed him for a bargain fee of £2,500 in December 1970. Yet the goalkeeper was to prove that there was still a great deal of footballing life left in him and he was approaching his 39th birthday before he decided that the time had come to retire. In the meantime, younger players, such as Peta Balac and Milija Aleksic, had developed their skills and were ready to replace him. Born in Clitheroe, Lancashire, Jim Furnell's first League club was Burnley. He then joined Liverpool but played second fiddle there, first to Bert Slater and then Tommy Lawrence, and it was not until Arsenal signed him in 1963 that his career really began to flourish. In just under five years at Highbury, he made nearly 150 League appearances and was their goalkeeper in the 1968 League Cup Final. He moved to Rotherham in 1968 and spent two years there before responding to Argyle's offer. Strongly built and decisive in his actions, he was a key figure in the team's League Cup run of 1973-4 and was voted Player of the Year by supporters in 1970-71, his first full season with the club.

	LEAGUE		*FA CUP*		*FL CUP*		*TOTAL*	
	App	*Gls*	*App*	*Gls*	*App*	*Gls*	*App*	*Gls*
1970-71	30	0	0	0	0	0	30	0
1971-72	23	0	1	0	2	0	26	0
1972-73	28	0	4	0	0	0	32	0
1973-74	43	0	3	0	7	0	53	0
1974-75	46	0	4	0	2	0	52	0
1975-76	13	0	0	0	0	0	13	0
	183	0	12	0	11	0	206	0

JIMMY GAULD

Although the name of Jimmy Gauld will always be tarnished in football because of his role at the centre of a bribes scandal which shook the game in the early 1960s, it is possible to consider his Plymouth Argyle career in isolation from those later, unsavoury, events. Indeed, many Argyle supporters still remember him best as the forward whose headlong dashes into the heart of opposing defences were among the highlights of the 1958-9 promotion season. A Scot, born in Aberdeen, Gauld first attracted the attentions of Football League clubs while playing for Waterford in the League of Ireland. Charlton Athletic gave him his chance in the First Division and he rewarded them with 21 goals in 47 appearances. It was a record which encouraged Everton to seek his transfer but his year with the Merseyside club was less productive and Jack Rowley was able to persuade Everton to release him in the autumn of 1957. Rowley wanted to fit Gauld into the team he was rebuilding to restore Plymouth to the Second Division. Gauld's spell at Home Park was relatively brief but dramatic. His attacking methods were simple. Once in possession of the ball he would take the shortest route to goal. The simplicity, however, was deceptive, for that style demands a high degree of skill in controlling the ball at speed and Jimmy Gauld had the knack of either retaining the ball when challenged, or else quickly regaining it if momentarily dispossessed. In that promotion year, Wilf Carter converted a number of penalties awarded after defenders had resorted to bringing down Gauld in full flight. He was, of course, an individualist but few supporters were troubled by his disregard for playing colleagues. The important factor was that goals were flowing and matches were being won. Gauld left Home Park for Swindon Town in August 1959 and later played for St Johnstone and Mansfield. It was with these clubs that he became involved in the corruption which eventually earned him a prison sentence.

	LEAGUE		*FA CUP*		*TOTAL*	
	App	*Gls*	*App*	*Gls*	*App*	*Gls*
1957-58	19	4	3	2	22	6
1958-59	45	21	4	1	49	22
	64	25	7	3	71	28

ARCHIE GORMAN

There was a touch of another Scottish half-back, Billy Bremner, in the way Archie Gorman played. Small but wiry, tenacious and indefatigable, he gave Argyle excellent playing service in the 1930s and was still fit enough to help shore up a disjointed side when the club resumed in the 1945-6 season. Born in Lochore, Gorman arrived at Home Park from Edinburgh City in 1931. The story is told of the newcomer being introduced to an Argyle director, who apparently expected to measure footballing value in pounds and inches. The director could hardly conceal his disappointment with the new addition to the staff: "Oh, he isn't very big is he? Still, never mind." For the next eight years, right up to the outbreak of World War Two, Archie Gorman was to demonstrate that height and weight are not all that matters in a footballer. On both flanks of the half-back line he was a regular choice and was one of the players who played in every match in the short-lived 1938-9 season. He was there again when the season was transformed into a regional league (27 out of 28 games) and was one of the former stalwarts Argyle called when an interim League was set up in 1945-6. After 15 years of professional football, however, Gorman's playing days were nearing an end and he was appointed assistant trainer to Bill Harper at the start of the 1946-7 season, a position he was to hold until the early 1950s.

	LEAGUE		*FA CUP*		*TOTAL*	
	App	*Gls*	*App*	*Gls*	*App*	*Gls*
1931-32	1	0	0	0	1	0
1932-33	19	0	1	0	20	0
1933-34	32	1	2	0	34	1
1934-35	41	1	2	0	43	1
1935-36	29	0	1	0	30	0
1936-37	38	0	2	0	40	0
1937-38	40	0	1	0	41	0
1938-39	37	0	1	0	38	0
1939-40	3	0	0	0	3	0
	240	2	10	0	250	2

Archie Gorman managed two goals for Plymouth Argyle. The first came in a 3-3 draw against Bury at Home Park in October 1933, the second helped Argyle to a 2-2 home draw against Bradford in September 1934.

ALEX GOVAN

Alex Govan was just 17 when, in the summer of 1946, he left his Glasgow home to seek fame and fortune as a professional footballer in Plymouth. He was not the only young Scot to arrive at Home Park with similar ambitions that summer but he was the only one to make the grade. In Glasgow he had been playing for Bridgeton Boys' Club; in Plymouth, after only six appearances in the Football Combination, he was selected to make his Second Division debut, against Coventry City. But that early promise was not to be sustained and over the next five years he made only sporadic appearances in the first team. In the modern game, with its pressures for instant success, it is just the sort of situation where patience is lost and club and player part company. Fortunately for Argyle, a different mood then prevailed and by the autumn of 1950 Govan, with National Service in the RAF behind him, was ready to take his place in the side. By then he had switched from inside-left to the wing and it was as specialist outside-left that he became a regular first-teamer for three seasons, winning a Third Division South championship medal in 1952. Govan was transferred to Birmingham City that summer and won a Second Division championship medal in 1955 as well as playing for the Blues in the 1956 FA Cup Final. He moved to Portsmouth in March 1958 but, six months later, was back in the green of Argyle, in time to assist the club to another climb from Division Three. He was now entering the final stage of his career and was by no means a regular choice, yet he proved a valuable asset and a useful deputy to the regular wingers, Harry Penk and Peter Anderson. Govan, who retired in 1960, was obviously left-footed and relied on his speed over short distances to get past defenders, usually attacking them on the outside. He was not a prolific scorer for Argyle (although he had a much better record with Birmingham) but his ability to whip the ball across goal from the goal-line set up many scoring chances for his colleagues.

	LEAGUE		*FA CUP*		*TOTAL*	
	App	*Gls*	*App*	*Gls*	*App*	*Gls*
1946-47	2	0	0	0	2	0
1947-48	2	0	0	0	2	0
1948-49	2	0	0	0	2	0
1949-50	1	0	0	0	1	0
1950-51	35	8	3	1	38	9
1951-52	35	9	1	0	36	9
1952-53	33	10	3	2	36	12
1958-59	20	6	1	0	21	6
1959-60	12	2	0	0	12	2
	142	35	8	3	150	38

During his Birmingham City days, Alex Govan proved quite a marksman. He made a goalscoring debut on the opening day of the 1953-4 season and was second-highest scorer the following season when Birmingham won promotion. In 1956-7 he scored five hat-tricks, a club record for a winger in a single campaign.

BILL HARPER

A place for Bill Harper in this gallery of Argyle's personalities is prompted not so much by his playing record for the club, which was not exceptional, but by his general service, spanning 50 years and including the roles of player, trainer, groundsman, laundryman and general factotum. Bill Harper's greatest football deeds were accomplished before he arrived in Plymouth. With Hibernian, he won nine Scottish caps and was Scotland's undisputed goalkeeper from 1923 to 1925 and he added two more to his collection after Arsenal had taken him south in 1926. Injury cost him a place in the Gunners' side which lost the 1927 Cup Final to Cardiff City, a famous Wembley Final which brought Bill's replacement, Dan Lewis, unwelcome notoriety as the goalkeeper whose fumble led to the only goal of the game and which took the Cup out of England for the first time. After a spell playing football in the United States, Harper returned to Arsenal and won a League Championship medal with the London club in 1930-31. After losing his Arsenal place to Frank Moss, he agreed to join Plymouth Argyle in December 1932 and he made his Argyle debut at Home Park on Boxing Day of that year, when Argyle celebrated with a 5-1 win over Bury. On Christmas Day, he had saved two penalties while appearing for the Reserves. He was the regular choice goalkeeper until 1934, when Harry Cann regained the position and the following year, Harper was appointed trainer in succession to Tommy Haynes, who had just retired from the job. His reappearance on the field was confined to a few games in 1938-9 and in 1940 when the club had difficulty in completing a team for their fixtures in the wartime South-West Regional League. These latter figures have not been added to his playing record alongside. Apart from Argyle, Bill Harper always had a warm spot for Arsenal. Soon after joining Argyle, he made a nostalgic return to Highbury as Argyle's goalkeeper in the fourth round of the Cup and it was Arsenal who again supplied the opposition when Argyle rewarded his services with a testimonial match in 1972. With his death in April 1989 at the age of 92, a great character passed from the Argyle scene but those using the training pitch, Harper's Park, will always have cause to remember the Scottish goalkeeper.

	LEAGUE		*FA CUP*		*TOTAL*	
	App	*Gls*	*App*	*Gls*	*App*	*Gls*
1931-32	20	0	2	0	22	0
1932-33	37	0	0	0	37	0
1933-34	14	0	2	0	16	0
1934-35	4	0	0	0	4	0
1938-39	3	0	0	0	3	0
	78	0	4	0	82	0

Bill Harper appeared in 11 out of the 12 full internationals played by Scotland between March 1923 and April 1926. He made his debut in a 1-0 win over Ireland in Belfast and bowed out in Scotland's famous 1-0 victory over England at Old Trafford. Indeed, Harper made four appearances against England and was never on the losing side. The only defeat he suffered on the international scene was a surprise 2-0 reverse at the hands of the Welsh at Cardiff in February 1924. Harper was blamed for the second goal, when he dropped the ball. Overall, though, these were great days for Scottish international football and Bill Harper enjoyed his share of the glory.

CHRIS HARRISON

Some players, either by virtue of their position in the team, their style of play or some particular physical characteristic, always get noticed. At the other end of the scale are those, equally if not more competent than their more flamboyant colleagues, whom the headlines constantly pass by. Chris Harrison comes into that latter category, his playing style and general demeanour on the pitch usually being the antithesis of the qualities which constitute the star footballer. Yet seven different managers (Waiters, Kelly, Allison, Saxton, Moncur, Hore and Smith), with different views on how the game ought to be played, all recognized Harrison's qualities. At 5ft 9in and 11st, he was not built to be the sort of defender who relies on physical strength to combat opposing forwards. Cover, anticipation, interception — these were the hallmarks of his game, allied to an ability to bring the ball quickly under control and use it to advantage. Born in Launceston, he became an Argyle apprentice at 18, in October 1974, and made his Football League debut at right-back in the last match of the 1975-6 season. In the next two seasons he alternated between a midfield and full-back role before apparently settling at full-back in 1979. For five seasons, he scarcely missed a game, either at full-back or as a central defender, a position he began to fill regularly from August 1981 onwards, and it was that position he occupied during Argyle's successful FA Cup run of 1983-4. The era in which he was an automatic choice for the team ended the following season when newcomers Adrian Burrows, Gerry McElhinney and Clive Goodyear were all in contention for the same positions. After some 300 games, Harrison lost his regular spot midway through that season and, in recognition of his past services, Argyle gave him a free transfer in order for him to get another club more easily. He had not long to wait. Swansea City offered him a contract and he played another 100 games for the Welsh club over three seasons, first as a central defender then at full-back, linking up in that side with another former Argyle Cornishman in Colin Sullivan. While with Swansea, he was also recognized as the team's penalty specialist and there were ten penalties in his 15 goals for the side. In the summer of 1988, with a free transfer from Swansea, he returned to the West Country and joined Saltash United.

	LEAGUE		*FA CUP*		*FL CUP*		*TOTAL*	
	App	*Gls*	*App*	*Gls*	*App*	*Gls*	*App*	*Gls*
1975-76	1	0	-	-	-	-	1	0
1976-77	21	1	1	0	1	0	23	1
1977-78	29/2	1	4	0	0	0	33/2	1
1978-79	22/2	1	0	0	1	0	23/2	1
1979-80	41	1	0/1	0	6	1	47/1	2
1980-81	45	0	3	0	1	0	49	0
1981-82	43	1	2	0	3	0	48	1
1982-83	41	1	3	0	2	0	46	1
1983-84	44	0	9	0	4	0	57	0
1984-85	28/5	1	3	0	3	0	34/5	1
	315/9	7	25/1	0	21	1	361/10	8

Chris Harrison's best season for Plymouth Argyle in terms of appearances was the 1980-81 campaign when he missed only one match, the 3-1 home win over Rotherham United on 6 December, when he was injured and John Uzzell stepped in. During the FA Cup run of 1983-4, Harrison's only absence was against Barking in the second round.

JACK HILL

The oldest generation of supporters generally agree that no finer centre-half ever pulled on an Argyle shirt than Jack Hill. Although dubbed 'Ginger' by most of his colleagues, a little more obscurely, some, with army backgrounds in World War One and memories of map reading, christened him 'Hill 60' in recognition of his height. To be 6ft 3in tall is a great advantage for a centre-half but it was not for his height alone that Jack Hill captured the attention. In 1920, he came into the side early in the season and after only a few matches had come to dominate the defence. 'What a wonder that youngster Hill is.' was the reported talk on the terraces as he strode about, doing 'the work of three men' as one observer liked to put it. Jack Hill was strong, as the local boxer with whom he got into a fight in a public-house brawl and was knocked out, could testify. But it was not simply for blunting the opposition attacks that he developed a reputation. His distribution, usually swinging the ball out to either wing, was first-class and he was not averse to moving forward to test the opposing goalkeeper. Not all of the ten goals he scored during his three seasons with Argyle came from set pieces. He scored three goals in his first Argyle season, an apparently trivial contribution. But when it is realized that the team failed to score in 20 matches that season, there was cause to be grateful to Jack Hill. Naturally enough, the big clubs began to take note and it was Burnley, then a First Division club, who prised him away from Argyle with a £6,000 offer in 1923. Three years later, he was in the England side and from 1926 to 1929 he made 11 appearances for his country, captaining the side on a number of occasions. After leaving Burnley, he went on to play for Newcastle United and Hull City. Hill had been a miner, playing for his native Durham City, when Robert Jack went north to persuade him to become a professional in an episode which would be incredible if transposed to the present. The manager offered Hill £5 a week wages; the player demanded £6. Robert Jack then suggested that they should spin a coin to decide on the sum. Hill agreed, lost, but accepted the luck of the toss with good grace.

	LEAGUE		*FA CUP*		*TOTAL*	
	App	*Gls*	*App*	*Gls*	*App*	*Gls*
1920-21	28	3	4	0	32	3
1921-22	37	4	2	0	39	4
1922-23	37	3	4	0	41	3
	102	10	10	0	112	10

KEVIN HODGES

The man who wins the Player of the Year award in his club's promotion season, when all the members of the team may be presumed to be close to their top form, clearly possesses some extra qualities. It was not simply for the fact that he was leading scorer that season that Kevin Hodges received the honour. It was for the consistency and all-round endeavour of his performances. 'A manager's dream' was how Dave Smith described him. Hodges was born in Bridport and that probably accounts for the fact that when Argyle reached the FA Cup semi-final in 1984, motor-coaches from Bridport, carrying passengers who sported Argyle favours, were amongst those converging on Villa Park. (Perhaps some enterprising statistician can discover how many natives of Bridport have appeared in an FA Cup semi-final?) Bridport's nearest League club is Bournemouth and the teenage Hodges first linked up with his 'local' side. But when economy measures forced Bournemouth to abandon their youth policy, he joined Argyle as an apprentice. That was in 1976 and he became a member of the side of that season which won the South West and Wales Youth Cup and included Mike Trusson, John Uzzell, Martin Hodge and Gary Megson amongst its members. Leigh Cooper was also an apprentice at the same time and gained first-team status the season after Hodges had made his League debut in 1978-9. His early games with Argyle were at right-back, but his qualities of good control of the ball at speed, a facility for wriggling past opponents and an ability to take up and capitalize on scoring opportunities, all pointed to his greater value in a forward position. For nine seasons, he was an almost automatic choice for the team, but in 1988-9 he was not at the peak of his form. At times, newcomers Calvin Plummer and David Byrne were both preferred to him and there is a significant figure in Hodges' statistics; he made nine substitute appearances, more than in any other season since he gained a place in the side. By the end of 1988-9, Kevin Hodges' total appearances had reached 468. Only Sammy Black has played more games for the club and, given a return to form, Hodges is still young enough to overtake the legendary Black and become the first Argyle player to make 500 appearances for the club.

	LEAGUE		*FA CUP*		*FL CUP*		*TOTAL*	
	App	*Gls*	*App*	*Gls*	*App*	*Gls*	*App*	*Gls*
1978-79	11/1	0	0	0	0	0	11/1	0
1979-80	41/3	5	2	1	4	0	47/3	6
1980-81	39/2	5	3	0	2	0	44/2	5
1981-82	46	11	2	0	4	0	52	11
1982-83	46	11	5	1	2	0	53	12
1983-84	41/2	4	10	1	4	0	55/2	5
1984-85	45	10	2	0	4	0	51	10
1985-86	46	16	4	0	2	0	52	16
1986-87	33/2	5	3	0	2	0	38/2	5
1987-88	35/2	6	3	0	2	0	40/2	6
1988-89	23/8	1	3	0	1/1	0	27/9	1
	406/20	74	37	3	27/1	0	470/21	77

JOHN HORE

John Hore's style of play was as reliable and unpretentious as the name suggests. Many spectators might well leave a match, not having noticed the contribution made by the curly-haired, ruddy-faced Cornishman, moving around in the heart of the defence, always alert to threatening danger, always ready to cover for a beaten colleague. Managers recognized his worth, however, and after totalling nearly 400 League appearances for Argyle, he had four more seasons and nearly 200 League appearances for Exeter City. Born in St Austell, Hore was discovered playing for East Cornwall Schools, signed for Argyle at the age of 17 and was given his first League chance by Malcolm Allison, when he played at left-back against Northampton Town at the end of the 1964-5 season. From the following season until the 1975-6 season, he was an almost automatic choice in defence, usually in the middle line but in later seasons at full-back and it was in that latter position that he mainly served Exeter City. His return to Home Park as manager is covered in another section of this book.

	LEAGUE		*FA CUP*		*FL CUP*		*TOTAL*	
	App	*Gls*	*App*	*Gls*	*App*	*Gls*	*App*	*Gls*
1964-65	1	0	0	0	0	0	1	0
1965-66	27/1	0	0	0	1	0	28/1	0
1966-67	25	1	1	0	0	0	26	1
1967-68	39	0	0	0	1	0	40	0
1968-69	33/5	2	1	0	3	0	37/5	2
1969-70	45	0	2	0	2	0	49	0
1970-71	46	3	1	0	1	0	48	3
1971-72	45	3	1	0	2	0	48	3
1972-73	44	4	4	0	1	0	49	4
1973-74	43	4	3	0	7	0	53	4
1974-75	33/1	0	4	0	2	0	39/1	0
1975-76	12	0	0	0	3	0	15	0
	393/7	17	17	0	23	0	433/7	17

Argyle have little experience against foreign sides but in 1933 they entertained the Austrian Cup and League winners, First Vienna, at Home Park. The match was drawn 1-1, Melaniphy scoring for Argyle and Wortman for the visitors. The teams were:

PLYMOUTH ARGYLE: Harper; Bland, Rae, Mackay, McKenzie, Gorman, Grozier, Bowden, Melaniphy, Leslie, Black.

FIRST VIENNA: Horeschafsy; Rainer, Schmaus, Kaller, Hofman, Machu, Brosenbauer, Adelbrecht, Sobotka, Wortman, Schonwetter.

~ ~

Another memorable encounter took place in March 1973 when Argyle defeated the Brazilian club Santos, who included the famous Pelé, 3-2. Dowling, Rickard and Hinch scored for Argyle, Pelé and Edu for Santos. The teams were:

PLYMOUTH ARGYLE: Furnell(Aleksic); Provan, Sullivan, Hore, Saxton, Hague, Dowling, Rickard, Hinch(Davey), Latcham, Welsh.

SANTOS: Claudio; Alberto, Murias, Hermes, Leo, Marcal, Jair, Brecha(Pitico[Vicente]), Alcindo, Pelé, Edu.

DAVID JACK

David Jack belongs to that group of players who have graced the scene at Home Park all too briefly and found fame after leaving Argyle. In more modern times, one can recall Tommy Briggs, never selected for a League match and given a free transfer by Argyle but who broke scoring records with the clubs he subsequently served. In David Jack's case, his departure from Plymouth was occasioned both by his own skill and also by a feeling that the manager's son did not always get the fairest of treatment from the crowd. David, the son of Robert Jack, was born in Bolton when his father was playing for the local Wanderers and when Robert Jack became Argyle's manager in 1910, he naturally brought the boy south with him. During World War One, he guested for Chelsea, who would have liked to have signed him, but Argyle had first call on his services. He became a regular choice in the first post-war season, when Argyle were playing in the Southern League, and had completed only 14 Football League appearances the following season when Bolton Wanderers persuaded Argyle to part with him for £3,000. Jack, the manager, had no doubts about releasing Jack, the player. Years afterwards, he advised a young local player that he should leave his home town if he wanted to make his mark as a player, citing the example of his own son. Jack played for Bolton in the 1923 and 1926 FA Cup Finals and was again at Wembley with Arsenal in 1930 and 1932. Arsenal, seeking a replacement for the legendary Charlie Buchan, paid Bolton a record fee for David Jack in 1928. By that time he was a regular choice for England and won a total of nine caps for his country. When the Arsenal offer came along, it was to Robert Jack in Plymouth that David turned for advice. Tall, slim and graceful in his movements, his skill with the ball was described by the former Arsenal player Bernard Joy: "He dribbled as though the ball was magnetized to the flow of his body." David Jack also had the distinction of being the first player to score in a Wembley Cup Final. All in all, the small group who could not appreciate his value to Argyle did the club a great disservice.

	S LEAGUE		*F LEAGUE*		*FA CUP*		*TOTAL*	
	App	*Gls*	*App*	*Gls*	*App*	*Gls*	*App*	*Gls*
1919-20	31	7	-	-	3	0	34	7
1920-21	-	-	14	3	0	0	14	3
	31	7	14	3	3	0	48	10

Four pairs of brothers have played for Argyle in the Football League. The first were the sons of manager Robert Jack with Rollo following his brother David into the team in the early-1920s. A third brother, Donald, did not get beyond the Reserves but later had League experience with Bolton. Bob and Dave Thomas had a brief, but very successful, scoring partnership with the club in the late-1940s and they were followed by the Langman brothers in the 1950s. In recent seasons, the Welsh-born Darren and Jason Rowbotham have appeared in the side although neither really established himself. At one stage the Argyle staff included identical twins. Local players Bob and Geoff Warren, centre-half and centre-forward respectively, joined the club in 1946. Bob played a few Second Division games but Geoff played only for the Reserves or 'A' teams.

BARRIE S. JONES

	LEAGUE		FA CUP		FL CUP		TOTAL	
	App	*Gls*	*App*	*Gls*	*App*	*Gls*	*App*	*Gls*
1964-65	36	4	2	2	5	0	43	6
1965-66	36	2	2	1	1	0	39	3
1966-67	26	3	1	0	1	0	28	3
	98	9	5	3	7	0	110	12

Malcolm Allison's team-building policy when he was appointed manager in 1964 was generally on a modest scale; Sykes and Dwyer for small fees, Book and Sanderson from the Southern League, Nicholas, Hore, Piper and Reynolds were youngsters already on the club's books. But for one player he apparently threw caution to the winds and committed the club to what was then its highest-ever payment, £45,000, to Swansea Town for their winger Barrie Jones. It was Jones' exceptional ball-control which Allison was seeking to incorporate into his team plans. Given the right conditions and the right service from his teammates, Barrie Jones could make even the most experienced full-backs look inept. The *Matches to Remember* section contains an account of one such afternoon at Swindon. But any team-planning which cast Jones in the role of goalgetter started with the wrong assumption. The two which he scored at Swindon that season and the brace which he had earlier registered in the home match against Derby were very much exceptional. In the three seasons he spent at Home Park, his seasonal goals' total never reached double figures. He had gained seven Welsh caps with Swansea, his home club, before joining Argyle and he won seven more with Cardiff City, whom he joined in March 1967, but for some reason, the fair-haired little winger was virtually ignored while with Plymouth and only one cap, in 1965, then came his way.

PAT JONES

It seems almost superfluous to praise the consistency of a player who made over 400 appearances for Plymouth Argyle and did not miss a single League match in five of the 12 seasons he spent with the club. Yet the adjectives 'consistent' and 'reliable' invariably attach themselves to Pat Jones, the Plymouth-born player who monopolized the number-three shirt at Home Park during that period. Born on 7 September 1920, he made his League debut in the first post-war season and began a career in which he experienced relegation, promotion and relegation again, retiring just before Argyle regained their Second Division place in 1959. He had first worn Argyle's colours before the war, turning out for the 'A' team before military service in the Devonshire Regiment ended his football ambitions for the duration. Signing as a professional in March 1947, Jones had made only nine appearances in the Football Combination side before being given his first-team chance. It was more his demeanour than his physique — he stood only 5ft 7ins tall and weighed 10st 7lbs — which presented a formidable barrier to opponents. Although an impassive character, he played each game with a fierce determination and could match most wingers for speed. He also knew the exact moment at which to launch a tackle and would almost always sweep the ball away from his opponent, once he had decided to go in. If he had a weakness it was that the quality of his passing did not match the rest of his game. Yet that slightly hunched, unsmiling figure at the heart of Argyle's defence, blunting the aspirations of many an attacker, compensated for any deficiencies in moving the ball forward. Pat Jones also had a distinction which may be unique among professional footballers, that of wearing a rugby scrum cap on the soccer pitch. It happened in the 1951 FA Cup game against Wolverhampton Wanderers. Jones, suffering a cut head, had been forced to leave the field. In modern football he would have been substituted but no such concession was then available so he returned to the field, his wound bandaged and the scrum cap giving added protection. He continued to give an immaculate display.

	LEAGUE		*FA CUP*		*TOTAL*	
	App	*Gls*	*App*	*Gls*	*App*	*Gls*
1946-47	3	0	0	0	3	0
1947-48	42	0	1	0	43	0
1948-49	42	0	1	0	43	0
1949-50	42	0	1	0	43	0
1950-51	46	0	4	0	50	0
1951-52	46	0	1	0	47	0
1952-53	42	0	3	0	45	0
1953-54	37	0	2	0	39	0
1954-55	18	0	0	0	18	0
1955-56	39	1	1	0	40	1
1956-57	44	1	2	0	46	1
1957-58	24	0	0	0	24	0
	425	2	16	0	441	2

Pat Jones had to wait until his tenth League appearance for Argyle before being on the winning side. By then, Argyle had conceded 26 goals, a run eventually relieved by a 1-0 victory over Barnsley at Home Park.

GEORGE KIRBY

For a player whose career total of League goals was 120, George Kirby had an uncharacteristically barren spell in his early career with Argyle. He did not score his first goal until his 14th game for the club, by which time the natives were beginning to get restless and enquiring what was the value of a centre-forward who could not find the net. By the end of that season, Kirby had only two goals to show for his 17 appearances. Matters were to improve in the following two seasons, however, and his record then was one of which any self-respecting striker would have been proud. It was certainly enough to attract Southampton's attention and they handed over a £17,000 cheque to Argyle for his services in the autumn of 1962. George Kirby soon rewarded his new club for their faith and in one game that November he scored three goals in four minutes. As a player who could regularly score (that early Argyle period being an exception), George Kirby was in constant demand and never seemed to spend longer than a couple of seasons with any of the five clubs who engaged him after he left Plymouth. He also had a spell in North American football before retiring from the League scene in the late 1960s. Liverpool-born Kirby started his professional career with Everton and had a few months with Sheffield Wednesday before being signed by Argyle as part of a double deal including Jimmy McAnearney. At 6ft and 12st, he was of a build to make his presence felt in any opposition goalmouth and strong and fearless enough to pursue vigorously any scoring chances which came his way.

	LEAGUE		*FA CUP*		*FL CUP*		*TOTAL*	
	App	*Gls*	*App*	*Gls*	*App*	*Gls*	*App*	*Gls*
1959-60	17	2	0	0	0	0	17	2
1960-61	33	18	1	0	7	1	41	19
1961-62	35	16	2	0	1	0	38	16
1962-63	8	2	0	0	0	0	8	2
	93	38	3	0	8	1	104	39

Plymouth Argyle line-up of the 1959-60 season, George Kirby's first with the club. Back row (left to right): J.S. Williams, Robertson, Fulton, Barnsley, Fincham, Newman. Front row: Anderson, Carter, Kirby, McAnearney, Wright.

NEIL LANGMAN & PETER LANGMAN

The good news for Argyle supporters listening to the BBC's *Sports Report* on the evening of 27 February 1954, was that local player Neil Langman had scored two goals on his Second Division debut for Argyle at Goodison Park. The bad news was that the visitors had been beaten 8-4 after having notched a convincing 4-0 win over Everton at Home Park earlier in the season. Such was the bitter-sweet introduction to League football experienced by the Bere Alston lad with the physique and face of a heavyweight boxer, one week after his 22nd birthday. Langman was to provide another headline-attracting feat later that season with a hat-trick at Derby in an unexpected 4-1 win for Argyle and by the end of the season had registered nine goals in as many League games. But although he was to score three more hat-tricks during his Argyle career (against Liverpool in 1956, Coventry in 1957 and Reading in 1957), Neil Langman never quite became the scoring sensation hoped for at Home Park although his record of 50 League goals in 128 League games for his next League club, Colchester United, is respectable to say the least. Curiously, both Neil Langman and his elder brother, Peter, played their last League games for Argyle on the same day in November 1957. Peter had been on the clubs' books as a centre-half two years before Neil joined the staff, both brothers having started their careers with Tavistock. It was not until the end of the 1954-5 season, however, that Peter Langman made his League debut and although he held his place at centre-half for virtually the whole of the following season, that was the period in which Argyle were relegated and a large number of reputations were dimmed. With Reg Wyatt taking over the first-team berth, Peter Langman returned to reserve-team football and left the club for Southern League Weymouth Town in 1958.

NEIL LANGMAN

	LEAGUE		*FA CUP*		*TOTAL*	
	App	*Gls*	*App*	*Gls*	*App*	*Gls*
1953-54	9	9	0	0	9	9
1954-55	17	5	1	0	18	5
1955-56	20	9	0	0	20	9
1956-57	32	17	2	1	34	18
1957-58	19	9	0	0	19	9
	97	49	3	1	100	50

PETER LANGMAN

	LEAGUE		*FA CUP*		*TOTAL*	
	App	*Gls*	*App*	*Gls*	*App*	*Gls*
1954-55	15	0	0	0	15	0
1955-56	34	0	1	0	35	0
1956-57	38	0	2	0	40	0
1957-58	3	0	0	0	3	0
	90	0	3	0	93	0

The Langman brothers' final appearance for Argyle was in the 2-0 defeat at Griffin Park, Brentford, on 9 November 1957. Argyle ended the season third in Division Three South.

JACK LESLIE

Jack Leslie, the *Football Herald* asserted in 1930, is "known throughout England for his skill and complexion". The Leslie skill would probably still attract admiration in today's game; the complexion would probably go unremarked, this term being an oblique reference to the fact that Jack Leslie was then a footballing rarity, a black player. Jack Leslie's father was a Jamaican but Jack himself was a Londoner born in Canning Town, and Argyle discovered him playing for Barking. In fact, Argyle were so impressed with Barking that they promptly signed three of their players (Frank Richardson and Alf Rowe being the others). Jack Leslie, enticed by the photographs of Plymouth and the surrounding area, arrived at Home Park in 1921. Richardson went straight into the first team and straight into the headlines for his scoring feats, but Leslie and Rowe had to wait a little longer for their first-team chances. How odd now to recall that when Leslie made his Argyle debut, on the left wing, the Press verdict was that he was no adequate substitute for the man he replaced, Billy Baker. Nowadays few can recall Baker, while Jack Leslie's name lives on, not least for the partnership which he formed with Sammy Black on the Argyle left flank. With two such players, both able to create and take goal openings, it was no wonder that Argyle had such a cutting edge to their attack in that period. Leslie's career with Argyle did not exactly match that of Black; he both started and finished earlier but together they were a peerless combination. On one occasion during his Argyle career, Robert Jack was informed that Leslie had been chosen for England. Club, player and city were all rejoicing but the celebrations proved to be premature. No formal confirmation of the choice was received and the only conclusion which could be drawn was that the selection had been withdrawn because the national selectors had discovered that Leslie's father was West Indian. Jack Leslie established his reputation with Argyle at inside-left but there were many good footballing judges who maintained that he was the best centre-half on the club's books. Certainly, when moved to that position to cover for an injury to another player during the course of a game, Leslie produced performances of the highest standard and occasionally Argyle selected him for that position. They soon realized, however, that such a move was not making the best use of their resources. There were other players on the books who could do a creditable job at centre-half but there were not many who could fill Jack Leslie's boots when goalscoring was required. Jack Leslie retired from the game in 1934 and, after a spell as a publican in Cornwall, returned to his roots in East London. After retiring from work as a boilermaker, he got a job with West Ham United, looking after the boots of the star players of the 1970s.

	LEAGUE		*FA CUP*		*TOTAL*	
	App	*Gls*	*App*	*Gls*	*App*	*Gls*
1921-22	9	0	0	0	9	0
1922-23	6	3	1	0	7	3
1923-24	17	5	0	0	17	5
1924-25	40	14	1	0	41	14
1925-26	40	17	1	0	41	17
1926-27	33	14	1	0	34	14
1927-28	41	15	1	0	42	15
1928-29	41	20	4	1	45	21
1929-30	32	8	4	0	36	8
1930-31	38	8	1	0	39	8
1931-32	41	20	2	1	43	21
1932-33	33	4	1	1	34	5
1933-34	11	2	0	0	11	2
1934-35	1	1	0	0	1	1
	383	131	17	3	400	134

Playing for, or supporting, Argyle was considered by many to be a deeply unpatriotic act in 1914 as is illustrated by the attitude expressed in this letter to the Western Morning News *which had decided to ignore the team's activities:*

"Sirs,

You have set a fine example when your directors decided to take no notice of football contests. At a time like this when we are fighting for our very existence, the seeking of pleasures is not in good taste."

JIMMY LOGAN

	S LEAGUE		F LEAGUE		FA CUP		TOTAL	
	App	Gls	App	Gls	App	Gls	App	Gls
1919-20	35	1	-	-	3	0	38	1
1920-21	-	-	40	2	5	0	45	2
1921-22	-	-	12	0	0	0	12	0
1922-23	-	-	24	0	4	0	28	0
1923-24	-	-	33	0	1	0	34	0
1924-25	-	-	42	3	1	0	43	3
1925-26	-	-	24	4	1	0	25	4
1926-27	-	-	26	4	1	0	27	4
1927-28	-	-	21	1	0	0	21	1
1928-29	-	-	6	0	0	0	6	0
	35	1	228	14	16	0	279	15

Jimmy Logan arrived at Home Park from Cowdenbeath in 1919 and had one season with Argyle in the Southern League before tasting Third Division football with his new colleagues the following year. He was virtually the undisputed choice at right-half for six seasons until the arrival of Bob Preston and Norman Mackay finally saw him lose his place. He had left League football for Yeovil Town by the time Argyle won promotion out of the Third Division. At 5ft 9ins and 12st Logan was of only average build but he had tremendous enthusiasm, good control and a hard shot. The latter quite frequently led to him being asked to fill forward positions and there were many followers of Argyle who felt that he was a better player when given an all out attacking role. Put another way, he was sometimes accused of neglecting his defensive duties, leaving gaps at the back in his enthusiasm to be where the ball was. He was awarded the match against Southampton in 1925 as his benefit game.

JAMES McANEARNEY

	LEAGUE		FA CUP		FL CUP		TOTAL	
	App	Gls	App	Gls	App	Gls	App	Gls
1959-60	17	3	0	0	0	0	17	3
1960-61	35	8	0	0	6	1	41	9
1961-62	34	11	2	0	1	0	37	11
1962-63	36	10	1	1	0	0	37	11
1963-64	13	2	0	0	2	1	15	3
	135	34	3	1	9	2	147	37

One of three footballing brothers from Dundee who started their professional careers with Sheffield Wednesday, Jimmy McAnearney was the brains of the Argyle attack in the early 1960s. Slightly built and inclined to be slow, he nevertheless had the ability to find midfield space and to bring his colleagues into the game with one of those 'carpet' passes in which the ball seemed to ripple from his foot. There was no doubt that the Argyle attack never functioned quite so smoothly when McAnearney was absent from the side. Unlike his brother, Tom, who was a regular choice for Sheffield Wednesday for a number of seasons, Jimmy made only sporadic appearances for the Wednesday during eight years with that club and so had everything to gain when he came west with teammate George Kirby in January 1960. The value of the newcomers was not immediately apparent but the following season the inside-forward combination of McAnearney, Carter and Kirby proved to be extremely successful and those three names headed the list of Argyle scorers. If McAnearney's record was not quite so impressive in this respect as the other two, he would certainly have figured prominently in any tally of goal-makers. He left Argyle for Watford in November 1963 and later had a couple of seasons with Bradford City.

NORMAN MACKAY

Norman Mackay had been a player with Aston Villa but dropped into non-League football with the Welsh club Lovells Athletic and was combining football for Lovells with a job selling toffees produced by the company when Argyle paid £200 for his signature in 1927. He started his Argyle career as a forward and made an immediate impact with a hat-trick against Coventry City in his first game for the club. Jimmy Logan was then the regular right-half but the following season he supplanted his fellow Scotsman in the number-four shirt and for six seasons after that was recognized as a wing-half, although he was occasionally restored to the forward line to meet a temporary emergency. He was one of the stalwarts of the side which first brought Second Division football to Plymouth in 1930 and went on to play for four Second Division seasons with Argyle before joining Southend United in 1934. Of medium height and stocky, he was renowned for his energy and terrier-like tackling. 'A hard nut, small but tough' was the brief but expressive description of him by a former clubmate.

	LEAGUE		*FA CUP*		*TOTAL*	
	App	*Gls*	*App*	*Gls*	*App*	*Gls*
1927-28	10	6	0	0	10	6
1928-29	36	4	4	0	40	4
1929-30	30	4	4	0	34	4
1930-31	42	0	1	0	43	0
1931-32	41	0	2	0	43	0
1932-33	35	0	1	0	36	0
1933-34	33	0	2	0	35	0
	227	14	14	0	241	14

Norman Mackay joined Aston Villa from Hibernian but managed only two games for the Midlanders, both in 1923-4, at centre-forward and inside-right respectively. There was stiff competition for forward places at Villa Park in those days, with players like Billy Walker on the books.

FRED McKENZIE

Whether in the centre or on one of the flanks, the name of Fred McKenzie was seldom absent from the Argyle half-back line of the late 1920s and he was one of the leading members of the side which brought promotion to Home Park in 1930. Born in Dundee, McKenzie began his Football League career with Newport County who signed him from the Scottish junior side, Lochee United, in the summer of 1924. Eighteen months later, he was on his way to Plymouth, Newport having been forced to sell him to Argyle because of their critical financial situation. A deterioration in the South Wales economy led to a decline in match attendances and therefore income at the Newport ground, and McKenzie's transfer to Argyle — at a record fee for the Welsh club — helped to ensure the County's survival. Newport's misfortune was Argyle's good luck and McKenzie was a regular Argyle choice for over four seasons. Although not fast, McKenzie was a good footballing half-back, always seeking to use the ball to advantage. In more settled times for the Welsh club, Fred McKenzie returned to Newport for a brief spell in 1934 but it was in Plymouth that he and his family settled when his playing days were over and a son, while at school in Devonport, was selected for England Schools at rugby.

Fred McKenzie came into the Argyle side for the first time against Reading at Home Park in February 1926. He kept his place for the rest of that season, scoring his first goal for the club in a 3-1 home win over Bristol Rovers in April. McKenzie added another goal before the end of the season, chipping in to help Plymouth become the League's leading scorers that season with 107 goals.

	LEAGUE		*FA CUP*		*TOTAL*	
	App	*Gls*	*App*	*Gls*	*App*	*Gls*
1925-26	14	2	0	0	14	2
1926-27	31	5	0	0	31	5
1927-28	42	3	1	0	43	3
1928-29	38	2	4	0	42	2
1929-30	37	1	4	0	41	1
1930-31	16	0	0	0	16	0
1931-32	3	0	0	0	3	0
1932-33	11	0	0	0	11	0
1933-34	11	0	2	0	13	0
	203	13	11	0	214	13

DAVID MacLAREN

Goalkeeping ran in the MacLaren family. Dave was the youngest of three brothers who had League experience in England. He played for Dundee for a season before coming down to England to join Leicester City for about £8,000 in January 1957. He had three seasons in the Midlands as a fairly regular choice before first injury, then the form of a rival in Gordon Banks, lost him his first-team place. Argyle paid £2,500 for MacLaren in the summer of 1960, but he was forced to work hard to gain a place in the League side at Home Park. Geoff Barnsley was the man in possession and he continued as first choice with MacLaren having to be content, for the most part, with Football Combination football. There was a marked physical difference between those two Argyle goalkeepers. Barnsley, at 5ft 10ins and 11st 6lbs, looked slight, even frail and relied on his agility and reflexes to defend his goal. After Barnsley had left Home Park for Norwich City the following summer, MacLaren became the automatic choice. He was four inches taller and over a stone heavier than his predecessor, almost identical in physique to Gordon Fincham, who played in front of him at centre-half, and the two presented a powerful physical barrier to opposition attacks, MacLaren's height and reach enabling him to take charge in the penalty area. He continued as first choice for three more seasons, until January 1965 when Andy Beattie, for whom he had played at Home Park, saw him as the goalkeeper who could help to save Wolverhampton Wanderers' First Division status. Noel Dwyer arrived from Swansea to replace him at Plymouth and MacLaren had two seasons with Wolves and another with Southampton. Ted Bates, then the Saints manager, was obviously not deterred by the fact that MacLaren had once conceded nine goals when playing for Wolves against Southampton. After leaving The Dell, he had a spell in the Southern League with Worcester City and later worked as a coach in Malaysia.

	LEAGUE		*FA CUP*		*FL CUP*		*TOTAL*	
	App	*Gls*	*App*	*Gls*	*App*	*Gls*	*App*	*Gls*
1960-61	11	0	1	0	1	0	13	0
1961-62	40	0	2	0	1	0	43	0
1962-63	28	0	1	0	1	0	30	0
1963-64	29	0	1	0	1	0	31	0
1964-65	23	0	0	0	5	0	28	0
	131	0	5	0	9	0	145	0

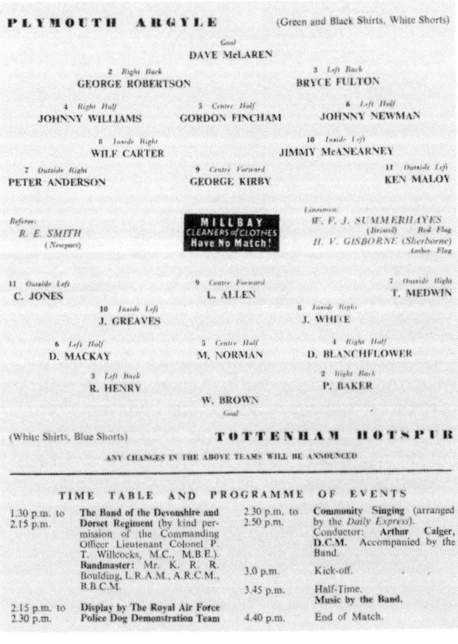

PLYMOUTH ARGYLE (Green and Black Shirts, White Shorts)

Goal
DAVE McLAREN

2 *Right Back* GEORGE ROBERTSON — 3 *Left Back* BRYCE FULTON

4 *Right Half* JOHNNY WILLIAMS — 5 *Centre Half* GORDON FINCHAM — 6 *Left Half* JOHNNY NEWMAN

8 *Inside Right* WILF CARTER — 10 *Inside Left* JIMMY McANEARNEY

7 *Outside Right* PETER ANDERSON — 9 *Centre Forward* GEORGE KIRBY — 11 *Outside Left* KEN MALOY

Referee: *R. E. SMITH* (*Newport*)

MILLBAY
CLEANERS of CLOTHES
Have No Match!

Linesmen: *W. F. J. SUMMERHAYES* (*Bristol*) *Red Flag*; *H. V. GISBORNE* (*Sherborne*) *Amber Flag*

11 *Outside Left* C. JONES — 9 *Centre Forward* L. ALLEN — 7 *Outside Right* T. MEDWIN

10 *Inside Left* J. GREAVES — 8 *Inside Right* J. WHITE

6 *Left Half* D. MACKAY — 5 *Centre Half* M. NORMAN — 4 *Right Half* D. BLANCHFLOWER

3 *Left Back* R. HENRY — 2 *Right Back* P. BAKER

W. BROWN
Goal

(White Shirts, Blue Shorts) **TOTTENHAM HOTSPUR**

ANY CHANGES IN THE ABOVE TEAMS WILL BE ANNOUNCED

TIME TABLE AND PROGRAMME OF EVENTS

1.30 p.m. to 2.15 p.m.	**The Band of the Devonshire and Dorset Regiment** (by kind permission of the Commanding Officer Lieutenant Colonel P. T. Willcocks, M.C., M.B.E.). **Bandmaster:** Mr. K. R. R. Boulding, L.R.A.M., A.R.C.M., B.B.C.M.
2.15 p.m. to 2.30 p.m.	**Display by The Royal Air Force Police Dog Demonstration Team**
2.30 p.m. to 2.50 p.m.	**Community Singing** (arranged by the *Daily Express*). Conductor: **Arthur Caiger, D.C.M.** Accompanied by the Band.
3.0 p.m.	Kick-off.
3.45 p.m.	Half-Time. **Music by the Band.**
4.40 p.m.	End of Match.

Team line-up page from the Argyle-Spurs FA Cup fourth-round tie at Home Park in January 1962. MacLaren had an unhappy day, letting in five goals as Spurs steamed on to retain the Cup.

PAUL MARINER

	LEAGUE		FA CUP		FL CUP		TOTAL	
	App	Gls	App	Gls	App	Gls	App	Gls
1973-74	41	14	3	2	6	1	50	17
1974-75	45/1	20	3	1	2	0	50/1	21
1975-76	38	15	2	0	2	0	42	15
1976-77	10	7	0	0	2	0	12	7
	134/1	56	8	3	12	1	154/1	60

The news from Portsmouth last summer that Paul Mariner had been given a free transfer by the club serves to emphasize how relatively short is life at the top for the professional footballer. To many Argyle supporters, it seems only yesterday that an unknown forward from Lancashire junior football, bearing a strong physical resemblance to the leader of the attack, Jimmy Hinch, arrived at Home Park. Mariner had been noted playing for Chorley by Verdi Godwin, then scouting for the club. A former professional centre-forward, Godwin had not made any great personal impact on the League scene, having played for ten clubs in as many seasons. But he could be relied on to know quality when he saw it. The 19-year-old Mariner came down to Plymouth, accompanied Argyle on a pre-season tour of Cornwall and did enough to convince manager Tony Waiters that he should be offered professional terms. Within weeks of the start of the new season, he had displaced Hinch and become recognized as one of the leading forwards in the Third Division and his scoring partnership with Billy Rafferty did much to ensure Argyle's promotion to the Second Division in 1975-6. It also attracted the attention of the First Division clubs and it was Bobby Robson, then manager of Ipswich Town, who made Argyle an offer which they did not refuse in October 1976. With seven goals in ten League games, Mariner had already demonstrated that he could get goals in the Second Division as well as the Third, and Argyle accepted Ipswich's valuation of the player — £220,000 including two Ipswich players, Terry Austin and John Peddelty. Robson's high opinion of Mariner continued after the former had left Ipswich to become manager of the national team and Mariner was awarded the first of his 35 caps some six months after moving to Ipswich and continued to receive the England call after he had been transferred to Arsenal in February 1984 for £150,000. Opinions about the exact position of Mariner in the ranks of England centre-forwards may legitimately differ although a player who scores 14 times for his country in 35 matches cannot be readily dismissed. There is little doubt, however, that he must rank as one of the best, if not the best ever to wear an Argyle shirt. For Argyle supporters, this is not a case of being wise after the event, of taking into account Mariner's achievements after he had left the club. In 1975, while still on the club's books, he was the popular choice for the number-nine shirt in a competition run by the *Sunday Independent* to choose a 'best-ever' team. The problem of how Mariner rated compared with Maurice Tadman was resolved by selecting both! In this writer's opinion, Mariner had the edge. For a big man, he was surprisingly nimble with his footwork and he had the ability to bring his fellow forwards into the game with deft flicks. His headwork was stronger than Tadman's; the shooting of both was on a par. Perhaps the greatest difference, however, was in confidence. Tadman, I believe, could have been an even better player with more self-confidence but there was always an element of diffidence in his play. Mariner did not appear to suffer any such inhibitions and his thrust and general liveliness served to inspire colleagues around him. The ideal team, as above, would have room for both men.

DUNCAN NEALE

Plymouth Argyle enjoyed good value for the few thousand pounds they paid Newcastle United for the stocky, fair-haired Duncan Neale in the summer of 1963. At half-back, inside-forward, a defensive 'sweeper' and finally as a conventional full-back, Neale, a strong player, could always be guaranteed to put his heart into the game. Born in Worthing, he had been playing for non-League Ilford when Newcastle convinced him that he ought to try his luck as a professional footballer. Neale signed for the Magpies in June 1959 and after making his League debut in the second match of the 1960-61 season, he won a regular place. Altogether, Neale made 98 League and Cup appearances for Newcastle and scored 12 goals. His place in the Gallowgate club's history was marked by the three goals he scored — from wing-half — in an FA Cup match against Fulham in 1961, when United won 5-0. He never produced anything really comparable for Argyle, although the two goals he scored against Portsmouth in 1955 — again from wing-half — came close to it. His League debut for Plymouth was hardly a happy experience, for it came in a 5-0 defeat at Ayresome Park, Middlesbrough, in the opening match of the 1963-4 season. These were times of struggle for Argyle but Neale never failed to give his all. Eventually he saw the club relegated to Division Three in 1968, but the following season he missed only one game as Argyle finished fifth in the table. Neale ended his professional career with Argyle and then joined Plymouth City.

	LEAGUE		*FA CUP*		*FL CUP*		*TOTAL*	
	App	*Gls*	*App*	*Gls*	*App*	*Gls*	*App*	*Gls*
1963-64	10	1	0	0	0	0	10	1
1964-65	36	4	2	0	7	0	45	4
1965-66	8/1	1	0	0	0	0	8/1	1
1966-67	11/3	1	0	0	1	1	12/3	2
1967-68	17	1	1	0	0	0	18	1
1968-69	45/1	0	1	0	3	0	49/1	0
1969-70	14	0	3	0	2	0	19	0
	141/5	8	7	0	13	1	161/5	9

JOHN NEWMAN

Honours came early to Johnny Newman and then proceeded to pass him by for the rest of his playing career. As a Birmingham City player, he won a Second Division championship medal in 1955 and a year later was on the losing side in the FA Cup Final. But there were no similar experiences later when he was with Leicester City and Argyle and it was not until he took up management and led Grimsby Town out of the Fourth Division in 1979 that fortune again smiled on him. A native of Hereford, Newman started as a teenager with the local United, signed for Birmingham City in 1951 and made his League debut for the club a year later. Although he was regarded mainly as a reserve half-back with the City, he did make enough appearances to qualify for a medal as Birmingham took the Second Division championship and it was to Newman that Birmingham turned when injury deprived the regular choice, Roy Warhurst, of a Cup Final appearance at Wembley. Former Argyle favourite, Len Boyd, then the Birmingham captain, was switched to left-half to allow Newman to come in on the right. A search for regular first-team football led him across the Midlands to Leicester City late in 1957 and he had spent two years with that club when Argyle, seeking to strengthen a failing team, made a sudden plunge into the transfer market in January 1960 and emerged with Newman, George Kirby and Jimmy McAnearney. Seven years service with Argyle brought Newman nothing in the way of personal honours but the club certainly benefited from the presence of a player who could fit into any defensive position and be relied on to bottle up the opposition. He was nearing 34 when he left Argyle in 1967 to become Exeter's player-manager and he later graduated to full-time management with Exeter, Grimsby, Derby and Hereford before joining the backroom staff at Notts County.

	LEAGUE		*FA CUP*		*FL CUP*		*TOTAL*	
	App	*Gls*	*App*	*Gls*	*App*	*Gls*	*App*	*Gls*
1959-60	17	1	0	0	0	0	17	1
1960-61	41	1	1	0	6	1	48	2
1961-62	40	1	2	0	1	0	43	1
1962-63	42	2	1	0	1	0	44	2
1963-64	35	0	1	0	3	0	39	0
1964-65	39	4	2	0	6	1	47	5
1965-66	40	0	2	0	1	0	43	0
1966-67	34	0	1	0	1	0	36	0
1967-68	10	0	0	0	1	0	11	0
	298	9	10	0	20	2	328	11

As a manager, John Newman did an excellent job for Grimsby Town, taking a run-down team back to the Third Division. He might have done as well at Derby, but there was no money available for new players. Good public relations was a hallmark of his management and he understood the importance of players getting out into the community.

GORDON NISBET

	LEAGUE		FA CUP		FL CUP		TOTAL	
	App	*Gls*	*App*	*Gls*	*App*	*Gls*	*App*	*Gls*
1980-81	19	0	0	0	0	0	19	0
1981-82	45	3	2	0	4	0	51	3
1982-83	46	2	4	0	2	0	52	2
1983-84	44	4	9	0	4	2	57	6
1984-85	46	2	3	0	4	0	53	2
1985-86	46	0	2	0	2	0	50	0
1986-87	35	3	3	0	2	1	40	4
	281	14	23	0	18	3	322	17

On 12 August 1969 Gordon Nisbet made his Football League debut for West Bromwich Albion in the First Division as an 18-year-old goalkeeper. The Albion lost 3-1 to a Willie Carr hat-trick at Coventry, regular goalkeepers John Osborne and Jim Cumbes took over for the rest of the season between the Albion posts and when Gordon Nisbet next appeared in the Football League — 18 December 1971 — he had been remodelled as a right-back. Apart from returning to goal in emergencies, it was as a right-back that Nisbet was to continue in a professional career lasting 18 years and totalling 622 League appearances. He was to remain Albion's first-choice right-back for three seasons until displaced in 1975 by the arrival of Irish international Paddy Mulligan at the Hawthorns. A year later, he moved on to Hull City and, after four seasons with the Yorkshire club, he was approaching his 200th League game for them when Argyle secured his transfer in December 1980 for £32,000. The rest is well-known to Argyle supporters. Nisbet liked Plymouth and the club; Argyle liked their new acquisition and for the next six and a half seasons, Gordon Nisbet was rarely absent from the Argyle team. As an attacking full-back, he had few equals, certainly not in the Third Division and he was a popular choice in the notional sides which were selected as representing the cream of the Division.

DAVID PHILLIPS

Wegberg, West Germany may seem a curious birthplace for a Welsh international but in David Phillips' case it does not signify that the Welsh selectors were desperately seeking someone with any kind of national qualification but that the young Phillips first saw the world in Germany because his Welsh father was stationed there with the RAF. He joined Argyle in 1981 as an apprentice and had his baptism in League football in the 1981-2 season, first as a substitute and later as a first-choice midfield player. He established himself in the side during the following season but really made his mark in 1983-4 during Argyle's FA Cup run. Wales selected him for three games at Under-21 level in 1984 and he did enough there to convince the national selectors that he was ready for senior honours. As at the end of 1987-8 season, he has won 20 Welsh caps, mostly in midfield but occasionally at full-back. Manchester City and Coventry City, for whom he subsequently played, have both appreciated his versatility and discovered that with the ball running for him David Phillips can take the best of goalkeepers by surprise with the strength of his snap shooting, a facet of his play which older Argyle supporters found reminiscent of Johnny Williams.

David Phillips played in every game for Argyle when they reached the FA Cup semi-final in 1984. Three years later, by now a Coventry player, he went even further in the Cup and was a member of the Sky Blues' team which beat Tottenham Hotspur 3-2 at Wembley in an extra-time thriller.

	LEAGUE		FA CUP		FL CUP		TOTAL	
	App	Gls	App	Gls	App	Gls	App	Gls
1981-82	6/2	1	1/1	0	0	0	7/3	1
1982-83	20/3	8	1	0	0	0	21/3	8
1983-84	39/3	6	10	0	2/1	0	51/4	6
	65/8	15	12/1	0	2/1	0	79/10	15

NORMAN PIPER

The late 1960s provided just the setting for Norman Piper's footballing talents to flourish. In earlier periods, his lack of specialist skills could well have led to him being ignored. But when Piper entered League football, the value of a player who would dovetail unobtrusively and effectively into any tactical formation was being recognized. So Malcolm Allison plucked this small, slight, dark-haired lad of 17 out of the Reserves and gave him what usually amounted to man-sized jobs, concentrating on stifling the threat of a particularly dangerous opposing forward, Mike Summerbee of Swindon and Mike Stringfellow of Leicester being two examples. For the rest of his Argyle career, a period of decline for the club, Norman Piper was virtually an automatic choice, fitting into whatever position best suited the team. He was just the sort of player valued by Alf Ramsey and it was hardly surprising that the England manager singled him out. From Youth international, he was then selected for overseas summer tours with the FA and then four England caps at Under-23 level. The first of those might have been inspired by the fact that the match was played at Plymouth, but the others were won without there being any suspicion of special treatment. Piper stepped up into the Second Division with Portsmouth in 1970 and he made over 300 League appearances for the Hampshire club during the next seven years but full England recognition never came his way. After leaving Portsmouth, he moved to the United States to participate in the growth of the game in that part of the world. Piper played for Fort Lauderdale in the NASL in 1977 and 1978, making 45 appearances and scoring eight goals altogether. He later coached in the United States.

	LEAGUE		*FA CUP*		*FL CUP*		*TOTAL*	
	App	*Gls*	*App*	*Gls*	*App*	*Gls*	*App*	*Gls*
1964-65	10	0	1	0	1	0	12	0
1965-66	35	6	2	1	1	0	38	7
1966-67	40	11	1	0	1	1	42	12
1967-68	41	6	1	0	1	0	43	6
1968-69	46	6	1	0	3	0	50	6
1969-70	43	6	3	0	2	0	48	6
	215	35	9	1	9	1	233	37

Norman Piper made his Football League debut in a 2-2 draw at Portman Road, Ipswich, on 16 January 1964. His final League appearance for Argyle came in the last match of the 1969-70 season, a 3-0 defeat at Gay Meadow, Shrewsbury.

JOHN PORTEOUS

Johnny Porteous came to Argyle in 1949 from Alloa Athletic with the reputation of being able to play at wing-half and inside or centre-forward but Argyle were so satisfied with his wing-half displays, particularly in the promotion side of 1951-2, that his versatility was overlooked until the spring of 1954. He was drafted into the forward-line which was then displaying a marked lack of punch. It would be an exaggeration to claim that Porteous immediately transformed the side but he brought to the positions of inside-left, outside-left and, on one occasion centre-forward, a much-needed zest and enthusiasm. Energy, in fact, was the hallmark of Porteous' play and his tenacity and refusal to be beaten brought an end to many opposition ambitions. Born in Motherwell, he served in the RAF during the war and although he joined his home-town team after demobilization he did not get a Scottish League game in two seasons with that club. It was not until he joined Alloa that he commanded a first-team place and it was his displays with that club which persuaded Jimmy Rae in 1949 that he was worth a fee of £2,000. When it is considered that in that same close season, Southend paid Argyle twice as much for one of their reserve players, Len Jones, then Argyle had a bargain indeed. Johnny Porteous left Argyle for Exeter City in March 1956 and had two seasons with that club before retiring from the game.

	LEAGUE		*FA CUP*		*TOTAL*	
	App	*Gls*	*App*	*Gls*	*App*	*Gls*
1949-50	35	1	0	0	35	1
1950-51	41	1	4	0	45	1
1951-52	34	0	0	0	34	0
1952-53	29	0	1	0	30	0
1953-54	41	3	2	0	43	3
1954-55	30	8	0	0	30	8
1955-56	5	0	0	0	5	0
	215	13	7	0	222	13

JOHN PULLEN

The list of players who have won international honours while playing for Argyle is not so large that the one cap Jack Pullen was awarded by Wales in 1926 can go without remark. Pullen's chance came during a rare absence from the Welsh side of the Cardiff City centre-half, Fred Keenor, who won 32 caps for his country between 1920 and 1933 and virtually monopolized the number-five shirt for his country. Born in Victoria, Monmouthshire, Jack Pullen arrived at Home Park in the summer of 1924 from Ebbw Vale and looked set to make the centre-half position his own with a string of fine performances towards the end of that season. Injuries then kept him out of the team for several seasons but he was back in harness to assist the club's promotion drive in 1929-30 and contested the position with Harry Bland and Fred McKenzie until deciding to retire from the game in 1935. At 6ft and over 12st, Jack Pullen was ideally built for his position and was a very strong centre-half of the stopper type. In particular, he was noted for never shirking a header, a facet of his play which should not be dismissed lightly in view of the fact that the leather balls of that period would absorb water on a wet pitch and provide a severe test for the thickness of the players' skulls.

John Pullen made his League debut for Plymouth Argyle in a 1-1 home draw with Millwall in January 1924. He scored his first goal for the club in a 2-2 draw at Ashton Gate, Bristol, three months later. Pullen's last appearance for Plymouth was on the opening day of the 1934-5 season when he was centre-half in the side that went down 3-0 against Fulham at Craven Cottage. For the next match he was replaced by David Hill, a recent recruit from Hamilton Academical.

	LEAGUE		*FA CUP*		*TOTAL*	
	App	*Gls*	*App*	*Gls*	*App*	*Gls*
1924-25	20	1	0	0	20	1
1925-26	32	2	1	0	33	2
1926-27	3	0	0	0	3	0
1927-28	2	0	0	0	2	0
1928-29	10	1	0	0	10	1
1929-30	22	7	0	0	22	7
1930-31	31	2	1	0	32	2
1931-32	35	4	2	1	37	5
1932-33	25	0	1	0	26	0
1933-34	13	0	0	0	13	0
1934-35	1	0	0	0	1	0
	194	17	5	1	199	18

Two Argyle players, Moses Russell and Jack Pullen, were in the Welsh team which beat England 3-1 at Selhurst Park in 1926. Russell and his former Argyle clubmate Jack Fowler were in the Welsh team which played England the previous year and they were opposed by Jack Hill who was in the England side.

JAMES RAE

Argyle liked the look of two players in the Partick Thistle team which came south in 1932 to play in a benefit match for Alec Hardie, so they promptly signed, left-back Jimmy Rae and centre-forward Jack Simpson. Simpson remained for only one season but Jimmy Rae became a fixture in the Argyle defence, up to the beginning of World War Two, through the first wartime season and he was again on hand for the intermediate season of 1945-6, although by that time his playing career was inevitably at an end. He was appointed assistant manager of the club, later taking over from Jack Tresadern. (See *The Argyle Managers*) Harry Roberts, normally Rae's full-back partner, was the hard man. Jimmy Rae always liked to apply skill to any defensive problem. There were times when he came under criticism for persisting in holding on to the ball before clearing his lines. In the opinion of some, a hefty clearance was often required but that sort of game was completely foreign to Jimmy Rae's footballing nature and the critics were often forced to eat their words and admit that the Rae method often achieved more in the long run. After captaining the Scottish schools side, Rae first signed professional forms for King's Park, went on to Partick Thistle in 1927-8 and came to Argyle, as has been noted, following that benefit game. Glasgow Rangers were also interested in signing him at the same time but the charms of Plymouth prevailed and he was to remain in the city until dismissed from his manager's post in 1954. He then moved to Solihull to manage a public house. Jimmy Rae never won the Scottish caps which many thought that he deserved but at that time the national selectors frequently announced their 'reserve' team, the players on whom they would call if the original choices had to withdraw. Jimmy had at least one consolation; he was chosen as a Scotland reserve on three occasions.

	LEAGUE		*FA CUP*		*TOTAL*	
	App	*Gls*	*App*	*Gls*	*App*	*Gls*
1932-33	37	0	1	0	38	0
1933-34	35	0	2	0	37	0
1934-35	37	0	2	0	39	0
1935-36	39	0	2	0	41	0
1936-37	30	0	1	0	31	0
1937-38	39	0	1	0	40	0
1938-39	29	0	1	0	30	0
1939-40	3	0	0	0	3	0
	249	0	10	0	259	0

Jimmy Rae's first appearance for Plymouth Argyle was on the opening day of the 1932-3 season, in a 3-1 defeat at Boundary Park, Oldham. His last appearance came in the aborted 1939-40 season.

PADDY RATCLIFFE

Best remembered at Home Park for his full-back partnerships with Pat Jones, Paddy Ratcliffe joined Plymouth Argyle in June 1947. Ratcliffe had to wait longer than Jones to win his first-team place, with either George Silk or Bobby Stuart being preferred at right-back until the latter part of the 1949-50 season. Then he finally won recognition and remained first choice, being ever-present in the 1951-2 promotion season. Born in Dublin on New Year's Eve 1919, Ratcliffe was under no obligation to fight for Britain during World War Two, yet he volunteered for the RAF and was serving as an air-gunner when his bomber was shot down over Essen. He parachuted to safety but was captured and spent two years in a PoW camp, with shrapnel in his left leg being one legacy from the incident. After being liberated he returned to Dublin but soon decided to leave the League of Ireland club, Bohemians, to try his luck with Notts County. Before League football resumed he was transferred to Wolves in June 1946, but his chances at Molineux were restricted and he made only two First Division appearances before Argyle signed him. Although the season had been extended to June, Argyle were unable to field him because they were involved in relegation matches. Ratcliffe retired from football in 1956 and emigrated with his family to the United States, where he died. A full-back able to combine the talents of both Ratcliffe and Jones would have been very rare indeed. To the opposition, their pairing of the 1950s must have appeared daunting. There was the unsmiling Jones, while Ratcliffe looked rather like a gangster from a Hollywood movie, one eye half closed and a twist to his mouth. Ratcliffe did not have a devastating tackle like Jones but he was probably a better user of the ball, often to be found moving up in support of his forwards and curling his foot around the ball to deliver a measured cross into the opposition's goalmouth. That careful placing of the ball was also to prove an asset when Argyle were awarded a penalty and most of his ten goals for the club were the result of carefully measured spot-kicks.

	LEAGUE		*FA CUP*		*TOTAL*	
	App	*Gls*	*App*	*Gls*	*App*	*Gls*
1947-48	19	0	0	0	19	0
1948-49	5	0	0	0	5	0
1949-50	21	1	2	0	23	1
1950-51	43	2	3	0	46	2
1951-52	46	3	1	0	47	3
1952-53	27	0	1	0	28	0
1953-54	27	2	2	0	29	2
1954-55	40	2	1	0	41	2
1955-56	8	0	0	0	8	0
	236	10	10	0	246	10

Paddy Ratcliffe endured an unforgettable League debut for Plymouth Argyle when they lost 6-1 at Newcastle on the opening day of the 1947-8 season. He had to wait for his seventh appearance before being on the winning side in a League game.

HARRY ROBERTS

Argyle's full-back pairing of the 1930s, Harry Roberts on the right and Jimmy Rae on the left, provided an interesting contrast in defensive styles; Rae skilful and correct, even gentlemanly, in his tackling, Roberts tough strong and, at times, impetuous according to some critics. Born in Crofton, Yorkshire, Roberts joined Leeds United as a boy and spent six years with that club before Robert Jack brought him to Plymouth. Not tall, but strongly built, Harry Roberts was one of the characters of the side. On one occasion, he turned in one of his best performances despite playing with enough alcohol in his system to fail a modern breathalyser test. He enjoyed the rough and tumble of a match but referees did not always smile benignly on his style of play and more than once with Argyle he was sent off and suspended while the other players dug into their pockets to compensate Harry for his lost wages. He had an excellent record from the penalty-spot, the source of his impressive (for a full-back) tally of 21 goals for the club. It was quite typical of his rumbustious approach to the game and to life that Harry was among the first to try his abilities at the then new fashion of all-in wrestling when it reached Plymouth. With Sam Kirkwood ready to take over the right-back spot, Argyle agreed to transfer Harry Roberts to Bristol Rovers in 1937. He was, in any case, nearing the end of his career but the outbreak of war effectively finished it.

	LEAGUE		*FA CUP*		*TOTAL*	
	App	*Gls*	*App*	*Gls*	*App*	*Gls*
1930-31	27	4	1	0	28	4
1931-32	38	6	2	0	40	6
1932-33	36	4	0	0	36	4
1933-34	42	1	2	0	44	1
1934-35	39	4	2	0	41	4
1935-36	40	2	2	0	42	2
1936-37	26	0	0	0	26	0
	248	21	9	2	257	21

After signing for Bristol Rovers, Harry Roberts made 77 League appearances for the Eastville club in the seasons 1937-8 and 1938-9, when they were struggling at the foot of the Third Division South. Despite his reputation as a penalty-taker for Plymouth, he did not immediately undertake the responsibility for Rovers, eventually scoring from the spot against Cardiff in April 1938. That proved to be his only goal for the club and thus he ended his career with 22 League goals from 325 appearances.

On 8 May 1926, Home Park saw probably the most remarkable football match ever staged there when a team of striking trade unionists met a team of policemen during the General Strike. A crowd of around 10,000 saw the strikers win 2-1, yet in the city centre there was another, more serious, confrontation going on between the sides. Tramcar managers were attempting to run some kind of service after drivers had gone on strike. A crowd of some 15,000 tried to block the trams and police were called to disperse them. Eventually the service was withdrawn and the danger of a full-scale riot averted. Of the action at Home Park, the Western Morning News & Mercury *commented: 'A match between policemen and strikers is, at least, strange.'*

GEORGE ROBERTSON

Few players can have had a more dispiriting introduction to the world of professional football than George Robertson when, still an amateur, he appeared at right-back in the Reserve team at Luton on the last day of the 1948-9 season. Argyle's defence that afternoon was torn to shreds as the home team won 9-0 and Robertson returned to his RAF unit in Wiltshire convinced that his football dreams had been shattered. After demobilization he returned to his native Scotland and was about to sign for his home-town team, Stenhousemuir, when out of the blue came an invitation to sign professional forms for Argyle. So began George Robertson's association with the club which lasted 14 years on the playing field and extended after that in the roles of groundsman and manager of the club's youth hostel. He was rewarded for his services to the club by a testimonial match against Blackburn Rovers in 1986. Early in his Argyle career, Robertson built up a reputation for himself in the Reserves as a centre-half and it was in that position that he made his League debut for Argyle but the availability of bigger, less mobile players for that position caused Argyle to switch him, first to wing-half and then, as successor to Paddy Ratcliffe, to that right-back position where he had that traumatic first encounter with the Luton forwards. Robertson positioned himself well, tackled strongly and used the ball to good effect. He was not a particularly fast mover and occasionally a left winger would appear who would give him a torrid 90 minutes. But Argyle never had a more wholehearted player than Robertson with his rather ungainly but wholly effective style.

	LEAGUE		*FA CUP*		*FL CUP*		*TOTAL*	
	App	*Gls*	*App*	*Gls*	*App*	*Gls*	*App*	*Gls*
1950-51	2	0	0	0	0	0	2	0
1951-52	0	0	0	0	0	0	0	0
1952-53	14	0	2	0	0	0	16	0
1953-54	41	0	2	0	0	0	43	0
1954-55	34	0	1	0	0	0	35	0
1955-56	41	1	1	0	0	0	42	1
1956-57	45	0	2	0	0	0	47	0
1957-58	45	0	3	0	0	0	48	0
1958-59	33	0	4	0	0	0	37	0
1959-60	13	0	0	0	0	0	13	0
1960-61	23	0	1	0	2	0	26	0
1961-62	37	1	2	0	1	0	40	1
1962-63	22	0	0	0	1	0	23	0
1963-64	9	0	0	0	1	0	10	0
	359	2	18	0	5	0	382	2

George Robertson made his League debut for Argyle in a 3-0 defeat at Colchester in March 1951. His final appearance for the club was in a 1-1 draw at Newcastle in December 1963. He scored two goals, against Lincoln City in January 1956 and against Liverpool in April 1962.

MOSES RUSSELL

There was no mistaking Moses Russell when Plymouth Argyle took the field in the years immediately after World War One. He was the one with no hair. Rheumatic fever in his youth had deprived Russell of most of his locks. Indirectly that was to Argyle's benefit because, when he was playing for his first club, Merthyr Tydfil, other clubs doubted whether one who looked so old could make a useful contribution to their cause. Argyle manager Robert Jack had no such reservations and in 1914 he paid £400 — at that time an Argyle club record fee for a full-back — to take Russell to Home Park. However, Jack took the precaution, after watching Russell play for Merthyr, of travelling to Tredegan and obtaining the player's birth certificate which showed that appearances were deceptive and that Russell was only 22. At that stage Russell had already won three Welsh caps, the first of them as a left-half. With Argyle he was to add 20 to that total, the last of his international appearances coming when he was 40 years old. At Plymouth he established full-back partnerships, first with Sep Atterbury, then with Billy Forbes, which were widely regarded as unequalled in the Third Division. He was a regular member of Argyle's side throughout that period in the 1920s when promotion to the Second Division proved so elusive. Thus, it was profoundly disappointing to him that he had lost his place to Fred Titmuss by the time the championship was finally won, in 1929-30. Russell was a robust player, good with his head, but he had to develop a thick skin to cope with the remarks of some opposing supporters. They either loved or hated him. His appearance could provoke derision and his style inspired malice. At Luton, in 1920, with Argyle reduced to ten men and clinging to a goal lead, Russell's tactics were to send the ball into touch at every opportunity. This so incensed one home supporter that he hurled a stone at the full-back. His aim was poor and it was goalkeeper Fred Craig who stopped the missile, sustaining a cut head. On another occasion, whilst touring Canada with the Welsh international team in 1929, Russell's tackling so outraged one spectator that he drew a gun and threatened the Plymouth man before being overpowered by police. On yet another occasion, he was actually assaulted by a spectator on leaving the pitch. The police, who moved in to arrest the attacker, unfortunately picked the wrong man. He left Argyle in 1930 to join the now-defunct Thames Association. Russell spent a couple of season's in East London, playing for Thames during their brief career in the Third Division South. He eventually returned to Plymouth and became manager of a public house in Union Street. He died in 1946.

	S LEAGUE		*F LEAGUE*		*FA CUP*		*TOTAL*	
	App	*Gls*	*App*	*Gls*	*App*	*Gls*	*App*	*Gls*
1914-15	25	0	-	-	2	0	27	0
1919-20	36	0	-	-	3	0	39	0
1920-21	-	-	36	1	5	1	41	2
1921-22	-	-	38	0	2	0	40	0
1922-23	-	-	32	1	4	0	36	1
1923-24	-	-	36	1	1	0	37	1
1924-25	-	-	36	2	1	0	37	2
1925-26	-	-	24	0	1	0	25	0
1926-27	-	-	34	0	1	0	35	0
1927-28	-	-	36	0	1	0	37	0
1928-29	-	-	35	0	4	0	39	0
1929-30	-	-	7	0	0	0	7	0
	61	0	314	5	25	1	400	6

BOBBY SAXTON

Few more wholehearted or enthusiastic players than Bobby Saxton have pulled on an Argyle shirt and it was not for any lack of effort on his part that his first season with the club should have been marked by relegation from the Second Division. Saxton had been bought from Derby County in February 1968 for £12,000 to help stave off the impending threat of a drop into the Third Division but although the half-back was to turn in an unbroken run of appearances, his team's fate was already sealed. Saxton's strong tackling was much in evidence during the following season as Argyle attempted to regain the Second Division but the player's plans and those of his club were thrown awry when he broke his leg in a car accident before the start of the 1969-70 season. The injury kept him out of action for a whole season but he returned to the team in August 1970 and did not miss a single League game that season. He was the driving force in the side which reached the semi-final of the League Cup in 1973-4 and gained promotion to the Second Division the following season. In September 1975 he signed for Exeter City, subsequently becoming player-manager there and returned to Plymouth as Argyle's manager in 1979. (See *The Argyle Managers*).

	LEAGUE		*FA CUP*		*FL CUP*		*TOTAL*	
	App	*Gls*	*App*	*Gls*	*App*	*Gls*	*App*	*Gls*
1967-68	18	0	0	0	0	0	18	0
1968-69	38/2	1	0	0	3	0	41/2	1
1970-71	46	2	0	0	0	0	46	2
1971-72	12/1	1	1	0	0	0	13/1	1
1972-73	29/2	3	4	0	0/1	0	33/3	3
1973-74	42	0	2	0	7	0	51	0
1974-75	38	0	4	0	0	0	42	0
1975-76	1/2	0	0	0	1/2	0	2/4	0
	224/7	7	11	0	11/3	0	246/10	7

Bobby Saxton, a South Yorkshireman, joined Derby County from Midland League club, Denaby United, in February 1962. After Brian Clough became manager at Derby in 1967, Saxton lost his place to Roy McFarland. But McFarland was ineligible for that season's League Cup and Saxton played in the run which took the Rams to the semi-final, where they lost to Leeds United.

BILL SHORTT

Many more spectacular goalkeepers than Bill Shortt have guarded the Argyle net over the years. Many have been taller, leaner, fitter, stronger; few have been as dependable. An excellent sense of positional play and timing and a very safe pair of hands were the assets which made Shortt master of the penalty area. When it is recalled that Shortt played in an era when goalkeepers received far less protection from referees than they do today — then a goalkeeper could, quite legitimately, be charged into the net provided that he was holding the ball — Shortt's ability in dealing with opposing forwards was all the more remarkable. There were times in a match when it seemed that he and opposing wingers had entered into some conspiracy to exclude all others from the game, so regularly did he pluck their crosses from the air, dodge the oncoming centre-forward and set his own attack away with a drop kick. For a period, of course, he was under the protection of Jack Chisholm and if referees were unwilling to defend Shortt against the attentions of marauding forwards, then Chisholm had no such inhibitions. Shortt was born in Wrexham on 13 October 1920 and it was Army service at the end of the war which brought him to Argyle's attention. Their regular goalkeeper, Matt Middleton, was having to make long trips to Plymouth from Derbyshire. Shortt was on the spot and his club, Chester, were happy to allow him to 'guest' for Argyle. Plymouth soon wanted the young Welshman permanently and a £1,000 fee persuaded Chester to agree to his transfer. In a team which conceded 120 goals that season, no Argyle goalkeeper could complain that he was not getting a fair share of the action. Shortt's displays were sufficient to attract the Welsh selectors and he won his first cap in a 'Victory' International against Northern Ireland. That international debut owed something to good fortune, for Wales' regular goalkeeper, Cyril Sidlow, was away on a club tour with Liverpool. Nevertheless, Shortt eventually won 12 full caps and was his country's goalkeeper when they won the Home International Championship in 1950-51 and beat a team representing the Rest of the United Kingdom. He was the longest-serving member of the Argyle team which won promotion in the 1951-2 season but also suffered the disappointment of relegation in 1955-6, after which he became a licensee in Plymouth.

	LEAGUE		*FA CUP*		*TOTAL*	
	App	*Gls*	*App*	*Gls*	*App*	*Gls*
1946-47	38	0	1	0	39	0
1947-48	42	0	1	0	43	0
1948-49	39	0	1	0	40	0
1949-50	37	0	2	0	39	0
1950-51	32	0	4	0	36	0
1951-52	44	0	1	0	45	0
1952-53	40	0	3	0	43	0
1953-54	16	0	0	0	16	0
1954-55	33	0	1	0	34	0
1955-56	21	0	0	0	21	0
	342	0	14	0	356	0

GEORGE SILK

	LEAGUE		FA CUP		TOTAL	
	App	Gls	App	Gls	App	Gls
1937-38	3	0	0	0	3	0
1938-39	6	0	1	0	7	0
1946-47	15	0	0	0	15	0
1947-48	3	0	0	0	3	0
1948-49	37	1	1	0	38	1
1949-50	20	0	1	0	21	0
1950-51	2	0	1	0	3	0
	86	1	4	0	90	1

More than any other player, George Silk marked the continuity between the Plymouth Argyle playing staffs of the pre and post-World War Two eras. A Liverpool man — he was born there on 18 October 1916 — Silk arrived at Home Park from Southport in 1937 and played in a few games before the League programme was suspended. He appeared in virtually all of Argyle's limited wartime programme and after the war he was either first-choice right-back, or on the fringes of selection, until he was replaced by Paddy Ratcliffe in 1950. Students of the art of polished full-back play would have wasted their time taking notes on the Silk method. His motto was: 'Make it simple, make it quick', although his interpretation of that saying was not quite in the same mould as Arthur Rowe's idea of 'push and run' football. As far as Silk was concerned, opposing wingers were there to be tackled, not shadowed. And in he went, sometimes to the point of recklessness. The local *Football Herald* liked to call it 'do or die tackling'. Modern referees would take a different view and be seen reaching for their notebooks. Having won the ball, Silk's next aim would be to dispatch it to the opposite end as quickly as possible, by the shortest available route. Cynics might argue that he was attempting just that in February 1949, when he shelled the West Ham goalmouth from a point half-way down the pitch near the right touch-line. Whatever his intention, the fact was that Hammers' goalkeeper Ernie Gregory misjudged the ball's flight and George Silk scored the only goal of his first-class career. Some supporters, believing that a powerful kick is the prime requirement for a centre-forward, would have given him further scoring opportunities and, when Argyle were finding it difficult to find the back of the net, the cry would go up for Silk to be tried up front. Although he had played centre-forward for Liverpool Schools, he was never a success on the infrequent occasions that Argyle experimented with him as leader of their attack. Quite simply, George Silk had been created to prevent goals, not to score them. He was the last survivor of Argyle's pre-war staff when he left in 1952 to join Newquay as player-manager. He died in 1969.

George Silk really came into his own during Plymouth Argyle's brief time in wartime soccer. In 1939-40, although he did not play in Argyle's three games of the abandoned Second Division season, he was an ever-present when they won the South-West Regional League championship. In 1945-6, he missed only one game — a 5-2 defeat at West Brom — as the Football League South got back to a 42-match programme in readiness for the resumption of normal League soccer.

FRANK SLOAN

	LEAGUE		*FA CUP*		*TOTAL*	
	App	*Gls*	*App*	*Gls*	*App*	*Gls*
1923-24	5	4	0	0	5	4
1924-25	31	8	1	0	32	8
1925-26	4	1	0	0	4	1
1926-27	7	1	0	0	7	1
1927-28	17	7	0	0	17	7
1928-29	12	2	0	0	12	2
1929-30	33	8	2	0	35	8
1930-31	10	1	0	0	10	1
1931-32	11	1	0	0	11	1
1932-33	12	1	0	0	12	1
1933-34	22	5	0	0	22	5
1934-35	35	8	2	0	37	8
1935-36	9	2	1	1	10	3
	208	49	6	1	214	50

There were often times when it seemed that the Argyle management could not make up its mind about Frank Sloan. For sheer ball control, he was in the very top of his class, but players with inferior technical skills were often preferred to him when it came to team selection. Although he made over 200 appearances for the club, in only three of his 13 seasons with Argyle could he be said to have been a regular choice. An inside forward, he often looked lethargic on the field but once in possession of the ball, he controlled it as though there was a magnetic attraction between ball and boots. The goal he scored against Tottenham on Easter Monday 1933 was still remembered over 30 years later by one who saw it. From the kick-off, he dribbled straight through the opposing defence, ran the ball into the net and then dribbled back to the centre of the field for the restart. There was an impish side to his character as well, as Jimmy Kirkpatrick, refereeing a practice game at Home Park, discovered. Concentrating on the play, he suddenly found his legs whipped from under him while Frank Sloan, the culprit, sauntered nearby, his expression the picture of innocence. Argyle have had few players to match his artistry and as late as 1947, the *Football Herald*, looking for words to praise a new arrival to the playing staff, could only comment that the newcomer brought back memories of Frank Sloan. A Scot, Sloan was born at Chapelhall, near Airdrie, and joined Argyle, his first League club, from Shieldmuir Celtic. The best of his playing days were spent at Home Park and although he left the city for Luton Town in 1936, he later returned as a member of the Argyle groundstaff.

BILL STRAUSS

It was fortunate for the game's journalists that Bill Strauss chose to make his football career as a winger. Those images of Strauss 'waltzing' around the opposition or 'dancing' his way along the touchline, so apt when it came to describing his his wing play, would have been totally inappropriate if applied to some dour, unyielding defender. But although Strauss' nimble footwork put many an opposing full-back to the test, he was never content to confine his skills to the extremities of the pitch. Bill Strauss cutting into the middle with the ball, or dashing in to meet a centre from the other wing, was one of the most cheering sights for Argyle supporters in the seasons just after World War Two. Indeed, at one point in 1946-7, he and his opposite wingman Sid Rawlings threatened to monopolize the scoring. Strauss, who scored 11 League goals that season, would have added more, had injury not forced him to miss half the season. Strauss was 30 when he joined Argyle from Aberdeen in 1946 and this meant that his career at Home Park was necessarily shortened. He effectively dropped out of the first-team reckoning in 1950, in favour of the younger Alex Govan, but he was still considered worthy of a couple of first-team games in 1953, at the age of 37. Strauss was born in Transvaal, South Africa, on 6 January 1916 and arrived in Britain on the SS Arundel Castle in December 1935, to begin his career in football with Aberdeen, the club to whom he had been recommended by a former Dons' player, Eddie Swan. Strauss broke into the first team at the start of 1936-7 and went on to play a major part in Aberdeen reaching the Scottish Cup Final for the first time. When war was declared he joined the Royal Signals and was later commissioned in the Commandos. He rejoined Aberdeen after the war and it was while he was playing for them in a Scottish League Cup semi-final that he was noticed by Plymouth manager Jack Tresadern, who had gone to check on another forward. So began Strauss' career at Home Park. His signing for Argyle also benefited other sports in the area, for he was an all-round games player who had starred at cricket and badminton whilst with Aberdeen. He played for Plymouth Cricket Club for a number of years and for Devon in the Minor Counties Championship, scoring a century against Surrey II at The Oval. After he retired from football in 1954, Bill Strauss became landlord of a public house in the Octagon, Union Street, Plymouth. He died in 1987.

	LEAGUE		*FA CUP*		*TOTAL*	
	App	*Gls*	*App*	*Gls*	*App*	*Gls*
1946-47	23	11	1	0	24	11
1947-48	41	5	1	0	42	5
1948-49	31	10	1	0	32	10
1949-50	37	10	2	0	39	10
1950-51	15	3	3	2	18	5
1951-52	9	1	0	0	9	1
1952-53	0	0	0	0	0	0
1953-54	2	0	0	0	2	0
	158	40	8	2	166	42

Bill Strauss appeared in 80 Scottish League games for Aberdeen before World War Two, scoring 42 goals. He scored 11 goals in 14 Scottish Cup appearances for the Dons.

COLIN SULLIVAN

Colin Sullivan was 16 years, eight months and 23 days old when he made his League debut for Argyle in March 1968, the youngest player to play for the club in League football. The Saltash-born full-back made the leap that season from Western League football to the Football Combination and then on to Division Two. He went on to make 11 League appearances that season and did not sign full-time professional forms until the close season. Even allowing for the fact that 1967-8 season saw Argyle's relegation from the Second Division and a large amount of turbulence in team selection, Sullivan's selection was achieved on merit. After one more season of consolidation at left-back, he established himself as a virtually automatic choice and was honoured by England at Youth level in 1969. He won two Under-23 caps in 1974 when he was also a key member of the side which got as far as the semi-final of the League Cup. His showing in that competition against some of the leading forwards in the First Division convinced Norwich City that he would be an asset and he played in their League Cup Final side in his first season with the East Anglian club. Having made such an early start, Colin Sullivan was on the League scene for some 20 years and had spells with Cardiff City, Hereford United, Portsmouth and Swansea City.

	LEAGUE		FA CUP		FL CUP		TOTAL	
	App	Gls	App	Gls	App	Gls	App	Gls
1967-68	11	0	0	0	0	0	11	0
1968-69	16/3	0	1	0	3	0	20/3	0
1969-70	39	1	3	0	1	0	43	1
1970-71	29/2	1	1	0	1	0	31/2	1
1971-72	39	3	0	0	1	0	40	3
1972-73	46	1	4	0	1	0	51	1
1973-74	45	1	3	0	7	0	55	1
	225/5	7	12	0	14	0	251/5	7

Colin Sullivan is the youngest player to make his first League appearance for Argyle at 16 years, eight months and 23 days, when he was selected in March 1968. Richard Reynolds was 16 years 11 months when he made his debut in 1965. The oldest is John Oakes, who was 41 years 11 months when he played against Newcastle United in August 1947. Oakes was also the oldest man to appear in an FA Cup Final at Wembley when he played for Charlton Athletic against Derby County in 1946.

JOHN SUTCLIFFE

	S League		W League		FA CUP		TOTAL	
	App	Gls	App	Gls	App	Gls	App	Gls
1904-05	4	0	-	-	0	0	4	0
1905-06	23	0	10	0	0	0	33	0
1906-07	32	0	9	0	1	0	42	0
1907-08	28	0	8	0	2	0	38	0
1908-09	23	0	11	0	0	0	34	0
1909-10	28	0	-	-	0	0	28	0
1910-11	25	0	-	-	1	0	26	0
1911-12	3	0	-	-	0	0	3	0
	166	0	38	0	4	0	208	0

It is hardly likely that there will ever again be a player like John Willie Sutcliffe who, at the end of the last century, had the distinction of playing for England at both soccer and Rugby Union. He was born in Shibden, near Halifax, in April 1868 and rugby was his first choice. From 1886 to 1887 he played as a full-back or centre three-quarter for his native Bradford. In 1888 he moved to another Yorkshire club, Heckmondwike, and while with that organization he played for Yorkshire, the North of England and, finally, England, winning his cap against the Maoris in 1889. Shortly afterwards, Sutcliffe's rugby career was cut short when the Heckmondwike club was suspended for alleged professionalism. He decided to switch codes and in September 1889 signed for Bolton Wanderers as a centre-forward. Bolton converted him to a goalkeeper and he soon won a regular first-team place. In 1894, Sutcliffe played for Wanderers in the FA Cup Final. By an odd coincidence Dai Davies, the next man to keep goal for Bolton in a Cup Final, was the last man to play both soccer and Rugby League for England. Sutcliffe won the first of his five soccer caps in 1893, making his last international appearance after moving to Southern League Millwall Athletic in April 1902. He was in competition for an England place with Jack Robinson, the man who preceded him in Argyle's goal. He joined Manchester United in 1903 but played only 28 League and Cup games for them before signing for Argyle in 1905. It was intended that he should be cover for the regular goalkeeper, 'Tich' Horne, and it was three months after signing before Sutcliffe visited Plymouth to make his Argyle debut, in March 1905. He and Horne, whom he matched in physique, alternated in the Argyle goal for the next seven years before Sutcliffe decided to end his playing career. In 1911-12 he was appointed coach to Southend United. During World War One he coached the Arnhem club in the Netherlands for a spell before returning to become Bradford City's trainer in 1919. He died in 1947, aged 79. Sutcliffe was a fine all-round sportsman in his day, excelling at cricket, billiards, cycling, running and even ice-skating. A Plymouth journalist once posed the question: Did he prefer soccer or Rugby Union? John Willie Sutcliffe had no doubts, replying, "Oh, soccer, every time."

MAURICE TADMAN

	LEAGUE		FA CUP		TOTAL	
	App	Gls	App	Gls	App	Gls
1947-48	19	7	1	0	20	7
1948-49	30	15	1	0	31	15
1949-50	29	9	2	0	31	9
1950-51	40	23	4	3	44	26
1951-52	44	27	1	0	45	27
1952-53	39	15	2	0	41	15
1953-54	32	11	2	1	34	12
1954-55	7	1	0	0	7	1
	240	108	13	4	253	112

Making a return visit to Plymouth some 20 years after his playing connection with Argyle had been severed, Maurice Tadman expressed genuine surprise that he was still remembered in the city. He might not have known, of course, that his 100 goals for the club gives him membership of a very select band of Plymouth footballers. Tadman cost Argyle £4,000 when he arrived from Charlton Athletic in the summer of 1947, but he had the misfortune to break his wrist on his debut. Born in Rainham, Essex, on 28 June 1921, he first played for Bexleyheath before joining Charlton, where his elder brother George was already on the playing staff, during the war. Maurice Tadman was a prolific scorer for Charlton Reserves — 38 goals in the first post-war season — but he had few opportunities in the First Division and after only three League games for the London club he was happy to move to Plymouth. His scoring rate in Argyle's last few seasons in Division Two was not spectacular but he came into his own during the two seasons they spent in the Third Division South at the beginning of the 1950s. In the autumn of 1950 he scored 14 goals in seven games, including four against Aldershot at Home Park and four at Brighton. Although he was well-built for a centre-forward, Tadman preferred finesse to power. A flick of the foot, a sidestep, a switch to the wings to unsettle defenders and a precisely-placed shot were all part of the Tadman repertoire. His heading ability was probably no more than average but when the ball was at his feet he could trouble even the best defenders. The image which persists in the mind of this writer is not of a Tadman goal but an incident in the 1951 FA Cup tie against Wolves. Tadman, apparently trapped by a burly Wolves defender near the right-wing corner-flag, simply slipped the ball through his opponent's legs and was clear. For skill, Tadman would not be out of place in any Argyle team of recent times but, in one respect at least, it is difficult to picture him at ease in the modern game. The exuberance of the typical modern goalscorer would have been quite foreign to Tadman, who contented himself with a brief congratulatory handshake for every one of that century of goals. He then got on with the game and his demeanour on the field was nonchalant almost to the point of indifference. Tadman left Argyle in 1955 and had a brief spell as manager of Belfast Distillery in the Irish League.

DAVID & BOB THOMAS

Brothers Dave and Bob Thomas achieved a remarkable similarity in their records during the season they were members of the same Argyle forward line. Each missed only one game and there was little to choose between their scoring rates, Dave netting 19 goals and Bob 17. DAVE THOMAS, born at Stepney on 6 July 1917, was the older by two years and was Jack Tresadern's first signing as Argyle manager. His previous club was Romford and he established himself in the number-nine shirt in 1939 after Bill Hullett had been transferred to Manchester United. The war interrupted Dave's best playing days and when he returned to Home Park after the conflict, his hair had receded and his waistline thickened. Nevertheless, he was the undisputed leader of Argyle's attack in that first post-war season of 1946-7, when he was particularly noted for his headwork and his habit of hurling himself horizontally to connect with a centre. One such dive, at Tottenham in 1946, sent the ball crashing past Ted Ditchburn and so impressed the Spurs' goalkeeper that he patted the Argyle man on the back for his effort. The arrival of Maurice Tadman in 1947 meant that Dave's opportunities at Home Park became more limited but he later gave good Third Division service to Watford and Gillingham. BOB THOMAS was also born in London, on 2 August 1919, and he arrived from Brentford just as the 1945-6 season was drawing to a close. It did not take him long to establish a reputation as an exciting player, whether setting off on one of his solo runs or testing opposing goalkeepers with a shot. One particularly memorable goal came on a September evening against Chesterfield. The shot was delivered with such force that the ball hit the stanchion and rebounded into play with goalkeeper Ray Middleton still in mid-air. Unfortunately for Argyle, Bob Thomas wanted to move back to his London home after only one season. Houses were difficult to obtain in post-war Plymouth and so, for Bob, every match was an away match. Fulham stepped in with an offer and he helped them win the Second Division championship in 1949 before ending his career with Crystal Palace. Reporting his transfer to Fulham, the *Evening Herald* curiously criticized him for having been only 'spasmodically' brilliant with Argyle. Perhaps that was a sort of compliment, implying that 'brilliance' had come to be expected of him. Many an Argyle manager, before and after Bob Thomas' time, would have been content to count on any kind of brilliance from an Argyle player, spasmodic or not.

DAVE THOMAS

	LEAGUE		*FA CUP*		*TOTAL*	
	App	*Gls*	*App*	*Gls*	*App*	*Gls*
1938-39	23	8	1	0	24	8
1946-47	41	19	1	0	42	19
1947-48	10	2	1	1	11	3
	74	29	3	1	77	30

BOB THOMAS

	LEAGUE		*FA CUP*		*TOTAL*	
	App	*Gls*	*App*	*Gls*	*App*	*Gls*
1946-47	41	17	1	0	42	17
	41	17	1	0	42	17

FREDDIE TITMUSS

	LEAGUE		FA CUP		TOTAL	
	App	Gls	App	Gls	App	Gls
1925-26	16	0	0	0	16	0
1926-27	25	0	1	0	26	0
1927-28	30	0	1	0	31	0
1928-29	25	0	3	0	28	0
1929-30	37	0	0	0	37	0
1930-31	22	0	0	0	22	0
1931-32	11	0	2	0	13	0
	166	0	7	0	173	0

Southampton-born Fred Titmuss spent five years with his home-town club before coming further south to join Argyle early in 1926. The years with Southampton were probably more memorable than those he was later to spend with Argyle for in that period the Hampshire club won promotion to the Second Division, taking the title because their goal average was superior to Argyle's, while Titmuss was personally honoured by England, being capped against Wales at left-back in 1922 and 1923 while a Second Division player. So he brought a lot of experience to Home Park when he linked up with Argyle and he achieved another Third Division medal with Plymouth and captained the side in 1929-30 when the full-back partnership of Harry Bland and Fred Titmuss played their full part in a side which lost only four of their 42 games. A master of the sliding tackle, Titmuss was the type of full-back who prefers to slip the ball to an unmarked colleague so that attacks can be started out of defence rather than bang it upfield in the hope that a teammate somewhere will fasten on to it. He retired from football in 1933 and became a publican in Plymouth.

TOMMY TYNAN

Scorer of over 100 goals, club captain, four times Player of the Year (three times in succession) — the casual onlooker could be forgiven for supposing that the Argyle team of the late 1980s consisted of Tommy Tynan and a supporting cast. While it would obviously be a distortion, such an observation does contain an element of truth, as the 1988-9 season seemed to confirm. With 24 League goals, Tynan scored nearly one half of the side's total for the season and was far ahead of his nearest challenger in the individual totals. Although it would be an exaggeration to claim that Tynan has found goalscoring easy since he entered the Football League, there is no doubt that he has been a consistent scorer with most of his clubs and his career total in League games now stands at 224 goals. Most of these goals have been scored in the lower divisions and he has not tested his abilities at the highest level. Nevertheless, it is a record which should not lightly be dismissed. At 5ft 10ins and 12st, Tynan is not a particularly big man nor is he renowned for the power of his shooting and heading. The most remarkable feature of his scoring technique is economy of effort as illustrated by the goal he scored at Birmingham on New Year's Day, 1987. A head-high cross from the left found him unmarked in front of goal and, seconds before the ball arrived, spectators in line of sight could see him pick his spot. If the City goalkeeper could also read the Tynan mind at that moment, it was not very apparent because he was moving in the wrong direction as the ball was carefully steered into the net. Add to this accuracy the fact that Tynan is never content to wait for the ball, but is constantly foraging to make scoring chances for himself and others, then his value to the team becomes even more apparent. A Liverpudlian, Tynan started his professional career as a 17-year-old with Liverpool but after four years he had only a short spell on loan to Swansea City to show in the way of League experience. His reputation as a scorer really dates from his transfer to Sheffield Wednesday, where he spent two years, and continued with Newport County, whom he joined after only a few months with his next club, Lincoln City. His record with the Welsh club in 1982-3, in partnership with John Aldridge, another Merseysider, encouraged Argyle to seek his transfer and, whatever other claims to Argyle fame, Bobby Moncur can take the credit for bringing Tynan to Plymouth. After a slow start, he began to demonstrate the scoring consistency which the club had been seeking. It was therefore a great disappointment that, after having scored 32 goals in 1984-5, he asked for a move for domestic reasons and was transferred to Rotherham United. The move did not prove to be successful for the player and his return to Home Park was straight out of the pages of boys' sports fiction. By April 1986 he had lost his place with Rotherham, who allowed him to return to Argyle on loan, just in time to assist the team's promotion drive over the last nine matches. Tynan played in all of those games and scored ten goals, with one of Argyle's victims in that period being Rotherham, whose manager, Norman Hunter, was to complain after the game that Dave Smith had violated a 'gentleman's agreement' not to play Tynan against the club which held his signature. Whatever the truth of that particular dispute, the experience was enough to persuade both Argyle and Tynan that their best interests required a reunion and he returned to Home Park in the summer of 1988 to resume where he had left off, a striker who can be depended on for double figures each season. At 33 it is unlikely that Tommy Tynan will get the chance to test his abilities in the First Division unless Argyle take him there, but 11 players of his calibre would certainly improve the chances of achieving that historical leap.

	LEAGUE		*FA CUP*		*FL CUP*		*TOTAL*	
	App	*Gls*	*App*	*Gls*	*App*	*Gls*	*App*	*Gls*
1983-84	35	12	10	3	4	1	49	16
1984-85	45	31	3	1	4	0	52	32
1985-86	9	10	0	0	0	0	9	10
1986-87	40	18	3	1	0	0	43	19
1987-88	42	16	3	0	1	1	46	17
1988-89	46	24	3	1	4	1	53	26
	217	111	22	6	13	3	252	120

JACK VIDLER

Jack Vidler belongs to that group of Argyle players, relatively small in number but generally talented, who arrived at Home Park via local football with Service teams. Gordon Astall, Bert Bowler, Charlie Twissell and Ernie Edds come to mind as representatives of the category. Not unnaturally, many of them had naval backgrounds. Jack Vidler, on the other hand, had been a soldier and Argyle's transfer fee in his case was to the Army in order to obtain his release. There was not a great deal of finesse about Jack Vidler but his bustle and dash could unsettle many defences and whether as a leader of the attack or in either of the two left side forward positions, he was not often out of the scoring limelight. Take, for example, his scoring spell in April 1930 when he scored three goals in one game and four in another, or his prominence in two famous Argyle wins of the 1930s, the record 8-1 defeat of Millwall and the 5-1 victory over West Bromwich. Vidler registered a hat-trick in both games, the second being particularly noteworthy because it marked his return to first-team football after being absent through injury for nearly four months. His Argyle career came to an end just before the outbreak of World War Two and although he played for his new club, Bristol City, throughout the first wartime season of 1939-40, the war virtually ended his professional career.

	LEAGUE		*FA CUP*		*TOTAL*	
	App	*Gls*	*App*	*Gls*	*App*	*Gls*
1928-29	2	0	0	0	2	0
1929-30	28	15	3	4	31	19
1930-31	17	6	0	0	17	6
1931-32	34	17	2	2	36	19
1932-33	27	8	0	0	27	8
1933-34	11	2	1	0	12	2
1934-35	42	21	2	0	44	21
1935-36	20	8	2	1	22	9
1936-37	35	13	2	1	37	14
1937-38	22	4	1	0	23	4
1938-39	5	1	0	0	6	0
	243	95	13	8	257	103

Jack Vidler made 30 appearances for Bristol City in 1939-40, including the three games of the aborted Third Division South season. His return to Home Park was hardly a happy one, for City lost there 6-0 in a Regional League South West Division match in October 1939. Later that season, Vidler was in the Bristol City team which lost 10-3 to Argyle on the same ground.

JOHN WILLIAMS

At one point in the late 1950s, Argyle fielded two half-backs named John Williams, one a Welshman, the other English. Opposing goalkeepers at least quickly learned to distinguish between the two. The latter was the one who would keep them on their toes with his shots at goal at the least provocation. Johnny Williams made his league debut for the Argyle team as an 18-year-old amateur from the dockyard side, EEM Department, in 1955 and was one of the few bright spots in that disjointed team which lost Argyle's Second Division status. The attacking promise was there from the start, but he also matched it with firmness in the tackle which marked him as a player with strong half-back potential. His career really sparked from the autumn of 1956 when Argyle moved him into the middle line and he went on to make more than 400 League appearances for the club over 11 seasons before rounding off his playing career with a couple of seasons with Bristol Rovers. For all his defensive qualities, he was an attacking player by instinct, always ready either to bring the ball forward himself or to pick up a loose opposition clearance and let fly at goal, a flair which brought him over 50 League and Cup goals, mostly from the midfield, during his Argyle career. This was the facet of his play which most delighted supporters and in the period 1958-60 he netted 15 League goals in two seasons with the club. National Service with the Army did no harm at all to Johnny Williams' career. He continued to play regularly for the club and was also selected for the Army XI, along with such notables as Bobby Charlton, Cliff Jones and John White. When it is realized that the Services then could select from the best of the young professionals, Johnny Williams' selection for the Army XI is all the more significant. The big clubs watched him on a number of occasions but were unwilling to agree with Argyle's valuation, reputedly set at £40,000, and he was past his peak when he finally left the club for Bristol in 1966 after a change of management had left him with no other prospect than reserve-team football. He rejoined Argyle for a brief spell in the late 1960s on the coaching staff and subsequently went into the garage business in Plymouth.

	LEAGUE		*FA CUP*		*FL CUP*		*TOTAL*	
	App	*Gls*	*App*	*Gls*	*App*	*Gls*	*App*	*Gls*
1955-56	23	3	1	0	0	0	24	3
1956-57	40	2	2	0	0	0	42	2
1957-58	44	3	2	0	0	0	46	3
1958-59	45	7	4	0	0	0	49	7
1959-60	42	8	1	0	0	0	43	8
1960-61	42	7	1	0	8	3	51	10
1961-62	42	4	2	1	1	1	45	6
1952-63	38	5	1	0	1	0	40	5
1963-64	39	3	1	0	2	1	42	4
1964-65	29	3	2	0	5	1	36	4
1965-66	27/1	3	2	0	0	0	29/1	3
	411/1	48	19	1	17	6	447/1	55

REGINALD WYATT

Reg Wyatt joined Argyle, his home-town club, in 1950 as an inside-forward, a position he had filled with both Plymouth Schoolboys and the Oak Villa club. But it was as a defender that he made his mark with the club. Joining Argyle as an 18-year-old, he served a six-year apprenticeship with the Reserves before finally being given a first-team chance in 1956. By that time, Wyatt had concluded that his future with the club was in defence but, although he made his debut at full-back, Argyle's forward weaknesses that year were so pronounced that he was asked to revert to his original inside-forward role before the season had finished. However, he was later to find his true position in the centre of the defence and he was the regular choice at centre-half until the arrival of competition in the shape of Gordon Fincham from Leicester City. Even then, he held off the challenge of his rival for some time and was to win a Third Division championship medal with the club in 1959. Tall and lean, Wyatt had neat ball control but he was a little too deliberate on the ball and lacking in the acceleration necessary to make a mark as an attacker. In defence, however, he could use his height to advantage and capitalize on his natural ball skills to play himself and the team out of trouble. He left Argyle in the autumn of 1964 and had three seasons with Torquay United before leaving the League scene in 1967.

When Argyle won the Third Division South championship in 1958-9, Reg Wyatt played in the first 33 League games of the season at centre-half before Gordon Fincham took over the number-five shirt for the remaining matches. Wyatt returned to finish the season at left-back, replacing Wally Bellett.

	LEAGUE		*FA CUP*		*FL CUP*		*TOTAL*	
	App	*Gls*	*App*	*Gls*	*App*	*Gls*	*App*	*Gls*
1955-56	11	1	0	0	0	0	11	1
1956-57	19	0	0	0	0	0	19	0
1957-58	45	0	3	0	0	0	48	0
1958-59	39	1	4	0	0	0	43	1
1959-60	28	0	0	0	0	0	28	0
1960-61	29	0	0	0	6	0	35	0
1961-62	3	0	0	0	0	0	3	0
1962-63	6	0	0	0	1	0	7	0
1963-64	21	0	1	0	0	0	22	0
1964-65	1	0	0	0	0	0	1	0
	202	2	8	0	7	0	217	2

Argyle Who's Who

The following section lists every player to have appeared in League or Cup football for Plymouth Argyle since they joined the Football League in 1920-21, with the exception of some 70 of the better-known players whose biographical details may be found in the section *Argyle Stars A-Z.*

GRAHAM ADAMS **Full-back**
Torrington-born, he played one match for Argyle in 1957-8 before moving to Headington (now Oxford) United.

BILL ADAMS **Full-back**
A Plymothian and one of the first recruits when Argyle was re-formed after World War Two. Although a stalwart performer for the Reserves, he received only one chance in the Football League side, on New Year's Day 1947.

MILIJA ALEKSIC **Goalkeeper**
Born in Staffordshire of a Yugoslav father and English mother, he was spotted by Argyle playing for Stafford Rangers and obtained for a £3,000 transfer fee. He took over in goal after Jim Furnell's retirement and later played for Luton Town and Tottenham Hotspur, winning an FA Cup medal with the latter in 1981. After losing his Spurs place to Ray Clemence, he emigrated to South Africa and was reported to be coaching there in 1987.

KEITH ALLEN **Forward**
Helped Stockport County and Luton Town to promotion before joining Argyle in 1970, but injury forced him to retire from the game after only two seasons at Home Park.

DOUG ANDERSON **Winger**
Signed by Dave Smith in August 1987 from Tranmere Rovers for £15,000 as a replacement for Gary Nelson, who had been transferred to Brighton. Born in Hong Kong, Anderson made his League debut for Oldham Athletic and played over 100 League games for Tranmere, but his Argyle form was disappointing. He lost his place in the side midway through 1987-8 and spent most of the next season on loan with Cambridge United and Northampton Town, leaving Argyle on a free transfer before the season ended to try his luck with the Hong Kong club, Double Flower.

BILL ARCHER **Wing-half**
Recruited from Coventry City in 1938, his Argyle career was cut short by the outbreak of war. He played for the team throughout the 1939-40 wartime season but was then called into the RAF and did not resume an association with the club when the war ended.

FRANK ARUNDEL **Outside-left**
Local player who made four appearances on Argyle's left wing in 1956 and later had a spell with Torquay United.

TERRY AUSTIN **Centre-forward**
Came to Home Park in 1976 as part of the deal which took Paul Mariner to Ipswich Town. He had two seasons with Argyle and later moved frequently around League clubs, playing for Walsall, Mansfield Town, Huddersfield Town, Doncaster Rovers and Northampton Town. He then dropped out of the Football League and was playing for Stamford in the United Counties League in 1984.

DOUG BAIRD **Full-back**
Brought to Home Park in 1963 by Andy Beattie, for whom he had played when the latter was managing Nottingham Forest. Baird won a Scottish Under-23 cap and was also chosen for the Scottish League team while with Partick Thistle, whom he left for Forest in 1960. He played over 150 games for Argyle in five seasons with the club, mostly at full-back but occasionally in the centre of defence.

GEORGE BAKER **Forward**
An Argyle recruit in 1955 from Welsh junior football, he joined the club as a winger but had his most successful spell as the deep-lying centre-forward of the 1958-9 promotion side, with Wilf Carter and Jimmy Gauld playing ahead of him as the strikers. The same period brought him selection for the Wales Under-23 team. He lost his place soon after Argyle began their Second Division programme and moved to Shrewsbury Town a year later.

BILLY BAKER **Outside-left**
A Woolwich-born winger who combined finesse and speed, he was signed from Derby County in 1921 and took over the left-wing spot from Arthur Dixon before relinquishing it in turn to Sammy Black. Playing second fiddle to that Argyle legend was not an attractive option and Baker retired from the game in 1927. Baker joined Derby from Dartford and played in the Rams team which won the Second Division title in 1914-15.

PETA BALAC **Goalkeeper**
Another Argyle goalkeeper of the early 1970s with a Yugoslav father (see Milija Aleksic). Exeter-born, he was spotted playing for Exeter Schools and brought to Home Park as an apprentice. He shared goalkeeping duties with Jim Furnell for two seasons and later had loan spells with Hereford United and Swansea City. He then played in South Africa but returned to Devon in 1986 to link up with John Hore at Torrington where the former Argyle half-back was manager.

GARY BALL **Full-back**
A Cornishman who began his Argyle career as an apprentice but made only one substitute appearance in 1979. He was later transferred to Lincoln City, for whom he played three games.

ALAN BANKS **Forward**
Began his League career with his home club, Liverpool, and found his way to Home Park via Cambridge United and Exeter City, returning to the latter after a season with Argyle.

BRUCE BANNISTER **Forward**
A Yorkshireman who had built a reputation as a goal-scorer with his home club, Bradford City, and then with Bristol Rovers. Argyle, whom he joined in 1976, had hopes that he might fill the vacancy left by Paul Mariner but his scoring record at Home Park was not impressive. He seemed to recover his form after moving back to Yorkshire with Hull City, after only a half season with Argyle.

PAUL BANNON **Forward**
A Dubliner, he made two substitute appearances for Argyle while on loan from Bristol Rovers in 1984.

GEOFF BANTON **Defender**
An apprentice with Bolton Wanderers before joining Argyle. He played a handful of games for the club in 1977-8 and then joined Fulham where he had a more sustained spell in League football.

MARTIN BARLOW **Winger**
Apprentice who was given his first-team opportunity at the end of the 1988-9 season. He impressed as a real prospect for the future and was offered professional terms.

BERNARD BARNES **Centre-forward**
A Plymothian, he scored twice against Watford in the FA Cup in 1957 but had few chances later with the Argyle first team and left the club a year later for Southern League Weymouth.

GEOFF BARNSLEY **Goalkeeper**
Goalkeeper in the 1958-9 promotion team. He made only one appearance for his first club, West Bromwich Albion, before joining Argyle, for whom he played nearly 150 games, in 1957. Lightly built but agile, he had one surprising limitation — he was a poor kicker of a dead ball. He left Argyle in 1961 for Norwich City but had only a few games for them and for Torquay United whom he later joined.

TOM BARRETT **Half-back**
Salford-born, he was one of the lesser-known 'Busby Babes' at Manchester United in the early 1950s. He joined that famous club at 18, but after five seasons was still awaiting his League debut, when Argyle's manager, Jack Rowley, returned to his old club in search of promising young players who could assist his new charge at Plymouth. Tom Barrett and Bryce Fulton were added to the Home Park staff as a result of that approach. After 27 games with Argyle, Barrett joined Chester in 1960.

PAUL BARRON **Goalkeeper**
Formerly with Slough Town, he had one season (1977-8) with Argyle before attracting Arsenal's attention and signed for the London club in 1978. Unable to win a permanent place at Highbury, he later had more successful spells with Crystal Palace, West Brom and Queen's Park Rangers and was in the West Brom goal in 1984 when Argyle pulled off their surprise fifth-round FA Cup victory at The Hawthorns. He left the Football League scene in the late 1980s and in 1988 was back playing for Welling, the club where he began.

BRIAN BASON **Full-back/midfield**
A £30,000 signing from Chelsea who had four seasons with Argyle in the late 1970s and gave the club good service in a variety of positions before moving to Crystal Palace. Given a free transfer by Reading at the end of 1982-3, he returned to the West Country to become manager of a hotel in Truro.

BERT BATTEN **Forward**
Had five seasons with Argyle, whom he joined in 1921 from Bristol City. Consistent displays with Argyle led to him being selected for the FA tour of Australia in the summer of 1925 where he created such a good impression that Everton were ready with an offer for him soon after the start of the new season. He did not really establish a place on Merseyside, however, and was transferred to Bradford City one season later.

BOBBY BELL **Inside-forward**
Loaned to Argyle by Partick Thistle in 1955 before the loan scheme became commonplace. Bell was doing his National Service with the Army in Wiltshire and was unable to return to Scotland every weekend for games. Argyle were struggling and badly in need of reinforcement. An agreement between the two clubs resulted in the young Scot playing twice for Argyle at the end of the 1955-6 season, too late unfortunately to be able to prevent the team's relegation from the Second Division.

WALLY BELLETT **Full-back**
A former England Youth international, the burly defender was part of a double signing from Chelsea by Jack Rowley in 1958 to strengthen Argyle's promotion bid. (Len Casey was the other player involved.) Neither player really established himself at Home Park and Bellett moved to Orient in 1961. He was a surprise — and unsuccessful — selection at centre-forward for Argyle in an FA Cup tie at West Brom in 1960.

FRED BINNEY **Centre-forward**
Plymouth-born, he arrived at Home Park towards the end of his League career after having played for Torquay, Exeter and Brighton. His most successful season for Argyle was 1978-9 (26 goals in 42 games including a hat-trick at Sheffield Wednesday) and he was a natural choice for Player of the Year. He ended his League career with Hereford United after leaving Argyle.

TONY BIRD **Forward**
Red-haired, powerfully-built Irishman who had four seasons with Argyle after joining them in 1930 from Dublin Bohemians. He was mostly regarded as a very useful reserve to have around when players like Jack Vidler, Ray Bowden and Jack Leslie were not available. He once scored six goals for the Reserves in a Southern League match. He later played for Newport County.

LEN BIRKS **Full-back**
Former Sheffield United player who made his debut for the club in February 1930 and for two more seasons competed with Fred Titmuss for the left-back position before retiring from the game.

TOMMY BLACK **Full-back/wing-half**
Scottish defender who came to Home Park under something of a cloud from his previous club Arsenal. On his only appearance for the London club, he had been a member of the side which suffered an FA Cup defeat at Walsall in 1933. He had, moreover, conceded the penalty by which Walsall scored one of their two winning goals. The net result was that he was virtually thrown out of the London club, their manager vowing that Black would never play for the team again. Argyle had few complaints about him and he spent seven seasons with them, playing mostly at left-half in front of Jimmy Rae. He was transferred to Southend United in 1939 and played in all three of their matches in the 1939-40 season before League football was suspended with the outbreak of war.

HARRY BLAND **Full-back/centre-half**
Another Argyle stalwart whose arrival at Home Park was due to the Navy who posted him to Plymouth. A hard and clean tackler, he was a member of the 1929-30 side which first took Argyle into the Second Division, having edged the ageing Moses Russell out of the side. He later played for Cardiff City.

PADDY BLATCHFORD **Outside-left**
The former Saltash United player gave up a job with the Admiralty in order to turn professional with Argyle, but Alex Govan's emergence in the 1950s denied him a permanent place and he left the club in 1951 for a more successful spell with Leyton Orient. Probably the best game he played for Argyle lies outside the official records; in a friendly match against Southampton in 1949. Time and again he swept past the visiting right-back, a player later to win fame for England as player, captain and manager — Alf Ramsey.

JIMMY BLOOMFIELD **Inside-forward**
A player of great skill. Regrettably the Home Park faithful did not see him at the peak of his career. He was 32 when Derek Ufton signed him for Argyle in 1966, by which time he had made over 400 League appearances with Brentford, Arsenal, Birmingham City, Brentford (again) and West Ham United. He had only one season with Argyle before accepting an offer to become player-manager with Orient. He died in 1983, aged 49.

CLARRIE BOURTON **Centre-forward**
Came to Argyle from Coventry City in October 1937 with a reputation of being a prolific goalscorer but his stay at Home Park was brief. Before his appearances had reached double figures, he was on his way again, to Bristol City, where he had a more successful spell and with whom he remained until the early years of the war.

BERT BOWLER **Forward**
A link with the Argyle of Southern League days, he remained with the club for three seasons after they had gained Football League status. Bob Jack discovered Bowler playing for the Army Cup winners, Sherwood Foresters, and, after the latter had obtained his discharge from the Army to turn professional, Argyle used him to good effect, both in the centre of the forward

line and on the left wing, and he was recognized as one of the best headers of the ball in the club. He was selected on a number of occasions for the Southern League representative side against the Football League and even played for England in an unofficial international against Scotland in Cairo during World War One. He retired from the game in 1923.

STUART BRACE **Winger**
A former Taunton Town player whose nine appearances for Argyle were spread over four seasons but who then went on to record nearly 400 League appearances with Watford, Mansfield, Peterborough, Grimsby and Southend. He has reappeared in West Country soccer in recent years as coach to Liskeard.

KEVIN BREMNER **Midfield**
Brother of former Aston Villa player Des Bremner, he made five appearances for Argyle while on loan from Colchester United in 1983 and has since given good service to Millwall, Reading and Brighton.

STEVE BRENNAN **Midfield**
Former Crystal Palace player who made six appearances for Argyle at the start of the 1978-9 season.

GEORGE BRIGGS **Inside-forward**
Heavily-built forward who arrived at Home Park from Birmingham City in 1933 and had just over two seasons with Argyle before deciding to retire from the game.

JOHN BRIMACOMBE **Defender**
Plymouth-born and a Saltash United player when he was working in the dockyard. He was given his professional opportunity at the age of 27 and justified the confidence placed in him. He missed only two League games in 1987-8 but injury restricted his appearances in 1988-9 when he was often tried in midfield roles.

TONY BRIMACOMBE **Inside-forward**
Plymouth-born schoolteacher who played as an amateur for Argyle from 1966 to 1968 — a period of great difficulty for Argyle — mostly in the Reserves but occasionally in the League side.

DAVID BROWN **Goalkeeper**
Loaned by Middlesbrough in 1979 to help Argyle over a goalkeeping problem which was to be solved soon afterwards by the signing of Geoff Crudgington.

HARRY BROWN **Goalkeeper**
A welcome addition to the Argyle staff in 1956 when the club had difficulty in filling the vacancy left by the retirement of Shortt and Major. Started his League career with Queen's Park Rangers, then played for Notts County, Derby and QPR again. During his first spell with Rangers, he came on as a substitute goalkeeper for Arsenal during their famous 1945 game in the London fog against Dinamo Moscow.

HENRY BROWN **Inside-forward**
A Scot who began his professional career with Hibernian, then moved south via Darlington and Chesterfield to join Argyle in 1936. He played just over two seasons for Argyle before moving to Reading. He joined Wolverhampton during the war years but played only a couple of wartime games for them before joining Hull City in 1946 where he had one season of Third Division North football.

JOHNNY BROWN **Inside-forward**
Former Wadebridge player who made his Argyle debut on the day Wilf Carter entered the record books by scoring five times in a match with Charlton Athletic. He made only a handful of further appearances for Argyle but became a regular choice over four seasons with Bristol Rovers, his next club, where he was affectionately known as 'Farmer' because of his rural background.

KENNY BROWN **Full-back**
Son of the Argyle manager who was given a free transfer by Norwich City (where he had been an apprentice under his father), at the end of 1987-8 after playing 25 League games for the Canaries. He came into the Argyle side in September 1988 and became first choice at right-back from that moment, showing that he has a good turn of speed and attacking ideas. At West Brom in April 1989 he scored his first League goal.

RONNIE BROWN **Winger**
Former Blackpool player, discovered by the seaside club in Durham junior football. He had two seasons with Argyle in the early 1970s and was later transferred to Bradford City.

ERIC BRYANT **Centre-forward**
A swarthy, black-haired player who was brought back into League football by Argyle in 1949 after he had starred in a notable FA Cup run by Yeovil Town. In his last season with Yeovil he scored 71 times and had netted 20 goals in ten games for the Somerset club at the time of his transfer. Before joining Yeovil, he had League experience with Aldershot and Mansfield. There always appeared to be a certain stiffness in his movement around the field and he was unable to reproduce such prolific scoring with either Argyle or Leyton Orient, whom he joined after only two seasons at Home Park.

COLIN BUCKINGHAM **Half-back**
Joined Argyle from school, first on the ground staff and then as an apprentice. He did not win a regular place in the Argyle League side, but later had more success with Exeter City.

JIMMY BUIST **Outside-left**
A pre-war player with Dundee and Raith Rovers, he arrived at Home Park from New Brighton but made only one League appearance for Argyle. That was when he was called into the side at the last minute in 1949 in order to replace a sick Bill Strauss in the match in which Neil Dougall made his Argyle debut. He later played Southern League football with Hereford United and Gloucester City.

REG BUNGAY **Forward**
Reading-born, former Tottenham Hotspur reserve who joined the London club from Oxford City. He made only one appearance in each of his two seasons with Argyle before being transferred to Bristol City in 1936. He later played for Mansfield Town.

ERIC BURGESS **Full-back**
Former Watford and Torquay United defender who came to Home Park on a free transfer in 1968 and was transferred to Colchester United two years later.

TONY BURNS **Goalkeeper**
Had a brief spell between the Argyle posts in 1978 before being supplanted by Martin Hodge. Formerly with Tonbridge, he had spent his career before joining Argyle with southern clubs — Arsenal, Brighton, Charlton, Crystal Palace and Brentford — as well as a period with Durban City in South Africa. He was managing Gravesend & Northfleet in 1984-5.

ADRIAN BURROWS **Central-defender**
A strongly-built and reliable defender who had one of his best seasons at the heart of the Argyle defence in 1988-9. He has now spent ten years in League football, having started with Mansfield Town. He then moved to Northampton Town and joined Argyle in the summer of 1984. At one point, his Argyle career appeared to be faltering and the club allowed him to have a spell on loan to Southend United at the start of 1987-8, but his form there was so impressive that he was recalled to Plymouth and he has been a regular in the middle of the defence since then.

HARRY BURROWS **Outside-left**
Lancashire-born winger who joined the Aston Villa ground staff on leaving school and was later offered professional terms, making his League debut in 1959. He had nearly 400 League games with Villa and Stoke City and an appearance for the England Under-23 team behind him when he arrived at Home Park in 1973. He retired from the game a year later.

PHIL BURROWS **Left-back**
Born in Stockport, he started his professional career with Manchester City but had to wait until moving to York City to make his League debut. He played over 300 games for York before being transferred for a £16,000 fee to Argyle, where he was a regular member of the promotion side of 1974-5. He had three seasons with Hereford United after leaving Argyle and then dropped out of the Football League. In 1983-4 he was reported to be playing in the Northern Premier League with Witton Albion.

DAVID BYRNE **Winger**
A free-transfer signing from Millwall in March 1989, he had been on loan to Blackburn Rovers and played against Argyle in the Ewood Park fixture. He took over the number-seven shirt soon after arriving at Home Park and looked to have plenty of pace and enthusiasm, also — shades of Gordon Astall — he could produce a surprisingly long throw-in. A Londoner, he began his professional career with Gillingham, whom he joined from Kingstonian, then moved to Millwall.

DAVID CAMPBELL **Midfield**
Northern Ireland international who played one match on loan to Argyle from Charlton Athletic in March 1989. Ken Brown was sufficiently impressed by him to begin negotiations for a permanent transfer, but the player was apparently more attracted by the offer from Bradford City, who also sought his services. Campbell won ten caps whilst with Charlton and Nottingham Forest, his first club.

GREGG CAMPBELL **Forward**
Son of the Chelsea manager Bobby Campbell, he was an apprentice with West Ham United and made a handful of Football League appearances with the Hammers whilst on loan to Brighton but was playing for Sparta Rotterdam when Ken Brown brought him back to England in the autumn of 1988. He was not really able to break the McCarthy-Tynan partnership and played more times as a substitute than as a full member of the side.

HARRY CANN **Goalkeeper**
A fearless, agile goalkeeper, Cann, apart from a period when he gave way to Bill Harper, guarded the Argyle goal after Fred Craig left the club in 1930 virtually up to the outbreak of World War Two. Born in Tintagel, he played for Tintagel and Cornwall County teams before signing for Argyle. His fearless plunges where the boots were flying often caused him painful injuries and on more than one occasion a colleague had to don the goalkeeping jersey while Harry Cann was carried off, having used his body to repel an opposition attack. Possibly his most memorable match was one which others associated with the club would want to forget. He was the goalkeeper at Everton at Christmas 1930 when a weary Argyle team were overwhelmed 9-1 by the home side. But the crowd recognized that the defeat could have been even heavier were it not for Cann's heroics in goal and the Argyle player received a standing ovation on leaving the field. At the end of his career, Argyle gave him a free transfer and he signed for Fulham in 1939. He played for them in the first of the wartime seasons but then retired from the game.

ERNIE CARLESS **Inside-forward**
One of a number of inside-forwards tried by Argyle in the 1946-7 season. He joined the club from Cardiff City during the previous season after having had the doubtful distinction of being a member of the City side hammered 10-1 by the touring Dinamo Moscow team. He was also employed on the Argyle ground staff. A Glamorgan cricketer whilst with Cardiff, he later played for Plymouth and Devon. He died in 1987.

MIKE CARTER **Forward**
Recruited for Argyle after having been given a free transfer by Bolton Wanderers, he played a few games in the 1982-3 season and was then transferred to Hereford United and subsequently to Wrexham.

BOB CARTER **Half-back**
Lancashire-born defender who looked like being a notable capture when he arrived at Home Park from Chelsea in April 1933, having played 16 First Division games in the previous season. He had three games for Argyle in 1933-4 but Harry Bland, Jack Pullen and Fred McKenzie were all in turn subsequently preferred to him and he left the club for Watford a year later.

LEN CASEY **Wing-half**
Signed from Chelsea by Jack Rowley in 1958, with Wally Bellett, in order to boost Argyle's promotion chances, he was immediately appointed team captain

and won a championship medal with the team. He was not so successful in the Second Division and lost his place when Johnny Newman was signed in 1960.

FRANCIS CASSIDY **Forward**
Made one appearance for Argyle in 1984, while on loan from Watford.

MIKE CAVE **Forward**
Scored four goals in eight appearances while on loan from Bournemouth in 1972. After returning to Bournemouth he continued his League career with York City and again with Bournemouth before going to the United States, where he was killed in an accident.

NEVILLE CHAMBERLAIN **Forward**
Brother of England forward Mark Chamberlain, he led the attack in the last six games of 1983-4 while on loan from Stoke City. Before signing for Stoke, he was with Port Vale and later played for Newport County, Mansfield Town, Cambridge United and Doncaster Rovers.

LEE CHAPMAN **Forward**
Made three appearances as a 19-year-old in 1978-9 whilst on loan from Stoke City. He has subsequently developed as a forward of First Division class with Stoke City, Arsenal, Sunderland, Sheffield Wednesday and Nottingham Forest.

PAUL CHAPMAN **Midfield**
Made only two appearances for Argyle in 1969-70. A cartilage operation forced his retirement from the game. He played for Plymouth and Devon Schools and had a trial for England Schools but, having been born in Cardiff, he qualified for recognition by Wales and won six caps for the Welsh Youth team.

PERCY CHERRETT **Centre-forward**
Came to Home Park in September 1923 from Portsmouth, having lost his place after three seasons with the Hampshire club. He made his debut for Argyle at Portsmouth and, although finishing on the losing side, had the satisfaction of scoring Argyle's only goal. It was a happy omen, for the centre-forward proved to be a consistent scorer for the club, netting 37 in 62 appearances. He lost his place in the side when Jack Cock arrived on the scene and was transferred to Crystal Palace in 1925.

STEVE CHERRY **Goalkeeper**
Former Derby County and Walsall goalkeeper who was unable to settle in the West Country and returned to his native Midlands to sign for Notts County for £70,000 early in the 1988-9 season. Argyle had seen him as the natural successor to Geoff Crudgington after he had given an excellent display for Derby at Home Park in the sixth round of the 1984 FA Cup. His departure left Argyle with a goalkeeping gap which they plugged up to the end of the season only by enlisting the services on loan of two Arsenal players.

WILF CHITTY **Winger**
Started his professional career with Chelsea after having played for Woking. He had three games on the Argyle left wing in December 1938 but moved to Reading the following year and played for the Berkshire club for two post-war seasons.

MARTIN CLAMP **Goalkeeper**
Played eight times for Argyle in the 1969-70 season as deputy for Pat Dunne. Coventry-born, he started his career with Coventry City but did not get a League chance with them. He joined Nuneaton Borough after leaving Home Park.

JIMMY CLARK **Centre-half**
World War Two interrupted this player's association with Argyle after he had been with the club for just over two seasons. With Sunderland, he won a League Championship medal in 1935-6 but was not selected for their FA Cup Final side in 1937 and was willing to leave the north to rebuild his career in the West Country. He was called into the RAF in 1939 but played a number of games for the club in the wartime 1939-40 League. He went to South Africa after the war and was reported to be managing a football club there in the 1960s.

COLIN CLARKE **Centre-back**
Scot who came to the fore with Oxford United for whom he played over 400 League games and shared in their successes after entering the Football League. He had a spell with Los Angeles Aztecs in the NASL before joining Argyle in the 1978-9 season. After finishing his Football League career, he was manager of Stafford Rangers and then player-coach of Launceston.

JOHN CLAYTON **Forward**
A Scottish Schools international, he joined Derby County as an apprentice, then left the Football League to join the Hong Kong side, Bulova, in 1982-3. Returning to this country, he played for Chesterfield and then for Tranmere Rovers where, in 1984-5, he made his mark as the country's leading scorer with 36 goals, his best performance in a season. Argyle added him to their staff in the summer of 1985, as a replacement for Tommy Tynan, but he later formed a forward partnership with Tynan when the latter returned to Home Park. His scoring record for Argyle, 22 goals in 77 games, was reasonable but not quite the spectacular return for which Argyle had been hoping and he left the club three years later for £65,000 to join the Dutch Division One club, Fortuna Sittard.

CRAWFORD CLELLAND **Inside-forward**
Of Scottish descent but born in New Jersey, USA. Signed from Aberdeen in 1955, he was included in the Argyle side for the first two matches of 1955-6, but did not hold a place in the team and returned to Scotland at the end of the season.

BILLY COBB **Inside-forward**
Brought to Home Park from Nottingham Forest with Doug Baird by Andy Beattie in 1963 in order to strengthen the relegation-threatened Argyle side. He had a capacity for hard work and made effective use of the ball which helped to stave off the prospect of a fall into the Third Division. Forest spotted him playing for the Newark works side, Ransome & Marles. He later played for Brentford and Lincoln City.

DOUG COLLINS **Inside-forward**
Started his League career with Grimsby Town, then had eight seasons with Burnley when the Lancashire side were in the First Division before coming to Home Park. A creative player, he made 22 appearances for Argyle in 1976-7 and later played for Sunderland and Rochdale.

JEREMY COLLINS **Midfield**
Local player who played four times for Argyle between 1980 and 1981, then left the League scene to play for Falmouth Town.

JACK CONNOR **Centre-forward**
Former Airdrieonians player who scored twice on his League debut for Argyle in September 1936 and went on to head the list for the club that season. The goal supply dried up the following season and with Fletcher, Hullett and Bourton being added to the staff, his first-team chances were much reduced and he was transferred to Swansea Town.

JEFF COOK **Forward**
Had an impressive goalscoring record — five goals in seven games — for Argyle when on loan from Stoke City in 1979 and returned to Home Park two years later on permanent transfer. He again showed the scoring touch although on this latter occasion the ratio of goals to appearances (21 in 58) was not quite so outstanding. He moved to Halifax Town in 1983.

BILL COOK **Goalkeeper**
Signed from Castleford Town with Joe Little in 1920, he had few opportunities to prove himself in the Argyle goal while Fred Craig was so reliable but he had two seasons as Brighton's regular goalkeeper after leaving Home Park.

JIMMY COOKSON **Centre-forward**
Began his League career as a full-back with Manchester City but really hit the high spots when tried at centre-forward with Chesterfield. He established individual scoring records in his first season with Chesterfield and also at his next club, West Bromwich Albion. With the latter, he was a member of the 1930-31 side which won both the FA Cup and promotion to the First Division and he was selected for the FA team touring Canada in the summer of 1931. He scored over 100 goals during his career with Albion, including six (five of them in 24 minutes of the second half) in a Division Two match against Blackpool in 1927. He maintained his reputation as a goalscorer in three seasons at Home Park where he had a scoring record — 38 goals in 48 games — which would be difficult to better. His great asset as a scorer was his readiness to shoot whenever chances presented themselves, his goal in the FA Cup against Huddersfield Town being a typical example. He moved to Swindon Town in 1935 and had a couple of seasons there before retiring from the game.

STEVE COOPER **Forward**
A native of Birmingham, his only League chance while on the books at St Andrew's was during a loan spell with Halifax Town. Birmingham transferred him to Newport County, from where he joined Argyle in exchange for Gordon Staniforth in 1985. He was a regular member of the promotion-winning side of 1985-6, but despite his natural athleticism — few could leap higher to head a ball than he — he never quite fulfilled his promise as a scorer. He was transferred to Barnsley for £100,000 in 1988.

DAVE CORBETT **Winger**
One of a number of talented young players who were on Swindon Town's books in the 1960s, he was brought to Home Park by Ellis Stuttard who had previously been on the management staff at Swindon. His speed and enthusiasm made him a popular figure and at one point there was a rumour that he was being seriously considered for a place in the England Under-23 side. Sadly, injury forced his early retirement from the game.

PATSY CORCORAN **Winger**
Tall for a winger, he was a little on the slow side, but he had excellent control and could shoot from narrow angles. A Scot, he was on Glasgow Celtic's books but it was from the junior side, Bathgate, that he joined Argyle in 1920, just in time for the club's entry into the Football League. He gave excellent service for six seasons, totalling nearly 200 appearances and being selected for a Scottish international trial while with Argyle. He had a benefit in 1926, when the opposition was provided by Everton who fielded former Argyle favourite, Bert Batten, in the side. He signed for Torquay United, not then a League club, in the summer of 1926 and within a few months for Luton Town, but did not make any League appearances for the latter.

FRED COSGROVE **Full-back**
Had 11 seasons with Argyle, his only professional club, whom he joined from Durham City in 1920. Patience had to be his chief virtue because he was forced to contend with some very capable rivals for a place in the side. With players like Moses Russell and Billy Forbes almost automatic choices at the start of his Argyle career, and Fred Titmuss appearing later, Cosgrove was regarded mainly as a most reliable reserve but he did have one season (1924-5) between the retirement of Forbes and the arrival of Titmuss when he was a regular partner for Russell.

RUSSELL COUGHLIN **Midfield**
A regular member of Argyle's 1985-6 promotion side. Swansea-born, he started his career with Manchester City, but did not make his League debut until joining Blackburn Rovers. He subsequently played for Carlisle United and had just over three seasons at Home Park before moving north again to Blackpool in 1987.

JOHN CRAVEN **Half-back**
Signed from Coventry City in 1977 in a bid to stop Argyle's slide into the Third Division. He started his League career with his home team, Blackpool, and was later with Crystal Palace before coming to Home Park. His spell there was relatively short and he afterwards went to Canada to play for Vancouver Whitecaps and then Calgary Boomers in the NASL.

JIMMY CRAWFORD **Inside-forward**
A Scot who had impressed the Argyle management while appearing at Home Park for Leicester City Reserves. However, he failed to reproduce his best form after joining Argyle in 1954 and made only spasmodic appearances for the side over three seasons.

TERRY DANN **Inside-forward**
Joined Argyle from Penzance in 1959 and played intermittently in the League team in the 1959-60 season.

PETER DARKE **Full-back**
Exeter-born defender who, like Peta Balac, was spotted playing for the Exeter Schools team. He made his Argyle debut at 18 and played just over 100 games for the club before moving to Torquay United in the summer of 1977. In recent seasons he has been managing Saltash United.

ARTHUR DAVIES **Goalkeeper**
Had two spells at Home Park with a brief season at Southport sandwiched between. Formerly with Exeter City, he was second choice to Harry Cann in 1935-6 and 1936-7 but was transferred to Southport at the end of the latter season. He had only a handful of League games in the north and rejoined Argyle at the start of 1938-9 to become one of four goalkeepers tried by the club that season. He died in 1939, before the outbreak of the war.

JACK DAVIES **Wing-half**
An unmistakable member of the Argyle side of the immediate post-war seasons — he was almost completely bald. A Welsh Schoolboy international, he was a pre-war player with Chester and Cardiff City. He spent two seasons with Argyle after arriving from Everton, playing mostly at left-half but occasionally at inside-forward. He was transferred to Bristol City in 1948.

MALCOLM DAVIES **Winger**
Joined Argyle in 1949 as an 18-year-old from Aberaman when the Welsh club was regarded as an Argyle 'nursery.' Slimly built and fast, he had five seasons with the club and was a fairly regular member of the side from 1954 to 1957 after the departures of Astall and Goven had opened the door for him. He returned to Wales to play for Llanelli at the end of his Argyle career.

ERIC DAVIS **Centre-forward**
Local player who was recruited from Tavistock in 1952 and made his debut for Argyle a year later. Tall and slim, he could be guaranteed to keep defenders at full stretch. For example, he provided an admittedly ageing Jack Chisholm with a number of problems during one Argyle pre-season public trial match when traditionally the first team was pitted against young aspirants. A contemporary of Neil Langman, he did not have quite the same scoring impact as his colleague, although his ball control was probably better. At one point, the two appeared to be rivals to take over the spot vacated by Maurice Tadman but Argyle later found that there was some advantage in playing both as a double spearhead in attack. In later seasons, he played for Scunthorpe (with whom he won a Third Division North championship medal), Chester and Oldham.

JACK DAVIS **Centre-forward**
Former Exeter City player who had one season (1927-8) and three games as leader of the Argyle attack, then retired from League football.

RICHARD DAVIS **Full-back**
A local player who graduated to the Argyle League side through the apprentice scheme. He made 25 appearances for the side from 1962 to 1964 before being transferred to Southampton. Davis later played for Bristol City and Barrow. He returned to the West Country after his League days were over, managed Falmouth Town and is now helping at Argyle's School of Excellence for young players.

LES DEACON **Half-back**
Came to Argyle from Devon County and was virtually a perpetual reserve during his eight seasons on Argyle's books. He was selected for first-team football on only five occasions and only once made more than one appearance during a League season.

JOHN DELVE **Midfield**
A Londoner, he began his League career with Queen's Park Rangers, cost Argyle £30,000 and made nearly 150 League appearances between 1974 and 1978. A busy, driving type of player, he was a regular member of the 1974-5 promotion side. He later had four seasons with Exeter City and was playing for Minehead in 1987-8.

JACK DEMMELWEEK **Outside-right**
Another product of Royal Navy football, he first played for Argyle as an amateur but found it difficult to establish a regular place in the team after turning professional. After only a handful of appearances over eight seasons, he reached double figures in his ninth and last season at Home Park but was transferred to Southend United, where he had more success the following season. He rejoined the Navy during World War Two and took part in the famous commando raid on St Nazaire, was captured and spent the rest of the war as a prisoner.

TONY DENNIS **Outside-left**
Another product of the apprentice scheme, he made a few appearances for Argyle in the early 1980s and later joined Exeter City. He then spent six years out of League football before returning to the senior game, signing for Cambridge United from Slough Town in 1989.

JOHN DEVINE **Full-back**
Came to Argyle from the Scottish junior side, Kilsyth Rangers. As a contemporary of Moses Russell and Billy Forbes, he had little chance to shine during his four years at Home Park and was transferred to Charlton Athletic in 1925.

JIMMY DICKINSON **Half-back**
Discovered by Argyle in a local Royal Navy team after World War One, he was an established member of the side before Argyle gained admittance to the Football League. He had five more seasons of League football with the club before being transferred to Wigan Borough in 1924.

ARTHUR DIXON **Winger**
A former Fulham player, he was signed by Bob Jack in 1910 and was a regular choice for the club, mainly on the left wing, up to and including Argyle's first season in the Football League. He made over 100 appearances for the side during his Home Park career but only 17 in the Football League. He was transferred to Barrow in 1921 but retired from the game after only three months with the northern side.

STAN DIXON **Centre-half**
A dependable pivot who joined Argyle just before the war and established himself in the side for the 1945-6 and 1946-7 seasons. Thereafter, he seemed to be regarded as a permanent understudy and he played second fiddle to Oakes, Goddard and Chisholm in turn, although at the point when Chisholm was signed, Dixon was keeping Ray Goddard out of the side. Although lacking some of the panache of his three rivals, he could always be relied on to give a sound display as a 'stopper' during their absence. He dropped out of the Football League on joining Poole Town in 1951 and settled in the Bournemouth area after retiring from the game.

HAROLD DOBBIE **Centre-forward**
Small but fast, he came to Home Park in 1950 from Middlesbrough in the hope that he could get the goals which the team needed. At the time of his transfer, Dobbie had been a prolific scorer with Middlesbrough Reserves but although his speed off the mark tended to leave colleagues and opponents floundering, he could not repeat that scoring form with Argyle and was regarded mostly as a deputy forward during his five seasons with the club. He was transferred to Torquay United in 1953, in an exchange deal which brought Ernie Edds back to Home Park, and had a much more successful four-season period at Plainmoor. He died in 1988.

TOMMY DOUGAN **Outside-right**
Came from the same small Scottish village as Tommy Ryan, although the two players reached Home Park by different routes. Argyle discovered him playing, as a 17-year-old, for Tunbridge Wells Rangers. His promise was such that after only a few games in the first team, he was being hailed as a future Scottish international. Manchester United stepped in with an offer for him in March 1939 and he played four games

for them before the season ended. As with so many players, the outbreak of war put an end to his dreams of football fame.

ERIC DOUGHTY **Full-back**
Somerset-born, he had only one League appearance to show for his ten-year career with three clubs. He was on Arsenal's books for seven years without getting a League game; he played once for Argyle in 1958 and had another 'nil' return after moving to Bristol City.

MIKE DOWLING **Midfield**
A Cornishman, discovered playing for East Cornwall and Cornwall Schoolboys, he made only occasional appearances for the Argyle League side over five seasons, but made a lasting impression on supporters with two blistering goals — against Yeovil in an FA Cup match in 1972 and against the Brazilian club, Santos, the following spring.

JACK DUGNOLLE **Half-back**
Like Dougan, he was discovered by Argyle whilst with Tunbridge Wells. He had a handful of games for the club in the two pre-war seasons and reappeared in the side in the two wartime seasons in which Argyle competed. He was transferred to Brighton before League football resumed in 1946 and had two seasons with the Goldstone club in post-war football.

NOEL DWYER **Goalkeeper**
Flamboyant and quite unpredictable Republic of Ireland international, capped 14 times for his country between 1960 and 1965. Wolves brought him to England and he played for West Ham United and Swansea Town before joining Argyle. At Home Park, he became the centre of a dispute between Malcolm Allison and his directors which led to Allison leaving the club. Allison thought highly of the player; the directors were less impressed and their insistence on Dwyer's omission from the side for one game caused a rift between the board and the manager. He stayed at Home Park some eight months after Allison's departure and then ended his League career with Charlton.

ALEC DYER **Left-back**
Came to Argyle's notice while playing against them on Crewe's left wing in a 1937 FA Cup tie. At Home Park he was converted to left-back before the war and did not return to the wing, although Jimmy Rae continued to be first choice for the number-three shirt. During the war, he played regularly for Army representative teams and when Argyle reopened in 1945-6 he travelled frequently from Aberdeen to claim his place in the side. He was a regular member of the team when League football resumed the following season and had one game in his old left-wing position but retired at the end of that season to enter business, resisting an invitation from Crewe to rejoin his old club. Fortunately for Argyle, they had a ready-made replacement for Dyer and Pat Jones then began his long, virtually unbroken association with the team.

PETER DYER **Goalkeeper**
Local player who made his Argyle debut as an 18-year-old in 1955 and was called on to fill the vacancy in goal caused by the double retirement of Shortt and Major the following season. He was in goal when the side crumbled 6-0 at home to Reading. At 5ft 7in he was on the small side to establish himself in League football and he was subsequently displaced by the more experienced Harry Brown.

CYRIL EASTWOOD **Half-back**
One of three players (Cook and Little were the others) signed by Argyle from Castleford Town in the summer of 1920, his career with the club was the most successful of the three. He was equally adept in filling any of the half-back positions, although he normally played in one of the wing-half berths, usually with Jimmy Dickinson on the other flank. He had four seasons at Home Park, then moved back north to join Preston North End.

ERNIE EDDS **Forward**
Discovered playing for an Army side in junior Plymouth football at the end of the war, he had two periods on the Argyle staff. In the first stage, he was regarded mainly as a centre-forward and enjoyed his most successful season in 1947-8 when he scored 14 goals in 23 games, including a hat-trick at Southampton towards the end of the season, which saved Argyle from relegation and also ended the home team's promotion chances. Both Blackburn Rovers and Torquay United, for whom he next played, used him on the left wing and it was in that position that he returned to Home Park in 1953 in exchange for Harold Dobbie in order to replace Alex Govan. He had just over a season with Argyle in that second period before moving on to Swindon Town. Small and lightly built, he did not fit the standard specification for a centre-forward of that period but he was quick on the turn and had an engaging habit of placing his shots out of the reach of opposition goalkeepers.

ALEC EDMUNDS **Outside-left**
Discovered by Argyle in Navy football, he played in five successive League games on the Argyle left wing in 1927 as a deputy for Sammy Black, then moved to Torquay United.

ARTHUR EGGLESTON **Inside-forward**
Signed from Bury in the summer of 1935, he had two seasons in the Argyle front line and two more with Sheffield United up to the outbreak of the war.

TOM ENGLISH — **Forward**
Had the curious distinction of scoring a League goal for Argyle in 1984 without playing a full game for the club, because all his four League appearances while on loan from Leicester City were as substitute. He had one full game in the League Cup.

KEITH ETHERIDGE — **Forward**
Born at Ivybridge, he arrived at Home Park from St Blazey and played intermittently in the League side for two seasons from 1966 to 1968 before dropping into Southern League football with Weymouth.

STEWART EVANS — **Forward**
A Dave Smith signing from West Bromwich Albion in March 1987, the Argyle manager having long admired the way this 6ft 4in attacker could trouble defences. A Yorkshireman, he was on Rotherham United's books as an apprentice but was allowed to drop out of the Football League. Sheffield United signed him from Gainsborough Trinity but did not give him a League opportunity. That came after he moved south to sign for Wimbledon, where the London club's style and his suited each other and he scored 50 goals there in 175 League games. West Brom was his next club but he had lost his first-team place at The Hawthorns when Dave Smith moved in for his transfer. His Argyle career was not marked with particular success and Rotherham United, who had originally rejected him, paid £40,000 for his transfer early in the 1988-9 season.

MIKE EVERITT — **Full-back**
Began his professional career with Arsenal but established himself with Northampton Town with whom, over six seasons, he played in all four divisions of the Football League and filled a number of positions, both forward and in defence. Derek Ufton signed him in the hope that he would be able to recapture with Argyle the promotion experience which he had known with Northampton. Unfortunately it was not to be and the last of his two seasons with the club saw them relegated to the Third Division. He had two seasons with Brighton before leaving League football.

KEITH FEAR — **Forward**
Bristol-born, he began his League career with Bristol City and played in over 100 games for that club, besides loan periods with Hereford United and Blackburn Rovers before coming to Home Park for just over two seasons in 1978. He returned to Bristol City as lottery manager in 1985 and in 1988 became assistant manager of the local Bristol club, Mangotsfield.

LEN FEATHERBY — **Inside-forward**
A signing from Merthyr Town on 16 March 1934, he went into the League side the following day, but in two seasons with Argyle he made only a limited number of appearances. He began his football career with King's Lynn and played for Norfolk County before entering the Football League with Merthyr, Wolves, Reading, Mansfield Town, Crewe Alexandra and then back again to Merthyr before arriving at Home Park. He was transferred to Notts County in the summer of 1935.

BILL FELLOWES — **Half-back**
A Devonian, formerly with Tavistock Town, he played only five times for Argyle in the Football League in as many years. He was transferred to Clapton Orient in 1932 but reappeared at Home Park in 1939 in order to assist the club in the Wartime League programme for that season.

GORDON FINCHAM — **Centre-half**
Well-built central defender — 6ft 2in and over 13st — who joined Argyle in the summer of 1958 but had to wait until the following spring to make his debut. He then played in the last 13 matches of Argyle's promotion season. Born in Peterborough, he joined Leicester City from a Peterborough junior side and played for Leicester in both First and Second Divisions but lost his place after a cartilage operation. After nearly 150 games for the club, he left Argyle in the summer of 1963 for Luton Town.

ALBERT FISHWICK — **Inside-forward**
Like Paul Mariner 50 years later, he was an Argyle capture from Chorley, but unlike Mariner he had only a few games for Argyle after arriving at Home Park in the summer of 1923. He was more successful after a transfer to Blackpool, playing for the Lancashire club for three seasons.

CHARLIE FLETCHER — **Forward**
Spent exactly a year with Argyle from November 1937 to November 1938. Signed from Burnley, he had 18 games for Argyle in 1937-8, either in the centre or on the left wing, and was then transferred to Ipswich Town for whom he played up to the outbreak of the war.

JOHN FOLEY — **Goalkeeper**
An Irishman from Cork with a big kick, he had been playing for Glasgow Celtic when he joined Argyle in January 1937. At one point, he looked to be permanently displacing Harry Cann but the Argyle veteran

won back his place and it was Foley who left Plymouth first, returning to Ireland to play for Cork City in 1938.

FRED FORBES **Forward**
Former Hearts player for whom Everton paid a big fee in 1922, but he did not get many chances at Goodison Park. He was transferred to Argyle with Jack Cock in 1925 and served the club for four more seasons, being a regular choice in a number of different forward positions. After appearing in nearly 150 games for Argyle he was transferred in 1929 to Bristol Rovers, but retired soon afterwards and returned to Edinburgh to set up a business.

DICK FORBES **Defender**
Schoolteacher, formerly with Woking and Exeter City, he had a few games in the Argyle defence in the 1983-4 season. Player-coach with Tiverton in 1987-8.

BILLY FORBES **Full-back**
Best known at Home Park for his full-back partnership with Moses Russell which began just before World War One and continued through four seasons after Argyle's entry into the Football League. He was capped for Scotland in a Junior international in 1912 and played for Denny Hibernians before coming south. Argyle was his only League club and he retired from the game in 1924.

CLEVERE FORDE **Forward**
Formerly with Hounslow, he had a handful of games for Argyle in 1978-9 but did not establish a place and returned to London football with Wealdstone. He was playing for Barnet in 1988.

GEORGE FORREST **Half-back**
Formerly with Peterhead, he made only three appearances in as many years at Home Park and was transferred to Mansfield Town in 1935.

WINSTON FOSTER **Centre-half**
Born in 1941 and named after the British Prime Minister, he had eight seasons and over 150 games with Birmingham City before arriving at Home Park on a free transfer from the Midlands club. He ably deputized for Fred Molyneux after the latter had been injured early in the 1969-70 season, but lost his place to a fit Molyneux the following season and moved out of League football on joining Chelmsford Town.

JACK FOWLER **Centre-forward**
A product of Welsh junior football, he joined Argyle from Mardy and made a big impact in 1922-3 with 17 goals in 22 League games. Seven goals in ten games the following season demonstrated that he was a scorer with more than ordinary capabilities. However, there were a number of followers who believed that Fowler did not receive sufficient recognition from the Argyle management, being dropped after a bad game whereas other players were given further chances. Swansea Town, promotion rivals, certainly liked his abilities when he appeared against them for Argyle and they paid what was then a club record fee of £1,280 for him in March 1924. The Welsh club certainly had reason to be pleased with the outcome of their expenditure. In seven years with Swansea, Fowler scored 100 goals — including nine hat-tricks, a five and a four — in 167 League games and was capped six times by Wales from 1926 to 1929. Argyle must have often regretted their decision to release him.

GEORGE FROST **Full-back**
Former Gillingham player, he appeared once at left-back in Argyle's first season of League football, then returned to Kent to link up with Chatham Town. He died in 1987, aged 97.

BRYCE FULTON **Full-back**
Heavily-built Scot who joined Manchester United as a 17-year-old straight from school but did not get a first-team chance with that club and was persuaded to come to Argyle by Jack Rowley in 1957. It was a good move for both player and club. He made nearly 200 first-team appearances for Argyle, winning a Third Division medal in 1958-9, and later had two seasons with Exeter City.

KEITH FURPHY **Winger**
Son of former Watford and Sheffield United manager Ken Furphy, he had six games on Argyle's left wing at the start of the 1987-8 season, having come on trial from American club Atlanta. He had previously been on Sheffield United and Queen's Park Rangers' books without getting a first-team chance. Argyle did not offer him a contract and he returned to the United States, but later came back to England to link up with Bath City.

TOMMY GALLOGLEY **Forward**
A pre-World War One signing from junior Scottish football, he won a regular place in the side in the last season before the war and regained it when Southern League football resumed, playing either on the wing or inside-forward. He had just over two League seasons with Argyle, then was transferred to Exeter City in 1922.

ALEC GARDEN **Inside-forward**
Aberdonian who qualifies for this section because of the one League Cup game he played for Argyle in the 1962-3 season. He returned to Home Park to play against Argyle for his new club, Corby Town, in an FA Cup match in 1965-6.

DARREN GARNER **Midfield**
Made his Football League debut late in the 1988-9 season and is one of the club's hopes for the future. It was an exciting period for the Argyle youngster, who also played for a Football League Under-18 team which toured Russia in April 1989.

JIMMY GEE **Goalkeeper**
One of the local goalkeepers tried by Argyle in the 1956-7 season in an attempt to plug the gap left by the retirements of Shortt and Major. Also a Devon County water polo player, he came from and returned to Launceston after only one Third Division game as an amateur.

REG GIBSON **Half-back**
A 1946 signing from Manchester United for whom he played one wartime game. He played in all three of Argyle's victories of 1945-6, but did not hold a place in the side when League football resumed the following season and was transferred to Exeter City with whom he had two seasons.

E.M. ('PAT') GLOVER **Centre-forward**
Won seven caps for Wales while playing for Grimsby Town from 1932 to 1939 and was Argyle's big scoring hope when the 1938-9 season opened. Alas, the war intervened after only three Second Division matches but he continued with the club in the 1939-40 South Western League and was again chosen for Wales — this time as an Argyle player — in a wartime international in November 1939. He did not resume his League career at the end of the war but took a public house at Tamerton Foliot and, not forgetting his old club, recommended Tommy Briggs to Grimsby Town when the burly ex-sailor was given a free transfer by Argyle in 1947.

RAY GODDARD **Half-back**
Formerly with Wolves and Chelsea, he arrived at Home Park in the summer of 1948 and was appointed centre-half and captain. He was troubled by injuries during his spell with Argyle and this partly accounted for the fact that Jimmy Rae continued to search for a pivot, who finally arrived in the unmistakable shape of Jack Chisholm. Realizing that there was no longer a regular place for him at Home Park, Goddard agreed to a move to Exeter City, where he had more success captaining the side and totalling nearly 150 games for that club in five seasons.

KEVIN GODFREY **Centre-forward**
Made a valuable contribution to Argyle's promotion bid of 1985-6 while on loan from Orient. Scored only one goal in his seven games but he brought pace and skill to an attack which was showing signs of faltering. After some 300 games for Orient he moved to Brentford in 1988-9.

WILL GODFREY **Half-back**
Formerly with Aberdeen, whom he joined from the Scottish junior club Alva Albion Rangers, he was a regular member of the Aberdeen side before being transferred to Argyle in 1933. He was unable to command a regular place in three seasons with the club, however, and was one of three Plymouth players to be transferred to Luton Town in February 1936.

RAY GOODING **Midfield**
Former Coventry player who came to Home Park and played a few games for the club at the beginning of the 1982-3 season.

CLIVE GOODYEAR **Defender**
Well-built defender who came to Argyle from Luton Town in 1984 and played in over 100 games, mostly as a central defender. Moved on to Wimbledon in 1987 and won an FA Cup-winners' medal at right-back with the London club against Liverpool in 1988.

BILL GOONEY **Half-back**
Like Godfrey, he was signed in 1936 from Argyle by Luton Town after failing to win a regular spot in the half-back line. He had only one season with the club, having arrived from Sheffield United the previous season.

MARK GRAVES **Forward**
Had four seasons in and out of the Argyle side from 1978 to 1981. A product of the apprentice scheme, he joined Wealdstone in 1982 and is believed to be still playing in non-League football in the London area.

MIKE GREEN **Centre-back**
Native of Carlisle who started his League career with his home team and then moved to Gillingham and Bristol Rovers, whom he helped to promotion from the Third Division in 1973-4. He gave a repeat performance for Argyle, who paid Rovers £20,000 for his signature. He captained the side which gained promotion in 1974-5 and played in every match — League, FA Cup and League Cup. He joined Torquay United as player-manager in 1977.

CLIVE GRIFFITHS **Centre-back**
Welsh Schools and Under-23 international who played for Argyle in the first ten games of 1974-5 while on loan from Manchester United. He later played for Tranmere Rovers.

TOMMY GROZIER **Outside-right**
Small but lively Scottish forward who established a first-team place in his third season with Argyle, having joined the club from Glencairn in 1927. He was an automatic choice for six seasons and totalled over 200 games for Argyle, mainly on the right wing, although he did turn in some excellent performances as an emergency half-back. He was not a remarkable scorer but he does have a special place in Argyle's scoring history as one of the few players to have scored four goals in a single game. Grozier's big moment was in December 1929, in a 6-1 home victory over Crystal Palace. He retired from the game in 1936.

NEIL HAGUE **Central defender**
Former England Youth international who started his League career with his home team, Rotherham United, for whom he played in almost every position. He joined Argyle in 1971 for £15,000, only 24 hours after heading the winning goal for Rotherham against Argyle. He was a regular member of the side which took Argyle to the League Cup semi-final in 1973-4 and was chosen Player of the Year in the previous season. He totalled over 100 games and scored some vital goals for the club. He left Home Park in the summer of 1974 and subsequently played for Bournemouth, Huddersfield Town and Darlington.

ALBERT HALL **Inside-forward**
Welsh Schoolboy international brought to Argyle in 1947 by Jack Tresadern who had managed him at Tottenham. He had been a Spurs player since he was 14 years old and a regular member of the side until the 1946-7 season when, after injury, he lost his place to Les Bennett. His form at Home Park was disappointing and he had played only nine games when another Welshman, Frank Squires, displaced him in the team. He moved out of League football at the end of the season.

BRIAN HALL **Inside-forward**
Came to Argyle in 1976 with a high reputation gained as a member of the Liverpool team of the late 1960s in which he and teammate Steve Heighway were both university graduates. His ambition, he announced, was to take Argyle into the First Division but without the backing to which he had become accustomed at Liverpool, he found that this was an aim beyond the capabilities of one individual and he remained at Home Park for only two seasons, during which the club dropped out of the Second Division and struggled in the Third. He returned to his native North Country with Burnley in 1977.

MIKE HAM **Central defender**
Local player who joined Argyle as an apprentice and made a handful of appearances for the club, spread over four seasons from 1981 before returning to junior Plymouth football with Saltash United.

JIM HAMILTON **Forward**
Scot who began his League career with Sunderland, played a handful of games for Argyle and Bristol Rovers, then established himself with Carlisle United. He then had a period in Australian soccer before returning to the UK and was reported to be playing for Gretna in 1984-5.

DAVID HANCOCK **Half-back**
Exeter-born, made two appearances for Argyle in the 1956-7 season. Did not get a League game while on loan to Gillingham but later became a regular player with Torquay United and Exeter City, thus joining the small group who have played for all three Devon clubs.

PETER HARDCASTLE **Midfield**
Gained England Amateur international honours while with Skelmersdale before joining Blackpool. He joined Argyle in 1974 and made a dozen appearances that season. Moved to Bradford City at the end of the following season.

ALEC HARDIE **Wing-half**
A regular half-back choice who hardly missed a game in five of the eight seasons he spent at Home Park and was always in contention for a place in the other seasons. A crisp tackler and smooth passer of the ball, this Scot from Kilsyth had played for Third Lanark before entering English League football with Charlton Athletic and was signed by Bob Jack for Argyle in March 1926. Nearly eight years and 250 games later, he moved to Exeter City where he finished his League career.

NEIL HARDS **Goalkeeper**
Former Argyle apprentice who had little chance to shine at Home Park with Geoff Crudgington in such consistent form. He saved a penalty on his debut for the club at 18 but made only six appearances in four seasons as Crudgington's deputy and left Argyle for Gloucester City in 1983, later playing for Cheltenham Town and Waterlooville.

ALAN HARRIS **Full-back**
Played for England at Schools and Youth level before joining brother Ron at Chelsea where he made his League debut when 17. He later went to Coventry, then back to Chelsea in time to play for them in the 1967 FA Cup Final, and to Queen's Park Rangers who transferred him to Argyle in 1971. He had three seasons at Home Park before signing for Cambridge United where he ended his playing career. More recently, he has been assistant manager to Terry Venables, first in Spain then with Tottenham Hotspur.

GEORGE HARRIS **Goalkeeper**
One of a group of players who joined Argyle in the late 1940s from Aberaman which, for a period, was regarded as Argyle's nursery. He was on Charlton Athletic's books during the war years without getting a first-team chance and his fortunes did not greatly improve during his time at Home Park. He deputized three times for Bill Shortt in 1948-9 but did not present a serious challenge to the latter and returned to Aberaman at the end of the season.

MIKE HARRISON **Outside-left**
The best buy of three forwards signed by Derek Ufton in 1967 in a bid to hold off relegation. Capped for England Schools, he also won three Under-23 caps whilst with Chelsea and had six seasons with Blackburn Rovers before coming to Home Park. He had only one part-season with Argyle, leaving them in the summer to play Third Division football with Luton Town, who had just been promoted.

JOHN HARTERY **Full-back**
Signed from Limerick in 1948, he played four times for the League of Ireland representative side and attracted attention particularly after his solid performance against Tom Finney when the Football League side were the visitors. He had two seasons at Home Park, playing regularly for the Reserves and many thought that he was worth more than the single first-team game which the club gave him in 1949. He returned to Irish football with Dublin Bohemians.

JIMMY HEALY **Winger**
A former teammate of Frank Sloan with Shieldmuir Celtic in Scottish junior football. Sloan came to Argyle; Healy first took the professional plunge with Glasgow Celtic but, although nominally on Celtic's books, he was on loan to Montrose for most of the 1924-5 season before coming south to join Argyle. Although being exceptionally fast, probably the fastest player on the books during his stay, he had difficulty in making an impact at Home Park and played in only 29 games during five seasons with the club and signed for Bristol City in 1929.

JIMMY HEEPS **Forward**
Another Scot, he had only one season with Argyle. Recruited from Scottish junior football in time for Argyle's entry into the Football League, he had a number of games either on the wing or at inside-forward and returned to Scotland to join Airdrieonians at the end of the season.

DAVID HILL **Centre-half**
A recruit from Hamilton Academical in 1934, he had ten games at half-back at the start of the 1934-5 season, but then lost his place to Johnny McNeil and played one game in each of the two following seasons at outside-right and centre-forward respectively. He was transferred to Southport in 1936.

JIMMY HINCH **Centre-forward**
Formerly with Portmadoc in the Welsh League, he entered League football with Tranmere Rovers, coming to Home Park a year later in exchange for Fred Molyneux. He made over 100 appearances for Argyle but lost his place in the side to Paul Mariner in 1973. He left Argyle for Hereford United and subsequently played for York City, Sheffield Wednesday and

Barnsley. After ending his League career, he went to the United States where, in 1985, he was reported to be running a successful insurance and property business in California and teaching soccer at a local college.

MARTIN HODGE **Goalkeeper**
Another successful product of Argyle's youth policy of the early 1970s. Born in Southport, he established himself in the Argyle goal at the age of 18 in 1978-9. Everton, recognizing his potential, paid £135,000 for him in the summer of 1979. Although his opportunities at Goodison Park were limited he had spells on loan to Preston, Oldham and Gillingham. He made his mark after being transferred to Sheffield Wednesday, making over 200 appearances for the Owls, captaining the side for a number of seasons. He joined Leicester City for £250,000 in the summer of 1988 and reappeared at Home Park playing for his new club in March 1989.

MICK HORSWILL **Midfield**
Busy, bustling player who started his League career with Sunderland, with whom he won an FA Cup-winners' medal in 1973. He then had a year with Manchester City before signing for Argyle in the summer of 1975 as part of Tony Waiters' plans to strengthen the side for the return to Second Division football. Spent three seasons at Home Park and tasted the bitterness of relegation with the club before moving on to Hull City in the close season of 1978. In 1982-3, he was playing for Barrow in the Gola League.

RON HOWELL **Goalkeeper**
Had one game in the Argyle goal in 1956 as deputy for Harry Brown. A native of Wolverhampton, he later joined Aston Villa but did not get a League game with the Midlands club.

BILL HULLETT **Centre-forward**
Liverpool-born, he was a reserve with Everton when signed by Argyle in October 1937 and soon impressed as a goalscorer with 20 goals in 28 games in his two seasons with the club. Manchester United signed him in March 1939 but he did not get into their first team by the time the outbreak of war had suspended the normal competition. He was linked with the Welsh club, Merthyr Tydfil, by the end of the war and played for Argyle in a friendly match in 1945-6, but the club subsequently decided against re-engaging him and he re-entered League football with Cardiff City, later playing for Nottingham Forest.

JIMMY HUNTER **Outside-right**
Signed from Mansfield Town in November 1935, he had nearly 100 games on the Argyle right wing in four pre-war seasons, signing for Preston North End in the summer of 1939. A fast and tricky winger, he was not particularly renowned as a scorer, but the goal he scored in a surprise Argyle victory at Manchester City in 1939 has frequently been recounted. Getting the ball on the half-way line, he cut into the middle, left four defenders floundering and then shot past Frank Swift as the England goalkeeper came out. It was a performance which even the home crowd rose to acclaim. He played once for Argyle as a guest in the 1945-6 season.

BILL HURST **Winger**
Joined Argyle just before the war but was regarded mainly as a reserve when League football resumed in 1946 and made only four appearances for the side in that first post-war season. Signed for the Lancashire Combination club Nelson in the summer of 1947 but Bury brought him back into League football within a month of the new season. He played only one League game each for Bury and for Accrington Stanley, his next club.

DON HUTCHINS **Outside-left**
Joined Leicester City from Stockton in 1966 but had few chances with the Midlands club. His fortunes changed when, after a strong recommendation to Argyle by Leicester manager Frank O'Farrell, he moved to Home Park for £5,000 in the summer of 1969. He contested the left-wing position with Aiden Maher during his first season with Argyle, but then made it his own for two seasons and headed the list of goalscorers in 1970-71. He later played for Blackburn Rovers and Bradford City, making over 250 appearances for the latter.

ROLLO JACK **Forward**
Second son of Argyle manager Bob Jack, he graduated to the League team via the juniors and had barely established himself in the side in November 1923 when Bolton Wanderers paid £1,500 to take him to Burnden Park, where he joined his brother, David. He did not make the same mark at Bolton as his elder brother, however, and later dropped out of First Division football to play for Clapton Orient (who later gave him a free transfer) and Swindon Town. He returned to Argyle in an adminstrative capacity in 1935 and was appointed acting secretary-manager when Jack Tresadern was called into the Army, but Argyle's demise during the war years made such a post virtually redundant.

ALEX JACKSON **Centre-forward**
A Glaswegian who had only a handful of games with his first League club, Birmingham City, but had four seasons in an Argyle shirt from 1959 to 1963, either in a centre or inside-forward position. A broken leg in 1963 kept him out of the side for half a season and he never fully recovered his best form after that. He moved to Weymouth in 1964 but reappeared in Devon football in 1985 when he was appointed lottery manager with Exeter City.

CLIFF JACKSON **Inside-forward**
Former England Schoolboys player who was scheduled for a trial with Chelsea before his home team, Swindon Town, realized the potential on their own doorstep and stepped in to sign him. He helped Swindon gain promotion to the Second Division in 1962-3, playing in every League game for the club that season. To the surprise of many Swindon supporters, he was allowed to move to Argyle and although he was unable to achieve promotion honours at Home Park he was a regular member of the squad which, under Malcolm Allison, took the club to the League Cup semi-finals. He fell out of favour during Derek Ufton's managership of the club and was transferred to Crystal Palace where he again tasted promotion success, helping that club into the First Division in 1968-9. He finished his League career with Torquay United.

TREVOR JACOBS **Full-back**
Played four games for Argyle in 1972, in between transferring his loyalties from Bristol City to Bristol Rovers.

TYRONE JAMES **Defender**
Londoner who joined Fulham at 18 and had a taste of League football with the London club before coming west for £15,000 in the spring of 1978. He had five seasons with Argyle but was a regular member of the side only in 1979-80. He joined Liskeard on leaving Argyle, and later played in Australia.

BRIAN JASPER **Full-back**
Local player who had a few games for the League side in 1957.

TED JELLY **Full-back**
Played for his home team Leicester City in 1949 FA Cup Final. He was signed by Jimmy Rae in the summer of 1951 but the consistent form of Paddy Ratcliffe gave him few first-team opportunities and he retired from the game in 1954.

REG JENKINS **Centre-forward**
Millbrook-born forward who joined Argyle in 1957 from Truro City. He was regarded at Home Park mainly as a reserve forward but his career took an upward turn with Exeter City, Torquay United and especially Rochdale, for whom he played over 300 games and scored over 100 goals.

NICKY JENNINGS **Outside-left**
Made his Argyle debut at 18 in 1964 and few teams in the mid-sixties could field a better pair of wingers than Argyle's Jennings and Barrie Jones. He made over 100 appearances for the club before being transferred to Portsmouth in 1967, apparently no longer having a place in Derek Ufton's plans for the club. He played over 200 games for the Hampshire club and then achieved another century with Exeter City with whom he ended his League career.

JOHN JOBSON **Half-back**
Formerly with the Durham mining team, Washington Colliery, he played once for Argyle in 1923 and was transferred to Hartlepools United the following year.

DENNIS JOHN **Full-back**
Had five seasons with Argyle whom he joined as a crewcut 17-year-old and another with his home club Swansea Town before achieving with Scunthorpe United and Millwall the real break into League football which he sought. He played in some 200 games for the last two teams before moving out of the Football League.

BRIAN JOHNSON **Winger**
Londoner who came to Home Park as an apprentice in 1972 and signed professional forms a year later. He spent eight seasons with the club and can count membership of the promotion side of 1974-5 and of the team which won national fame in the League Cup the previous season among the highlights of that career. He also experienced life in the doldrums of the Third Division but throughout the period was one of the most reliable members of the squad and ended his Argyle career with over 200 first-team appearances to his credit.

BILL JOHNSTONE **Inside-forward**
Another one-game player for Argyle, his sole appearance being in 1933. He arrived at Home Park earlier that season from the Scottish junior side, Irvine Meadow, and was later transferred to Coventry City.

LEN JONES **Wing-half**
Born in Barnsley, he had three seasons with his local club before dropping out of League football. Argyle signed him from Chelmsford City and he played in the opening match of the short-lived 1939-40 season. He was a fairly regular member of the side for the first two post-war seasons before losing his first-team place and moving to Southend United who later transferred him to Colchester United. Argyle regarded him mainly as a wing-half but his later clubs played him on the right wing where, such was his skill with the ball, that at one point he was known as 'The Stanley Matthews of the Third Division.' In one other respect he resembled the latter; he was 40 before he ended his League career.

MIKE KEARNS **Goalkeeper**
Born in Banbury, he had an Irish qualification which brought him 18 Republic of Ireland caps. Played once for Argyle in 1972 while on loan from Oxford United.

PETER KEARNS **Inside-forward**
Joined Argyle at 19 from his home-town club, Wellingborough, and won a first-team place early into the 1956-7 season. Lost his place when Jimmy Gauld arrived from Everton and played only a handful of games for Argyle after that but remained at Home Park until December 1962 when he was transferred to Aldershot where he stayed for six seasons before moving to Lincoln City.

BILLY KELLOCK — **Forward**

A signing from Stockport County in 1913, he was nearing the end of his Argyle career when the club gained admission to the Football League, and made only half a dozen appearances that first Third Division season. He was then transferred to Torquay United.

TONY KELLOW — **Centre-forward**

Cornishman who had three spells with Exeter City and also played for Blackpool, Newport County and Swansea City. In the context of his whole professional career, his period with Argyle, who paid only £5,000 for him, was a minor interlude of 11 full games and two goals in 1983-4. In 1986 he became manager of a public house in Exeter.

DAVID KEMP — **Centre-forward**

A proven goalscorer whose 24 goals for Argyle in 1980-81 had much to do with the club's attainment of a respectable seventh position in the Third Division. No other player on the staff reached double figures in the scoring list that season and it could therefore reasonably be argued that he was the inevitable choice as Player of the Year. Formerly with Slough Town, he entered League football with Crystal Palace and played for Portsmouth and Carlisle United before coming to Plymouth for £75,000 in 1979. He had just over two seasons at Home Park, played for a number of teams in North American football and then became manager of a Swedish side.

HARRY 'JAZZO' KIRK — **Inside-forward**

Not a well-remembered name at Home Park but he gave Exeter City good service after leaving Argyle in 1922 with one Third Division game to his credit. He had previously played for Bristol City.

SAM KIRKWOOD — **Full-back**

Burly Irish defender who replaced Harry Roberts as full-back partner to Jimmy Rae in 1937, permitting Argyle to release the latter to join Bristol Rovers. A strong tackler with a tendency to lose his temper in the heat of a game, he was previously with Arsenal but did not win a First Division place there. He remained with Argyle until 1940, playing in the early part of the wartime South Western League, but then returned to his native Belfast, where he had a business, and did not return to Home Park in 1946.

JIMMY KIRKPATRICK — **Outside-right**

A regular in the Argyle side from 1911 until the end of Argyle's first season in the Football League, after which the emergence of Patsy Corcoran restricted his chances. He made over 100 appearances for Argyle's Southern League side in those earlier years and would surely have almost doubled that total, had not World War One intervened. Argyle signed him from Dumfries and transferred him to Torquay United in 1924. His football career over and, unemployed, he was given a job on the Home Park ground staff in the 1930s.

ARNOLD KNIGHT — **Inside-forward**

A Jack Tresadern signing for Argyle in the summer of 1947. He played under Tresadern at Tottenham, whom he joined in 1936, spending two seasons at White Hart Lane before moving to Leeds United in 1937-8. He was a regular member of Leeds wartime sides but did not win a place in the post-war line-up. He started brightly with Argyle but faded soon after and, with the arrival of George Dews and Frank Squires, had little further chance to shine at Home Park. He was transferred to Bradford City after only six months in the West Country.

HARRY LANE — **Winger**

A Midlander, he started with his home-town team, Hednesford, before entering the professional ranks with Birmingham and was later transferred to Southend United. After five seasons with the latter, he came to Home Park in March 1938 and was a regular member of the team, mainly at inside-forward but occasionally as a winger, for a season and a half before returning to the Essex club during the war. He resumed his career with Southend at the end of the war and had three post-war seasons before retiring from the game.

LES LATCHAM — **Inside-forward**

Came to Argyle in 1971 on a free transfer from Burnley. He had spent 11 years at Turf Moor during a period when the Lancashire club was a major force in both English League and European football. A model passer of the ball, he was a regular member of the Argyle side for two seasons but returned to Yorkshire to play for Bradford City in 1973. He became manager of the North West Counties League side, Nelson, in 1983.

NICKY LAW — **Defender**

A £40,000 signing from Blackpool in 1987, he was sold to Notts County for a £30,000 profit early in 1988-9. Greenwich-born, he was on Arsenal's books as an apprentice but had to move north in order to break into the Football League. He made over 100 appearances for Barnsley before joining Blackpool. Argyle used him mainly as a central defender but the consistent form of Adrian Burrows who displaced him from the side after returning from loan to Southend in the autumn of 1987 led Argyle to conclude that they could afford to release him.

TREVOR LAWLESS **Centre-half**
Former schoolteacher who had been playing as an amateur for Worcester City and asked for an Argyle trial while on holiday in the Plymouth area at Easter 1955. After only two games for the Reserves that season, he made his League debut as centre-half and captain of the side in the following August. It was not, however, a comfortable period for either Argyle or the player and, after only eight games, he lost his place to Peter Langman. He later had League experience with Oldham, Aldershot and Southport without making a real mark at any club.

DAVID LEAN **Defender**
Gave up a job as a garage mechanic to try his fortunes as a footballer. He was a regular in the defence in 1969-70 but had only a limited spell in the side the following season and returned to local junior football. He came back to Home Park as John Hore's assistant when the latter was appointed manager in 1983 and resigned when Hore was dismissed some months later. He then became manager of St Blazey and has subsequently managed Launceston and Saltash United.

ARTHUR LEE **Goalkeeper**
Local player who played four times as an amateur, deputizing for Fred Craig, from 1926 to 1928.

JOHN LEIPER **Goalkeeper**
Scot who reputedly suffered badly from pre-match nerves. Formerly with Aberdeen East End, he had seven seasons with Argyle but was first-choice goalkeeper in only one of these — 1965-6. He was involuntarily drawn into the dispute between the directors and Malcolm Allison over team selection at Easter 1965 when the board overruled the manager and insisted on Leiper being chosen for a game instead of Noel Dwyer. One match later Dwyer was back in the side. Leiper left Argyle for Chelmsford City in 1968.

TONY LEVY **Forward**
Londoner, former apprentice at Home Park. Made one substitute appearance in 1978 and later joined Torquay United. He was with the Isthmian League side, Hendon, in 1983 and was reported to be playing in New Zealand in 1987.

ARTHUR LEWIS **Outside-right**
Signed from Grimsby Town in the summer of 1939, he had made only one appearance for Argyle when war was declared. He did not resume a professional career after the war.

MICKY LILL **Winger**
England Youth international. A Londoner, he was with West Ham United as an amateur but turned professional with Wolves and scored for them in the first minute of his League debut game. He was later transferred to Everton for £25,000. Signed by Argyle in the summer of 1962 for only half of that fee, he did not spend a full season at Home Park, but was transferred to Portsmouth in the following spring.

JOE LITTLE **Outside-left**
Formerly with Castleford Town, he made seven appearances in four seasons with Argyle from 1920 to 1924.

DUGGIE LIVINGSTONE **Full-back**
Former Celtic player who spent five years with Everton, for whom he played 100 times, before joining Argyle in February 1926. He was then in contention for a first-team place with Moses Russell and Fred Titmuss and remained with the club for only two half-seasons before returning to his native Scotland to join Aberdeen. In 1930 he signed for Tranmere and was later trainer at Exeter City and Sheffield United before managing Sheffield Wednesday, Sparta (Holland), Newcastle United, Fulham and Chesterfield. He also managed the Republic of Ireland and Belgian national teams and was Belgium's manager when they drew 4-4 with England in the 1954 World Cup Finals.

FRANK LORD **Centre-forward**
Spent ten years in the lower reaches of the Football League with Rochdale and Crewe Alexandra before Argyle signed him in 1963 to help stave off the threat

of relegation. He was not a scoring sensation at Home Park, his most notable feat being the six goals he scored during the club's League Cup run in 1964-5. On leaving Argyle in 1966, he played for three clubs — Stockport County, Blackburn Rovers and Chesterfield — in 18 months before returning to Plymouth in 1967 to play a few more games for the club before being offered a coaching appointment. After ending his playing career, he had periods as manager with Hereford United, Penang State and Capetown.

RAY LUGG **Midfield**
Formerly with Middlesbrough, he came to Home Park from Watford, having been a member of the Watford squad which reached the semi-finals of the FA Cup in 1969-70. He had one season with Argyle and later had lengthy spells with Crewe Alexandra and Bury.

TOM McARTHUR **Centre-half**
Former Scots Guardsman who was signed from Leicester City in 1954 as understudy and eventual successor to Jack Chisholm. His form, however, did not match his promise, and he made only two Second Division appearances for the club and left Argyle a year later to return to the Leicester area with Loughborough Sports.

HUGH McAULEY **Outside-left**
Spent over four years with his home team, Liverpool, but the only League experience he had was a period on loan to Tranmere Rovers when Argyle signed him for £12,000 in the autumn of 1974. He was a regular choice at Home Park for two seasons and afterwards served Charlton Athletic, Tranmere Rovers and Carlisle United. He returned to the Merseyside area after leaving League football to play for Formby and later took a post with the Merseyside Youth Association at a sports centre in Liverpool.

SEAN McCARTHY **Forward**
Tommy Tynan's striking partner in 1988-9, this burly young forward was signed from Swansea City the previous summer for £50,000, having headed the Welsh club's list of scorers in 1987-8. Before signing for Swansea, he played for his home team, Bridgend, a town more renowned for producing rugby players. He left it late to demonstrate his scoring form in 1988-9 with six of his eight League goals coming in the last 11 matches. At 21, he still has time to develop into the reliable scorer Argyle will need when Tynan's playing days finally come to an end.

MIKE McCARTNEY **Defender**
Scottish Schoolboy international who began his English League career as an apprentice with West Bromwich Albion but did not get a first-team chance until his move to Carlisle United. He played at Carlisle under Bobby Moncur and it was the latter who brought him to Home Park in 1981 from Southampton. He had two seasons with Argyle and returned to Carlisle in 1983. Crossing the border, he became manager of the Scottish junior side, Gretna, in 1988.

JIM McCOLGAN **Half-back**
Had been playing at half-back for the Reserves when called on for his only first-team appearance for Argyle at centre-forward in February 1939, as a deputy for Dave Thomas. An Irishman, he was playing for the Scottish junior club, St Anthony's, when signed by Argyle in 1937. He was transferred to Queen's Park Rangers in 1939 and played for them in the first wartime season.

SAM McCRORY **Inside-forward**
Swansea Town brought him into League football from Linfield in 1946 and he helped both Swansea and Ipswich Town to promotion out of the Third Division before joining newly-promoted Argyle in the summer of 1952. Although not fast, he was a skilful user of the ball. Competition for inside-forward places was strong during his three seasons at Home Park, the team's fortunes declined and he never became an automatic choice. His career revived somewhat after his transfer to Southend United in 1955 and, at the age of 33, he received his sole international cap for Northern Ireland, scoring in a rare win over England in 1957. For Southend, he made over 200 appearances and scored nearly 100 goals.

GERRY McELHINNEY **Centre-half**
A regular member of the promotion side of 1985-6. He left Distillery to come into the Football League with Bolton Wanderers in 1980. He won six Northern Ireland caps and made over 100 appearances for the Lancashire club before coming to the West Country for £32,500. He was reaching the landmark of 100 appearances for Argyle when he lost his place in the team and was transferred to Peterborough United for £10,000 in 1988.

FRANK MACEY **Inside-forward**
English Amateur international. The first time he had ever seen a professional match was when he made his one appearance for Argyle in February 1926. He was then about to leave the Army, where he was a Lance Corporal, but declined the possibility of turning professional with Argyle, preferring to remain with the Kingstonian amateur club, for domestic reasons.

ALEC MACHIN **Wing-half**
A signing from Chelsea in the summer of 1948 with plenty of First Division experience, he had an unhappy start to his Argyle career as a forward and was dropped from the side, but he began to show his abilities when tried at wing-half after Len Boyd's transfer to Birmingham City. Unfortunately, he broke a leg playing against Coventry City in 1949 and although he made a recovery from that injury and played a few games two seasons later, he never regained a permanent place and left the club in 1952 to join St Austell in the South Western League.

ERNIE MACHIN **Inside-forward**
A Lancastrian, he cost Argyle £35,000 in 1973 and created so favourable an impression among supporters that he was chosen as Player of the Year during his only full season at Home Park. He entered League football with Coventry City, where he spent ten years, sharing in that club's rise from the Third to the First Division and making over 250 League appearances. After requesting a move from Argyle in the summer of 1974 he had two seasons with Brighton before leaving League football.

HUGH McJARROW **Forward/half-back**
A Scot from Motherwell, he had established a reputation as a scorer with Chesterfield, Sheffield Wednesday and Luton Town when signed by Jimmy Rae for Argyle in December 1953 in an attempt to boost Argyle's scoring rate. He was not particularly successful in that sphere but he played some of his best football for the club after being tried at wing-half. He had three seasons at Home Park before being transferred to Peterborough United, then an ambitious non-League club, in 1956.

PAT McKENNA **Full-back**
A former teammate at Aberdeen of Bill Strauss, George Taylor and Stan Williams, he was signed in the summer of 1952, but the form of Ratcliffe and Jones restricted his Football League experience with Argyle to only one game (the last match of the 1952-3 season), and he returned to Scottish football with Arbroath a year later.

GEORGE McKENZIE **Goalkeeper**
Born in Dublin, his father was the Irish half-mile champion five times. It was, however, from the Scottish club Arthurlie that he joined Argyle in 1934. He was nicknamed 'Vice' at Home Park because of the strength of his grip but he made only one appearance in goal and was transferred to Southend United in the summer of 1935.

JOHNNY McNEIL **Centre-half**
Another Bob Jack capture from Scottish junior football, he came from Inverness Caledonians in 1934 and, taking over the centre-half position from another Scot, Dave Hill, in the autumn of that year, was the regular choice for four seasons until displaced by the arrival of Jimmy Clark in the 1938-9 season. Given a free transfer by Argyle he signed for Clapton Orient in 1939. He began the season interrupted by war with the London club, but returned to Home Park to play one match as a guest for Argyle in the Wartime League of 1939-40.

BRIAN McNEILL **Full-back**
Newcastle-born, his first professional club was Bristol City where he began as an apprentice but he had made only three substitute appearances for that club when Argyle signed him for £15,000 in 1978. He had just over two seasons at Home Park before linking up with Hearts in 1981.

PETER McPARLAND **Winger/centre-forward**
He was one of the best-known names in football for his exploits with Aston Villa and Northern Ireland when he came west from Wolverhampton Wanderers to join Argyle in 1963. He made over 300 appearances and scored over 100 goals for Villa, whom he joined from Newry in 1952, and gained a reputation as a fast, direct winger. He played only one season for Wolves and two seasons for Argyle, who often preferred to play him in the centre of the attack. His 14 goals for the club included a hat-trick against Leeds United in April 1963.

TONY McSHANE **Half-back**
Belfast-born, he played in Ireland for Belfast Celtic, Bangor and Brantwood before successfully completing a trial at Home Park, making his League debut for Argyle on the same day as Jack Chisholm. An attacking half-back, he made good use of the ball when on the attack but his defensive work was not always to the same standard. He was, at one time, team captain but as a contemporary of Neil Dougall and Johnny Porteous, he was never an automatic choice and the 34 appearances which he made in 1951-2 and which qualified him for a Third Division championship medal were mainly as deputy to either of his two rivals. He played twice as many games for the Reserves as for the first team and in one Football Combination match completed a hat-trick of penalties. He moved to Swindon Town in 1955 and later had managerial experience with Goole Town, Scunthorpe United and Chesterfield.

AIDEN MAHER **Outside-left**
English Schoolboy international who signed for his home team, Everton, at 18 but made only one League appearance at Goodison Park. He was a regular on the Argyle left wing for two seasons from 1968 to 1970 until losing his place to Don Hutchins. He returned to his native Merseyside to play for Tranmere Rovers, but had little more success there than he had with Everton, playing in only two full League games.

JIM MAILEY **Outside-left**
Came across the Irish Sea from Dundalk to join Argyle in 1937 and had a spell of 11 consecutive games on the Argyle left wing in the spring of 1939. He was transferred to Swindon Town just before the war but was called into the Army before being able to make much contribution to the fortunes of his new club.

LES MAJOR **Goalkeeper**
Had impressed the Argyle management with some fine displays at Home Park while playing for Leicester City. That club was well endowed with good goalkeepers and were willing to release him. Thus, Les Major started on a seven-season career with Argyle. Unfortunately for him, most of that period coincided with the peak of Bill Shortt's career and his opportunities were mostly

restricted to periods when Shortt was either injured or on international duty. Just when Shortt's retirement from the game seemed to provide the opening for which he had waited, injury forced Major to leave the game.

KEN MALOY **Outside-left**
A Londoner who joined Argyle from Ilford in 1959 as a 19-year-old, he had spells in and out of the side over four seasons at Home Park. He also played for Peterborough United and Aldershot and then crossed the Channel to play for ten years in Belgian football.

JOE MANTLE **Centre-forward**
Former Burnley player who appeared briefly for Argyle in 1931 and 1932. He left Home Park for Chester and subsequently played for Stockport County and Hearts.

NICK MARKER **Midfield**
An automatic choice since he joined Argyle from his home team, Exeter City, in November 1987 for £95,000 plus the promising Darren Rowbotham. He had made over 200 League appearances for the City, whom he joined as an apprentice, before going further south. The number-five shirt, which he normally wears for Argyle, belies the fact that he is not a central defender but more like the left-half of previous ages. Despite the publicity which he received for the tackle which put Ossie Ardiles out of the game when the latter played at Home Park for Blackburn Rovers in March 1987, Marker's value to the side lies as much in the support which he provides to his own attack as in stifling the opposition. The eight goals which he scored during 1988-9 made him Argyle's third-highest scorer, behind Tynan and McCarthy.

ALF MATTHEWS **Outside-right**
A regular choice on the Argyle right wing from 1926 to 1929, he remained with the club for four more seasons after losing his first-team place to Tommy Grozier and had a benefit match against Exeter City in 1933. It was from Exeter that he came to Argyle in March 1926 after making 117 consecutive appearances for City. For Argyle, he made nearly 150 appearances. Born in Bristol, he entered League football as an amateur with Bristol City before signing professional forms.

JOHN MATTHEWS **Midfield**
The injury at Everton in January 1989, which put Kevin Summerfield out of the side for the rest of the season, placed the burden of controlling Argyle's midfield on this 33-year-old player, in his 15th year of League football. Not always being able to last the pace of a 90-minute match, he was substituted 11 times during the season. A Londoner, he received his League baptism with Arsenal, made over 100 appearances for Sheffield United and then played for Mansfield Town and Chesterfield before coming to Home Park in the summer of 1985 in time to assist Argyle's successful bid to regain the Second Division. With another century of appearances behind him, he left Home Park in the 1989 close season on a free transfer in recognition of his past services.

GARY MEGSON **Midfield**
Son of former Sheffield Wednesday captain Don Megson, he came to Argyle as an apprentice in 1977, his father approving of the fact that Gary would be developing under Tony Waiters. Over two and a half seasons he made such progress with Argyle that Everton paid £250,000 for him in February 1970, a fee which is still an Argyle record. Despite the size of that fee, his chances with Everton were somewhat limited and were even more curtailed during a brief spell with Nottingham Forest where he and manager Brian Clough failed to see eye to eye. Nevertheless, he established his First Division credentials during two periods with Sheffield Wednesday and a season with Newcastle United. More recently, Manchester City have concluded that his midfield drive and bite in the tackle can help them regain their First Division place.

EUGENE MELANIPHY **Forward**
'Miffy' to those supporters who found pronouncing his full name too difficult. He joined Argyle as an amateur from Finchley in 1932 and, after turning professional, remained with the club for five seasons, playing in various forward positions as the need arose. Although mainly regarded as a very useful reserve player, he averaged a goal in every two games he played for the club. He was transferred to Cardiff City in December 1936 and guested for York City and Tranmere Rovers in wartime football.

BARRIE MEYER **Centre-forward**
Well-known to the modern cricket follower as a Test umpire, he combined football with cricket for Gloucestershire in his playing days. He developed with Bristol Rovers for whom he played for ten years before coming to Plymouth. In his six months at Home Park he scored eight goals in ten games — a goals-to-matches ratio which few can match — including an FA Cup hat-trick against Gillingham in 1958, and had done for the club all that could have been asked of him. Unfortunately, however, he was unable to settle in the city and asked for a transfer nearer his Bristol home. He subsequently played for Newport County and for Bristol City where he ended his League career. He now lives near Derby.

MATT MIDDLETON **Goalkeeper**
Probably travelled more miles to play at Home Park than any other goalkeeper who has served the club. He joined Argyle from Sunderland in the summer of 1939 and had played only three League games for the club when war was declared and he was drafted into the mines. He played for Argyle in both the 1939-40 and 1945-6 provisional leagues and, in the interim, regularly kept goal as a guest player for Middlesbrough and also appeared for Carlisle United and Darlington. However, he found that resuming his Argyle career while remaining a coal-miner in Derbyshire imposed a heavy travel burden, especially when the club had a home game. Fortunately for the club, an Army posting brought Bill Shortt to the Plymouth area and his form was so impressive that the management decided that they could afford to release Middleton, who then went on to make over 150 League appearances for Bradford City and York City. Pre-war, he entered League football with Southport after playing for the mining team, Boldon Colliery Welfare. Younger brother Ray, also a goalkeeper, had a distinguished professional career with Chesterfield and Derby County.

PETER MIDDLETON **Inside-forward**
His must rank as one of the most tragic stories among the hundreds of players who have worn the Argyle colours. He arrived at Home Park in 1972 from Bradford City in an exchange deal with Ronnie Brown, scored a spectacular solo goal for Argyle in his debut match and the following week was knocked down by a car. The accident left him with a back injury which both ended his footballing career and was the source of the depression which later caused him to take his own life.

ALAN MILLER **Goalkeeper**
This 19-year-old goalkeeper won much praise for his performances in the Argyle goal during a 13-match spell while on loan from Arsenal in the middle of the 1988-9 season. Indeed, it is no secret that Argyle would have liked to have kept the player permanently at Home Park, but looking to their own future, Arsenal were unwilling to release him. He is not yet the finished product but many clubs would be happy with his potential. Although he has yet to make his League debut for Arsenal, he already has an appearance for England's Under-21 team to his credit, coming on as a substitute in the match against Morocco in 1988. He has West Country connections, his father having played for St Blazey & Bugle, although Alan was born in Epping and joined Arsenal as a trainee.

ALF MILLER **Wing-half**
Appointed Argyle's captain on his League debut after League football resumed in 1946. He came to Plymouth from Southport in 1939 but was almost immediately called into the Army, where he served as a PT instructor. Injury restricted the number of appearances he made in Argyle colours and he retired from playing after a season and linked up with Colchester United as trainer. Brother-in-law of Bob Royston.

CHARLIE MILLER **Full-back**
Scot from Bellshill Athletic who had a few games as stand-in for Moses Russell from 1924 to 1926. He was later transferred to Exeter City where he was a regular member of the side for two seasons.

JOHN MILNE **Full-back**
Another Scot from Scottish junior football, this time from the Highland League side, Fraserburgh, he had one game in each of the three seasons from 1934 to 1936 and was then transferred to Southend United.

KEN MITCHELL **Centre-forward**
Recommended to Argyle while playing for Whitby Rovers, he made eight appearances over two seasons in 1956 and was later on the books of both Hartlepools United and Darlington without getting a League game with either club.

FRED MITCHESON **Inside-forward/wing-half**
Born in Newcastle, he joined Argyle from Port Vale in November 1935 and was a regular member of the side, either at inside-forward or wing-half, until he left for Ipswich Town in the summer of 1939 after playing nearly 100 games for Argyle. He played in all three of Ipswich's fixtures in the short 1939-40 season and, although Ipswich did not compete in any of the Wartime Leagues, he remained on their books until the end of the war when he joined Yeovil & Petters United. He returned to Home Park in 1948 for a brief spell with the training and groundstaff but did not play again for the first team. His best performance for Argyle was in January 1939 when his hat-trick at Luton brought the side a surprise 4-3 victory.

JOHN MITTEN **Outside-left**
Son of Charles Mitten, left winger in the famous Manchester United side of the late 1940s. An England Schools and Youth international, he arrived at Home Park in 1967 from Coventry City after having been with a string of clubs — Mansfield Town, Newcastle United, Leicester City and Manchester United — without making a real mark with any of them. His two seasons at Home Park coincided with a low period in Argyle's fortunes and he later spent three seasons with Exeter City. He also played cricket for Leicestershire.

FRED MOLYNEUX **Centre-half**
Brought to Home Park from his old club, Southport, for £7,500 by manager Billy Bingham in 1969. Formerly with Liverpool, where he was reserve to the giant Ron Yeats and never made a League appearance, he made over 100 appearances for Southport and during the summer acted as a lifeguard at the New Brighton resort. Thigh and cartilage injuries interrupted his progress during his three seasons with Argyle and after two games on loan to Exeter City, he returned to Merseyside to finish his League career with Tranmere Rovers and Southport.

ARTHUR MORGAN **Full-back/inside-forward**
An Argyle signing from Swansea Town in 1953. The plan seemed to be that he would be groomed to succeed Pat Jones, but the latter was in no mood to relinquish his place in the side and Morgan had to be content with spasmodic appearances. Jones in fact was still playing strongly for Argyle when Morgan left the club for Barry Town, having in the meantime given evidence of some versatility by showing up well when tried as an inside-forward.

MORTON MORGAN **Winger**
Joined Argyle from Torquay United in September 1937 and had 11 games on both flanks for the team that season. Transferred to Bristol City the following year.

ANDY MORRISON **Defender**
Born 650 miles from Home Park, at Inverness, he nevertheless played his primary school football in Plymouth and joined Argyle as an apprentice, making his League debut at 17, coming on as a substitute at Villa Park in April 1988. He had two games towards the end of the 1988-9 season and, if Mark Smith persists in his announced intention to leave Home Park, Morrison could get an early chance to establish himself in the side.

DONAL MURPHY **Outside-left**
Dublin-born forward who entered League football as an apprentice with Coventry City and arrived at Home Park via Torquay United for £65,000. He was a regular in the number-11 shirt for Argyle in 1980-81 but moved to Blackburn Rovers a year later.

MARCUS MURPHY **Inside-forward**
Small, balding player who lost his best footballing years to World War Two. Well-known in local Plymouth football before the war, he started in the Argyle side which resumed League football in 1946 but lost his place as the season advanced. With Reserve-team football the only realistic prospect, he dropped out of the League and moved to Chelmsford Town in 1948.

JOHN MURRAY **Half-back**
Powerfully-built player, normally a centre-half, he had four games for Argyle in the last full pre-war season after arriving at Home Park from East Stirling in 1937 and was transferred to Rotherham United in 1939.

ROY NAIL **Centre-forward**
A prolific scorer for St Blazey in Cornish football, he had been a professional for only a matter of weeks when plunged into a struggling Argyle side in 1947. It was a measure of the club's desperation at the time that Argyle were looking to him to work a scoring miracle which more seasoned professionals had failed to produce. It was hardly surprising, therefore, that he looked completely out of his depth in what proved to be his only League game. He returned to Cornish junior football a year later and at that level continued to look a good player.

ANDY NELSON **Centre-half**
A Londoner whose displays for London and Essex Youth sides persuaded West Ham United to sign him as a professional in 1953. After nearly six years at Upton Park and intermittent appearances for the League team, he moved to Ipswich Town for £8,000 and became a leading figure in their side which rose from the Third Division and won the League Championship in 1961-2. He had two seasons with Orient before being brought to Home Park for £4,000 by Derek Ufton in 1965. He was one short of 100 appearances for Argyle when he ended his playing career. He was later manager of Gillingham and Charlton Athletic.

GARY NELSON **Outside-left**
A leading figure in the promotion side of 1985-6, his eye for a scoring chance brought him 13 goals. He entered League football with his local club, Southend United, and then played for Swindon Town before arriving at Home Park. He had only two seasons with Argyle before disappointing the club by requesting a move which took him to Brighton where, in the 1987-8 season, he excelled himself with 22 goals in 42 games.

GLYN NICHOLAS **Forward**
Dartmouth-born, signed as an Argyle apprentice at 18 but had only three first-team games in two years at Home Park before moving to Torquay United.

JOHN OAKES **Centre-half**
Jack Tresadern shocked the football world in the summer of 1947 by signing 42-year-old Oakes on a free transfer from Charlton Athletic and appointing him team captain. Not unreasonably, Oakes had concluded that his playing days were over but he was willing to face the new challenge. It was certainly not the veteran's fault that Argyle had a dismal season; his shrewd positional play and timing frequently brought opposing attacks to nought but, at that age, he could not be considered a long-term investment and he had only one season at the heart of the Argyle defence. He was a centre-forward with Nottingham Forest, Southend and Aldershot in pre-war football but switched to centre-half after joining Charlton and was a leading member of the side which won promotion to the First Division. He also played in the Charlton side beaten by Derby County in the 1946 FA Cup Final.

TONY OBI **Outside-left**
A former member of the England Youth team, he played five games on the Argyle left wing in the promotion season of 1984-5 whilst on loan from Aston Villa, but did not do enough to persuade Argyle that he would be worth a long-term engagement. He later moved to Bristol Rovers.

BILL OLVER **Inside-forward**
A Cornishman from Launceston who played twice for Argyle in 1938-9 and once in the 1945-6 interim season, then returned to junior football in Cornwall with St Austell.

ALAN O'NEILL **Inside-forward**
Changed his surname from Hope after joining his home club Sunderland in 1955. He was Sunderland's leading scorer in 1957-8 and had a couple of seasons with Aston Villa before joining Argyle in 1962. From December 1962 to the following November, he played in almost every Argyle match, but with the team facing difficulties he lost his place and was transferred to Bournemouth a few months later.

HARRY OSMAN **Outside-left**
Born in Alton, Hampshire, he was discovered by Argyle playing for Poole Town and made his League debut for Argyle in 1936. He had five games on the Argyle left wing and then returned to Hampshire to join Southampton in 1938. Transferred to Millwall in 1942, he resumed League football with the London club after the war and ended his League career with Bristol City.

BERNARD OXLEY **Forward**
Formerly with Chesterfield and Sheffield United, Oxley came to Argyle in September 1935 from Sheffield Wednesday and played 15 times in 1935-6, either in the centre or on the right wing, without getting on the score-sheet. He was transferred to Stockport County in 1937.

GEOFF PEACH **Inside-forward**
A local player, he linked up with Millwall and played for the Reserve team as an amateur whilst on National Service. Despite a good scoring record in the Football Combination, he received only one first-team opportunity — in 1957 — for Argyle and returned to Cornish football.

JOHN PEACHEY **Forward**
Formerly with Hillingdon, he started his League career with York City, had a very successful spell with Barnsley and a shorter period with Darlington before coming to Home Park on a free transfer in 1980. He could not force his way into the Argyle side, however, and played only one full League game before dropping out of League football and joining Barnstaple. In 1988 he was playing for Frickley Athletic in the Northern Premier League.

ALAN PEACOCK **Centre-forward**
A local Middlesbrough discovery whose scoring partnership with Brian Clough in the late 1950s and early 1960s made the Teesside club the envy of many of their rivals. Both players were capped by England, Peacock six times and Clough twice. Leeds United paid £53,000 for him in February 1964 and his reputation was such that there were high hopes, when he joined a struggling Argyle side in 1967 for £10,000, that he would be able to produce the goals which the side so obviously needed. Unfortunately, the plan did not work. Injuries restricted him to a dozen appearances for Argyle and eventually forced his retirement from the game.

IAN PEARSON **Forward**
A schoolteacher and part-time professional, he had two spells at Home Park. Argyle introduced him to League football when they signed him from Goole Town in 1974. He made ten appearances in two seasons and returned to non-League football, then had a new lease of life in the Football League with Millwall and Exeter City. He returned to Home Park from Exeter in 1983 but again failed to establish a first-team place and left League football once more, this time for Bideford Town as player and assistant manager.

JOHN PEDDELTY **Central-defender**
A former England Youth international, he came to Argyle in 1974 as part of the deal which took Paul Mariner to Ipswich Town. At Ipswich he had been regarded as a very good future prospect and he soon settled into the Argyle side but, after some 30 games for the club, he suffered a head injury and the specialist medical advice was that it would be dangerous for him to continue to play football.

NORMAN PENGELLY **Half-back**
A former carpenter who was captain of the Looe and Cornwall teams, he arrived at Home Park in the summer of 1947 and stepped into the League side at centre-half after only four games with the Reserves. Cartilage problems caused him to lose his place and finally to retire from the game.

GARY PENHALIGON **Goalkeeper**
Eighteen-year-old who became the first member of Argyle's Centre of Excellence to taste League football when he made his debut at Birmingham in October 1988. He kept a clean sheet then but had a more unhappy experience, being beaten six times against Chelsea in the Simod Cup a few matches later.

HARRY PENK **Winger**
Tiny (5ft 4in) but sturdy winger who could operate with equal facility on either wing, an attribute which proved particularly useful during Argyle's promotion season of 1958-9 when he and Peter Anderson would frequently switch flanks and confuse defences. He spent all of his League career with seaside clubs. Portsmouth signed him from Wigan Athletic. He joined Argyle in 1957 and made over 100 appearances for the club before moving on to Southampton, where he finished his career, three years later.

JOHN PENNY **Winger**
Local player who joined Argyle from school and had seven games for the first team in the period from 1955 to 1959, then joined Penzance.

STEVE PERRIN **Forward**
Londoner who began his League career with Crystal Palace. Had two seasons with Argyle from 1978 then moved to Portsmouth. He was playing for Wycombe Wanderers in 1984.

FORBES PHILLIPSON-MASTERS **Central defender**
Started League football as an 18-year-old apprentice with Southampton and gained further experience on loan to Exeter City, Bournemouth and Luton Town before being signed by Argyle. He formed a central defensive partnership with George Foster from 1979 to 1982 and made over 100 appearances for both Argyle and his next club, Bristol City. After leaving League football, he played for Yeovil Town and in 1987-8 was coach at Weston-super-Mare.

DAVE PHILP **Goalkeeper**
Former Newquay and Cornwall player who joined Argyle in 1984. Geoff Crudgington's consistent form gave him few opportunities to shine but he did not let the side down when standing in for Crudgington during Argyle's promotion season of 1984-5.

OWEN PICKARD **Forward**
Supporters who had been clamouring for this young

player from North Devon to be given a chance were heeded in March 1989 when he was selected for two games, first as a substitute, then as an initial choice. He scored over 30 goals in the Western League in 1988-9 and was voted Young Player of the Year.

CALVIN PLUMMER **Winger**
A £30,000 signing from Nottingham Forest in September. He was then in his second spell with Forest, whom he had joined as an apprentice. He made his League debut at Forest in his first period, then left to play for Chesterfield, Derby County and Barnsley before returning to Forest. He made a good start at Home Park but later lost form and his place in the side, although he was used frequently as a substitute in the latter part of 1988-9.

ALF POWELL **Winger**
Formerly with Bolton Wanderers, he made two appearances for Argyle in 1935 but returned to the north to join Leeds United a year later.

GEORGE POYSER **Full-back**
A pre-war player with Wolves, Mansfield and Port Vale, he joined Argyle from Brentford in 1946 with Bob Thomas in a double transfer. At the age of 36 his contribution to Argyle's fortunes was always likely to be limited and he made only three appearances for the club, leaving at the end of the season to become player-manager of Dover Town. He later reappeared on the League scene as manager of Notts County and Manchester City.

FRED PRESKETT **Forward**
Had three seasons from 1935 to 1937 with Argyle who brought him into League football from Woking Town but he played only a handful of games. He was transferred to Torquay United in 1937.

BOB PRESTON **Centre-half**
Born in Edinburgh, he started his professional career with Heart of Midlothian and later came south to join Torquay United. Argyle bought him from their neighbours to replace Jack Hill in 1923 and he gave them excellent service for five seasons, first at centre-half and later, with the emergence of Jack Pullen and Fred McKenzie, on the flanks. He returned to Torquay at the end of his Argyle career and had two seasons at Plainmoor.

WALTER PRICE **Full-back**
Came to Argyle from his home team Aberdare in December 1924 in exchange for John Smith. He was a fairly regular member of the Argyle side for one and a half seasons, but then spent four more seasons with the club up to and including Argyle's promotion to the Second Division, when he had only a handful of games. He was transferred to Bristol Rovers the following season.

NEIL PRICE **Full-back**
Played once for Argyle in 1984 while on loan from Watford. He later went on permanent transfer to Blackpool and Swansea City.

DAVE PROVAN **Defender**
A bargain signing for Argyle — he came on a free transfer from Crystal Palace — after a distinguished career in Scottish football during which he shared in many of Glasgow Rangers' European triumphs and won five Scottish caps. His career also contained its share of setbacks in that he twice suffered a broken leg. Originally he commuted to Plymouth from London, but later settled in the city and completed well over 100 appearances before returning to Scotland with St Mirren. His ten goals for Argyle came mainly from the penalty-spot. He was chosen as Player of the Year in 1971-2. Latterly, he has been manager of East Stirling and Albion Rovers.

GORDON QUINN **Inside-forward**
A tall, slim player with good ball control, he was signed by Jack Rowley from Queen's Park Rangers in 1956 as part of the Argyle manager's attempt to rebuild the side which had dropped into the Third Division. He had only one season with Argyle and failed to win a permanent first-team place.

BILLY RAFFERTY **Forward**
Well-built native of Glasgow, best remembered at Home Park for the scoring partnership he formed with Paul Mariner which helped to take Argyle back to the Second Division in 1974-5. Rafferty scored 23 League goals that season and Mariner 20. A player of his scoring ability is always in demand and Rafferty moved around a great deal after joining Coventry City as an apprentice. He joined Argyle from Blackpool for £25,000 and later played for Carlisle, Wolves, Newcastle, Portsmouth and Bournemouth. He was reported to be playing in Portugal during 1987.

NEIL RAMSBOTTOM **Goalkeeper**
Had only one season in Argyle's goal — 1976-7, between Milija Aleksic and Paul Barron — but it was enough for supporters to elect him Player of the Year. Cynics might argue that in that relegation year it was the goalkeeper who saw most of the action! Obviously, however, no blame for the team's fate that season was laid on the last line of defence. After seven years at Bury, he served a whole string of clubs, all in the north, apart from Argyle, spending little more than a season with each.

COLIN RANDELL **Midfield/full-back**
Two spells on the Argyle playing staff brought his total of appearances for the club to 277. Capped for Wales at Schoolboy, Youth and Under-23 levels, he joined Coventry City as an 18-year-old apprentice but did not get a League game there and had to wait for three years, until his arrival at Home Park, to make his debut. In his first period there, he figured in both of the team's successes of the mid-1970s, the League Cup run of 1973-4 and promotion in the following season. He was allowed to leave Argyle for Exeter City in 1977 for a fee of £10,000 and after two seasons with the latter came back at £60,000 to become a regular choice for the side for three seasons. Bobby Saxton, appointed Blackburn's manager, took him to Ewood Park in 1982 for £40,000. His period at Blackburn included a spell on loan to Newport County and it was in his native Wales that he finished his League career with Swansea City. He took up a post as manager of the Welsh club Britton Ferry Athletic in 1988.

PETER RATTRAY **Inside-forward**
The only newcomer to the team which had previously been relegated, he was the tallest member of the promotion-winning attack of 1951-2 and the one upon whom Argyle mainly relied to head for goal when Astall or Govan swung across their centres. The 19 goals he scored that season made a significant contribution towards the side's total of over 100. He came to Argyle from Dundee in 1950 in exchange for Stan Williams, took a season to settle at Home Park, then became an indispensable member of the attack. He did not accompany Argyle into the Second Division, having requested a move, and was transferred to Norwich City for £12,000. His performances with that club, however, were never as impressive as during his Argyle days and he moved back to Scotland to join Stirling Albion after just over a season in East Anglia.

SID RAWLINGS **Outside-right**
Son of Bill Rawlings, who played twice for England in 1922 whilst with Southampton. Sid was 33 when he came to Plymouth, having played for Preston, Northampton, West Brom, Millwall and Everton. He had only one full season with the club before retiring, but he scored 17 goals and became renowned for his cross-wing play with Bill Strauss and his accuracy from the penalty-spot.

HARRY RAYMOND **Inside-forward**
Local player who was captain of Mutley Grammar School team and played for Woodland Villa before joining Argyle in 1908. He established a place in the first team in the following year and won three England Amateur caps in 1914. He later turned professional and was a regular member of the Argyle side which entered the Football League in 1920. He was still in the first-team squad for the next two seasons but, having lost some of the pace he displayed when younger, was no longer such an automatic choice and in 1924 — after 16 years with Argyle — he accepted an offer to become player-manager of Torquay United, but not before taking a benefit with Argyle when the famous amateur side, Corinthians, provided the opposition.

GEORGE REED **Half-back**
Born in Leeds, he came to Home Park from Leeds United and from 1931 to 1933 vied with Alec Hardie and later Archie Gorman for the left-half position. He was transferred to Crystal Palace in the summer of 1934. In the early 1950s he returned to Argyle as assistant trainer, coincidentally replacing Archie Gorman, the man who had taken his playing place in the Argyle side.

HUGH REED **Winger**
Came to Argyle in 1971 after having had a handful of First Division games with West Bromwich Albion. The latter discovered him playing for the same Glasgow junior side as Asa Hartford, who went on to win international honours for Scotland. The tiny Hughie was to have nowhere near so impressive a career. Argyle bought him from West Brom for £12,000 but after a dream start, in which he scored eight goals in his first nine games for the club, he lost his place in the side, appeared only intermittently for the next two seasons and then made modest contributions to the playing fortunes of Brentford, Crewe Alexandra, Huddersfield Town and Hartlepool.

MIKE REEVES **Full-back**
Joined Argyle as a teenager. His 100 or so appearances for the club were spread over eight seasons and in only three of those could it be said that he was an established member of the side. Curiously, his most successful spell was near the end of his career with Argyle, when in 1968-9 the team's full-backs were usually Mike Reeves and Colin Sullivan, both of them born in Saltash.

RICHARD REYNOLDS **Forward/half-back**
Made his Argyle debut in the League Cup semi-final in January 1965, a month short of his 17th birthday, leading the attack as deputy to the injured Frank Lord. It was, as manager Malcolm Allison admitted, a gamble but it proved to be justified. The Cornishman was a burly young man, not physically dominated by any opponent and selection for the England Youth team soon followed. He played six seasons for Argyle, initially as a striker but later gave some fine performances when switched to a midfield role. He was transferred to Portsmouth in the summer of 1971, joining up with his former Argyle teammate, Norman Piper. He remained in football after his League career ended and was at one point manager of Fareham Town.

LEN RICH **Winger**
A local player with Co-op United and Torpoint, he made his Football League debut as an amateur with Bournemouth in 1934 before returning to junior football with Torpoint, from which club he joined Argyle. He had three Second Division games from August 1935 to January 1936 and was transferred to Luton Town the following month. He was again recruited by Argyle for the 1939-40 South West League and, playing at centre-forward, scored four times in two games, including a hat-trick against Bristol Rovers.

PERCY RICHARDS **Centre-forward**
Signed from Burnley in January 1928, he displayed plenty of dash and vigour when leading the Argyle forwards. He scored ten times in 18 games in his first Argyle season, including a hat-trick in ten minutes against Torquay United in March 1928. The development of Ray Bowden restricted his first-team

appearances in the following seasons and he finally dropped out of the League scene when joining Tunbridge Wells in 1931. He later played for Folkestone.

FRANK RICHARDSON **Centre-forward**
One of three players signed from Barking by Bob Jack in 1921 (Jack Leslie and Alf Rowe were the others), he had a sensational start in League football with a hat-trick on his debut and a total of 31 League goals, including two more hat-tricks, in that first season. For good measure, he also scored four goals in an FA Cup tie the following season. Although his early form for Argyle was more impressive than the latter period, his overall record for the club — 41 goals in 67 games — can hardly be faulted and inevitably aroused the interest of other clubs seeking a scorer. However, he was never able to reproduce that form after leaving Home Park when he played for Stoke City, West Ham United, Swindon Town, Reading and Swindon again before retiring from the game in 1931. He died in 1987, aged 90.

DEREK RICKARD **Forward**
Local player who made so big an impact after only half a season in 1969-70 that supporters voted him Player of the Year by a big margin. Started with the club as a part-timer but gave up his job in the dockyard when it was evident that he could make the grade as a full-time professional. He spent five seasons with Argyle, making nearly 150 appearances and scoring 41 goals, then had two seasons with Bournemouth.

NEIL RIOCH **Central defender**
Younger brother of the Scottish international Bruce Rioch and an England Youth international in 1969. Like his brother, he began his professional career with Luton Town, but found it more difficult to break into first-team football. Without any League experience with Luton, he moved to Aston Villa in 1969 but in six years made only rare appearances for that club and had been on loan to Northampton Town and York City before coming to Argyle. His experiences at Home Park were equally disappointing and he made only three full and two substitute appearances for the club.

DAVID ROBBIE **Winger**
Nearing the end of his League career when he arrived at Home Park from Bury, he had three games on the right wing at the start of the 1935-6 season and moved to Manchester United a year later.

DAVID ROBERTS **Full-back**
Plymouth-born former apprentice who made infrequent appearances over three seasons at Home Park and then entered South Western League football with St Austell.

ALAN ROGERS **Winger**
Not to be confused with Andy (below). A Plymothian, he signed for Argyle as an apprentice in 1970 and as a full-time professional three years later. He made his debut in 1973-4 and was a member of the squad which advanced to the semi-finals of the League Cup that season. He was with Argyle for six seasons, mostly on the left wing, but sometimes at left-back, and had played over 100 games for the club when he was transferred to Portsmouth in 1979. He made over 150 appearances for the latter and then had spells with Southend United and Cardiff City before returning to the West Country to sign for Falmouth Town in 1988.

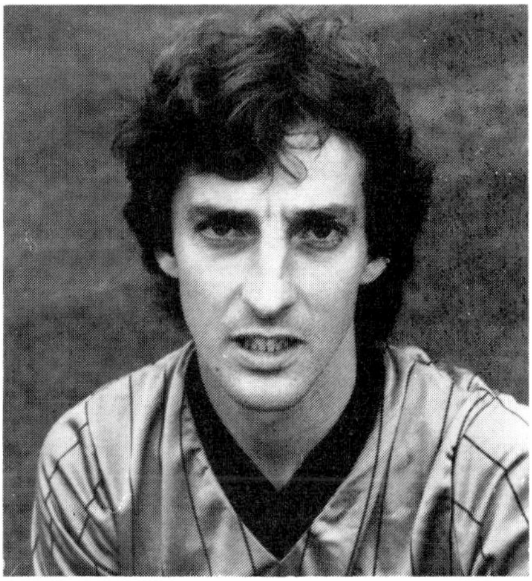

ANDY ROGERS **Winger**
Excelled during Argyle's FA Cup run of 1983-4. Not so much for the goal (direct from a corner and 'an absolute fluke' according to the scorer) which beat Derby County in the sixth-round replay, as for his all-round wing play which kept First Division defenders at full stretch as Argyle advanced in the competition. Started his League career with his local club, Peterborough United, and had a spell with Southampton, making only substitute appearances before coming to Argyle for £50,000 in 1981. Had four seasons as an Argyle regular and was transferred to Reading for £15,000 in 1985. In a game with Reading in 1986 he swallowed his tongue after a collision on the field and his life was saved by prompt work from the team's trainer. A transfer to Southend United for £10,000 followed in 1985. He became a probation officer at the end of his professional career in 1988.

BOB ROSS **Half-back**
Former Stenhousemuir player who played twice for Argyle in 1924 and was then transferred to Coventry City and had 20 games for that club in his first season there.

TONY ROUNSEVELL **Defender**
Cornish-born product of the Argyle apprentice scheme. He had five seasons with the club but in only two — 1963-4 and 1966-7 — did he have any notable spells in the League side. He joined Weymouth Town after leaving Argyle.

BARRY ROWAN **Winger**
A Londoner who had ten seasons in League football before arriving at Home Park. He had played for a number of clubs in the south-east, Watford, Brentford, Millwall, Colchester and Reading, but had made a mark only with Millwall. He had two short periods in the Argyle team of 1969-70 but had more success after joining Exeter City in the summer of 1970.

DARREN ROWBOTHAM **Forward**
One of two Cardiff-born brothers who came to Home Park by means of the YTS scheme, he holds the record for the highest number of substitute appearances for the club. A former captain of the Welsh Youth team, he was transferred to Exeter City in 1987 as part of the deal which brought Nick Marker to Argyle.

JASON ROWBOTHAM **Full-back**
Younger brother of Darren and, like him, became an Argyle player after being engaged by the club under the YTS scheme. He made his debut in 1987-8 and had a couple more games for the club when deputizing for Kenny Brown in 1988-9.

ALF ROWE **Half-back**
Relatively the least successful of the trio of players signed from Barking Town by Bob Jack in 1921. Whereas Frank Richardson attained instant fame and Jack Leslie, after a slower start, became an Argyle legend, Rowe spent four seasons at Home Park without ever becoming an automatic choice and the run of games he had in the side in the first half of the 1924-5 season represented his best achievement. In search of regular first-team football, he moved to Queen's Park Rangers in 1925 but found League fame just as elusive there.

MARK ROWE **Midfield**
Slim, neat player, another product of Argyle's apprentice scheme. He had four seasons in and out of the Argyle side, his most successful season being 1983-4, although he had lost his place by the time that the club began to make significant progress in the FA Cup competition. He dropped out of League football to join Saltash in 1985 but is still young enough to make a comeback in the professional sphere if the chance arises.

JACK ROWLEY **Forward**
Came to Home Park in 1955 as player-manager at the end of a career which started before World War Two with his home team, Wolves, then took him to Bournemouth and finally to his greatest successes with Manchester United where, in the post-war years, he won FA Cup and League Championship medals and became renowned for his scoring abilities — 163 post-war League goals. He won six England caps between 1949 and 1952, scoring four goals in one match against Northern Ireland. He was nearing the end of his playing career when he joined Argyle and, whereas with Manchester United he had played at the head of the attack, he preferred to drop further back where he could have more effect on the course of play during the three seasons he continued to play for Argyle. (See *The Argyle Managers*)

BOB ROYSTON **Full-back**
World War Two intervened to rob this player of what would have been the best years of his professional career; and playing in wartime football for the Portsmouth, Aldershot and Army sides was not an adequate compensation. Born in Newcastle, he played for Durham County as a schoolboy and later signed for Sunderland. The latter gave him a free transfer

and he joined Southport in 1936, playing nearly 100 League matches for them. Signed by Argyle in 1939, he played five games for the club before the outbreak of war. After the war he was the regular choice at right-back in 1946-7 and he ended the season captaining the side, but early into the new season he decided to retire from the game and entered business.

SID RUNDLE **Half-back**
Member of a well-known St Blazey sporting family, he joined Argyle at the end of the war and was a member of the squad of mainly local players from whom Argyle selected a side to compete in the 1945-6 FA Cup and League South competitions. He had seven post-war seasons at Home Park but had difficulty in holding a regular place in the side and his most successful season was 1947-8 when he and Len Boyd were the wing-halves for much of the season. His younger brother, Charles, played for Tottenham Hotspur and Crystal Palace in the same period. Sid died in 1987 aged 65.

TOMMY RYAN **Half-back**
From the same small Scottish village as Tommy Dougan, he was an Argyle recruit from Glasgow Celtic in 1935. He spent three seasons at Home Park but was only rarely called on for first-team duty and was transferred to Swindon Town in 1939. He remained on the Wiltshire club's books throughout the war years and, according to their records, was transferred to Torquay United in 1945 but did not make any first-team appearances for the Plainmoor club.

KEITH SANDERSON **Midfield**
Former Cambridge soccer 'Blue' who came to Malcolm Allison's attention when the latter was coaching the University team. When Allison entered club management, Sanderson followed him, first to Bath City then to Argyle where he became a part-time professional. Sanderson had his Home Park critics, some arguing that as a part-timer he ought not to receive full wages, but he was championed by the manager who maintained that the player's value to the side was not appreciated from the terraces and that he was the best retriever of the ball in the club. He did not remain with Argyle after Allison's departure but for a £5,000 fee moved to Queen's Park Rangers, for whom he played over 100 games and won a Football League Cup medal in 1967. He expressed his disenchantment with the modern game in a recent letter to *The Times*.

CHARLES SARGEANT **Winger**
Another player whose Argyle career was prematurely ended by the outbreak of World War Two. He arrived from Stockport County in the summer of 1939 and played in the three games of the 1939-40 season. He was a regular member of the side in the first Wartime League (1939-40) but was then called into the Army. During his brief spell at Home Park he had caught the eye as a fast winger with a strong shot and it is a matter for regret that post-war supporters did not get the opportunity to see his skills for themselves.

ALAN SEALEY **Winger**
One of Derek Ufton's three panic forward buys in the autumn of 1967 when the side had lost seven of the first ten League games. A Londoner, he joined Orient at 17 but did not establish a regular League place until joining West Ham United. He played over 100 games for West Ham and gained a European Cup-winners' Cup medal with them in 1965. Argyle paid £9,000 for him but he had played only four games for the club when injury caused his retirement from the League scene.

LES SEALEY **Goalkeeper**
Alan Sealey's cousin. Had six games with Argyle while on loan from Luton Town in 1984 as cover while Geoff Crudgington recovered from a broken finger. At that point he had been temporarily displaced in the Luton goal by Andy Dibble but has since regained his position and has played over 200 games for Luton.

PETER SHEARING **Goalkeeper**
Londoner and former paratrooper who arrived at Home Park in 1966 via West Ham United, Portsmouth and Exeter City but had established a regular League place only with the last-named club. He replaced John Leiper in the Argyle goal but before the season had finished he had in turn lost his place to Pat Dunne. He returned to Exeter City and had another three years there before moving on to Bristol Rovers and Gillingham.

GEORGE SHEFFIELD **Centre-forward**
Stockily-built forward who arrived at Home Park from Loughborough in the spring of 1920 and, with five goals in eight appearances for Argyle, looked to be a very promising prospect, but his later form was less impressive and after being in and out of the side in the following season, Argyle's first in the Football League, he was transferred to Kettering Town.

TREVOR SHEPHERD **Winger**
Had just over a season on the Argyle right wing in the early 1970s. Nottinghamshire-born, he was on Forest's books as a teenager but was allowed to link up with Coventry City. He had First Division experience with the latter but could not command a regular place and had a successful period on loan to Torquay United before joining Argyle for £9,000 in the summer of 1969. He entered non-League football with Nuneaton after leaving Argyle.

DAVE SHIPPERLEY **Centre-half**
Had been a regular in the Charlton Athletic side when he played one game on loan to Argyle in the latter part of the 1973-4 season.

BARRY SILKMAN **Midfield**
A talented player whose relatively brief spell of five months on Argyle's books was fairly typical of the pattern of a career in which he did not seem to settle anywhere for long. He played for Hereford United and Crystal Palace before joining Argyle and for Manchester City, Brentford, Queen's Park Rangers, Orient, Southend United and Crewe Alexandra after leaving Home Park. Add to that list a period on loan to Luton Town and his playing record is one of service with ten different League clubs. In 1987-8 he joined Staines Town, presumably signifying that his Football League career had ended. He is well-known in greyhound racing circles as a trainer.

JOHN SILLETT **Full-back**
Comes from a footballing family. Father was a pre-war professional and elder brother Peter, also a full-back, won three England caps in 1955 while with Chelsea. John followed Peter, first to their home club, Southampton, then to Chelsea. He made over 100 appearances for the London club and was chosen for the Football League team before joining Coventry City in 1962. He marked up another century of appearances there before joining Argyle in the summer of 1966, playing mostly in defence but occasionally at centre-forward. He had two seasons with the club, leaving Home Park for a training job with Bristol City after Argyle had been relegated. After entering club management he guided Coventry City to an FA Cup win in 1987.

JOHN SIMPSON **Centre-forward**
Former teammate of Jimmy Rae at Partick Thistle. Both players had caught Bob Jack's eye while playing for the Scottish club at Home Park in a benefit match for Alec Hardie at the end of the 1931-2 season. Both were transferred to Argyle that summer and both went straight into the side for the opening of the new season, but whereas Rae became a fixture in the team over many seasons, Simpson had only a handful of games in two seasons for Argyle.

PETER SIMPSON **Inside-forward**
Recruited from the Scottish club, Fraserburgh, with full-back John Milne in the summer of 1933, he made his League debut for Argyle in the following February and had half a dozen games in two seasons with the club.

JOHN SIMS **Forward**
In four seasons with Argyle from 1979 to 1983 he was virtually an automatic choice as attack leader. His scoring record of just under a goal for every three games played is not particularly remarkable but the bare figures do not reveal the extent of his toil. A Derbyshire man, he started his career with Derby County but did not really begin to make a mark in League football until he joined Notts County three years later. He then moved to Exeter City where he played under Bobby Saxton and the latter brought him to Home Park for £22,000 when he took over as Argyle's manager. After he left Argyle to join Torquay United, he played for all three of Devon's professional sides. He had two more spells with both Exeter City and Torquay and the latter gave him a chance as player-manager but dismissed him after only eight games in charge of the side. He then became a licensee in the resort.

KEVIN SMART **Full-back**
A product of Argyle's apprentice scheme, he had a virtually unbroken run in the League side from March to December 1977, then lost his place to Chris Harrison. He moved to Wigan Athletic the following summer and had two seasons with the Lancashire side.

ARTHUR SMITH **Inside-forward**
One of the two players recruited by Argyle to replace Peter Rattray when the team returned to the Second Division in 1952 (Sam McCrory being the other). A small but speedy player whose first professional club was Leicester City, he was then transferred to West Bromwich Albion and was a regular member of the Albion side which gained promotion to the First Division in 1948-9. He played in just over half of Argyle's 1952-3 games and was transferred to Crewe Alexandra the following summer.

ERNIE SMITH **Inside-forward**
Signed from Rotherham United in November 1938, he remained on the club's books throughout the war and played a few games in the 1945-6 season but did not resume a professional career after the war had ended.

JACK SMITH **Full-back**
Local player who had only three games for Argyle in four years but then had six seasons as a regular member of the Torquay United team. He was the younger brother of Bill Smith, who played at centre-forward for Argyle in a few games in 1945-6 and then was allowed to leave the club. His subsequent career was to prove how mistaken that decision was, for as a wing-half, inside-forward and finally full-back, he had 14 more years in League football, playing for Reading, Northampton Town, Birmingham City, Blackburn Rovers and Accrington Stanley.

JACKIE SMITH **Inside-forward**
Arrived at Home Park in the summer of 1935 and remained until 1946 when, after assisting the club in that League South season, he decided to retire from the game. He carried on scouting for Argyle in northern football into the late-1940s.

JAMES SMITH **Centre-forward**
Formerly with Clydebank, he had one game for Argyle in January 1922 before returning to the Scottish club.

JOHN SMITH **Centre-forward**
Formerly with Bristol City, he scored four times in six games for Argyle in the latter part of the 1923-4 season and toured Argentina with the team the following summer. Moved to Aberdare Athletic in exchange for Walter Price the following season.

LINDSAY SMITH **Centre-half**
Fair-haired and uncompromising defender at the heart of the Argyle defence during the FA Cup run of 1983-4. Started in League football as an apprentice with Colchester United and played over 200 games for them before moving to Cambridge United where he recorded over 100 appearances. He came to Argyle for £20,000 and played for two seasons with the club but he and his wife could not settle in the area and he was transferred to Millwall in 1984, where he spent two more seasons before returning to Cambridge United. That he spent most of 1988-9 on loan to Bury Town suggests that his League career is drawing to a close.

MARK SMITH **Central defender**
Argyle paid their record fee of £170,000 to Sheffield Wednesday in the summer of 1987 for Mark Smith and the tall defender was an automatic choice for the side from then on. His decision towards the end of 1988-9 to seek a transfer in order to return to the north was a big blow to Ken Brown's team-building plans. Sheffield-born, he joined Wednesday as an apprentice and played nearly 300 games for them and had won five caps for the England Under-21 team before coming to Plymouth.

MARK SMITH **Full-back**
Redruth-born defender who played three games at left-back in 1984. He had previously been on Bristol City's books but dropped out of League football and was playing for Exmouth Town when recruited by Argyle. He had only a season with Argyle, but later played for the Newcastle (Australia) side managed by former Argyle favourite, Mike Trebilcock.

MIKE SMITH **Inside-forward**
A Scot who had a rapid rise to football prominence and an equally rapid fall. After being on trial from his local Scottish junior side, Preston Athletic, he signed for Argyle in February 1948. He made his League debut two months later and three months after that was signed by First Division Chelsea, who regarded him as an extremely promising player. His hopes were to be dashed, however, and he did not get a first-team game with the London club and left League football.

BOB SMITH **Half-back**
Born in Walkden, Lancashire, he joined Argyle from Manchester City and had almost a full season (1925-6) as Argyle's left-half until the arrival of Alec Hardie and the latter's consistency restricted his opportunities. He was then transferred to Torquay United.

FRANK SQUIRES **Inside-forward**
Former Welsh Schoolboy international, a master of the swerve and feint, he had the unfortunate experience of serving three clubs who lost their Second Division status. After Swansea Town, his home team, had been relegated in 1947, he was signed by Argyle for £5,000 a few months later. Three years later, it was Argyle's turn to be relegated. Squires was transferred that summer to Grimsby Town only to find his new club meeting the same fate by the end of the season. He then returned to Wales and played for a period with Merthyr Tydfil. Although he played for Wales in a wartime international, he never received the full cap which his talents deserved, although lesser players than he were so honoured by their country. Supporters with long memories might recall the brilliant individual goal he registered in a surprise win at Sheffield Wednesday in 1950 when his skill inside the penalty area outwitted four defenders before he slipped the ball into the net.

TERRY STACEY **Full-back**
Won six England Amateur international caps when with Carshalton. He also played for Chelsea's youth team but entered the professional world with Argyle. He broke into the first team relatively quickly and played 16 games in his first season with the club (1959-60) but later lost his place and made only isolated appearances for the next two seasons. He was transferred to Watford in the summer of 1962 but had not played a single match for them before moving to Gillingham a year later.

GEORGE STANBURY **Gaolkeeper**
Local player, formerly with Torpoint and Devon County, whose five seasons at Home Park were spent mostly as an understudy, first to Fred Craig and then to Harry Cann. In 1927-8, however, he made more appearances than any other of the four goalkeepers tried that season. He moved to Gillingham in 1933 but played only once for his new club before returning to the Plymouth area and taking over a public house.

GORDON STANIFORTH **Forward**
Tommy Tynan's striking partner during Argyle's FA Cup run of 1984-5. He played for England Schoolboys and joined his home team, Hull City, as a 17-year-old apprentice. He did not get many League opportunities with Hull but his career blossomed first with York City and then with Carlisle United. He joined Argyle in 1983 in a part-exchange deal involving Mike McCartney plus £5,000 and had three seasons at Home Park, being elected Player of the Year for 1983-4, before being transferred to Newport County in the summer of 1985 in exchange for Steve Cooper. He retired from League football to become a publican in his native Yorkshire but continued playing to assist North Ferriby United to the semi-finals of the 1988-9 FA Vase competition.

ARTHUR STENNER **Winger**
Born in Yeovil, he turned professional with Bristol City but had to wait for his League debut until arriving at Home Park in 1955. He made only occasional appearances in the Argyle first team and did not make much more impression with the clubs he later served Norwich City, Exeter City and Oldham Athletic.

MARK STUART **Winger**
A £150,000 signing from Charlton Athletic in November 1988, he brought speed and skill to the left-wing spot which had not been satisfactorily filled for the club since the departure of Gary Nelson. Born in London, he had been on Queen's Park Rangers' books as a schoolboy but did not make his League debut until joining Charlton. He played over 100 games for the latter before being persuaded to come south by Ken Brown.

BOBBY STUART **Full-back**
A full-back of the old school, even to the bow legs, he arrived at Home Park as part of the double transfer deal with Middlesbrough which also brought George Dews to the West Country. Stuart was the more surprising element in the deal because at the age of 34, and after 19 years with Middlesbrough, he could hardly be considered an investment for the future. Although when compared with his team captain John Oakes, Stuart was but a youngster, he played for only half a season with Argyle before the club discovered that George Silk and Paddy Ratcliffe were as competent and younger (although in the former case by only a few years).

ELLIS STUTTARD **Half-back**
Probably better known at Home Park in the capacities of manager, trainer or coach than as the player who first came to Plymouth in 1938 from Burnley, where he had been playing in the 'A' team. He made a few appearances for Argyle in the 1939-40 Wartime League but was then called in to the RAF. He resumed his association with the club after the war and played in a number of defensive positions in the first post-war season, then had three seasons with Torquay United before leaving the League scene as a player. After his links with Argyle had been severed, he moved back to his native Burnley and died there in 1984. (See *The Argyle Managers*).

KEVIN SUMMERFIELD **Midfield**
The tackle which broke his leg in the FA Cup replay at Everton in 1989 not only ended Argyle's Cup hopes but also caused more long-term damage to the team's fortunes because the side's midfield plans revolved around Summerfield. With Argyle, he was having one of the best periods of his League career, having moved around from West Bromwich Albion (where he was an apprentice) to Birmingham City, Walsall and Cardiff City without having made a real mark with any of those clubs before arriving at Home Park in 1985.

DAVE SUTTON **Centre-half**
Comes from the Preston area but was overlooked by the northern clubs and began his professional career as an apprentice with Argyle. He had five seasons with the club, his most sustained spell in the first team being during Argyle's stay in the Second Division from 1975 to 1977. Having lost his place, he was transferred a year later to Huddersfield Town, for whom he played over 200 games. He registered over 100 appearances for his next club, Bolton Wanderers, and remained in the north when subsequently moving to Rochdale. During 1988-9, his playing career was ended through injury but he remained with Rochdale, first as coach and later as caretaker manager.

BRADLEY SWIGGS **Midfield**
Son of Bob Swiggs, he became the first son of a former player to represent the club in the League since the days of the Jack family. He made his only full appearance in the spring of 1984.

BOB SWIGGS **Centre-forward**
Had three games in the struggling Argyle side of the mid-1950s after demonstrating his goalscoring potential with St Blazey. Repeating those performances at the higher level, however, proved to be more difficult and he later dropped into Southern League football with Weymouth Town.

NORMAN SYKES **Half-back**
Bristolian who played for England at Schoolboy and Youth levels before joining Bristol Rovers at 17. He had played over 200 games for the Eastville club but there was some doubt about his fitness when Derek Ufton signed him for £2,000 in 1964. A persistent knee injury and an arthritic hip made his signing something of a gamble and he played only three games for Argyle. But he kept fit enough to play three more seasons of League football with Stockport County and Doncaster Rovers.

BRIAN TAYLOR **Half-back**
A native of Gateshead, he entered professional football with Coventry City but did not get his League chance until moving to Walsall for whom he made over 200 appearances before coming to Argyle in 1977. After just over a season at Home Park, he was transferred to Preston North End for £35,000 a year later.

GEORGE TAYLOR **Half-back**
As immaculate in his tackling and passing as in his appearance, he was nearing the end of his professional career when he joined Argyle in 1948 at the age of 35. His best footballing years had been spent with Aberdeen with whom he won a Scottish Cup medal in 1947. He had two seasons in the Argyle side before retiring as a player but his association with the club as trainer and, briefly, manager lasted for nearly 20 years.

JOHN TEDESCO **Forward**
Born in Modbury; signed professional forms for Argyle in 1966 after having been with the club as an apprentice. Made a total of 37 appearances over four seasons, then moved to Bristol Rovers but did not get a first-team opportunity with them.

GEORGE TEPPER **Outside-right**
Did not have the best of luck during his one season with Argyle. Given a first-team chance, late in the 1933-4 season, he was hit in the eye by the ball and considerably handicapped for the rest of the game and was unable to take a place in the side for the last game of the season. He left Argyle for Bath City in the close season.

KEITH THOMAS **Winger**
Jimmy Rae's choice as the successor to Gordon Astall after the latter had been transferred to Birmingham

City. He spent three years with Sheffield Wednesday and Cardiff City before coming west in 1953 but his Argyle career gave him his first real opportunity to make a mark on the League scene. He had two seasons at Home Park, then two with Exeter City. After that, his career took an unusual turn. A qualified teacher, he applied for and was granted a commission in the RAF and, as Flying Officer Thomas, he subsequently appeared for RAF representative teams.

JOHN THOMSON **Goalkeeper**
Splendid displays against Argyle for Brentford by this Glasgow-born goalkeeper persuaded Bob Jack to obtain his transfer in the summer of 1926. In the previous season, he had missed only two matches for Brentford and previously had Scottish League experience with Alloa Athletic and Partick Thistle. He played seven times for Argyle in 1926 but Fred Craig then regained and held his place and Thomson moved to Aberdare Athletic the following year.

ADRIAN THORNE **Forward**
Has a place in the Brighton record books as the man who scored six goals against Watford in 1957-8 in a game which ensured that Brighton won the Third Division championship title. His career at Home Park brought no such record-breaking and two and a half years and a dozen games later he moved to Exeter City. He later played a couple of games for Orient.

ALBERT THORPE **Half-back**
Joined Argyle as an amateur from Loughborough and played in the last three games of Argyle's first Football League season. Later joined Burnley.

REX TILLEY **Wing-half**
None of football's honours came the way of this red-haired half-back. He left the club the season before they won the Third Division championship in 1958-9 but his teammates rated him highly, particularly Johnny Williams who usually operated on the other flank of the half-back line and took advantage of the crossfield passes which Tilley provided. Argyle brought him into League football from Chippenham Town. He took three seasons to establish himself in the side but then went on to make over 100 appearances for the club before ending his League career with Swindon Town.

JOHN TIMMINS **Full-back**
Former Wolves junior and reserve player who had not made his League debut when he signed for Argyle in 1958. He had played only five games for Argyle when, eight months later, he was on his way again, unable to settle in Plymouth. He failed to make an impact with Bristol Rovers, his next club, and dropped out of League football.

LUKE 'LOU' TINKLER **Outside-left**
One of the few playing successes of the 1945-6 League South season. The little (5ft 6in) winger had played for Birmingham Schools and was on West Brom's books when conscripted into the Navy in 1942. A naval posting in 1945 brought him to Plymouth and to the attention of both Argyle and the Navy's soccer selectors. Jack Tresadern, who used to sing Lou Tinkler's praises, nevertheless bought Bill Strauss to fill the outside-left position when the Football League programme resumed in 1946, but Tinkler still played in about half of that season's fixtures, sometimes replacing the injured Strauss and occasionally at inside-forward to the latter. He was transferred to Walsall two years later but spent only one season with the Midlands club.

WILLIAM TOMS **Centre-forward**
Bustling, hard-working type of player who was a reserve at Manchester United before coming west in 1920. He had one season with Argyle, alternating between the centre and inside-forward positions, before moving on to Tranmere Rovers.

GEORGE TOOTILL **Half-back**
Tall player, a product of the Lancashire club Chorley, he had occasional games for Argyle in the two seasons encompassed by 1937, mostly as a half-back but on one occasion at centre-forward. He was transferred to Sheffield United in January 1938 and remained with the Yorkshire club during the early years of the war, but did not resume a professional career when peace was restored.

DANNY TRAINOR **Forward**
Had been with Belfast Crusaders for five years and had Northern Ireland Amateur, Under-23 and one full international caps to his credit when he joined Argyle in 1968 but he did not make a great impact and he went back across the Irish Sea to join Waterford after only one season at Home Park.

MIKE TREBILCOCK **Forward**
Malcolm Allison once predicted that the little Gunnislake-born forward, formerly with Tavistock, would score a hatful of goals. He never quite became the goalscoring machine thus implied, but he did become nationally known when he scored two of the goals by which Everton beat Sheffield Wednesday in the 1966 FA Cup Final. Everton had paid Argyle £23,000 for him the previous New Year's Eve and their manager Harry Catterick took a calculated risk by preferring Trebilcock to international Fred Pickering for the Wembley game. It was a brief glory for the little Cornishman, who found it difficult to win a regular place among the stars at Goodison Park and had only 14 League and Cup games for them in two seasons — he could have done the struggling Argyle side much more good at that time. He later had more success with Portsmouth before ending his League career back in the West Country with Torquay United. More recently, he has been managing a soccer club in New South Wales, Australia.

MIKE TRUSSON **Forward**
Well-built Londoner who was an apprentice with the club before signing professional forms in 1977. He scored twice on his League debut for Argyle at 18. He had four seasons as a fairly regular member of the side, then played over 100 games each for Sheffield United and Rotherham United. He is now with Brighton where he has been used mainly in a midfield role.

CHARLIE TWISSELL **Winger**
Very fast player, both with and without the ball, he was discovered by Argyle playing in local Navy football and made his Argyle debut as an amateur in 1955. His appearances for Argyle attracted the attention of the selectors and he won five England Amateur caps. He continued playing as an amateur, even after buying his discharge from the Navy to pursue a career in football, in order to play for Great Britain's soccer team in the 1956 Olympic Games. He finally turned professional, had two seasons with Argyle, three more with York City and is believed to have gone into business in the York area.

COLIN UPTON **Midfield**
Former apprentice who made two full and one substitute appearance for the club in the 1978-9 season.

JOHN UZZELL **Defender**
This tall defender's decision not to accept Argyle's terms for 1989-90 meant that he was likely to end his 12-year association with the club. He was not a regular choice throughout that period and certainly in recent seasons has had long spells out of the side, apparently being regarded as a second choice. The injury to Leigh Cooper in November 1988 brought him a recall to the left-back position which he occupied for most of the rest of the season, bringing his total appearances for the club to near the 300 mark. Plymouth-born, he joined Argyle as an apprentice and graduated to the League side via the Youth team and the Reserves. He shared in the glamour of the side's FA Cup run of 1984 but was not a regular member of the side which regained the club's place in the Second Division. His performances may lack the polish of some of his rivals but he is strong and wholehearted and for sheer defensive power, at his best he has few equals.

BARRIE VASSALLO **Midfield**
Newport-born, he had a season with Arsenal but did not play League football until arriving at Home Park for £10,000. He had a few games with the promotion side of 1974-5, none with Aldershot, his next club, but later had a more successful spell with Torquay United whom he joined via Barnstaple Town in 1977. He ended his footballing career with Kidderminster, Merthyr Tydfil and Gloucester City before injury forced his retirement from the game.

RON WALDOCK **Forward**
Served six League clubs in ten years, his four-month spell with Argyle coming towards the end of his career. He played for Coventry City, Sheffield United and Scunthorpe before joining Argyle and for Middlesbrough and Gillingham afterwards. He was Scunthorpe's leading scorer when they won the Third Division North championship in 1957-8. His scoring record with Argyle (six goals in 18 games) cannot lightly be dismissed but, as is evident from his short stay, he did not settle at Home Park.

JIMMY WALKER **Inside-forward**
Never a regular member of the side in four seasons at Home Park, he came west from the Scottish club, Rutherglen Waverley, in 1922 and left Argyle in 1925 for Exeter City.

BRUCE WALLACE **Winger**
Formerly with Hamilton Academical, he had one game on the Argyle right wing in 1925 and was transferred to Torquay United at the end of the season.

BOB WALLACE **Full-back**
Another Scot, previously with Bolton Wanderers, who arrived at Home Park in August 1935 from Swindon Town, with whom he had spent the previous season. He had nine games as deputy for Jimmy Rae in the following season and was then transferred to Exeter City.

BOB WARREN **Centre-half**
At one point, it seemed that Warren, one of identical twins, had a bright future in professional football. He and brother, Geoff, joined Argyle when 18 and after only three League games for the club, Bob was signed by First Division Chelsea. He was given only one chance in the Chelsea first team, however, but more surprisingly, failed to establish himself in the Third Division with Torquay United when he returned west three years later.

ALAN WATKINS **Midfield**
Better known to the sporting public as a Glamorgan and England cricketer, he was added to Argyle's staff while serving with the Navy at the end of Word War Two and played five times for the club in the 1946-7 season. He had earlier been on Cardiff City's books and although, after being released at his own request, he was transferred back to Cardiff in 1948, his sights were really set on a cricketing career and it was in order to safeguard that ambition that he relinquished professional football. Whether he could have reached international standards at both sports, had he continued in football, must remain a matter

for conjecture, but he had a weight problem which would have been a big handicap on the soccer field.

JOHN WEBB **Full-back**
Former Liverpool apprentice who did not make any League appearances for that club and had a brief spell on loan to Argyle in 1973. He was transferred to Tranmere Rovers after his return to Liverpool.

ALAN WELSH **Winger**
Edinburgh-born forward who entered League football with Millwall from a Scottish junior club. He made only a handful of appearances in two years with Millwall but his career brightened when he joined Torquay United for £5,000 in 1967. Five years and 150 games later his value had trebled and Ellis Stuttard paid £15,000 for his services. He finished his first season with Argyle as the leading scorer and he also impressed by his displays during the club's long run in the League Cup the following season. He was transferred to Bournemouth in 1974 and ended his stay in English football when he returned to his first club, Millwall, 18 months later.

RALPH WETTON **Half-back**
Former Spurs player who had five seasons with the London club, mainly as reserve to such talented players as Bill Nicholson, Ron Burgess and Tony Marchi. A move to Home Park in 1955 seemed to offer him the chance to break out of the understudy role but, although he was a regular choice in his first season with Argyle, it was an unhappy period for the club, culminating in relegation, while Wetton experienced the indignity of being ordered off early in his second game for Argyle (and first at Home Park), after having intervened in a brawl originally involving other players. He was transferred to Aldershot midway through the following season and had two more seasons there.

JACKIE WHARTON **Winger**
Small but lively forward, discovered playing in junior football in his home town of Bolton by Argyle, who gave him his League debut as an 18-year-old in 1938. He showed such great promise in his first season (1938-9) that First Division Preston North End secured his transfer just before the war. He established his place with Preston during the war and was young enough to rebuild his career after 1946. In post-war games he played over 250 times for Preston, Manchester City, Blackburn Rovers and Newport County. His son, Terry, also a winger, played for Wolves, Bolton Wanderers, Crystal Palace and Walsall in the late 1960s and early 1970s.

PETER WHISTON **Midfield**
Widnes-born player who made his League debut for Argyle towards the end of 1988-9.

PAUL WILKINSON **Forward**
The two games he played for Argyle while on loan from Norwich City in 1970-71 were his only appearances in the Football League.

JOHN LLOYD WILLIAMS **Wing-half**
Welshman popularly known as 'Cardiff' Williams during his Argyle career in order to distinguish him

from the other more famous and contemporary half-back, Johnny Williams. The nickname derived from his previous club, whom he joined as a 17-year-old but for whom he never made a League appearance. He had four seasons with Argyle but was a consistent choice only in the first, the 1958-9 promotion season. Probably the most attention he received from the media was in December 1961 when he found himself cast in the role of the man who had to mark Jimmy Greaves when the England forward played his first game for Spurs, at Home Park in the Football Combination after returning from Milan. That Greaves scored twice in the visitors' 4-1 victory that day does not necessarily reflect badly on JL; better players than he had their work cut out to keep Greaves off the scoring list. Williams had three seasons with Torquay United after leaving Argyle.

KEITH WILLIAMS **Forward**
Former Everton junior who did not get a League chance at Goodison Park but who began to attract attention after linking up with Tranmere Rovers with a scoring average of a goal every other game during his 161 League appearances. He had ended the previous season with 28 goals for Tranmere when he joined Argyle in the summer of 1961 but his spell with the club was brief. Six months later he was off again, to Bristol Rovers, having lost his first-team place with Argyle. His tally of 15 goals in 14 games for the Reserves, however, showed that in those less exacting settings he still had the scoring flair.

STAN WILLIAMS **Outside-left**
South African forward who had one season with Argyle, mainly on the left wing, but occasionally in the middle, after having been signed from Aberdeen for £6,000 in 1949. He had been on the Scottish club's books for 14 years and was a playing colleague of both Bill Strauss and George Taylor. While a guest player with Clyde, he was capped for Scotland against England in a wartime international in October 1941. He had good ball control and speed but he did not enjoy his period at Home Park, partly because of the attitude of a section of the crowd who were vociferous in condemning his tactics of holding on to the ball in a season when goals for the side proved to be in very short supply. He was transferred to Dundee in 1950 in the exchange deal which brought Peter Rattray to Home Park.

GEORGE WILLIS **Inside-forward**
A whole-hearted player who made up in energy and enthusiasm for any technical deficiencies. He was sometimes specifically chosen for first-team duty because his ability to annoy and unsettle defenders tended to create openings for his forward colleagues. A former miner, he signed for Wolves at 17 and had five years with that club, followed by two seasons with Brighton before coming to Argyle in the summer of 1949. He spent seven seasons at Home Park, rarely as a consistent choice and became one of the victims of the wholesale clearance of staff when 1955-6 ended with Argyle being relegated from the Second Division. He then had two seasons with Exeter City.

RHYS WILMOT **Goalkeeper**
Followed his Arsenal teammate Alan Miller to Home Park on loan in 1988-9 and played most of the rest of the season between the Argyle posts after Miller had been recalled to Highbury. Newport-born, he has more League experience than his teenage Arsenal colleague but has been second-choice to John Lukic at Highbury and in addition to his spell at Home Park, he has also been on loan to Hereford and Orient. One unusual feature of his play is that he kicks a dead ball with his left foot and drop-kicks with his right. Argyle were satisfied with his displays but Arsenal's reported asking price of £200,000 seems excessive for a player who does not seem to have an important role in Arsenal's long-term plans.

ANDREW WILSON **Winger**
Played three times on the Argyle right wing in 1922-3, having been recruited from the Scottish club Dunipace Athletic, but returned to Scottish football with Alloa Athletic at the end of the season. His son, Ronnie, was on Argyle's staff in the early 1950s as a full-back and played regularly for the Reserves.

JIMMY WILSON **Inside-forward**
Born in Edinburgh and formerly with Swindon Town. He played twice for Argyle in 1931 and was transferred to Cowdenbeath two years later.

JOHN WINGATE **Centre-foward**
Played once for Argyle in 1968 as an amateur and then joined Dawlish but was offered professional terms by Exeter City and proved his qualities in over 250 games and eight seasons at St James' Park, broken by one season with Bournemouth.

STEVE WOOLDRIDGE **Full-back**
Londoner who came to Argyle in 1970 from Crystal Palace at the age of 19, first on loan then on a permanent transfer. He had one season in the Argyle first team and was later transferred to Colchester United.

GEORGE WRIGHT **Goalkeeper**
Tall, fair-haired Plymothian, the son of a Devon rugby player, he joined Argyle in 1937 and made his League debut in 1938 when 17½. He was still available during Argyle's two wartime seasons and again when League football resumed in 1946 but, not being assured of recognition even as a second choice, he asked to leave the club. Given a free transfer, he signed for Colchester United and re-entered League football when that club was elected to the Third Division in 1950. Returning to Home Park with Colchester in October 1950 he found the homecoming distinctly unfriendly as an Argyle side, firing on all cylinders, crashed seven goals past him. The second visit the following season was slightly better with Argyle winning 3-1, but George finally had his revenge, keeping a clean sheet in the return fixture at Colchester which the home team won 1-0. He played five seasons of League football for Colchester before being replaced by the former Bury goalkeeper Jimmy Kirk, who later played for Torquay United.

VIC WRIGHT **Forward**
Former Liverpool player who was a regular choice for Argyle in the early part of 1937-8 but lost his place in the second part of the season and then dropped out of League football on signing for Chelmsford City in 1938.

BILL WRIGHT **Forward**
A famous name in soccer but the Argyle player was an attacker, unlike his Wolves' namesake. He started his career at 19 with his home team, Blackpool, and played for Leicester City and Newcastle United before joining the Argyle staff for the return to the Second Division in the summer of 1959. He had two seasons in the Argyle attack, either on the left wing or in the middle, and was transferred to Millwall in the summer of 1961.

ROBINSON (BOB) WYLLIE **Goalkeeper**
A former Dundee United player, he had some Football League experience with Blackpool and West Ham United before joining Argyle in the summer of 1958. Geoff Barnsley was first-choice goalkeeper that 1958-9 season but Wyllie was able to play a small, but significant, part in the team's winning of the Third Division championship as deputy for the injured Barnsley in some of the critical matches towards the end of the season. He moved on to Mansfield Town in the following autumn and became the regular choice for that club for over two seasons.

Action from a Second Division game between Argyle and Coventry City in 1949-50. Top picture shows Coventry's Allen heading wide from a Lockhart cross. Argyle men are (from left) Chisholm, Porteous, Dougall and Shortt. Bottom picture shows Chisholm watching a shot from Lockhart go wide of the goal. This season Argyle finished 21st and dropped into the Third Division South.

Match to Remember 1 — 29 April 1925

Plymouth Argyle 6 Southend United 0

TOP of the division, their season's programme completed, yet not confirmed as champions, that was the position in which Argyle found themselves on the evening of 29 April 1925. Devon neighbours, Exeter City, held the key to whether Argyle would be promoted. Three days later they were due to play at Swansea and the home side lay second in the table, one point behind Argyle. Swansea needed an outright win to be sure of winning promotion; Argyle's superior goal-average would ensure that they took the title in the event of a draw.

The Argyle players, therefore, took the field against Southend, highly conscious that, in the final analysis, goal-averages could be crucial. They went all out from the start to improve their total. Southend, although not having anything much at stake, had their own ideas about the way the match should progress and the first half ended with the advantage only slightly in Argyle's favour, Forbes having scored after five minutes following brilliant inter-passing between Jack Leslie and Sammy Black.

It was not until the second half that Argyle began to take control of the game and Southend's resistance began to crumble. Patsy Corcoran scored in the second minute, from a Black centre, and when Jack Cock was fouled in the Southend penalty area, Sammy Black stepped up to fire in goal number-three from the spot. By this time, Argyle were moving smoothly and with purpose. Black lifted over another centre, Corcoran shot and Hayes in the Southend goal blocked the ball but, before he could recover, Jack Leslie had forced it over the line.

Argyle's pressure at this point could be measured in the number of corner-kicks which fell to the home side and from one of these, placed by Fred Forbes, Corcoran scored his second goal of the game. The sixth fell to Cock, who had joined the club only in the previous month, just in time for the promotion run-in. Argyle had played their hearts out but, as the future was to show, all in vain. From Swansea on the Saturday evening came the result which Argyle supporters had been dreading — Swansea 2 Exeter 1 — and the Plymouth side knew that they must resign themselves to another season in the Third Division South.

Plymouth Argyle: Craig; Price, Russell, Logan, Pullen, Preston, Corcoran, Forbes, Cock, Leslie, Black.
Southend United: Hayes; Gates, Donnelly, Jewhurst, O'Rowe, Edwards, Johnson, Dobson, Hick, Slater, McDonald.

Four months after hammering Southend for six goals, Plymouth beat them again, this time by 6-2 on the opening day of the following season. This picture shows Jack Leslie scoring the first of his side's goals that day. Plymouth went on to become the League's leading scorers with 107 goals that season.

Fred Titmuss (left) took over in goal and Jack Leslie (right) switched to centre-half as Argyle reshuffled following Harry Cann's injury.

Match to Remember 2 — 6 December 1930

Plymouth Argyle 2 Tottenham Hotspur 0

BEFORE substitutes were permitted, a team losing a player during the course of a match was at an obvious disadvantage. If the missing man was the goalkeeper, the outcome was usually disastrous. This was a match in which Argyle proved that the conventional wisdom need not be a dogma.

As one of the leading sides in the Second Division, Tottenham looked like being a difficult enough proposition even before the 30th minute of the game when Harry Cann, following his natural instincts, plunged forward at the feet of an advancing Spurs forward. Cann's forehead and the forward's boot came into collision and the Argyle goalkeeper was led from the field, blood streaming from a head wound. As a result, Argyle had to make a major team reshuffle. Fred Titmuss took over in goal, Jack Pullen moved to fill his place at left-back and Jack Leslie was withdrawn from the forward line to fill the centre-half position.

The most that supporters could hope for was that Argyle would be able to hold out until Cann's return or until the end of the match if he did not come back. Yet, within six minutes of Cann's departure, Argyle were in the lead, Tommy Grozier heading in a centre from Sammy Black on the other wing and two minutes later, Black added a second after clever footwork by Bowden had opened up the Spurs defence. Argyle continued to make chances without adding to the score. Grozier completely miskicked with the goal at his mercy, Tony Bird hesitated too long when in a scoring position and Ray Bowden — who otherwise had his best game of the season — shot wide with only Cyril Spiers to beat.

Yet the traffic was not all in the direction of the Tottenham goal. Argyle's tactics were obviously to keep Spurs away from their stand-in goalkeeper for as long as possible and no one was more successful in that aim than Leslie, a revelation in the unusual position, for him, of centre-half. Leslie completely commanded the defence, always ready to move where danger threatened and to protect Titmuss. Even when Spurs were able to breach that Argyle defence, the gods smiled on the home team. Goal-bound shots from the Spurs forwards rebounded off both the crossbar and posts as Spurs' efforts to turn the match grew more and more desperate.

Five minutes from time, Cann, his head bandaged, returned to the pitch and Argyle reverted to their original formation. By that time, Tottenham knew that their best chances had gone and that, against all the odds, Argyle had pulled off one of the surprises of the season.

Plymouth Argyle: Cann; Roberts, Titmuss, Mackay, Pullen, Hardie, Grozier, Bird, Bowden, Leslie, Black.
Tottenham Hotspur: Spiers; Lyons, Hodgkinson, Skitt, Messer, Meads, Davies, O'Callaghan, Harper, Cooke, Bellamy.

Attendance: 24,549

Match to Remember 3 — 31 January 1931

Plymouth Argyle 5 West Bromwich Albion 1

IN the history of West Bromwich Albion, the 1930-31 season is one of the major milestones, the season in which they completed a remarkable double success, winning both the FA Cup and promotion to the First Division. 'A wonderful season, the most heart-warming in the club's history.' So wrote Peter Morris in a history of the club published in 1965.

With so much cause for rejoicing, it is not surprising that Albion should wish to avert their gaze from the fact that twice that season they were humbled by an Argyle side which was knocked out of the Cup at the first hurdle, suffered the heaviest defeat to date in the club's history (9-1 at Everton) and finished the season in 18th position.

Argyle had already inflicted a home defeat on West Brom and the Midlands side travelled to Plymouth that January day, hoping for revenge. Albion had demonstrated that they could be formidable opponents even away from home and had produced a number of impressive victories — 6-3 at Cardiff, 4-0 at Charlton and 6-1 at Nottingham Forest.

One factor which had not figured in West Brom's plans for the game was the weather. Torrential, driving rain had turned the pitch into a sea of mud and a gusting wind added to the discomfort of players and spectators alike. It was probably not the sort of afternoon that Jack Vidler would have chosen to make a return to the first team after having been out of action through injury since October, but by the end of the match, with a hat-trick to his credit, he was glad that he had come.

At least part of the explanation for this remarkable reversal of form can be attributed to the conditions. They just did not suit Albion's style of play. West Brom's short passes got stuck in the mud while Argyle, swinging the ball around more vigorously, obtained and retained possession.

It is no exaggeration to claim that Argyle could have won the game by a much bigger margin. Tommy Grozier in particular threw away three golden chances, and half an hour had passed before Vidler scored the goal which Argyle had been threatening to obtain for some time.

Four minutes later, Sammy Black had made it 2-0, picking up a pass from Jack Pullen and taking the ball right up to the Albion goalkeeper before placing it into the net while the visiting defenders appealed in vain for an offside verdict. Just before the interval, ground conditions again proved to be West Brom's undoing. Trentham's attempted back-pass to his goalkeeper stuck in the mud and a grateful Ray Bowden seized on the ball and drove it past Pearson.

Albion's misery continued for another 45 minutes, during which Vidler completed his hat-trick, the first of the two goals coming by courtesy of some persistent wing play by Black and the second being a solo effort by the Argyle leader. Wood's reply for West Brom, coming between those last two Vidler goals, did nothing to affect the outcome of a match in which Argyle had utilized the conditions while the Albion had been overcome by them.

Plymouth Argyle: Cann; Roberts, Titmuss, Mackay, Pullen, Hardie, Grozier, Bowden, Vidler, Leslie, Black.
West Bromwich Albion: Pearson; Shaw, Trentham, Magee, W.Richardson, Edwards, Glidden, Carter, W.G Richardson, Sandford, Wood.

Attendance: 9,319

Tommy Grozier scores Argyle's second goal. Players (from left) are Silcock (lying on ground), Hilditch, Vidler, Black, Mellor and Steward, the United goalkeeper. The goalscorer is out of picture.

Match to Remember 4 — 9 January 1932

Plymouth Argyle 4 Manchester United 1

THE modern Argyle supporter might well be surprised to learn that this FA Cup third-round game went very much as predicted. Argyle were on the crest of a wave; United were a mid-table side who had already lost 3-1 in a League match at Home Park that season. So, when the day of the match turned out to be very wet and windy, many potential supporters thought it not worth showing up.

That, at least, was the fairly reasonable explanation for the fact that the attendance of 28,000 was, by the standards of the time, rather disappointing. Argyle won as expected. Even one of the United directors admitted to his Plymouth counterparts that he envied the home side and wished Manchester United were as good.

According to some observers, the main difference between the teams was that Argyle were young and energetic, their opponents more mature and 'sedate' as one reporter put it. Certainly the younger, fitter Argyle team made light of conditions difficult enough to test the stamina of any side. At times, players sank up to their ankles in the mud of Home Park and on one occasion Tommy Grozier, sent flying into a pool of mud and water, emerged virtually unrecognizable beneath his covering of mud.

But the Argyle's footwork continually had the United defenders struggling to turn as the ball was manœuvred past them. It therefore came as no surprise when Argyle took the lead in the opening minutes. Grozier fired across the face of the United goal, Sammy Black retrieved the ball from the other side and when goalkeeper Steward could only parry the winger's cross-cum-shot, Jack Vidler quickly put the ball into the net.

Grozier added number two after 23 minutes and Argyle could well have left the field at the interval with a 3-0 lead had not Black, of all people, missed an open goal.

Although the rain continued to pour and the ground became slippier and heavier, Argyle kept up their momentum in the second half. Twelve minutes after the interval, Grozier hit his second goal, probably the best of the game, when he volleyed in a pass from Jack Leslie. And with ten minutes to go, Jack Pullen moved upfield for a corner from Grozier and fastened on to the ball for number four. The goal which Reid scored for United three minutes after that was only a token effort.

Plymouth Argyle: Harper; Roberts, Titmuss, Mackay, Pullen, Reed, Grozier, Bowden, Vidler, Leslie, Black.
Manchester United: Steward; Mellor, Silcock, Bennion, Hilditch, McLenahan, Spence, Johnston, Ridding, Reid, McLachlan.

Attendance: 28,000

Match to Remember 5 16 January 1932

Plymouth Argyle 8 Millwall 1

THE record has stood for nearly 60 years — the biggest victory in Argyle's League history. And what a confidence booster for a side which the following week was due to meet mighty Arsenal in the fourth round of the FA Cup, having already eliminated Manchester United (then in the Second Division) from the competition.

Arsenal manager Herbert Chapman was among those who witnessed the astonishing performance, particularly in the second half, from the Argyle men. But the signs had been there just before the first half closed. Argyle mounted a siege on the Millwall goal but had only a goal by Jack Vidler, breaking clear from the half-way line, to show for their efforts.

But after the interval, it was all-out attack by Argyle with the half-backs adding themselves to the forwards' thrusts to make it a nightmare occasion for Wilson in the Millwall goal. Half a dozen corners in succession were proof that Argyle could not easily be deflected from the Millwall end and from the last of these, Jack Leslie turned Tommy Grozier's kick into the Lions' net. Bond gave Millwall some hopes of a recovery when the visitors found Argyle's defence in disarray but the home side, adopting the motto that attack was the best form of defence, were soon swarming again around the Londoners' goal.

Attack after attack was the Argyle response to that slight reversal and Vidler, Ray Bowden and Sammy Black brought the score up to five. Number six came by courtesy of Millwall, full-back Pipe deflecting a shot into his own net, and before the game was over Bowden and Vidler had added more goals.

It was an exhilirating display by Argyle and yet it might have worked to their disadvantage. The performance convinced Herbert Chapman that Arsenal should take nothing for granted when the teams met in the Cup.

Plymouth Argyle: Harper; Roberts, Titmuss, Mackay, Pullen, Reed, Grozier, Bowden, Vidler, Leslie, Black.
Millwall: Wilson; Sweetman, Pipe, Newcombe, Hancock, Graham, Bloxham, Landells, Bond, Higgins, Poxton.

Attendance: 15,799

Ray Bowden (left) scored twice against Millwall while Sammy Black (right) netted once in Argyle's record victory in League football.

Argyle players claimed that Jack Lambert was offside when he scored Arsenal's second goal but the referee ignored their protests.

Match to Remember 6 — 23 January 1932

Arsenal 4 Plymouth Argyle 2

IT was one of those classic FA Cup confrontations — the current champions at home to a leading Second Division side. The previous Saturday, Argyle had demolished Millwall 8-1 in a League game and six train loads of fans went up from Plymouth to see their side's return to London.

The Underground stopped accepting bookings for Arsenal station after 2.20pm and over 65,000 packed into Highbury, most of them hoping to see Arsenal emulate their performance in the previous round when they beat Darwen 11-1.

They were rewarded with an exciting, fluctuating contest in which Argyle took the lead after only five minutes. A raid down the right by Tommy Grozier caused Arsenal all kinds of confusion and after Jack Leslie's shot smacked against the crossbar, Jack Vidler forced the ball past Moss.

Argyle continued as though they believed that they could win. Twice their appeals for penalties were ignored. Bob John surely handled the ball in the penalty area? Sammy Black was surely fouled? Then Black hit another shot against the Arsenal bar.

After 33 minutes, Arsenal were level. Jack Pullen was penalized for a foul on James, unjustly so it seemed because James appeared to have fallen with the ball between his legs and to be preventing the Argyle centre-half from touching it. Hapgood placed the free-kick in the goalmouth and Lambert back-headed the ball past Bill Harper, an Arsenal player only a month earlier.

Worse was to follow for Argyle. Pullen and George Reed left the field for short spells with head wounds, then two quick goals for Arsenal put the Gunners in a seemingly impregnable position. Jack, the former Argyle boy star, instigated the first with a pass which put Lambert away. Despite Argyle protests that he was offside, Lambert forced the ball past Harper and four minutes later Hulme scored Arsenal's third.

Argyle, though, were not finished and a minute later Leslie got to a Grozier cross and made it 3-2. Eleven minutes from time, though, Harry Roberts, harried by Lambert and Jack, put the ball into his own net. Argyle were left to reflect on what might have been.

Arsenal: Moss; Parker, Hapgood, Jones, Roberts, John, Hulme, Jack, Lambert, James, Bastin.
Plymouth Argyle: Harper; Roberts, Titmuss, Mackay, Pullen, Reed, Grozier, Bowden, Vidler, Leslie, Black.

Attendance: 65,386

Match to Remember 7 — 14 January 1934

Plymouth Argyle 1 Huddersfield Town 1

SO often the Argyle story is a tale of the chances that were missed, a side just on the edge of a great achievement, and this match was a classic illlustration. Here were Huddersfield, one of the leading teams in the country — runners-up to Arsenal in the First Division that season — reduced to a very ordinary level by an outstanding Argyle display.

This was not simply the view of Argyle followers, blind to everything but the displays of their favourites. It was also the opinion of the Town manager Clem Stephenson, relieved to find his side drawing level in the last two minutes of the match: 'We are thankful to have forced a replay. Argyle were the better team.'

So great was the local interest in the game that only one match was played that afternoon in the Plymouth & District League and there were nearly 45,000 people to see Argyle come within a hair's breadth of creating one of the sensations of the round. Far from being overawed by the reputation of the Yorkshire visitors, they played like men inspired. Sammy Black in particular gave Huddersfield's international full-back Roy Goodall — an England regular at the time — a most uncomfortable afternoon. After the match, Clem Stephenson admitted that it was the first time he had ever seen Black play but that he thought the Argyle winger was 'quite outstanding'.

It was Black who set up the chance for the Argyle goal in the 20th minute. Huddersfield had failed to clear an Argyle corner and Sammy returned the ball into the middle. Before the Town defenders could move to block the danger, Jimmy Cookson hit the ball high into the net and Argyle were ahead. Black was again at the centre of a second-half move which seemed to have confimed Argyle's superiority as he switched to the middle to pick up a Cookson pass and drive the ball past Turner, only to see the referee rule him offside. Had the goal been allowed, an Argyle victory must surely have been assured but the referee's decision gave Huddersfield a lifeline and, with the minutes ticking away, Bott centred and McLean forced the ball past Bill Harper from close range. This time, Argyle protests that the Huddersfield player was offside fell on deaf ears.

The Huddersfield equalizer was a bitter disappointment for Argyle and another blow was the absence of Sammy Black from the side which travelled to Yorkshire the following week for the replay. Having had first-hand experience of their opponents capabilities, the home side were in no mood to give anything away and Plymouth were brought down to earth by a 6-2 defeat.

Argyle once more had nothing to show for all their endeavours except praise as in this enthusiastic verdict on the first match by a Huddersfield reporter: 'Argyle's display has been an amazing revelation to us. They are good enough to beat the ten lowest teams in the First Division on any ground and they would give the others a run as well. They would give Sheffield United three goals start and a beating!'

Plymouth Argyle: Harper; Roberts, Rae, Mackay, McKenzie, Gorman, Grozier, Melaniphy, Cookson, Briggs, Black.
Hudderfield Town: Turner; Goodall, Roughton, Carr, Young, Campbell, W.Smith, McLean, J.Smith, Luke, Bott.

Attendance: 44,526

Match to Remember 8 — 10 October 1936

Plymouth Argyle 2 Aston Villa 2

RELEGATED from the First Division in 1934-6 and regaining their place in 1937-8, Aston Villa could have been said to be just passing through the Second Division when, in the intervening season, they played two pulsating matches against Argyle. The Home Park fixture drew over 43,000, a ground record (and unlikely to be broken in today's safety-conscious age), so great was the crowd-pulling power of the Villa side with six international players in their team.

It was in response to the atmosphere generated by that packed ground that the players reacted as though the FA Cup and the League championship all depended on that one fixture. If Aston Villa were showing the polish in the early stages, Argyle were no less inferior in terms of enthusiasm and commitment. But it was Villa who took the lead in the ninth minute, when Frank Broome, later to be capped by England, sped past three opponents to find the Argyle net.

Argyle's hopes of at least squaring the game appeared to have receded when injury forced Harry Roberts to the right wing and Archie Gorman into his place at right-back. But Argyle not only held their opponents, they also began to carry the fight to them and just as the first half was closing, Sammy Black produced his own brand of trickery to level the scores.

Inevitably, the second half could not match the first for speed and excitement and those who concluded that the players had probably burned themselves out in the first 45 minutes were not far from the mark. But the teams had two more goals to share before the match was over. Welsh international Dai Astley restored Villa's lead early in the second half and within three minutes Jack Connor had produced Argyle's reply, fastening on a loose ball to beat Biddlestone, who afterwards claimed that he had been blinded by the sun.

Not content with a share of the points, Argyle recharged their batteries and pressed for a win. Hunter hit a post with Biddlestone beaten and another shot from Connor looked to be the winner until Biddlestone turned it aside.

Plymouth Argyle: Cann; Roberts, Rae, Gorman, McNeil, T.Black, Hunter, Smith, Connor, Vidler, S.Black.
Aston Villa: Biddlestone; Griffiths, Cobley, Gardner, Allen, Hardy, Astley, Massie, Broome, Dix, Houghton.

Attendance: 43,596

Archie Gorman (above) switched to right-back when Roberts was injured. Jimmy Rae (opposite) had a good game against Dai Astley, although the Welshman restored Villa's lead.

Match to Remember 9 — 13 February 1937

Aston Villa 5 Plymouth Argyle 4

THOSE privileged to witness the return encounter at Villa Park that season saw another thrilling game from which Argyle emerged with much credit and praise but no tangible reward. For the first half-hour, Argyle outplayed the Villa, shooting at every opportunity, but some of their fire died after Eric Houghton had converted two penalties in reply to Jack Vidler's goal.

The home side led 2-1 at the interval and Frank Broome gave the Argyle side another reminder of his scoring potential when he added a third shortly into the second half. Argyle's chances appeared to have vanished but two goals by Jack Connor and another by Jackie Hunter put Argyle into an incredible 4-3 lead. Broome struck again to tie the scores and three minutes from the end Houghton moved into the centre, fastened on to a centre from Haycock and shot past Foley for his third goal of the afternoon. Beaten, but far from disgraced, Argyle won themselves many new friends by that spirited performance.

Aston Villa: Morton; Cobley, Cummings, Massie, Griffiths, Iverson, Maund, Haycock, Broome, Starling, Houghton.
Plymouth Argyle: Foley; Roberts, Rae, Gorman, Kirkwood, T.Black, Hunter, Smith, Connor, Mitcheson, Vidler.

Attendance: 42,000

Jackie Hunter (left) helped Argyle to a remarkable recovery. Fred Mitcheson (right) was one of the architects behind the Plymouth goals.

Match to Remember 10 — 16 March 1946

Birmingham City 0 Plymouth Argyle 1

THE Birmingham City side which took the field to confront Argyle on this March afternoon just after the end of the war could be forgiven for a certain complacency in their approach to the match. They headed the Football League (South) — a division comprising First and Second Division clubs from Derby southwards — and had advanced to the FA Cup semi-finals.

Against them, Argyle were having what can only be described as a season of disasters. At that point they had made an early exit from the Cup and had won only one of their 30 League matches. Birmingham fielded their settled side; Argyle were the usual patchwork team, comprising those members of the staff who were available and anyone else who could be spared by his club to make up the team. A guest player that afternoon was Horace Cumner, a Welsh international but surplus to Arsenal's immediate requirements.

With hardly an awesome test in view, Birmingham proceeded to the inevitable dismemberment of their visitors. In retrospect, it was easy to see that they could be faulted for having played at half-pace. At the time, they were content with smoothly moving into the attack and forcing Argyle to pack their goal. Bill Shortt performed heroics beneath the Argyle bar — 'Bonnie Shortt of Argyle,' was one sub-editor's description of him that day — and all the Birmingham forwards saw goalbound shots beaten away by the Argyle goalkeeper. On two occasions when he was beaten, George Silk's lusty clearances despatched the ball from the line.

Silk and Dixon in fact were at full stretch all afternoon attempting and mostly succeeding in containing the Birmingham wingers and Argyle were rarely seen as an attacking force, although Cumner gave the home team one anxious moment when his shot hit a post and rebounded across the goal.

Then, with four minutes to go and Argyle achieving a goalless draw seeming the most likely outcome, the unbelievable happened. In a rare Plymouth attack, a centre from Cumner found Paddy Brown, Argyle's leading scorer that season, in front of goal and he directed a header past Merrick.

As a wartime match, this result does not figure in most records of the game, but at the time it caused a sensation in the football world.

Like many sensations, however, it proved to be short-lived and it had little effect on the fortunes of either club during the remainder of the season. Birmingham, although losing the division leadership to Charlton that afternoon, went on to win the title, although they lost their Cup semi-final to Derby, the eventual winners. Argyle achieved only one more victory by the time the season ended and Paddy Brown, the hero of the hour, failed to get a single first-team game when League football resumed the following season.

Birmingham City: Merrick; Duckhouse, Jennings, Harris, Turner, Dearson, Mulraney, Dougall, C.W.Jones, Bodle, Edwards.
Plymouth Argyle: Shortt; Silk, Dixon, L.Jones, Gibson, Gorman, Stephenson, Carless, Brown, Cumner, Tinkler.

Attendance: 22,000

Many Argyle followers will recognize the familiar name of Neil Dougall in the Birmingham side. The result did no damage to his personal career. A month later, he was chosen to play for Scotland against England at Hampden Park.

Match to Remember 11 — 31 August 1946

Plymouth Argyle 3 West Ham United 1

FOR the 25,000 or so spectators who assembled at Home Park on the last day of August 1946, there was pleasure at the resumption of League football after a wartime suspension, but little optimism that Argyle would achieve much.

The preparatory season of 1945-6 had been little short of disastrous with only three of the 42 games being won. Furthermore, Jack Tresadern's original first-choice side had been tested the previous week against Third Division club, Bristol City, and had crashed to an ignominious 6-3 defeat.

Apparently more out of desperation than inspiration, Plymouth switched five of that team with five from the Reserves for their opening fixture of the new season against West Ham United. The Hammers, who had won the corresponding fixture in the short-lived 1939-40 season, included in their line-up Archie Macaulay, regarded by Tresadern as a model inside-forward.

When winger Jackie Wood opened the scoring for the visitors in the 18th minute, it seemed that the old familiar pattern of defeat was to start a new cycle. But the Argyle defenders began to get a grip on their opponents and the men in front began to respond to the confidence displayed behind them.

It was the new wingers, Bill Strauss and Sid Rawlings, who transformed the game as Argyle first drew level and then went ahead. First Rawlings and Dave Thomas interchanged passes, then Thomas switched the ball across the goal and Strauss moved in to shoot past the advancing Medhurst. Minutes later, it was Rawlings who was on the spot to net after the Hammers' defence had failed to clear a Miller free-kick.

A 2-1 interval lead was cheer enough for the Argyle followers but when Strauss popped up to score again in the second half to clinch a 3-1 victory, they began to experience the unusual sensation of supporting a winning side. A new period in Argyle's history had begun in the right style.

As for the potential threat of Macaulay, it never materialized and Alec Dyer, in particular, played an outstanding part in nullifying the West Ham attack. The old pattern of defeat had been broken.

Plymouth Argyle: Shortt; Royston, Dyer, Stuttard, Dixon, Miller, Rawlings, R.Thomas, D.Thomas, Murphy, Strauss.
West Ham United: Medhurst; Bicknell, Cater, Corbett, Walker, Attwell, Wood, Hall, Small, Macaulay, Woodgate.

Attendance: 25,659

Despite their winning start to the 1946-7 season, Plymouth Argyle did not enjoy the best of times overall. They suffered five defeats on the trot around Christmas, five in a row in the run-up to Easter and then ended the season with six successive reverses. The final game was lost 5-1 at Nottingham Forest and that left Argyle in 19th place, four points ahead of next-to-bottom Swansea Town and ten in front of wooden-spoonists Newport County.

Match to Remember 12 — 20 December 1947

Plymouth Argyle 3 Newcastle United 0

ONCE League football had resumed after the war, Newcastle United made no secret of their determination to get back into the First Division. If players on the staff were not good enough to achieve that aim, then they were ready to spend heavily to buy the best. So it was that some of the leading footballers in the British Isles, Frank Brennan, Roy Bentley and Len Shackleton, were added to the squad being assembled at St James' Park.

On the very first day of the 1947-8 season they gave notice that promotion was their aim by crushing the visiting Argyle side 6-1.

As the year drew to its close, they were lying third in the table while Argyle, although strengthened since the August fixture by the arrival of George Dews, Frank Squires and Bobby Stuart, were still firmly fixed to the bottom of the table.

Even Argyle supporters could hope for little more than good entertainment out of the match. After all, 42-year-old John Oakes, at the centre of the Argyle defence, could hardly be expected to offer any serious opposition to Newcastle centre-forward Jackie Milburn, whose speed off the mark was once described by Shackleton as being 'like a whippet out of the trap'.

But the match never developed in the manner predicted. In footballing terms, Oakes might have been old. Jack Davies, with his bald head, might have looked old, but those two Argyle half-backs played right on top of the two Newcastle dangermen, Shackleton and Milburn, and the expected threat was stifled. United might have fielded a half-back line composed of burly six-footers but the relatively small Argyle forwards kept finding a way past them.

Newcastle's threat to the Argyle peace of mind seemed to evaporate after 15 minutes. It was then that Squires seized on an opening set up by Dews and Strauss to fire a low shot into the Newcastle net to give Argyle the lead.

Newcastle began to come back into the game in the second half, but another thrust by Argyle completely demoralized them. Fifteen minutes into the half, a Billy Strauss centre from the left wing found Dave Thomas standing with his back to the United goal.

The Argyle centre-forward had never been renowned for skilled footwork but on this occasion, without hesitation, he hooked the ball back over his shoulder and into the net past a dumfounded Jack Fairbrother. Faced with a goal like that, Newcastle could well have decided that it was not to be their day, and when, ten minutes from time, Dews took the ball up to and past the giant Brennan to score Argyle's third goal it was evident that the afternoon's entertainment had been provided, not by the expensive visitors, but by the humbler Argyle team.

Newcastle won their promotion that season. By its conclusion Argyle had crept up the table to a safe 17th position, but if promotion and relegation issues could be decided on one single match, it would have been Argyle that most independent observers that December afternoon would have chosen to grace the First Division.

Plymouth Argyle: Shortt; Stuart, Jones, Boyd, Oakes, Davies, Tadman, Squires, Thomas, Dews, Strauss.
Newcastle United: Fairbrother; Fraser, Craig, Harvey, Brennan, Dodgin, Sibley, Shackleton, Milburn, Stobbart, Pearson.

Attendance: 27,069

Match to Remember 13 — 29 October 1949

Plymouth Argyle 1 Preston North End 0

BEFORE the domestic television became commonplace, the heroes of the game had to be seen in the flesh or not at all. And if one lived in the far south-west of Britain, the opportunity might occur only rarely, perhaps never. There was no doubt, therefore, that it was the presence of Tom Finney in the visiting Preston side which drew a crowd of over 32,000 to Home Park on this afternoon.

That Preston were also fielding another England winger on the left flank in Bobby Langton was a bonus for the crowd, but was not the centre of their attention. Finney it was whom the crowd wanted to see. Finney, the man whom the England selectors had preferred to the undoubted genius of Stanley Matthews. And it was Finney whose talent Argyle would have to suppress if they were to stand any chance of collecting vital points from the game.

By a coincidence, the Argyle coach, Hugh Ross, had held a similar position with Preston and knew Finney's capabilities intimately. His view was that if Finney had possession he could cause havoc in the Plymouth defence. Pat Jones, his direct opponent, was strong, fearless and reliable but in a personal duel with the England player would he succeed where proven international backs had failed?

The solution advanced by Ross therefore was that Finney should be denied possession of the ball, and if he did get it, Jones was to hold off from tackling while the rest of the defence organized in the goalmouth. Telling Pat Jones not to tackle was like telling a greyhound not to chase a rabbit, but the Argyle back reined in his natural instincts for the sake of the plan.

George Taylor was another key figure in the project and he was required to clamp down on Bobby Beattie, Finney's partner, so that the famous winger did not receive his normal service.

In practice, the plan succeeded, or at least well enough. Finney was left isolated for long periods and when he did receive the ball, Pat Jones, following his instructions to the letter, contented himself with shadowing and crowding his opponent and keeping himself between the ball and the goal. In the goalmouth, the Argyle defenders set up a barrier to deny the Preston attack opportunities.

The Argyle forwards, however, were having as much difficulty in penetrating Preston's defence, and just when a stalemate seemed to be the most likely outcome, Maurice Tadman for once eluded the Preston pivot, Paddy Waters, and shot Plymouth into the lead. His goal, five minutes from the end, provoked a furious Preston counter-attack which forced Bill Shortt to hold on to a Finney shot and Pat Jones to head off the line with Shortt beaten.

Whether or not Argyle had a plan to counter Bobby Langton as well has not been disclosed. The left winger was badly shaken by a challenge from George Silk early in the match and was subdued afterwards.

There is an interesting sequel to this match. In the return game at Preston, Pat Jones, playing in his usual style, gave a virtually faultless performance, his positioning, tackling and kicking all being of the highest quality. Was, then, that Argyle tactical plan rather superfluous? Could Finney have been contained by less complex methods? A glance at the team sheet for that second fixture provides a clue to the answer. Preston, on that occasion, were without Tom Finney, and his number-seven shirt was filled by an understudy.

Plymouth Argyle: Shortt; Silk, Jones, Porteous, Dixon, Taylor, Strauss, Squires, Tadman, Dews, Williams.
Preston North End: Gooch; Kane, Cunningham, Horton, Waters, Robertson, Finney, Beattie, Brown, Morrison, Langton.

Attendance: 32,802

FULL SOCCER COVERAGE

Best for Football News and Forecasts

SPORTING RECORD

The Family All-Sports Weekly, 3d

29th OCT., 1949
Kick-off 3-15 p.m.

FOOTBALL LEAGUE DIVISION II

Plymouth Argyle

versus

Preston North End

OFFICIAL PROGRAMME 3d

PALE A ALE

The Best Bitter in the West of England

Brewed only by

THE PLYMOUTH BREWERIES LTD.

Printed by Clarke, Doble & Brendon, Ltd., Oakfield Press, Plymouth
Published by Plymouth Argyle Football Co., Ltd.

Match to Remember 14 7 January 1950

Plymouth Argyle 1 Wolverhampton Wanderers 1

THE history of the FA Cup is full of stories of teams who, faced with superior opposition, have raised their sights, drawn on latent reserves of energy and strength, and matched or even overcome their opponents. Less common are instances in which the underdog has matched the adversary in footballing skill since, almost by definition, no such equality exists.

The Wolves side of the late 1940s and early 1950s was a vastly different proposition from its modern successors who have fought their way out of the Fourth Division. At Home Park in 1950, the current FA Cup holders paraded the trophy around the ground before the start of this Cup game, and although the manner in which it was carried — on an ambulance stretcher — detracted somewhat from the dignity of the object itself, the significance of the ceremony was not lost on the crowd. They were witnessing one of the great teams of the land about to go into action.

But it was Argyle who, freed for 90 minutes from relegation worries, began to demonstrate the skills of a leading side. Neil Dougall and John Porteous time and again brought the ball through in support of their forwards, and on the left wing tiny Stan Williams made the beefy McLean look clumsy as he repeatedly sped past him. It therefore seemed only natural when in the first half, Argyle took the lead when Frank Squires unleashed a shot at the Wolves goal. England goalkeeper Bert Williams parried it but, before he could recover, Williams had driven the ball into the net.

Despite frantic efforts by the Wolves' forwards, and despite the urging of England skipper Billy Wright, that lead was preserved until well into the second half, with the Argyle defenders proving that the international pedigrees of their opponents held no fears for them. Then, in the final quarter of the game, Wolves flung everything into a last attempt to salvage the game and following, a succession of corners, their Irish international Sammy Smyth forced the ball past Bill Shortt.

The cold light of reason insists that this was not an Argyle victory. Indeed, if the replay at Wolverhampton the following week is taken into account, Argyle lost the tie 4-1 on aggregate. Yet the 40,000 present that afternoon somehow felt that the home team had made a point, that they had proved they could hold their heads high when faced with the best in the country.

Plymouth Argyle: Shortt; Ratcliffe, Jones, Dougall, Chisholm, Porteous, Strauss, Squires, Tadman, Dews, S.Williams.
Wolverhampton Wanderers: B.Williams; McLean, Pritchard, Crook, Chatham, Wright, Hancocks, Swinbourne, Pye, Smyth, Mullen.

Attendance: 40,000

Argyle players take the air in preparation for their FA Cup meeting with Wolves. From left: Porteous, McShane, Squires, Astall, Govan, Willis (partly hidden), Shortt, Tadman, Ratcliffe, Taylor, Jones, Dews (partly hidden), Strauss and Ross (trainer).

JANUARY 7th, 1950 — Kick-off 2.15 p.m.

F.A. Challenge Cup, 3rd round

PLYMOUTH ARGYLE

versus

WOLVERHAMPTON WANDERERS

Official Souvenir Programme 6d.

Published by Plymouth Argyle Football Co., Ltd.
Printed by Clarke, Doble & Brendon, Ltd., Oakfield Press, Plymouth

Maurice Tadman completed his hat-trick as Walsall were hammered.

Match to Remember 15 — 22 December 1951

Walsall 2 Plymouth Argyle 5

IF it is one of the marks of true champions that they are able to win away from home by convincing margins, then Argyle's claim to the championship of the Third Division South in 1951-2 was truly laid half-way through their programme.

It was not simply that Argyle won the game, nor even the size of the victory which impressed observers; it was the manner in which the game was won. Defenders, especially in the Third Division, might feel that they are entitled to the occasional mistake without being punished too severely. Argyle were in no mood that pre-Christmas afternoon to be charitable and Jack Lewis in the home goal had to work overtime to try to atone for the lapses of colleagues in front of him.

But Lewis alone could not resist the inevitable as Argyle forced the home defence into mistakes and when Walters misdirected a clearance after a quarter of an hour, Alex Govan ran on to open the Argyle score. Seven minutes later Russon, the home centre-half, ran the ball into his own net in trying to clear a Maurice Tadman centre; and in the 35th minute another Walters blunder again let Govan through. This time the winger passed to Gordon Astall, who transferred the ball to Tadman and Argyle were three up and looking to be cruising to an easy victory, an impression which grew stronger when Tadman added another goal just before the interval to send Argyle into the dressing-room with a 4-0 lead.

Walsall's Bridgett briefly raised his side's hopes with a goal at the start of the second half, but Argyle were soon back in command and in the 62nd minute Tadman completed his hat-trick. With the Walsall defence having been completely opened up by an Argyle attack, Lewis was forced to leave his goal to confront Astall and the winger simply slipped the ball across for Tadman to turn it into an empty net.

Bridgett's second goal, five minutes from time, helped to restore some of Walsall's pride but Argyle's superiority throughout the match could not be disputed.

Walsall: Lewis; Holding, Green, Aston, Russon, Walters, Bowen, Evans, Bridgett, O'Neill, Giles.
Plymouth Argyle: Shortt; Ratcliffe, Jones, Dougall, Chisholm, Porteous, Astall, Dews, Tadman, Rattray, Govan.

Attendance: 7,991

Match to Remember 16 — 11 February 1956

Plymouth Argyle 4 Liverpool 0

THIS Liverpool team of 1956 bore little resemblance to the side which has dominated English football for the last decade, although it contained one link with the present set-up in Ronnie Moran, now on the Liverpool training staff. Nevertheless, the Merseysiders were one of the leading Second Division teams. Moreover, they had reached the FA Cup fifth round and had Scottish international Billy Liddell looking for his 150th League goal.

Argyle, in contrast, were worried by the prospect of relegation and their team selection suggested desperation. The spearhead of the attack was entrusted to the two relatively inexperienced local players, Eric Davis and Neil Langman; and Arthur Morgan, originally signed from Swansea as Pat Jones's successor, was asked to take on the role of forward schemer.

Why then did this apparently ill-matched contest result in Liverpool's heaviest defeat of the season? Perhaps it was the conditions. A rock-hard pitch, a biting wind and intense cold forced both goalkeepers to wear tracksuit trousers, while Liverpool's centre-half Hughes wore gloves. And the Liverpool players may have had half a mind on the forthcoming Cup tie against Manchester City.

A third explanation, though, is equally plausible. Liverpool could not contain the Argyle attack in which Morgan displayed unsuspected craft and Neil Langman could not be shaken off the ball. No one could ever describe Langman as an elegant player, but on this surface, his control was exceptional.

Morgan opened the scoring three minutes before the interval, scooping the ball over Underwood's head, but the second half belonged to Langman who recorded a hat-trick and had another shot kicked off the line. His second goal might have been freakish — his downward header bouncing up to shoot over Underwood's head — but Argyle could claim that they deserved some luck that season.

It was a good day all round for the Langman family, for while Neil was getting the goals at one end, centre-half Peter was keeping a watch on Billy Liddell which ensured that the Scottish international would have to wait before reaching that scoring landmark.

Plymouth Argyle: Major; Robertson, Jones, Dougall, P.Langman, Wetton, Twissell, N.Langman, Davis, Morgan, Rowley.
Liverpool: Underwood; Molyneux, Moran, Saunders, Hughes, Twentyman, Payne, Arnell, Liddell, Evans, A'Court.

Attendance: 10,250

Argyle pictured in 1955-6. Back row (left to right): Ratcliffe, Robertson, P.Langman, Shortt, Wetton, Jones, G.Taylor (trainer). Front row: Davies, Dougall, Davis, Willis, Stenner.

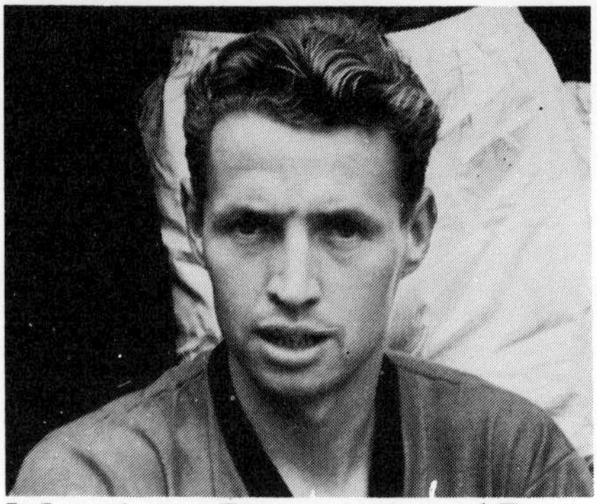

Wilf Carter got amongst the goals from the penalty-spot.

Match to Remember 17 — 7 March 1959

Plymouth Argyle 8 Mansfield Town 3

BY the coming of spring in 1959, Argyle's drive for promotion to the Second Division appeared to be faltering. Vital home points had been dropped and in the last four home matches before this Argyle-Mansfield fixture, two had been lost and two drawn. Mansfield, in contrast, had lost only one of their last ten games.

It was, therefore, both a delight and relief to home supporters when Argyle, apparently resolving to wipe out the memories of past failures, went into a 3-0 lead over their visitors within the first 20 minutes of the game. There was possibly an element of luck about the first, visiting centre-half Terry Swinscoe turning the ball past his own goalkeeper in the second minute, but wingers Alex Govan and Harry Penk followed up with two quick goals which were clear-cut enough. Mansfield, though, had concluded that it was too early in the game to bid farewell to two points and by half-time they had narrowed the Argyle lead to 3-2, Ripley and Downie having scored from corner-kicks expertly placed by winger Lindy Delaphena.

The Argyle defence, with Bob Wyllie and Gordon Fincham both making Argyle debuts in key positions, was looking distinctly shaky at this stage and when, just after half-time, Downie scored a second goal to bring the scores level, a section of the crowd, sensing the prospect of more points being lost, began to barrack the home team.

It was not until the final quarter of the match that Argyle's fortunes suddenly and dramatically changed for the better. Jimmy Gauld, who could never be neglected by defences, forced his way along the Mansfield goal-line from the left wing. His obvious move was to slip the ball back to a colleague in a better position. Instead, he chose to shoot and, in defiance of all the known laws of geometry, the ball found a spot just inside a post.

This seemed to convince Argyle that the match could be won after all and they set up another three goals in a 20 minute spell, two goals by Johnny Williams sandwiching a Carter penalty. At 7-3 to Plymouth, with time running out and the defence beginning to show much more confidence, the crowd was at last content but Swinscoe set the seal on Argyle's victory by once more crashing the ball past his own 'keeper.

Compared with the Mansfield game, the remainder of Argyle's fixtures that season were relatively sedate affairs in which they never exceeded two goals. More to the point, they took the Third Division championship. To what extent the Mansfield result contributed towards that final triumphant phase can only be guessed at. It can, however, be fairly confidently asserted that a defeat by or a draw with Mansfield that afternoon would have severely damaged the team's morale and self-belief in that crucial final stage of the season.

Plymouth Argyle: Wyllie; Fulton, Bellett, Williams, Fincham, Casey, Penk, Gauld, Carter, Baker, Govan.
Mansfield Town: Statham; Toon, Savin, Williams, Swinscoe, Ripley, Delaphena, Uphill, Thomas, Downie, Nugent.

Attendance: 17,597

Match to Remember 18 — 30 April 1960

Plymouth Argyle 3 Aston Villa 0

ACCORDING to the plan, this last match of the season was to revolve around Villa celebrations on winning the Second Division championship. A group of Villa shareholders had even chartered an aircraft to take them to Plymouth in support of their team. Argyle were to form a guard of honour as the Villa players came on to the pitch — and presumably were respectfully to admire the skills displayed by the champions during the game — and before the match a League official was to present Villa with the championship trophy. Argyle fulfilled their role in welcoming the visitors but the plan for the presentation had to be shelved because no League official was available to perform the ceremony.

The more superstitious of Villa supporters might have regarded this as an omen because by the end of the game Villa were looking anything but champions. They were given their first shock of the afternoon in the 21st minute. Argyle were awarded a free-kick just outside the penalty area and the Villa team lined to form their customary barrier to the goal. But they were then completely bemused as first Johnny Williams and then Alex Jackson feinted to take the kick but left it to Johnny Newman to curl the ball over the defenders for George Kirby to stride in and drive it past Sims. That sort of trick is common in modern football, but it was then sufficiently novel to leave the Villa defence flatfooted.

Another free-kick led to the second Argyle goal. No special tricks were employed this time. Peter Anderson simply floated the ball across and up soared Bill Wright to head past the Villa goalkeeper.

If these two goals were not sufficiently disrespectful to the champions, Argyle were to strike again before the first half had been completed. Williams, moving forward, found the ball at his feet five minutes before half-time. The gap between defenders and goal was a narrow one but Williams found it and Argyle were three up.

Teams have been known to recover from being three down, but the Villa side that afternoon was not one of them. Ron Wylie did once get the ball into the Argyle net but Gerry Hitchens was in an offside position and the 'score' was not allowed. Argyle could hold that they were equally unlucky when a powerful second-half drive from Kirby thudded against the Villa crossbar.

After the match, Aston Villa officials were unanimous in declaring that their side had given its worst performance of the season. They might reasonably have added that Villa were only allowed to play as well as Argyle let them. On that afternoon, it was the champions who were made to look the inferior side.

Plymouth Argyle: Barnsley; Wyatt, Fulton, Williams, Robertson, Newman, Anderson, Jackson, Kirby, McAnearney, Wright.
Aston Villa: Sims; Lynn, Neal, Crowe, Dugdale, Saward, Adam, Thomson, Hitchens, Wylie, McParland.

Attendance: 29,895

Johnny Newman laid on a goal for George Kirby with a clever free-kick.

Match to Remember 19 — 27 December 1960

Plymouth Argyle 6 Charlton Athletic 4

ONLY rarely can one individual be said to have dominated a match but there is little question that this was Wilf Carter's game, the Argyle marksman setting up an individual scoring record for the club in League matches by netting five times against Charlton Athletic.

It was in fact a Christmas to remember for Argyle followers because, only the previous day, Charlton had trounced Argyle at The Valley by exactly the same score. Carter seemed to have taken it upon himself to avenge that defeat. On paper, Argyle looked, if anything, slightly weaker than on the previous day, injury having deprived them of Carter's striking partner, George Kirby. So Carter was asked to wear the number-nine shirt and a young Cornishman, Johnny Brown, making his League debut, was brought in to fill the gap.

As the match progressed, it became obvious that the changes were having no harmful effect on Argyle's performance. Brown worked hard and contributed some useful passes in Argyle's attack but the main attention was drawn to Carter, who was in explosive form in the middle. Charlton tried everything to contain him, close-marking the Plymouth leader, attempting to ensnare him in the offside trap, all to no avail. His speed off the mark and his nose for an opening left his markers repeatedly stranded.

Although Carter showed that afternoon how moves should be finished, he did not function alone. It was Brown whose pass split the Charlton defence for the first goal, Johnny Williams who set up numbers two and three and Terry Stacey, bursting down the wing, who provided the opening for number four. Then, when a quarter of an hour from time, Argyle were awarded a penalty, what more natural than for Wilf Carter to step up and take it and win a place in Argyle's history? For the record, Argyle's other goal was scored by Alec Jackson, with Edwards and Leary scoring twice for Charlton, but somehow on that day the other scorers seemed irrelevant. It was Carter's match.

Plymouth Argyle: MacLaren; Wyatt, Stacey, Williams, Fincham, Newman, Anderson, Brown, Carter, Jackson, Maloy.
Charlton Athletic: Duff; Hewie, Townsend, Tocknell, Hinton, Bailey, Lawrie, Edwards, Leary, White, Summers.

Attendance: 23,335

Charlton supporters were less surprised than Plymothians by those two ten-goal encounters that Christmas. Charlton developed something of a habit of getting involved in high-scoring games. In October they beat Portsmouth 7-4 and Brighton 5-3, then drew 6-6 with Middlesbrough and in January they beat Swansea 6-1 and lost 5-3 to Stoke. It could almost be said that Carter's scoring feat was just waiting to happen against Charlton.

Match to Remember 20 — 6 January 1962

Plymouth Argyle 3 West Ham United 0

ARGYLE'S present manager Ken Brown is presumably aware that, with some occasional exceptions, his team's record in the FA Cup is generally mediocre. As a member of the West Ham side which met Argyle in this third-round match in January 1962, he might have found that record difficult to believe. West Ham were one of the leading First Division sides. Argyle were then having one of their more successful spells in the Second Division and Ken Brown filled the centre-half spot for the visitors, flanked by two players who were to become internationally famous for their parts in England's 1966 World Cup victory, Geoff Hurst and Bobby Moore.

The match revealed a contrast in styles with West Ham showing fluent, interchanging football revolving around their Welsh international forward, Phil Woosnam; but the West Ham approach work came to a stop when it ran up against an Argyle defence which displayed covering, marking and anticipation of the highest order.

And as the West Ham attacks foundered, so the Argyle counter-attacks moved into top gear with little time being lost in switching the ball to the other end. Those who had seen Argyle score three times in six minutes in the previous week's game were hopeful of a repeat performance when Wilf Carter headed home a corner-kick from Ken Maloy. Within the next five minutes a 'goal' by Johnny Williams was disallowed and West Ham's John Bond had to be at full stretch to prevent a shot from Carter crossing the goal-line. At half-time, Argyle led by Carter's 14th-minute goal.

Nine minutes after the restart, however, Argyle added another. Jim McAnearney set up the chance and Johnny Williams hit one of his 25-yard scorching shots past goalkeeper Lawrie Leslie. West Ham tried desperately to get back in the game as the minutes ticked away. Bond appeared to have scored when Dave MacLaren somersaulted to grab a ball which had already passed him; Geoff Hurst thundered a shot against the Argyle crossbar and Ron Tindall was inches wide with a header.

But the visitors' chances of victory receded completely five minutes from the end when Maloy switched into the middle and beat Leslie from some 30 yards. It was a wholly convincing performance by Argyle and a thoroughly deserved victory, but any thoughts which they might have entertained of travelling to Wembley that year were rudely shattered by their visitors in the next round of the Cup. Tottenham Hotspur, who had achieved the League and Cup double the previous season, restored the honour of London football with an emphatic 5-1 win.

Early in the following season, Argyle were drawn against West Ham at Upton Park in the Football League Cup. Seven of the Hammers' side defeated in the Home Park game played in that match and must have derived some satisfaction and feelings of revenge in defeating their visitors 6-0.

Plymouth Argyle: MacLaren; Robertson, Fulton, J.Williams, Fincham, Newman, Anderson, Carter, Kirby, McAnearney, Maloy.
West Ham United: Leslie; Kirkup, Bond, Hurst, Brown, Moore, Crawford, Woosnam, Tindall, Dick, Musgrove.

Attendance: 26,915

Johnny Williams (left) worked on the right flank as Argyle countered Swindon's threat. Barrie Jones (right) scored twice and made a goal for Trebilcock.

Match to Remember 21 — 20 March 1965

Swindon Town 2 Plymouth Argyle 3

MALCOLM Allison encountered a certain amount of criticism for his team selections and tactical plans during his first, brief, spell in charge of Plymouth Argyle. But this was one occasion when the Allison judgement was triumphantly vindicated. Swindon had a reputation as a young, talented side, and players like Mike Summerbee, Don Rogers and Ernie Hunt were already receiving covetous glances from the major clubs.

Allison's way of dealing with the problem was to strengthen the left flank of the Argyle defence and to concentrate the attacks down the right wing. Purists might object that such a strategy would unbalance the side. So it did — but it worked. Norman Piper wore a number-11 shirt but his task was really to act as an auxiliary left-back in order to counter the menace of Summerbee. Cliff Jackson and Keith Sanderson patrolled the centre of the field and Johnny Williams joined them on the right flank to collect and distribute the ball.

And if this meant that Argyle rarely functioned as an attacking force down the left, it did not matter because Barrie Jones made full use of the wealth of possession which came his way.

With the centre of the field having the consistency of a cake mixture, Jones had firmer ground over which to operate on the wing and he revelled in the workload thrust upon him. John Trollope, his direct opponent, was no soft option, as his record 767 League appearances for Swindon testify. But on that rainy afternoon he was made to look a novice by Jones. If he lunged into the tackle, Jones would whisk the ball out of his reach; if he stood off, Jones would deliver his centres just the same.

Jones also revealed himself as a goal-taker as well as a maker and after half an hour was on hand to shoot a Jackson centre past Hicks. Roger Smart brought Swindon level five minutes later but Jones was in the picture on either side of the interval. With only one minute left in the first half, he crossed the ball and Mike Trebilcock found himself alone and able to choose the spot for his header into the Swindon goal. Two minutes after the restart, it was Jones again, this time himself tucking a low shot inside the Swindon post.

Argyle continued to dominate the game, playing calmly and intelligently against a Swindon side which began to look increasingly desperate and whose second goal from Summerbee served only to give a false impression of the margin of the Argyle victory.

Swindon Town: Hicks; Dawson, Trollope, Smart, McPherson, Atherton, Summerbee, Hunt, Brown, Atkins, Rogers.
Plymouth Argyle: Dwyer; Book, Reeves, Neale, Baird, Williams, Jones, Sanderson, Trebilcock, Jackson, Piper.

Attendance: 12,175

Match to Remember 22 — 11 September 1965

Plymouth Argyle 6 Birmingham City 1

TACTICS mainly won this game for Argyle — Birmingham's tactics. Before the match, Blues' manager Joe Mallett decided that his side would adopt a defensive policy and so it proved. Centre-forward Thomson spent the greater part of the game in the intermediate line, thereby releasing Welsh international Terry Hennessey to act as a defensive sweeper.

It was, as some observed, a waste of Hennessey's creative talents to use him in this manner but it would have been justified if it had worked. The scoreline shows that it failed. Why such caution should have been considered necessary remains a mystery. At that stage in the season, with six matches played, Birmingham were still unbeaten while Argyle had only one victory to show for their labours.

By the half-way mark, Mallett was feeling reasonably satisfied. Although only three of his forwards had been left upfield to threaten the Argyle goal, his defenders, skilfully exploiting the offside regulations, had taken away any sting the Argyle forwards might have possessed. Mike Trebilcock, however, had put Argyle one up, his shot from 30 yards deceiving Jim Herriot in flight.

But the game was transformed in the second half. Birmingham's defensive plan fell apart and the advantage swung Argyle's way. Johnny Williams fired in goal number-two and in the last third of the game, Trebilcock completed a hat-trick and Frank Lord and Nicky Jennings also scored to add to Herriot's unhappy afternoon.

At the other end, Noel Dwyer had one of his more inspired games, dealing with almost every test the Birmingham forwards could try on him. Two drives from Vowden, another from Thomson and a powerful Hennessey header were all turned aside. Vowden eventually got one past him but too late to affect the result.

Plymouth Argyle: Dwyer; Book, Newman, Williams, Baird, Hore, Jones, Piper, Lord, Trebilcock, Jennings.
Birmingham City: Herriot; Fraser, Green, Wylie, Foster, Hennessey, Jackson, Vowden, Thomson, Beard, Thwaites.

Attendance: 10,606

Mike Trebilcock (left) scored a hat-trick against the Blues and Frank Lord (right) weighed in to compound Jim Herriot's misery.

Geoff Crudgington (right) created a goal for Tommy Tynan (left) with a huge clearance. Tynan later scored a second with a brave header.

Match to Remember 23 — 29 April 1986

Plymouth Argyle 4 Bristol City 0

SIXTY-ONE years to the day after their 1925 failure, Argyle faced another promotion-deciding match. The ground was packed and Argyle's target was clear. Victory over Bristol City that April evening would ensure a return to the Second Division after an absence of nine years.

Anything less and the future was uncertain, depending as much on the performance of Argyle's promotion rivals as themselves. It was just the sort of situation when many teams have been overcome by the occasion and too paralysed by nerves to do themselves justice. Fortunately, it did not happen that evening.

Perhaps the promise by the Bristol City manager that his team would play an attacking game induced Argyle to cast off any inhibitions which they might have felt. Whatever the reason, the victory was emphatic, just the sort of result that promotion winners look for.

It was, however, after over half an hour's play that Argyle finally got the goal which they had been threatening when a huge clearance by Geoff Crudgington caught the City defence unawares. Gary Nelson forced the bouncing ball into the penalty area and Tommy Tynan deftly steered it past Waugh to give Argyle a 1-0 interval lead.

The same two players were again involved when Argyle increased their lead in the eighth minute of the second half. This time it was Tynan, operating in the middle of the field, who made the pass and Nelson who ran on to lob the ball over Waugh. The third, Bristol might complain, was a fluke. Waugh and Llewellyn between them had kept out a Kevin Summerfield header at the expense of a corner. Russell Coughlin's corner-kick from the left was a long in-swinger and it passed over defender and attacker alike to nestle in the corner of the goal.

Finally, came the best goal of the evening. A centre from Nelson was blocked but Kevin Hodges regained possession, spun around at the edge of the penalty area and crossed for Tommy Tynan to hurl himself forward and complete Argyle's victory.

A crowd of 20,000, the vast majority of them Argyle fans, were there that evening to witness an historic occasion. How odd, therefore, that the average attendance the following season, when Argyle were in the Second Division, was only half that number.

Plymouth Argyle: Crudgington; Nisbet, L.Cooper, Goodyear, McElhinney, Matthews, Hodges, Coughlin, Tynan, Summerfield, Nelson.
Bristol City: Waugh; Llewellyn, Williams, Curle, Moyse, Riley, Pritchard, Newman, Moore, Walsh, Neville.

Attendance: 20,000

Match to Remember 24 — 5 November 1988

Plymouth Argyle 4   Blackburn Rovers 3

ABOVE all this has to be remembered as Tommy Tynan's match as the striker produced a solo performance which gave Argyle the edge in a seven-goal thriller. There were portents for the future after only 11 seconds when Sean McCarthy headed into the Blackburn net. The effort was ruled offside and the Argyle man's protests earned him a booking, an action which was to have a crucial bearing on the course of the game.

Blackburn, fielding a reserve centre-half, looked invitingly open at the back and Argyle wingers Calvin Plummer and newcomer Mark Stuart began to create the holes in the Blackburn defence which Tynan was eager to exploit. Within six minutes, after a nonchalant bout of passing with Leigh Cooper, he drove a left-footed shot into the corner of the net and before the half was over, he had completed his hat-trick. In the 39th minute it was his right foot which seized on a Blackburn defensive slip to despatch the ball into the net and a minute later, he was again on the spot when the Rovers failed to get an Argyle corner away from the danger area. Three goals ahead at half-time, Argyle looked to be heading for a record win, particularly as Blackburn had caused Steve Cherry no trouble at all.

But the balance of the game began to shift after the interval. The second half was no more than five minutes old when a slick four-man move by Blackburn left Cherry flat-footed as Reid headed in Garner's left-wing centre. Then McCarthy, already cautioned, took revenge on a Blackburn defender who had fouled him and was promptly dismissed from the game. The development appeared to put new heart into the visitors. They swarmed around the Argyle goal and leading scorer Garner netted with a low drive.

With the Argyle lead reduced to one goal and the team down to ten men, it seemed as though the home side might have problems in salvaging a point but Tynan was again to intervene decisively. A run by full-back Kenny Brown ended in a long centre. Stuart headed the ball back and Tynan slipped past his marker, Hill, and prodded the ball under goalkeeper Gennoe. This appeared to deflate Blackburn and although they scored again in the last minute, when late substitute Kennedy forced the ball over the line from a prone position, Argyle played as though assured of their victory. Thanks to Tynan's marksmanship they ended the game confidently, playing out time, even by working the ball in the Rovers' penalty area.

Plymouth Argyle: Cherry; Brown, Cooper, Burrows, Marker, Uzzell, Plummer, Summerfield, Tynan, McCarthy, Stuart.
Blackburn Rovers: Gennoe; Atkins, Millar(Ainscow), Dawson, Hill, Mail, Gayle, Reid, Curry(Kennedy), Garner, Sellars.

Attendance: 7,823

Heads high in front of the Blackburn goal.

Match to Remember 25 — 28 January 1989

Plymouth Argyle 1 Everton 1

THIS FA Cup fourth-round tie was a game which Argyle could and should have won. They had the appetite, the territorial domination and, at one stage, the lead. But for the inexplicable 'hand in the air' by Adrian Burrows when there seemed little danger, Everton would not have had their penalty chance and the opportunity for a second contest with home advantage. On the day, their costly team, with nine full international players on display, just could not raise their game.

In every department, Argyle had heroes, none more so than Kevin Hodges whose penetrating runs caused Pat Van den Hauwe many problems. On the other flank, Mark Stuart showed First Division poise and there were enthusiastic displays by Kenny Brown in support of his attack and by John Uzzell, who rarely gave Steven an inch. At the heart of the defence, Mark Smith and Brown neutralized the dual threat of the partially-fit Sharp and the dangerous Cottee. Nick Marker and Sean McCarthy were lively in going forward but, possibly because of all the pre-match publicity concerning him, Tommy Tynan was closely watched in the middle by the uncompromising Watson. Despite his inexperience, Alan Miller in goal could not be faulted and made an outstanding one-handed save from McCall when the latter let fly from 20 yards.

In both halves, Argyle had caused Southall, Everton's Welsh international goalkeeper, some anxieties, notably when he was forced to divert a Kevin Summerfield shot for a corner with his knee. Southall was finally beaten in the 62nd minute. McCarthy both started and finished the move. He ran at the defence and slipped the ball to Stuart in the clear. The latter's low centre flashed across the goal, beating both Southall and Tynan before Kevin Hodges retrieved the ball and turned it back. Southall could only divert it into the path of McCarthy and the Argyle forward's shot from ten yards found the net off the legs of a defender.

Unfortunately for Argyle, the reverse seemed to inspire Everton to greater efforts and they began to press on the Argyle goal. Even so, the home team might have held on to their lead, had not Burrows, leaping among a group of players in the penalty area, handled the ball with 12 minutes of the match remaining. Up stepped Kevin Sheedy, who gave Miller no chance to save his penalty-kick.

The disappointment to the home crowd resulting from that equalizer was compounded by the news from Everton a few days later that, not only had Everton soundly beaten Argyle 4-0 in the replay, but also that Summerfield had fractured his leg. Supporters with long memories or good record books would have found in that replay result echoes of the matches against Huddersfield in 1934 and Wolves in 1950. The precise results might have differed, but the outcome in all three matches had been the same — Argyle, just a whisker away from being 'giantkillers' in one game, but clearly beaten in the replay.

Plymouth Argyle: Miller; Brown, Uzzell, Burrows, Marker, Smith, Summerfield, McCarthy, Tynan, Hodges, Stuart.
Everton: Southall; Snodin, Van den Hauwe, Ratcliffe, Watson, Bracewell, Steven, McCall, Sharp, Cottee, Sheedy.

Attendance: 27,566

Sean McCarthy in action against Everton.

McCarthy puts Argyle in front.

Argyle goalkeeper Geoff Crudgington watches Lindsay Smith clear a Watford attack in the FA Cup semi-final at Villa Park in 1984.

FA Cup 1983-84

THERE was little indication in the early rounds of this competition that Argyle were destined to have their best-ever season in the FA Cup and to come within one match of a Wembley appearance. In the first round, a replay was necessary to dispose of Southend United, who were relegated by the end of the season. Even then, the second match at Home Park went to extra-time before Argyle finally settled the issue with an own-goal by the Southend defender Stead and another from Tommy Tynan.

Barking, from the Isthmian League, at Home Park in the second round looked on paper a much easier proposition, but Argyle made heavy weather of the task and Lindsay Smith's header from a corner-kick which brought Argyle victory owed something to a deflection from Barking's John Reeves.

Two attempts were also needed to get past the obstacle posed by Newport County in the third round. At Home Park, Newport were leading 2-1 well into injury time when the referee awarded Argyle a penalty for a foul on Hodges. Tynan scored from the spot but Argyle could hardly claim that they deserved their replay opportunity. Victory at Somerton Park was also left until a late stage in the game; there were only six minutes remaining when Andy Rogers netted a low cross.

Despite a home advantage, Argyle also laboured somewhat to beat Fourth Division Darlington in the fourth round. The visitors took the lead in the 28th minute and played impressive football throughout. John Uzzell headed in his first goal of the season to bring the scores level and a goal in the 81st minute by Gordon Staniforth denied the northern side the opportunity of a replay.

Paradoxically, as they advanced in the FA Cup and encountered more formidable opposition, Argyle's performance improved. The draw for the fifth round took them to West Bromwich. If the pre-match build-up can influence the result of a game, then Argyle would have been doomed to failure before taking the field. It so happened that their arrival coincided with the return to The Hawthorns of Johnny Giles as manager. Giles engaged Nobby Stiles and Norman Hunter as his assistants and all three received an ecstatic welcome from the home crowd when they presented themselves for approval before the kick-off

The Argyle match was to have marked the start of a glorious new chapter in West Bromwich's history. Unfortunately for the homesters it did not work out as planned. Albion attacks were constantly pegged back by the tight Plymouth marking and Andy Rogers posed many questions to the Albion defence. It was Tommy Tynan who put the ball into the Albion goal in the 58th minute, but it was Gordon Staniforth who provided the chance. The little forward picked up a pass on the left wing and drew out the former Argyle goalkeeper, Paul Barron, before squaring thc ball for Tynan to chest it down and fire into the net. The home crowd had anticipated an Albion victory but drifted quietly away when they thought it was unlikely. Johnny Giles was forced to admit to the post-match Press conference that he had a lot of problems on his hands.

John Hore, on the other hand, in his first spell of League management, must have thought that he possessed the Midas touch. The quarter-final tie with Derby County went to a replay, as did some of those earlier fixtures. But the Argyle team by this stage was no longer the struggling, hesitant group which had stuttered through the earlier rounds. Derby, strengthened by experienced if somewhat ageing international players in Archie Gemmill, Kenny Burns and Dave Watson, spent most of the time on the defensive at Home Park and it was mainly inspired goalkeeping by Steve Cherry, later to join Argyle, which kept the home team at bay. It was

Cherry who foiled Gordon Staniforth, eight minutes from time, when the the latter's shot hit both uprights before rebounding to safety.

If luck favoured Derby on that occasion, it swung round to Argyle's side in the replay at the Baseball Ground. The goal which took Argyle on to a semi-final appearance was, as even scorer Andy Rogers admitted, a fluke. Rogers' intention was to place his corner-kick into the middle of the goal, but something went wrong with his aim and the ball soared over the goalmouth players to drop inside the far post with Cherry floundering. The goal might have been fortunate but the overall Argyle display merited victory and Lindsay Smith could well have complained that Lady Luck had deserted him when he saw a volley hit the bar and a header come back off the post.

For regular Argyle supporters — and about 20,000 more who discovered or rediscovered their backing for the Plymouth team — the semi-final appearance at Villa Park against Watford was an occasion not to be missed. Argyle were, after all, only 90 minutes away from a Wembley appearance and Watford did not appear to be the most formidable of opponents. Regular supporters, however, would not have been unaware that in the interval between winning at Derby and arriving at Villa Park, Argyle's League form had been most unimpressive. Of the seven games played, they had won only one and drawn two and the defeats included a 5-0 collapse at Oxford in which they were completely outplayed. All doubts, however, could be put into suspension for the great day, because, as every football follower knows, League form is no true guide to Cup performance.

That warm, sunny afternoon at Villa Park will always be remembered by the Argyle fans who were there. Many of them will also remember the moment when the team's Wembley dreams were shattered. Watford's reputation for fast, long-ball attacks was well known, and in the 13th minute, they demonstrated just how it was done. It was John Barnes who carved the opening, much in the same way as he has more recently been doing for Liverpool. Receiving the ball on the left wing, he flashed past Gordon Nisbet and delivered a centre of such precision that his 6ft 3in centre-forward, George Reilly, was able to head it past Crudgington with equal speed.

Argyle were not to know it then, but it was the *coup de grace*. Although they continued to battle away, although Lindsay Smith gave Reilly few further opportunities and although Andy Rogers twisted and turned and did everything possible to send the Watford defenders dizzy, an Argyle equalizer, let alone a winner, always seemed a rather improbable prospect.

In retrospect, it was a strange sequence of Cup matches. Taken as a group, the later matches, including to some extent the semi-final, had no continuity with the earlier rounds or with Argyle's general League form. It was as though, for one set of games only, some form of inspiration descended upon the side which enabled them to transcend their normal form. There seems to be no other easy explanation for the situation in which at selected intervals a struggling Third Division side was able to perform so confidently against nominally superior opposition.

FA Cup 1983-84

First Round
19 November 1983
Southend United 0 Plymouth Argyle 0
Southend United: Keeley; Stead, Collins, Pennyfather, Turner, Moody, Ferguson, Kellock(Pountney), McDonough, Shepherd, Phillips.
Plymouth Argyle: Crudgington; Nisbet, Uzzell, Harrison, Smith, Cooper, Hodges, Rowe, Tynan, Kellow, Phillips.

Replay
22 November 1983
Plymouth Argyle 2 *(Stead og, Tynan)* **Southend United 0**
Plymouth Argyle: Crudgington; Nisbet, Uzzell, Harrison, Smith, Cooper, Hodges, Rowe, Tynan, Kellow, Phillips.
Southend United: Keeley; Stead, Collins, Pennyfather(Clark), Turner, Moody, Ferguson, Pountney, McDonough, Shepherd, Phillips.

Second Round
10 December 1983
Plymouth Argyle 2 *(Rowe, Smith)* **Barking 1** *(Groom)*
Plymouth Argyle: Crudgington; Nisbet, Uzzell, Ham, Smith, Phillips, Hodges, Rowe, Tynan(Staniforth), Kellow, Rogers.
Barking: Root; Wright, Watts, Cooper, Groom, Reeves, Shirt, Keen, Armstrong (Rolph), Tappin, Crown.

Third Round
7 January 1984
Plymouth Argyle 2 *(Hodges, Tynan)* **Newport County 2** *(Aldridge 2)*
Plymouth Argyle: Crudgington; Nisbet, Uzzell, Harrison, Smith, Cooper, Hodges, Phillips, Tynan, Staniforth, Rogers.
Newport County: Kendall; V.Jones, Relish, Reid, Boyle, Matthewson, Micallef, Aldridge, Chamberlain, Carter, Lewis.

Replay
10 January 1984
Newport County 0 Plymouth Argyle 1 *(Rogers)*
Newport County: Kendall; V.Jones, Relish, Reid, Boyle, Matthewson(Woodruff), Micallef, Aldridge, Chamberlain, Carter, Lewis.
Plymouth Argyle: Crudgington; Phillips, Uzzell, Harrison, Smith, Cooper, Hodges, Forbes(Pearson), Tynan, Staniforth, Rogers.

Fourth Round
28 January 1984
Plymouth Argyle 2 *(Uzzell, Staniforth)* **Darlington 1** *(Todd)*
Plymouth Argyle: Crudgington; Nisbet, Uzzell, Harrison, Smith, Cooper, Hodges, Phillips, Tynan, Staniforth, Rogers.
Darlington: Barber; Craggs, Johnson, Honour(Davies), Smith, Barton, Cartwright, Todd, Gilbert, Walsh, McLean.

Fifth Round
18 February 1984
West Bromwich Albion 0 Plymouth Argyle 1 *(Tynan)*
West Bromwich Albion: Barron; Whitehead, Statham, Zondervan, McNaught, Bennett, Jol, Thompson, Perry(Luke), MacKenzie, Morley.
Plymouth Argyle: Crudgington; Nisbet, Uzzell, Harrison, Smith, Cooper, Hodges, Phillips, Tynan, Staniforth, Rogers.

THE MANAGER SAYS...

Plymouth Argyle Football Club

Registered Office: Home Park, Plymouth. Tel. Plymouth 52561 2 3
President: George Gillin
Chairman: S.W. Dawe
Vice Chairman: P.D. Bloom
Directors: R. Burroughs ARICS, B.L. Hooper, G.E. Jasper, J.F.C. Kent
Life Vice-Presidents: T.H Deans, C.W. Crookes, C. Harvey
Hon. Vice-Presidents: S.J. Rendell, R. Harding
Company Secretary: Graham Little
Commercial Manager: Bill Pearce
Team Manager: John Hore
Coach: Martin Harvey
Hon. Orthopaedic Surgeon: Mr. M.H. Saiz FRCS
Hon. Medical Officers: Dr. B.M. Walker, Dr. P.N. Grannum
Head Groundsman: George Robertson
Club Colours: Green shirts with black trim, Black shorts, white stockings
Magazine Editor: Bill Pearce
Photography: Bernard Prince
Printed by: Norwood, Roose & Co. Ltd.
Cover Design by: Taylor Art & Design
The views expressed by independent contributors are not necessarily the views of Plymouth Argyle Football Company Ltd.

"MEMORIES ARE MADE OF THIS!"

NO one here today will need reminding that this is a very special event in the history of Plymouth Argyle.

It's special for everyone connected with the club – the players, all the staff behind the scenes, the directors and, of course, our supporters descending on Home Park from all over the West Country.

We are all making history together by seeing the Pilgrims compete in the quarter-finals of the F.A. Cup and we all have our part to play in obtaining the maximum advantage from this unique occasion.

Club secretary Graham Little and his overworked office staff have had a thankless task coping with the demand for tickets. It's impossible to please everyone but I know they have played their part with superb efficiency.

The players will be keyed up and striving to produce their absolute best to negotiate one giant step closer to Wembley.

I can't stress enough how much YOU can help, too, by cheering the team on as loudly and as often as you can through the 90 minutes. Your encouragement is more important today than ever before. With powerful backing from all parts of the gound you could be helping to make our dreams come true. . .

We are pleased to welcome the management, players and supporters of Derby County to the West Country. We know they will be as determined and as enthusiastic as us about the challenge they face.

Whatever the outcome of this contest, I hope you enjoy this special day and that the game itself will bring back happy memories for years to come.

GOOD LUCK!

Sixth Round
10 March 1984
Plymouth Argyle 0 Derby County 0
Plymouth Argyle: Crudgington; Nisbet, Uzzell, Harrison, Smith, Cooper, Hodges, Phillips, Tynan, Staniforth, Rogers.
Derby County: Cherry; Barton, Buckley, Gemmill, Burns, Powell, Futcher, Davison, Wilson, Hooks(Watson), Robertson.

Replay
14 March 1984
Derby County 0 Plymouth Argyle 1 *(Rogers)*
Derby County: Cherry; Barton, Buckley, Gemmill, Burns, Powell, Futcher, Davison(Watson), Wilson, Plummer, Robertson.
Plymouth Argyle: Crudgington; Nisbet, Uzzell, Harrison, Smith, Cooper, Hodges, Phillips, Tynan, Staniforth, Rogers.

Semi-final (at Villa Park)
14 April 1984
Plymouth Argyle 0 Watford 1 *(Reilly)*
Plymouth Argyle: Crudgington; Nisbet, Uzzell, Harrison, Smith, Cooper, Hodges, Phillips, Tynan, Staniforth, Rogers.
Watford: Sherwood; Bardsley, Price, Taylor, Terry(Jobson), Sinnott, Callaghan, Johnston, Reilly, Rostron, Barnes.

Action from the 1984 FA Cup semi-final at Villa Park. Above: Steve Terry of Watford gets in a tackle on Argyle's Kevin Hodges. Below: Terry (left) challenges David Phillips.

Football League Cup 1964-65

THE League Cup was a relatively new competition when Argyle, under their new manager Malcolm Allison, attained heights hitherto undreamed of in the winter of 1964-5. Centre-forward Frank Lord was the hero of the hour in the earlier rounds. His two second-half goals put paid to First Division Sheffield United in the second round and he was again on target in the fourth round against another First Division side, Stoke City.

At Stoke, Lord had put Argyle into a 1-0 interval lead but home forward John Ritchie equalized in the second half to force a replay. This provided the setting for Lord to score a hat-trick, one goal in the first half and two in the second, to shock the previous season's runners-up. At that stage in the competition, Lord had scored six of Argyle's seven goals, the other having been snatched by defender Doug Baird in the third-round match at Bury.

It was another defender, Johnny Newman, who scored the goal in the fifth round by which Argyle defeated visiting Northampton Town. Northampton at the time were pushing for (and eventually gained) promotion from the Second Division so defeat might not have been entirely unwelcome.

The Northampton victory brought Argyle to the semi-final, played on a two-leg basis, against Leicester City, the League Cup holders. Allison's tactical thinking was much in evidence in the first game at Leicester with Argyle playing a 4-3-3 formation and Norman Piper being handed the key duty of sticking close to Mike Stringfellow, who was reckoned to be Leicester's dangerman. Frank Lord was absent from the Argyle side and Argyle's manager gambled on 16-year-old Richard Reynolds to lead the attack. Reynolds considerably troubled the home defence and Argyle twice took the lead, only to see Leicester cancel the advantage and finally get the winner.

It was a Johnny Williams special which set Plymouth on what they thought was the path to victory and even so fine a goalkeeper as Gordon Banks had no chance as the Argyle half-back thundered the ball in from some 30 yards in the 35th minute. But Williams' jubilation turned to despair in the second half when he turned a McDerment shot into his own net to equalize for Leicester. Mike Trebilcock restored Argyle's lead within minutes but with 20 minutes to go Bobby Roberts brought Leicester level again and, as the match drew to a close, Stringfellow began to show why Allison had identified him as the main danger. Twice he hit the Argyle bar and then, five minutes from time, centred for Gibson to net Leicester's winning goal.

It was a goal by defender John Sjoberg in the second leg at Plymouth which put the issue beyond doubt and took Leicester to their fourth Cup Final in five years. Frank Lord was back in the Argyle side for the match but could not produce his scoring touch and Sjoberg's 15th-minute goal proved to be enough to give Leicester a 4-2 aggregate win.

Football League Cup 1964-65

Second Round
23 September 1964
Plymouth Argyle 2 *(Lord 2)* **Sheffield United 1** *(Birchenall)*
Plymouth Argyle: MacLaren; Book, Baird, Neale, Sykes, Jackson, Brace, Trebilcock, Lord, Cobb, Jennings.
Sheffield United: Hodgkinson; Badger, B.Shaw, Richardson, Mallender, Matthewson, Docherty, T.Wagstaff, Jones, Birchenall, Hartle.

Third Round
14 October 1964
Bury 0 Plymouth Argyle 1 *(Baird)*
Bury: Harker; Gallagher, Eastham, Turner, Bunner, Atherton, Claxton, Bell, Griffin, Leech, Alston.
Plymouth Argyle: MacLaren; Book, Baird, Williams, Newman, Neale, Jones, Trebilcock, Lord, Jackson, Jennings.

Fourth Round
4 November 1964
Stoke City 1 *(Ritchie)* **Plymouth Argyle 1** *(Lord)*
Stoke City: Leslie; Asprey, Allen, Palmer, Skeels, Bloor, Bridgwood, Ritchie, Viollet, Philpott, Dobing.
Plymouth Argyle: MacLaren; Book, Reeves, Neale, Newman, Jackson, Jones, Trebilcock, Lord, Williams, Jennings.

11 November 1964
Plymouth Argyle 3 *(Lord 3)* **Stoke City 1** *(Dobing)*
Plymouth Argyle: MacLaren; Book, Reeves, Williams, Newman, Neale, Jones, Trebilcock, Lord, Jackson, Jennings.
Stoke City: Leslie; Asprey, Allen, Bloor, Kinnell, Skeels, Dobing, Philpott, Ritchie, McIlroy, Bebbington.

Fifth Round
25 November 1964
Plymouth Argyle 1 *(Newman)* **Northampton Town 0**
Plymouth Argyle: MacLaren; Book, Reeves, Neale, Newman, Jackson, Jones, Trebilcock, Lord, Sanderson, Jennings.
Northampton Town: Harvey; Foley, Cockroft, Leck, Branston, Kiernan, Walden, Martin, Livesey, Lines, Robson.

Semi-final (first leg)
20 January 1965
Leicester City 3 *(Williams og, Roberts, Gibson)* **Plymouth Argyle 2** *(Williams, Trebilcock)*
Leicester City: Banks; Chalmers, Norman, McDerment, Sjoberg, Appleton, Goodfellow, Roberts, Cross, Gibson, Stringfellow.
Plymouth Argyle: Dwyer; Book, Reeves, Neale, Newman, Williams, Corbett, Trebilcock, Reynolds, Piper, Nicholas.

Semi-final (second leg)
10 February 1965
Plymouth Argyle 0 Leicester City 1 *(Sjoberg)*
Plymouth Argyle: Dwyer; Book, Reeves, Neale, Newman, Williams, Jones, Trebilcock, Lord, Jackson, Jennings.
Leicester City: Banks; Sjoberg, Norman, Roberts, King, Appleton, Hodgson, Cross, Goodfellow, Gibson, Stringfellow.

Rodney Marsh gets in a header against Argyle in the League Cup semi-final first leg at Home Park in January 1974. Jim Furnell appears to be beaten but the ball went over the bar.

Football League Cup 1973-74

THE stars had decreed that 1974 should be a year of Argyle attainment. At least that seemed to be the most natural interpretation of a prophecy in *Old Moore's Almanac* that a team wearing green and black would appear at Wembley that year. Considering the rarity of that particular colour combination among League clubs, Argyle seemed to be the obvious candidates. And as the competition progressed, some esoteric explanation seemed to be needed for the phenomenon in which a Third Division side, in the lower half of the table, should register a string of victories on the grounds of illustrious First Division opponents.

So, while the country as a whole braced itself for that famous 'winter of discontent' caused by the miners' strike — electricity cuts, a three-day working week and darkened roads and houses — in one corner of the British Isles, hopes were high that Plymouth Argyle would achieve an historic appearance at Wembley before the season had finished.

Fourth Division neighbours Torquay United were the first barrier to Argyle's League Cup progress that season, but two goals by Steve Davey ended any threat from that quarter and the next round brought Second Division Portsmouth to Home Park. At that point, Portsmouth had been having difficulty in getting away from the lower end of the table. Argyle's clear-cut 4-0 victory did nothing to strengthen their self-confidence.

Victory over Pompey brought Argyle to that sequence of wins at First Division clubs. Burnley were third in the First Division at the end of October when they received their Argyle visitors. Ray Hankin's goal for them in the 16th minute seemed to be the beginning of an expected victory but, 17 minutes later, their centre-half, Colin Waldron, turned an Ernie Machin free-kick into his own net. Burnley's anticipation of an easy passage into the next round was ended when, three minutes from time, Neil Hague moved upfield for a corner and got a touch to Colin Sullivan's kick to give Argyle a surprise victory.

Queen's Park Rangers held seventh position in Division One when Argyle met them in late November and they had not been beaten at home for a year. Again, this fixture had looked to be an almost certain home win. Again, though, Argyle upset the form-book and produced a decisive result which had even the home manager, Gordon Jago, admitting that his side had been beaten by the better team. If any player deserved to be singled out in that Argyle side it was winger Alan Welsh, who not only scored twice but was also a constant menace to the Rangers' defence.

But Ernie Machin and Steve Davey were not far behind Welsh in the ability to cause problems for the home defenders and the Argyle attack, quick and incisive, was constantly threatening Rangers' goal. Welsh opened the scoring in the 53rd minute, dribbling the ball to within a few yards of the goalposts. Then, with colleagues and opponents alike expecting him to pass, he drove the ball past McLintock and Parkes into the net.

Ten minutes later, a fluent move between Hore, Machin and Mariner put Steve Davey clear for the second goal and with the minutes running out, Davey burst through to the edge of the penalty-area and screwed the ball back for Welsh to notch his second goal of the evening.

With victories over two leading First Division clubs, Argyle were not at all perturbed at being drawn away again in the fifth round at Birmingham City, then 20th in the First Division. Despite going behind to a Birmingham goal in the ninth minute, when Hatton touched in a shot from Bob Latchford, Argyle maintained their sequence of victories and the scorers in the Queen's Park Rangers match were again on target.

By half-time, first Welsh and then Davey had beaten goalkeeper Dave Latchford to give the visitors a lead which they did not surrender in spite of second-half pressure by the home side. And when Jim Furnell made a superb save from Kenny Burns' half-volley in the 65th minute, Argyle realized that another victory was well within their grasp.

The Manchester City side which former Argyle stalwart Tony Book brought to Home Park for the first-leg of the semi-final included a forward line which sparkled with talent — Mike Summerbee, Colin Bell, Francis Lee, Denis Law, Rodney Marsh — a select group from a footballing equivalent of *Debrett's Peerage.* Yet their reputations appeared to make little impression on the Argyle men who tore into their more famous visitors. Heavy morning rain had turned the pitch into a gluey, slippery mess; the sort of surface on which defenders are prone to mistakes, and when City's Scottish international left-back Willie Donachie slipped in moving for the ball, Steve Davey saw the opening and had put the ball past MacRae in a flash.

Argyle had a dominant first half, but after the interval the heavy pitch seemed to sap their energy and, as Booth and Doyle in the centre of the Manchester defence began to get a grip on Davey and Paul Mariner, their forward colleagues began to display their individual skills. Nevertheless, they found the Argyle defence in an unyielding mood and it took a Booth header from a corner-kick to level the scores.

The return game at Maine Road was the point at which the prophecy foundered. Perhaps 'Old Moore' had not allowed for the fact that Argyle would be without leading scorer Steve Davey on that occasion. Whatever the reason, Argyle's challenge to Manchester City gradually faded after first Francis Lee, with a fierce shot in the tenth minute, and Colin Bell, with an early second-half goal, put City into a clear lead. For the Manchester side, jubilation was mingled with relief. Their path to the League Cup Final had been somewhat laborious, three games being needed to beat Walsall and two each to defeat York, Coventry and Plymouth. For Argyle came the inevitable disappointment and a warning not to put too much faith in mysterious predictions.

Football League Cup 1973-74

First Round
29 August 1973
Torquay United 0 Plymouth Argyle 2 *(Davey 2)*
Torquay United: Mahoney; Twitchin, P.Sandercock, K.Sandercock, Boulton, Stocks, Morrall, Rowles, Lucas, Myers, Stuckey.
Plymouth Argyle: Furnell; Dowling, Sullivan, Hore, Saxton, Provan, Johnson, Davey, Hinch, Machin, Burrows.

Second Round
9 October 1973
Plymouth Argyle 4 *(Machin, Davey 2, Mariner)* **Portsmouth 0**
Plymouth Argyle: Furnell; Webb, Sullivan, Hore, Saxton, Hague, Welsh, Davey, Mariner, Machin, Rogers.
Portsmouth: Milkins; Roberts, Wilson, Piper, Stephenson, Hand, Marinello, Kellard, Davies, Lewis, Hiron.

Third Round
30 October 1973
Burnley 1 *(Hankin)* **Plymouth Argyle 2** *(Waldron og, Hague)*
Burnley: Stevenson; Noble, Newton, Dobson, Waldron, Thomson, Nulty, Hankin, Fletcher, Collins, James.
Plymouth Argyle: Furnell; Randell, Sullivan, Hore, Saxton, Hague, Welsh, Davey, Mariner, Machin, Rogers.

Fourth Round
20 November 1973
Queen's Park Rangers 0 Plymouth Argyle 3 *(Welsh 2, Davey)*
Queen's Park Rangers: Parkes; Clement, Hazell, Venables, Mancini, McLintock, Thomas, Francis, Busby, Bowles, Givens.
Plymouth Argyle: Furnell; Randell, Sullivan, Hore, Saxton, Hague, Welsh, Davey, Mariner, Machin, Rogers.

Fifth Round
19 December 1973
Birmingham City 1 *(Hatton)* **Plymouth Argyle 2** *(Welsh, Davey)*
Birmingham City: D.Latchford; Martin, Gallagher(Taylor), Pendrey, Hynd, Roberts, Burns, Francis, R.Latchford, Hatton, Hendrie.
Plymouth Argyle: Furnell; Randell, Sullivan, Hore, Saxton, Hague, Welsh(Rickard), Davey, Mariner, Machin, Rogers.

Semi-final (first leg)
23 January 1974
Plymouth Argyle 1 *(Davey)* **Manchester City 1** *(Booth)*
Plymouth Argyle: Furnell; Randell, Sullivan, Hore, Saxton, Hague, Welsh, Davey, Mariner, Machin, Rogers.
Manchester City: MacRae; Barrett, Donachie, Doyle, Booth, Towers, Summerbee, Bell, Lee, Law(Leman), Marsh.

Semi-final (second leg)
30 January 1974
Manchester City 2 *(Lee, Bell)* **Plymouth Argyle 0**
Manchester City: MacRae; Barrett, Donachie, Doyle, Booth, Towers, Summerbee, Bell, Lee(Leman), Oakes, Carrodus.
Plymouth Argyle: Furnell; Randell, Sullivan, Hore, Saxton, Hague, Welsh, Richard, Mariner, Machin, Rogers.

Associate Members Cup

1983-84
Round 1
Feb 21 v Torquay United (h) 5-1
Tynan 2, Hodges 2, Rogers
Crudgington; Nisbet, Uzzell, Harrison, Smith(Price), Cooper(Cassidy), Hodges, Phillips, Tynan, Staniforth, Rogers.
Att: 3,962
Round 2
Mar 26 v Brentford (h) 2-0
Tynan 2
Crudgington; Nisbet, Uzzell(Swiggs), Harrison, Ham, Cooper, Rowe(M.Smith), Phillips, Tynan, Chamberlain, Rogers.
Att: 2,308
Quarter-finals
Apr 24 v Exeter City (h) 2-1
Smith, Phillips
Philp; Nisbet, Uzzell(Rogers), Harrison, Smith, Cooper, Ham, Phillips, Swiggs, Chamberlain(Hodges), Rowe.
Att: 3,715
Semi-finals
May 17 v Millwall (h) 0-1
Crudgington; Nisbet, Uzzell, Harrison, Smith, Cooper(Rowe), Hodges(Tynan), Phillips, Chamberlain, Staniforth, Rogers.
Att: 4,531

Freight/Rover Trophy

1984-85
Round 1 (1st leg)
Jan 22 v Bournemouth (h) 2-1
Staniforth, Cooper
Crudgington; Nisbet, Harrison, Ham, McElhinney, Cooper, Rogers, Hodges(Rowbotham), Summerfield, Staniforth, Coughlin.
Att: 2,995
Round 1 (2nd leg)
Feb 5 v Bournemouth (a) 0-2
Crudgington; Nisbet, Uzzell, Ham(Rowe), McElhinney, Cooper, Rogers, Hodges, Tynan, Staniforth, Goodyear.
Att: 2,748
Bournemouth won 3-2 on aggregate.

1985-86
Jan 14 v Bristol City (a) 0-0
Crudgington; Nisbet, Uzzell, Goodyear(Burrows), McElhinney, Matthews, Hodges, Coughlin, Summerfield, Clayton, Nelson.
Att: 2,402
Jan 21 v Walsall (h) 0-1
Crudgington; Nisbet, L.Cooper, Goodyear, McElhinney, Matthews, Hodges, Coughlin, Summerfield(S.Cooper), Clayton, Nelson.
Att: 3,198

Simod Cup

1987-88
Round 1
Nov 10 v Manchester City (a) 2-6
Tynan, Coughlin
Cherry; Brimacombe, L.Cooper, Matthews, Marker, Smith, Hodges(Law), Coughlin, Tynan, Evans(Clayton), Anderson.
Att: 5,051

1988-89
Round 1
Nov 9 v Chelsea (a) 2-6
Stuart, McCarthy
Penhaligon; Brown, Cooper, Burrows, Marker, Uzzell, Plummer, Brimacombe(Matthews), Tynan(McCarthy), G.Campbell, Stuart.
Att: 4,767

Watney Cup

1973-74
Round 1
Aug 11 v Stoke City (h) 0-1
Furnell; Provan, Sullivan, Hore, Saxton, Hague, Welsh, Davey, Hinch(Rogers), Machin, Richard.
Att: 17,501

Football League Group Cup

1981-82
Aug 15 v Bournemouth (h) 0-0
Crudgington; Nisbet, McCartney, Harrison, James, Hodges, Cooper, Kemp, Sims, Randell, Murphy.
Att: 2,707
Aug 18 v Newport County (a) 1-2
Sims
Crudgington; Nisbet, McCartney, Harrison, Phillipson-Masters, Hodges, Cooper, Kemp, Sims, Randell, Murphy.
Att: 2,316
Aug 19 v Torquay United (a) 1-1
Kemp
Crudgington; Nisbet, McCartney, Phillipson-Masters, Foster, Cooper(Collins), Hodges, Kemp, Sims, Randell, Murphy.
Att: 3,088

Anglo-Scottish Cup

1977-8
Preliminary Competition Group 'B'
Jul 30 v Bristol Rovers (a) 1-0
Austin
Barron; Smart, Uzzell, Horswill, Peddelty, Craven, Johnson, Delve, Austin, Trusson.
Att: 2,786

Aug 6 v Birmingham City (h) 1-1
Austin
Barron; Smart, Uzzell, Horswill, Peddelty(Foster), Craven, Johnson, Delve, Austin, Trusson, Rodgers.
Att: 5,176
Aug 9 v Bristol City (h) 0-2
Barron; Smart, Uzzell, Horswill, Sutton, Craven, Johnson(Foster), Delve, Austin, Trusson, Rodgers.
Att: 4,648
Argyle finished in third place in their group and did not qualify for the quarter-finals.

1979-80
Preliminary Competition Group 'D'
Aug 4 v Fulham (a) 0-1
Hards; James, Harrison, Phillipson-Masters, Foster, Bason, Megson, Graves(Hodges), Johnson, Randell, Perrin.
Att: 2,067
Aug 6 v Birmingham City (h) 1-1
Johnson
Hards; James, Harrison, Phillipson-Masters, Foster, Bason, Megson, Randell, Johnson, Graves, Perrin.
Att: 3,137
Aug 8 v Bristol City (h) 0-0
Hards; James, Harrison, Phillipson-Masters, Foster, Hodges, Megson, Johnson, Binney, Randell, Perrin.
Att: 2,848
Argyle finished third in the group and did not qualify for the quarter-finals.

Argyle pictured before the start of the 1970-71 season. Back row (left to right): John Hore, Derek Rickard, Bobby Saxton, Winston Foster, Paul Chapman, David Burnside. Middle row: Bryan Edwards (coach), Fred Molyneux, Keith Allen, Pat Dunne, Gordon Robinson, Richard Reynolds, Mike Bickle, Ellis Stuttard (manager). Front row: Don Hutchins, Trevor Shepherd, Steve Davey, David Lean, Colin Sullivan, Aiden Maher.

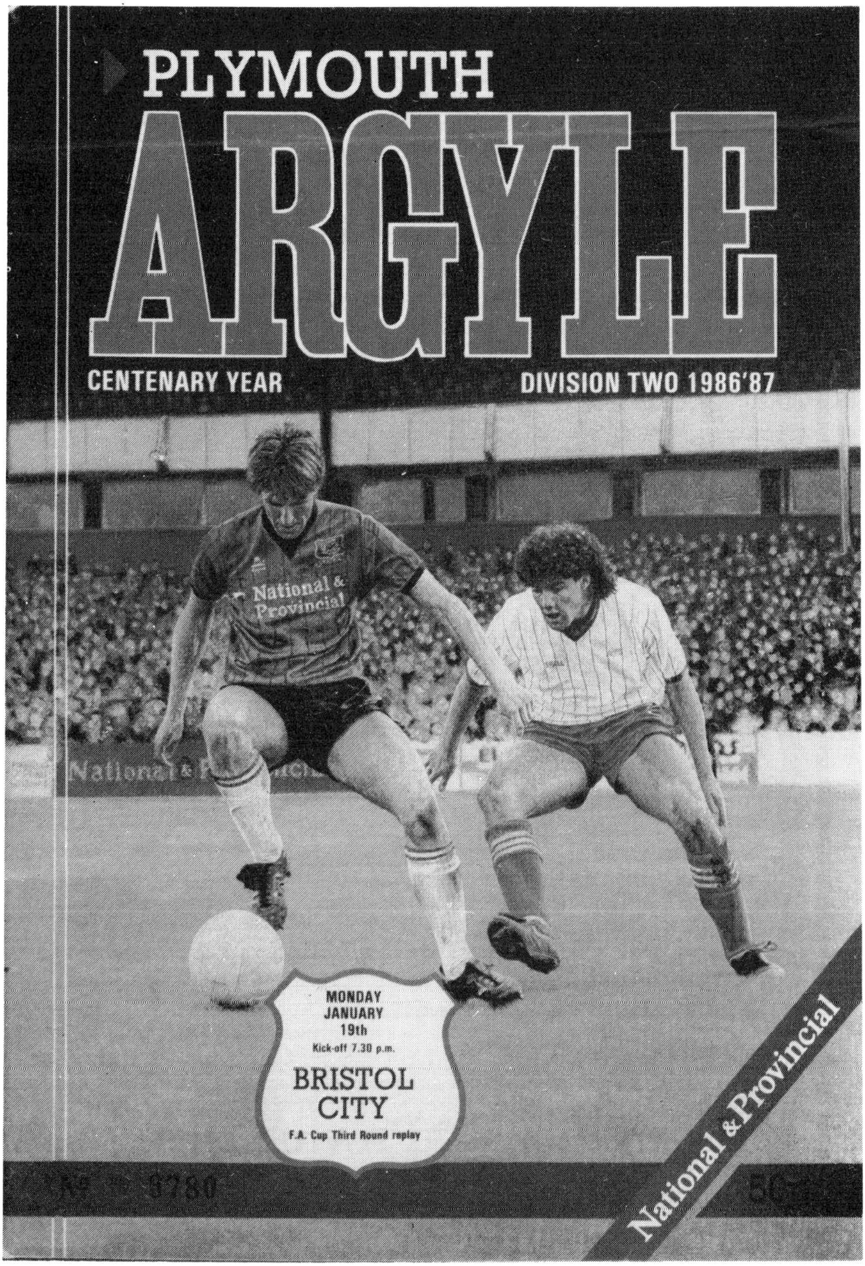
PLYMOUTH
ARGYLE
CENTENARY YEAR
DIVISION TWO 1986'87
National &
Provincial
MONDAY
JANUARY
19th
Kick-off 7.30 p.m.
BRISTOL
CITY
F.A. Cup Third Round replay
National & Provincial

1903-04

Manager: Frank Brettell

1	Sep	5	(h)	Northampton T	W 2-0	Peddie, Picken
2		12	(a)	Brentford	L 0-1	
3		19	(h)	West Ham U	W 2-0	Winterhalder, Peddie
4		26	(a)	Tottenham H	W 2-0	Anderson, Leech
5	Oct	3	(h)	Luton T	D 0-0	
6		10	(a)	New Brompton	D 0-0	
7		17	(h)	Kettering T	W 5-1	Dalrymple, Picken 2, Peddie 2
8		24	(a)	Southampton	W 5-3	Jack 2, Dalrymple, Anderson, Picken
9	Nov	7	(a)	Millwall	L 0-1	
10		11	(h)	Fulham	W 1-0	Picken
11		21	(a)	Swindon T	L 0-2	
12	Dec	5	(h)	Wellingborough	W 4-1	Anderson 3, Jack
13		19	(h)	Brighton & HA	W 4-2	Peddie, Winterhalder, Dalrymple, Anderson
14		25	(h)	Reading	L 0-1	
15		26	(a)	Bristol R	W 2-1	Dalrymple, Anderson
16		28	(a)	Portsmouth	D 0-0	
17	Jan	2	(a)	Northampton T	L 0-1	
18		9	(h)	Brentford	D 2-2	Anderson, Dalrymple
19		16	(a)	West Ham U	D 1-1	Peddie
20		23	(a)	Tottenham H	L 1-3	Anderson
21		30	(a)	Luton T	D 1-1	Jack
22	Feb	13	(a)	Kettering T	L 0-3	
23		20	(a)	Brighton & HA	D 0-0	
24		27	(a)	Fulham	L 0-1	
25	Mar	5	(h)	Millwall	L 2-3	Dalrymple, Wheaton
26		9	(h)	Southampton	L 0-2	
27		12	(a)	Queen's Park R	L 0-1	
28		16	(h)	New Brompton	W 1-0	Banks
29		19	(h)	Swindon T	D 0-0	
30	Apr	1	(h)	Bristol R	D 0-0	
31		2	(a)	Wellingborough	W 3-1	Picken 2, Peddie
32		4	(a)	Reading	W 3-1	Picken 2, Peddie
33		13	(h)	Queen's Park R	D 1-1	Picken
34		23	(h)	Portsmouth	W 2-0	Buck, Peddie

FINAL LEAGUE POSITION: 9th in Southern League

Appearances
Goals

FA Cup

Q1	Oct	31	(h)	Whiteheads	W 7-0	Dalrytmple 2, Peddie 2, Winterhalder 2, Anderson	1,870
Q2	Nov	14	(h)	Freemantle	W 5-1	Peddie 2, Winterhalder, Picken 2	2,500
Q3		28	(h)	Swindon T	W 2-0	Dalrymple, Peddie	5,000
I1	Dec	12	(a)	Brentford	D 1-1	Clark	8,000
R		16	(h)	Brentford	W 4-1	Dalrymple, Anderson, Winterhalder 2	4,000
1	Feb	6	(h)	Sheffield W	D 2-2	Dalrymple, Peddie	20,103
R		10	(a)	Sheffield W	L 0-2		18,845

Appearances
Goals

Western League

1	Sep	1	(a)	West Ham U	W 1-0	Peddie
2		9	(a)	Portsmouth	W 2-1	Leach, Anderson
3		14	(a)	Queen's Park R	D 1-1	Picken
4		30	(h)	Portsmouth	W 3-1	Peddie, Anderson, Dalrymple
5	Oct	12	(a)	Bristol R	L 0-3	
6	Nov	18	(h)	Southampton	W 2-0	Peddie 2
7	Jan	4	(a)	Southampton	W 2-1	Banks, Dalrymple
8	Feb	14	(h)	Queen's Park R	L 0-1	
9		29	(a)	Tottenham H	D 1-1	Fitchett
10	Mar	23	(h)	Brentford	D 0-0	
11		26	(a)	Reading	L 1-2	Dalrymple
12	Apr	5	(a)	Brentford	W 1-0	Dalrymple
13		9	(h)	Bristol R	D 2-2	Picken 2
14		20	(h)	Tottenham H	D 0-0	
15		27	(h)	West Ham U	W 3-2	Buck, Dalrymple, Picken
16		30	(h)	Reading	W 4-0	Peddie, Picken, Dalrymple

Appearances
Goals

Robinson	Fitchett	Clark A	Leech	Goodall	Digweed	Dalrymple	Anderson	Peddie	Picken	Jack	Banks	Winterhalder	Hare	Clark C	Edwards	Broad	Pinnell	Crabtree	Wyatt	Wheaton	Cleghorn	Chadburn	Buck	Mackie	Horne	Pethick	Andrews	Langhan	Pilot	
1	2	3	4	5	6	7	8	9	10	11																				1
1	2	3	4	5	6		8	9	10	11		7																		2
1	2	3		5	6			9	10	11	4	7	8																	3
1		3	4	2			8	9	10	11	6	7		5																4
1		3	4	2	6	7	8	9	10	11				5																5
1		3	4	2			8	9	10	11	6	7		5																6
1	2	3	4		6	7	8	9	10	11				5																7
1	2	3	4		6	7	8	9	10	11				5																8
1		3	4	2	6	7	8	9	10	11				5																9
1	2	3	4		6		8	9	10	11		7		5																10
1	2	3	4		6		8	9	10	11		7		5																11
1	2	3	4		6	10	8	9		11		7		5																12
1		3				10	8	9		11	6	7		5	2	4														13
	2	3	4		6	10	8	9		11		7		5			1													14
1	2	3	4		6	10	8	9		11		7		5																15
1	2	3	4		6	10	8	9		11		7		5																16
1	2	3	4		5	10	8	9		11	6	7																		17
1	2	3	4			7	8	9	10	11	6			5																18
	4	3			6	7	8	9	10	11	5						1	2												19
		3	4		6	7	8	9	10	11				5			1	2												20
		3			6	7	8	9	10	11	4			5				2							1					21
1	2		4		6	9	8		10	11		7		5				3												22
	2	3	4		6	7	8		10	11	9			5			1													23
	2	3	4			9	8		10	11	6	7		5			1													24
	2		6			8		9	10	11				5					3	7					1	4				25
	2	3	4			8		9	10	11		7		5							6				1					26
1	2	3	4						10	11		7	9	5							6						8			27
1	2	3	4			8			10	11	6	7	9	5																28
1	2	3	4			8			10	11	6	7	9	5																29
1	2	3	4					9	10	11	6			5								7	8							30
1	2	3	4			7		9	10	11				5								6	8							31
1	2		4			7		9	10	11				5								3	8	6						32
1	4	3				7		9	10		6			5								2	8	11						33
1	2	3	4			7		9	10	11	6			5									8							34
26	27	31	29	7	19	26	23	28	28	33	15	18	4	29	1	1	5	4	1	1	2	4	5	2	3	1	1			
			1			6	9	9	10	4	1	2								1			1							

Robinson	Fitchett	Clark A	Leech	Goodall	Digweed	Dalrymple	Anderson	Peddie	Picken	Jack	Banks	Winterhalder	Hare	Clark C	Edwards	Broad	Pinnell	Crabtree	Wyatt	Wheaton	Cleghorn	Chadburn	Buck	Mackie	Horne	Pethick	Andrews	Langhan	Pilot	
1	2	3	4		6	10	8	9		11		7		5																Q1
1	2	3	5				8	9	10	11	6	7				4														Q2
1		3	4		6	10	8	9		11		7		5	2															Q3
1	2	3	4		6	7	8	9		11	10			5																I1
1	2	3	4		6	10	8	9		11		7		5																R
1	2	3	4		6	7	8	9	10	11				5																1
1	2	3	4		6	9	8		10	11		7		5																R
7	6	7	7		6	6	7	6	3	7	2	5		6	1	1														
						5	2	6	2			5		1																

Robinson	Fitchett	Clark A	Leech	Goodall	Digweed	Dalrymple	Anderson	Peddie	Picken	Jack	Banks	Winterhalder	Hare	Clark C	Edwards	Broad	Pinnell	Crabtree	Wyatt	Wheaton	Cleghorn	Chadburn	Buck	Mackie	Horne	Pethick	Andrews	Langhan	Pilot	
1	2	3	4	5	6	7	8	9	10	11																				1
1	2	3	4	5	6		8	9	10	11		7																		2
1	2	3	4	5	6		8	9	10	11		7																		3
1		3	4	2		7	8	9	10	11	6			5																4
1		3	4	2			8	9	10	11	6	7		5																5
1	2	3	4		6		8	9	10	11		7		5																6
1	4	3			6	10	8	9		11	5	7			2															7
	3		4		6		8	9	10	11	2	7		5			1													8
1	3	3	4			9			10	11	6	7		5							8							2		9
1	2	3	4			9		10		11	6			5								7	8							10
1	2	3	4			9		10			6	11		5								7	8							11
1	2	3				9			10	11		7		5							4	6	8							12
1	2	3	4			7		9	10	11				5								6	8							13
1		3	4			9				10	6	7		5								2	8	11						14
1	5	3	4			9			10	11	6											7	8						2	15
1	5	3	4			7		9	10	11	6											2	8							16
15	13	15	14	5	6	11	8	12	12	15	10	10		10	1		1				2	7	7	1				1	1	
	1		1			6	2	5	5		1												1							

1904-05

Manager: Frank Brettell

1	Sep	3	(a)	Queen's Park R	L	1-2	C.Clark
2		10	(h)	Millwall	W	5-0	Picken 2, Dalrymple, McLuckie, Buck
3		17	(a)	Tottenham H	L	0-2	
4		24	(h)	Luton T	W	3-0	Buck, Picken 2
5	Oct	1	(a)	Swindon T	L	0-4	
6		8	(h)	New Brompton	W	3-2	Picken 3
7		15	(a)	Wellingborough	W	5-0	Jack, Wright, Buck 2, McLuckie
8		22	(h)	Southampton	W	1-0	McLuckie
9		29	(a)	Fulham	D	0-0	
10	Nov	5	(h)	Watford	D	0-0	
11		19	(a)	West Ham U	L	1-2	McLuckie
12		26	(a)	Reading	L	0-2	
13	Dec	3	(a)	Bristol R	L	0-4	
14		10	(h)	Northampton T	D	2-2	Owens 2
15		17	(a)	Portsmouth	L	2-3	Buck, Dalrymple
16		24	(h)	Brentford	W	1-0	Picken
17		31	(h)	Queen's Park R	W	3-1	Cox, Buck 2
18	Jan	7	(a)	Millwall	L	1-2	Buck
19		21	(a)	Luton T	W	2-0	Picken, Wright
20		28	(h)	Swindon T	W	3-0	Picken 2, Buck
21	Feb	11	(h)	Wellingborough	W	3-1	Hodgkinson, Chadburn, Wright
22		18	(a)	Watford	L	1-3	C.Clark
23		25	(h)	Fulham	D	1-1	McLuckie
24	Mar	11	(a)	Brighton & HA	L	0-2	
25		18	(h)	West Ham U	W	2-0	McLuckie, Wright
26		25	(h)	Reading	W	1-0	Picken
27		27	(a)	New Brompton	D	1-1	Hodgkinson
28	Apr	1	(h)	Bristol R	W	3-1	Owens, Tait (og), Hodgkinson
29		5	(h)	Tottenham H	W	2-1	Wright, Hodgkinson
30		8	(a)	Northampton T	W	2-0	Leech, Picken
31		10	(a)	Southampton	W	3-0	Buck, Dalrymple, Picken
32		15	(h)	Portsmouth	W	2-1	Buck, Walker (og)
33		21	(h)	Brighton & HA	W	3-1	Picken, Dalrymple, Wright
34		22	(a)	Brentford	L	0-1	

FINAL LEAGUE POSITION: 4th in Southern League

Appearances
Goals

FA Cup

Q	Jan	14	(h)	Barnsley	W	2-0	McLuckie, Buck	10,515
1	Feb	4	(a)	Newcastle U	D	1-1	Dalrymple	28,000
R		8	(h)	Newcastle U	D	1-1	McLuckie	17,641
2R		13	(n*)	Newcastle U	L	0-2		16,000

*Played at Plumstead

Appearances
Goals

Western League

1	Sep	1	(a)	Brentford	D	1-1	Buck
2		5	(a)	Millwall	D	1-1	Banks
3		14	(h)	Brentford	W	6-1	Buck, Banks, Cox 3, Davidson (og)
4		19	(a)	Southampton	W	2-1	Picken, Buck
5		28	(h)	Southampton	W	4-1	Dalrymple 2, Picken 2
6	Oct	5	(a)	Portsmouth	L	1-2	Dalrymple
7		12	(h)	Queen's Park R	W	3-0	McLuckie 3
8		19	(h)	Tottenham H	W	5-0	Picken 3, C.Clark, Jack
9		26	(h)	Portsmouth	W	3-1	McLuckie 2, Picken
10		31	(a)	Queen's Park R	W	4-2	Picken, McLuckie, Leech, Buck
11	Nov	9	(h)	West Ham U	D	2-2	Picken, McLuckie
12		21	(a)	Tottenham H	L	0-2	
13		30	(h)	Millwall	W	1-0	Dalrymple
14	Dec	26	(h)	Reading	W	4-0	Picken 2, Buck, Dalrymple
15	Mar	6	(a)	West Ham U	D	1-1	Dalrymple
16		13	(a)	Fulham	W	4-0	McLuckie, Buck, Hodgkinson 2
17		22	(h)	Bristol R	W	5-1	Buck 2, Picken, Dalrymple, Hodgkinson
18		29	(h)	Fulham	L	0-1	
19		24	(a)	Reading	W	3-0	Owens, Cox, Picken
20	Apr	17	(h)	Bristol R	W	2-1	Dalrymple, Picken

Appearances
Goals

Robinson	Ashby	Clark A	Saul	Leech	Clark C	Dalrymple	Buck	McLuckie	Picken	Jack	Banks	Cox	Horne	Hodgkinson	Wright	Owens	Mortimer	Wyatt	Gleghorn	Chadburn	Sutcliffe	Northey	
1	2	3	4	5	6	7	8	9	10	11													1
1	2	3	6	4	5	7	8	9	10	11													2
1	2	3	4	6	5	7	8	9	10	11													3
1	2	3	4		5	7	8		10	11	6	9											4
	2		3	4	5			9	10	11		8	1		6					7			5
	2	3		4	5	7	8		10		6	9	1	11									6
	2	3	5	4		7	8	9		11	6		1		10								7
	2	3		4	5	7		9	10	11	6		1		8								8
	2	3	6	4	5	7	8	9	10	11			1										9
	2	3	6	4	5	7	8	9	10	11			1										10
	2	3	6	4	5	7	8	9	10	11			1										11
	2	3	6	4	5		7	9		11			1		10	8							12
	2	3	4		5	7	8	9	10	11	6		1										13
1	2	3		4	5	7	8		10	11						9	6						14
	2	3		4	5	7	8		10	11		9	1			6							15
	2	3		4	5	7	8		10	11		9	1			6							16
	2	3		4	5	7	8		10	11		9	1			6							17
	2	3	4		5	7	8	9			6		1	11	10								18
	2	3		4	5	7	8	9		11	6		1		10								19
	2	3		4	5	7	8	9	10	11	6		1										20
	2						8					9	1	11	10	5	6	3	4	7			21
	2		3	4	5	7	8	9	6				1	11	10								22
		3	2	4	5	7	8	9	10		6		1	11									23
		3	2	4	5	7		9			6	8	1	11	10								24
		3	2	4	5	7	8	9			6			11	10						1		25
		3	2	4	5	7	8		9		6			11	10						1		26
	2	3	4		5	7						8		11	10	9	6				1		27
		3	2		5		8		6		4			11		9		10		7	1		28
		3	2	4	5	7	8		9		6			11	10						1		29
		3	2	4	5	7	8		9		6			11	10						1		30
		3	2	4	5	7	8		9		6			11	10						1		31
	2			4	5	7		9	8		6			11	10	3					1		32
	2			4	5	7		9			6	8		11	10	3					1		33
	2	3	5	4								10		11		9	6			7	1	8	34
5	26	29	23	28	31	29	27	20	24	18	18	11	19	16	17	11	4	2	1	4	10	1	
				1	2	4	11	6	15	1		1		4	6	3				1			

2 own-goals

	2	3		4	5	7	8	9	10	11	6		1										Q
		3	2	4	5	7	8	9	10	11	6		1										1
		3	2	4	5	7	8	9	10	11	6		1										R
		3	2	4	5	7	8	9	10	11	6		1										2R
	1	4	3	4	4	4	4	4	4	4	4		4										
							1	1															

1	2	3		4	5	7	8	9	10	11	6												1
1	2	3	4	8	5	7		9	10	11	6												2
1	2	3	4		5	7	8			11	6	9			10								3
1		3	2	4	5	7	8		9	11	6				10								4
1	2		3	4	5	7	8	9	10	11	6												5
	2	3		4	5	7	8	9	10	11	6		1										6
	2	3	5	4				9	10		6		1	11	8	7							7
	2	3		4	5	7	8	9	10	11	6		1										8
	2	3	6	4	5			9	10	11			1		8	7							9
	2	3	6	4	5	7	8	9	10	11			1										10
	2	3	6	4	5		8	9	10	11			1	7									11
	2	3	6	4	5	7	8	9	10	11			1										12
	2	3	6		5	7	8	9					1	11	10		4						13
	2	3		4	5	7	8		10	11		9	1				6						14
		3	2	4	5	7		9	10		6		1	11	8								15
		3	2	4	5	7	8	9	10		6		1	11									16
		3	2	4	5	7	8		9		6			11	10						1		17
	2	3	4		5	7	8	9	10	11	6										1		18
		3	2	4	5				8		6	9		11	10	7					1		19
	2	3		4	5	7			8		6			11	10	9					1		20
5	15	19	15	17	19	16	14	14	18	13	14	3	11	8	9	4	2				4		
				1	1	8	8	8	14	1	2	4		3		1							

1 own-goal

1905-06

Manager: Robert Jack

1	Sep	2	(h)	Norwich C	W 2-0	Jack, Buck
2		4	(a)	Luton T	D 0-0	
3		9	(a)	Northampton T	W 4-1	Buck 4
4		23	(h)	Reading	W 2-1	Wilcox 2
5		30	(a)	Watford	W 2-0	Wilcox, Buck
6	Oct	7	(h)	Brighton & HA	W 1-0	C.Clark
7		14	(a)	West Ham U	L 1-2	Leech
8		21	(h)	Fulham	D 0-0	
9		28	(a)	Queen's Park R	L 0-2	
10	Nov	4	(h)	Bristol R	L 1-2	Briercliffe
11		11	(h)	New Brompton	D 1-1	Wilcox
12		18	(h)	Portsmouth	W 3-1	Wilcox 2, Buck
13		25	(a)	Swindon T	L 1-2	Buchanan
14	Dec	2	(h)	Millwall	W 2-0	Briercliffe, Buck
15		16	(h)	Totttenham H	W 2-1	Owens, Briercliffe
16		23	(a)	Brentford	L 0-1	
17		25	(h)	Southampton	D 0-0	
18		30	(a)	Norwich C	L 1-2	Corrin
19	Jan	6	(h)	Northampton T	L 0-2	
20		27	(a)	Reading	L 1-3	Buck
21	Feb	10	(a)	Brighton & HA	D 0-0	
22		17	(h)	West Ham U	W 4-2	Buck, Wilcox 2, Saul
23		24	(a)	Fulham	L 1-3	Wilcox
24	Mar	3	(h)	Queen's Park R	D 1-1	Buck
25		10	(a)	Bristol R	W 5-1	Wilcox 2, Buck, Leech, Wright
26		17	(h)	New Brompton	W 5-0	Saul, Briercliffe, Wilcox 2, Buck
27		24	(a)	Portsmouth	D 1-1	Buck
28		31	(h)	Swindon T	W 3-0	Briercliffe, Wright, Corrin
29	Apr	7	(a)	Millwall	W 1-0	Wright
30		14	(h)	Luton T	W 2-0	A.Clark, Buck
31		16	(a)	Southampton	L 0-1	
32		21	(a)	Tottenham H	W 1-0	Buck
33		25	(h)	Watford	L 2-3	Wright, Jack
34		28	(h)	Brentford	W 2-0	Wilcox, C.Clark

FINAL LEAGUE POSITION: 5th in Southern League

Appearances
Goals

FA Cup

Q	Jan	13	(a)	New Crusaders	W 6-3	Banks, Wilcox 3, Briercliffe, Saul	
1	Feb	3	(a)	Aston Villa	D 0-0		22,843
R		7	(h)	Aston Villa	L 1-5	Buck	

Appearances
Goals

Western League

1	Sep	11	(a)	Brentford	D 0-0	
2		16	(a)	Southampton	D 1-1	Bauchop
3		27	(h)	Queen's Park R	W 2-1	Buchanan, C.Clark
4	Oct	2	(a)	Tottenham H	W 2-0	Wright, Wilcox
5		11	(a)	Portsmouth	D 0-0	
6		30	(a)	Millwall	L 1-2	Wilcox
7	Nov	13	(a)	Fulham	D 2-2	Wright 2
8		29	(h)	West Ham U	W 3-2	Leech, Wilcox 2
9	Dec	6	(h)	Portsmouth	D 2-2	Wilcox, Briercliffe
10		9	(h)	Reading	L 1-2	Wilcox
11		26	(a)	Bristol R	D 3-3	Owens, Saul, Buck
12	Jan	1	(a)	West Ham U	L 2-3	Owens 2
13		20	(h)	Southampton	W 2-1	Buck, Corrin
14		24	(h)	Fulham	D 1-1	Wilcox
15	Feb	14	(h)	Brentford	W 4-0	Corrin 2, Wilcox, Buck
16		28	(a)	Reading	W 2-1	Owens 2
17	Mar	21	(h)	Tottenham H	D 0-0	
18		28	(h)	Millwall	W 4-1	Briercliffe 2, Godley 2
19	Apr	13	(h)	Bristol R	W 2-0	Briercliffe, Owens
20		17	(a)	Queen's Park R	L 0-1	

Appearances
Goals

Sutcliffe	Saul	Clark A	Leech	Clark C	Mortimer	Briercliffe	Buck	Wilcox	Wright	Jack	Buchanan	Corrin	Owens	Bauchop	McNeil	Black	Horne	Godley	Banks	
1	2	3	4	5	6	7	8	9	10	11										1
1	2	3	4	5	6	7	8	9			10	11								2
1	2	3	4	5		7	8	9	10	11		6								3
1	2	3	4	5		7	8	9	10			11	6							4
1	2	3	4	5		7	8	9	10			11	6							5
1			4	5		7		9	10		6			11	2	3		8		6
1	2	3	4	5		7		9	10		6	11						8		7
1	2	3	4	5		7		9	10	11	8	6								8
1	2	3	4	5		7	8	9	10		6	11								9
1	2		4	5		7	8	9	10	11	6				3					10
1	2	3	4	5		7	8	9	10		6	11								11
1	2	3	4	5		7	8	9	10		6	11								12
1	2	3	4	5		7	8	9	10		6	11								13
1	2	3	4	5		7	8	9	10		6	11								14
	2	3	4	5		7		8	10		6	11	9				1			15
	2		4			7	8	5	10	6		11	9		3		1			16
	3		4			7	8	5	10			11	9		2		1		6	17
	3		4			7	8	5	10			11	9		2		1		6	18
1			4	5		7	8		10	11		6	9		2	3				19
	2	3		5		7	8	9	10		6	11	4				1			20
	2		4	5		7	8	6			10	11	9			3	1			21
	3		4	5			8	9	10		6	11	7		2		1			22
	3		4	5			8	9	10		6	11	7		2		1			23
	2		4	5		7	8	6	10			11	9		3		1			24
	2	3	4	5		7	8	9	10			11					1		6	25
	2	3	4	5		7	8	9	10			11					1		6	26
1	2	3		5		7	8	4				11	9					10	6	27
1	2	3	4	5		7	8	9	10			11							6	28
1	2	3	4	5		7	8	9	10			11							6	29
1	2	3	4			7	8	5	10			11	9						6	30
1	2	3		5		7		9		11	4	10						8	6	31
1	2	3	4	5		7	8	9	10			11							6	32
1	2	3	4	5				9	10	11			7	8					6	33
1	2		4	5				9	10	11	6		7	8	3					34
23	32	23	31	30	2	30	27	33	30	9	17	29	16	3	10	3	11	4	11	
	2	1	2	2		5	16	14	4	2	1	2	1							

	2	3	4	5		7	8	9	10			11					1		6	Q
	2	3	4	5		7	8	6	10			11	9				1			1
	2	3	4	5		7	8	6	10			11	9				1			R
	3	3	3	3		3	3	3	3			3	2				3		1	
	1					1		3											1	

1		3	4	5		7	8	9	10	11		6			2					1
1	6	3	4	5			8		10	11			9	7	2					2
1		3	4	5		7		9			10		6	11	2			8		3
1	2	3	4	5		7	8	9	10	11	6									4
1	2	3	4	5		7		9		11	6	10						8		5
1	2	3	4	5		7	8	9		11	6	10								6
1	2		4	5		7	8	9	10		6	11			3					7
	2	3	4	5		7		9	10		6	11	8				1			8
	2	3	4	5		7		9	10		6	11		8			1			9
	2	3	4	5		7	8	9	10			11	6				1			10
	3		4			7	8	5	10			11	9		2		1		6	11
						7	4	5	10	11		6	9		2	3	1	8		12
	2	3	4	5		7	8	9	10			11					1		6	13
	3			5			8	4			10	11	9	7	2		1		6	14
	2		4	5			8	9	10		6	11	7		3		1			15
	2		4	5		7		8	10	11	6		9			3	1			16
	2	3	4	5		7	8	9	10			11					1		6	17
1	2	3	4	5		7		9	10			11						8	6	18
1	2	3	4			7	8	5	10		6	11	9							19
1	2	3	4	5		7		9	10		8	11							6	20
10	17	14	18	17		17	13	19	16	7	12	16	10	4	8	2	10	4	6	
	1		1	1		4	3	8	3		1	3	6	1				2		

1906-07

Manager: William Fullerton

1	Sep	1	(a)	Portsmouth	L	0-4	
2		8	(h)	New Brompton	W	2-1	McLaughlin, McKenzie
3		15	(h)	Bristol R	W	3-0	Smith, McKenzie, Wright
4		22	(a)	Brighton & HA	L	1-4	Thorpe
5		24	(a)	Millwall	L	0-4	
6		29	(h)	Reading	W	4-0	Smith, McKenzie 3
7	Oct	6	(a)	Watford	D	2-2	Smith, McKenzie
8		13	(h)	Northampton T	D	1-1	Thorpe
9		20	(a)	Queen's Park R	D	0-0	
10		27	(h)	Fulham	D	1-1	Briercliffe
11	Nov	3	(a)	Southampton	L	1-3	Swann
12		10	(a)	West Ham U	D	0-0	
13		14	(h)	Millwall	L	2-3	Swann, McKenzie
14		17	(a)	Tottenham H	L	2-4	McKenzie, Smith
15		24	(h)	Swindon T	D	2-2	Smith, Coaker
16	Dec	1	(a)	Norwich C	W	1-0	Smith
17		8	(h)	Luton T	D	0-0	
18		15	(a)	Crystal P	W	2-0	Swann, Smith
19		22	(h)	Brentford	D	2-2	Swann, Thorpe
20		25	(h)	Leyton	W	3-0	Garrett, Briercliffe, Swann
21	Jan	5	(a)	New Brompton	W	2-0	Swann, McKenzie
22		19	(a)	Bristol R	L	0-2	
23		26	(h)	Brighton & HA	D	0-0	
24	Feb	2	(a)	Reading	L	1-2	Wright
25		9	(h)	Watford	L	1-2	McKenzie
26		16	(a)	Northampton T	L	0-1	
27		23	(h)	Queen's Park R	W	2-1	Briercliffe, Thorpe
28	Mar	2	(a)	Fulham	L	0-2	
29		9	(h)	Southampton	W	1-0	Burch
30		16	(a)	West Ham U	D	0-0	
31		23	(h)	Tottenham H	D	0-0	
32		27	(h)	Portsmouth	L	0-1	
33		30	(a)	Swindon T	L	0-1	
34	Apr	1	(a)	Leyton	L	1-2	Swann
35		6	(h)	Norwich C	W	2-0	Swann, Briercliffe
36		13	(a)	Luton T	L	2-3	Smith 2
37		20	(h)	Crystal P	D	0-0	
38		27	(a)	Brentford	L	1-2	Wright

FINAL LEAGUE POSITION: 15th in Southern League

Appearances
Goals

FA Cup

1	Jan	12	(a)	Millwall	L	0-2		14,230

Appearances
Goals

Western League (Section B)

1	Sep	3	(a)	Tottenham H	D	0-0	
2	Oct	3	(h)	Portsmouth	W	1-0	Briercliffe
3		10	(h)	Southampton	W	1-0	Burch
4		24	(a)	Portsmouth	L	0-1	
5		31	(h)	Millwall	W	5-0	Swann 5
6	Nov	5	(a)	Millwall	D	0-0	
7	Dec	3	(a)	Southampton	W	2-1	Garrett, Wright
8		12	(h)	Tottenham H	D	2-2	Swann, Thorpe
9		26	(a)	West Ham U	L	2-6	Briercliffe, Swann
10	Mar	29	(h)	West Ham U	W	3-0	Swann, Thorpe, Garrett

Appearances
Goals

Sutcliffe	Noon	Orrell	Smith	Clark	Thorpe	Garrett	Swann	McKenzie	Wright	Corrin	Black	Fullerton	Briercliffe	McLoughlin	Coaker	Brown	Burch	Johnson	Lintott	Haynes	Simmons	Cudlipp	Hughes	
1	2	3	4	5	6	7	8	9	10	11														1
1		2	8	4	5			9	10		3	6	7	11										2
1		2	8	4	5			9	10		3	6	7	11										3
1	3	2	8	4	5			9	10			6	7	11										4
1	3	2	8	4	5			9	10			6	7	11										5
1	3	2	8	4	5			9				6	7	10	11									6
1	3	2	8	5	4		10	9				6	7	11										7
1	6	2	8		5			9			3	4	7	10	11									8
1	2		8	4	5			9	10			6	7	11		3								9
1	2	3	8	6	5			9	10			4	7	11										10
1		3	4	6	5		9	8	10			2	7	11										11
1	2	3	4		5	7	9	10		11		6	8											12
1	4	3		6	5		9	11					7	10		2	8							13
1	2	3	8	6	5			9				4	7	10	11									14
1	2	3	8	6	5			9	10			4	7		11									15
1	6	2	8		5	7	9		10		3	4		11										16
1	4	2	8	6	5	7	9		10		3			11										17
1	4	2	8	6	5	7	9		10		3			11										18
	2		8	6	5	7	9	10			3	4		11				1						19
1	2	3		4	5	7	9	10				6	8	11										20
		2		6	5	7	9	10				3	8	11				1	4					21
1	2	3		6	5	7		9	10			4	8	11										22
1	2			6	5	7	9		10		3	4	8	11										23
1	2	3		6	5	7	9		10			4	8	11										24
	2	3	8	6	5			9	10			4	7	11				1						25
	2	3		6	5	7	9		10			4	8	11				1						26
1	2	3		6	5	7	9		10			4	8							11				27
1	2	3		6	5	7	9		10			4	8							11				28
1			4	6	5	7	9		10		2	3	8				11							29
1		2	8	6	5	7	9		10		3	4					11							30
1		2	8	6	5	7	9		10		3	4					11							31
1		3	4	6		7	9					5	8	10			11					2		32
1	2	3	4	5		7	9		10			6	8	11										33
1	2	3	6	5		7	9		10			4	8	11										34
1	2	3		5		7			10			6	8	11			9				4			35
1	2	3	4	5		7			10			6	8	9			11							36
	2	3	4	5		7			10			6	8	9			11	1						37
	2	3	4	5		7			10			6	8	9				1		11				38
32	30	35	28	35	31	24	22	20	28	2	11	34	31	30	4	2	8	6	1	3	1	1		
			9		4	1	8	10	3				4	1	1		1							

1	2	3		6	5	7	9	10				4	8	11										1
1	1	1		1	1	1	1	1				1	1	1										

1	3		6	5	4	11		9			2		7	10			8							1
1	2	3	8	4	5			9	10			6	7	11										2
1	2	3	8		5	7		9				4		11			10						6	3
1	2	3	4	5				9	10			6	7	8			11							4
1		3	8	6	5		9		10			2	7	11					4					5
1		3	4	6	5		9	8	10			2	7	11										6
1	4	3	8		5	7	9		10		2	6		11										7
1	2	3	4	6	5	7	9		10					8	11									8
	2	3		6	5	7	9	10				4	8	11				1						9
1	2	3	4	6	5	7	9	10	6				8				11							10
9	8	9	9	8	9	6	6	7	1		2	7	7	9	1		4	1	1				1	
					2	2	8						2				1							

1907-08

Manager: None

1	Sep	2	(a)	Northampton T	W	1-0	Stirling
2		7	(h)	Swindon T	W	2-0	Stirling, Ingham
3		14	(a)	Crystal P	W	4-0	Leonard 2, Ingham, Morris
4		21	(h)	Luton T	W	2-1	Ingham 2
5		28	(a)	Brighton & HA	W	2-1	Ingham, Leonard
6	Oct	5	(h)	Portsmouth	W	2-1	Morris, Leonard
7		12	(a)	Bradford	D	0-0	
8		19	(h)	Millwall	D	0-0	
9		26	(a)	Brentford	L	1-2	Morris
10	Nov	2	(h)	Bristol R	W	4-2	Leonard 2, Morris, Leavey
11		9	(a)	Leyton	D	1-1	Leavey
12		16	(h)	Reading	W	3-0	McCormick 2, Leonard
13		23	(a)	Watford	L	0-3	
14		30	(h)	Norwich C	W	1-0	Leavey
15	Dec	14	(h)	Southampton	W	2-0	Ingham 2
16		21	(h)	New Brompton	W	1-0	Stirling
17		25	(a)	Queen's Park R	D	0-0	
18		28	(a)	West Ham U	D	1-1	McIntyre
19	Jan	4	(a)	Swindon T	L	0-1	
20		18	(a)	Luton T	D	0-0	
21		20	(a)	Tottenham H	W	1-0	Morris
22		25	(a)	Brighton & HA	L	2-3	McCormick, Burch
23	Feb	8	(h)	Bradford	W	2-1	Allman 2
24		15	(a)	Millwall	L	0-2	
25		22	(h)	Brentford	W	2-1	Stirling, Allman
26		29	(a)	Bristol R	L	0-1	
27	Mar	7	(h)	Leyton	W	3-0	Ingham 2, Morris
28		14	(a)	Reading	W	1-0	Ingham
29		21	(h)	Watford	D	1-1	Allman
30		25	(a)	Portsmouth	L	0-3	
31		28	(h)	Norwich C	L	1-2	Allman
32	Apr	4	(h)	Northampton T	D	1-1	Leonard
33		8	(h)	Crystal P	D	1-1	Ingham
34		11	(a)	Southampton	D	1-1	Holden
35		17	(h)	Queen's Park R	D	1-1	Holden
36		18	(a)	New Brompton	W	3-0	Morris, Clark, Stirling
37		20	(h)	Tottenham H	W	1-0	Ingham
38		25	(h)	West Ham U	W	2-0	Holden, Allman

FINAL LEAGUE POSITION: 2nd in Southern League

Appearances
Goals

FA Cup

1	Jan	11	(h)	Barnsley	W	1-0	Leonard	17,539
2	Feb	1	(h)	Crystal P	W	2-3	Ingham, Morris	17,830

Appearances
Goals

Western League

1	Sep	9	(a)	Leyton	L	1-3	Stirling
2		16	(a)	Southampton	L	1-2	Morris
3		18	(h)	Leyton	W	3-0	McCormick, Burch, Morris
4	Oct	2	(h)	Southampton	W	1-0	Ingham
5		9	(h)	Brighton & HA	D	0-0	
6		14	(a)	Queen's Park R	W	1-0	Holden
7	Nov	13	(a)	Portsmouth	L	1-3	Leavey
8		20	(h)	Queen's Park R	L	0-2	
9		25	(a)	Brentford	D	0-0	
10	Dec	4	(h)	Brentford	W	2-0	Leonard, Nugent
11		11	(a)	Brighton & HA	L	2-3	Leonard, Allman
12	Jan	1	(h)	Portsmouth	W	2-1	Nugent 2

Appearances
Goals

Sutcliffe	Butler	Atterbury	McCormick	Clark	McIntyre	Stirling	Leonard	Ingham	Morris	Holden	Burch	Wake	Black	Leavey	Allman	Nugent	Haynes	Evans	Horne	Cudlipp	Wheaton	
1	2	3	4	5	6	7	8	9	10	11												1
1	2	3	4	5	6	7	8	9	10	11												2
1	2	3	4	5	6		8	9	10	11	7											3
1	2	3	4	5	6		8	9	10	11	7											4
1	2	3	4	5	6	7	8	9	10	11												5
1	2	3	4	5	6		8	9	10	11	7											6
1	2	3	4	5	6		8	9	10	11	7											7
1	2	3	4	5	6	7	8	9	10		11											8
1	2	3	4	5			8	9	10	11	7	6										9
	2		4	5	6		8	9	10		7		3	11					1			10
1	2	3	4	5	6		8	9	10		7			11								11
1	2	3	4	5	6		8	9	10		7			11								12
1	2	3	4	5	6		8	9	10		7			11								13
1	2	3	4		5		8	10			7	6		11		9						14
1	2	3	4	5	6	7		8	10					11	9							15
1	2	3	4	5	6	7	8	10		11					9							16
1	2	3	4	5	6	7	8	9	10					11								17
1	2	3	4	5	6	7	8	9	10					11								18
1	2	3	4	5	6	7	8	10						11	9							19
1	2	3	4	5		7	8	9	10	11		6										20
1	2	3	4	5	6		8		10	11	7				9							21
1	2	3	4	5	6		8			11	7				10	9						22
	2	3	4	5	6	7	8	10		11					9				1			23
	2	3	4	5	6	7	8	10		11					9				1			24
		3	4	5	6	7		8		11			2		9				1			25
	2	3	4	5	6	7	8	10		11					9				1			26
	2	3	4	5	6			8	10	11				7		9			1			27
	2	3	4	5	6			8	10	11				7	9				1			28
	2	3	4	5	6			8	10	11				7	9				1			29
	2	3	4		6	9		8	10	11				7	5				1			30
	2		4	5	6			8	10	11			3	7	9				1			31
1	2	3	4	5	6		8	9		11				7	10							32
1	2	3	4	5	6		8	9	10	11				7								33
1	2		4		6		8	9		11		5	3	7	10							34
1	2	3	4	5	6			8	10	11				7	9							35
1		3		5	6	7	8		10	11		4	2		9							36
1	2	3	4	5	6			10	8	11					9		7					37
1	2	3	4	5	6	7		8		11					10			9				38
28	36	35	37	35	36	16	28	35	27	28	13	5	5	18	19	3	1	1	10			
			3	1	1	5	8	12	7	3	1			3	6							

1	2	3	4	5	6		8	9	10		7			11								1
1	2	3	4	5	6		8	9	10	11	7											2
2	2	2	2	2	2		2	2	2	1	2			1								
							1	1	1													

1	2	3	4	5				9	10	11	7	6				8						1
1	2	3	4	5	6			9	10	11	7					8						2
1	2	3	4	5	6		8	9	10	11	7											3
1	2	3	4	5	6		8	9	10	11	7											4
1	2	3	4	5	6		8	9	10		7					11						5
1		3	4	5				9	10	11	7	6				8				2		6
1	2	3	4	5	6		8	10			7			11		9			1			7
1		3	4	5	6	7	8		10		9			11						2		8
1	2	3	4	5	6	7		9	10					11							8	9
	2	3		5	4	7	8	10				6		11					1		9	10
	2	3	5		4	7	8	10				6		11	9				1			11
	2		4	5					10	11	7	6	3		9	8			1			12
8	10	11	11	11	9	4	7	10	9	6	9	5	1	5	2	6			4	2	2	
			1			1	2	1	2	1	1			1	1	3						

1908-09

Manager: None

1	Sep	5	(a)	Millwall	W	1-0	Hakin
2		12	(h)	Brentford	L	0-1	
3		19	(a)	Queen's Park R	L	0-1	
4		26	(h)	Crystal P	D	0-0	
5	Oct	3	(a)	Coventry C	W	2-0	Wilcox, Hakin
6		10	(h)	Brentford	W	2-0	Holden 2
7		17	(a)	Bristol R	L	0-2	
8		24	(h)	Luton T	D	1-1	Warburton
9		31	(a)	Watford	D	1-1	Evenson
10	Nov	7	(h)	Swindon T	D	1-1	Holden
11		11	(a)	Exeter C	L	1-2	Clark
12		14	(a)	Norwich C	D	0-0	
13		21	(h)	Portsmouth	L	1-2	Holden
14		28	(a)	Reading	D	0-0	
15	Dec	5	(h)	West Ham U	W	2-0	Wilcox, Ingham
16		12	(a)	Soauthampton	L	2-4	Hakin 2
17		19	(h)	Northampton T	L	0-2	
18		25	(a)	New Brompton	W	2-1	Wilcox, Warburton
19		28	(a)	West Ham U	L	0-4	
20	Jan	2	(h)	Millwall	L	0-3	
21		9	(a)	Brighton & HA	W	2-1	Warburton, Leavey
22		23	(h)	Southend U	W	2-1	Wilcox, Hindmarsh
23		30	(a)	Crystal P	W	1-0	Hakin
24	Feb	10	(h)	Coventry C	W	4-1	Hakin, Holden, Hindmarsh, Warburton
25		13	(a)	Brentford	L	0-1	
26		27	(a)	Luton T	W	3-1	Hakin 2, Hindmarsh
27	Mar	6	(h)	Watford	W	2-0	Hakin, Ingham
28		10	(h)	Exeter C	W	4-0	Hakin 3, Hindmarsh
29		13	(a)	Swindon T	L	0-5	
30		15	(a)	Leyton	D	1-1	Hindmarsh
31		17	(h)	Bristol R	L	0-1	
32		20	(h)	Norwich C	W	2-1	Wilcox, Warburton
33		27	(a)	Portsmouth	L	0-2	
34	Apr	3	(h)	Reading	D	1-1	Atterbury
35		9	(h)	New Brompton	D	1-1	Leavey
36		10	(h)	Crystal P	W	2-0	Ingham 2
37		13	(a)	Southend U	L	1-2	Hakin
38		17	(h)	Southampton	D	0-0	
39		21	(h)	Leyton	W	3-0	Wilcox, Ingham, Evans
40		24	(a)	Northampton T	L	1-2	Hakin

FINAL LEAGUE POSITION: 10th in Southern League

Appearances
Goals

FA Cup

1	Jan	16	(h)	Swindon T	W	1-0	Hindmarsh	21,388
2	Feb	6	(h)	Exeter C	W	2-0	Hindmarsh, Leavey	18,624
3		20	(a)	Derby C	L	0-1		22,500

Appearances
Goals

Western League

1	Sep	7	(a)	Brentford	W	2-1	Hindmarsh, Hakin
2		16	(h)	Brentford	W	1-0	Wilcox
3		21	(a)	Bristol C	W	1-0	Ingham
4		30	(h)	Bristol R	L	1-2	Wilcox
5	Oct	5	(a)	West Ham U	W	1-0	Hakin
6		14	(h)	Portsmouth	W	1-0	Holden
7		21	(a)	Portsmouth	L	0-3	
8		28	(h)	West Ham U	W	2-1	Wilcox 2
9	Nov	4	(h)	Southampton	L	0-1	
10		16	(a)	Southampton	L	0-1	
11	Dec	7	(a)	Millwall	L	2-3	Warburton, Wilcox
12		16	(h)	Millwall	D	1-1	Hakin

Appearances
Goals

Sutcliffe	Butler	Atterbury	McCormick	Clark	McIntyre	Leavey	Ingham	Hindmarsh	Hakin	Holden	Black	Cook	Wilcox	Evenson	Cudlipp	Warburton	Raymond	Horne	Simmons	Evans	Peard	Johnson	Carmen	
1	2	3	4	5	6	7	8	9	10	11														1
1	2		4	5	6	7	8	9	10	11	3													2
1	2		4	5	6		10		9	11	3	7	8											3
1	2	3		5	6		9	10		11		7	8	4										4
1	2		5		6				10	11		7	8	4	3	9								5
1	2	3	4		6				10	11		7	8	5		9								6
1	2	3	4		6		8		10	11		7		5		9								7
1	2	3	4		6	7			9	11			8	5		10								8
1	2	3	4	5		7			8	11			9	6		10								9
1	2	3		5	6	7	8	9		11			4			10								10
1		3	4	5	6		8			11		7	9		2		10							11
1	2	3		5	6	7	8		9	11			4			10								12
1	2	3		5	6	7	8		9	11			4			10								13
1	2	3	9	5		7	10			11			8	4		6								14
1	2	3		5	6	7	8			11			9	4		10								15
1	2	3		5	6	7	8		9	11				4		10								16
		3	4	5	6	11	8		9	10		7				2		1						17
		3	4	5		7	8			11			9	6	2	10		1						18
		3	4	5		7	8			11			9	6	2	10		1						19
1		3	4	5		7	8		10	11			9		2	6								20
	2	3	4	5		7		9		11			6	8		10		1						21
1	2	3	4	5		7		9		11			8	6		10								22
1		3	4		6	7			9	11			8	5	2	10								23
1	2	3	4		6	7		9	8	11				5		10								24
1		3	4		6	7		9	8	11				5	2	10								25
	2	3	4			7		9	8	11			6	5		10		1						26
	2	3	4			7	9		8	11			6	5		10		1						27
	2	3	4			7		9	8	11			6	5		10		1						28
		3					10	9	8	11		7	4	5	2	6		1						29
		3					10	9	8	11		7	4	5		2		1	6					30
	2	3					8		9	11		7	4	5		10		1	6					31
		3				7	10		8	11	2		4	5		9		1	6					32
		3		5		7		9	8	11			4	6		10		1	2					33
	2	3		5		7		9	8	11			4	6		10		1						34
	2	3	6			7		9	8	11			4	5		10		1						35
	2	3	4			7	10		8	11			6	5				1		9				36
1		3		5		7	10		8	11			4	6					2	9				37
1		3	4	5		11	8		7				9	6	2	10								38
	2	3	4			11	8						6	5		10		1		9	7			39
		3	4	5					8				10	6		9		1			7	2	11	40
23	26	37	27	23	18	30	25	15	30	37	3	10	33	31	8	33	1	17	5	3	2	1	1	
		1		1		2	5	5	14	5			6	1		5				1				

	2	3	4	5		7		9		11			8	6		10		1						1
	2	3	4		6	7		9	8	11				5		10		1						2
	2	3	4		6	7		9	8	11				5		10		1						3
	3	3	3	1	2	3		3	2	3			1	3		3		3						
						1		2																

1	2	3	4	5	6	7		9	10	11			8											
1	2		4		6		8		10	11	3	7	9	5										1
1	2		3	5	6		9			11		7	8	4			10							2
1	2		3	5	6	11	9			10		7	8	4										3
1	2				6		8		10	11		7	4	5	3	9								4
1	2	3	4		6	7			10	11			8	5		9								5
1	2	3	4		6	7		9	10	11			8	5										6
1	2	3	4	5		7				11			8	6		9	10							7
1	2	3		5		7	8		9	11			4			6	10							8
1	2	3		5	6	7	8		9	11			4			10								9
1	2	3		5	6	7	8			11			9	4		10								10
			4	5	6	11	8		9	10		7			2	3		1						11
11	11	7	8	8	10	9	8	2	8	12	1	5	11	8	2	7	3	1						
							1	1	3	1			5			1								

1909-10

Manager: None

1	Sep	1	(a)	Southampton	L 0-1	
2		4	(h)	New Brompton	L 1-2	Burch
3		8	(h)	Southampton	D 1-1	Leavey
4		11	(a)	Northampton T	L 1-5	Lamb
5		18	(h)	Queen's Park R	L 0-2	
6		25	(a)	Luton T	L 2-3	Evans, Burch
7	Oct	2	(h)	Swindon T	D 0-0	
8		9	(a)	Crystal P	L 0-3	
9		11	(a)	Brentford	D 2-2	Hindmarsh, Atterbury
10		16	(h)	Brighton & HA	D 2-2	Atterbury, Raymond
11		20	(h)	Millwall	W 2-0	Wood, Hindmarsh
12		23	(a)	West Ham U	L 1-4	Raymond
13		25	(a)	Millwall	L 0-2	
14		30	(h)	Portsmouth	W 2-0	McCormick, Raymond
15	Nov	6	(a)	Bristol R	D 0-0	
16		13	(h)	Norwich C	W 1-0	Hindmarsh
17		20	(h)	West Ham U	D 0-0	
18		27	(h)	Coventry C	W 6-0	Raymond 2, Atterbury, Wood, Butler, Griffiths
19	Dec	18	(a)	Southend U	D 0-0	
20		25	(h)	Exeter C	W 1-0	Burch
21		27	(a)	Exeter C	W 4-2	Burch 2, Griffiths 2
22	Jan	8	(a)	New Brompton	D 1-1	Hindmarsh
23		22	(h)	Northampton T	L 0-1	
24		29	(a)	Queen's Park R	L 1-2	McCormick
25	Feb	5	(h)	Luton T	W 4-2	Hindmarsh 2, Atterbury, Raymond
26		12	(a)	Swindon T	L 1-4	Hindmarsh
27		19	(h)	Crystal P	W 2-0	Hindmarsh, Griffiths
28		26	(a)	Brighton & HA	L 0-1	
29	Mar	12	(a)	Portsmouth	L 0-4	
30		16	(h)	Reading	D 0-0	
31		19	(h)	Bristol R	W 2-0	Hindmarsh, Wood
32		25	(a)	Leyton	L 0-2	
33		26	(a)	Norwich C	W 4-2	Hindmarsh, Burch 2, McCormick
34		30	(h)	Leyton	W 4-0	Hindmarsh, Raymond, Lamb, Newton (og)
35	Apr	2	(h)	Brentford	W 3-0	McCormick, Lamb, Griffiths
36		6	(h)	Croydon Common	W 4-0	Burch, Hindmarsh 2, Lamb
37		9	(a)	Coventry C	D 2-2	Lamb, Hindmarsh
38		16	(h)	Watford	W 2-0	Raymond, Burch
39		20	(a)	Watford	L 0-3	
40		23	(a)	Reading	D 2-2	Atterbury, Evans
41		27	(a)	Croydon Common	L 0-1	
42		30	(h)	Southend U	W 3-0	Raymond, Hindmarsh 2

FINAL LEAGUE POSITION: 11th in Southern League

Appearances
Goals

FA Cup

1	Jan	15	(h)	Tottenham H	D 1-1	Griffithss	11,437
R		19	(a)	Tottenham H	L 1-7	Burch	16,000

Appearances
Goals

Sutcliffe	Butler	Atterbury	McCormick	Evenson	Wilcox	Griffiths	Wood	Hindmarsh	Burch	Lamb	Fagen	Broome	Boyd	Leavey	Simmons	Baker	Horne	Evans	Raymond	Tomlinson	Caddy	
1	2	3	4	5	6	7	8	9	10	11												1
1	3		4	5	6		8	9	7	11	2	10										2
1	2	3	5		4		8	9	7			10	6	11								3
1	2	3	4		5		8	9	7	11		10			6							4
1	2	3			5		8	9	7	11		10	6			4						5
	2	3			5		10	9	7				6	11		4	1	8				6
	2	3	5		4	9	10		7					11		6	1	8				7
	2	3			4	8	10	9	7				6	11		5	1					8
	2	3			5		10	9	7				6	11		4	1		8			9
1	2	3	5		4		10	9	7					11		6			8			10
	2	3	5		4		10	9	7					11		6	1		8			11
	2	3	5		4		10	9	7					11		6	1		8			12
	2	3	5		4		10	9	7					11		6	1		8			13
1	2	3	5		4	7	10	9	11							6			8			14
1	2	3	4		5	7	10	9	11							6			8			15
	2	3	4		5	7		9	11							6	1		8	10		16
	2	3	4		5	7	10	9		11						6	1		8			17
	2	3	4		5	7	10	9		11						6	1		8			18
	2	3	4	6	5	7	10	9		11							1		8			19
1	2	3	4		5	7		9	10	11						6			8			20
		3	4		5	7		9	10	11	2					6	1		8			21
		3	4		5	7		9	10	11	2					6	1		8			22
1	3			5	4	7	9		8	11	2					6					10	23
1		3	4		5	7	8	9	10	11	2					6						24
1		3		5	4	7		9	10	11	2					6			8			25
1		3	8	5	4	7		9	10	11	2					6						26
1	2	3	4	5	8	7		9	10	11						6						27
1	2		4	5				9	10	11	3			7		6			8			28
	2	3	4		5			9	10	11				7		6	1		8			29
1	2	3		5	4			9	10	11				7		6			8			30
1	2	3	4		5		10	9		11				7		6			8			31
1		3	4	5	8		10	9	7	11	2					6						32
1		3	4	5	8		10	9	7	11	2					6						33
1	3		4	5	8			9	7	11	2					6			10			34
1	3		4		5	7		9	8	11	2					6			10			35
1	3		4		5	7		9	8	11	2					6			10			36
1	3		4		5	7		9	8	11	2					6			10			37
1	2	3	4		5	7		9	8	11						6			10			38
1	2	3	4		5	7		9	8	11						6					10	39
1	2	3	4	5	10	7		9	8	11						6						40
1	2	3	4	5	10	7		9	8	11						6						41
1	2		4	5	8	7		9		11	3					6			10			42
28	35	34	36	15	41	25	23	40	37	30	15	4	5	13	1	37	14	2	25	1	2	
	1	5	4			5	3	16	9	5				1				2	9			

1 own-goal

	2	3	4		5	7	8	9	10	11						6	1					I
	2	3	4		5		8	9	10	11				7		6	1					R
	2	2	2		2	1	2	2	2	2				1		2	2					
						1			1													

1910-11

Manager: Robert Jack

1	Sep	3	(a)	Portsmouth	D	0-0	
2		10	(h)	Northampton T	D	0-0	
3		17	(a)	Brighton & HA	L	1-2	Holden
4		24	(h)	Exeter C	D	0-0	
5	Oct	1	(a)	Swindon T	L	0-4	
6		8	(h)	Bristol R	L	1-2	Baker
7		15	(a)	Crystal P	L	1-6	Burch
8		22	(h)	Brentford	W	2-0	Wood, Walker
9		29	(a)	Leyton	L	0-1	
10	Nov	5	(h)	Watford	L	0-2	
11		12	(h)	Norwich C	W	1-0	Raymond
12		19	(a)	Southampton	L	0-5	
13		26	(h)	Southend U	L	0-1	
14	Dec	3	(a)	Coventry C	L	1-6	Burch
15		10	(h)	New Brompton	W	3-0	Raymond, Dixon, Malcolm
16		17	(a)	Millwall	W	1-0	Boden
17		24	(h)	Queen's Park R	D	1-1	Dixon
18		26	(a)	West Ham U	L	0-4	
19		27	(h)	West Ham U	W	1-0	Burch
20		31	(h)	Portsmouth	W	4-0	Raymond 2, Dixon, Malcolm
21	Jan	7	(a)	Northampton T	W	1-0	Dixon
22		21	(h)	Brighton & HA	D	2-2	Burch, Raymond
23		28	(a)	Exeter C	W	3-1	Raymond, Boden 2
24	Feb	11	(a)	Bristol R	W	3-1	Boden, Burch, Raymond
25		18	(h)	Crystal P	W	5-1	Dixon, Boden, Raymond 2, Burch
26		25	(a)	Brentford	W	2-1	Dixon, Boden
27	Mar	4	(h)	Leyton	W	2-1	Raymond, Burch
28		11	(a)	Watford	L	0-2	
29		18	(a)	Norwich C	L	1-3	Burch
30		25	(h)	Southampton	D	1-1	Boden
31		29	(h)	Swindon T	D	1-1	Raymond
32	Apr	1	(a)	Southend U	L	2-3	Raymond, Boden
33		8	(h)	Coventry C	W	6-0	Boden 2, Wilcox 2, Dixon, McCormick
34		14	(h)	Luton T	W	4-0	Green, Holden, Griffiths, Burch
35		15	(a)	New Brompton	D	1-1	Worden
36		17	(a)	Luton T	D	0-0	
37		22	(h)	Millwall	W	3-2	Dixon, Boden, Holden
38		29	(a)	Queen's Park R	L	0-1	

FINAL LEAGUE POSITION: 8th in Southern League

Appearances
Goals

FA Cup

1	Jan	14	(a)	Derby C	L	1-2	Dixon	16,000

Appearances
Goals

Sutcliffe	Butler	Atterbury	Barton	Wilcox	Baker	Griffiths	Raymond	Burch	Wood	Holden	Hosking	Boden	Black	Walker	Burgoyne	Caddy	Horne	Jack	Malcolm	Dixon	Green	Haynes	Crews	Worden	McCormick	
1	2	3	4	5	6	7	8	9	10	11																1
1		3		5	6	7	8	9	10	11	4		2													2
		3		5	6	7	8	9	10	11		4	2				1									3
1		3		5	6	7	8	9	10	11		4	2													4
1		3		5	6		8	7	10	11		4	2	9												5
1		3		5	6		8	7	10	11		4	2	9												6
1	2	3		5	6		8	7		11		4			9	10										7
	2	3		5	4		8	7	10	11		6		9			1									8
	2			5	4		8	7	10	11		6	3	9			1									9
	2			5	4		8	7	10	11		6	3	9			1									10
	2			5	4		8	7	10	11		6	3	9			1									11
	2			5	4		8	7	10	11		6	3	9			1									12
1	2	3		5	4	9	8	7	10	11		6														13
1	2	6		9	4		8	7		11		5	3					10								14
1	2	3		5			8	7		11		6							9	10					4	15
	2	3		5		7				11		6					1		9	10	8				4	16
	2	3		5		7	8			11		6					1		9	10					4	17
	1	3		5	6		8	4		11				9						10		7			2	18
1	2	3		5		7	8	9		11		6								10					4	19
1	2	3		5			8	7		11		6							9	10					4	20
1	2	3		5	4			7		11		6							9	10	8					21
	2	3		5	6		8	7		11		9					1			10					4	22
1	2	3		5	6		8	7		11		9								10					4	23
1	2	3		5	6		8	7		11		9								10					4	24
1	2	3		5	6		8	7		11		9								10					4	25
1	2	3		5	6		8	7		11		9								10					4	26
1	2	3		5	6		8	7		11		9								10					4	27
1		3		5	6	7		8		11		9	2							10					4	28
1		3		5			8	7		11		6	2	9						10					4	29
1		3		5	6		8	7		11		9	2							10					4	30
1		3		5	6		8	7		11		9								10			2		4	31
1		3		5	6		8	7		11		9								10			2		4	32
1	2	3		5	6		8	7		11		9								10					4	33
1	2	3		5	6	8		9		11										10	7				4	34
	2	3		5	6			7	8	11							1			10				9	4	35
	2	3		5	6			7		11							1			10	8			9	4	36
	2	3		5	6		8	7	9	11							1			10					4	37
1	2	3		5				7	8	11		6		9						10					4	38
25	28	34	1	38	31	10	31	36	15	38	1	30	13	10	1	1	12	1	5	24	4	1	2	2	23	
				2	1	1	12	9	1	3		11		1					2	8	1			1	1	

Sutcliffe	Butler	Atterbury	Barton	Wilcox	Baker	Griffiths	Raymond	Burch	Wood	Holden	Hosking	Boden	Black	Walker	Burgoyne	Caddy	Horne	Jack	Malcolm	Dixon	Green	Haynes	Crews	Worden	McCormick	
1	2	3		5	6		8	7		11		9								10					4	1
1	1	1		1	1		1	1		1		1								1					1	
																				1						

1911-12

Manager: Robert Jack

1	Sep	2	(h)	Queen's Park R	L	0-1	
2		9	(a)	Millwall	D	1-1	Boden
3		16	(h)	West Ham U	D	0-0	
4		23	(a)	Bristol R	D	1-1	Dixon
5		30	(h)	Swindon T	D	1-1	Malcolm
6	Oct	6	(a)	Northampton T	L	1-4	Raymond
7		14	(h)	Brighton & HA	W	1-0	Burch
8		24	(a)	Stoke	L	1-2	Burch
9		28	(h)	Coventry C	W	4-1	Boden 2, McCormick, Dixon
10	Nov	4	(a)	Leyton	W	4-0	Burch, Dixon, McCormick, Raymond
11		11	(h)	Norwich C	W	3-0	Burch, Hampson (og), McCormick
12		25	(h)	Southampton	W	1-0	Dixon
13	Dec	2	(a)	Luton T	W	3-0	McCormick, Boden 2
14		9	(a)	Reading	D	1-1	Bartholomew (og)
15		16	(h)	Watford	W	5-1	Raymond, Boden 2, Burch 2
16		23	(a)	New Brompton	W	1-0	Dixon
17		25	(h)	Exeter C	W	3-1	McCormick 2, Burch
18		26	(a)	Exeter C	W	1-0	Boden
19		27	(a)	Swindon T	L	0-2	
20		30	(a)	Queen's Park R	L	0-2	
21	Jan	6	(h)	Millwall	W	2-0	Malcolm, Bowler
22		20	(a)	West Ham U	W	2-0	Boden 2
23		27	(h)	Bristol R	W	2-0	Malcolm 2
24	Feb	10	(h)	Northampton T	W	2-0	Malcolm, Burch
25		17	(a)	Brighton & HA	L	0-1	
26		24	(h)	Stoke	W	3-0	Malcolm, Raymond 2
27		28	(a)	Crystal P	W	1-0	Malcolm
28	Mar	2	(a)	Coventry C	L	1-4	Raymond
29		9	(h)	Leyton	W	3-1	Malcolm 2, Boden
30		16	(a)	Norwich C	D	1-1	Boden
31		23	(h)	Crystal P	W	3-1	Boden 2, Dixon
32		30	(a)	Southampton	L	0-1	
33	Apr	5	(a)	Brentford	L	0-4	
34		6	(h)	Luton T	W	2-0	Boden, Burch
35		8	(h)	Brentford	W	1-0	Dixon
36		13	(h)	Reading	W	4-0	Boden 3, Dixon
37		20	(a)	Watford	W	2-0	Dixon, McCormick
38		27	(h)	New Brompton	W	2-0	Raymond, Boden

FINAL LEAGUE POSITION: 2nd in Southern League

Appearances
Goals

FA Cup

1	Jan	13	(a)	Sunderland	L	1-3	Burch	28,317

Appearances
Goals

Horne	Butler	Atterbury	McCormick	Wilcox	Baker	Burch	Malcolm	Boden	Dixon	Holden	Raymond	Kirkpatrick	Forbes	Sutherland	Bowler	Thom	Sutcliffe	
1	2	3	4	5	6	7	8	9	10	11								1
1	2	3	4	5	6	7		9	10	11	8							2
1	2	3	4	5	6		9		10	11	8	7						3
1		3	4	5	6		9		10	11	8	7	2					4
1	2	3	4	5	6		9		10	11	8	7						5
1	3		4	5	6		9			11	10	7	2	8				6
1	3		4	5	6	8	9		11		10	7	2					7
1	2	3	4	5	6	8	9		11		10	7						8
1	2	3	4	5	6	8		9	11		10	7						9
1	2	3	4	5	6	8		9	11		10	7						10
1	2	3	4	5	6	8		9	11		10	7						11
1	2	3	4	5	6	7		9	11		10	8						12
1	2	3	4	5	6	8		9	11		10	7						13
1	2		4	5	6	8		9	11		10	7	3					14
1	2	3	4	5	6	8		9	11		10	7						15
1	2	3	4	5	6	8		9	11		10				7			16
1	2	3	4	5	6	8		9	11		10	7						17
1	2	3	4	5	6	8		9	11		10	7						18
1	2	3	4	5	6	8		9	11		10	7						19
1	2		4	5	6	8	10	9				7	3		11			20
1	2		4	5	6		8	9				7	3		11	10		21
1	2	3	4	5	6	8	10	9				7			11			22
1	2		4	5	6	8		9			10	7	3		11			23
1	2	3	4	5	6	8	9		11		10	7						24
1	2	3	4	5	6	8	9		11		10	7						25
	2	3	4	5	6	8	9		11		10				7		1	26
1	2	3	4	5	6	8	9		11		10				7			27
1	2	3	4	5	6	8	9		11		10				7			28
1	2	3	4	5	6	8	10	9	11						7			29
1	2	3		5	6	8	4	9	10			7			11			30
1	2	3		5	6	8	4	9	11		10				7			31
1	2	3	4	5	6		10	9	11		8				7			32
1	2	3	4	5	6		8	9			10	7			11			33
	2	3	4	5		8	6	9	11		10				7		1	34
		3	4	5		8	6	9	11		10		2		7		1	35
1		3	4	5		8	6	9	11		10		2		7			36
1	2	3	4	5		8	6	9	11		10				7			37
1	2	3	4	5		8	6	9	11		10				7			38
35	35	32	36	38	33	31	25	27	32	6	32	24	9	1	18	1	3	
			7			9	9	19	9		7				1			

2 own-goals

1	2	3	4	5	6	8		9			10	7			11			1
1	1	1	1	1	1	1		1			1	1			1			
						1												

1912-13

Manager: Robert Jack

1	Sep	2	(a)	Queen's Park R	L	1-2	Burch
2		7	(h)	Bristol R	W	3-1	Wilcox, Dixon, Boden
3		14	(h)	Swindon T	W	3-1	Raymond 2, Burch
4		21	(a)	Portsmouth	D	0-0	
5		28	(h)	Exeter C	W	3-0	Bowler, Raymond, Burch
6	Oct	5	(a)	West Ham U	L	1-3	Burch
7		12	(h)	Brighton & HA	W	1-0	McCormick
8		19	(a)	Coventry C	W	3-2	McCormick, Harris (og), Burch
9		26	(h)	Watford	D	0-0	
10	Nov	2	(a)	Merthyr T	L	2-3	Burch, McCormick
11		9	(h)	Crystal P	D	0-0	
12		16	(h)	Stoke	W	4-0	Bowler 3, Burch
13		23	(a)	Southampton	L	0-2	
14		30	(h)	Reading	L	0-1	
15	Dec	7	(a)	Norwich C	W	3-0	Raymond, Bowler, Dixon
16		21	(h)	Northampton T	D	1-1	Burch
17		26	(a)	Brentford	D	2-2	Burch, Bowler
18		28	(h)	Bristol R	W	3-1	Dixon, Bowler, McCormick
19	Jan	4	(a)	Swindon T	D	2-2	Burch 2
20		18	(h)	Portsmouth	W	2-0	Bell, Burch
21		25	(a)	Exeter C	L	0-1	
22	Feb	8	(h)	West Ham U	L	0-2	
23		15	(a)	Brighton & HA	W	4-1	Kirkpatrick, Burch, Bowler, Dixon
24		22	(h)	Coventry C	W	4-1	Bowler 2, Burch 2
25	Mar	1	(a)	Watford	W	1-0	Dixon
26		8	(h)	Merthyr T	W	5-0	Burch 3, Bowler, Russell (og)
27		12	(h)	Brentford	W	3-0	Burch 2, Wilcox
28		15	(a)	Crystal P	L	0-1	
29		21	(h)	Millwall	W	2-1	Bowler, Dixon
30		22	(a)	Stoke	W	2-0	Bowler, Bell
31		24	(a)	Millwall	L	1-2	Wilson (og)
32		29	(h)	Southampton	W	6-1	Bell, Burch 4, Dixon
33	Apr	5	(a)	Reading	W	2-0	Burch, Bell
34		12	(h)	Norwich C	W	3-1	Bowler 2, Burch
35		19	(h)	Gillingham	W	4-0	Burch 2, Bowler, Bell
36		23	(h)	Queen's Park R	W	2-0	Bowler, Burch
37		26	(h)	Northampton T	W	2-0	Bell, Burch
38		30	(a)	Gillingham	L	2-4	Bell, Bowler

FINAL LEAGUE POSITION: 1st in Southern League

Appearances
Goals

FA Cup

1	Jan	11	(h)	Preston NE	W	2-0	McCormick, Bell	14,345
2	Feb	1	(h)	Manchester U	L	0-2		20,711

Appearances
Goals

Horne	Butler	Atterbury	McCormick	Wilcox	Malcolm	Bowler	Burch	Boden	Raymond	Dixon	Baker	Tainsh	Thom	Craig	Bell	Paltridge	Kirkpatrick	Prout	Forbes	Reed	McLaren	
1	2	3	4	5	6	7	8	9	10	11												1
1	2	3		5	6	7	8	9	10	11	4											2
1	2	3		5	6	7	8	9	10	11	4											3
1	2	3		5	6	7	8	9	10	11	4											4
1	2	3	4	5	6	7	8	9	10	11												5
1	2	3	4	5	6	7	8	9	10	11												6
1	2	3	9	5	6	7	8		10	11	4											7
1	2	3	9	5	6	7	8		10	11	4											8
1	2	3	9	5	6	7	8		10	11	4											9
1	2	3	9			7	8		10	11	4	5	6									10
	2	3		5		7	8		10	11	4		6	1	9							11
1	2	3	5			10	9		8	11	4					6	7					12
1	2	3	5			10	7		8	11	4					6		9				13
1	2	3	5			7	10		8	11	4					6		9				14
1	2	3	5			10	9		8	11	6						7	4				15
1	2	3	4	5		10	9		8	11	6						7					16
1	2	3	4	5		10	9			11	6				8		7					17
	2	3	4	5		10	9		8	11	6			1			7					18
	2		4	5		10	9		8	11	6			1			7		3			19
1	2		4	5		10	9			11	6				8		7		3			20
1		3	4	5		10			8	11	6				7			9	2			21
1	2	3	4	5			9		8		6				10		7			11		22
1	2		4	5		10	9		8	11	6						7		3			23
1	2		4	5		10	9		8	11	6						7		3			24
1		3	4	5		10	9		8	11	6						7		2			25
1	2	3	4	5		10	9		8	11	6						7					26
1	2	3	4	5		10	9		8	11	6						7					27
1	2		4	5		10	9		8	11	6						7		3			28
1	2	3	4	5		10	9		8	11	6						7					29
1	2	3	4	5		10	9			11	6				8		7					30
1	2	3	4	5			9			11	6				8		7				10	31
1	2	3	4	5		10	9			11	6				8		7					32
1	2	3	4	5		10	9			11	6				8		7					33
1	2	3	4	5		10	9			11	6				8		7					34
1	2	3	4	5		10	9				6				8		7			11		35
1	2	3	4	5		10	9			11	6				8		7					36
1	2	3	4	5		10	9			11	6				8		7					37
	2	3	4			11	9				6	5		1	8		7				10	38
34	36	33	34	32	9	36	37	6	27	35	35	2	2	4	14	3	24	4	7	2	2	
			4	2		18	30	1	4	7					7		1					

3 own-goals

1	2	3	4	5		10	9			11	6				8		7	1
1	2	3	4	5			9		8	11	6				10		7	2
2	2	2	2	2		1	2		1	2	2				2		2	
			1												1			

1913-14

Manager: Robert Jack

1	Sep	3	(a)	Portsmouth	W 2-0	Burch, Bell
2		6	(h)	Cardiff C	W 2-1	Bowler, Kirkpatrick
3		13	(a)	Swindon T	L 1-4	Burch
4		20	(h)	Bristol R	D 1-1	Burch
5		24	(a)	Gillingham	L 0-4	
6		27	(h)	Merthyr T	L 0-1	
7	Oct	4	(h)	West Ham U	W 3-0	Bowler 2, Burch
8		11	(a)	Queen's Park R	D 0-0	
9		18	(a)	Southampton	W 2-1	Burch, Blott
10		25	(h)	Reading	W 1-0	Bowler
11	Nov	1	(a)	Crystal P	D 2-2	Rutter, Burch
12		8	(h)	Coventry C	L 0-3	
13		15	(a)	Watford	W 1-0	Gallogley
14		22	(h)	Norwich C	W 2-0	Rutter 2
15	Dec	6	(h)	Northampton T	W 2-0	Rutter, Raymond
16		20	(h)	Brighton & HA	D 2-2	Bowler 2
17		25	(a)	Millwall	L 0-4	
18		26	(h)	Millwall	W 1-0	Bowler
19		27	(a)	Cardiff C	L 1-2	Bowler
20	Jan	3	(h)	Swindon T	W 3-1	Blott, Wilcox, McCormick
21		17	(a)	Bristol R	W 4-1	Raymond, Burch 3
22		24	(h)	Merthyr T	W 1-0	Bowler
23	Feb	7	(a)	West Ham U	L 1-2	Kirkpatrick
24		14	(h)	Queen's Park R	W 2-0	Bowler, Raymond
25		18	(a)	Southend U	L 1-2	Burch
26		21	(h)	Southampton	D 1-1	Bowler
27		28	(a)	Reading	D 2-2	Burch 2
28	Mar	7	(h)	Crystal P	D 0-0	
29		14	(a)	Coventry C	D 1-1	Bowler
30		21	(h)	Watford	D 1-1	Raymond
31		28	(a)	Norwich C	D 1-1	Burch
32	Apr	4	(h)	Gillingham	W 1-0	Rutter
33		10	(h)	Exeter C	D 0-0	
34		11	(a)	Northampton T	D 2-2	Kellock, Blott
35		13	(a)	Exeter C	D 0-0	
36		18	(h)	Southend U	L 0-1	
37		22	(h)	Portsmouth	W 2-1	Rutter, McCormick
38		25	(a)	Brighton & HA	L 0-1	

FINAL LEAGUE POSITION: 5th in Southern League

Appearances
Goals

FA Cup

1	Jan	10	(h)	Lincoln C	W 4-1	Raymond 2, Burch, Butler	18,260
2		31	(a)	Sunderland	L 1-2	Bowler	37,000

Appearances
Goals

Horne	Butler	Atterbury	McCormick	Wilcox	Baker	Kirkpatrick	Bell	Burch	Bowler	Blott	Thompson	Forbes	Raymond	Dixon	Rutter	Gallogley	Reed	Craig	Paltridge	Tainsh	Kellock	
1	2	3	4	5	6	7	8	9	10	11												1
1	2		3	5	6	7	8	9	10	11	4											2
1	2		3	5	6	7	8	9	10	11	4											3
1	2		4	5	6	7	8	9	10	11		3										4
1	2		4	5	6	7		9	10	11		3	8									5
1	2		4	5	6	7	8	9	10	11		3										6
1	2	3	4	5	6	7		9	10	11			8									7
1	2	3	4	5	6	7		9		11			8	10								8
1	2	3	4	5	6	7		9	10	11			8									9
1	2	3	4	5	6	7		9	10				8				11					10
	2	3	4	5	6	7		9		11			8		10			1				11
	2	3	4	5	6	7		9	10	11					8			1				12
	2	3	4	5	6	7		9	10	11						8		1				13
	2	3	4	5	6	7			10	11			8		9			1				14
	2	3		5	6	7			10	11	4		8		9			1				15
	2	3		5	6	7		4	10	11			8		9			1				16
	2	3		5	6	7		4	10	11			8		9			1				17
	2	3		5	6	7		9	10				8	11				1	4			18
	2	3		5	6	7		9	10	4			8	11				1				19
1	2	3	4	5	6	7			10	11			8		9							20
1	2	3	4	5	6	7		9	10	11			8									21
1	2	3	4	5	6	7		9	10	11			8									22
1	2	3		5	6	7			10	11					9	8				4		23
1	2	3		5	6	7		9	10				8	11					4			24
1	2	3		5		7		9	10		6		8	11					4			25
1	2	3		5	6	7		9	10				8	11					4			26
1	2	3		5	6	7		9	10	11		4	8									27
1	2	3		5	6	7		9	10	11		4	8									28
1	2	3	4	5	6	7		9	10				8	11								29
1	2	3	5		6	7		9	10			4	8	11								30
	2	3	5		6	7		9		10		4	8	11				1				31
1	2	3	5		6	7				10		4	8	11	9							32
1	2	3	5		6	7			11	10			8		9					4		33
1	2		5		6	7		9		4		3	10	11							8	34
1	2		5		6	7		9		4		3	10	11							8	35
1	2	3	5		6	7						4	10	11	9						8	36
1	2	3	5			7		9		6		4	10	11	8							37
1		3	5		6	7		9		4		2	10	11	8							38
28	37	31	27	29	36	38	5	31	29	30	4	13	30	15	13	2	1	10	4	2	3	
			2	1		2	1	13	12	3			4		7	1					1	

1	2	3	4	5	6	7		9	10	11			8									1
1	2	3	4	5	6	7		9	10	11			8									2
2	2	2	2	2	2	2		2	2	2			2									
								1	2				2									

1914-15

Manager: Robert Jack

1	Sep	2	(h)	Brighton & HA	W	2-0	Burch, Kirkpatrick
2		5	(a)	Luton T	L	1-2	Burch
3		9	(a)	Brighton & HA	D	2-2	Bowler, Woodhouse (og)
4		12	(h)	Portsmouth	D	2-2	Bowler 2
5		19	(a)	Swindon T	L	2-3	Burch, Davis
6		26	(h)	Southend U	W	1-0	Rutter
7	Oct	3	(a)	Queen's Park R	D	1-1	Kirkpatrick
8		10	(h)	Millwall	D	0-0	
9		17	(a)	Bristol R	L	2-3	Kirkpatrick, Gallogley
10		24	(h)	Croydon Common	L	1-2	Kirkpatrick
11		31	(a)	Reading	L	0-2	
12	Nov	7	(h)	Southampton	W	6-2	Bowler 4, Raymond, Gallogley
13		14	(a)	Northampton T	D	1-1	Gallogley
14		21	(h)	Watford	D	1-1	Gallogley
15		28	(h)	Crystal P	L	1-4	Blott
16	Dec	5	(a)	West Ham U	L	0-2	
17		12	(h)	Norwich C	D	2-2	Burch 2
18		19	(a)	Gillingham	D	0-0	
19		25	(h)	Cardiff C	W	2-0	Bowler, Kirkpatrick
20		26	(a)	Cardiff C	L	0-2	
21	Jan	2	(h)	Luton T	D	3-3	Burch, Dixon 2
22		23	(a)	Swindon T	W	3-1	Burch 3
23		30	(a)	Portsmouth	L	1-3	Burch
24	Feb	6	(h)	Queen's Park R	D	1-1	Burch
25		20	(h)	Bristol R	W	3-0	Burch, Dixon, Blott
26		27	(a)	Croydon Common	D	2-2	Gallogley, Dixon
27	Mar	1	(a)	Millwall	D	1-1	McCormick
28		6	(h)	Reading	D	1-1	Dixon
29		13	(a)	Southampton	L	1-2	Gallogley
30		20	(h)	Northampton T	L	0-1	
31		27	(a)	Watford	L	0-2	
32	Apr	2	(h)	Exeter C	L	1-3	Burch
33		3	(a)	Crystal P	L	1-2	Gallogley
34		5	(a)	Exeter C	D	1-1	Strettle (og)
35		10	(h)	West Ham U	W	1-0	Bowler
36		17	(a)	Norwich C	L	0-2	
37		24	(a)	Gillingham	W	3-2	Burch, Forbes, Gallogley
38	May	1	(a)	Southend U	L	1-3	Burch

FINAL LEAGUE POSITION: 17th in Southern League

Appearances
Goals

FA Cup

1	Jan	9	(a)	Bury	D	1-1	Bowler	8,510
R		16	(h)	Bury	L	1-2	Raymond	12,501

Appearances
Goals

Horne	Forbes	Russell	McCormick	Wilcox	Baker	Kirkpatrick	Raymond	Burch	Bowler	Blott	Rutter	Dixon	Durnin	Gallogley	Craig	Atterbury	Butler	Gosling	Kellock	Bates	Turnbull	Jennings	Davis	
1	2	3	4	5	6	7	8	9	10			11												1
1	2	3	4	5	6	7	8	9	10	11														2
1	2	3	4	5	6				10	11	9			8				7						3
1	2	3	4	5	6		8	7	10		9	11												4
1	2	3		5	6	7		9	10			11		8									4	5
	4	3		5	6	7			10		9	11		8	1	2								6
1	4	3	8	5	6	7			10	11	9					2								7
1	4	3		5	6	7			10		9	11		8		2								8
1	3			5	6	7			10	11			4	8			2		9					9
1	3		2	5	6	7			10				4	8				11	9					10
1	3			5	6	7				11		10	4	8					9	2				11
1	3			5	6	7	9		10	11			4	8			2							12
1	9			5	6	7			10	11			4	8		3	2							13
1	4			5	6	7	9		10	11				8		3	2							14
1	4		9	5					10	11			6	8		3	2	7						15
	2		9	5	6					11		10	4	8	1	3		7						16
	4	5						9				11	6	8	1	3	2	7			10			17
	4	5				7		9				11		8	1	3	2				10		6	18
	4	5			6	7		9	10			11		8	1	3	2							19
	4	5			6	7		9	10			11		8	1	3	2							20
	4	3	2	5		7		9			10	11	6	8	1									21
		2		5	6	7		9		11		10	4	8	1	3								22
	6	2	5			7		9		11		10	4	8	1	3								23
		2		5	6	7	10	9		11			4	8	1	3								24
	6	2		5		7		9		11		10	4	8	1	3								25
	6	2		5		7		9		11		10	4	8	1	3								26
		6	9	5		7				11		10	4	8	1	3	2							27
	6	2	9	5		7				11		10	4	8	1	3								28
	6	2		5		7		9				10	4	8	1	3					11			29
	6	3		5		7	9					11	4	8	1		2					10		30
	6	3	9	5		7						11	4	8	1		2	10						31
	6			5		7		9				11	4	8	1	3	2	10						32
	6		9	5		7						10	4	8	1	3	2	11						33
	10			5	6	7		9					4	8	1	3	2	11						34
			4	5		7	10	9	11				6	8	1	3	2							35
	10	6	4	5				9		7		11		8	1	3	2							36
	6	3		5		7	10	9	11				4	8	1		2							37
	10		7	5	6			9		4		11		8	1	3	2							38
14	34	25	17	33	21	31	9	21	18	19	6	25	24	34	24	25	19	9	3	1	3	1	2	
	1		1			5	1	15	9	2	1	5		8										

2 own-goals

Horne	Forbes	Russell	McCormick	Wilcox	Baker	Kirkpatrick	Raymond	Burch	Bowler	Blott	Rutter	Dixon	Durnin	Gallogley	Craig	Atterbury	Butler	Gosling	Kellock	Bates	Turnbull	Jennings	Davis	
	4	3		5	6	7		9	10			11		8	1		2							1
	4	6		5		7	8	9		10		11			1	3	2							R
	2	2		2	1	2	1	2	1	1		2		1	2	1	2							
							1		1															

1919-20

Manager: Robert Jack

1	Aug	30	(h)	Swindon T	W	3-0	Dixon 2, Gallogley	11,595
2	Sep	1	(h)	Queen's Park R	D	0-0		9,500
3		6	(a)	Millwall	D	1-1	Kellock	10,804
4		8	(a)	Queen's Park R	L	0-1		5,000
5		13	(h)	Brighton & HA	W	1-0	Dixon	11,000
6		20	(a)	Newport C	L	1-2	Gallogley	
7		27	(h)	Portsmouth	L	1-2	Kellock	15,000
8	Oct	4	(a)	Northampton T	W	4-0	Bowler 2, Kellock, Blott	
9		6	(a)	Gillingham	W	2-0	Kellock, Dixon	4,000
10		11	(h)	Crystal P	D	0-0		
11		18	(a)	Southend U	L	0-1		
12		25	(h)	Norwich C	W	4-0	Kellock, Bowler 2, Dixon	12,000
13	Nov	1	(a)	Brentford	D	0-0		
14		8	(h)	Merthyr T	W	3-0	Gallogley, Bull, Bowler	11,000
15		15	(a)	Watford	L	0-3		5,000
16		22	(a)	Bristol R	L	0-2		12,000
17		29	(h)	Reading	D	0-0		12,711
18	Dec	6	(a)	Southampton	D	2-2	Dickinson, Blott	8,000
19		13	(h)	Luton T	W	1-0	Kellock	6,336
20		25	(h)	Exeter C	W	3-1	Jack, Flood, Kellock	14,000
21		26	(a)	Exeter C	W	1-0	Flood	10,000
22		27	(h)	Swansea T	L	0-1		14,000
23	Jan	3	(a)	Swindon T	L	0-2		
24		17	(h)	Millwall	W	3-0	Bowler 2, Kellock	
25		24	(a)	Brighton & HA	L	0-1		
26	Feb	7	(a)	Portsmouth	D	1-1	Kellock	20,000
27		14	(h)	Northampton T	W	4-0	Dixon 2, Jack 2	12,000
28		28	(h)	Southend U	D	0-0		12,000
29	Mar	3	(a)	Crystal P	L	0-1		4,000
30		6	(a)	Norwich C	W	3-2	McCormick, Kellock 2	
31		13	(h)	Brentford	W	3-2	Kellock, Dixon, Flood	8,853
32		20	(a)	Merthyr T	W	2-0	Logan, Dixon	
33		27	(h)	Watford	D	1-1	Bowler	10,563
34	Apr	2	(h)	Cardiff C	W	1-0	Jack	19,950
35		3	(h)	Bristol R	W	2-0	Jack, Sheffield	11,440
36		5	(a)	Cardiff C	W	2-0	Sheffield 2	24,000
37		10	(a)	Reading	D	0-0		
38		14	(h)	Newport C	W	3-0	Griffin (og), Jack, Sheffield	3,528
39		17	(h)	Southampton	L	0-1		13,943
40		24	(a)	Luton T	W	2-1	Dixon 2	
41		26	(h)	Gillingham	W	2-0	Sheffield, Jack	8,000
42	May	1	(a)	Swansea T	L	0-1		

FINAL LEAGUE POSITION: 5th in Southern League

Appearances
Goals

FA Cup

1	Jan	10	(h)	Reading	W	2-0	Jack 2	18,480
2		31	(h)	Barnsley	W	4-1	Jack 2, Bowler 2	27,193
3	Feb	21	(a)	Huddersfield T	L	1-3	Jack	35,000

Appearances
Goals

Craig	Russell	Atterbury	McCormick	Wilcox	Forbes	Blott	Gallogley	Jack	Raymond	Dixon	Kirkpatrick	Logan	Kellock	Roadley	Dickinson	Bowler	Davies	Bull	Flood	Hastie	Kay	Sheffield	Symons	
1	2	3	4	5	6	7	8	9	10	11														1
1	2	3	4	5	6		8	9	10	11	7													2
1	2	3	5		6		8		10	11	7	4	9											3
	2	3	5		6		8		10	11	7	4	9	1										4
	2	3	5		6		8		10	11	7	4	9	1										5
1	2	3		5	6	11	8	7	10				9		4									6
1	2	3	5		6			7	8	11		4	9			10								7
1	2	3	5		6	7	8			11		4	9			10								8
1	2	3	5		6	7	8			11		4	9			10								9
1		3	5		6	7	8			11		4	9			10	2							10
1	2	3		5	6	7	8			11		4	9			10								11
1	2	3	5		6		8			11		4	10			7		9						12
1	2	3	5		6		8	7		11		4	9			10								13
1	2	3	5		6		8	7		11		4				10		9						14
1	2	3	5		6		8	7		11		4	9			10								15
1	2		5		3	7		8	10	11		4	9		6									16
1	2		5		3	7		8	10	11		4	9		6									17
1	2		5		3	7		8	10	11		4			6				9					18
1	2	3	5		4	7		8	10	11			9		6									19
1	2	3	5		4		7	8		11			10		6				9					20
1	2	3	5		4		7	8		11			10		6				9					21
1	2	3	5		8		7			11		4	10		6				9					22
1	2	3	5		6		7	8		11		4	10		9									23
1	5	3			2			8		11	7	4	10		6	9								24
1		3	5		2	11	7	8	10			4			6					9				25
1		3			2	6	7	8	10			4	11		5					9				26
1		3	5		2	4	7	8	10	11			9		6									27
1	2	3	5		6		7	8	10	11		4				9								28
1		3	5		2		8			11	7	4	10		6						9			29
1		3	5		2		8			11	7	4	10		6						9			30
1	2	3	5		6			8		11	7	4	10						9					31
1	2	3			6			8	10	11	7	4	9		5									32
1	2						9	8		11	7	4	10		6	5	3							33
1	2	3	5					8		11	7	4			6	10						9		34
1	2	3	5					8		11	7	4			6	10						9		35
1	2	3	5					8	10		7	4			6	11						9		36
1	2		5		3			8	10	11	7	4			6							9		37
1	2		5		3			8		11	7	4			6	10						9		38
1	2		5		3			8	10	11	7	4			6							9		39
1	2	3			6		10	8		11	7	4			5							9		40
1	2				3	6		8		11	7	4			5							9	10	41
1	2		5		3		10	8		11	7	4			6							9		42
40	36	33	34	4	38	14	27	31	19	38	19	35	27	2	26	16	2	2	5	2	2	9	1	
			1			2	3	7		11		1	12		1	8		1	3			5		

1 own-goal

1	2	3	5		6		7	8		11		4	10			9								1
1	2	3	5		6		7	8	10	11		4				9								2
1	2	3	5		6		7	8	10	11		4				9								3
3	3	3	3		3		3	3	2	3		3	1			3								
							5									2								

1920-21

Manager: Robert Jack

1	Aug	28	(h)	Norwich C	D 1-1	Heeps	17,356
2	Sep	1	(a)	Crystal P	D 0-0		9,000
3		4	(a)	Norwich C	D 0-0		
4		8	(h)	Crystal P	L 0-1		
5		11	(h)	Newport C	W 5-1	Gallogley, Sheffield 2, Dixon, Raymond	
6		18	(a)	Newport C	D 0-0		
7		25	(h)	Gillingham	W 3-1	Jack, Raymond 2	
8	Oct	2	(a)	Gillingham	W 1-0	Hill	
9		9	(h)	Swindon T	D 0-0		
10		16	(a)	Swindon T	D 1-1	Sheffield	11,974
11		23	(h)	Watford	L 0-2		
12		30	(a)	Watford	D 1-1	Toone (og)	
13	Nov	6	(h)	Brighton & HA	W 5-0	Kellock, Jack 2, Corcoran, Toms	19,000
14		13	(a)	Brighton & HA	L 0-1		
15		20	(h)	Northampton T	L 0-2		
16		27	(a)	Northampton T	D 1-1	Hill	
17	Dec	4	(a)	Southend U	L 1-2	Toms	
18		11	(h)	Southend U	D 0-0		
19		18	(a)	Merthyr T	D 0-0		
20		25	(h)	Exeter C	D 0-0		18,000
21		27	(a)	Exeter C	D 1-1	Russell	14,000
22	Jan	1	(h)	Merthyr T	W 2-1	Dixon, Sheffield	
23		15	(h)	Grimsby T	D 0-0		12,000
24		22	(a)	Grimsby T	D 1-1	Hill	
25	Feb	5	(a)	Portsmouth	D 1-1	Toms	
26		12	(h)	Queen's Park R	W 1-0	Raymond	
27		26	(h)	Swansea T	W 1-0	Milne (og)	
28	Mar	5	(a)	Swansea T	L 0-3		8,000
29		12	(h)	Luton T	W 1-0	Bowler	
30		17	(a)	Queen's Park R	L 0-4		
31		19	(h)	Luton T	D 1-1	Raymond	
32		25	(h)	Millwall	L 0-2		
33		26	(a)	Southampton	L 0-1		
34		28	(a)	Millwall	D 0-0		
35	Apr	2	(h)	Southampton	D 0-0		
36		9	(a)	Reading	D 1-1	Raymond	
37		13	(h)	Portsmouth	W 2-0	Corcoran, Raymond	10,000
38		16	(h)	Reading	D 1-1	Bowler	16,000
39		23	(a)	Bristol R	L 0-2		
40		30	(h)	Bristol R	W 2-1	Logan 2	
41	May	2	(a)	Brentford	D 0-0		5,000
42		7	(h)	Brentford	W 1-0	Gallogley	

FINAL LEAGUE POSITION: 11th in Division Three South

Appearances
Goals

FA Cup

1	Jan	8	(h)	Rochdale	W 2-0	Sheffield, Russell	24,287
2		29	(a)	Swansea T	W 2-1	Bowler, Toms	22,539
3	Feb	19	(h)	Chelsea	D 0-0		27,749
R		24	(a)	Chelsea	D 0-0		45,000
2R		28	(n*)	Chelsea	L 1-2	Toms	22,000

*Played at Bristol

Appearances
Goals

Craig	Russell	Atterbury	Logan	Dickinson	Forbes	Kirkpatrick	Jack	Bowler	Heeps	Dixon	Sheffield	Hill	Little	Kellock	Eastwood	Gallogley	Raymond	Toms	Corcoran	Cosgrove	Frost	Thorpe	
1	2	3	4	5	6	7	8	9	10	11													1
1	2	3	4	5	6	7	8	9	10	11													2
1	2	3	4	5	6	7	8		10	11	9												3
1	2	3	4	6		7	8				9	5	11	10									4
1	2	3	4	5		7				11	9				6	8	10						5
1	2	3	4	5		7				11	9				6	8	10						6
1	2	3	4	5		7	8			11					6		10	9					7
1	2	3	4			7	8			11	9	5			6		10						8
1	2	3	4			7	8			11		5			6		10	9					9
1	2	3	4				8			11	9	5			6	7	10						10
1	2	3	4	5	6		8			11						7	10	9					11
1	2	3	4		6		8					5		11		7	10	9					12
1	2	3	4		6		8					5		11			10	9	7				13
1	2	3	4		6		8					5		11			10	9	7				14
1	2	3	4		6		8			11		5					10	9	7				15
1	2	3	4		6				10			5		11		8		9	7				16
1	2	3	4		6				10	11		5				8		9	7				17
1	2	3	4		6		8	11				5					10	9	7				18
1	2		4	6	3					11	9	5				8	10		7				19
1	2		4	6	3			11			9	5				8	10		7				20
1	2	3	4		6			11			9	5				8	10		7				21
1	2	3	4							11	9	5			6	8	10		7				22
1	2		4		3				10	11	9	5			6		8		7				23
1	2		4		3				10	11	9	5			6		8		7				24
1	2		4		3	7				11	9	5			6		8	10					25
1		3	4		2	7		9				5			6		8	10	11				26
1		·	4	6		7					9	5				8		10	11	2	3		27
1	5	3		4		7		9	11						6	8		10		2			28
1	2	3	4	6		7		9	11						5		8	10					29
1	2	3	4	6		7		9	11						5		8	10					30
1	2	3	4	6		7			11		9				5		8	10					31
1	2	3	4	6		7			11		9				5		8	10					32
1	2	3	4	6		7			11						5	8	10	9					33
1		3		6		7			11		9				5	4	8	10		2			34
1	2		4		3	7		9	11			5			6	8	10						35
1		3	4		2	7			10		9	5			6		8		11				36
1		3	4	6	2	7					9	5				8	10		11				37
1	3		4	6	2	7		9				5				8	10		11				38
1	3		4	6	2	7						5		9		8		10	11				39
1	3		9	6	2	7						5				8		10	11			4	40
1	3		9	6		7						5				8		10	11	2		4	41
1			9	6	2	7						5				8		10	11	3		4	42
42	36	30	40	24	25	27	14	11	16	17	19	28	1	6	20	22	30	24	21	5	1	3	
	1		2				3	2	1	2	4	3		1		2	7	3	2				

2 own-goals

1	3		4		2					11	9	5			6	8	10		7				1
1	3		4		2	7		9		11		5			6		8	10					2
1	3		4		2	7		9				5			6		8	10	11				3
1	2	3	4			7		9				5			6		8	10	11				R
1	2	3	4	5		7		9							6		8	10	11				2R
5	5	2	5	1	3	4		4		2	1	4			5	1	5	4	4				
	1							1			1							2					

1921-22

Manager: Robert Jack

1	Aug	27	(a)	Bristol R	W 3-1	Richardson 3
2		29	(h)	Norwich C	D 1-1	Bowler
3	Sep	3	(h)	Bristol R	W 1-0	Bowler
4		8	(a)	Norwich C	D 1-1	Raymond
5		10	(a)	Gillingham	W 2-1	Gallogley 2
6		17	(h)	Gillingham	W 3-0	Richardson 2, Bowler
7		24	(a)	Luton T	L 0-1	
8	Oct	1	(h)	Luton T	W 2-0	Richardson 2
9		8	(a)	Reading	W 1-0	Richardson
10		15	(h)	Reading	W 2-0	Richardson, Gallogley
11		22	(a)	Newport C	D 0-0	
12		29	(h)	Newport C	W 1-0	Richardson
13	Nov	5	(a)	Swindon T	W 2-1	Richardson 2
14		12	(h)	Swindon T	W 1-0	Richardson
15		19	(h)	Merthyr T	D 0-0	
16		26	(a)	Merthyr T	W 1-0	Richardson
17	Dec	3	(h)	Portsmouth	D 0-0	
18		10	(a)	Portsmouth	L 1-3	Abbott (og)
19		17	(h)	Southend U	W 4-0	Bowler 2, Fowler, Hill
20		24	(a)	Southend U	L 0-1	
21		26	(a)	Exeter C	W 2-0	Richardson 2
22		27	(h)	Exeter C	D 0-0	
23		31	(h)	Swansea T	W 3-1	Richardson 3
24	Jan	14	(a)	Swansea T	L 0-3	
25		21	(a)	Brentford	L 1-3	Richardson
26		28	(h)	Brentford	W 4-1	Richardson 3, Bowler
27	Feb	4	(a)	Aberdare A	D 0-0	
28		11	(h)	Aberdare A	W 3-0	Hill, Baker, Gallogley
29		18	(a)	Brighton & HA	D 1-1	Corcoran
30		25	(h)	Brighton & HA	W 3-1	Gallogley, Richardson, Baker
31	Mar	4	(a)	Watford	W 1-0	Hill
32		11	(h)	Watford	W 3-0	Baker, Richardson 2
33		18	(h)	Charlton A	W 3-0	Corcoran 2, Richardson
34		25	(a)	Charlton A	D 0-0	
35	Apr	1	(h)	Northampton T	W 2-0	Corcoran 2
36		8	(a)	Northampton T	W 3-1	Raymond, Baker, Corcoran
37		14	(a)	Millwall	D 1-1	Richardson
38		15	(h)	Southampton	W 1-0	Gallogley
39		17	(h)	Millwall	W 2-0	Baker, Richardson
40		22	(a)	Southampton	D 0-0	
41		29	(h)	Queen's Park R	W 4-0	Gallogley, Richardson 2, Hill
42	May	6	(a)	Queen's Park R	L 0-2	

FINAL LEAGUE POSITION: 2nd in Division Three South

Appearances
Goals

FA Cup

1	Jan	7	(h)	Fulham	D 1-1	Baker	29,965
R		11	(a)	Fulham	L 0-1		28,300

Appearances
Goals

Craig	Cosgrove	Russell	Logan	Hill	Eastwood	Kirkpatrick	Kirk	Gallogley	Richardson	Bowler	Little	Forbes	Dickinson	Corcoran	Raymond	Leslie	Batten	Rowe	Fowler	Cook	Devine	Smith	Deacon	Baker	
1	2	3	4	5	6	7		8	9	10	11														1
1	2	3	4		5	7		8	9	10	11		6												2
1		3		5	6		8		9	10		2	4	7										11	3
1		3		5	6				9	10		2	4	7	8									11	4
1		3		5	6			8	9	10		2	4	7										11	5
1		2		5	6			8	9	10		3	4	7										11	6
1		2		5	6			8	9	10		3	4	7										11	7
1		2		5	6	7		8	9	10		3	4											11	8
1		2		5	6	7		8	9	10		3	4											11	9
1		2		5	6	7		8	9	10		3	4											11	10
1		2	4	5		7		8	9	10		3	6											11	11
1		2	4	5				8	9	10		3	6	7										11	12
1		2	4	5				8	9	10		3	6	7										11	13
1		3	4	5				8	9	10		2	6	7										11	14
1		3	4	5				8	9	10		2	6	7		11									15
1		3	4	5				8	9			2	6	7		11	10								16
1		3	4	5				8	9			2	6	7		11	10								17
1		3	4	5				8	9			2	6	7		11	10								18
1		3		5					9	10		2	4	7		11		6	8						19
1		3		5					9	10		2	4	7		11		6	8						20
1		3		5					9	10		2	4	7		11		6	8						21
1		3			5				9			2	4	7		11	10	6	8						22
			5		6			8	9			2	4	7	10					1	3			11	23
			5		6			8				2	4	7	10					1	3	9		11	24
	2			5	6				9	10		3	4	7	8					1				11	25
		3		5	6				9	10		2	4	7	8					1				11	26
	2	3		5	6				9				4	7	8				10	1				11	27
		3		5	6			8	9			2	4	7	10					1				11	28
1		3		5	6			8	9			2	4	7	10									11	29
1		3		5	6			8	9			2	4	7	10									11	30
1		3		5	6			8	9	10		2	4	7										11	31
1		3		5	6			8	9			2	4	7	10									11	32
1		3			6			8	9	10		2	4	7									5	11	33
1		3		5	6			8	9	10		2	4	7										11	34
1				5	6			8	9	10		2	4	7							3			11	35
1	2	3		5	6				9				4	7	8		10							11	36
1	2	3		5	6				9				4	7	8		10							11	37
1		3		5	6			8	9			2	4	7			10							11	38
1		3		5	6			8	9			2	4	7	10									11	39
1		3		5	6			8	9			2	4	7	10									11	40
1		3		5	6			8	9			2	4	7	10									11	41
1		3		5	6			8	9			2	4	7	10	11									42
36	6	38	12	37	31	6	1	31	41	24	2	37	41	36	16	9	7	4	5	6	3	1	1	31	
				4				7	31	6				6	2				1					5	

1 own-goal

1		3		5	6			8	9	10		2	4	7										11	1
1		3		5	6			8	9	10		2	4	7										11	R
2		2		2	2			2	2	2		2	2	2										2	
																								1	

1922-23

Manager: Robert Jack

1	Aug	26	(a)	Millwall	D 0-0	
2		28	(h)	Bristol C	W 5-1	Richardson 2, Bowler, Corcoran, Banfield (og)
3	Sep	2	(h)	Millwall	W 1-0	Hill
4		4	(a)	Bristol C	L 0-2	
5		9	(h)	Merthyr T	W 2-0	Bowler 2
6		16	(a)	Merthyr T	W 1-0	Batten
7		23	(a)	Reading	W 1-0	Baker
8		30	(h)	Reading	W 3-0	Hill 2, Batten
9	Oct	7	(a)	Portsmouth	W 2-1	Fowler, Batten
10		14	(h)	Portsmouth	W 2-0	Fowler, Batten
11		21	(a)	Luton T	L 1-2	Fowler
12		23	(a)	Charlton A	L 0-1	
13		28	(h)	Luton T	W 4-0	Richardson 2, Batten, Corcoran
14	Nov	4	(h)	Bristol R	W 3-0	Corcoran, Richardson, Bowler
15		11	(a)	Bristol R	W 1-0	Batten
16		25	(h)	Southend U	D 1-1	Baker
17	Dec	9	(h)	Charlton A	W 2-0	Richardson, Bowler
18		16	(a)	Watford	L 0-1	
19		23	(h)	Watford	W 1-0	Bowler
20		25	(h)	Northampton T	W 1-0	Bowler
21		26	(a)	Northampton T	L 0-1	
22	Jan	6	(a)	Brentford	L 0-2	
23		20	(h)	Norwich C	D 1-1	Batten
24		27	(a)	Norwich C	L 0-1	
25	Feb	10	(h)	Queen's Park R	W 2-0	Corcoran, Batten
26		17	(a)	Gillingham	L 0-1	
27	Mar	3	(a)	Brighton & HA	L 0-1	
28		10	(h)	Brighton & HA	D 2-2	Corcoran, Deacon
29		15	(a)	Queen's Park R	W 3-2	Fowler, Devine 2
30		17	(h)	Swindon T	W 2-0	Fowler, Batten
31		24	(a)	Swindon T	L 1-2	Fowler
32		30	(h)	Exeter C	W 5-1	Jack, Fowler 3, Corcoran
33		31	(h)	Aberdare A	W 2-0	Fowler 2
34	Apr	2	(a)	Exeter C	D 0-0	
35		7	(a)	Aberdare A	D 2-2	Fowler, Batten
36		9	(a)	Southend U	L 1-2	Fowler
37		14	(h)	Swansea T	W 2-0	Fowler 2
38		18	(h)	Gillingham	W 2-0	Fowler, Leslie
39		21	(a)	Swansea T	D 1-1	Raymond
40		28	(h)	Newport C	W 1-0	Russell
41	May	2	(h)	Brentford	W 3-0	Fowler, Leslie 2
42		5	(a)	Newport C	L 0-1	

FINAL LEAGUE POSITION: 2nd in Division Three South

Appearances
Goals

FA Cup

1	Jan	13	(h)	Notts C	D 0-0		27,344
R		17	(a)	Notts C	W 1-0	Gallogley	16,422
2	Feb	3	(h)	Bradford	W 4-1	Richardson 4	24,500
3		24	(a)	West Ham U	L 0-2		30,525

Appearances
Goals

Cook	Forbes	Russell	Logan	Hill	Eastwood	Corcoran	Gallogley	Richardson	Bowler	Baker	Craig	Dickinson	Kirkpatrick	Fowler	Devine	Raymond	Batten	Cosgrove	Jack	Wilson	Jobson	Rowe	Walker	Deacon	Leslie	Little	
1	2	3	4	5	6	7	8	9	10	11																	1
	2	3	4	5	6	7	8	9	10	11	1																2
	2	3	4	5	6		8	9	10	11	1		7														3
	2	3		5	6			9	10	11	1	4	7	8													4
	2	3		5	6		8	9	10	11	1	4	7														5
	2			5	6	7			10	11	1	4		9	3	8											6
	2	3		5	6	7			10	11	1	4		9		8											7
	2	3		5	6	7	8	9		11	1	4					10										8
		3		5	6	7		9		11	1	4		8			10	2									9
	2	3		5	6	7		9		11	1	4		8			10										10
	2	3		5	6	7		9		11	1	4		8			10										11
	2			5	6	7		9	10	11	1	4		8	3												12
	2			5	6	7		9	10	11	1	4			3		8										13
	2			5	6	7		9	10	11	1	4			3		8										14
	2			5	6	7		9	10	11	1	4			3		8										15
	2	3		5	6	7		9	10	11	1	4					8										16
	2	3		5	6	7		9	10	11	1	4					8										17
	2	3		5	6	7		9	10	11	1	4					8										18
	2	3		5	6	7			10	11	1	4					9		8								19
	2	3	5		6	7			10	11	1	4					9		8								20
	2	3		5	6	7			10	11	1	4					9		8								21
	2	3	4	5	6	7		8	10	11	1						9										22
	2	3	4	5	6		8				1			9			10			7					11		23
	2		4	5		7	8	9	11		1				3		10				6						24
	2	3	4	5	6	7	8	9		11	1						10										25
	2	3	4	5	6	7	8	9		11	1						10										26
	2	3		5		7		9		11	1						10		8			4	6				27
	2	3	4			7		9		11	1					8	10					6		5			28
	2	5	4			7				11	1			9	3	8	10					6					29
			4	5		7				11	1			9	3	8	10	2				6					30
	2	3	4	5		7				11	1			9		8	10					6					31
	2	3	4	5		7				11	1			9			10		8			6					32
	2	3	4	5	6	7				11	1			9		8	10										33
	2	3	4		6	7				11	1	5		9		8							10				34
	2	3	4	5	6					11	1			9		8	10			7							35
	2	3	4	5	6					11	1			9		8	10			7							36
	2		4	5	6	7				11	1			9	3	8	10										37
		3	4	5	6	7					1			9		8		2							10	11	38
			4	5	6	7				11	1			9	3	8		2							10		39
	2	3	4	5	6	7				11	1			9		8									10		40
	2	3	4			7				11	1	5		9		8							6		10		41
	3		5			7				11	1	6		9	2	8							4		10		42
1	38	32	24	36	33	36	9	22	19	39	41	21	3	22	11	16	28	4	5	3	1	6	4	1	6	1	
		1		3		6		6	7	2				17	2	1	10		1					1	3		

1 own-goal

	2	3	4	5	6		7		10	11	1						9		8								1
	2	3	4	5	6		8				1			9			10		7						11		R
	2	3	4	5	6	7	8	9		11	1						10										2
	2	3	4	5	6	7	8	9		11	1						10										3
	4	4	4	4	4	2	4	2	1	3	4			1			4		2						1		
							1	4																			

1923-24

Manager: Robert Jack

1	Aug	25	(h)	Portsmouth	L 1-2	Fowler
2		27	(a)	Brentford	D 1-1	Jack
3	Sep	1	(a)	Portsmouth	L 1-2	Cherrett
4		3	(h)	Brentford	W 4-1	Jack, Cherrett 2, Batten
5		8	(a)	Norwich C	W 1-0	Cherrett
6		15	(h)	Norwich C	W 2-0	Jack, Cherrett
7		22	(a)	Swindon T	W 1-0	Fowler
8		29	(h)	Swindon T	L 1-3	Baker
9	Oct	6	(a)	Watford	W 1-0	Cherrett
10		13	(h)	Watford	W 1-0	Cherrett
11		20	(h)	Swansea T	W 2-0	Eastwood, Batten
12		27	(a)	Swansea T	L 0-1	
13	Nov	3	(h)	Northampton T	D 0-0	
14		10	(a)	Northampton T	L 0-1	
15		17	(a)	Gillingham	L 0-1	
16		24	(h)	Gillingham	W 3-0	Fowler 2, Batten
17	Dec	1	(a)	Queen's Park R	L 2-3	Fowler, Cherrett
18		8	(h)	Queen's Park R	W 2-0	Cherrett 2
19		15	(a)	Newport C	W 2-1	Cherrett 2
20		22	(h)	Newport C	W 3-2	Cherrett 2, Eastwood
21		25	(h)	Exeter C	W 4-0	Cherrett 2, Eastwood, Leslie
22		26	(a)	Exeter C	W 4-0	Cherrett 2, Corcoran, Preston
23		29	(h)	Merthyr T	D 1-1	Preston
24	Jan	5	(a)	Merthyr T	L 0-1	
25		19	(h)	Bristol R	D 2-2	Fishwick, Russell
26		26	(a)	Bristol R	D 1-1	Fowler
27	Feb	9	(a)	Brighton & HA	L 1-4	Baker
28		16	(h)	Luton T	D 0-0	
29		23	(a)	Luton T	W 2-0	Walker, Fowler
30	Mar	1	(h)	Reading	W 2-1	Smith, Corcoran
31		8	(a)	Reading	W 2-1	Cherrett 2
32		15	(a)	Bournemouth	D 0-0	
33		22	(h)	Bournemouth	W 4-0	Smith 3, Cherrett
34		29	(a)	Millwall	L 0-1	
35	Apr	5	(h)	Millwall	D 1-1	Batten
36		12	(a)	Aberdare A	W 2-1	Corcoran, Cherrett
37		18	(h)	Charlton A	D 1-1	Batten
38		19	(h)	Aberdare A	W 2-0	Leslie, Cherrett
39		21	(a)	Charlton A	W 1-0	Cherrett
40		26	(a)	Southend U	W 2-0	Baker, Cherrett
41		30	(h)	Brighton & HA	W 3-0	Leslie, Baker, Sloan
42	May	3	(h)	Southend U	W 7-1	Sloan 3, Leslie 2, Cherrett 2

FINAL LEAGUE POSITION: 2nd in Division Three South

Appearances
Goals

FA Cup

1	Jan	12	(a)	Manchester U	L 0-1		26,342

Appearances
Goals

Craig	Forbes	Russell	Logan	Deacon	Eastwood	Corcoran	Raymond	Fowler	Leslie	Little	Cosgrove	Dickinson	Jack	Preston	Cherrett	Batten	Baker	Walker	Kirkpatrick	Rowe	Fishwick	Smith	Ross	Sloan	
1	2	3	4	5	6	7	8	9	10	11															1
1	3		5		6	7		9	10	11	2	4	8												2
1	3				6	7				11	2	4	8	5	9	10									3
1	2	3			6	7						4	8	5	9	10	11								4
1	2	3			6							4	8	5	9	10	11		7						5
1	2	3	4		6	7							8	5	9	10	11								6
1	2	3	4		6	7		8						5	9	10	11								7
1	2	3	4		6			8						5	9	10	11		7						8
1		3	4		6	7					2		8	5	9		11	10							9
1	2	3	4		6	7							8	5	9	10	11								10
1	2	3	4		6	7	10						8	5	9	11									11
1	2	3	4		6	7	10						8	5	9	11									12
1	2	3			6	7	10					4	8	5	9	11									13
1		3	4			7					2	6		5	9	11		10			8				14
1		3	4			7					2	6		5	9	11		10			8				15
1	2	3	4			7		9				6		5	8	11		10							16
1	2	3	4			7		9				6		5	8	11		10							17
1	2	3	8		6	7			10			4		5	9	11									18
1	3		8		6	7			10		2	4		5	9	11									19
1	2	3	8		6	7			10			4		5	9	11									20
1	2	3	8		6	7			10			4		5	9	11									21
1	2	3	8		6	7			10			4		5	9	11									22
1	2	3			6	7	8		10			4		5	9	11									23
1	2	3	8		6	7		9				4		5	10	11									24
1	2	3	4	5		7						6			9	11		10			8				25
1	2	3	5			7		9				4			8	11		10		6					26
1	2	3	4			7						6		5	8	10	11					9			27
1	3				6	7		9	10		2	4		5	8		11								28
1	2	3	4			7		9						5	8	11		10					6		29
1	2	3	4			7								5	8	11		10				9	6		30
1	2	3	4			7								5	8	11		10		6		9			31
1	3		4			7					2			5	8	11		10		6		9			32
1	2	3	4											5	8	11		10	7	6		9			33
1	2	3	4											5	8	11		10	7	6		9			34
1	2	3			6	7			10			4		5	9	11					8				35
1	3				6	7			10		2	4		5	9	11					8				36
1	2	3			6	7			10			4		5	9	11					8			8	37
1		3	4			7			10		2			5	9		11			6				8	38
1		3	4			7			10		2			5	9		11			6				8	39
1		3	4			7			10		2			5	9		11			6				8	40
1		3	4			7			10		2			5	9		11			6				8	41
1		3	4			7			10		2			5	9		11			6				5	42
42	34	36	33	2	24	38	5	10	17	3	14	23	10	38	40	33	14	13	4	10	6	6	2	4	
		1			3	3		7	5				3	2	27	5	4	1			1	4			

1	2	3	4			7		8				6		5	9	11		10	1
1	1	1	1			1		1				1		1	1	1		1	

1924-25

Manager: Robert Jack

1	Aug	30	(a)	Norwich C	D 1-1	Sloan
2	Sep	1	(a)	Swindon T	L 0-1	
3		6	(h)	Brentford	W 7-1	Corcoran 2, Leslie 2, Batten 2, Black
4		8	(h)	Swindon T	W 2-0	O'Neill (og), Batten
5		13	(a)	Millwall	D 0-0	
6		20	(h)	Luton T	W 4-0	Batten 3, Black
7		24	(h)	Queen's Park R	W 1-0	Leslie
8		27	(a)	Gillingham	W 3-0	Cherrett 2, Sloan
9	Oct	4	(h)	Bournemouth	W 2-0	Cherrett 2
10		11	(a)	Brighton & HA	W 3-2	Leslie 2, Sloan
11		18	(h)	Bristol R	W 3-2	Leslie 2, Russell
12		25	(a)	Newport C	D 0-0	
13		27	(a)	Aberdare A	L 1-3	Black
14	Nov	8	(a)	Watford	L 0-1	
15		15	(h)	Northampton T	W 2-1	Russell, Batten
16		22	(a)	Charlton A	L 1-2	Cherrett
17	Dec	6	(a)	Merthyr T	W 2-1	Cherrett, Black
18		13	(h)	Aberdare A	W 2-0	Black, Sloan
19		20	(a)	Swansea T	L 0-2	
20		25	(h)	Exeter C	D 1-1	Batten
21		26	(a)	Exeter C	L 0-3	
22		27	(h)	Norwich C	W 5-0	Batten, Black 3, Cherrett
23	Jan	3	(a)	Brentford	L 0-1	
24		17	(h)	Millwall	D 1-1	Batten
25		24	(a)	Luton T	D 1-1	Cherrett
26		31	(h)	Gillingham	W 2-0	Logan, Cherrett
27	Feb	7	(a)	Bournemouth	W 1-0	Sloan
28		14	(h)	Brighton & HA	W 1-0	Sloan
29		21	(a)	Bristol R	D 1-1	Sloan
30		28	(h)	Newport C	L 0-2	
31	Mar	7	(a)	Southend U	W 3-0	Logan 2, Black
32		14	(h)	Watford	W 1-0	Black
33		21	(a)	Northampton T	L 2-5	Preston, Cock
34		28	(h)	Charlton A	W 3-2	Cock 2, Sloan
35	Apr	4	(a)	Queen's Park R	W 1-0	Black
36		10	(h)	Bristol C	W 7-1	Leslie 3, Forbes 2, Black, Cock
37		11	(h)	Merthyr T	W 2-0	Leslie 2
38		13	(a)	Bristol C	D 2-2	Pullen, Cock
39		18	(a)	Reading	D 0-0	
40		20	(h)	Reading	W 2-0	Leslie, Cock
41		25	(h)	Swansea T	D 1-1	Forbes
42		29	(h)	Southend U	W 6-0	Forbes, Corcoran 2, Black, Leslie, Cock

FINAL LEAGUE POSITION: 2nd in Division Three South

Appearances
Goals

FA Cup

1	Jan	10	(a)	Swansea T	L 0-3		13,272

Appearances
Goals

Craig	Cosgrove	Russell	Logan	Preston	Rowe	Corcoran	Sloan	Cherrett	Leslie	Batten	Black	Dickinson	Price	Walker	Pullen	Fishwick	Wallace	Forbes	Cock	Miller	
1	2	3	4	5	6	7	8	9	10	11											1
1	2	3	4		6	7	8	9	10	11					5						2
1	2	3	4	5	6	7	8		10	9	11										3
1	2	3	4	5	6	7	8		10	9	11										4
1	2	3	4	5	6	7	8		10	9	11										5
1	2		4	5	6	7	8		10	9	11									3	6
1	2	3	4	5	6	7	8		10	9	11										7
1	2	3	4	5	6	7	8	9	10		11										8
1	2	3	4	5	6	7	8	9	10		11										9
1	2	3	4	5	6	7	8		10	9	11										10
1	2	3	4	5	6	7	8	9	10		11										11
1	2	3	4	5	6	7	8	9	10		11										12
1	2	3	4	5	6	7	8	9	10		11										13
1	2	3	4	5		7	8		10	9	11	6									14
1	2	3	4	5		7	8		10	9	11	6									15
1	2	3	4	5	6	7		8	10	9	11										16
1	2	3	4	5	6	7	8	9	10		11										17
1	2	3	4	5	6	7	8	9	10		11										18
1	2	3	4	5	6	7	8	9	10		11										19
1	2		4	5	6	7	8		10	9	11		3								20
1	2		4	5	6	7		8		9	11		3	10							21
1	2		4	5	6	7	8	9		10	11		3								22
1	2	3	4	5	6	7	8		10	9	11										23
1		3	4	6		7	8		10	9	11		2		5						24
1		3	4	6		7		9	11	10			2		5	8					25
1		3	4	6		7	8	9	10		11		2		5						26
1	2	3	4	6		7	8	9	10		11				5						27
1	2		4	6		7	8	9	10		11		3		5						28
1	2	3	4	6		7	8	9	10		11				5						29
1	2		4	6		7	8	9	10		11		3		5						30
1	2	3	9	6			8		10		11			4	5		7				31
1	2	3	4	6			8		10		11				5			7	9		32
1	2	3	4	6			8		10		11				5			7	9		33
1	2	3	4	6			8		10		11				5			7	9		34
1		3	4	6		7			10		11		2		5			8	9		35
1		3	4	6		7			10		11		2		5			8	9		36
1		3	4	6		7		9	10		11		2		5			8			37
1		3	8	6					10		11		2	4	5			7	9		38
1		3	4	6		7			10		11		2		5			8	9		39
1		3	4	6		7		8	10				2		5			11	9		40
1		3	4	6		7			10		11		2		5			8	9		41
1		3	4	6		7			10		11		2		5			8	9		42
42	31	36	42	41	21	37	31	21	40	17	38	2	16	3	20	1	1	11	10	1	
		2	3	1		4	8	9	14	10	13				1			4	7		

1 own-goal

1	2	3	4	5	6	7	8		10	9	11	1
1	1	1	1	1	1	1	1		1	1	1	

1925-26

Manager: Robert Jack

1	Aug	29	(h)	Southend U	W 6-2	Leslie, Cock 3, Black, Corcoran	15,000
2	Sep	2	(h)	Crystal P	W 6-2	Cock 2, Leslie 2, Forbes, Black	14,000
3		5	(a)	Norwich C	W 3-0	Leslie, Black, Cock	11,000
4		12	(h)	Millwall	W 2-0	Cock, Leslie	16,748
5		19	(a)	Northampton T	L 1-2	Black	6,344
6		23	(h)	Brentford	W 4-0	Black, Cock, Corcoran, Whitton (og)	8,384
7		26	(h)	Aberdare A	W 7-2	Pullen, Forbes, Cock 2, Corcoran, Leslie, Black	14,000
8	Oct	3	(a)	Brighton & HA	W 2-1	Jenkins (og), Cock	14,000
9		10	(h)	Watford	W 2-1	Forbes, Black	12,000
10		17	(a)	Reading	D 1-1	Pullen	17,000
11		24	(h)	Bournemouth	W 7-2	Black 2, Leslie 2, Cock 2, Corcoran	8,000
12		31	(a)	Bristol R	W 3-2	Black, Corcoran, Cock	25,000
13	Nov	7	(h)	Swindon T	D 1-1	Leslie	10,000
14		14	(a)	Merthyr T	D 1-1	Logan	11,000
15		21	(h)	Newport C	W 3-0	Smith (og), Cock, Black	11,000
16		28	(a)	Crystal P	D 5-5	Corcoran, Forbes, Cock 2, Black	15,000
17	Dec	5	(h)	Queen's Park R	W 3-1	Cock, Black, Forbes	12,000
18		19	(h)	Gillingham	W 2-1	Leslie, Black	7,000
19		25	(a)	Exeter C	L 0-4		10,000
20		26	(h)	Exeter C	D 2-2	Cock 2	20,000
21		28	(a)	Luton T	D 1-1	Healy	10,000
22	Jan	2	(a)	Southend U	L 0-2		8,000
23		16	(h)	Norwich C	W 6-3	Leslie, Cock 4, Sloan	10,000
24		23	(a)	Millwall	D 0-0		20,000
25		30	(h)	Northampton T	L 2-4	Healy, Forbes	12,000
26	Feb	6	(a)	Aberdare A	L 1-6	Black	6,000
27		13	(h)	Brighton & HA	W 5-3	Forbes, Black, Batten, Cock 2	12,000
28		20	(a)	Watford	W 1-0	Forbes	8,000
29		27	(h)	Reading	L 1-3	Healy	22,000
30	Mar	6	(a)	Bournemouth	W 2-1	Leslie 2	7,000
31		13	(h)	Bristol R	L 1-2	Cock	17,000
32		20	(a)	Swindon T	L 0-2		6,000
33		25	(a)	Charlton A	W 5-0	Forbes, Cock, Leslie 2, Matthews	5,162
34		27	(h)	Merthyr T	W 3-0	Leslie, Matthews, Logan	12,000
35	Apr	2	(h)	Bristol R	W 3-1	McKenzie, Forbes, Matthews	27,000
36		3	(a)	Newport C	W 3-0	Black, Logan 2	12,000
37		5	(a)	Bristol C	L 1-2	Black	25,000
38		10	(h)	Luton T	W 4-3	Forbes 2, Cock 2	15,000
39		17	(a)	Queen's Park R	W 4-0	McKenzie, Leslie, Black, Cock	8,000
40		24	(h)	Charlton A	W 1-0	Matthews	15,000
41		26	(a)	Brentford	D 2-2	Matthews, Forbes	10,123
42	May	1	(a)	Gillingham	L 0-2		10,651

FINAL LEAGUE POSITION: 2nd in Division Three South

Appearances
Goals

FA Cup

1	Jan	9	(a)	Chelsea	L 1-2	Cock	31,025

Appearances
Goals

Craig	Price	Russell	Logan	Pullen	Preston	Corcoran	Forbes	Cock	Leslie	Black	Smith	Cosgrove	Miller	Healy	Walker	Sloan	Livingstone	Titmuss	Batten	McKenzie	Macey	Matthews	Hardie	
1	2	3	4	5	6	7	8	9	10	11														1
1	2	3	4	5		7	8	9	10	11	6													2
1	2	3	4	5		7	8	9	10	11	6													3
1	2	3	4	5		7	8	9	10	11	6													4
1	3		4	5		7	8	9	10	11	6	2												5
1	3		4	5		7	8	9	10	11	6	2												6
1	2	3	4	5		7	8	9	10	11	6													7
1	2	3	4	5		7	8	9	10	11	6													8
1	2	3	4	5		7	8	9	10	11	6													9
1	2	3	4	5		7	8	9	10	11	6													10
1	2	3	4	5		7	8	9	10	11	6													11
1	3			5	4	7	8	9	10	11	6	2												12
1	2	3	4	5		7	8	9	10	11	6													13
1	2	3	4	5		7	8	9	10	11	6													14
1	2	3		5	4	7	8	9	10	11	6													15
1	2	3		5	4	7	8	9	10	11	6													16
1	2		4	5		7	8	9	10	11	6		3											17
1	2	3	4	5		7	8	9	10	11	6													18
1	2	3	4	5		7	8	9	10	11	6													19
1	2	3	4	5		7	8	9	10	11	6													20
1	2	3	4	5					10	11	6			7		8			9					21
1	2	3	4	5			8	9	11		6			7	10									22
1	2	3		5	4		11	9	10		6			7		8								23
1	2			5	4		11	9	10		6	3		7		8								24
1	2		8	5	4		11		10		6		3	7					9					25
1	2			5	4		8	9	10	11	6		3	7										26
1				5	4		8	9		11	6			7			2	3	10					27
1	2			5	4		8	9	10	11	6			7				3						28
1		2		5			8	9		11	6			7				3		4	10			29
1		2		4			9		10	11	6			7		8		3		5				30
1		2		4			8	9	10	11	6							3		5		7		31
1				4			8	9	10	11							2	3		5		7	6	32
1					4		8	9	10	11							2	3		5		7	6	33
1			9		4		8		10	11							2	3		5		7	6	34
1			9		4		8		10	11							2	3		5		7	6	35
1			9		4		8		10	11							2	3		5		7	6	36
1			9		4		8		10	11							2	3		5		7	6	37
1		2			4		8	9	10	11								3		5		7	6	38
1					4		8	9	10	11							2	3		5		7	6	39
1					4		8	9	10	11							2	3		5		7	6	40
1					4		8	9	10	11							2	3		5		7	6	41
1		2			4		8	9	10	11								3		5		7	6	42
42	27	24	24	32	20	20	41	35	40	38	30	4	3	10	1	4	10	16	3	14	1	12	11	
			4	2		6	13	31	17	19				3		1			1	2		5		

3 own-goals

1	2	3	4	5	6		8	9	10	11				7										1
1	1	1	1	1	1		1	1	1	1				1										
								1																

1926-27

Manager: Robert Jack

1	Aug	28	(a)	Newport C	L 1-2	Cock	12,000
2	Sep	1	(h)	Northampton T	W 3-0	McKenzie, Cock, Forbes	12,000
3		4	(h)	Aberdare A	W 2-0	Leslie, Cock	15,000
4		8	(h)	Bournemouth	D 1-1	Leslie	12,000
5		11	(a)	Gillingham	L 1-4	Cock	5,000
6		18	(h)	Watford	W 4-0	Cock 3, Leslie	10,000
7		22	(a)	Bristol C	L 2-4	Cock, Leslie	19,346
8		25	(a)	Cyrstal P	D 1-1	Sloan	17,000
9	Oct	2	(h)	Coventry C	W 3-0	McKenzie, Cock 2	11,000
10		9	(a)	Queen's Park R	L 2-4	Smith, Cock	14,000
11		16	(h)	Southend U	W 2-1	Cock, Forbes	9,000
12		23	(a)	Merthyr T	L 1-5	Cock	4,000
13		30	(h)	Swindon T	W 3-1	Matthews, McKenzie, Leslie	17,000
14	Nov	6	(a)	Bristol R	D 2-2	Matthews, Cock	9,000
15		13	(h)	Millwall	D 1-1	Forbes	6,000
16		20	(a)	Brentford	D 0-0		8,000
17	Dec	4	(a)	Brighton & HA	W 2-1	Cock, Black	14,000
18		11	(h)	Queen's Park R	W 2-0	Forbes, Leslie	10,000
19		18	(a)	Luton T	D 3-3	Forbes, Cock, Black	9,000
20		25	(h)	Exeter C	W 2-0	Leslie, Forbes	14,000
21		26	(a)	Exeter C	W 2-0	Black, Matthews	16,000
22	Jan	1	(a)	Bournemouth	L 2-6	Logan, Cock	7,000
23		15	(h)	Newport C	W 4-1	Forbes, Cock, Craig, Black	9,000
24		22	(a)	Aberdare A	W 6-5	Matthews, Leslie, Cock 2, Black 2	3,000
25		29	(h)	Gillingham	D 0-0		7,000
26	Feb	5	(a)	Watford	W 4-1	Cock 3, Matthews	6,000
27		12	(h)	Crystal P	W 7-1	Hardie, Leslie 3, Black, Cock 2	13,000
28		19	(a)	Coventry C	W 3-2	Black, Forbes, Cock	17,000
29	Mar	5	(a)	Southend U	W 2-1	Matthews, Andrews (og)	6,000
30		12	(h)	Merthyr T	D 1-1	Leslie	9,000
31		19	(a)	Swindon T	W 2-1	Cock 2	14,000
32		26	(h)	Bristol R	W 3-2	Forbes 2, Cock	7,000
33	Apr	2	(a)	Millwall	W 3-1	Cock 2, Black	20,000
34		9	(h)	Brentford	W 2-1	Logan, Craig	9,000
35		15	(h)	Charlton A	W 3-1	Craig, Leslie 2	20,000
36		16	(a)	Northampton T	L 1-2	Forbes	12,000
37		18	(a)	Charlton A	D 1-1	McKenzie	8,711
38		23	(h)	Brighton & HA	W 2-0	Matthews, Forbes	15,000
39		25	(h)	Norwich C	W 2-1	Matthews, Forbes	5,723
40		30	(a)	Norwich C	W 2-0	Cock, Forbes	9,000
41	May	4	(h)	Bristol C	W 4-2	Logan 2, Black, Forbes	15,800
42		7	(h)	Luton T	W 1-0	McKenzie	10,000

FINAL LEAGUE POSITION: 2nd in Division Three South

Appearances
Goals

FA Cup

1	Jan	8	(a)	South Shields	L 1-3	Cock	9,210

Appearances
Goals

Craig	Livingstone	Russell	Preston	McKenzie	Hardie	Matthews	Forbes	Cock	Leslie	Black	Titmuss	Baker	Sloan	Thomson	Pullen	Smith	Bowden	Price	Lee	Demmelweek	Cosgrove	Logan	
1	2	3	4	5	6	7	8	9	10	11													1
1	2	3	4	5	6	7	8	9	10	11													2
1	2	3	4	5	6	7	8	9	10	11													3
1	2		4	5	6	7	8	9	10	11	3												4
1	3		4	5	6	7	8	9	10			11									2		5
1	3		4	5	6	7	11	9	10				8								2		6
1	3		4	5	6	7	11	9	10				8								2		7
	3		4	5	6	7	11	9	10				8	1							2		8
	2	3	4	5	6	7	11	9	10				8	1									9
	2	3	4		6	7	11	9					8	1	5	10							10
	2	3	4	5	6	7	10	9		11			8	1									11
	3	2	4	5	6	7	10	9		11			8	1									12
		2		5	6	7	8	9	10	11	3			1								4	13
		2			6	7	8	9	10	11	3			1	5							4	14
1		2			6	7	8	9	10	11	3				5							4	15
1		5			6	7	8	9	10	11	3										2	4	16
1		5			6	7	8	9	10	11	3										2	4	17
1		5			6	7	8	9	10	11	3										2	4	18
1		5			6	7	8	9	10	11	3										2	4	19
1		5			6	7	8	9	10	11	3										2	4	20
1		5			6	7	8	9	10	11	3										2	4	21
1		5			6	7	8	9	10	11	3										2	4	22
1		5			6	7	8	9	10	11	3										2	4	23
1		2		5	6	7	8	9	10	11	3											4	24
1		2		5	6	7	8	9	10	11	3											4	25
1		2		5	6	7	8	9	10	11	3											4	26
1		2		5	6	7	8	9	10	11	3											4	27
1		2		5	6	7	8	9	10	11	3											4	28
1				5	6	7	8	9	10	11	3										2	4	29
1			6	5		7	8		10	11	3						9				2	4	30
1		2	4	5	6	7	8	9	10	11	3												31
1		2	4	5	6	7	8	9	10	11	3												32
1		2	4	5	6	7	10	9		11	3											8	33
1		2	4	5	6	7	10	9		11	3											8	34
1		2	4	5	6	7	8	9	10	11	3												35
1			4	5	6	7	10	9		11	3										2	8	36
		3	6	5		7	10	9		11								2	1	8		4	37
1		3	4	5	6	7	8	9	10	11								2					38
1		3	4	5	6	7	10	9		11											2	8	39
1		3	4	5	6	7	10	9		11											2	8	40
1		3	4	5	6	7	8		10	11											2	9	41
1		3	4	5	6	7	8		10	11											2	9	42
34	12	34	25	31	40	42	42	39	33	36	25	1	7	7	3	1	1	2	1	1	19	26	
3				5	1	8	15	32	14	10			1			1						4	

1 own-goal

1		5			6	7	8	9	10	11	3										2	4	1
1		1			1	1	1	1	1	1	1										1	1	
								1															

1927-28

Manager: Robert Jack

1	Aug	27	(h)	Merthyr T	W	5-0	Forbes 4, Leslie	9,000
2		31	(h)	Bristol R	W	4-1	Sloan 3, Black	10,084
3	Sep	3	(a)	Walsall	L	1-2	Leslie	12,000
4		7	(a)	Bristol R	L	1-3	Black	9,013
5		10	(h)	Gillingham	D	2-2	Cock, Black	9,000
6		17	(a)	Coventry C	D	1-1	Black	12,000
7		24	(h)	Newport C	W	2-0	Leslie, Black	8,000
8	Oct	1	(a)	Swindon T	D	2-2	Black, Cock	6,000
9		8	(h)	Queen's Park R	W	3-0	Leslie, Black, Sloan	14,000
10		15	(a)	Watford	W	2-1	Leslie, Black	15,000
11		22	(a)	Northampton T	L	1-2	Leslie	12,000
12		29	(h)	Norwich C	W	4-2	Leslie, Forbes 3	9,000
13	Nov	5	(a)	Torquay U	W	2-1	Forbes, Black	11,000
14		12	(h)	Southend U	W	3-2	Forbes, Matthews, Black	11,000
15		19	(a)	Brighton & HA	L	1-4	Forbes	7,000
16	Dec	3	(a)	Brentford	W	2-0	Black, Logan	20,000
17		10	(h)	Millwall	D	3-2	Matthews, Leslie, Bland	14,000
18		17	(a)	Millwall	L	0-2		20,000
19		24	(h)	Crystal P	W	5-1	Forbes, Black 2, McKenzie, Bland	10,000
20		26	(a)	Exeter C	L	0-2		9,000
21		27	(h)	Exeter C	L	1-2	Leslie	12,000
22	Jan	7	(h)	Walsall	W	2-1	Matthews, Sloan	7,361
23		14	(a)	Merthyr T	W	4-1	Forbes, McKenzie, Richards 2	1,500
24		21	(a)	Gillingham	L	1-3	Richards	5,000
25		28	(h)	Coventry C	W	4-0	Mackay 3, Leslie	6,000
26	Feb	4	(a)	Newport C	D	1-1	Leslie	5,000
27		11	(h)	Swindon T	W	3-0	Richards, Forbes, Leslie	15,000
28		18	(a)	Queen's Park R	W	1-0	Mackay	15,000
29		25	(h)	Watford	L	0-1		15,000
30	Mar	3	(h)	Northampton T	D	3-3	Richards, Mackay, Leslie	15,000
31		10	(a)	Norwich C	L	0-2		8,000
32		17	(h)	Torquay U	W	4-1	Richards 3, Matthews	10,000
33		24	(a)	Southend U	L	0-3		5,000
34		31	(h)	Brighton & HA	W	2-0	Richards, Black	15,000
35	Apr	6	(a)	Charlton A	L	0-2		10,000
36		7	(a)	Luton T	D	1-1	Sloan	10,000
37		9	(h)	Charlton A	W	2-0	Leslie, Black	10,000
38		14	(h)	Brentford	W	1-0	McKenzie	5,000
39		21	(a)	Bournemouth	D	2-2	Bowden 2	6,000
40		25	(h)	Bournemouth	W	3-1	Leslie, Richards, Forbes	5,519
41	May	2	(h)	Luton T	W	4-0	Mackay, Bowden 2, Black	4,719
42		5	(a)	Crystal P	W	2-0	Sloan, Craig	15,000

FINAL LEAGUE POSITION: 3rd in Division Three South

Appearances
Goals

FA Cup

1	Nov	26	(a)	Gillingham	L	1-2	Matthews	9,000

Appearances
Goals

Craig	Russell	Titmuss	Preston	McKenzie	Hardie	Matthews	Sloan	Forbes	Leslie	Black	Cock	Stanbury	Logan	Cosgrove	Davis	Healy	Bland	Edmunds	Richards	Mackay	Price	Pullen	Lee	Bowden	Grozier	Cann	
1	2	3	4	5	6	7	8	9	10	11																	1
1	2	3	4	5	6	7	8	9	10	11																	2
1	2	3	4	5	6	7	8	9	10	11																	3
1	2	3	4	5	6	7	8	9	10	11																	4
1	2	3	4	5	6	7		8	10	11	9																5
	2	3	4	5	6	7		8	10	11	9	1															6
	2	3	4	5	6	7		8	10	11	9	1															7
	2	3	4	5	6	7		8	10	11	9	1															8
	2	3		5	6	7	8	9	10	11		1	4														9
	2	3		5	6	7	8	9	10	11		1	4														10
	2	3		5	6	7	8	9	10	11		1	4														11
		3		5	6	7		8	10	11	9	1	4	2													12
	2	3		5	6	7		8	10	11	9	1	4														13
	2	3		5	6	7		8	10	11		1	4		9												14
	2	3	4	5	6	7		11	10			1	8		9												15
	2	3	4	5	6			8	10	11		1	9			7											16
	2	3	4	5	6	7		9	10	11		1					8										17
		3	4	5	6	7		9	10	11		1		2			8										18
	2	3	4	5	6	7		9	10	11		1					8										19
	2		4	5	6	7		9	10			1		3			8	11									20
	2			5	6	7		9	10				4	3			8	11					1				21
	2	3		5	6	7	8	9	10			1					4	11									22
	2	3		5	6	7		8	10			1	4					11	9								23
	2	3		5	6	7		8	10			1	4					11	9								24
	2	3		5	6	7		11	10			1	4						9	8							25
	2	3		5	6	7		11	10			1	4						9	8							26
	2	3		5	6	7		11	10			1	4						9	8							27
	2			5	6	7		11	10			1	4						9	8	3						28
	2			5	6			7	10	11		1	4						9	8	3						29
	2			5	6			11	10			1				7	4		9	8	3						30
				4	6			11	10			1		2		7			9	8	3	5					31
	2			4	6	7			10	11		1							9	8	3	5					32
	3			5	6	7	8		10	11			4	2					9				1				33
1	3			5	6	7	8		10	11			4	2					9								34
1	3			5	6	7	8		10	11			4	2					9								35
1	3			5	6	7	8		10	11			4	2					9								36
1	3		4	5	6	7	8		10	11				2					9								37
		3	4	5	6		8		10	11				2					9				1		7		38
		3	4	5	6		8	7	10	11				2										9		1	39
1	2	3		5	6		8	7	10				4						9						11		40
1	2	3	4	5	6				10	11						7				8				9			41
1		3	4	5	6		8		10	11				2		7			9	10							42
12	36	30	19	42	42	33	17	33	41	29	6	26	21	13	2	5	7	5	18	10	5	2	3	2	2	1	
1				3		4	7	14	15	16	2		1				2		10	6				4			

	2	3	4	5	6	7		8	10	11		1			9												1
	1	1	1	1	1	1		1	1	1		1			1												
						1																					

1928-29

Manager: Robert Jack

1	Aug	25	(h)	Merthyr T	W	4-0	Matthews, Bowden 2, Leslie	10,000
2		29	(h)	Swindon T	W	3-0	Black 2, Leslie	11,557
3	Sep	5	(a)	Fulham	L	2-5	Hardie, Leslie	20,000
4		1	(a)	Swindon T	D	0-0		7,711
5		8	(h)	Queen's Park R	L	1-2	Leslie	12,000
6		15	(a)	Bristol R	W	1-0	McKenzie	12,000
7		17	(a)	Northampton T	L	0-3		7,110
8		22	(h)	Watford	W	2-0	Bowden 2	10,000
9		29	(a)	Walsall	D	1-1	Forbes	8,000
10	Oct	6	(h)	Newport C	W	5-2	Bowden, Forbes, Pugh (og), Leslie 2	11,000
11		13	(a)	Crystal P	W	4-1	Leslie, Bowden, Mackay, McKenzie	20,000
12		20	(h)	Southend U	D	1-1	Bowden	12,000
13		27	(a)	Exeter C	W	2-1	Black, Matthews	10,000
14	Nov	3	(h)	Brighton & HA	W	1-0	Leslie	10,000
15		10	(a)	Norwich C	W	3-0	Bowden 2, Matthews	10,000
16		17	(h)	Charlton A	D	2-2	Bowden 2	11,000
17	Dec	1	(h)	Coventry C	W	3-0	Bowden, Leslie 2	12,000
18		15	(h)	Brentford	W	4-0	Richards, Hardie, Matthews, Forbes	10,000
19		22	(a)	Bournemouth	L	1-4	Forbes	7,000
20		25	(h)	Gillingham	W	3-0	Leslie 2, Richards	16,000
21		26	(a)	Gillingham	L	0-2		5,000
22		29	(a)	Merthyr T	D	2-2	Bowden, Matthews	3,000
23	Jan	5	(h)	Fulham	W	4-2	Black 2, Bowden, Leslie	15,000
24		19	(a)	Queen's Park R	L	0-2		20,000
25	Feb	2	(a)	Watford	L	3-6	Bowden, Mackay, Black	6,000
26		9	(h)	Walsall	D	2-2	Black, Matthews	9,000
27		23	(h)	Crystal P	D	1-1	Matthews	10,000
28	Mar	2	(a)	Southend U	D	1-1	Bowden	7,000
29		9	(h)	Exeter C	D	0-0		10,000
30		11	(a)	Luton T	D	2-2	Sloan, Leslie	
31		16	(a)	Brighton & HA	L	1-2	Mackay	8,000
32		23	(h)	Norwich C	W	4-0	Black, Bowden, Leslie 2	10,000
33		29	(h)	Torquay U	W	4-0	Richards 3, Mackay	15,000
34		30	(a)	Charlton A	L	1-2	Matthews	15,000
35	Apr	1	(a)	Torquay U	D	2-2	Forbes, Pullen	6,000
36		6	(h)	Northampton T	D	1-1	Leslie	12,000
37		13	(a)	Coventry C	W	4-1	Healy, Leslie, Sloan, Bowden	12,000
38		28	(a)	Newport C	L	0-1		3,499
39		20	(h)	Luton T	W	2-0	Black 2	8,000
40		27	(a)	Brentford	W	2-0	Leslie 2	8,000
41	May	1	(h)	Bristol R	W	2-0	Forbes, Bowden	7,422
42		4	(h)	Bournemouth	W	2-0	Bowden, Leslie	5,000

FINAL LEAGUE POSITION: 4th in Division Three South

Appearances
Goals

FA Cup

1	Nov	4	(a)	Yeovil T	W	4-1	Bowden 2, Leslie, Matthews	Unknown
2	Dec	8	(a)	Brentford	W	1-0	Forbes	9,482
3	Jan	12	(h)	Blackpool	W	3-0	Black 3	30,358
4		18	(h)	Bradford	L	0-1		38,159

Appearances
Goals

Craig	Russell	Titmuss	Logan	McKenzie	Hardie	Matthews	Sloan	Bowden	Leslie	Black	Cann	Forbes	Mackay	Cosgrove	Richards	Bland	Deacon	Healy	Pullen	Vidler	Grozier	Price	
1	2	3	4	5	6	7	8	9	10	11													1
1	2	3	4	5	6	7	8	9	10	11													2
1	2	3	4	5	6	7	8	9	10	11													3
1	2	3	4	5	6	7	8	9		11		10											4
1	2	3	4	5	6	7	8		10	11		9											5
	2	3		5	6	7		9	10	11	1	8	4										6
	2	3		5	6	7		9	10	11	1	8	4										7
1	2	3		5	6	7		9	10	11		8	4										8
1		3		5	6	7			10	11		8	4	2	9								9
1	2	3		5	6	7		9	10	11		8	4										10
1	2	3		5	6	7		9	10	11		8	4										11
1	2	3		5	6	7		9	10	11		8	4										12
1	2	3		5	6	7		9	10	11		8	4										13
1	2	3		5	6	7		9	10	11		8	4										14
1	2	3		5	6	7		9	10	11		8	4										15
1		3		5	6	7		9	10	11		8	4	2									16
1	2	3	7	5	6			9	10	11		8	4										17
1	2	3		5	6	7			10	11		8	4		9								18
1	2	3			6	7			10	11		8	4		9	5							19
1	2	3			6	7			10	11		8	4		9	5							20
1	2	3		5	6	7			10	11		8			9	4							21
1	2	3		5		7		9	10	11		8	4				6						22
1	2	3		5	6			9	10	11		8	4					7					23
1	3			5	6			9	10	11		8	4			2		7					24
1	3			5	6			9	10	11		8	4			2		7					25
1	2	3			6	7	8	9	10	11			4						5				26
1	3			5	6	7		9	10	11		8	4			2							27
1	3			5	6	7		9	10	11			4			2				8			28
1	3			5	6	7			10	11		8	4			2					9		29
1	3			5	6	7	8		10				4		9	2				11			30
1	3			5	6	7		8	10	11			4		9	2							31
1	3			5	6	7		9	10	11		8	4			2							32
1	3			5		7	8		10	11			4		9	2			6				33
1				5		7	8		10	11			4		9	2			6			3	34
1	5					7	8		10	11			4		9	2			6			3	35
1	2			5			8		10	11		9	4			6		7				3	36
1				6			8	9	10	11			4			2		7	5			3	37
1	2			6					10	11		8	9			4		7	5			3	38
1				6				9	10	11		8	4			2		7	5			3	39
1				6				9	10	11		8	4			2		7	5			3	40
1				6				9	10	11		8	4			2		7	5			3	41
1	2	3		6				9	10	11		8	4					7	5				42
40	35	25	6	38	31	31	12	29	41	41	2	31	36	2	10	20	1	10	10	2	1	8	
				2	2	8	2	21	20	10		6	4		5			1	1				

1 own-goal

1	2	3		5	6	7		9	10	11		8	4						1
1	2	3		5	6	7			10	11		8	4		9				2
1	2	3		5	6			9	10	11		8	4					7	3
1	3			5	6			9	10	11		8	4			2		7	4
4	4	3		4	4	2		3	4	4		4	4		1	1		2	
						1		2	1	3		1							

1929-30

Manager: Robert Jack

1	Aug	31	(a)	Clapton O	W 2-0	Bowden, Black	18,054
2	Sep	4	(a)	Torquay U	W 4-3	Craig, Matthews, Bowden, Leslie	8,299
3		7	(h)	Brentford	D 1-1	Bowden	12,161
4		11	(h)	Torquay U	W 5-0	Leslie 2, McKenzie, Sloan, Black	9,827
5		14	(a)	Bristol R	W 3-2	Bowden, Leslie, Black	11,787
6		21	(h)	Brighton & HA	D 1-1	Vidler	11,530
7		25	(a)	Watford	W 2-0	Black 2	7,015
8		28	(a)	Swindon T	W 2-1	Grozier, Bowden	8,663
9	Oct	5	(h)	Gillingham	W 3-0	Pullen, Grozier, Bowden	5,777
10		12	(h)	Merthyr T	W 2-1	Pullen, Black	12,392
11		19	(a)	Northampton T	D 1-1	Leslie	21,102
12		26	(h)	Exeter C	W 4-1	Bowden 3, Black	15,427
13	Nov	2	(a)	Southend U	D 1-1	Bowden	10,966
14		9	(h)	Luton T	W 6-1	Vidler 2, Grozier, Sloan, Bowden, Black	15,073
15		16	(a)	Bournemouth	D 1-1	Bowden	13,667
16		23	(h)	Walsall	D 1-1	Bowden	12,543
17	Dec	7	(h)	Fulham	W 3-1	Black 2, Leslie	15,653
18		21	(h)	Crystal P	W 6-1	Grozier 4, Mackay, Vidler	15,728
19		25	(a)	Coventry C	L 0-1		26,400
20		26	(h)	Coventry C	W 3-0	Mackay, Leslie, Black	27,975
21		28	(h)	Clapton O	W 3-0	Black 2, Vidler	7,001
22	Jan	4	(a)	Brentford	L 0-3		20,511
23		18	(h)	Bristol R	W 3-0	Mackay, Grozier, Leslie	11,610
24	Feb	8	(a)	Gillingham	D 0-0		4,905
25		15	(a)	Merthyr T	W 3-0	Bowden 2, Sloan	2,968
26		22	(h)	Northampton T	W 1-0	Grozier	15,376
27	Mar	1	(a)	Exeter C	D 1-1	Vidler	17,742
28		8	(h)	Southend U	W 1-0	Grozier	13,998
29		13	(a)	Queen's Park R	W 2-1	Grozier, Black	8,758
30		15	(a)	Luton T	L 2-5	Black, Miller (og)	9,051
31		22	(h)	Bournemouth	W 2-1	Black 2	14,226
32		26	(h)	Swindon T	W 5-0	Bowden 2, Pullen, Sloan, Vidler	14,931
33		29	(a)	Walsall	W 3-1	Grozier, Bowden, Black	7,213
34	Apr	2	(a)	Brighton & HA	W 1-0	Vidler	9,791
35		5	(h)	Queen's Park R	W 4-0	Vidler 3, Pullen	18,897
36		12	(a)	Fulham	W 3-1	Pullen 2, Sloan	22,994
37		18	(h)	Newport C	W 3-1	Sloan 2, Mackay	26,409
38		19	(h)	Norwich C	W 4-1	Vidler 4	19,899
39		21	(a)	Newport C	W 2-0	Black 2	10,766
40		26	(a)	Crystal P	L 0-3		18,649
41		28	(a)	Norwich C	W 2-1	Pullen, Grozier	13,736
42	May	3	(h)	Watford	W 2-1	Sloan, Black	23,459

FINAL LEAGUE POSITION: 1st in Division Three South

Appearances
Goals

FA Cup

1	Nov	30	(a)	Dulwich H	W 4-1	Bowden 2, Black 2	Unknown
2	Dec	14	(a)	Watford	D 1-1	Bland	9,235
R		18	(h)	Watford	W 3-1	Vidler 3	18,929
3	Jan	11	(h)	Hull C	L 3-4	Vidler, Leslie, Black	28,929

Appearances
Goals

Craig	Russell	Titmuss	Mackay	Pullen	McKenzie	Matthews	Sloan	Bowden	Leslie	Black	Hardie	Bland	Healy	Grozier	Vidler	Price	Richards	Cosgrove	Fellowes	Cann	
1	2	3	4	5	6	7	8	9	10	11											1
1		3	4		5	7	8	9	10	11	6	2									2
1	2	3	4		5	7	8	9	10	11	6										3
1		3	4		5		8	9	10	11	6	2	7								4
1		3	4		5		8	9	10	11	6	2	7								5
1		3	4		5		8		10	11	6	2		7	9						6
1		3		5	4		8		10	11	6	2		7	9						7
1		3		5	4		8	9	10		6	2		7	11						8
1		3		5	4		8	9	10		6	2		7	11						9
1		3	4	5			8	9	10	11	6	2		7							10
1		3	4	5		7	8	9	10		6	2			11						11
1		3	4	5			8	9	10	11	6	2		7							12
1		3	4	5			8	9	10	11	6	2		7							13
1		3	4	5			8	9		11	6	2		7	10						14
1		3	8	5	4			9		11	6	2		7	10						15
1		3	4	5	6			9		11		2		7	10		8				16
1		3	4		5			9	10	11		6		7	8	2					17
1		3	8		5			9		11	6	4		7	10	2					18
1		3			5			9	10	11	6	4		7	8	2					19
1	2	3	8		5				10	11	6	4		7	9						20
1	2	3	8		5					11	6	4	7	10	9						21
1	2	3	8		5			9	10		6	4		7	11						22
1	3		4		5		8	9	10	11	6	2		7	11						23
1	3		4		5		8	9	10	11	6	2		7							24
1			4		5		8	9	10	11	6	3		7				2			25
1		3	4		5		8	9	10	11	6	2		7							26
1		3	4		5		8		10	11	6	2		7	9						27
1		3	4		5		8		10	11	6	2		7	9						28
1		3	4		5		8	9	10	11	6	2		7							29
1		3	4		5		8	9	10	11	6	2		7							30
		3	4		5		8	9	10	11	6	2		7						1	31
		3		5	4		8	9		11	6	2		7	10					1	32
		3		5	4		8	9		11	6	2		7	10					1	33
		3		5	4		8		10	11	6	2		7	9					1	34
		3		5	4		8		10	11	6	2		7	9					1	35
		3		5	4	7	8	9		11	6	2			10					1	36
		3	9	5	4		8			11	6	2		7	10					1	37
		3	8	5	4	7				11	6	2		10	9					1	38
		3	6	5	4		8		10	11		2		7	9					1	39
				5	4		8		10	11		6		7	9	3		2		1	40
				5	4		8		10	11		2		7	9	3			6	1	41
		3		5	4		8		10	11		2		7	9				6	1	42
30	7	37	30	22	37	6	33	28	32	37	35	40	3	35	28	5	1	2	2	12	
1			4	7	1	1	8	18	8	21				13	15						

1 own-goal

1			4		5		8	9	10	11		6		7		2					1
1			4		5	8			10	11		6		7	9	2					2
1			8		5				10	11	6	4		7	9	2					R
1			4		5		8		10	11	6	2		7	9						3
4			4		4	1	2	1	4	4	2	4		4	3	3					
								2	1	3		1			4						

1930-31

Manager: Robert Jack

1	Aug	30	(h)	Everton	L 2-3	Grozier, Leslie	34,236
2	Sep	3	(a)	Bristol C	L 1-2	Sloan	19,225
3		6	(a)	Bury	L 0-2		11,898
4		10	(h)	Barnsley	W 4-0	Black 2, Grozier, Matthews	18,560
5		13	(h)	Southampton	L 2-3	Black 2	19,610
6		20	(h)	Swansea T	D 0-0		12,688
7		22	(a)	Cardiff C	L 1-4	Black	6,615
8		27	(a)	West Brom A	W 2-1	Vidler, Grozier	19,821
9	Oct	4	(h)	Port Vale	W 2-1	Grozier, Vidler	20,243
10		11	(a)	Bradford C	L 0-1		15,661
11		18	(a)	Preston NE	L 1-2	Black	17,434
12		25	(h)	Burnley	L 1-2	Leslie	18,494
13	Nov	1	(a)	Bradford	L 1-7	Black	9,697
14		8	(h)	Stoke C	L 1-2	Black	15,372
15		15	(a)	Nottingham F	D 1-1	Black	8,433
16		22	(h)	Oldham A	D 1-1	Leslie	14,940
17		29	(a)	Millwall	L 1-4	Roberts	13,077
18	Dec	6	(h)	Tottenham H	W 2-0	Grozier, Black	24,549
19		13	(a)	Reading	W 2-1	Leslie, Black	8,235
20		20	(h)	Wolves	W 3-2	Bowden, Grozier 2	22,049
21		26	(h)	Cardiff C	W 5-1	Black 2, Pullen, Leslie, Bird	31,106
22		27	(a)	Everton	L 1-9	Black	37,018
23	Jan	1	(a)	Barnsley	W 4-0	Bird 2, Pullen, Grozier	8,438
24		3	(h)	Bury	L 3-6	Grozier, Chester (og), Bowden	19,749
25		17	(a)	Southampton	D 3-3	Bowden 2, Grozier	13,745
26		24	(a)	Swansea T	L 0-2		9,598
27		31	(h)	West Brom A	W 5-1	Vidler 3, Bowden, Black	9,319
28	Feb	7	(a)	Port Vale	L 1-2	Black	10,236
29		14	(h)	Bradford C	L 0-2		15,539
30		21	(h)	Preston NE	L 1-2	Vidler	16,382
31		28	(a)	Burnley	D 2-2	Leslie, Bowden	4,986
32	Mar	7	(h)	Bradford	D 0-0		13,123
33		14	(a)	Stoke C	D 0-0		8,490
34		21	(h)	Nottingham F	W 1-0	Roberts	18,075
35		28	(a)	Oldham A	L 1-2	Bowden	88,458
36	Apr	3	(h)	Charlton A	L 1-3	Black	23,554
37		4	(h)	Millwall	W 5-0	Black, Bowden 2, Bird, Grozier	16,685
38		6	(a)	Charlton A	W 3-1	Bowden, Bird, Grozier	12,675
39		11	(a)	Tottenham H	D 1-1	Black	33,546
40		18	(h)	Reading	W 3-1	Roberts, Leslie, Mantle	20,804
41		25	(a)	Wolves	L 3-4	Leslie, Bowden, Roberts	3,569
42	May	2	(h)	Bristol C	W 5-3	Black, Grozier 3, Hardie	19,423

FINAL LEAGUE POSITION: 18th in Division Two

Appearances
Goals

FA Cup

3	Jan	10	(a)	Everton	L 0-2		33,000

Appearances
Goals

Cann	Bland	Titmuss	Mackay	McKenzie	Hardie	Grozier	Sloan	Vidler	Leslie	Black	Bowden	Pullen	Cosgrove	Bird	Roberts	Birks	Mantle	Matthews	
1	2	3	4	5	6	7	8	9	10	11									1
1	2	3	4	5	6	7	8	10		11	9								2
1	2	3	8	4	6	7		9	10	11		5							3
1	2	3	4		6	8		9	10	11		5						7	4
1	2	3	4		6	8		9	10	11		5						7	5
1	2	3	4	5	6	8		9	10	11								7	6
1	2	3	4	6		7		9	10	11	8	5							7
1	2	3	4	5	6	7		9	10	11	8								8
1		3	4	5	6	7		9	10	11	8		2						9
1	2	3	4	5	6	7	8		10	11	9								10
1	2	3	8	4	6	7			10	11	9	5							11
1	2	3	8	4	6	7			10	11	9	5							12
1	2	3	4	5	6	7			10	11	9			8					13
1	3		4	5	6		8		10	11		9	2					7	14
1	3		4		6	7	8		10	11		5		9	2				15
1	3		4		6	7	8		10	11		5		9	2				16
1	3		4		6	7	8		10	11		5		9	2				17
1		3	4		6	7			10	11	8	5		9	2				18
1		3	4		6	7			10	11	8	5		9	2				19
1	2	3	4		6	7	8			11	10	5		9					20
1		3	4		6	7		10		11	8	5		9	2				21
1		3	4		6	7			10	11	8	5		9	2				22
1	3		4		6	7			10	11	8	5		9	2				23
1	3		4		6	7	8		10	11	9	5			2				24
1		3	4	6		7			10	11	8	5		9	2				25
1		3	4		6	7			10	11	8	5		9	2				26
1		3	4		6	7		9	10	11	8	5			2				27
1			4	5	6	7		9	10	11	8	3			2				28
1	6		4			7	8	10		11	9	5	3		2				29
1		3	4		6			9	10	11	8	5			2			7	30
1			4		6			9	10	11	8	5			2	3		7	31
1			4		6	7		9	10	11	8	5			2	3			32
1			4		6	7			10	11	8	5			2	3	9		33
1			4		6	7			10	11	8	5			2	3	9		34
1			4		6	7			10	11	8	5			2	3	9		35
1			4		6	7		9	10	11	8	5			2	3			36
1			4	5	6	7			10	11	8			9	2	3			37
1			4	5	6	7			10	11	8			9	2	3			38
1			4		6	7			10	11	8	5		9	2	3			39
1	5		4		6	7			10	11	8				2	3	9		40
1			4		6	7			10	11	8	5			2	3	9		41
1	5		4		6	7			10	11	8				2	3	9		42
42	22	22	42	16	39	39	10	17	38	42	33	31	3	15	27	12	6	6	
					1	15	1	6	8	20	11	2		5	4		1	1	

1 own-goal

1	3		4		6	7			10	11	8	5		9	2				1
1	1		1		1	1			1	1	1	1		1	1				

1931-32

Manager: Robert Jack

1	Aug	29	(h)	Port Vale	L	1-3	Bowden	21,749
2		31	(a)	Chesterfield	W	2-1	Bird, Black	13,471
3	Sep	5	(a)	Millwall	W	3-1	Black 2, Leslie	18,328
4		12	(h)	Bradford C	D	3-3	Leslie 3	19,282
5		16	(h)	Bristol C	W	2-1	Pullen, Roberts	16,276
6		19	(a)	Leeds U	D	0-0		10,782
7		23	(a)	Bristol C	W	2-0	Bowden, Black	7,021
8		26	(h)	Swansea T	W	4-2	Roberts, Vidler 2, Black	23,514
9	Oct	3	(a)	Barnsley	D	0-0		6,182
10		10	(h)	Notts C	L	3-4	Black, Grozier, Leslie	22,655
11		17	(h)	Nottingham F	W	5-1	Leslie 4, Grozier	20,425
12		24	(a)	Tottenham H	W	1-0	Bowden	22,863
13		31	(h)	Manchester U	W	3-1	Mantle, Bowden, Grozier	22,555
14	Nov	7	(a)	Burnley	D	1-1	Black	9,461
15		14	(h)	Wolves	D	3-3	Vidler, Bowden 2	18,870
16		21	(a)	Charlton A	L	0-2		12,462
17		28	(h)	Stoke C	D	1-1	Roberts	20,953
18	Dec	5	(a)	Southampton	W	6-0	Bowden 3, Vidler 2, Black	12,509
19		12	(h)	Preston NE	W	2-1	Leslie, Vidler	20,867
20		19	(a)	Bradford	L	0-2		11,900
21		26	(h)	Bury	W	5-1	Vidler 3, Bowden, Demmelweek	36,344
22	Jan	1	(a)	Bury	D	2-2	Bowden 2	13,197
23		2	(a)	Port Vale	L	0-2		7,731
24		16	(h)	Millwall	W	8-1	Vidler 3, Leslie, Bowden 2, Black, Pipe (og)	15,799
25		27	(a)	Bradford C	D	3-3	Matthews, Bowden, Pullen	10,762
26		30	(h)	Leeds U	W	3-2	Black, Vidler, Leslie	28,426
27	Feb	6	(a)	Swansea T	L	1-4	Vidler	14,191
28		13	(h)	Barnsley	W	3-0	Black 2, Vidler	16,251
29		20	(a)	Notts C	L	0-3		11,434
30		27	(a)	Nottingham F	L	2-3	Pullen, Leslie	9,823
31	Mar	5	(h)	Tottenham H	W	4-1	Leslie 2, Vidler, Black	18,903
32		12	(a)	Manchester U	L	1-2	Sloan	24,827
33		19	(h)	Burnley	W	4-0	Grozier, Roberts, Vidler, Reed	16,838
34		25	(a)	Oldham A	W	3-1	Black, Bowden 2	13,817
35		26	(a)	Wolves	L	0-2		27,552
36		28	(h)	Oldham A	W	5-0	Leslie 2, Melaniphy 2, Roberts	20,237
37	Apr	2	(h)	Charlton A	D	1-1	Bowden	15,412
38		9	(a)	Stoke C	L	2-3	Bowden, Pullen	7,651
39		16	(h)	Southampton	L	1-2	Mantle	13,653
40		23	(a)	Preston NE	L	2-5	Leslie, Mantle	5,051
41		30	(h)	Bradford	W	4-1	Mantle 2, Leslie, Bowden	9,356
42	May	7	(h)	Chesterfield	W	4-0	Mantle, Leslie, Roberts, Black	11,556

FINAL LEAGUE POSITION: 4th in Division Two

Appearances
Goals

FA Cup

3	Jan	9	(h)	Manchester U	W	4-1	Grozier 2, Vidler, Pullen	27,000
4		23	(a)	Arsenal	L	2-4	Vidler, Leslie	65,386

Appearances
Goals

Cann	Roberts	Birks	Mackay	McKenzie	Hardie	Grozier	Bowden	Bird	Leslie	Black	Pullen	Mantle	Reed	Sloan	Vidler	Wilson	Stanbury	Matthews	Harper	Demmelweek	Bland	Melaniphy	Titmuss	Gorman	
1	2	3	4	5	6	7	8	9	10	11															1
	2	3	4		6	7		8	10	11	5	9					1								2
1	2	3	4		6	7		8	10	11	5	9													3
1	2	3	4			7			10	11	5		6	8	9										4
1	2	3	4			7			10	11	5			8	9									6	5
1	2	3	4			7			10	11	5		6	8	9										6
1	2	3	4			7	8		10	11	5		6		9										7
1	2	3	4			7			10	11	5		6	8	9										8
1	2	3	4			7			10	11	5		6	8	9										9
1	2	3	4			7			10	11	5		6	8	9										10
1	2	3	4			7	9		10	11			6			8					5				11
1	2	3	4		6	7	9		10	11						8					5				12
1	2		4		6	7	8		10	11		9									5		3		13
1	2	3	4		6	7	8		10	11		9									5				14
1	2	3	4		6	7	8		10	11	5				9										15
		3	4		6	7	8		10	11	5				9		1				2				16
	2	3	4			7	8			11	5	9	6		10		1								17
	2	3	4			7	8		10	11	5		6		9		1								18
	2	3	4				8		10	11	5		6		9		1	7							19
	2	3	4				8		10	11	5		6		9		1	7							20
	2	3	4				8		10	11	5		6		9				1	7					21
		3	4			7	8		10	11	5		6		9				1		2				22
		3	4						10	11	5		6	8	9				1	7	2				23
	2		4			7	8		10	11	5		6		9				1				3		24
	2				6		9		10		5			8	11			7	1		4		3		25
	2		4			7		8	10	11	5		6		9				1				3		26
	2		4			7		9	10		5		6	8	11				1				3		27
	2		4			7			10	11	5		6	8	9				1				3		28
	2		4			7	8		10	11	5		6		9				1				3		29
	2		4			7	8		10	11	5		6		9				1				3		30
	2	3	4		6	7	8		10	11	5				9				1						31
	2	3	4		6	7			10	11	5			8	9				1						32
	2	3	4			7	8		10	11	5		6		9				1						33
	2	3	4			7	8		10	11	5		6		9				1						34
	2	3	4		6	7	8		10	11	5				9				1						35
	2		4	5	6	7	8		10						11				1			9	3		36
	2	3	4	5		7	8		10	11			6		9				1						37
		3	4		6	7	8		10		5				11				1		2	9			38
	2	3	4		6	7	8		10		5	9			11		1								39
	2	3	4		6	7	8		10		5	9			11				1						40
1	2		4				8		10		5	9	6		11			7					3		41
	2		4		6		8		10	11	5	9						7	1				3		42
15	38	31	41	3	17	35	29	5	41	35	35	9	24	11	34	2	7	5	20	2	9	2	11	1	
	6					4	20	1	20	15	4	6	1	1	17			1		1		2			

1 own-goal

	2		4			7	8		10	11	5		6		9				1				3		3
	2		4			7	8		10	11	5		6		9				1				3		4
	2		2			2	2		2	2	2		2		2				2				2		
						2			1		1				2										

1932-33

Manager: Robert Jack

1	Aug	27	(a)	Oldham A	L 1-3	Simpson	9,934
2		31	(h)	Grimsby T	W 4-0	Grozier, Black 2, Leslie	20,760
3	Sep	3	(h)	Preston NE	W 5-0	Black, Matthews 2, Vidler 2	13,318
4		6	(a)	Grimsby T	W 3-2	Roberts, Grozier, Black	9,140
5		10	(a)	Burnley	D 1-1	Grozier	12,438
6		17	(h)	Bradford	W 3-2	Leslie, Roberts, Grozier	21,240
7		24	(a)	Swansea T	W 1-0	Grozier	16,075
8	Oct	1	(a)	Nottingham F	D 1-1	Black	9,786
9		8	(h)	Charlton A	W 6-1	Black 3, Grozier, Bowden, Vidler	20,253
10		15	(a)	Stoke C	L 0-2		20,473
11		22	(h)	Bradford C	W 2-1	Barkas (og), Bowden	26,945
12		29	(a)	Chesterfield	D 1-1	Grozier	6,224
13	Nov	5	(h)	Fulham	L 2-3	Melaniphy, Bowden	24,021
14		12	(a)	Notts C	L 1-4	Melaniphy	10,479
15		19	(h)	Southampton	D 1-1	Leslie	20,667
16		26	(a)	Bury	L 1-2	Vidler	9,610
17	Dec	3	(h)	Lincoln C	L 0-3		18,347
18		10	(a)	Millwall	L 0-2		10,121
19		17	(h)	Port Vale	W 3-1	Bowden 2, Black	15,567
20		24	(a)	West Ham U	D 2-2	Bowden 2	21,312
21		26	(h)	Manchester U	L 2-3	Vidler 2	33,776
22		31	(h)	Oldham A	W 2-1	Grozier, Black	12,614
23	Jan	2	(a)	Manchester U	L 0-4		30,257
24		7	(a)	Preston NE	L 0-3		8,730
25		21	(h)	Burnley	W 4-0	Bowden 2, Black, Melaniphy	11,527
26	Feb	1	(a)	Bradford	L 0-1		3,708
27		4	(h)	Swansea T	W 1-0	Vidler	11,135
28		11	(h)	Nottingham F	D 1-1	Roberts	13,794
29		18	(a)	Charlton A	L 1-4	Grozier	11,283
30		25	(h)	Stoke C	W 1-0	Simpson	17,747
31	Mar	4	(a)	Bradford C	W 3-2	Grozier, Roberts, Bird	10,763
32		11	(h)	Chesterfield	W 1-0	Grozier	16,893
33		18	(a)	Fulham	L 1-3	Vidler	23,776
34		25	(h)	Notts C	L 0-2		11,609
35	Apr	1	(a)	Southampton	L 0-2		6,649
36		8	(h)	Bury	W 1-0	Black	12,713
37		14	(a)	Tottenham H	D 0-0		44,483
38		15	(a)	Lincoln C	L 0-2		9,012
39		17	(h)	Tottenham H	D 2-2	Sloan, Melaniphy	21,461
40		22	(h)	Millwall	D 0-0		11,934
41		29	(a)	Port Vale	L 1-4	Black	3,364
42	May	6	(h)	West Ham U	W 4-1	Melaniphy, Grozier, Leslie, Chalkley (og)	10,444

FINAL LEAGUE POSITION: 14th in Division Two

Appearances
Goals

FA Cup

3	Jan	14	(a)	Bradford	L 1-5	Leslie	10,509

Appearances
Goals

1927-28 names

Harper	Roberts	Rae	Mackay	Pullen	Hardie	Grozier	Bowden	Simpson	Leslie	Black S	Reed	Bird	Vidler	Matthews	McKenzie	Demmelweek	Melaniphy	Cann	Fellowes	Gorman	Birks	Sloan	Bland	Johnstone	Black T	
1	2	3	4	5	6	7	8	9	10	11																1
1	2	3	4	5		7			10	11	6	8	9													2
1	2	3	4	5		8			10	11	6		9	7												3
1	2	3	4	5		8			10	11	6		9	7												4
1	2	3	4	5		8			10	11	6		9	7												5
1	2	3	4			8			10	11	6		9		5	7										6
1	2	3	4			8		11	10		6		9		5	7										7
1	2	3	4			8	9		10	11	6				5	7										8
1	2	3	4		6	7	8		10	11			9		5											9
1	2	3	4	5		7	8		10	11	6		9													10
1	2	3	4	5		7	8		10	11	6		9													11
1	2	3	4	5	6	7	8		10	11			9													12
1	2	3	4	5	6	7	8		10	11							9									13
1	2		4	5	6	7	8		10	11							9				3					14
	2	3	4		6	8	9		10	11					5	7		1								15
1	2	3	4	5	6	7	8		10	11			9													16
1	2	3	4	5		7	8		10	11		9			6											17
1	2	3	4	5	6	7	8		10	11			9													18
1	2	3		5			8		10	11			9	7					4	6						19
1	2	3					8		10	11			9	7	5				4	6						20
1	2	3					8		10	11			9	7	5				4	6						21
		3	4	5		7	8			11			10				9	1		6	2					22
		3	4	5		7	8		10	11							9	1		6	2					23
		3	4	2		7	8		5	10			11				9	1		6						24
1	2	3	4			7	8		10	11					5		9			6						25
1	2	3			6	7				11			10		5		9			4		8				26
1	2	3			6	7	8			11			9		5					4		10				27
1	2			5	6	7	8			11			9							4	3	10				28
1	2				6	7	8			11			9							4	3	10	5			29
1	2	3	4			7	8	9	10	11										6			5			30
1	2	3	4			7		9		11		8	10							6			5			31
1	2	3	4			7		9		11		8								6			5	10		32
1	2	3	4			7				11		8	9							6		10	5			33
1		3	4	5		8				11				7			9			6		10	2			34
1		3	4	5		7			10	11			9							6		8	2			35
1		3	4		6	7			10	11			9				8						5		2	36
1	2	3	4		6	7			10	11			9									8	5			37
1	2	3	4	5		7			10	11							9			6		8				38
	2		4	5		7			10	11							9	1		6		8			3	39
1	2		4	5	6	7			10	11			9								3	8				40
1	2	3	4	5	6				10	11						7	9					8				41
1	2	3	4	5	6	8			10	11						7	9									42
37	36	37	35	25	17	38	23	5	33	41	9	5	27	7	11	6	13	5	3	19	6	12	9	1	2	
	4					12	9	2	4	13		1	8	2			5					1				

2 own-goals

	3	4	5		7	8		10	11			9					1		6	2		3
	1	1	1		1	1		1	1			1					1		1	1		
								1														

1933-34

Manager: Robert Jack

1	Aug	26	(h)	Manchester U	W	4-0	S.Black 2, Cookson 2	25,700
2		30	(h)	West Ham U	D	4-4	Cookson 2, Grozier, S.Black	24,312
3	Sep	2	(a)	Bolton W	L	0-2		11,388
4		4	(a)	West Ham U	L	1-5	Grozier	16,004
5		9	(h)	Brentford	D	1-1	Leslie	20,945
6		16	(a)	Burnley	D	2-2	S.Black, Leslie	11,609
7		23	(h)	Oldham A	W	1-0	Cookson	17,825
8		30	(a)	Preston NE	D	1-1	Vidler	13,814
9	Oct	7	(h)	Bradford	W	4-1	S.Black, Melaniphy 3	18,127
10		14	(a)	Grimsby T	L	1-5	Melaniphy	8,394
11		21	(a)	Lincoln C	D	1-1	Melaniphy	6,024
12		28	(h)	Bury	D	3-3	Cookson, Roberts, Gorman	12,966
13	Nov	4	(a)	Hull C	L	4-5	Cookson 2, Sloan, S.Black	12,281
14		11	(h)	Fulham	W	4-0	Grozier, Cookson 2, S.Black	18,993
15		18	(a)	Southampton	W	1-0	Cookson	12,333
16		25	(h)	Blackpool	L	0-3		21,533
17	Dec	2	(a)	Bradford C	W	4-3	Briggs, Sloan, Cookson 2	9,229
18		9	(h)	Port Vale	W	3-0	Grozier, S.Black, Cookson	13,672
19		16	(a)	Notts C	L	1-2	Cookson	7,590
20		23	(h)	Swansea T	D	2-2	S.Black, Cookson	14,872
21		25	(h)	Nottingham F	W	4-3	Cookson 2, Melaniphy, Sloan	21,446
22		26	(a)	Nottingham F	L	1-2	Melaniphy	17,293
23		30	(a)	Manchester U	W	3-0	Cookson, Melaniphy, Demmelweek	12,206
24	Jan	6	(h)	Bolton W	W	3-0	Cookson 2, Grozier	18,348
25		20	(a)	Brentford	L	0-3		17,566
26		27	(h)	Burnley	W	1-0	S.Black	13,952
27	Feb	3	(a)	Oldham A	D	1-1	Cookson	3,961
28		10	(h)	Preston NE	D	0-0		15,429
29		17	(a)	Bradford	L	1-4	Cookson	9,428
30		24	(a)	Grimsby T	L	0-2		8,394
31	Mar	3	(h)	Lincoln C	W	3-0	Sloan, Grozier, Cookson	10,913
32		10	(a)	Bury	L	0-4		4,715
33		17	(h)	Hull C	D	1-1	Melaniphy	6,068
34		24	(a)	Fulham	L	2-3	Cookson, Briggs	12,417
35		30	(a)	Millwall	D	0-0		20,302
36		31	(h)	Southampton	D	0-0		12,616
37	Apr	2	(h)	Millwall	W	1-0	Sloan	11,988
38		7	(a)	Blackpool	D	1-1	Vidler	13,994
39		14	(h)	Bradford C	W	3-0	S.Black, Cookson 2	8,981
40		21	(a)	Port Vale	L	0-4		4,956
41		28	(h)	Notts C	W	1-0	Melaniphy	7,465
42	May	5	(a)	Swansea T	L	1-2	S.Black	7,030

FINAL LEAGUE POSITION: 10th in Division Two

Appearances
Goals

FA Cup

3	Jan	13	(h)	Huddersfield T	D	1-1	Cookson	43,426
R		17	(a)	Huddersfield T	L	2-6	Briggs 2	18,000

Appearances
Goals

Harper	Roberts	Rae	Mackay	Carter	Reed	Grozier	Briggs	Cookson	Leslie	Black S	Pullen	Melaniphy	Godfrey	Bungay	Cann	Forrest	Demmelweek	McKenzie	Bland	Gorman	Sloan	Black T	Vidler	Bird	Simpson	Featherby	Tepper	
1	2	3	4	5	6	7	8	9	10	11																		1
1	2	3	4		6	7	8	9	10	11	5																	2
1	2	3	4	5	6	7	8		10	11		9																3
1	2	3	4	5		7	8		10	11			6	9														4
1	2	3	4			7	8		5	11		9	6	10														5
	2	3	4				8		10	11			6		1	5	7						9					6
	2	3	4				8	9	10	11			6		1		7	5										7
	2	3	4		6		8	9	10						1		7		5				11					8
	2	3			6				10	11		9			1		7		5	4	8							9
	2	3			6				10	11		9			1		7		5	4	8							10
	2				6		7		10	11		8			1				5	4		3	9					11
	2				6		7	9		11		10			1				5	4	8	3						12
	2		4		6	7	10	9		11					1				5		8	3						13
1	2	3			6	7	10	9		11									5	4	8							14
	2	3			6	7	10	9		11					1				5	4	8							15
	2	3			6	7	10	9		11					1				5	4	8							16
1	2	3	4			7	10	9		11									5	6	8							17
1	2	3	4			7	10	9		11									5	6	8							18
1	2	3	4			7	10	9		11									5	6	8							19
1	2	3	4				10	9		11							7		5	6	8							20
1	2	3	4				10	9		11		7							5	6	8							21
1	2	3	4		6		10	9		11		7						5			8							22
1	2	3	4				10	9		11		8					7	5		6								23
1	2	3	4			7	10	9		11		8						5		6								24
	2	3	4			7	10	9		11		8			1			5		6								25
	2	3	4			7	10	9		11		8			1			5		6								26
	2	3	4			8	10	9		11					1		7	5		6								27
	2	3	4			7	10	9		11					1			5		6				8				28
	2		4			7	10	9		11					1			5		6		3			8			29
	2	3	4				7	9		11					1			5		6	10				8			30
	2	3	4			7		9		11	5				1					6	10				8			31
	2	3	4			7		9		11	5				1					6	10				8			32
	2	3	4			7		9		11	5	8			1					6						10		33
	2	3	4				1	9		11	5				1					6	8					10		34
	2	3	4				10			11	5	7			1					6	8		9					35
	2	3					10			11	5	7			1				4	6	8		9					36
	2	3	4				10			7	5	9			1					6	8		11					37
	2	3	4				7			10	5	9			1					6	8		11					38
	2	3					7	9		10	5	8			1			4		6			11					39
	2		4				7	9		10	5	8			1					6		3	11					40
	2		4							11	5	8			1					6		3	9			10	7	41
	2		4				7			11	5	8			1					6	10	3	9					42
14	42	35	33	3	13	21	36	29	11	41	13	21	4	2	28	1	8	11	15	32	22	7	11	1	4	3	1	
	1					6	2	27	2	12		10					1			1	5		2					

Harper	Roberts	Rae	Mackay	Carter	Reed	Grozier	Briggs	Cookson	Leslie	Black S	Pullen	Melaniphy	Godfrey	Bungay	Cann	Forrest	Demmelweek	McKenzie	Bland	Gorman	Sloan	Black T	Vidler	Bird	Simpson	Featherby	Tepper	
1	2	3	4			7	10	9		11		8						5		6								3
1	2	3	4			8	10	9									7	5		6			11					R
2	2	2	2			2	2	2		1		1					1	2		2			1					
							2	1																				

1934-35

Manager: Robert Jack

1	Aug	25	(a)	Fulham	L 0-3		21,748
2		29	(h)	Hull C	W 6-4	Vidler 3, Sloan, Cookson, Melaniphy	17,234
3	Sep	1	(h)	Bradford	D 2-2	Melaniphy, Gorman	17,298
4		8	(a)	Port Vale	D 2-2	Cookson 2	10,133
5		10	(a)	Hull C	D 1-1	Melaniphy	7,533
6		15	(a)	Norwich C	L 0-3		17,474
7		22	(h)	Newcastle U	L 1-3	Vidler	13,404
8		29	(a)	West Ham U	L 1-2	Melaniphy	20,484
9	Oct	6	(h)	Blackpool	L 1-2	Vidler	8,286
10		13	(a)	Bury	L 1-2	Simpson	8,078
11		20	(h)	Barnsley	W 3-1	Briggs, Melaniphy 2	12,891
12		27	(a)	Sheffield U	W 2-1	Melaniphy, Grozier	14,041
13	Nov	3	(h)	Bradford C	W 3-1	Vidler, Grozier, Melaniphy	14,378
14		10	(a)	Notts C	W 3-1	Melaniphy, Sloan, S.Black	10,927
15		17	(h)	Southampton	W 4-0	Vidler 2, Melaniphy, Roberts	17,201
16		24	(a)	Bolton W	L 2-3	Melaniphy, Vidler	18,210
17	Dec	1	(h)	Oldham A	W 2-0	Sloan, Melaniphy	12,299
18		8	(a)	Burnley	W 2-1	Grozier, Roberts	11,072
19		15	(h)	Swansea T	W 3-2	S.Black 2, Davies (og)	13,780
20		22	(a)	Manchester U	L 1-3	S.Black	24,896
21		25	(a)	Brentford	D 0-0		23,786
22		26	(h)	Brentford	D 1-1	Roberts	32,509
23		29	(h)	Fulham	W 3-1	S.Black, Leslie, Grozier	17,888
24	Jan	5	(a)	Bradford	D 2-2	Melaniphy, Sloan	8,836
25		19	(h)	Port Vale	W 2-1	Briggs 2	14,041
26	Feb	2	(a)	Newcastle U	L 0-3		23,317
27		6	(h)	Norwich C	L 0-1		6,314
28		9	(h)	West Ham U	L 0-1		10,841
29		16	(a)	Blackpool	L 1-4	Vidler	7,484
30		23	(h)	Bury	W 3-0	Vidler, Featherby, Melaniphy	8,445
31	Mar	2	(a)	Barnsley	W 4-1	Roberts, Sloan, S.Black, Vidler	7,609
32		9	(h)	Sheffield U	W 2-0	S.Black, Vidler	10,657
33		16	(a)	Bradford C	W 1-0	Vidler	5,798
34		23	(h)	Notts C	W 4-0	Grozier 2, Sloan, Vidler	8,691
35		30	(a)	Southampton	L 0-1		7,271
36	Apr	6	(h)	Bolton W	W 1-0	Vidler	16,238
37		13	(a)	Oldham A	D 1-1	Briggs	7,374
38		19	(a)	Nottingham F	W 3-1	Vidler, Briggs, Grozier	10,316
39		20	(h)	Burnley	D 2-2	Vidler 2	11,929
40		22	(h)	Nottingham F	W 5-2	Briggs, Vidler 2, Sloan 2	14,436
41		27	(a)	Swansea T	L 0-3		6,562
42	May	4	(h)	Manchester U	L 0-2		10,767

FINAL LEAGUE POSITION: 8th in Division Two

Appearances
Goals

FA Cup

3	Jan	12	(a)	Brentford	W 1-0	S.Black	24,000
4		26	(h)	Bolton W	L 1-4	Briggs	41,403

Appearances
Goals

Cann	Roberts	Rae	Grozier	Pullen	Gorman	Briggs	Melaniphy	Cookson	Featherby	Vidler	Hill	Godfrey	Sloan	Harper	Demmelweek	McKenzie	Simpson	Black S	McNeil	Forrest	Bungay	Black T	Milne	Kirkwood	Leslie	
1	2	3	4	5	6	7	8	9	10	11																1
1	2	3	7		4		8	9		11	5	6	10													2
1	2	3	7		4		8	9		11	5	6	10													3
	2	3			4		8	9		11	5	6	10	1	7											4
	2	3			4		8	9		11	5	6	10	1	7											5
	2	3			4		8	9		11	5	6	10	1	7											6
	2	3			4		8	9		11	5	6	10		7	1										7
	2	3			4	8	9			11	5	6	10	1	7											8
1	2	3			4	10				9	5	6			7		8	11								9
1	2	3	4		6	10				9	5				7		8	11								10
1	2	3	4		6	8	9			10					7			11	5							11
1	2	3	7		6	8	9			11								10	5	4						12
1	2	3	7		6		9			11	4		8					10	5							13
1	2	3	7		4		9			11		6	8					10	5							14
1	2	3	7		6		9			11			8					10	5	4						15
1	2	3	7		4		9			11		6	8					10	5							16
1	2	3	7		4		9			11			8					10	5		6					17
1	2	3	7		4		9			11			8					10	5			6				18
1	2	3	7		4		9			11			8					10	5			6				19
1	2	3	7		4		9			11			8					10	5			6				20
1	2	3	7		4		9			11			8					10	5			6				21
1	2	3	7		4		9			11	5		8					10				6				22
1	2	3	7		4					11			8					10	5			6			9	23
1		3	7		4		9			11			8					10	5			6	2			24
1	2	3	7			9				11			8		4			10	5			6				25
1		3	6		4	9				11			8		7			10	5					2		26
1		3	6		4		9			11			8		7			10	5					2		27
1	2	3	6		4	10	9			11			8					7	5							28
1	2	3	7		4	10				9			8					11	5			6				29
1	2	3	7		4		8		10	9								11	5			6				30
1	2	3	7		4				10	9			8					11	5			6				31
1	2	3	7		4		8		10	9								11	5			6				32
1	2	3	7		6				10	9	4		8					11	5							33
1	2	3	7		4	10				9			8					11	5			6				34
1	2	3	7		4		10			9			8					11	5			6				35
1	2	3	7		4	10				9			8					11	5			6				36
1	2	3	7		4	10				9			8					11	5			6				37
1	2		7		6	10				9			8		4			11	5			3				38
1	2		4		6	10				9			8		7			11	5			3				39
1	2		4		6	10				9			8		7			11	5			3				40
1	2		4		6	10				9			8		7			11	5			3				41
1	2				4	10	7			9			8					11	5			6		3		42
37	39	37	35	1	41	18	27	7	5	42	12	10	35	4	15	1	2	34	31	2	1	21	1	3	1	
	4		7		1	6	14	3	1	21			8				1	7							1	

1 own-goal

Cann	Roberts	Rae	Grozier	Pullen	Gorman	Briggs	Melaniphy	Cookson	Featherby	Vidler	Hill	Godfrey	Sloan	Harper	Demmelweek	McKenzie	Simpson	Black S	McNeil	Forrest	Bungay	Black T	Milne	Kirkwood	Leslie	
1	2	3	7		4	9				11			8						10	5			6			3
1	2	3	6		4	9				11			8		7				10	5						4
2	2	2	2		2	2				2			2		1				2	2			1			
						1													1							

1935-36

Manager: Robert Jack

1	Aug	31	(h)	Manchester U	W	3-1	Vidler, Eggleston 2	22,366
2	Sep	2	(h)	Bradford C	L	0-1		19,195
3		7	(a)	Port Vale	L	0-2		9,718
4		9	(a)	Bradford C	D	2-2	Rich, Roberts	8,722
5		14	(h)	Fulham	W	2-0	S.Black, Vidler	17,663
6		21	(a)	Burnley	W	1-0	Smith	10,631
7		28	(h)	Charlton A	W	4-2	Eggleston 2, S.Black, Smith	17,819
8	Oct	5	(a)	Hull C	L	1-2	Roberts	4,990
9		12	(h)	Barnsley	W	7-1	S.Black 3, Briggs 2, Cookson 2	16,301
10		19	(h)	West Ham U	W	4-1	Cookson 2, S.Black, Vidler	19,140
11		26	(a)	Bury	L	0-2		6,952
12	Nov	2	(h)	Doncaster R	L	1-3	Cookson	16,734
13		9	(a)	Blackpool	L	1-3	Eggleston	12,415
14		16	(h)	Nottingham F	W	3-1	Hunter, Vidler, Sloan	14,268
15		23	(a)	Leicester C	L	0-2		16,251
16		30	(h)	Southampton	D	0-0		12,232
17	Dec	7	(a)	Sheffield U	D	0-0		12,867
18		14	(h)	Bradford	W	2-0	Eggleston 2	14,673
19		21	(a)	Norwich C	D	0-0		12,867
20		25	(a)	Tottenham H	W	2-1	S.Black, Eggleston	34,510
21		26	(h)	Tottenham H	W	2-1	S.Black, Mitcheson	34,426
22		28	(a)	Manchester U	L	2-3	McNeil, Sloan	20,894
23	Jan	1	(a)	Newcastle U	L	0-5		19,630
24		4	(h)	Port Vale	W	4-1	S.Black 4	13,779
25		18	(a)	Fulham	D	2-2	Eggleston, Vidler	15,326
26		29	(h)	Burnley	W	2-0	Richmond (og), S.Black	8,566
27	Feb	1	(a)	Charlton A	D	1-1	S.Black	22,776
28		8	(h)	Hull C	L	0-1		12,604
29		19	(a)	Barnsley	W	2-1	McNeil, S.Black	5,849
30		22	(a)	West Ham U	L	2-4	Melaniphy, McNeil	19,518
31	Mar	7	(a)	Nottingham F	W	1-0	Smith	7,524
32		11	(h)	Sheffield U	D	1-1	Mitcheson	15,916
33		14	(h)	Blackpool	W	3-2	Eggleston, Vidler, Briggs	13,761
34		21	(a)	Doncaster R	W	2-1	Vidler 2	12,279
35		28	(h)	Leicester C	W	2-1	Eggelston, Hunter	17,208
36	Apr	4	(a)	Southampton	L	0-2		5,882
37		10	(h)	Swansea T	L	1-2	Mitcheson	20,411
38		11	(h)	Bury	W	3-0	Mitcheson 2, Melaniphy	11,653
39		13	(a)	Swansea T	L	0-2		9,975
40		18	(a)	Bradford	D	2-2	Hunter, Mitcheson	5,774
41		25	(h)	Norwich C	W	5-1	Mitcheson 2, Cookson 2, Smith	6,601
42	May	2	(h)	Newcastle U	W	1-0	Preskett	12,933

FINAL LEAGUE POSITION: 7th in Division Two

Appearances
Goals

FA Cup

3	Jan	11	(a)	Stockport C	W	3-2	S.Black, Eggleston, Sloan	16,844
4		25	(a)	Chelsea	L	1-4	Vidler	53,704

Appearances
Goals

Davies	Roberts	Rae	Gorman	McNeil	Black T	Robbie	Smith	Vidler	Eggleston	Black S	Gooney	Powell	Rich	Kirkwood	Oxley	Cann	Cookson	Godfrey	Melaniphy	Grozier	Mitcheson	Hunter	Sloan	Hill	Briggs	Milne	Osman	Preskett	
1	2	3	4	5	6	7	8	9	10	11																			1
1	2	3		5	6	7	8	9	10		4	11																	2
1	2	3		5	6	7	8	9	10		4		11																3
1	2	3			6		8	9			4		11	5						7			10						4
1	2	3			6		8	9	10	11	4			5	7														5
1	2	3	4				8	9	10	11	6			5	7														6
	2	3	4				8	9	10	11	6			5	7	1													7
	2	3	4	5			8			10	6	11			7	1				9									8
	2	3	4	5			8			11	6					1	9			7					10				9
	2	3	4	5			8	10		11	6					1	9			7									10
	2	3	4	5			8	10		11	6					1	9			7									11
	2	3			6		7			11				5		1	9	4	8						10				12
	2	3	4				8	9	10	11	6			5		1						7							13
	2	3	4	5	6			9	10	11						1						7	8						14
1	2		6	5	3		8	9	10	11											4	7							15
	2		4	5	3		8			11	6					1	9				10	7							16
	2	3	4	5	6		8		10	11						1					9	7							17
	2	3		5	6		8		10	11					9	1					4	7							18
	2	3		5	6		7		10	11					9	1					4		8						19
	2	3		5	6		7		10	11					9	1					4		8						20
	2	3		5	6		7		10	11					9	1					4		8						21
	2	3		5	6		7		10	11					9	1					4		8						22
	2			5	3		8		10	11	6		7			1	9				4								23
	2	3	6						10	11	5					1	9				4		8	7					24
	2	3		5	6			9	10	11					7	1					4		8						25
	2	3		5	6		8	9	10	11						1					4	7							26
	2	3	4	5	6		8		10	11					9	1						7							27
	2	3	4	5	6				10	11					9	1						7	8						28
	2	3	4	5	6		8		10	11						1			9			7							29
	2	3	4	5	6		8		10	11						1			9			7							30
	2	3	4	5	6		8	9		11						1						7			10				31
	2	3	4	5	6		7	9	10	11						1					8								32
	2	3	6	5				9	10	11					7	1					4				8				33
	2	3	4	5	6			9	10	11						1					8	7							34
	2	3	4	5	6		8	9	10	11						1						7							35
1	2	3	4	5	6		7	9	10	11											8								36
	5	3	4		6		7		10	11					9	1			9		8					2			37
	2	3	4	5	6		8			11						1			9		10	7							38
	2	3	4	5	6		8			11						1			9		10	7							39
		3	4	5	6		8							2		1	9				10	7					11		40
		3	4	5	6		8							2		1	9				10	7					11		41
1	2	3	4	5	6					10							9					7					11	8	42
9	40	39	29	34	33	3	35	20	29	37	14	2	3	8	14	33	10	1	5	5	21	19	9	1	4	1	3	1	
	2			3			4	8	11	15			1				7		2		8	3	2		3			1	

1 own-goal

	2	3	5		6			9	10	11					7	1					4		8						3
	2	3		5	6		8	9	10	11						1					4	7							4
	2	2	1	1	2		1	2	2	2					1	2					2	1	1						
								1	1	1													1						

1936-37

Manager: Robert Jack

1	Aug	29	(a)	Fulham	D	2-2	Vidler, Mitcheson	22,000
2		31	(a)	Bradford C	D	1-1	Vidler	9,694
3	Sep	5	(h)	Doncaster R	W	7-0	Smith 3, S.Black, Hunter, Vidler 2	21,302
4		9	(h)	Bradford C	D	4-4	Vidler 2, S.Black, Mitcheson	17,715
5		12	(a)	Coventry C	L	0-2		15,000
6		14	(a)	Burnley	L	0-2		8,000
7		19	(h)	Leicester C	W	2-1	Eggleston 2	20,542
8		26	(h)	Nottingham F	W	4-1	Conner 2, S.Black, Vidler	18,000
9	Oct	3	(a)	Chesterfield	W	1-0	S.Black	14,382
10		10	(h)	Aston Villa	D	2-2	S.Black, Connor	43,596
11		17	(a)	West Ham U	D	1-1	Vidler	28,000
12		24	(h)	Norwich C	W	2-0	Connor, Mitcheson	18,560
13		31	(a)	Newcastle U	D	1-1	Hunter	29,000
14	Nov	7	(h)	Bradford	W	2-0	Connor, Vidler	11,513
15		14	(a)	Barnsley	W	3-1	Vidler, Mitcheson 2	8,000
16		21	(h)	Sheffield U	W	2-0	Connor, Hunter	22,000
17		28	(a)	Tottenham H	W	3-1	Smith, McNeil, Connor	33,000
18	Dec	5	(h)	Blackpool	L	1-3	Smith	25,131
19		12	(a)	Blackburn R	W	3-2	Eggleston 2, Vidler	8,000
20		19	(a)	Bury	W	3-0	Eggleston, Connor, Hunter	25,263
21		25	(h)	Swansea T	D	0-0		23,263
22		26	(h)	Fulham	L	0-3		37,242
23		28	(a)	Swansea T	W	1-0	Mitcheson	10,000
24	Jan	2	(a)	Doncaster R	L	1-2	Connor	12,000
25		9	(h)	Coventry C	W	1-0	Mitcheson	22,000
26		23	(a)	Leicester C	L	2-3	Connor 2	20,000
27	Feb	3	(a)	Nottingham F	W	3-2	Brown, Vidler, Hunter	4,000
28		6	(h)	Chesterfield	D	1-1	Brown	21,000
29		13	(a)	Aston Villa	L	4-5	Vidler, Connor 2, Hunter	42,000
30		20	(h)	West Ham U	W	2-0	Brown, Connor	19,500
31		27	(a)	Norwich C	W	2-1	Connor, McNeil	18,000
32	Mar	6	(h)	Newcastle U	D	1-1	Connor	19,000
33		13	(a)	Bradford	D	0-0		6,000
34		20	(h)	Barnsley	L	1-2	McNeil	14,737
35		26	(h)	Southampton	W	3-1	Mitcheson 2, Brown	24,116
36		27	(a)	Sheffield U	L	0-2		20,000
37		29	(a)	Southampton	D	0-0		21,000
38	Apr	3	(h)	Tottenham H	D	2-2	Brown 2	19,000
39		10	(a)	Blackpool	D	1-1	Dyer	22,000
40		17	(h)	Blackburn R	W	2-0	Dyer, Connor	17,577
41		24	(a)	Bury	L	0-2		8,000
42	May	1	(h)	Burnley	L	0-1		9,950

FINAL LEAGUE POSITION: 5th in Division Two

Appearances

Goals

FA Cup

3	Jan	16	(a)	Crewe A	W	2-0	Vidler, McNeil	11,542
4		30	(a)	Tottenham H	L	0-1		42,430

Appearances

Goals

Cann	Kirkwood	Rae	Gorman	McNeil	Black T	Smith	Mitcheson	Vidler	Eggleston	Black S	Roberts	Wallace	Hunter	Osman	Hill	Connor	Milne	Davies	Foley	Brown	Dyer	Ryan	Dougen	Tootill	
1	2	3	4	5	6	7	8	9	10	11															1
1		3	4	5	6	7	8	9	10	11	2														2
1			4	5	6	8		9	10	11	2	3	7												3
1			6	5	3	8	4	9	10	11	2		7												4
1	5		4		6	8		9		10	2	3	7	11											5
1	5		4		6	8		10		11	2	3	7		9										6
1		3	4	5	6	8		9	10	11	2		7												7
1		3	4	5	6			8	10	11	2		7			9									8
1		3	4	5	6			8	10	11	2		7			9									9
1		3	4	5	6	8		10		11	2		7			9									10
1		3	4	5	6	8		10		11			7			9	2								11
	2	3	4	5	6	8	10	11					7			9		1							12
	2	3	4	5	6	8	10	11					7			9		1							13
	2	3	4	5		8	10	11	6				7			9		1							14
	2	3	4	5	6	8	10	11					7			9		1							15
	2	3	4	5	6	8	10	11					7			9		1							16
	2	3	4	5	6	8	10	11					7			9		1							17
	2	3	4	5	6	8	10	11					7			9		1							18
		3	4	5		8	6	11	10		2		7			9		1							19
1		3	2	5	6	8	4	11	10				7			9									20
			4	5	6		10	11			2	3	7			9		1		8					21
			4	5	6	8			10		2	3	7	11		9		1							22
	2		4	5	6	8	10	11				3	7			9		1							23
	2		4	5	6		10	11				3	7			9		1		8					24
	2		4	5	6	8	10	11				3	7			9			1						25
	2	3	4	5	6	8	10	11					7			9			1						26
	2	3	4	5	6			9	10				7						1	8	11				27
	2	3	4	5	6	7		9	10										1	8	11				28
	5	3	4		6	8	10	11			2		7			9			1						29
		3	4	5	6		10	11			2		7			9			1	8					30
		3	4	5			10	11			2		7			9			1	8		6			31
				5	6		4	11	10		2	3	7			9			1	8					32
	3			5	6			11	10		2		7			9			1	8		4			33
	3			5	6	8	10	11			2		7			9			1			4			34
		3	4	5	6		8	11			2		7			9			1	10					35
		3	4	5	6		8	11			2		7			9			1	10					36
		3	4	5	6				10		2					9			1	8	11		7		37
		3	4		6		8				2					9			1	10	11		7	5	38
		3		5	6		8				2					9			1	10	11		7	4	39
		3	4	5	6		8				2		7			9			1	10	11				40
		3	4		6		8				2		7			9			1	10	11			5	41
		3	4	5	6		8				2								1	10	11		7	9	42
12	19	30	38	37	39	25	29	35	16	11	26	9	35	2	1	32	1	12	18	16	8	3	4	4	
				3		5	9	13	5	5			6			17				6	2				

	2		4	5	6		10	11				3	7			9		1		8					3
	2	3	4	5	6	8	10	11					7			9			1						4
	2	1	2	2	2	1	2	2				1	2			2		1	1	1					
				1				1																	

1937-38

Manager: Robert Jack

1	Aug	28	(h)	Fulham	W 4-0	Wright 2, Dougan, Brown	24,691
2		30	(a)	Blackburn R	L 1-2	Dougan	10,000
3	Sep	4	(a)	Bury	L 0-2		10,000
4		8	(h)	Blackburn R	D 2-2	Connor, Dyer	20,106
5		11	(a)	Chesterfield	L 0-2		17,684
6		15	(a)	Southampton	D 0-0		12,000
7		18	(h)	Swansea T	D 2-2	McNeil, Connor	18,355
8		25	(a)	Norwich C	L 0-4		23,000
9	Oct	2	(h)	Aston Villa	L 0-3		32,936
10		9	(a)	Bradford	L 0-2		12,748
11		16	(h)	Burnley	L 2-3	Wright, Vidler	15,609
12		23	(a)	Tottenham H	L 2-3	Morgan, Wright	23,000
13		30	(h)	Sheffield U	W 2-0	Wright, Vidler	21,392
14	Nov	6	(a)	Manchester U	D 0-0		18,000
15		13	(h)	Stockport C	W 2-1	Bourton, Morgan	21,168
16		20	(a)	Newcastle U	L 1-3	Bourton	21,000
17		27	(h)	Luton T	L 2-4	Vidler, Fletcher	18,559
18	Dec	4	(a)	Barnsley	L 2-3	Hullett, Wright	6,000
19		11	(h)	Nottingham F	W 1-0	Hullett	13,672
20		18	(a)	Coventry C	L 0-4		25,000
21		25	(h)	Sheffield W	L 2-4	Bourton, Brown	17,389
22		27	(a)	Sheffield W	D 1-1	McNeil	21,000
23	Jan	1	(a)	Fulham	W 3-2	Wright, McNeil, Vidler	13,215
24		15	(a)	Bury	W 2-1	McNeil, Brown	11,686
25		26	(h)	Chesterfield	D 1-1	Dougan	6,300
26		29	(a)	Swansea T	L 0-1		8,729
27	Feb	5	(h)	Norwich C	D 1-1	Mitcheson	14,050
28		19	(h)	Bradford	W 1-0	Dougan	15,349
29		23	(a)	Aston Villa	L 0-3		21,214
30		26	(a)	Burnley	W 2-0	Fletcher 2	9,315
31	Mar	9	(h)	Tottenham H	D 2-2	Brown 2	15,724
32		12	(a)	Sheffield U	D 0-0		22,708
33		19	(h)	Manchester U	D 1-1	Hullett	20,311
34		26	(a)	Stockport C	W 3-1	Beardshaw (og), Mitcheson, Fletcher	13,794
35	Apr	2	(h)	Newcastle U	W 2-1	McNeil, Brown	22,810
36		9	(a)	Luton T	D 1-1	Mitcheson	11,516
37		15	(a)	West Ham U	W 1-0	Hullett	21,947
38		16	(h)	Barnsley	D 2-2	Hullett, Mitcheson	21,406
39		18	(h)	West Ham U	W 2-1	Lane, Hullett	21,805
40		23	(a)	Nottingham F	L 0-1		13,696
41		30	(h)	Coventry C	W 3-1	Crawley (og), Lane, Hullett	20,662
42	May	7	(h)	Southampton	W 4-0	Hullett 3, Fletcher	15,574

FINAL LEAGUE POSITION: 13th in Division Two

Appearances
Goals

FA Cup

3	Jan	8	(a)	New Brighton	L 0-1		10,576

Appearances
Goals

Foley	Kirkwood	Rae	Gorman	McNeil	Black T	Dougan	Smith	Wright	Brown	Vidler	Tootill	Mitcheson	Connor	Dyer	Black S	Morgan	Hunter	Preskett	Mailey	Clark	Bourton	Hullett	Fletcher	Silk	Lane	Ryan	Cann	
1	2	3	4	5	6	7	8	9	10	11																		1
1	2	3	4	5	6	7	8	9	10	11																		2
1	2	3	4		6	7	8	9		11	5	10																3
1	2	3	4		6	7	8		10		5		9	11														4
1	2	3	4	5	6	7		8	10				9	11														5
1	2	3	4	5	6	7	8		10				9		11													6
1	2	3	4	5	6	7	8		10			6	9		11													7
1	2	3	4	5	6			8		10			9		11	7												8
1	2	3	4	5	6				10	11		8	9				7											9
1	2	3	4		6					10	5		9	11		7		8										10
1	2	3	4		6			9		10	5					7		8	11									11
	2	3	4		6			9		10		8				7			11	5							1	12
	2	3	4		6			8		10						7			11	5	9						1	13
	2	3	4		6			8		10						7				5	9		11				1	14
	2	3	4		6			8		10						7				5	9		11				1	15
	2	3	4		6			8		10						7				5	9		11				1	16
	2	3	4		6			8		10						7				5	9		11				1	17
1	2	3	4	5	6	7		8							10							9	11					18
1	2	3	4	5	6	7		8							10							9	11					19
1	2		4		6	7			8		5				10							9	11	3				20
1	2	3	4	5	6	7		10	8												9		11					21
1			2	5	6	7		8		10					11						9			3				22
1		3	2	5	6	7		8		9					11						10							23
1	2	3	4	5	6				10	11		8					7					9						24
1	2	3	4	5		7		8	10	9					11					6								25
1	2	3	4	5	6	7			10	9		8			11													26
1	2	3	4	5	6	7			10	11		8	9															27
	2	3	4	5	6	7	8			11		10	9														1	28
	2	3	4	5	6	7	8			11			9										10				1	29
	2	3	4	5	6	7	8		10							11							9				1	30
	2	3	4	5	6	7	8		10							11							9				1	31
	2	3		5	6	7			10	8		4											9		11		1	32
	2	3		5	6	7			8			4										10	9		11		1	33
	2	3	4	5	6	7			10			8											9		11		1	34
	2	3	4	5	6	7			10			8											9		11		1	35
	2	3	4	5		7			10			8											9		11	6	1	36
	2	3	4	5		7			10			8										9			11	6	1	37
	2	3	4	5		7			10			8										9			11	6	1	38
	2	3	4	5	6	7			10			8										9			11		1	39
	2	3	4	5	6	7			10			8										9			11		1	40
	2	3	4	5	6							8					7					9	11		10		1	41
	2		4	5	6							8					7					9	11	3	10		1	42
21	40	39	40	31	37	29	10	18	24	22	5	21	10	3	10	11	4	2	3	7	8	11	18	3	11	3	21	
				5		4		7	6	4		4	2	1		2					3	10	5		2			

2 own-goals

1		3	2	5	6	7		8		9		4									10		11					3
1		1	1	1	1	1		1		1		1			.						1		1					

1938-39

Manager: Jack Tresadern

1	Aug	27	(a)	Newcastle U	L	1-2	Lane	38,000
2		31	(h)	Nottingham F	W	3-0	Hullett 3	18,664
3	Sep	3	(h)	West Brom A	W	2-1	Wharton 2	26,092
4		10	(a)	Norwich C	L	1-2	Hullett	15,800
5		14	(a)	Southampton	L	1-2	Hullett	12,000
6		17	(h)	Luton T	W	4-1	Hullett 3, McNeil	14,666
7		24	(a)	Millwall	L	0-3		32,000
8	Oct	1	(a)	Sheffield U	W	1-0	Hullett	25,800
9		8	(h)	Burnley	W	1-0	Mitcheson	17,306
10		15	(h)	Manchester C	D	0-0		24,710
11		22	(a)	Bradford	D	2-2	Lane, Fletcher	10,807
12		29	(h)	Fulham	D	0-0		24,390
13	Nov	5	(a)	Chesterfield	L	1-3	Dougan	11,000
14		12	(h)	Tranmere R	W	3-1	Hullett, Lane, Dougan	14,059
15		19	(a)	West Ham U	L	1-2	E.Smith	25,600
16		26	(h)	Bury	L	0-1		17,128
17	Dec	3	(a)	Sheffield W	W	2-1	Chitty, Lane	22,000
18		10	(h)	Swansea T	D	0-0		·12,754
19		17	(a)	Blackburn R	L	0-4		12,400
20		24	(h)	Newcastle U	L	0-1		17,861
21		26	(a)	Coventry C	W	2-1	Hunter, E.Smith	13,428
22		27	(h)	Coventry C	L	0-2		27,776
23		31	(a)	West Brom A	L	2-4	Thomas, Hunter	20,000
24	Jan	21	(a)	Luton T	W	4-3	Mitcheson 3, Thomas	12,716
25		28	(h)	Millwall	D	2-2	Lane, Vidler	14,897
26	Feb	4	(h)	Sheffield U	L	0-1		18,659
27		11	(a)	Burnley	L	0-1		8,000
28		18	(a)	Manchester C	W	3-1	Mailey, Thomas, Hunter	25,000
29		25	(h)	Bradford	W	4-1	Hunter 2, Thomas, Kirkwood	14,564
30	Mar	4	(a)	Fulham	W	2-1	Thomas, Hunter	10,000
31		11	(h)	Chesterfield	D	0-0		14,000
32		18	(a)	Tranmere R	L	0-2		6,000
33		25	(h)	West Ham U	D	0-0		14,437
34	Apr	1	(a)	Bury	L	0-3		7,904
35		7	(a)	Tottenham H	L	0-1		33,896
36		8	(h)	Sheffield W	D	1-1	Lane	17,649
37		10	(a)	Tottenham H	L	0-1		16,000
38		15	(a)	Swansea T	L	1-2	E.Smith	6,000
39		22	(h)	Blackburn R	W	1-0	E.Smith	14,483
40		29	(a)	Nottingham F	L	1-2	Thomas	7,700
41	May	3	(h)	Norwich C	W	1-0	Thomas	7,694
42		6	(h)	Southampton	W	2-0	Thomas, E.Smith	6,000

FINAL LEAGUE POSITION: 15th in Division Two

Appearances
Goals

FA Cup

3	Jan	7	(a)	Sunderland	L	0-3	25,000

Appearances
Goals

Davies	Kirkwood	Black T	Gorman	McNeil	Mitcheson	Hunter	Smith J	Hullett	Lane	Fletcher	Clark	Mailey	Wharton	Brown	Thomas	Vidler	Cann	Rae	Smith E	Dougan	Dyer	Ryan	Archer	Wright	Chitty	Murray	Olver	Silk	McColgan	Dugnolle	Stuttard	Royston	Harper	
1	2	3	4	5	6	7	8	9	10	11																								1
1	2	3	4		6	7	8	9	10		5	11																						2
1	2	3	4		6	7	8	9	10		5		11																					3
1	2	3	4		6	7		9	10		5		11	8																				4
1	2	3	4		8	7		9			5			6	10	11																		5
	2	6	4	5	8	7		9		11			10				1	3																6
	2	6	4	5	8	7		9		11			10				1	3																7
	2	6	4				10	9	8		5						1	3		7	11													8
	2		4		10	7		9	8		5			6			1	3			11													9
1	2	6	4		10	7		9	8		5							3			11													10
1	2	6	4			7		9	8	11	5			10				3																11
1	2	6	4			7		9	8	11	5			10				3																12
1	2		4			7		9	8		5					11		3		10		6												13
	2	6	4			7		9	8		5						1	3	10	11														14
	2	6	4			7		9	8		5						1	3	10	11														15
	2		4			7		9	8		5						1	3	10	11			6											16
	2		4		10	7		9	8		5							3					6	1	11									17
	2		4		10	7			8		5							3		9			6	1	11									18
	2		4					9	8									3	10	7			6	1	11	5								19
	2		4						8						9			3		7	11		6	1		5	10							20
	5	6			8	7									9		1	3	10				4				11	2						21
	5	6			8								11		9		1	3	10	7			4					2						22
			4		8	7			11		5				9		1	3	10				6					2						23
		3	4		8	7			10		5				9	11							6	1				2						24
		3	4	5	8	7			10						9	11							6	1				2						25
	2		4		8	7			10		5				9	11		3					6	1										26
	2	6	4	5		7						11			8			3					10	1					9					27
	2		4			7	8		10		5	11			9		1	3												6				28
	2		4			7	8		10		5	11			9		1	3												6				29
	2		4			7	8		10		5	11			9		1	3					6											30
	2		4			7	8		10		5	11			9		1	3					6											31
	2		4				8		10		5	11	7		9		1	3					6											32
1	2				8	7			10		5	11			9			3					6								4			33
1	2				8	7			10		5	11			9			3					6							4				34
1	2		4		8	7			10		5	11			9			3					6											35
	2		4		8	7			10		5	11			9			3					6										1	36
	4	6			8	7			10		5	11			9						3											2	1	37
1	5		4			7			11				10						8		3							9		6		2		38
	5	6	4			7			10				11		9				8		3											2	1	39
1	5	6	4			7			10				11		9				8		3					2								40
	2	6	4			7			10		5		11		9		1		8		3													41
	2	3	4			7			10		5		11		9		1		8							6								42
14	39	23	37	5	22	37	9	18	36	5	30	12	11	5	23	5	17	29	12	9	9	1	19	8	3	4	2	6	1	4	1	3	3	
	1			1	4	6		10	6	1		1	2		8	1			5	2					1									

			4		8		7		11		5				9		1	3	10				6					2						3
			1		1		1		1		1				1		1	1	1				1					1						

1939-40

Manager: Jack Tresadern

Football League Division Three

1	Aug	26	(h)	West Ham U	L	1-3	Sargeant	18,628
2		28	(a)	Millwall	W	2-0	Sargeant, Lane	14,359
3	Sep	2	(a)	Sheffield W	W	1-0	Glover	12,088

FINAL LEAGUE POSITION: League abandoned

Appearances
Goals

South West Regional League

1	Oct	21	(h)	Torquay U	W	4-0	Archer, J.Smith, Sargeant 2	2,866
2		28	(h)	Bristol C	W	6-0	Glover 3, Sargeant, Lane, J.Smith	3,635
3	Nov	4	(a)	Cardiff C	L	0-1		4,000
4		11	(h)	Swansea T	W	3-0	Lane, Thomas, Sargeant	3,420
5		18	(h)	Swindon T	W	2-1	Smith, Thomas	2,415
6		25	(a)	Bristol R	W	2-1	Dugnolle, Thomas	1,000
7	Dec	2	(h)	Newport C	W	2-0	Sargeant, Thomas	4,048
8		9	(a)	Torquay U	L	2-5	Thomas, J.Smith	
9		16	(a)	Bristol C	L	0-1		1,400
10		23	(h)	Cardiff C	W	6-2	J.Smith, McDonald, Stuttard, Glover 2, Sargeant	2,671
11		26	(h)	Torquay U	D	1-1	McDonald	4,619
12		30	(a)	Swansea T	L	0-1		3,000
13	Jan	6	(a)	Swindon T	L	0-2		3,801
14		13	(h)	Bristol R	W	2-0	J.Smith, McDonald	2,187
15		27	(a)	Torquay U	L	0-1		1,200
16	Feb	3	(h)	Bristol C	W	10-3	Townsend 3, Olver, J.Smith 4, McDonald 2	896
17		10	(a)	Cardiff C	D	0-0		2,000
18		17	(h)	Swansea T	W	3-1	Townsend 2, J.Smith	2,100
19		24	(h)	Swindon T	W	4-1	Townsend 3, Archer	3,912
20	Mar	2	(a)	Bristol R	D	1-1	J.Smith	2,000
21		9	(h)	Newport C	W	3-0	Archer 3	3,436
22		23	(a)	Bristol C	W	4-3	Sargeant, McDonald, Olver, Archer	2,500
23		30	(h)	Cardiff C	W	4-1	Townsend, Sargeant 2, McDonald	3,541
24	Apr	6	(a)	Swansea T	L	2-0	Townsend, Fellowes	6,000
25	May	11	(a)	Swindon T	D	2-2	Rich, Archer	
26		13	(h)	Bristol R	W	4-1	Rich 3, McDonald	
27	Jun	7	(a)	Newport C	L	3-6	Archer, Fellowes 2	
28		8	(a)	Newport C	L	2-5	Archer, Sargeant	

FINAL LEAGUE POSITION: 1st in South West Regional League

Appearances
Goals

League Cup

	Apr	20	(h)	Bournemouth	L	0-1		6,404
		27	(a)	Bournemouth	L	1-4	J.Smith	6,800

Appearances
Goals

Middleton	Kirkwood	Rae	Gorman	Clark	Archer	Lane	Jones	Glover	McDonald	Sargeant	Royston	Smith	Dugnolls	Lewis	Silk	Thomas	Stuttard	Parnaby	Mitcheson	Olver	Fellowes	Townsend	Rosenthal	Simpson	Harper	Dixon	Wright	Rich	McNeil	Williams	Hurst	Hastie	
1	2	3	4	5	6	7	8	9	10	11																							1
1	5	3	4		6	7		9	10	11	2	8																					2
1	3	3	4			10		9		11	2	8	6	7																			3
3	3	3	3	1	2	3	1	3	2	3	2	2	1	1																			
						1		1		2																							

1	5	3	4		7	10		9		11		8	6		2																		1
1	5	3	4		7	10		9		11		8	6		2																		2
1	5	3	4		7	10				11		8	6		2	9																	3
1	5	3	4		7	10			6	11		8			2	9																	4
1	2		4	5	6	7			10	11		8			3	9																	5
1	5	3			4	7			10	11		8	6		2	9																	6
1	5	3	4		7	10				11		8	6		2	9																	7
1	5	3	4		6	7				11		8	10		2	9																	8
1	5	3	4		6	7		9	10	11		8			2																		9
1	5	3	4		7			9	10	11		8			2		6																10
1	5	3	4		7			9	10	11		8	6		2																		11
1	5		4		7				9	11		8	6		2		3	10															12
1	5		4		7				10	11		8	6		3		2							9									13
1		3	4		6				9	11		7			2				8	10									5				14
			4	5	6			10	7	11		8			3						2	9			1								15
		3	4	5	6				7			8			2			10		11		9			1								16
		3	4	5	6				7	11		8			2			10					9				1						17
		3	4	5	6				7	11		8			2				10			9					1						18
		3	4	5	6				7	11		8			2				10			9					1						19
		3	4	5	6				7	11		8			2			10				9					1						20
		3	4	5	9				7	11		8	6		2			10									1						21
			4	5	9				7	11		8	6		2					10					1	3							22
			4	5	6				7	11		8			2			10				9				3	1						23
		3	4	5					7			8	6		2			11			10	9					1						24
		3	4	5	10				7	11		8	6		2												1	9					25
		3	4	5	10				7	11					2			6			8						1	9					26
			4	5	8				10	11					2		6				9					3	1				7		27
			4	5	8				10	11					2		6				9					3	1			7			28
14	13	20	27	15	27	9		6	23	26		25	13		28	6	5	8	3	3	5	7	1	1	3	4	11	2	1	1	1		
					9	2		5	8	10		12	1			5	1			2	3	10						4					

		3	4	5	6				7	11		8			2							9					1					10	
		3	4	5	9				7	11		8	6		2							10					1						
		2	2	2	2				2	2		2	1		2							2					2					1	
												1																					

1945-46

Manager: Jack Tresadern

1	Aug	25	(a)	Southampton	D 5-5	D.Thomas 2, R.Brown 3	10,000
2	Sep	1	(h)	Southampton	L 0-3		12,000
3		8	(h)	Derby C	L 0-4		12,000
4		12	(a)	Portsmouth	L 1-6	Tinkler	13,000
5		15	(a)	Derby C	L 1-3	D.Thomas	12,000
6		17	(a)	Nottingham F	L 0-2		10,000
7		22	(h)	Leicester C	L 2-3	Tinkler, R.Brown	15,000
8		29	(a)	Leicester C	D 2-2	Tinkler, D.Thomas	24,000
9	Oct	6	(a)	Coventry C	L 1-3	D.Thomas	12,750
10		13	(h)	Coventry C	D 1-1	D.Thomas	18,000
11		20	(h)	Luton T	D 1-1	D.Thomas	13,000
12		27	(a)	Luton T	D 0-0		10,000
13	Nov	3	(h)	Aston Villa	L 0-3		33,000
14		10	(a)	Aston Villa	L 2-4	D.Thomas, D.Brown	25,000
15		17	(a)	Arsenal	L 0-3		14,479
16		24	(h)	Arsenal	L 0-4		29,000
17	Dec	1	(a)	Charlton A	L 0-4		20,000
18		8	(h)	Charlton A	L 1-5	D.Thomas	12,000
19		15	(a)	Fulham	L 0-4		15,000
20		22	(h)	Fulham	L 0-2		2,000
21		25	(h)	Swansea T	L 1-3	Prescott	11,000
22		26	(a)	Swansea T	D 0-0		20,000
23		29	(h)	Portsmouth	L 1-3	W.Smith	15,000
24	Jan	12	(h)	Newport C	L 0-3		14,000
25		19	(a)	Newport C	L 1-2	R.Brown	8,000
26	Feb	2	(h)	Wolves	W 3-2	R.Brown 3	10,000
27		9	(h)	West Ham U	L 1-2	R.Brown	20,000
28		16	(a)	West Ham U	L 0-7		15,000
29		23	(a)	West Brom A	L 2-5	R.Brown, Tranter (og)	12,000
30	Mar	2	(h)	West Brom A	L 0-4		20,000
31		16	(a)	Birmingham C	W 1-0	R.Brown	22,000
32		23	(a)	Tottenham H	L 0-2		20,789
33		30	(h)	Tottenham H	L 0-1		25,000
34	Apr	1	(h)	Birmingham C	L 2-3	R.Brown 2	
35		6	(h)	Brentford	D 1-1	Hurst	20,000
36		13	(a)	Brentford	L 2-3	Tinkler, R.Brown	13,200
37		19	(a)	Chelsea	L 0-2		30,000
38		20	(a)	Millwall	L 1-6	Carless	13,000
39		22	(h)	Chelsea	L 1-4	Swinscoe	27,000
40		27	(h)	Millwall	L 1-2	R.Brown	15,000
41		29	(a)	Wolves	D 1-1	R.Brown	17,000
42	May	4	(h)	Nottingham F	W 3-2	R.Brown, Hurst, R.Thomas	18,000

FINAL LEAGUE POSITION: 22nd in Football League South

Appearances
Goals

FA Cup

3	Jan	5	(a)	Aldershot	L 0-2		7,800
		9	(h)	Aldershot	L 0-1		5,000

Appearances
Goals

GUEST PLAYERS

Robert Brown (Queen's Park), G.Cole (Chester), E.Carless (Cardiff City), J.Court (Cardiff City), H.Cumner (Arsenal), J.Dryden (Charlton Athletic), R.Ferrier (Oldham Athletic), J.Gardiner (Wolves), K.Griffiths (Cardiff City), R.Haddington (Bradford), F.Haycock (Aston Villa), J.Hunter (Preston North End), J.Kirkham (Bournemouth), A.Kerr (Aston Villa), L.Latham (Aston Villa), J.Logie (Arsenal), J.Prescott (Hull City), T.Swinscoe (Chesterfield), F.Scrine (Swansea Town), F.Sargent (Tottenham Hotspur), A.Squires (Preston North End), D.Smale (Chelsea), R.Sinclair (Chesterfield), E.Taylor (Newcastle United), J.Tivendale (Watford), A.Tomlinson (Blackburn Rovers), W.Whittaker (Charlton Athletic).

Wright	Rundle	Silk	Adams	Gardiner	Jones	Prescott	Brown Ron	Thomas D	Tinkler	Beeson	Fullbrook	Came	Stephenson	Royston	Smith W	Tomlinson	Shortt	Dyer	Dugnolle	Tivendale	Smith E	Dixon	Brown D	Middleton	Gorman	Tugwell	Gibson	Butler	Hurst	Carless	Howshall	Swinscoe	Thomas R	
1	2	3	5	6	7	8	9	10	11																									1
	2	3	5	6	7		9	8	11	10																								2
	2	3		6	7		9	8	11		4																							3
1		2	5				9		11	10		6	8																					4
1		3	5		4			9	11	10	6			2																				5
1		3	5		7				11		6			2	9																			6
1		3		6			9		11		4		8			2																		7
		5			4			9	11				8			2	1	3	6	7	10													8
1		5			4			9	11				8			2		3	6	7	10													9
	6	5			4			10	11		2		8		9					7														10
		5			4		7	10		11	2					3	1					6												11
	6	9			4			10				8				2		3				5		1										12
		5			4			9								2		3		7	8	6		1										13
		2			4			9			6	8						3			10	5	7	1										14
		2			4			10										3	6			5	7	1										15
		2						9	11						8			3	6			5	7	1	4									16
		2							11		8								6			3	7	1	4									17
		2		6				9	11													5		1	4									18
		2	4		8			9										3				5		1										19
		3	4			8	9	10	11													5		1	6	2								20
		3	4	6		10			11			8	9							7		5		1		2								21
		3	4	6		10			11						9					7		5		1		2								22
		8	4	6		10			11						9			3		7		5		1		2								23
		6	4										10	2				3		7				1	6									24
		3	4		7		9		11					2							10	5		1	6									25
		3			7		9		11					2			1				10	4			6		5	8						26
		3			7		9		11					2			1				10	4					5	8						27
		3			6		9		11					2			1				10	5					4	7						28
			8		4		9		11							2	1					3					5	7						29
		3	2		8		9		11								1		6	7					4		5		10					30
		2			4		9		11				7				1					3			6		5			8				31
		2			4		9						7				1					3			6				11	8				32
		2			4		9						7	3			1										5		11	8	6			33
		2			4		9		11				7				1					3					5	8		10	6			34
		2					9						7	4			1					3					5		11	8	6			35
		2			8		9		11				7	4			1					3			6		5			10				36
		2			8		9		11				7	4			1					3			6		5			10				37
		2			8		9		11				7	4			1								6		5			10				38
		2			8				11				7	4			1					3			6		5			10		9		39
		2					9		11				7				1					5			6		4				10		8	40
		2					9										1					5			6		4		11	10			8	41
1		2			6		9															5					4		11	10			8	42
7	5	41	14	8	29	5	24	16	30	4	8	4	17	13	5	7	18	10	6	9	8	28	4	14	16	4	16	5	6	11	4	1	3	
						1	17	9	4						1								1						2	1		1	1	

1 own-goal

		2	4			8		10	11						9			3				5		1	6									3
		3	4			9			11			10	8	2								5		1	6									
		2	2			2		1	2			1	1	1	1			1				2		2	2									

Squires played number 4 in Matches 1 & 6; Bob Brown played number 1 in Matches 2, 3 & 10, Roberts played number 4 in Match 2 & number 5 in Matches 7 & 17; Latham played number 5 in Match 3; Ferrier played number 10 in Match 3; Rae played number 3 in Matches 4 & 18; Court played number 4 in Match 4, number 8 in Match 5, number 10 in Match 7 & number 11 in Match 17; Griffiths played number 7 in Matches 4 & number 10 in Match 6; Hazlett played number 7 in Matches 5 & 7 and number 8 in Match 6; Stuttard played number 3 in Match 10; Taylor played number 8 in Match 11 & number 10 in Match 13; Kirkham played number 9 in Match 11; Hunter played number 7 in Match 12; Scrine played number 11 in Matches 12 & 13; Smale played number 11 in Matches 14 & 15 and number 10 in Match 16; Dryden played number 8 in Match 15; Dryden played number 8 in Match 15; Harris played number 9 in Match 15; Haddington played number 9 in Match 17, number 8 in Match 18 & number 10 in Match 36; Kerr played number 7 in Matches 18, 19 & 20; Northover played number 10 in Match 18; Whittaker played number 6 in Match 19; Haycock played number 10 in Match 19; Olver played number 11 in Match 19; Hodge played number 8 in Match 22 & number 7 in both legs of the FA Cup; Warren played number 5 in Matches 24 & 32; Sargent played number 8 in Match 24; Case played number 9 in Match 24; Clark played number 11 in Match 24; J.Smith played number 8 in Matches 25 & 28; Cole played number 6 in Match 29; Gallagher played number 10 in Match 29; Cumner played number 10 in Matches 31 & 33; Logie played number 10 in Match 32; Jenkins played number 3 in Match 38; Poyser played number 3 in Matches 40, 41 & 42; Carter played number 7 in Match 41; Sinclair played number 7 in Match 42.

1946-47

Manager: Jack Tresadern

1	Aug	31	(h)	West Ham U	W 3-1	Strauss 2, Rawlings	25,659
2	Sep	2	(a)	Millwall	D 1-1	Rawlings	17,200
3		7	(a)	Sheffield W	L 1-2	Rawlings	27,326
4		11	(h)	Chesterfield	W 1-0	R.Thomas	26,331
5		14	(h)	Fulham	D 2-2	Strauss, Rawlings	25,451
6		21	(a)	Bury	D 3-3	R.Thomas 2, Strauss	14,853
7		28	(h)	Luton T	W 2-1	Strauss, Rawlings	28,031
8	Oct	5	(h)	Coventry C	D 2-2	Rawlings, D.Thomas	28,634
9		12	(a)	Leicester C	L 1-4	Strauss	20,177
10		19	(h)	Nottingham F	W 2-0	Strauss, Rawlings	20,623
11		26	(a)	Southampton	L 1-5	Rawlings	24,000
12	Nov	2	(h)	Newport C	W 4-1	R.Thomas 2, Rawlings, Boyd	22,435
13		9	(a)	Barnsley	W 3-1	D.Thomas 2, Dixon	18,200
14		16	(h)	Burnley	D 2-2	Tinkler, R.Thomas	29,362
15		23	(a)	Tottenham H	L 1-2	D.Thomas	41,760
16		30	(h)	Swansea T	W 2-1	R.Thomas 2	20,757
17	Dec	7	(a)	Newcastle U	L 2-3	D.Thomas, Tinkler	45,000
18		14	(h)	West Brom A	W 2-1	D.Thomas, R.Thomas	27,495
19		21	(a)	Birmingham C	L 1-6	Tinkler	30,000
20		25	(a)	Manchester C	L 3-4	Rawlings 2, D.Thomas	24,532
21		26	(h)	Manchester C	L 2-3	D.Thomas, Stuttard	29,256
22		28	(a)	West Ham U	L 1-4	R.Thomas	24,770
23	Jan	1	(a)	Chesterfield	L 1-4	D.Thomas	17,000
24		4	(h)	Sheffield W	W 4-1	D.Thomas, R.Thomas, Strauss, Rawlings	21,698
25		18	(a)	Fulham	L 1-3	D.Thomas	24,068
26		25	(h)	Bury	W 3-1	D.Thomas, Rawlings	18,093
27	Feb	1	(a)	Luton T	W 4-3	D.Thomas 2, R.Thomas, Rawlings	16,000
28		16	(h)	Leicester C	W 4-0	D.Thomas, Tinkler, S.Smith (og), D.Jones (og)	18,298
29	Mar	1	(h)	Southampton	L 2-3	D.Thomas, Watkins	24,077
30		15	(h)	Barnsley	W 3-2	D.Thomas, Rawlings, Boyd	6,950
31		22	(a)	Burnley	L 1-2	D.Thomas	30,000
32		29	(h)	Tottenham H	L 3-4	D.Thomas, Rawlings, Nicholson (og)	22,516
33	Apr	5	(a)	Swansea T	L 1-3	Strauss	22,000
34		7	(h)	Bradford	L 2-4	Boyd, Rawlings	23,533
35		12	(h)	Newcastle U	L 0-1		32,460
36		19	(a)	West Brom A	W 5-2	R.Thomas 3, Strauss 2	25,000
37		26	(h)	Birmingham C	L 0-2		24,949
38	May	3	(h)	Millwall	L 0-2		12,494
39		10	(a)	Newport C	L 0-2		9,100
40		17	(a)	Coventry C	L 0-1		16,713
41		26	(a)	Bradford	L 2-3	R.Thomas, Murphy	7,994
42		31	(a)	Nottingham F	L 1-5	R.Thomas	11,944

FINAL LEAGUE POSITION: 19th in Division Two

Appearances
Goals

FA Cup

3	Jan	11	(a)	Chester	L 0-2		16,900

Appearances
Goals

Shortt	Royston	Dyer	Stuttard	Dixon	Miller	Rawlings	Thomas R	Thomas D	Murphy	Strauss	Poyser	Gibson	Govan	Boyd	Jones L	Rundle	Hurst	Tinkler	Edds	Carless	Wright	Adams	Silk	Watkins	Davies	Jones P	Warren	
1	2	3	4	5	6	7	8	9	10	11																		1
1	2	3	4	5	6	7	8	9	10	11																		2
1	2	3	4	5	6	7	8	9	10	11																		3
1	2	3	4	5	6	7	8	9	10	11																		4
1	2		4	5	6	7	8	9	10	11	3																	5
1	2		4	3	6	7	8	9	10	11		5																6
1	2	3	4	5	6	7	8	9	10	11																		7
1	2	3		5	6	7	8	9		11		4	10															8
1	2		3	5		7	8	9	10	11		4		6														9
1	2		6	5		7	10	9		11	3				4	8												10
1	2	11	6	5		7	10	9			3				4	8												11
1	2	3	6	5		7	10	9						8	4			11										12
1	2	3	6	5			10	9						8	4		7	11										13
1	2	3	6	5		7	10	9						8	4			11										14
1	2	3	6	5		7	8	10							4			11	9									15
1	2	3	6	5		7	10	9							4			11		8								16
	2	3	6	5		7	10	9							4			11		8	1							17
	2	3	6	5		7	10	9							4			11		8	1							18
	2	3	6	5		7	10	9		8					4			11			1							19
1	2	3	6	5		7	10	9		8					4			11										20
1	2	3	6			7	8	9		11				5	4			10										21
1	2	3	6	5		7	8	9		11					4			10										22
						7	10	9				5		4			11			8	1	2	3	6				23
1	2	3		5		7	8	9		11				4				10						6				24
1	2	3	4	5		7	10	9	8	11														6				25
1	2	6		5		7	10	9						8	4			11					3					26
1	2	6		5		7	10	9						8	4			11					3					27
1	2	6		5		7	10	9						8	4			11					3					28
1	2	6		5		7	10	9							4			11					3	8				29
1	2	3		5		7	10	9						8	4			11							6			30
1	2	3		5		7	10	9						8	4			11							6			31
1	2	3		5		7	10	9		11				8	4										6			32
1		3	5			7		9		10				8	4			11					2		6			33
1		3	5			7	10	9				4		8				11					2		6			34
1	2		5			7	10	9						8	4			11					3		6			35
1	2		4	5		10	8	9		7							11						3		6			36
1	2		4	5		10	8	9		7								11					3		6			37
1	2		5			10	9		8	7					4		11						3		6			38
1	2	6				7	10	9	8	11		5											3		4			39
1		6				7	10	9	8	11													2		4	3	5	40
1		6				7	8	9	10				11										2		4	3	5	41
1		6					7	9	10						8			11					2		4	3	5	42
38	36	33	28	32	8	40	41	41	14	23	3	6	2	16	24	2	4	22	1	4	4	1	15	4	13	3	3	
			1	1		17	17	19	1	11				4				4						1				

3 own-goals

1	2	3		5		7	8	9		11					4			10						6				3
1	1	1		1		1	1	1		1					1			1						1				

1947-48

Manager: Jack Tresadern/Jimmy Rae

1	Aug	23	(a)	Newcastle U	L	1-6	Tadman	52,642
2		25	(a)	Leicester C	L	1-2	Thomas	19,845
3		30	(h)	Birmingham C	L	0-3		25,672
4	Sep	3	(h)	Leicester C	D	0-0		17,060
5		6	(a)	West Brom A	D	1-1	Rawlings	38,000
6		10	(a)	Leeds U	L	0-5		30,000
7		13	(h)	Barnsley	W	1-0	Rawlings	18,930
8		17	(h)	Leeds U	W	1-0	Strauss	21,686
9		20	(a)	Cardiff C	L	0-3		35,000
10		27	(a)	Luton T	D	0-0		19,184
11	Oct	4	(h)	Brentford	D	0-0		24,672
12		11	(h)	Sheffield W	L	0-2		21,215
13		18	(a)	Tottenham H	L	0-2		35,249
14		25	(h)	Millwall	D	1-1	Strauss	22,399
15	Nov	1	(a)	Chesterfield	D	1-1	G.Milburn (og)	13,000
16		8	(h)	West Ham U	D	1-1	Edds	29,111
17		15	(a)	Bury	D	0-0		14,823
18		22	(h)	Southampton	W	3-1	Squires, Tadman, Strauss	21,501
19		29	(a)	Doncaster R	L	0-2		15,478
20	Dec	6	(h)	Nottingham F	D	1-1	Rawlings	21,225
21		13	(a)	Bradford	L	0-3		14,851
22		20	(h)	Newcastle U	W	3-0	Squires, Thomas, Dews	27,069
23		25	(a)	Fulham	D	1-1	Tadman	16,800
24		26	(h)	Fulham	W	3-2	Edds, Tadman 2	25,157
25	Jan	3	(a)	Birmingham C	D	1-1	Tadman	36,000
26		17	(h)	West Brom A	W	2-1	Tadman, Strauss	18,050
27		31	(a)	Barnsley	L	1-2	Strauss	21,000
28	Feb	7	(h)	Cardiff C	W	3-0	Dews, Sherwood (og), Edds	25,034
29		14	(h)	Luton T	L	1-3	Edds	25,520
30		21	(a)	Brentford	D	0-0		13,714
31		28	(a)	Sheffield W	D	1-1	Edds	27,083
32	Mar	6	(h)	Tottenham H	D	1-1	Edds	33,538
33		13	(a)	Millwall	L	0-2		28,000
34		20	(h)	Chesterfield	L	1-2	Astall	21,272
35		27	(a)	West Ham U	D	1-1	Edds	22,000
36		29	(h)	Coventry C	W	1-0	Edds	26,000
37		30	(a)	Coventry C	D	0-0		20,000
38	Apr	3	(h)	Bury	D	0-0		20,232
39		10	(a)	Southampton	W	3-2	Edds 3	20,000
40		17	(h)	Doncaster R	D	2-2	Edds 2	21,887
41		24	(a)	Nottingham F	D	1-1	Edds	17,288
42	May	1	(h)	Bradford	D	2-2	L.Jones, Squires	20,801

FINAL LEAGUE POSITION: 17th in Division Two

Appearances
Goals

FA Cup

3	Jan	10	(h)	Luton T	L	2-4	Dews, Thomas	36,195

Appearances
Goals

Shortt	Ratcliffe	Jones P	Jones L	Oakes	Davies	Rawlings	Hall	Tadman	Knight	Strauss	Miller	Boyd	Thomas	Rundle	Pengelly	Murphy	Edds	Tinkler	Nail	Squires	Dews	Stuart	Astall	Dixon	Smith M	Govan	Silk	
1	2	3	4	5	6	7	8	9	10	11																		1
1	2	3		5	6	7			10	11	4	8	9															2
1	2	3		5	6	7			10	11		8	9	4														3
1	2	3	4	5	6	7	8		10	11			9															4
1	2	3	4	5		7	8		10	11			9	6														5
1	2	3	4			7			10	11			9	6	5	8												6
1	2	3	4		6	7	8		10						5		9	11										7
1	2	3	7		10		8			11		4		6	5		9											8
1	2	3	7		10		8			11		4		6	5		9											9
1	2	3	7		10		8	9		11		4		6	5													10
1	2	3	7	5	10		8	9		11		4		6														11
1	2	3	7	5	10		8	9		11		4		6														12
1	2	3	8	5		7		9		11		4		6			10											13
1	2	3	8	5		7		10		11		4		6					9									14
1	2	3		5		7		9		11		4		6						8	10							15
1		3		5		7				11		4		6			9			8	10	2						16
1		3		5		7		9		11		4		6						8	10	2						17
1		3		5	6	7		9		11		4								8	10	2						18
1		3		5	6	7		9		11		4								8	10	2						19
1		3		5	6	7		9		11		4								8	10	2						20
1		3		5	6	7		9		11		4								8	10	2						21
1		3		5	6			7		11		4	9							8	10	2						22
1		3		5	6			7		11		4	9							8	10	2						23
1		3		5	6			7		11		4	9				10			8		2						24
1		3		5	6			7		11		4	9				10			8		2						25
1		3		5	6			7		11		4	9				10				8	2						26
1		3		5				7		11		4		6			9			8	10	2						27
1		3		5				7		11		4		6			9			8	10	2						28
1		3		5						11		4		6			9			8	10	2	7					29
1		3		5						11		4		6			9			8	10	2	7					30
1	2	3		5						11		4		6			9			8	10		7					31
1	2	3		5						11		4		6			9			8	10		7					32
1	2	3		5						11		4		6			9			8	10		7					33
1	2	3		5	6					11		4					9			8	10		7					34
1		3		5						11		4		6			9			8	10	2	7					35
1		3		5						11		4		6			9			8	10	2	7					36
1		3								11		4		6						8	10		7	5	9		2	37
1		3		5						11		4		6			9			8	10	2	7					38
1		3		5						11		4		6			9			8	10	2	7					39
1		3		5						11		4		6			9			8	10	2	7					40
1		3	4	5						11		6					9			8			7			10	2	41
1		3	4	5						11		6					9			8			7			10	2	42
42	19	42	14	36	20	16	9	19	7	41	1	37	10	26	5	1	23	1	1	27	24	20	14	1	1	2	3	
			1			3		7		5			2				14			3	2		1					

2 own-goals

1		3		5	6			7		11		4	9							8	10	2						3
1		1		1	1			1		1		1	1							1	1	1						
													1								1							

1948-49

Manager: Jimmy Rae

1	Aug	21	(a)	Barnsley	D 0-0		15,549
2		23	(h)	Southampton	L 1-2	Astall	21,501
3		28	(h)	Grimsby T	L 0-2		24,744
4	Sep	1	(a)	Southampton	L 0-2		20,000
5		4	(a)	Nottingham F	L 0-1		19,000
6		8	(h)	Bradford	W 3-0	Edds, Strausss, Astall	18,914
7		11	(h)	Fulham	W 3-1	Strauss, Squires 2	25,322
8		15	(a)	Bradford	D 2-2	Strauss, Squires	10,642
9		18	(a)	West Ham U	L 0-3		22,000
10		25	(a)	Blackburn R	L 1-2	Strauss	24,400
11	Oct	2	(h)	Cardiff C	L 0-1		29,346
12		9	(h)	Bury	W 1-0	Dews	21,500
13		16	(a)	West Brom A	L 0-3		30,000
14		23	(h)	Chesterfield	D 2-2	Tadman 2	20,151
15		30	(a)	Lincoln C	W 2-1	Astall 2	15,027
16	Nov	6	(h)	Sheffield W	W 3-2	Astall, Edds, Tadman	22,458
17		13	(a)	Coventry C	D 1-1	Dews	14,153
18		20	(h)	Leeds U	W 2-1	Edds, Tadman	24,576
19		27	(a)	Leicester C	D 1-1	Tadman	24,350
20	Dec	4	(h)	Brentford	W 1-0	Tadman	26,188
21		11	(a)	Tottenham H	L 0-3		41,950
22		18	(h)	Barnsley	W 3-0	Tadman 2, Edds	19,778
23		25	(a)	Luton T	L 1-3	Strauss	17,109
24		27	(h)	Luton T	D 1-1	Boyd	33,325
25	Jan	1	(a)	Grimsby T	D 2-2	Strauss 2	12,000
26		22	(a)	Fulham	L 1-6	L.Jones	25,000
27		29	(h)	Nottingham F	W 1-0	Tadman	17,292
28	Feb	5	(h)	West Ham U	W 2-0	Silk, Goddard	18,494
29		19	(h)	Blackburn R	W 3-0	Dews, Tadman 2	20,198
30		26	(a)	Cardiff C	L 0-1		25,000
31	Mar	12	(h)	West Brom A	L 1-2	Dews	26,011
32		19	(a)	Chesterfield	D 0-0		11,806
33		26	(h)	Lincoln C	D 0-0		18,176
34	Apr	2	(a)	Sheffield W	L 1-2	Dews	30,000
35		9	(h)	Coventry C	L 2-3	Tadman, Taylor	17,083
36		15	(a)	Queen's Park R	L 1-2	Squires	20,140
37		16	(a)	Leeds U	L 0-1		24,000
38		18	(h)	Queen's Park R	W 3-1	Strauss 2, Tadman	22,000
39		23	(h)	Leicester C	D 1-1	Strauss	25,654
40		27	(a)	Bury	D 1-1	Squires	10,124
41		30	(a)	Brentford	D 2-2	Tadman 2	13,709
42	May	7	(h)	Tottenham H	L 0-5		22,900

FINAL LEAGUE POSITION: 20th in Division Two — Appearances / Goals

FA Cup

3	Jan	8	(h)	Notts C	L 0-1		40,000

Appearances

Goals

Shortt	Silk	Jones P	Boyd	Goddard	Taylor	Astall	Squires	Edds	Machin	Strauss	Dews	Rundle	Tadman	Blatchford	Govan	Jones L	Dougall	Buist	Harris	Dixon	Ratcliffe	Pengelly	
1	2	3	4	5	6	7	8	9	10	11													1
1	2	3	4	5	6	7	8	9	10	11													2
1	2	3	4	5	6		8	11	9	7	10												3
1	2	3	4	5		7		9	8	11	10	6											4
1	2	3	4	5		7		9	8	11	10	6											5
1	2	3	4	5		7	8	9		11	10	6											6
1	2	3	4	5		7	8	9		11	10	6											7
1	2	3	4	5		7	8	9		11	10	6											8
1	2	3	4	5		7	8	9		11	10	6											9
1	2	3	4	5		7	8	9		11	10	6											10
1	2	3	4	5	6	7	8			11	10		9										11
1	2	3	4	5	6	7	8	9		11	10												12
1	2	3	4	5	6	7	8	9		11	10												13
1	2	3	4	5	6	7	8			11	10		9										14
1	2	3	4	5	6	7	8			11	10		9										15
1	2	3	4	5	6	7		10		11	8		9										16
1	2	3	4	5	6	7		10			8		9	11									17
1	2	3	4	5	6	7		10			8		9	11									18
1	2	3	4	5		7		10	6		8		9		11								19
1	2	3	4	5		7		10	6		8		9	11									20
1	2	3	4	5		7		10	6	11	8		9										21
1	2	3	4	5		7		10	6	11	8		9										22
1	2	3	4	5		7		10	6	11	8		9										23
1	2	3	4	5		7		10	6	11	8		9										24
1	2	3	4	5		7		10	6	11	8		9										25
1	2	3		5		7		10	6		8		9	11		4							26
1	2	3		5	6	7	8		4		10		9	11									27
1	2	3		5	6	7	8		4		10		9	11									28
1	2	3		5	6	7	8		4	11	10		9										29
1	2	3		5	6	7	8		4	11	10		9										30
1	2	3		5	6	7			4		10		9				8	11					31
1	2	3		5	6	7		11	4		10		9				8						32
	2	3		5		7		10	4	11	6		9				8		1				33
	2	3		5	6	7	8	11	4		10		9						1				34
	2	3		5	6	7	8		4		10		9		11				1				35
1	2	3			6	7	8			11	10		9							5		4	36
1	2	3			6		8	11		7	10		9							5		4	37
1		3			6		8	11		7	10	4	9							5	2		38
1		3			6		8	11		7	10	4	9							5	2		39
1		3			6		8	11		7	10	4	9							5	2		40
1		3		4	6		8	11		7	10		9							5	2		41
1		3		4	6	7	8	10		11			9							5	2		42
39	37	42	25	37	26	36	26	32	22	31	39	10	30	6	2	1	3	1	3	7	5	2	
	1		1	1	1	5	5	4		10	5		15			1							

1	2	3	4	5		7		10	6	11	8		9										3
1	1	1	1	1		1		1	1	1	1		1										

1949-50

Manager: Jimmy Rae

1	Aug	20	(h)	Bradford	D	1-1	Hepworth (og)	24,767
2		22	(a)	Tottenham H	L	1-4	Williams	41,882
3		27	(a)	Chesterfield	L	0-2		14,805
4		31	(h)	Tottenham H	L	0-2		25,242
5	Sep	3	(h)	West Ham U	L	0-3		23,521
6		10	(h)	Sheffield W	L	0-1		20,008
7		14	(a)	Bury	L	1-5	Strauss	12,614
8		17	(a)	Hull C	L	2-4	Strauss, Tadman	40,000
9		24	(h)	Brentford	W	2-0	Strauss, Tadman	17,810
10	Oct	1	(a)	Blackburn R	L	0-1		24,300
11		8	(a)	Sheffield U	D	1-1	Strauss	26,134
12		15	(h)	Grimsby T	W	4-2	Strauss, Tadman, Dews, Taylor	24,276
13		22	(a)	Queen's Park R	W	2-0	Tadman 2	15,981
14		29	(h)	Preston NE	W	1-0	Tadman	32,802
15	Nov	5	(a)	Swansea T	D	2-2	Tadman, Squires	27,000
16		12	(h)	Leeds U	L	1-2	Tadman	22,281
17		19	(a)	Southampton	D	3-3	Dews, Williams, Strauss	25,129
18		26	(h)	Coventry C	L	1-2	Williams	20,995
19	Dec	3	(a)	Luton T	D	1-1	Porteous	13,273
20		10	(h)	Barnsley	D	2-2	Dews 2	17,315
21		17	(a)	Bradford	L	2-3	Strauss, Williams	7,708
22		24	(h)	Chesterfield	W	2-1	Tadman, Squires	19,864
23		26	(h)	Cardiff C	D	0-0		29,000
24		27	(a)	Cardiff C	L	0-1		35,000
25		31	(a)	West Ham U	D	2-2	Strauss, Dews	19,000
26	Jan	14	(a)	Sheffield W	W	4-2	Squires 2, Strauss, Dews	39,316
27		21	(h)	Hull C	L	1-3	Squires	29,591
28	Feb	4	(a)	Brentford	D	0-0		22,343
29		11	(a)	Leicester C	D	0-0		27,912
30		18	(h)	Blackburn R	D	0-0		23,139
31		25	(h)	Sheffield U	L	0-1		21,761
32	Mar	4	(a)	Grimsby T	D	2-2	Dews 2	17,000
33		11	(h)	Queen's Park R	L	0-2		23,380
34		18	(a)	Preston NE	D	0-0		21,000
35		25	(h)	Swansea T	L	0-1		20,132
36	Apr	1	(a)	Coventry C	L	0-3		20,882
37		8	(h)	Luton T	D	0-0		17,191
38		10	(h)	Leicester C	W	2-1	Strauss, Dews	14,576
39		15	(a)	Leeds U	D	1-1	Ratcliffe	24,000
40		22	(h)	Southampton	D	0-0		22,873
41		29	(a)	Barnsley	L	1-4	Bryant	4,399
42	May	6	(h)	Bury	W	2-0	Bryant, Blatchford	12,614

FINAL LEAGUE POSITION: 21st in Division Two

Appearances
Goals

FA Cup

3	Jan	7	(h)	Wolves	D	1-1	Williams	40,000
R		10	(a)	Wolves	L	0-3		43,835

Appearances
Goals

Shortt	Silk	Jones P	Porteous	Goddard	Taylor	Squires	Dougall	Tadman	Williams	Strauss	Willis	Astall	Dews	Govan	Major	Pengelly	Hartery	Dixon	Ratcliffe	Edds	Bryant	Chisholm	McShane	Dobbie	Blatchford	
1	2	3	4	5	6	7	8	9	10	11																1
1	2	3	4	5	6	7	8		9	11	10															2
1	2	3	4	5	6		8		9			7	10	11												3
	2	3	4	5	8	9			11	7			10		1	6										4
	2	3	4	5		8	9		11	7			10		1	6										5
		3	4		6			9	11	7			8		1		2	5		10						6
		3	4	5	6		8	9	10	7					1				2	11						7
		3	4		6	8		9	11	7			10		1			5	2							8
1	2	3	4		6	8		9	11	7			10					5								9
1	2	3	4		6	8		9	11	7			10					5								10
1	2	3	4		6	8		9	11	7			10					5								11
1	2	3	4		6	8		9	11	7			10					5								12
1	2	3	4		6	8		9	11	7			10					5								13
1	2	3	4		6	8		9	11	7			10					5								14
1	2	3	4		6	8		9	11	7			10					5								15
1	2	3	4		6	8		9	11	7			10					5								16
1	2	3	4		6	8		9	11	7			10					5								17
1	2	3	4		6	8			11	7			10					5			9					18
1	2	3	4		6		8		11	7			10					5		9						19
1	2	3	4		6		8	9	11	7			10					5								20
1	2	3			6	8	4	9	11	7			10					5								21
1	2	3				8	4	9	11	7			10									5	6			22
1	2	3				8	4	9	11	7			10									5	6			23
1		3				8	4	9	11			7	10						2			5	6			24
1		3				8	4	9	11	7			10						2			5	6			25
1		3				8	4	9		11		7	10						2			5	6			26
1		3				8	4	9		11		7	10						2			5	6			27
1		3	6		8		4	9	11	7			10						2			5				28
1		3	6		8		4	9	11			7	10						2			5				29
1		3	6		8		4			11		7	10						2		9	5				30
1		3	6			8	4			11		7	10						2		9	5				31
1		3	6			8	4			11		7	10						2			5		9		32
1		3	6			8	4		11			7	10						2			5		9		33
1		3	6			8	4			11		7	10						2			5		9		34
1		3	6			8	4	11		7			10						2			5		9		35
1		3	6				4	9	10	11									2			5		8	7	36
1		3	6			8	4	9	11	7			10						2			5				37
1		3	6			8	4	9	11	7			10						2			5				38
1		3	6			8	4	9	11	7			10						2			5				39
1		3	6			8	4	9	11	7			10						2			5				40
1		3	6			8	4		11	7									2		9	5		10		41
1		3	6			8	4		10			7							2		9	5			11	42
37	20	42	35	6	22	33	30	29	35	37	1	11	36	1	5	2	1	15	21	3	5	21	6	6	2	
			1		1	5		9	4	10			9						1		2				1	

1 own-goal

Shortt	Silk	Jones P	Porteous	Goddard	Taylor	Squires	Dougall	Tadman	Williams	Strauss	Willis	Astall	Dews	Govan	Major	Pengelly	Hartery	Dixon	Ratcliffe	Edds	Bryant	Chisholm	McShane	Dobbie	Blatchford	
1		3				8	4	9	11	7			10						2			5	6			3
1	2					8	4	9	11	7			10						3			5	6			R
2	1	1				2	2	2	2	2			2						2			2	2			
									1																	

1950-51

Manager: Jimmy Rae

1	Aug	19	(h)	Leyton O	W 2-1	Bryant 2	20,900
2		24	(a)	Walsall	D 1-1	Machin	14,278
3		26	(a)	Ipswich T	L 0-2		13,000
4		30	(h)	Walsall	D 1-1	Porteous	12,000
5	Sep	2	(h)	Port Vale	W 1-0	Blatchford	19,390
6		6	(a)	Nottingham F	L 1-4	Dews	17,596
7		9	(h)	Reading	W 2-0	Dews, Rattray	15,592
8		13	(h)	Nottingham F	L 0-2		19,939
9		16	(a)	Southend U	L 0-1		14,500
10		23	(h)	Exeter C	L 0-1		25,424
11		30	(a)	Bournemouth	W 2-0	Dougall, Govan	14,878
12	Oct	7	(a)	Torquay U	W 3-1	Tadman 2, Dews	17,000
13		14	(h)	Aldershot	W 5-1	Tadman 4, Dougall	19,081
14		21	(a)	Swindon T	W 2-1	Tadman, Dews	16,783
15		28	(h)	Colchester U	W 7-1	Tadman 2, Strauss 2, Govan, Dews, Dougall	20,727
16	Nov	4	(a)	Bristol R	L 1-3	Tadman	29,654
17		11	(h)	Crystal P	W 4-0	Dews 2, Govan, Harding (og)	18,229
18		18	(a)	Brighton & HA	W 6-0	Tadman 4, Strauss, Rundle	8,000
19	Dec	2	(a)	Norwich C	L 0-1		26,841
20		23	(h)	Ipswich T	W 2-1	Ratcliffe, Feeney (og)	13,860
21		25	(a)	Bristol C	L 0-1		19,948
22		26	(h)	Bristol C	W 2-0	Astall, Dews	26,306
23	Jan	10	(h)	Watford	W 3-1	Astall, Dougall, Tadman	7,000
24		13	(a)	Reading	L 0-4		17,298
25		20	(h)	Southend U	W 2-0	Tadman, Astall	14,187
26		27	(a)	Watford	D 1-1	Dougall	9,107
27	Feb	3	(a)	Exeter C	L 2-3	Dews 2	20,000
28		10	(h)	Newport C	D 1-1	Dougall	13,267
29		17	(h)	Bournemouth	W 3-1	Tadman, Dews, Govan	13,102
30		24	(h)	Torquay U	W 1-0	Tadman	19,102
31	Mar	3	(a)	Aldershot	D 2-2	Tadman, Dews	8,500
32		5	(a)	Port Vale	L 1-2	Willis	5,000
33		10	(h)	Swindon T	W 5-1	Tadman, Dews, Govan, Willis, Ratcliffe	11,636
34		17	(a)	Colchester U	L 0-3		8,746
35		23	(a)	Millwall	D 1-1	Astall	23,000
36		24	(h)	Bristol R	D 0-0		21,066
37		26	(h)	Millwall	D 2-2	Dews, Govan	16,204
38		31	(a)	Crystal P	W 1-0	Astall	10,461
39	Apr	7	(h)	Brighton & HA	D 3-3	Dobbie 2, Govan	9,594
40		9	(h)	Northampton T	W 4-1	Govan, Tadman, Astall, Dobbie	7,515
41		14	(a)	Newport C	L 0-2		11,967
42		18	(h)	Gillingham	W 2-0	Dobbie, Tadman	11,373
43		21	(h)	Norwich C	W 2-1	Dews 2	20,500
44		26	(a)	Leyton O	W 2-1	Dobbie, Tadman	8,092
45		28	(a)	Northampton T	W 3-1	Astall, Govan, Dews	6,297
46	May	5	(a)	Gillingham	W 2-1	Rattray 2	13,000

FINAL LEAGUE POSITION: 4th in Division Three South

Appearances
Goals

FA Cup

1	Nov	25	(a)	Gainsborough T	W 3-0	Tadman 3	Unknown
2	Dec	9	(a)	Crewe A	D 2-2	Govan, Strauss	11,366
R		13	(h)	Crewe A	W 3-0	Dews 2, Strauss	17,500
3	Jan	6	(h)	Wolves	L 1-2	Dews	40,000

Appearances
Goals

Shortt	Ratcliffe	Jones	Dougall	Chisholm	Porteous	Astall	Dews	Bryant	Machin	Blatchford	Rundle	Dixon	McShane	Rattray	Tadman	Govan	Dobbie	Strauss	Silk	Major	Robertson	Smith	Willis	
	2	3	4	5	6	7	8	9	10	11										1				1
	2	3	4	5	6	7	8	9	10	11										1				2
	2	3	8	5	6	7	10	9		11	4									1				3
	2	3	4		6	7	8	9	10	11		5								1				4
	2	3	4		10	7		9		11		5	6	8						1				5
1	2	3	4			7	10			11		5	6	8	9									6
1	2	3	4		6	7	10			11		5		8	9									7
1	2	3	4		6	7	10			11		5		8	9									8
1	2	3	4	5	6	7	10							8	9	11								9
1	2	3	4	5	6		10	9							7	11	8							10
1	2	3	8	5	6		10				4				9	11		7						11
1	2	3	8	5	6		10				4				9	11		7						12
1	2	3	8	5	6		10				4				9	11		7						13
1	2	3	8	5	6		10				4				9	11		7						14
1	2	3	8	5	6		10		4						9	11		7						15
1	2	3	8	5	6		10				4				9	11		7						16
1	2	3	8	5	6		10				4				9	11		7						17
1	2	3	8	5	6		10				4				9	11		7						18
1	2	3		5	6		8			11	4				9			7					10	19
1	2	3		5	6		8				4			10	9	11		7						20
1	2	3	8	5	6		10				4				9	11		7						21
1		3	8	5	6	7	10				4				9	11			2					22
1		3	8	5	6	7	10						4		9	11			2					23
	2	3	8	5	6	7	10						4		9	11				1				24
	2	3	8	5	6	7	10						4		9	11				1				25
	2	3	8	5	6	7	10						4		9	11				1				26
	2	3	8	5	6	7	10						4		9	11				1				27
1	2	3	8	5	6	7	10						4		9	11								28
1	2	3	4	5	6		10								9	11		7					8	29
1	2	3	4	5			10						6		9	11		7					8	30
1	2	3	4	5			10			11			6		9			7					8	31
1	2	3	4	5			10						6		9	11		7					8	32
1	2	3	4	5	6	7	10								9	11							8	33
1	2	3	4		6	7	10									11	9				5		8	34
1	2	3	4	5	6	7	10								9	11	8							35
1	2	3	4	5		7	10						6		9	11	8							36
1	2	3	4	5	6	7	10								9	11	8							37
1	2	3	4	5	6	7	10								9	11	8							38
1	2	3	4	5	6	7	10								9	11	8							39
	2	3			6	7							4	10	9	11	8			1	5			40
1	2	3		5	6	7							4	10	9	11	8							41
		3	4	5	6	7								10	9	11	8			1		2		42
1	2	3	4	5	6	7	8							10	9	11								43
	2	3	4	5	6	7								10	9	11	8			1				44
	2	3	4	5	6	7	8							10	9	11				1				45
	2	3	4	5	6	7				11				10	9					1			8	46
32	43	46	42	39	41	30	40	6	4	11	12	5	14	13	40	35	11	15	2	14	2	1	8	
	2		6		1	7	17	2	1	1	1			3	23	9	5	3					2	

2 own-goals

1	2	3		5	6		8				4				9		11	7					10	1
1	2	3	8	5	6		10				4				9	11		7						2
1	2	3	8	5	6		10				4				9	11		7						R
1		3	8	5	6	7	10						4		9	11			2					3
4	3	4	3	4	4	1	4				3		1		4	3	1	3	1				1	
							3								3	1		2						

1951-52

Manager: Jimmy Rae

1	Aug	18	(a)	Leyton O	L 0-1		15,000
2		22	(h)	Crystal P	W 5-0	Dews 2, Astall, Strauss, Rattray	14,388
3		25	(h)	Walsall	W 3-0	Tadman 2, Astall	12,991
4		29	(a)	Crystal P	W 1-0	Rattray	14,037
5	Sep	1	(a)	Shrewsbury T	W 3-1	Dews, Tadman, Ratcliffe	12,720
6		5	(h)	Colchester U	W 3-1	Dews, Tadman, Ratcliffe	17,892
7		8	(h)	Aldershot	W 2-1	Dews, Rattray	18,201
8		13	(a)	Colchester U	L 0-1		8,105
9		15	(a)	Watford	W 3-1	Astall, Govan, Tadman	12,000
10		22	(h)	Bristol R	L 1-2	Govan	25,593
11		29	(a)	Ipswich T	D 2-2	Dews, Rattray	15,633
12	Oct	6	(h)	Port Vale	W 3-0	Astall, Govan, Rattray	18,867
13		13	(a)	Northampton T	L 1-3	Chisholm	14,661
14		20	(h)	Reading	W 3-2	Astall 2, Dews	18,116
15		27	(a)	Newport C	D 3-3	Tadman 2, Astall	10,065
16	Nov	3	(h)	Southend U	W 2-0	Dougall, Tadman	17,627
17		10	(a)	Bournemouth	W 2-1	Dews, Govan	18,618
18		17	(h)	Millwall	W 5-0	Astall, Rattray, Tadman, Dews, Govan	21,849
19	Dec	1	(h)	Gillingham	W 4-2	Rattray 2, Astall, Dougall	18,609
20		8	(a)	Torquay U	L 2-3	Rattray 2	10,000
21		22	(a)	Walsall	W 5-2	Tadman 3, Govan, Russon (og)	7,991
22		25	(h)	Bristol C	D 2-2	Rattray 2	17,498
23		26	(a)	Bristol C	D 1-1	Tadman	23,365
24		29	(h)	Shrewsbury T	W 6-1	Dews 2, Rattray 2, Tadman, Govan	16,840
25	Jan	5	(a)	Aldershot	W 2-1	Dews, Tadman	7,800
26		12	(h)	Exeter C	W 2-1	Dews, Rattray	25,494
27		16	(h)	Norwich C	W 3-1	Astall 2, Dews	15,293
28		19	(h)	Watford	W 3-1	Tadman 2, Astall	20,381
29		26	(a)	Bristol R	W 2-1	Rattray, Dougall	28,937
30	Feb	9	(h)	Ipswich T	W 2-0	Dews, Rattray	19,039
31		13	(h)	Swindon T	W 3-0	Astall, Dews, Tadman	13,257
32		16	(a)	Port Vale	L 0-1		10,600
33		27	(a)	Swindon T	D 2-2	Dews 2	8,000
34	Mar	1	(h)	Northampton T	W 2-0	Rattray, Tadman	22,046
35		8	(a)	Reading	L 0-2		28,161
36		15	(h)	Newport C	W 5-0	Astall 2, Tadman 2, Dews	17,939
37		19	(h)	Leyton O	W 3-0	Astall, Rattray, Tadman	15,508
38		22	(a)	Southend U	D 1-1	Tadman	15,000
39		29	(h)	Bournemouth	W 4-1	Dews 2, Astall, Govan	11,994
40	Apr	5	(a)	Millwall	W 2-0	Dews, Tadman	25,810
41		12	(h)	Brighton & HA	D 2-2	Ratcliffe, Tadman	31,755
42		14	(a)	Exeter C	L 0-1		19,000
43		19	(a)	Gillingham	W 2-1	Dews, Tadman	14,639
44		23	(a)	Brighton & HA	W 3-2	Dews, Govan, Astall	28,000
45		26	(h)	Torquay U	D 2-2	Dews, Tadman	28,728
46		30	(a)	Norwich C	L 0-3		20,179

FINAL LEAGUE POSITION: 1st in Division Three South

Appearances
Goals

FA Cup

1	Nov	25	(a)	Millwall	L 0-1		26,490

Appearances
Goals

Shortt	Ratcliffe	Jones	McShane	Chisholm	Porteous	Astall	Willis	Dobbie	Rattray	Govan	Dews	Tadman	Strauss	Dougall	Major	Rundle	
1	2	3	4	5	6	7	8	9	10	11							1
1	2	3	4	5	6	7			10		8	9	11				2
1	2	3	4	5	6	7			10		8	9	11				3
1	2	3	4	5	6	7			10		8	9	11				4
1	2	3	4	5	6	7					10	9	11	8			5
1	2	3	4	5	6	7					10	9	11	8			6
1	2	3	4	5	6	7			10		8	9	11				7
1	2	3	4	5	6	7					10	9	11	8			8
1	2	3	4	5	6	7				11	10	9		8			9
1	2	3	6	5		7			10	11	8	9		4			10
1	2	3	6	5		7			10	11	8	9		4			11
1	2	3	6	5		7			10	11	8	9		4			12
1	2	3	6	5		7			10	11	8	9		4			13
	2	3	6	5		7	10		9	11	8			4	1		14
1	2	3	6	5		7			10	11	8	9		4			15
1	2	3	6	5		7			10	11	8	9		4			16
1	2	3	6	5		7			10	11	8	9		4			17
1	2	3	6	5		7			10	11	8	9		4			18
1	2	3	6	5		7			10	11	8	9		4			19
1	2	3	6	5		7			10	11	8	9		4			20
1	2	3		5	6	7			10	11	8	9		4			21
1	2	3		5	6	7			10	11	8	9		4			22
1	2	3		5	6	7			10	11	8	9		4			23
1	2	3	4	5	6	7			10	11	8	9					24
1	2	3	4	5	6	7			10	11	8	9					25
1	2	3		5	6	7			10	11	8	9		4			26
1	2	3		5	6	7			10	11	8	9		4			27
1	2	3		5	6	7			10	11	8	9		4			28
1	2	3		5	6	7			10	11	8	9		4			29
1	2	3		5	6				10	11	8	9	7	4			29
1	2	3	6	5		7			10	11	8	9		4			30
1	2	3	4	5	6	7			10	11	8	9					31
1	2	3		5	6	7			10	11	8	9		4			32
1	2	3		5	6	7			10		8	9	11	4			33
1	2	3		5	6	7			10	11	8	9				4	34
1	2	3		5	6	7			10	11	8	9				4	35
	2	3	4	5	6	7			10	11	8	9			1		36
1	2	3	4	5	6	7			10	11	8	9					37
1	2	3	4	5	6	7		10		11	8	9					38
1	2	3	4	5	6	7		11	10		8	9					39
1	2	3	4	5	6	7		11	10		8	9					40
1	2	3	4	5	6	7		11	10		8	9					41
1	2	3	4	5	6	7			10	11	8	9					42
1	2	3	4	5	6	7			10	11	8	9					43
1	2	3	4	5	6	7			10	11	8	9					44
1	2	3	4	5	6	7		10	8	11		9					45
44	46	46	34	46	34	45	2	6	41	35	44	44	9	26	2	2	46
	3			1		18			19	9	25	27	1	3			

1 own-goal

1	2	3	6	5		7			10	11	8	9		4			1
1	1	1	1	1		1			1	1	1	1		1			

1952-53

Manager: Jimmy Rae

1	Aug	25	(h)	Luton T	W 2-1	Tadman, McCrory	29,021
2		27	(a)	Southampton	W 3-2	Tadman 2, Astall	20,099
3		30	(a)	Leeds U	D 1-1	Govan	25,000
4	Sep	3	(h)	Southampton	W 3-1	Astall, Govan, Smith	26,440
5		6	(h)	Sheffield U	W 5-2	Smith 2, Govan, Astall, Willis	31,456
6		13	(h)	Rotherham U	W 4-3	Tadman 2, Smith 2	28,628
7		17	(h)	Bury	D 0-0		22,849
8		20	(a)	Fulham	L 1-2	Smith	35,000
9		27	(h)	West Ham U	D 1-1	Tadman	28,154
10	Oct	4	(a)	Leicester C	L 0-2		33,036
11		11	(a)	Barnsley	W 3-0	Dews, Yuell (og), Astall	14,794
12		18	(h)	Lincoln C	D 0-0		21,932
13		25	(a)	Hull C	W 1-0	Astall	31,776
14	Nov	1	(h)	Blackburn R	W 3-1	Astall, Govan, Tadman	23,795
15		8	(a)	Nottingham F	L 1-2	Dews	24,006
16		15	(h)	Everton	W 1-0	Dougall	22,354
17		22	(a)	Brentford	W 2-1	Tadman, Dews	18,000
18		29	(h)	Doncaster R	D 0-0		12,939
19	Dec	6	(a)	Swansea T	D 2-2	Govan, Smith	24,000
20		13	(h)	Huddersfield T	L 0-2		33,228
21		20	(a)	Luton T	L 0-1		13,055
22		25	(a)	Birmingham C	L 0-4		20,800
23		27	(h)	Birmingham C	W 2-1	Govan, Tadman	25,050
24	Jan	1	(a)	Bury	L 2-3	Smith, Bardsley (og)	13,785
25		3	(h)	Leeds U	L 0-1		22,926
26		17	(a)	Sheffield U	L 0-5		35,000
27		24	(a)	Rotherham U	W 3-2	Smith, Dobbie, Govan	14,843
28	Feb	7	(h)	Fulham	W 3-1	Tadman 2, Dews	21,199
29		18	(a)	West Ham U	W 1-0	Tadman	8,000
30		21	(h)	Leicester C	W 2-1	Dougall, Willis	19,181
31		28	(h)	Barnsley	W 4-0	Astall 2, Govan, Tadman	16,786
32	Mar	7	(a)	Lincoln C	D 0-0		14,235
33		14	(h)	Hull C	L 1-2	Davies	19,553
34		21	(a)	Blackburn R	W 3-1	Dougall, Davis, Dews	21,200
35		28	(h)	Nottingham F	L 0-3		14,538
36	Apr	3	(a)	Notts C	W 4-0	Govan 2, Astall, Tadman	18,322
37		4	(a)	Everton	L 0-2		38,974
38		6	(h)	Notts C	D 2-2	Astall, Chisholm	18,172
39		11	(h)	Brentford	W 1-0	Dougall	19,985
40		18	(a)	Doncaster R	D 1-1	Anderson	12,286
41		25	(h)	Swansea T	W 3-2	Tadman, Anderson, McCrory	20,893
42	May	2	(a)	Huddersfield T	L 0-2		19,624

FINAL LEAGUE POSITION: 4th in Division Two

Appearances
Goals

FA Cup

3	Jan	10	(h)	Coventry C	W 4-1	Dews, Smith, Astall, Govan	23,799
4		31	(h)	Barnsley	W 1-0	Govan	26,800
5	Feb	14	(h)	Gateshead	L 0-1		29,736

Appearances
Goals

Shortt	Ratcliffe	Jones	Dougall	Chisholm	Porteous	Astall	McCrory	Tadman	Smith A	Govan	Rundle	Willis	Dews	Dobbie	Major	McShane	Robertson	Jelly	Davies	Tilley	Davis	Smith J	Anderson	McKenna	
1	2	3	4	5	6	7	8	9	10	11															1
1	2	3	4	5	6	7	8	9	10	11															2
1	2	3	4		6	7		9	10	11	5	8													3
1	2	3	4	5	6	7		9	10	11		8													4
1	2	3	4	5	6	7		9	10	11		8													5
1	2	3	4	5	6	7		9	10	11		8													6
1	2	3	4	5	6	7		9	10	11		8													7
1	2	3	4	5	6	7		9	10	11		8													8
1	2	3	4	5	6	7	8	9	11				10												9
1	2	3	4	5	6	7	8	9					10	11											10
1	2	3	4	5	6	7	8	9	11				10												11
	2	3	4	5	6	7		9	10	11			8		1										12
1	2	3	4	5	6	7		9	10	11			8												13
1	2	3	4	5	6	7		9	10	11			8												14
1	2	3	4	5	6	7		9	10	11			8												15
1	2	3	4	5	6	7		9	10	11			8												16
1	2	3	4	5	6	7		9	10	11			8												17
1	2	3	4	5	6	7		9	10	11			8												18
1	2	3	4	5	6	7		9	10	11			8												19
1	2	3	4	5	6	7		9	10	11			8												20
1	2	3	4	5	6	7		9	10	11			8												21
1	2	3	4	5	6	7		9		11		10	8												22
1	2	3	4	5		7	8	9	10	11						6									23
1	2	3	4			7		9	10	11			8			6	5								24
1	2	3	4		6	7	8	9	10	11							5								25
1	2	3	4	5		7		9	10	11			8			6									26
	2	3	4	5		7			10	11			8	9	1	6									27
1		3		5		7		9		11		10	8			6	4	2							28
1		3	4	5		7		9				10	8			6		2	11						29
1		3	4	5		7		9				10	8			6		2	11						30
1		3	4	5		7	8	9		11			10				6	2							31
1		3	4	5		7	8	9		11			10				6	2							32
1		3	4	5			8	9		11			10				6	2	7						33
1		3	8	5						11			10	7			6	2		4	9				34
1		3	8	5						11			10	7			6			4	9	2			35
1		3	4	5		8		9		11			10				6	2	7						36
1		3	4	5	6	8		9		11			10						7			2			37
1		3	4	5	6	8	10	9		11							2		7						38
1		3	4		6	8		9					10				5	2	7				11		39
1		3	4		6	8		9					10				5	2	7				11		40
1		3	4	5	6	8	10	9						7			2						11		41
1		3	4		6	7	10	9									5			8			11	2	42
40	27	42	41	36	29	39	13	39	25	33	1	10	29	5	2	7	14	10	8	3	2	2	4	1	
			4	1		10	2	15	9	10		2	5	1					1		1		2		

2 own-goals

1	2	3	4	5	6	7		9	10	11			8												3
1		3		5		7				11		10	8	9		6	4	2							4
1		3		5		7		9	10	11			8			6	4	2							5
3	1	3	1	3	1	3		2	2	3		1	3	1		2	2	2							
						1			1	2			1												

1953-54

Manager: Jimmy Rae

1	Aug	19	(h)	Bury	D	1-1	McCrory	16,732
2		22	(a)	Nottingham F	L	0-3		16,746
3		24	(h)	Birmingham C	D	2-2	Davis, Tadman	20,800
4		29	(h)	Luton T	D	2-2	Davis, Tadman	22,094
5	Sep	2	(a)	Birmingham C	L	0-3		22,000
6		5	(a)	Oldham A	D	1-1	McCrory	22,114
7		7	(h)	Leeds U	D	1-1	Willis	20,725
8		12	(a)	Swansea T	W	1-0	Willis	22,000
9		16	(a)	Leeds U	D	1-1	McCrory	20,000
10		19	(h)	Rotherham U	L	0-2		20,037
11		26	(a)	Leicester C	L	2-4	Davis 2	24,495
12	Oct	3	(h)	Stoke C	D	1-1	Dews	22,642
13		10	(h)	Everton	W	4-0	Astall, McCrory, Davis, Edds	26,148
14		17	(a)	Hull C	L	0-2		24,633
15		24	(h)	Notts C	D	3-3	McCrory 2, Edds	16,456
16		31	(a)	Lincoln C	L	0-2		13,217
17	Nov	7	(h)	Bristol R	D	3-3	Dews 2, McCrory	23,724
18		14	(a)	Brentford	L	0-1		17,300
19		21	(h)	Derby C	W	3-2	Thomas, Tadman, Dews	19,436
20		28	(a)	Blackburn R	W	3-2	Tadman 2, McCrory	21,000
21	Dec	3	(h)	Doncaster R	D	0-0		19,644
22		12	(a)	Bury	L	0-3		10,144
23		19	(h)	Nottingham F	W	1-0	Thomas	17,491
24		25	(a)	Fulham	L	1-3	Dews	12,000
25		26	(h)	Fulham	D	2-2	Thomas, Tadman	15,000
26	Jan	2	(a)	Luton T	L	1-2	Thomas	9,694
27		16	(h)	Oldham A	W	5-0	Edds, McJarrow, Dews 2, Brierley (og)	16,222
28		23	(h)	Swansea T	D	1-1	Tadman	18,756
29	Feb	6	(a)	Rotherham U	L	1-2	Tadman	12,135
30		13	(h)	Leicester C	L	0-3		17,020
31		20	(a)	Stoke C	L	2-3	Langman, Ratcliffe	5,806
32		27	(a)	Everton	L	4-8	Langman 2, Davies, McCrory	44,496
33	Mar	6	(h)	Hull C	D	2-2	Langman, Ratcliffe	17,950
34		13	(a)	Notts C	L	0-2		12,000
35		20	(h)	Lincoln C	L	1-2	Dews	14,036
36		27	(a)	Derby C	W	4-1	Langman 3, Porteous	9,382
37	Apr	3	(h)	Blackburn R	D	1-1	Porteous	20,404
38		10	(a)	Bristol R	L	1-3	Crawford	23,799
39		16	(a)	West Ham U	D	2-2	Tadman 2	16,500
40		17	(h)	Brentford	W	3-2	Tadman, Thomas 2	23,286
41		19	(h)	West Ham U	W	2-1	McShane, Porteous	20,938
42		24	(a)	Doncaster R	D	3-3	Langman 2, Edds	7,316
				FINAL LEAGUE POSITION: 19th in Division Two				Appearances
								Goals

FA Cup

3	Jan	9	(h)	Nottingham F	W	2-0	McJarrow, Tadman	21,630
4		30	(h)	Doncaster R	L	0-2		24,226
								Appearances
								Goals

Major	Robertson	Jones	Dougall	Chisholm	Porteous	Astall	McCrory	Tadman	Smith A	Anderson	Davies	Davis	Willis	McShane	Dobbie	Ratcliffe	Edds	Thomas	Jelly	McJarrow	Langman N	McArthur	Crawford	Morgan	Shortt	Dews	Strauss	
1	2	3	4	5	6	7	8	9	10	11																		1
1	2	3	4	5	6	8		9	10	11	7																	2
1	2	3	4	5	6	8		11			7	9	10															3
1	2	3	4	5	6	8		11			7	9	10															4
1	2	3	4	5	6	8		11			7	9	10															5
1	2	3	4	5	6	7	8	11				9	10															6
	2	3	4	5	6	7	8	11				9	10												1			7
	2	3	4	5	6	7	8	9					10												1		11	8
	2	3	4	5	6	7	8	9					10												1		11	9
	2	3		5	6	7	8	9						4	11										1	10		10
	5	3	4		6	7	8					9			11	2									1	10		11
	5	3	4		6	7	8					9				2	11								1	10		12
	2	3	4	5	6	7	8					9					11								1	10		13
	2	3	4	5	6		8					9					11	7							1	10		14
	2	3	4	5	6		8	9									11	7							1	10		15
	2	3	4	5	6		8	9	10								11	7							1			16
	5		4		6		8	9								3	11	7	2						1	10		17
	2		4	5	6		8	9								3	11	7							1	10		18
	5	3	4		6		8	9								2	11	7							1	10		19
	5	3	4		6		8	9								2	11	7							1	10		20
	5	3	4		6		8	9								2	11	7							1	10		21
	5	3	4		6		8	9								2	11	7							1	10		22
1	4	3		5	6		8									2	11	7		9						10		23
1	4	3		5	6		8	7								2		11		9						10		24
1	4	3		5	6		8	7								2		11		9						10		25
1	4	3		5	6		8	7								2		11		9						10		26
1	4	3		5	6			9								2	11	7		10						8		27
1	4	3		5	6			9								2	11	7		10						8		28
1	4	3	8	5	6			9								2		7		10						11		29
1	4	3	8	5	6					11						2		7		9						10		30
1	2	3	4	5	6		8				7							11			9					10		31
1	4	3			6						7					2		11			9	5	9			10		32
1		3	4		6			11			7					2					9	5	8			10		33
1	6	3	4	5				11			7					2					9		8			10		34
1	4	3		5	10			7						6		2	11				9		8					35
1	4	3		5	10			7						6		2	11				9		8					36
1	4	3		5	10			7						6		2	11				9		8					37
1	4			5	10			9						6		2	11	7					8	3				38
1	4	3		5	10			9						6		2	11	7								8		39
1	4		8	5	10			9		11				6		2		7						3				40
1	4			5	10									6		2	11	7			9		8	3				41
1	4	3		5	6						7					2	11				9		8	10				42
26	41	37	27	33	41	13	23	32	3	4	9	9	7	8	2	27	21	23	1	8	9	2	9	4	16	25	2	
					3	1	9	11			1	5	2	1		2	4	6		1	9		1			8		

1 own-goal

1	4	3		5	6			9								2	11	7		10						8		3
1	4	3		5	6			9								2	11	7		10						8		4
2	2	2		2	2			2								2	2	2		2						2		
								1												1								

1954-55

Manager: Jimmy Rae/Jack Rowley

1	Aug	21	(h)	Middlesbrough	D 2-2	N.Langman, Ratcliffe	26,900
2		23	(h)	Liverpool	W 1-0	Thomas	27,011
3		28	(a)	Port Vale	L 0-1		25,600
4	Sep	1	(a)	Liverpool	D 3-3	Thomas, Dews, Porteous	32,777
5		4	(h)	Doncaster R	L 1-2	Porteous	20,504
6		9	(a)	Notts C	L 0-2		15,000
7		11	(a)	Derby C	D 2-2	Porteous 2	12,592
8		15	(h)	Notts C	L 1-3	Crawford	16,230
9		18	(h)	West Ham U	D 1-1	Tadman	18,370
10		25	(a)	Blackburn R	D 2-2	Davies, Dews	23,300
11	Oct	2	(h)	Fulham	W 3-2	Elliott (og), Porteous, McShane	23,077
12		9	(h)	Hull C	L 1-2	Dews	21,666
13		16	(a)	Luton T	L 1-3	Porteous	15,059
14		23	(h)	Nottingham F	L 1-2	Anderson	16,771
15		30	(a)	Leeds U	L 2-3	Porteous, Anderson	20,500
16	Nov	6	(h)	Bury	L 2-4	Davis, Anderson	15,099
17		13	(a)	Lincoln C	L 2-3	N.Langman, Ratcliffe	11,818
18		20	(h)	Birmingham C	W 1-0	Davies	19,184
19		27	(a)	Ipswich T	L 1-2	Dews	12,826
20	Dec	4	(h)	Rotherham U	W 2-1	N.Langman, Davies	14,956
21		11	(a)	Stoke C	L 1-3	Davies	17,397
22		18	(a)	Middlesbrough	L 1-4	Anderson	18,000
23		25	(h)	Swansea T	D 2-2	N.Langman, Dews	14,416
24		27	(a)	Swansea T	L 2-4	Anderson, N.Langman	24,000
25	Jan	1	(h)	Port Vale	D 0-0		14,371
26		15	(a)	Doncaster R	L 2-3	Davis, Dougall	6,000
27		22	(h)	Derby C	W 1-0	Anderson	13,492
28	Feb	5	(a)	West Ham U	L 1-6	Davis	18,200
29		12	(h)	Blackburn R	L 0-2		16,625
30		19	(a)	Fulham	W 3-2	Davis, Davies, Anderson	12,000
31		26	(a)	Hull C	W 2-0	Rowley, Davies	14,921
32	Mar	5	(h)	Luton T	W 2-1	Davis 2	25,995
33		12	(a)	Nottingham F	L 0-2		9,947
34		19	(h)	Leeds U	W 3-1	Willis, Anderson, Davis	19,968
35		26	(a)	Bury	L 1-3	Davis	7,348
36	Apr	2	(h)	Lincoln C	W 1-0	Willis	9,802
37		8	(a)	Bristol R	L 1-3	Rowley	26,010
38		9	(a)	Birmingham C	L 1-3	McJarrow	25,058
39		11	(h)	Bristol R	L 0-1		26,134
40		16	(h)	Ipswich T	W 2-0	Porteous, Willis	20,040
41		23	(a)	Rotherham U	L 0-2		16,700
42		30	(h)	Stoke C	W 2-0	Willis, McJarrow	23,844

FINAL LEAGUE POSITION: 20th in Division Two — Appearances

Goals

FA Cup

3	Jan	8	(h)	Newcastle U	L 0-1		29,865

Appearances

Goals

Major	Ratcliffe	Morgan	Tilley	Robertson	McShane	Thomas	McCrory	Langman N	Porteous	Edds	Shortt	Jones	Dougall	Crawford	Dews	Tadman	Davies	Davis	Baker	McJarrow	Willis	Langman P	Rowley	Anderson	
1	2	3	4	5	6	7	8	9	10	11															1
	2	3	4	5	6	7	8	10	11	1															2
1	2		4	5	6	7	8	9	10	11		3													3
1	2			5	6	7		9	11			3	4	8	10										4
	2	3	4	5	6	7		9	11		1		10	8											5
1	2	3	4	5	6	7			11					8	10	9									6
1	2	3	4	5	6	7	10		11					8		9									7
1	2	3	4	5	6	7	10		11					8		9									8
	2	3	4	5					6		1			8	10	9	7							11	9
	2	3	4	5	6				10		1				8		7	9						11	10
	2	3	4	5			9	10		1				8		7								11	11
	2	3	4	5			9	10		1				8	7									11	12
1	2	3	4	5	6			9	10						8	7								11	13
	2	3	4	5					10		1		6		8			9	7					11	14
	2	3	4	5					10		1		6		8		7	9						11	15
1	2	3	4	5					10				6		8		7	9						11	16
1	2	3	4	5		7		9	10				6		8									11	17
	2		4	5	6			9	10		1		3		8		7							11	18
	2		4	5	6			9	10		1		3		8		7							11	19
	2		4	5	6			9	10		1		3		8		7							11	20
	2		4	5	6			9	10		1		3		8		7							11	21
	2		4	5				9	6		1		3	8	10		7							11	22
	2		4	5				9	10		1		3		8		7			6				11	23
	2		4	5			8	9	10		1		3				7			6				11	24
	2		4	5			8	9	10		1		3				7			6				11	25
	2		4			7	8				1	3	5					9		6	10			11	26
	2		4			7	8				1	3	5					9		6	10			11	27
				2							1	3	4		10		7	9		6	8	5		11	28
	2		4				10				1	3				7		9		6	8	5		11	29
	2		4								1	3					7	9		6	8	5	10	11	30
	2		4								1	3					7	9		6	8	5	10	11	31
	2	3	4								1						7	9		6	8	5	10	11	32
	2		4								1	3					7	9		6	8	5	10	11	33
	2		4	6							1	3					7	9			8	5	10	11	34
	2		4								1	3					7	9		6	8	5	10	11	35
	2			4							1	3					7	9		6	8	5	10	11	36
	2			4			10				1	3					7			6	8	5	9	11	37
	2			4			8		10		1	3					7			6		5	9	11	38
	2			4			8		6	11	1	3			10							5	9	7	39
	2			4					6		1	3			10		7				8	5	9	11	40
				2			8		6	11	1	3					7			9		5	10		41
	2	11		4					6		1	3					7			9	8	5	10		42
9	40	17	34	34	16	11	14	17	30	5	33	18	17	7	20	7	26	15	1	17	14	15	13	32	
	2				1	2		5	8				1	1	5	1	6	8		2	4		2	8	

1 own-goal

	2		4	5		7	8	9			1		3							6	10			11	3
	1		1	1		1	1	1			1		1							1	1			1	

1955-56

Manager: Jack Rowley

1	Aug	20	(a)	Sheffield W	L 2-5	Anderson 2	31,716
2		22	(h)	Doncaster R	D 2-2	Willis, Rowley	21,236
3		27	(h)	Nottingham F	L 1-2	Willis	17,955
4	Sep	1	(a)	Doncaster R	L 1-3	Anderson	10,000
5		3	(a)	Hull C	W 1-0	Anderson	17,815
6		5	(h)	Stoke C	L 0-1		21,000
7		10	(h)	Blackburn R	W 1-0	Rowley	20,500
8		12	(a)	Stoke C	L 1-4	Rowley	17,179
9		17	(a)	Lincoln C	L 0-1		13,466
10		24	(h)	Leicester C	L 0-1		19,454
11	Oct	1	(a)	Liverpool	L 1-4	Williams	34,397
12		8	(a)	West Ham U	L 0-4		19,750
13		15	(h)	Port Vale	D 1-1	Rowley	16,879
14		22	(a)	Barnsley	W 2-1	Rowley 2	11,246
15		29	(h)	Swansea T	L 0-1		24,070
16	Nov	5	(a)	Notts C	L 0-3		12,500
17		12	(h)	Leeds U	W 4-3	Willis, Williams, Davis, Dougall	18,852
18		19	(a)	Fulham	L 1-2	Dougall	23,000
19		26	(h)	Bury	L 1-4	Twissell	15,474
20	Dec	3	(a)	Rotherham U	D 0-0		11,488
21		10	(h)	Middlesbrough	W 4-0	Wetton, Davis, Robinson (og), Stenner	11,415
22		17	(h)	Sheffield W	D 1-1	Jones	16,500
23		24	(a)	Nottingham F	L 1-3	Twissell	10,003
24		26	(h)	Bristol C	W 5-0	Davies, Crawford 2, Davis, Williams	22,096
25		27	(a)	Bristol C	L 0-6		27,490
26		31	(h)	Hull C	D 1-1	Twissell	20,130
27	Jan	14	(a)	Blackburn R	L 1-2	Willis	18,200
28		21	(h)	Lincoln C	L 1-4	Robertson	12,586
29	Feb	4	(a)	Leicester C	L 1-4	Davis	25,000
30		11	(h)	Liverpool	W 4-0	Morgan, N.Langman 3	10,250
31		18	(h)	Fulham	D 0-0		16,962
32		25	(a)	Port Vale	L 1-3	N.Langman	14,236
33	Mar	3	(h)	Barnsley	W 3-0	Morgan, N.Langman, Davies	11,200
34		10	(a)	Middlesbrough	D 2-2	Davies, N.Langman	23,000
35		17	(h)	Notts C	D 1-1	Morgan	19,616
36		24	(a)	Leeds U	L 2-4	Mitchell 2	12,000
37		30	(a)	Bristol R	L 1-2	N.Langman	27,814
38		31	(h)	West Ham U	L 0-1		17,555
39	Apr	2	(h)	Bristol R	L 0-1		19,181
40		7	(a)	Bury	L 1-7	Wyatt	8,936
41		14	(h)	Rotherham U	W 3-1	N.Langman 2, Morgan	6,661
42		21	(a)	Swansea T	D 2-2	Davies, Bell	15,500

FINAL LEAGUE POSITION: 21st in Division Two

Appearances
Goals

FA Cup

3	Jan	7	(a)	Leyton O	L 0-1		15,619

Appearances
Goals

Major	Robertson	Jones	Clelland	Lawless	Wetton	Thomas	Crawford	McJarrow	Rowley	Anderson	Dougall	Willis	Davis	Shortt	Davies	Langman N	Porteous	Williams	Langman P	Stenner	Tilley	Ratcliffe	Twissell	Baker	Dyer	Swiggs	Morgan	Mitchell	John	Bell	Wyatt	
1	2	3	4	5	6	7	8	9	10	11																						1
1	2	3		5	6		10		11	7	4	8	9																			2
1	2	3	10	5	6					11	4	8			7	9																3
1	2	3		5	6					11	4	8			7	9	10															4
	2	3		5	6					11	4	8		1	7	9	10															5
	2	3		5	6				11	7	4	8	9	1			10															6
	2	3		5	6			9	11		4	8	7	1				10														7
	2	3		5	6			9	11		4	8		1	7			10														8
	4	3			6		8		10					1	7	9	11		5											2		9
	4	3			6		8		10					1	7	9			5	11										2		10
	4	3			6				10			8		1	7			9	5	11										2		11
	2	3			6				10		4		9	1	7				5	11	8											12
	4	3			10				11		6			1				9	5		8	2	7									13
		3			10			6	11		4			1				9	5		8	2	7									14
	4	3			10				11		6			1				9	5		8	2		7								15
	4	3							11		6			1		8		9	5		10	2		7								16
	4	3									6	10	9	1				8	5			2	7	11								17
	4	3									6	10	9	1				8	5			2	7	11								18
1	4	3									6	10	9					8	5			2	7	11								19
1	4	3									6	8	9					10	5			2	7	11								20
	2	3			6						4	8	9	1				10	5	11				7								21
	2	3			6						4		9	1				8	5		10		11	7								22
	2	3			6						4		9	1				8	5		10		11	7								23
	2	3			6		8				4		9	1	7			10	5				11									24
	2	3			6		10				4		9	1	7			8	5				11									25
	2	3			6		10				4				7			8	5				11		1	9						26
1	2				6						4	10			7		9	8	5				11								3	27
1	2	3			6		8				4				7			10	5				11			9						28
1	2				6		8				4		9			10			5	11			7								3	29
1	2	3			6						4		9		7	8			5	11							10					30
1	2	3			6				11		4		9			8			5				7				10					31
1	2	3			6				11		4		9			8			5				7				10					32
1	2	3			6				11		4				7	9		8	5								10					33
1	2	3			6										7	9		8	5		4		11				10					34
1	2	3			6										7	9		8	5		4		11				10					35
1	2				6										7	8			5	11	4						10	9			3	36
1	2	3			6											9			5	11	4		7				10				8	37
	2	3			6									1	7	9		8	5		4		11				10					38
	4	3			6								9	1	7	8			5		10		11								2	39
	2	3						6							7				5	11	4				1		10	9			8	40
	4	3			6										7	9			5						1		11		2	10	8	41
	4	3			6										7	9			5						1		11		2	10	8	42
17	41	39	2	8	36	1	9	5	16	6	29	14	18	21	23	20	5	23	34	9	14	8	21	9	4	2	12	2	2	2	11	
	1	1			1		2		6	4	2	4	4		4	9		3		1			3				4	2		1	1	

1 own-goal

1	2	3			6		10				4		9		7			8	5				11									3
1	1	1			1		1				1		1		1			1	1				1									

1956-57

Manager: Jack Rowley

1	Aug	18	(a)	Brentford	L 1-4	Davies	13,700
2		20	(h)	Queen's Park R	L 1-2	Mitchell	15,278
3		25	(h)	Reading	L 0-6		11,498
4		27	(a)	Queen's Park R	L 0-3		8,424
5	Sep	1	(a)	Newport C	L 1-4	Mitchell	12,098
6		5	(a)	Southend U	W 1-0	Twissell	7,020
7		8	(h)	Colchester U	D 2-2	Rowley, Kearns	9,702
8		10	(h)	Southend U	D 0-0		14,000
9		15	(a)	Norwich C	L 0-3		15,877
10		17	(a)	Northampton T	L 0-2		7,736
11		22	(h)	Coventry C	D 0-0		11,722
12		24	(h)	Northampton T	W 4-3	Twissell, Dougall 2, Kearns	13,250
13		29	(a)	Southampton	D 2-2	Twissell 2	17,192
14	Oct	6	(a)	Watford	W 1-0	Rowley	11,586
15		13	(h)	Shrewsbury T	D 1-1	Rowley	14,534
16		20	(a)	Walsall	L 0-1		10,113
17		27	(h)	Ipswich T	L 1-2	Rowley	12,079
18	Nov	3	(a)	Bournemouth	L 1-2	N.Langman	11,587
19		10	(h)	Torquay U	D 0-0		20,357
20		24	(h)	Brighton & HA	W 2-0	Davis, N.Langman	11,534
21	Dec	1	(a)	Gillingham	W 3-0	Davis 2, Anderson	7,000
22		15	(h)	Brentford	W 2-0	Davis, N.Langman	6,203
23		22	(a)	Reading	L 2-3	Davis 2	6,342
24		26	(a)	Exeter C	L 1-2	N.Langman	10,301
25	Jan	5	(h)	Exeter C	W 5-0	Davis 2, N.Langman, Rowley, Harvey (og)	9,857
26		12	(a)	Colchester U	L 1-2	Rowley	7,732
27		19	(h)	Norwich C	W 3-2	N.Langman, Dougall, Barnes	11,254
28		26	(a)	Crystal P	L 1-2	N.Langman	10,656
29	Feb	2	(a)	Coventry C	W 4-1	Davis, N.Langman 3	12,668
30		9	(h)	Southampton	W 2-1	Dougall, Davis	17,281
31		16	(h)	Watford	D 3-3	Jones, Quinn, N.Langman	13,355
32		23	(a)	Shrewsbury T	L 1-3	Dougall	5,777
33	Mar	2	(h)	Walsall	L 2-4	Dougall, Quinn	13,638
34		9	(a)	Swindon T	W 3-0	Dougall 2, Cross (og)	8,864
35		11	(h)	Crystal P	L 0-1		12,293
36		16	(h)	Bournemouth	W 2-0	Williams, Anderson	10,497
37		23	(a)	Torquay U	D 1-1	N.Langman	12,038
38		30	(h)	Millwall	D 0-0		11,284
39	Apr	6	(a)	Brighton & HA	L 1-3	Anderson	12,444
40		10	(h)	Newport C	W 3-2	N.Langman 2, Davis	8,688
41		13	(h)	Gillingham	W 2-0	Davis, N.Langman	9,107
42		19	(a)	Aldershot	W 2-0	Davies, N.Langman	6,102
43		20	(a)	Ipswich T	L 1-2	Dougall	16,758
44		22	(a)	Aldershot	D 2-2	N.Langman, Wetton (og)	12,476
45		27	(a)	Millwall	D 2-2	Williams, Twissell	8,680
46		29	(h)	Swindon T	W 1-0	Twissell	9,052

FINAL LEAGUE POSITION: 18th in Division Three South

Appearances
Goals

FA Cup

1	Nov	17	(a)	Exeter C	W 2-0	N.Langman, Rowley	15,000
2	Dec	8	(a)	Torquay U	L 0-1		15,830

Appearances
Goals

Dyer	Wyatt	Jones	Robertson	Langman P	Tilley	Davies	Langman N	Davis	Williams	Twissell	Mitchell	Kearns	John	Anderson	Gee	Brown	Morgan	Rowley	Swiggs	Arundel	Quinn	Howell	Barnes	Peach	Baker	Hancock	Jasper	Dougall	
1	2	3	4	5	6	7	8	9	10	11																			1
1	2	3	4	5	6	7		8	11	9	10																		2
1	8	3	5		6	7			10		9		2	11														4	3
	2	3	4	5	6	7	9				10			11	1													8	4
	2	3	4	5	6	7	9				8			11		1	10												5
	2	3	4	5	6	7				11	9	10				1		8											6
	2	3	4	5	6	7		9		11		10				1		8											7
	2	3	4	5	6	7		9		11		10				1		8											8
	2	3	4	5	6	7		9				8		11		1		10											9
		3	2	5	6	7			4	11	9	10				1		8											10
		3	2	5	6				4	7		10				1			9	11								8	11
1		3	2	5	6				4	7		10						9		11								8	12
		3	2	5	6				4	7						1		9		11	10							8	13
		3	2	5	6				4	7		11				1		9			10							8	14
	2			5	6	7			4			11					3	9			10	1						8	15
	8	3	2	5	6				4	7		11				1		9			10								16
		3	2	5	6	7			4			8				1		9		11	10								17
	3		2	5	6		9		4	7		8				1	11	10											18
		3	2	5	6		9	8	4			10				1		11										7	19
		3	2	5	6	7	9	8	4			10		11		1													20
		3	2	5	6		9	8	4			10		11		1		7											21
		3	2	5	6		9	8	4			10		11		1												7	22
		3	2	5	6		9	8	4			10		11		1												7	23
		3	2	5	6		9	8	4			10		11		1												7	24
		3	2	5	6		9	8	4			10				1		11										7	25
		3	2	5	6		9	8	4			10				1		11										7	26
		3	2	5	6		8		4			10				1		11					9					7	27
		3	2	5	6		8		4			10				1		11					9					7	28
		3	2	5	6		9	8	4							1		11			10							7	29
		3	2	5	6		9	8	4							1		11			10							7	30
		3	2	5	6		9	8	4							1		11			10							7	31
		3	2	5	6		9		4							1					10			8	11			7	32
		3	2	5	6		9		4					11		1					10				7			8	33
	5	3	2				9		4			10		11		1									7	6		8	34
	5	3	2				9		4			10		11		1									7	6		8	35
		3	2	5	6		9		4					11		1		10							7			8	36
		3	2	5	6		9		4					11		1		10							7			8	37
		3	2	5	6		9		4					11		1		10							7			8	38
		3	2	5	6		9		4					11		1		10			8				7				39
		3	2	5	6	7	8	9	4					11		1		10											40
		3	2	5	6	7	9	8	4					11		1		10											41
	5	3	2		6	7	9	8	4			10		11		1													42
	5	3	2		6	7	9		4			10		11		1												8	43
	5	3	2		6	7	9	8	4			10		11		1													44
	5	3	4		6		9		8	7		10		11		1											2		45
	5	3	4		6		9		8	7		10		11		1											2		46
4	19	44	45	38	44	18	32	19	40	14	6	30	1	23	1	40	3	27	1	4	11	1	2	1	8	2	2	26	
		1				3	17	11	2	6	2	2		3				6			2		1					9	

3 own-goals

		3	2	5	6	7	9	8	4			10				1		11											1
		3	2	5	6		9	8	4			10				1		11										7	2
		2	2	2	2	1	2	1	2			2				2		2										1	
							1											1											

1957-58

Manager: Jack Rowley

1	Aug	24	(a)	Shrewsbury T	L	0-2		10,092
2		26	(h)	Reading	W	1-0	N.Langman	20,123
3		31	(h)	Aldershot	W	4-2	Anderson, Carter 2, Kearns	20,423
4	Sep	4	(a)	Reading	W	3-1	N.Langman 3	10,568
5		7	(a)	Swindon T	L	0-1		11,305
6		12	(a)	Brighton & HA	L	2-3	N.Langman, Kearns	13,408
7		14	(h)	Millwall	W	1-0	Carter	18,385
8		16	(h)	Brighton & HA	W	2-1	Williams, Carter	18,883
9		21	(a)	Gillingham	L	0-1		9,555
10		25	(a)	Southampton	W	1-0	Carter	14,251
11		28	(h)	Exeter C	W	1-0	N.Langman	23,418
12		30	(h)	Southampton	W	4-0	Anderson, Carter 2, Kearns	25,600
13	Oct	5	(a)	Queen's Park R	L	0-1		11,222
14		9	(h)	Colchester U	D	1-1	N.Langman	22,550
15		12	(a)	Northampton T	L	0-5		9,422
16		19	(h)	Watford	W	2-1	N.Langman 2	17,901
17		26	(a)	Crystal P	L	0-3		14,532
18	Nov	2	(h)	Torquay U	W	1-0	Gauld	23,765
19		9	(a)	Brentford	L	0-2		15,600
20		23	(a)	Norwich C	L	0-1		20,776
21		30	(h)	Bournemouth	W	3-1	Rule (og), Gauld, Hughes (og)	16,892
22	Dec	14	(h)	Coventry C	W	4-0	Anderson, Carter 3	14,539
23		21	(h)	Shrewsbury T	D	2-2	Carter, Barrett	13,638
24		25	(a)	Newport C	W	2-0	Baker, Gauld	10,680
25		26	(h)	Newport C	W	1-0	Carter	25,936
26		28	(a)	Aldershot	D	3-3	Carter 2, Baker	5,767
27	Jan	11	(h)	Swindon T	D	2-2	Carter, Baker	16,797
28		18	(a)	Millwall	W	1-0	Baker	11,338
29	Feb	1	(h)	Gillingham	W	2-1	Anderson, Carter	17,566
30		8	(a)	Exeter C	L	2-4	Penk, Gauld	13,598
31		15	(h)	Queen's Park R	W	3-1	Carter 3	17,068
32		22	(h)	Northampton T	W	3-0	Williams, Carter, Baker	16,517
33	Mar	1	(a)	Watford	W	2-0	Williams, Baker	10,508
34		3	(a)	Walsall	W	2-0	Carter, Penk	9,393
35		8	(h)	Cystal P	W	1-0	Anderson	18,719
36		15	(a)	Torquay U	W	2-0	Carter, Kearns	14,609
37		22	(h)	Norwich C	L	0-1		17,018
38		29	(a)	Coventry C	D	1-1	Carter	11,563
39	Apr	4	(h)	Port Vale	W	1-0	Kearns	22,258
40		5	(h)	Brentford	D	0-0		19,581
41		7	(a)	Port Vale	D	0-0		11,059
42		12	(a)	Bournemouth	D	0-0		16,705
43		16	(a)	Southend U	L	1-2	Morrison (og)	10,000
44		19	(h)	Walsall	W	2-1	Carter, Baker	19,081
45		21	(h)	Southend U	L	2-3	Carter, Baker	22,000
46		26	(a)	Colchester U	W	2-1	Carter, Baker	8,593

FINAL LEAGUE POSITION: 3rd in Division Three South

Appearances
Goals

FA Cup

1	Nov	16	(h)	Watford	W	6-2	Anderson, Barnes 2, Carter 2, Gauld	20,875
2	Dec	7	(h)	Dorchester T	W	5-2	Penk, Carter 3, Gauld	18,305
3	Jan	4	(h)	Newcastle U	L	1-6	Carter	38,129

Appearances
Goals

Brown	Robertson	Jones	Williams	Wyatt	Tilley	Penk	Carter	Langman N	Dougall	Anderson	Kearns	Twissell	Quinn	Penny	Langman P	Barrett	Gauld	Barnsley	Barnes	Baker	Adams	Timmins	Fulton	Jasper	
1	2	3	4	5	6	7	8	9	10	11															1
1	2	3	4	5	6	7	8	9		11	10														2
1	2	3	4	5	6	7	8	9		11	10														3
1	2	3	4	5	6	7	8	9			10	11													4
1	2	3	4	5	6	7	8	9			10	11													5
1	2	3	4	5	6	7	8	9			10	11													6
1	2	3	4	5	6		8	9			11	7	10												7
1	2	3	4	5	6		8	9			11	7	10												8
1	2	3	4	5	6		8	9			11	7	10												9
1	2	3	4	5	6	7	8	9		11	10														10
1	2	3		5	6	11	8	9	4		10			7											11
1	2	3	4		6	7	8	9		11	10				5										12
1	2	3	4	5	6	7	8	9		11	10														13
1	2	3	4	5		7	8	9	6	11	10														14
1	2	3	4	5		7	8	9	6	11						10									15
1	2	3	4	5	6	7	8	9		11	10														16
1	2	3	4	5	6	7	8	9		11							10								17
1	2		4	3	6	7	8	9		11					5		10								18
1			4	3	6	7	8	9	2	11					5		10								19
	2		4	5	6	7	8		3	11							10	1	9						20
	2		4	5	6	7	8		3	11							10	1	9						21
	2		4	5		7	9			11	10					6	8	1			3				22
	2			5	4	7	9		3	11	10					6	8	1							23
	2		4	5	6	7	8		3	11							10	1		9					24
	2		4	5	6	7	8		3	11							10	1		9					25
	2		4	5	6	7	8		3	11							10	1		9					26
	2		4	5	6	7	8			11							10	1		9		3			27
	2		4	5		7	8			11						6	10	1		9		3			28
	2		4	5		7	8			11						6	10	1		9		3			29
	2		4	5	6	7	8			11							10	1		9		3			30
	2		4	5		7	8			11	10					6		1		9			3		31
	2		4	5		11	8			7	10					6		1		9			3		32
	2		4	5		11	8			7	10					6		1		9			3		33
	2		4	5		11	8			7	10					6		1		9			3		34
	2		4	5		11	8			7	10					6		1		9			3		35
	2		4	5		11	8			7	10					6		1		9			3		36
	2		4	5		11	8			7	10					6		1		9			3		37
	2		4	5		11	8			7	10					6		1		9			3		38
	2	3	4	5		11	8			7	10					6		1		9					39
1	2	3	4	5		11	8			7	10					6				9					40
1	2	3	4	5	6	11			8	7	10									9					41
1	2	3	4	5	6	11			7		10						8			9					42
1	2	3	4	5	6	11	7				10						8			9					43
1	2	3	4	5			8				10					6	9			7		11			44
1	2	3	4	5		11	10			7						6	8			9					45
1	2		4	5		11	10			7						6	8			9			3		46
26	45	24	44	45	28	42	44	19	13	36	30	6	3	1	3	18	19	20	2	23	1	5	9		Apps
			3			2	26	9		5	5					1	4			9					Goals

3 own-goals

Brown	Robertson	Jones	Williams	Wyatt	Tilley	Penk	Carter	Langman N	Dougall	Anderson	Kearns	Twissell	Quinn	Penny	Langman P	Barrett	Gauld	Barnsley	Barnes	Baker	Adams	Timmins	Fulton	Jasper	
	2		4	5	6	7	8		3	11							10	1	9						1
	2			5	4	7	8			11						6	10	1	9					3	2
	2		4	5	6	7	8		3	11							10	1		9					3
	3		2	3	3	3	3		2	3						1	3	3	2	1				1	Apps
						1	6			1							2		2						Goals

1958-59

Manager: Jack Rowley

1	Aug	23	(a)	Hull C	D	1-1	Gauld	14,318
2		25	(a)	Rochdale	W	2-0	Carter, Penk	8,442
3		30	(h)	Tranmere R	W	4-0	Carter 2, Baker, Gauld	22,518
4	Sep	4	(h)	Rochdale	W	2-0	Carter, Williams	26,961
5		6	(a)	Stockport C	D	2-2	Penk, Gauld	11,300
6		8	(a)	Bury	D	1-1	Anderson	12,188
7		13	(h)	Reading	D	2-2	Carter, Penk	25,966
8		18	(h)	Bury	W	3-0	Meyer 2, Gauld	27,589
9		20	(a)	Colchester U	L	0-2		10,038
10		22	(h)	Doncaster R	W	4-0	Carter 2, J.S.Williams, Govan	24,827
11		27	(h)	Bournemouth	W	3-1	Dougall, Meyer, Wyatt	24,822
12	Oct	2	(a)	Doncaster R	W	6-4	Anderson 3, Meyer 2, Penk	5,300
13		4	(a)	Norwich C	D	1-1	Carter	22,200
14		8	(h)	Southend U	W	3-1	Costello (og), J.S.Williams, Gauld	25,349
15		12	(h)	Swindon T	W	3-2	Carter, Gauld 2	26,051
16		18	(a)	Mansfield T	W	4-1	Carter 3, Anderson	12,488
17		25	(h)	Notts C	W	3-0	Baker, Gauld, Penk	25,910
18	Nov	1	(a)	Chesterfield	W	2-1	Baker, Carter	10,976
19		8	(h)	Newport C	W	3-2	Baker, Gauld 2	23,482
20		22	(h)	Wrexham	D	2-2	Penk, Gauld	21,056
21		29	(a)	Southampton	L	1-5	Carter	21,830
22	Dec	13	(a)	Bradford C	D	0-0		11,908
23		20	(h)	Hull C	D	1-1	Carter	20,305
24		26	(h)	Queen's Park R	W	3-2	Carter, Gauld 2	30,036
25		27	(a)	Queen's Park R	L	1-2	Gauld	15,656
26	Jan	17	(h)	Stockport C	W	2-1	Govan, Baker	10,099
27		24	(a)	Southend U	D	0-0		12,410
28		31	(a)	Reading	W	2-0	Govan, Baker	13,595
29	Feb	7	(h)	Colchester U	D	1-1	J.S.Williams	22,686
30		14	(a)	Bournemouth	D	1-1	Govan	15,107
31		21	(h)	Norwich C	L	0-1		24,532
32		28	(a)	Swindon T	W	4-3	Gauld 3, Anderson	13,090
33	Mar	4	(h)	Accrington S	L	2-4	Gauld, Penk	12,022
34		7	(h)	Mansfield T	W	8-3	Govan, Penk, J.S.Williams 2, Gauld, Carter, Swinscoe 2 (2 og's)	17,597
35		14	(a)	Notts C	W	2-1	Gauld 2	7,369
36		16	(a)	Tranmere R	L	0-2		15,811
37		21	(h)	Chesterfield	W	2-0	Jenkins, Carter	17,334
38		27	(a)	Brentford	L	0-3		29,000
39		28	(a)	Newport C	W	1-0	Carter	8,108
40		30	(h)	Brentford	D	1-1	Govan	27,073
41	Apr	4	(h)	Halifax T	D	1-1	Carter	19,571
42		11	(a)	Wrexham	D	1-1	J.S.Williams	8,817
43		18	(h)	Southampton	W	1-0	Carter	23,775
44		20	(a)	Halifax T	W	1-0	Anderson	8,523
45		25	(a)	Accrington S	D	1-1	Penk	4,000
46		29	(h)	Bradford C	D	1-1	Carter	26,717

FINAL LEAGUE POSITION: 1st in Division Three

Appearances
Goals

FA Cup

1	Nov	15	(h)	Gillingham	D	2-2	Carter, Anderson	21,759
R		19	(a)	Gillingham	W	4-1	Meyer 3, Gauld	10,459
2	Dec	6	(a)	Coventry C	W	3-1	Baker, Carter 2	27,295
3	Jan	10	(h)	Cardiff C	L	0-3		36,247

Appearances
Goals

Barnsley	Robertson	Doughty	Williams JS	Wyatt	Barrett	Anderson	Gauld	Baker	Carter	Penk	Dougall	Williams JL	Meyer	Govan	Fulton	Bellett	Casey	Jenkins	Wyllie	Fincham	
1	2	1	4	5	6	7	8	9	10	11											1
1	2		4	5	6	7	8	9	10	11	3										2
1	2		4	5	6	7	10	9	8	11	3										3
1	2		4	5	6	7	10	9	8	11	3										4
1	2		4	5	6	11	8	9	10	7	3										5
1	2		4	5	6	7	8	9	10	11	3										6
1	2		4	5	6	7	8	9	10	11	3										7
1	2		4	5			8		10	7	3	6	9	11							8
1	2		4	5			8		10	7	3	6	9	11							9
1	2		4	5			8		10	7	3	6	9	11							10
1	2		4	5			10		8	7	3	6	9	11							11
1	2		4	5		7	10		8	11	3	6	9								12
1	2		4	5		7	8		10	11	3	6	9								13
1	2		4	5		7	10		8	11	3	6	9								14
1	2		4	5		7	10	9	8	11	3	6									15
1	2		4	5		7	10	9	8	11	3	6									16
1	2		4	5		7	10	9	8	11	3	6									17
1	2		4	5		7	10	9	8	11	3	6									18
1	2		4	5		7	10	9	8	11	3	6									19
1	2		4	5		7	8	9		11	3	6	10								20
1	2		4	5		7	8	9	10	11		6			3						21
1	2			5	4	7	10	9	8	11	3	6									22
1	2		4	5		7	10	9	8							3	6				23
1	2		4	5		7	10	9	8					11		3	6				24
1	2		4	5		7	10	9	8					11		3	6				25
1	2		4	5			10	9	8	7				11		3	6				26
1	2		4	5			10	9	8	7				11		3	6				27
1	2		4	5			10	9	8	7				11		3	6				28
1			4	5			10	9	8	7				11	2	3	6				29
1			4	5			10	9	8	7				11	2	3	6				30
1			4	5		11	10	9	8	7					2	3	6				31
1			4	5		11	10		8	7					2	3	6	9			32
1			4	5		11	10		8	7					2	3	6	9			33
			4				8	10	9	7				11	2	3	6		1		34
			4				8	10	9	7				11	2	3	6		1	5	35
			8			7	10		9			4		11	2	3	6		1	5	36
			4			11	8		9	7					2	3	6	10	1	5	37
			4	3			8	7	9					11	2		6	10	1	5	38
1			10				8	7	9			4		11	2	3	6			5	39
1			10				8	7	9			4		11	2	3	6			5	40
1			8			10		7	9			4		11	2	3	6			5	41
1	2		10	3			8	7	9			4		11			6			5	42
1	2		10	3			8	7	9			4		11			6			5	43
1	2		10	3		7	8		9	11		4					6			5	44
1	2		10	3		7	8		9	11		4					6			5	45
1	2		10	3		7	8		9	11		4					6			5	46
41	33	1	45	39	8	30	45	32	45	37	20	24	8	20	14	18	24	4	5	13	
			7	1		7	21	6	22	9	1		5	6				1			

3 own-goals

1	2		4	5		7	10	9	8	11	3	6									1
1	2		4	5		7	8	9		11	3	6	10								R
1	2		4	5		7	10	9	8	11	3	6									2
1	2		4	5			10	7	8				9	11		3	6				3
4	4		4	4		3	4	4	3	3	3	3	2	1		1	1				
						1	1	1	3				3								

1959-60

Manager: Jack Rowley/Neil Dougall & George Taylor

1	Aug	22	(a)	Hull C	L	1-3	Kearns	17,319
2		24	(h)	Scunthorpe U	W	4-0	Carter 2, Baker, Penk	25,729
3		29	(h)	Sheffield U	D	1-1	J.S.Williams	29,776
4	Sep	3	(a)	Scunthorpe U	L	0-2		12,165
5		5	(a)	Middlesbrough	L	2-6	Carter, Bellett	22,338
6		7	(h)	Rotherham U	W	1-0	Carter	24,684
7		12	(h)	Derby C	L	0-5		21,956
8		16	(a)	Rotherham U	D	1-1	Govan	9,197
9		19	(a)	Brighton & HA	D	2-2	Carter 2	23,163
10		26	(a)	Liverpool	L	1-4	Jenkins	29,278
11	Oct	3	(h)	Charlton A	W	6-4	Carter 3, Govan, Wright, Anderson	25,176
12		10	(h)	Stoke C	L	2-3	Waldock, Carter	20,807
13		17	(a)	Portsmouth	L	0-1		20,698
14		24	(h)	Sunderland	D	0-0		21,990
15		31	(a)	Aston Villa	L	0-2		35,000
16	Nov	7	(h)	Lincoln C	L	0-2		17,205
17		14	(a)	Leyton O	W	3-2	Penk, Carter, Waldock	11,169
18		21	(h)	Huddersfield T	L	1-3	Carter	18,250
19		28	(a)	Ipswich T	D	3-3	Waldock, Penk, Anderson	11,347
20	Dec	5	(h)	Bristol R	W	5-3	Carter 2, Anderson, Jenkins, J.S.Williams	16,675
21		12	(a)	Swansea T	L	1-6	Carter	15,000
22		19	(h)	Hull C	W	3-2	Carter 2, Waldock	8,550
23		26	(h)	Bristol C	L	1-4	Waldock	18,377
24		28	(a)	Bristol C	L	1-2	Waldock	22,331
25	Jan	1	(a)	Sheffield U	L	0-4		16,100
26		16	(h)	Middlesbrough	D	2-2	McAnearney, J.S.Williams	20,981
27		23	(a)	Derby C	L	0-1		15,529
28		30	(h)	Cardiff C	D	1-1	Milne (og)	22,554
29	Feb	6	(h)	Brighton & HA	W	3-2	McAnearney, Carter 2	18,668
30		13	(h)	Liverpool	D	1-1	Carter	16,966
31		20	(a)	Charlton A	L	2-5	J.S.Williams, Carter	12,151
32		27	(a)	Stoke C	L	0-1		9,961
33	Mar	5	(h)	Portsmouth	D	1-1	J.S.Williams	20,550
34		12	(a)	Sunderland	L	0-4		16,783
35		19	(h)	Ipswich T	W	3-1	J.S.Williams, Jackson, Newman	14,782
36		26	(a)	Lincoln C	W	1-0	J.S.Williams	7,010
37	Apr	2	(h)	Leyton O	W	1-0	McAnearney	11,911
38		9	(a)	Huddersfield T	L	0-2		10,660
39		16	(h)	Swansea T	W	3-1	Kirby, Wright 2	21,961
40		19	(a)	Cardiff C	W	1-0	Carter	30,000
41		23	(a)	Bristol R	L	0-2		17,073
42		30	(h)	Aston Villa	W	3-0	Kirby, Wright, J.S.Williams	29,895

FINAL LEAGUE POSITION: 19th in Division Two

Appearances
Goals

FA Cup

3	Jan	10	(a)	West Brom A	L	2-3	Anderson, Penk	26,150

Appearances
Goals

Barnsley	Robertson	Bellett	Williams JS	Fincham	Casey	Penk	Carter	Baker	Kearns	Govan	Anderson	Wright	Fulton	Williams JL	Penny	Dann	Jenkins	Stacey	Wyatt	Waldock	Newman	Kirby	McAnearney	Jackson	
1	2	3	4	5	6	7	8	9	10	11															1
1	2	3	4	5	6	7	8	9	10		11														2
1	2	3	4	5	6	7	8	9	10			11													3
1	2	3	4	5	6		8	9	10		7	11													4
1		3	4	5	6		8			11	7	9	2				10								5
1		3	8	5	6		9					11	2	4	7	10									6
1		3	4	5	6		8					11	2		7	10	9								7
1		3	4				8			11	7			6		10	9	2	5						8
1		3	4				8			11	7			6		10	9	2	5						9
1		3	4				8			11	7			6			9	2	5	10					10
1		3	4				8			11	7	9		6				2	5	10					11
1		3	4				8			11	7	9		6				2	5	10					12
1		3	4		6		8			11	7	9						2	5	10					13
1		3	4		6		8	9		11	7							2	5	10					14
1		3	4		6	7	8		10	11								2	5	9					15
1		3	4		6	7	8				11					10		2	5	9					16
1		3	4		6	7	8				11						10	2	5	9					17
1	2	3	4		6	7	8				11						10		5	9					18
1	2	3	4		6	7	8				11						10		5	9					19
1	2	3	4		6	7	8				11						10		5	9					20
1	2	3	4		6	7	8				11						10		5	9					21
1	2	3	4		6	7	8					11					10		5	9					22
1	2	3	4		6	7	8					11					10		5	9					23
1			4	5	6	7	8					11	3			10		2		9					24
1			4	5	6	7	8					11	3			10		2		9					25
1			4	5		11	8						3					2		7	6	9	10		26
1			4	5		11	8						3					2		7	6	9	10		27
1			4	5		11	8				7		3					2			6	9	10		28
1			4	5		11	8				7		3					2			6	9	10		29
1	2		4	5		7	8				11		3								6	9	10		30
1	2		4	5			8			11			3		7				2		6	9	10		31
1			4	5						11			3		7	10			2		6	9	8		32
1			4	5		11	8						3		7				2		6	9	10		33
1			4	5		11	8						3		7				2		6	9	10		34
1			4	5		11					7		3						2		6	9	10	8	35
1			4	5		11					7		3						2		6	9	10	8	36
1			4	5		11					7		3						2		6	9	10	8	37
1			4	5		11					7		3						2		6	9	10	8	38
1			4	5			8				7	11	3						2		6	9	10		39
1			4	5			8				7	11	3						2		6	9	10		40
1			4	5			8				7	11	3						2		6	9	10		41
1	5		4								7	11	3						2		6	9	10	8	42
42	13	23	42	25	20	25	36	5	5	12	27	16	22	6	6	8	12	16	28	18	17	17	17	5	
		1	8			3	22	1	1	2	3	4					2			6	1	2	3	1	

1 own-goal

Barnsley	Robertson	Bellett	Williams JS	Fincham	Casey	Penk	Carter	Baker	Kearns	Govan	Anderson	Wright	Fulton	Williams JL	Penny	Dann	Jenkins	Stacey	Wyatt	Waldock	Newman	Kirby	McAnearney	Jackson	
1		9	4	5	6	7	8				11		3					2		10					3
1		1	1	1	1	1	1				1		1					1		1					
						1					1														

1960-61

Manager: Neil Dougall & George Taylor/Neil Dougall

1	Aug	20	(h)	Stoke C	W 3-1	Kirby, Carter, Wright	21,138
2		23	(a)	Sheffield U	L 0-3		16,364
3		27	(a)	Swansea T	W 2-1	Carter 2	16,000
4		31	(h)	Sheffield U	W 2-0	Kirby, Wright	24,873
5	Sep	3	(h)	Luton T	D 1-1	Kirby	21,408
6		7	(a)	Norwich C	L 0-1		32,212
7		10	(a)	Lincoln C	L 1-3	Kirby	8,650
8		14	(h)	Norwich C	W 3-0	Jackson, McAnearney, J.S.Williams	23,147
9		17	(h)	Portsmouth	W 5-1	Kirby 3, Jackson, Anderson	20,243
10		24	(a)	Huddersfield T	W 5-1	Newman, Kirby 2, Wright, McAnearney	14,154
11	Oct	1	(h)	Sunderland	W 1-0	Wright	24,464
12		8	(h)	Middlesbrough	D 3-3	Kirby, Jackson, McAnearney	19,854
13		15	(a)	Leeds U	L 1-2	Jackson	12,000
14		22	(h)	Southampton	L 1-3	Anderson	23,017
15		29	(a)	Rotherham U	D 0-0		8,318
16	Nov	5	(h)	Liverpool	L 0-4		17,641
17		12	(a)	Bristol R	W 5-2	Purdon (og), Carter, Kirby, J.S.Williams, McAnearney	17,005
18		19	(h)	Derby C	W 4-2	Maloy, Carter 2, J.S.Williams	18,510
19	Dec	3	(h)	Scunthorpe U	W 3-1	J.S.Williams, McAnearney, Kirby	11,925
20		10	(a)	Ipswich T	L 1-3	Kirby	11,790
21		17	(a)	Stoke C	L 0-9		6,479
22		26	(a)	Charlton A	L 4-6	Kirby 2, Anderson, J.S.Williams	11,196
23		27	(h)	Charlton A	W 6-4	Carter 5, Jackson	23,335
24		31	(h)	Swansea T	W 1-0	Fincham	15,617
25	Jan	14	(a)	Luton T	L 2-3	Kirby, J.S.Williams	13,873
26		21	(h)	Lincoln C	D 1-1	Carter	12,671
27	Feb	4	(a)	Portsmouth	W 2-0	J.S.Williams, Carter	9,178
28		11	(h)	Huddersfield T	W 2-1	McAnearney, Carter	12,876
29		22	(a)	Sunderland	L 1-2	Carter	34,333
30		25	(a)	Middlesbrough	L 1-3	Maloy	16,396
31	Mar	6	(h)	Leeds U	W 3-1	Carter 3	14,878
32		7	(a)	Leyton O	D 1-1	Fincham	9,637
33		11	(a)	Southampton	D 1-1	Fincham	18,949
34		18	(h)	Ipswich T	L 1-2	Carter	9,626
35		24	(a)	Liverpool	D 1-1	McAnearney	25,350
36		31	(a)	Brighton & HA	L 0-2		19,330
37	Apr	1	(h)	Leyton O	W 3-2	Carter, McAnearney, Wright	14,814
38		3	(h)	Brighton & HA	L 1-2	Jennings (og)	14,826
39		8	(a)	Derby C	L 1-4	Carter	12,098
40		15	(h)	Bristol R	W 5-0	Anderson, Kirby 2, Carter 2	14,026
41		22	(a)	Scunthorpe U	L 0-2		5,762
42		29	(h)	Rotherham U	D 3-3	Jackson 2, Carter	11,690

FINAL LEAGUE POSITION: 11th in Division Two — Appearances / Goals

FA Cup

3	Jan	7	(h)	Bristol C	L 0-1		13,087

Appearances
Goals

FL Cup

1	Oct	12	(h)	Southport	W 2-0	McAnearney, Jackson	10,400
2	Nov	2	(a†)	Torquay U	D 1-1	Carter	9,855
R		7	(h)	Torquay U	W 2-1	Maloy, J.S.Williams	7,982
3		14	(a)	Birmingham C	D 0-0		15,300
R		16	(h)	Birmingham C	W 3-1	Carter, Kirby, Jackson	14,132
4	Dec	13	(a)	Aston Villa	D 3-3	Carter, Anderson, J.S.Williams	12,117
R		19	(h)	Aston Villa*	D 0-0		11,006
2R	Feb	6	(h)	Aston Villa	L 3-5	Carter, Newman, J.S.Williams	13,548

†Played at Home Park. *Match abandoned after 90 minutes. — Appearances / Goals

Barnsley	Wyatt	Fulton	Williams JS	Fincham	Newman	Anderson	Carter	Kirby	McAnearney	Wright	MacLaren	Jackson	Stacey	Robertson	Maloy	Brown	Williams JL	Leiper	Casey	
1	2	3	4	5	6	7	8	9	10	11										1
1	2	3	4	5	6	7	8	9	10	11										2
1	2	3	4	5	6	7	8	9	10	11										3
1	2	3	4	5	6	7	8	9	10	11										4
1	2	3	4	5	6	7	8	9	10	11										5
1	2	3	4	5	6	7	8	9	10	11										6
	2	3	4	5	6	7	8	9	10	11	1									7
1	2	3	4	5	6	7		9	10	11		8								8
1	2	3	4	5	6	7		9	10	11		8								9
1	2	3	4	5	6	7		9	10	11		8								10
1		3	4	5	6	7		9	10	11		8	2							11
1	2	3	4		6	7		9	10	11		8		5						12
	2	3	4		6	7		9	10	11	1	8		5						13
	2	3	4		6	7		9	10	11	1	8		5						14
	2	3	4	5	6	7		9	10	11	1	8								15
1	2	3	4	5		7	8	9				10		6	11					16
1	2	3	4	5	6	7	8	9	10						11					17
1		3	4	5	6		7	9	10			8		2	11					18
1		3	4	5	6	7	8	9	10	11				2						19
1		3	4	5	6	7	8	9	10	11				2						20
1		3	4	5	6	7	8		10			9		2	11					21
1	2	3	4	5	6	7	8	9				10			11					22
	2		4	5	6	7	9				1	10	3		11	8				23
			4	5	6	7	9				1	10	3	2	11	8				24
1	5	3	4		6	7	8	9	10	11				2						25
1	5	3	4		6	7	8	9	10	11				2						26
1	5	3	4		6	7	8	9	10	11				2						27
1	5	3	4		6	7	8	9	10	11				2						28
1	5	3	4		6		8	9	10			7		2	11					29
1	5	3	4		6		8	9	10			7		2	11					30
1	5	3	8		6		10	9				7		2	11		4			31
1		3	4	5	6	7	8	9						2	11	10				32
1	2	3	4	5	6	7	8	9	10						11					33
1	2	3	4	5	6	7	8	9	10						11					34
	2	3	4	5	6		9		10	11	1	8					7			35
	2	3	4	5	6	7	9		10	11	1	8								36
		3	4	5	6	7	8		10	11	1	9		2						37
		3	4	5	6	7	8	9			1	10		2	11					38
		3	4	5	6	7	8		10		1	9		2	11					39
		3	4	5	6	11	8	9	10			7		2				1		40
		3	4	5	6	7	8		10	11		9		2				1		41
		3	4	5	6	7	8		10	11		9		2				1		42
29	29	40	42	32	41	37	32	33	35	26	11	25	3	23	15	3	2	3		
			7	3	1	4	24	18	8	5		7			2					

2 own-goals

			4	5	6		7	9		11	1	10	3	2		8				3
			1	1	1		1	1		1	1	1	1	1		1				

	2	3	4	5	6	7		9	10	11	1	8								1
1	2	3	4	5		7	8	9	10						11				6	2
1	2	3	8	5		7	10	9						6	11		4			R
1	2	3	4	5	6		7	9	10			8			11					3
1	2	3	4	5	6		7	9	10			8			11					R
1		3	4	5	6	7	8	9	10	11				2						4
1	2	3	8	5	6	7	9					10			11		4			R
1		3	4	5	6	7	8	9	10	11				2						2R
7	6	8	8	8	6	6	7	7	6	3	1	4		3	5		2		1	
			3		1	1	4	1	1			2			1					

1961-62

Manager: Neil Dougall/Ellis Stuttard

1	Aug	19	(a)	Southampton	W	2-1	Kirby, McAnearney	16,505
2		23	(a)	Huddersfield T	L	1-5	Carter	13,730
3		26	(h)	Luton T	L	0-3		15,490
4		30	(h)	Huddersfield T	W	4-2	Carter, Kirby, Anderson, Thorne	14,065
5	Sep	2	(a)	Newcastle U	W	2-0	Kirby, Carter	27,841
6		9	(h)	Middlesbrough	D	1-1	Kirby	16,240
7		16	(a)	Walsall	L	0-1		14,848
8		20	(h)	Preston NE	W	1-0	Jackson	17,174
9		23	(h)	Derby C	L	2-3	Maloy, Jackson	13,803
10		26	(a)	Preston NE	D	1-1	K Williams	11,911
11		29	(a)	Leyton O	W	2-1	K.Williams 2	13,398
12	Oct	7	(h)	Leeds U	D	1-1	Maloy	10,144
13		14	(a)	Bristol R	L	3-4	Brown, Maloy, J.S.Williams	14,435
14		21	(h)	Stoke C	W	3-1	Kirby, Brown, Carter	10,288
15		28	(a)	Sunderland	L	0-5		30,202
16	Nov	4	(h)	Rotherham U	L	2-5	Carter 2	10,685
17		11	(a)	Scunthorpe U	L	1-5	Carter	8,780
18		18	(h)	Charlton A	W	2-1	Kirby, K Williams	8,742
19		25	(a)	Bury	D	1-1	Kirby	7,129
20	Dec	2	(h)	Brighton & HA	W	5-0	Kirby, J.. Williams, Maloy, Carter, McAnearney	10,414
21		9	(a)	Liverpool	L	1-2	J.S.Williams	32,534
22		16	(h)	Southampton	W	4-0	Carter 2, McAnearney, Kirby	13,531
23		23	(a)	Luton T	W	2-0	Carter, McAnearney	8,400
24		26	(a)	Norwich C	W	2-0	McAnearney, Kirby	18,363
25		30	(h)	Norwich C	W	3-1	Kirby, Anderson, Carter	15,924
26	Jan	13	(h)	Newcastle U	D	1-1	Maloy	17,457
27		20	(a)	Middlesbrough	D	1-1	McAnearney	10,962
28	Feb	3	(h)	Walsall	W	2-1	J.S.Williams, McAnearney	12,044
29		10	(a)	Derby C	D	2-2	Carter, McAnearney	15,217
30		17	(h)	Leyton O	W	2-1	Newman, McAnearney	20,531
31		24	(a)	Leeds U	W	3-2	McAnearney, Fincham, Kirby	8,534
32	Mar	3	(h)	Bristol R	W	3-1	Maloy, Kirby 2	15,350
33		10	(a)	Stoke C	L	0-2		18,033
34		17	(h)	Sunderland	W	3-2	Kirby, Carter 2	16,726
35		24	(a)	Rotherham U	W	3-1	Carter 2, Maloy	8,438
36		31	(h)	Scunthorpe U	W	3-1	Anderson, Kirby, Corbett	15,913
37	Apr	7	(a)	Charlton A	L	1-3	Carter	20,093
38		14	(h)	Bury	L	1-2	McAnearney	15,104
39		21	(a)	Brighton & HA	L	2-3	Carter, Maloy	13,016
40		23	(h)	Swansea T	D	0-0		11,135
41		25	(a)	Swansea T	L	0-5		12,000
42		28	(h)	Liverpool	L	2-3	Jackson, Robertson	13,427

FINAL LEAGUE POSITION: 5th in Division Two

Appearances
Goals

FA Cup

3	Jan	6	(h)	West Ham U	W	3-0	Carter, J.S.Williams, Maloy	26,915
4		27	(h)	Tottenham H	L	1-5	Anderson	40,040

Appearances
Goals

FL Cup

1	Sep	11	(a)	West Ham U	L	2-3	Maloy, J.S.Williams	12,178

Appearances
Goals

MacLaren	Stacey	Fulton	Williams JS	Fincham	Newman	Anderson	Williams RK	Kirby	McAnearney	Thorne	Carter	Jackson	Robertson	Maloy	Williams JL	Brown	Leiper	Wyatt	Roberts	Corbett	Casey	
1	2	3	4	5	6	7	8	9	10	11												1
1	2	3	4	5	6	7	8		10	11	9											2
1	2	3	4	5	6	7	10			11	8	9										3
1		3	4	5	6	7		9	10	11	8		2									4
1		3	4	5	6	7		9	10	11	8		2									5
1		3	4	5	6	7		9	10	11	8		2									6
1		3	4	5	6	7		9	10		8		2	11								7
1		3	4	5	6	7	8		10			9	2	11								8
1		3	4	5		7	8		10			9	2	11	6							9
1		3	4	5		7	8		10			9	2	11	6							10
1		3	4	5	6	7	8		10			9	2	11								11
1		3	4	5	6	7	8		10			9	2	11								12
1		3	4	5	6			9			8	7	2	11		10						13
1		3	4	5	6			9			8	7	2	11		10						14
1		3	4	5	6			9			8	7	2	11		10						15
1		3	4	5	6			9	10	11	8	7	2									16
		3	4		6	7	10	9		11	8		2				1	5				17
		3	4		6	7	10	9		11	8		2				1	5				18
1		3	4		6	7		9	10		8		2	11				5				19
1		3	4	5	6	7		9	10		8		2	11								20
1		3	4	5	6	7		9	10		8		2	11								21
1		3	4	5	6	7		9	10		8		2	11								22
1		3	4	5	6	7		9	10		8		2	11								23
1		3	4	5	6	7		9	10		8		2	11								24
1		3	4	5	6	7		9	10		8			11					2			25
1		3	4	5	6	7		9	10		8		2	11								26
1		3	4	5	6	7		9	10		8		2	11								27
1		3	4	5	6	7		9	10		8		2	11								28
1		3	4	5	6	7		9	10		8		2	11								29
1		3	4	5	6	7		9	10		8		2	11								30
1		3	4	5	6	7		9	10		8		2	11								31
1		3	4	5	6	7		9	10		8		2	11								32
1		3	4	5	6	7		9	10		8		2	11								33
1		3	4	5	6	7		9	10		8		2	11								34
1		3	4	5	6	7		9	10		8		2	11								35
1		3	4	5	6	11		9	10		8		2							7		36
1		3	4	5	6	11		9	10		8		2							7		37
1		3	4	5	6	11		9	10		8		2							7		38
1		3	4	5	6			9	10		8		2	11						7		39
1		3	4	5	6	11		9	10		8								2	7		40
1		3	4	5	6	10		9				8	2	11						7		41
1		3	4	5	6	10		9		11		8	2							7		42
40	3	42	42	39	40	37	10	35	34	10	34	12	37	28	2	3	2	3	2	7		
			4	1	1	3	4	16	11	1	19	3	1	8		2				1		

1		3	4	5	6	7		9	10		8		2	11								3
1		3	4	5	6	7		9	10		8		2	11								4
2		2	2	2	2	2		2	2		2		2	2								
			1			1					1			1								

1		3	4		5	7		9	10		8		2	11							6	1
1		1	1		1	1		1	1		1		1	1							1	
			1											1								

1962-63

Manager: Ellis Stuttard

1	Aug	18	(h)	Grimsby T	W	2-0	Carter 2	16,736
2		22	(h)	Preston NE	W	7-1	Williams, Carter 2, Lill 2, McAnearney 2	20,701
3		25	(a)	Norwich C	L	1-2	Kirby	21,392
4		28	(a)	Preston NE	D	0-0		15,400
5	Sep	1	(h)	Walsall	W	3-0	McAnearney 2, Anderson	16,543
6		8	(a)	Newcastle U	L	1-3	Kirby	34,375
7		12	(a)	Portsmouth	W	2-1	McAnearney, Jackson	22,661
8		15	(h)	Derby C	W	2-1	Williams, Anderson	16,647
9		19	(h)	Portsmouth	W	2-0	Williams, Jackson	23,544
10		22	(a)	Middlesbrough	L	0-3		17,608
11		29	(h)	Huddersfield T	D	1-1	Jackson	20,125
12	Oct	6	(a)	Scunthorpe U	D	2-2	Neale (og), Carter	8,497
13		13	(h)	Bury	D	0-0		18,069
14		20	(a)	Rotherham U	L	2-3	Lill, Jackson	9,215
15		27	(h)	Charlton A	W	6-1	McAnearney, Carter 3, Jackson 2	14,629
16	Nov	3	(a)	Stoke C	D	2-2	Lill, McAnearney	24,281
17		10	(h)	Sunderland	D	1-1	Lill	18,622
18		17	(a)	Leeds U	L	1-6	Jackson	15,301
19		24	(h)	Swansea T	W	1-0	Lill	12,326
20	Dec	1	(a)	Chelsea	D	1-1	O'Neill	29,829
21		8	(h)	Luton T	W	3-1	O'Neill 2, Jackson	8,891
22		15	(a)	Grimsby T	D	1-1	Lill	8,612
23		22	(h)	Norwich C	W	1-0	Jackson	15,466
24		26	(h)	Cardiff C	W	4-2	McAnearney 2, Jackson 2	18,602
25	Jan	19	(h)	Newcastle U	L	0-2		11,940
26	Feb	9	(h)	Middlesbrough	L	4-5	Williams, Carter, O'Neill, McNeil (og)	12,444
27		23	(h)	Scunthorpe U	L	2-3	McAnearney, Carter	11,519
28	Mar	3	(a)	Bury	W	2-1	Corbett, Carter	10,074
29		9	(h)	Rotherham U	D	2-2	Newman, McParland	7,351
30		16	(a)	Charlton A	L	3-6	Carter, McParland 2	10,406
31		20	(a)	Derby C	L	2-3	O'Neill, Carter	10,633
32		23	(h)	Stoke C	L	0-1		22,056
33		26	(a)	Walsall	D	2-2	McParland, Carter	7,846
34		30	(a)	Sunderland	D	1-1	O'Neill	30,276
35	Apr	1	(a)	Huddersfield T	L	2-4	O'Neill, McParland	8,452
36		6	(h)	Leeds U	W	3-1	McParland 3	8,992
37		12	(h)	Southampton	W	2-1	Williams, Trebilcock	18,207
38		13	(a)	Swansea T	L	1-2	McParland	8,000
39		15	(a)	Southampton	D	1-1	McParland	22,422
40		20	(h)	Chelsea	W	2-1	McParland, O'Neill	16,864
41		27	(a)	Luton T	L	0-3		6,937
42	May	1	(a)	Cardiff C	L	1-2	Newman	9,340

FINAL LEAGUE POSITION: 12th in Division Two

Appearances
Goals

FA Cup

3	Jan	5	(h)	West Brom A	L	1-5	McAnearney	21,901

Appearances
Goals

FL Cup

2	Sep	26	(a)	West Ham U	L	0-6		9,714

Appearances
Goals

MacLaren	Robertson	Fulton	Williams	Fincham	Newman	Corbett	Carter	Kirby	McAnearney	Lill	Anderson	Jackson	Wyatt	Reeves	O'Neill	McParland	Leiper	Buckingham	Roberts	Davis	Brown	Trebilcock	Brace	Maloy	Garden	Thorne	
1	2	3	4	5	6	7	8	9	10	11																	1
1	2	3	4	5	6	7	8	9	10	11																	2
1	2	3	4	5	6	7	8	9	10	11																	3
1	2	3	4	5	6	7	8	9	10		11																4
1	2	3	4	5	6	7	8	9	10		11																5
1	2	3	4	5	6	7	8	9	10	11																	6
1	2	3	4	5	6	7		9	10	11		8															7
1	2	3	4	5	6			9	10	11	7	8															8
1	2	3	4	5	6	7	9		10		11	8															9
1	2	3	4	5	6	7	9		10		11	8															10
1	2	3	4	5	6	7	8		10	11		9															11
1	2	3	4	5	6	7	8		10	11		9															12
1	2	3	4	5	6	7	8		10	11		9															13
1	2	3	4	5	6	7	8		10	11		9															14
1	2	3	4	5	6	7	8		10	11		9															15
1	2		4	5	6	7	8		10	11		9	3														16
1	2		4	5	6	7	8		10	11		9	3														17
1	2		4	5	6	7	8		10	11		9	3														18
1		3	4	5	6	7	8			11		9		2							10						19
1		3	4	5	6	7	8			11		9		2	10												20
1		3	4	5	6	7	8			11		9		2	10												21
1		3	4	5	6	7	8			11		9		2	10												22
1		3	4	5	6	7			8	11		9		2	10												23
1		3	4	5	6	7			8	11		9		2	10												24
1		3	4	5	6	7			8	11				2	10	9											25
1		3	4	5	6	7	9		8					2	10	11											26
	2	3	4	5	6	7	9		8						10	11	1										27
	2	3	4		6	7	9		8				5		10	11	1										28
	2	3	4		6	7	9		8				5		10	11											29
1	2	3			4	7	9		8				5		10	11		6									30
					5	7	9		8					4	10	11	1	6	2	3							31
					5	7	9		8					4	10	11	1	6	2	3							32
					5	7	9		8					4	10	11	1	6	2	3							33
			4		5	7	9							2	10	11	1	6		3	8						34
			4		5	7	9							2	10	11	1	6		3	8						35
			4		5	7	9		8					2	10	11	1	6		3							36
			4		5	7			8					2	10	11	1	6		3		9					37
			4		5	7			8					2	10	11	1	6		3		9					38
			4		5	7			8					2	10	11	1	6		3		9					39
			4		5				8					2	10	11	1	6		3		9	7				40
			4		5				8					2	10	11	1	6		3		9	7				41
1			4		5				8					2	10	11		6		3		9	7				42
28	22	27	38	27	42	38	31	8	36	21	5	18	6	20	23	18	14	13	3	12	3	6	3				
			5		2	1	14	2	10	7	2	11			8	11						1					

MacLaren	Robertson	Fulton	Williams	Fincham	Newman	Corbett	Carter	Kirby	McAnearney	Lill	Anderson	Jackson	Wyatt	Reeves	O'Neill	McParland	Leiper	Buckingham	Roberts	Davis	Brown	Trebilcock	Brace	Maloy	Garden	Thorne	
1		3	4	5	6				8	7		9		2	10									11			3
1		1	1	1	1				1	1		1		1	1									1			
									1																		

MacLaren	Robertson	Fulton	Williams	Fincham	Newman	Corbett	Carter	Kirby	McAnearney	Lill	Anderson	Jackson	Wyatt	Reeves	O'Neill	McParland	Leiper	Buckingham	Roberts	Davis	Brown	Trebilcock	Brace	Maloy	Garden	Thorne	
1		3	4		6	7					11	8	5						2						9	10	2
1		1	1		1	1					1	1	1						1						1	1	

1963-64

Manager: Ellis Stuttard / Andy Beattie

1	Aug	24	(a)	Middlesbrough	L	0-5		18,678
2		28	(h)	Leyton O	D	2-2	McParland, Carter	15,746
3		31	(h)	Newcastle U	L	3-4	O'Neill 2, McAnearney	14,061
4	Sep	3	(a)	Leyton O	L	0-1		14,923
5		7	(a)	Huddersfield T	L	3-4	Neale, O'Neill, Carter	12,977
6		9	(a)	Preston NE	D	0-0		17,000
7		14	(h)	Derby C	D	0-0		12,297
8		18	(h)	Preston NE	L	0-2		13,156
9		21	(a)	Bury	D	2-2	McAnearney, Corbett	8,713
10		28	(a)	Charlton A	L	0-1		13,404
11	Oct	2	(h)	Sunderland	D	1-1	A.Jackson	13,484
12		5	(h)	Grimsby T	W	3-2	Maloy, C.Jackson, O'Neill	9,595
13		9	(a)	Manchester C	D	1-1	O'Neill	13,456
14		12	(h)	Northampton T	L	0-3		13,094
15		19	(a)	Sunderland	L	0-1		36,787
16		26	(h)	Swindon T	L	2-4	C.Jackson, O'Neill	19,281
17	Nov	2	(a)	Rotherham U	L	1-3	C.Jackson	7,100
18		9	(h)	Portsmouth	L	0-4		12,150
19		16	(a)	Scunthorpe U	L	0-1		5,512
20		23	(h)	Norwich C	L	1-2	Thorne	11,093
21		30	(a)	Cardiff C	L	1-3	Corbett	11,500
22	Dec	7	(h)	Leeds U	L	0-1		9,918
23		14	(h)	Middlesbrough	W	2-0	Carter 2	8,456
24		21	(a)	Newcastle U	D	1-1	McParland	23,680
25		26	(a)	Southampton	W	2-1	Lord 2	21,778
26		28	(h)	Southampton	D	1-1	Lord	17,914
27	Jan	11	(h)	Huddersfield T	D	0-0		9,842
28		18	(a)	Derby C	L	1-3	McParland	6,964
29	Feb	1	(h)	Bury	W	1-0	Carter	8,473
30		8	(h)	Charlton A	D	1-1	Carter	11,031
31		15	(a)	Grimsby T	D	1-1	Carter	6,522
32		18	(a)	Northampton T	D	0-0		8,961
33		29	(h)	Scunthorpe U	W	3-1	Jennings, Lord 2	10,145
34	Mar	7	(a)	Swindon T	L	1-2	Corbett	13,743
35		14	(h)	Manchester C	W	2-1	Lord, Corbett	11,586
36		21	(a)	Portsmouth	W	2-1	Jennings, Williams	10,374
37		30	(h)	Swansea T	W	3-2	Lord 2, Jennings	17,428
38		31	(a)	Swansea T	L	1-2	Williams	11,929
39	Apr	4	(a)	Norwich C	D	1-1	C.Jackson	10,851
40		11	(h)	Cardiff C	D	1-1	Williams	14,821
41		18	(a)	Leeds U	D	1-1	Jennings	34,725
42		24	(h)	Rotherham U	D	0-0		17,383

FINAL LEAGUE POSITION: 20th in Division Two — Appearances / Goals

FA Cup

3	Jan	4	(h)	Huddersfield T	L	0-1		13,883

Appearances
Goals

FL Cup

1	Sep	25	(h)	Huddersfield T	D	2-2	A.Jackson 2	6,423
R	Oct	21	(a)	Huddersfield T	D	3-3	Maloy, Williams, McAnearney	5,429
2R		28	(n*)	Huddersfield T	L	1-2	Maloy	3,000

*Played at Villa Park, Birmingham. — Appearances / Goals

Leiper	Reeves	Davis	Williams	Newman	Neale	Corbett	Jackson A	Carter	O'Neill	McParland	Fulton	MacLaren	Wyatt	Robertson	McAnearney	Maloy	Roberts	Rounsevell	Trebilcock	Jackson C	Baird	Cobb	Brace	Thorne	Lord	Jennings	Buckingham	
1	2	3	4	5	6	7	8	9	10	11																		1
1	2		4		6			9	10	7	3		5		8	11												2
1			4		6			9	10	7	3		5		8	11	2											3
		3	4	5	6			9	10	7		1			8	11	2											4
		3	4	5	6			9	10	7		1			8	11	2											5
		3	4	5	6			9	10	7		1			8	11	2											6
		3	4		6	7		9	10	11		1					2	5	8									7
		3	4	5	6	7			10	11		1					2		9	8								8
	4			6		7					3	1		2	10	11		5	9	8								9
1			4	6		7	9	3	10					2		11		5		8								10
1				6	4		9	3	10	7				2		11		5		8								11
1				6	4	7	9	3	10					2		11		5		8								12
1			4	6				3	8	7				2	10	11		5		9								13
1			4	6				3	8	7				2	10	11		5		9								14
1			4					3	8	7					10	11		5		9	2	6						15
1			4						8	7	2				10	11		5		9	3	6						16
1			4					3	8	7					10	11		5		9	2	6						17
1			4			7	9	3							10	11		5			2	6	8					18
			4	6			9	3				1		5	8	11					2	10	7					19
		3	4	6					8			1		5		11					2	10		7	9			20
		3	4	6		7	8					1				11		5			2	10			9			21
		3	4	6		7		8				1				11		5			2	10			9			22
			4	6		7		8		11	3	1	5								2	10			9			23
			4	6		7		8		11	3	1		5							2	10			9			24
			4	6		7		8		11	3	1	5								2	10			9			25
			4	6		7		8		11	3	1	5								2	10			9			26
		3	4	6		7		8		11		1	5								2	10			9			27
		3	4	6		7		8		11		1	5								2	10			9			28
			4	6		7		8			3	1	5								2	10			9	11		29
			4	6		7		8			3	1	5								2	10			9	11		30
			4	6		7		8			3	1	5								2	10			9	11		31
			4	6		7		8			3	1	5								2	10			9	11		32
			8	4		7		10			3	1	5								2				9	11	6	33
			8	4		7		10			3	1	5								2	6			9	11		34
			8	4		7					3	1	5						10		2	6			9	11		35
			8	4		7					3	1	5						10		2	6			9	11		36
			8	4		7					3	1	5						10		2	6			9	11		37
			8	4		7		10			3	1	5								2	6			9	11		38
			8	4		7					3	1	5							10	2	6			9	11		39
1			8	4		7					3		5							10	2	6			9	11		40
			8	4		7					3	1	5							10	2	6			9	11		41
			8	4		7					3	1	5							10	2	6			9	11		42
13	3	11	39	35	10	29	7	30	17	20	22	29	21	9	13	19	6	13	6	14	28	27	2	1	23	14	1	
			3		1	4	1	7	6	3					2	1				4				1	8	4		

Leiper	Reeves	Davis	Williams	Newman	Neale	Corbett	Jackson A	Carter	O'Neill	McParland	Fulton	MacLaren	Wyatt	Robertson	McAnearney	Maloy	Roberts	Rounsevell	Trebilcock	Jackson C	Baird	Cobb	Brace	Thorne	Lord	Jennings	Buckingham	
			4	6		7		9	8	11	3	1	5								2	10						3
			1	1		1		1	1	1	1	1	1								1	1						

Leiper	Reeves	Davis	Williams	Newman	Neale	Corbett	Jackson A	Carter	O'Neill	McParland	Fulton	MacLaren	Wyatt	Robertson	McAnearney	Maloy	Roberts	Rounsevell	Trebilcock	Jackson C	Baird	Cobb	Brace	Thorne	Lord	Jennings	Buckingham	
	4			6		7	9	3	10			1		2		11		5		8								1
1			4	6				3	8	7	2				10	11		5		9								R
1		3	4	6		7			8		2				10	11		5		9								2R
2	1	1	2	3		2	1	2	3	1	2	1		1	2	3		3		3								
			1				2								1	2												

1964-65

Manager: Malcolm Allison

1	Aug	22	(a)	Coventry C	L	0-2		34,650
2		26	(h)	Huddersfield T	D	0-0		17,841
3		29	(h)	Cardiff C	W	3-1	Lord, Neale, Trebilcock	14,367
4	Sep	2	(a)	Huddersfield T	W	2-1	Atkins (og), Lord	9,478
5		5	(a)	Preston NE	W	3-1	Sanderson 2, Lord	18,425
6		12	(h)	Ipswich T	D	1-1	Lord	20,539
7		16	(a)	Newcastle U	L	1-2	Jackson	29,000
8		19	(a)	Crystal P	L	1-2	Newman	21,740
9		26	(a)	Bolton W	L	1-6	Trebilcock	13,479
10		30	(h)	Newcastle U	W	2-1	Jackson, Trebilcock	21,639
11	Oct	3	(h)	Middlesbrough	W	1-0	Newman	18,161
12		6	(a)	Bury	W	2-0	Lord, Jones	8,176
13		10	(h)	Norwich C	W	1-0	Trebilcock	17,167
14		17	(a)	Rotherham U	L	2-4	Jackson, Lord	10,820
15		24	(h)	Swansea T	W	2-1	Williams (og), Lord	16,105
16		31	(a)	Derby C	L	2-3	Williams, Trebilcock	11,648
17	Nov	7	(h)	Swindon T	W	2-0	Trebilcock, Jackson	16,215
18		14	(a)	Portsmouth	W	1-0	Lord	9,050
19		21	(h)	Manchester C	W	3-2	Trebilcock 2, Lord	19,468
20		28	(a)	Charlton A	L	2-3	Lord, Bailey (og)	11,096
21	Dec	5	(h)	Leyton O	D	1-1	Jennings	14,528
22		12	(h)	Coventry C	L	2-3	Trebilcock, Jones	13,892
23		19	(a)	Cardiff C	L	0-4		9,877
24		26	(a)	Southampton	L	0-5		21,891
25	Jan	2	(h)	Preston NE	L	0-1		13,266
26		16	(a)	Ipswich T	D	2-2	Trebilcock, Jackson	12,107
27		23	(h)	Crystal P	D	1-1	Reynolds	15,582
28	Feb	6	(h)	Bolton W	L	1-3	Trebilcock	14,273
29		13	(a)	Middlesbrough	W	3-1	Book, Jackson, Neale	10,165
30		17	(h)	Southampton	W	4-0	Trebilcock 2, Book, Jennings	14,813
31		20	(a)	Norwich C	L	0-3		19,597
32		27	(h)	Rotherham U	D	1-1	Williams	11,969
33	Mar	13	(h)	Derby C	D	1-1	Newman	9,526
34		20	(a)	Swindon T	W	3-2	Jones 2, Trebilcock	12,175
35		27	(h)	Portsmouth	W	2-1	Neale 2	10,405
36		31	(a)	Leyton O	L	0-2		9,081
37	Apr	3	(a)	Manchester C	L	1-2	Trebilcock	10,929
38		10	(h)	Charlton A	L	1-5	Lord	9,545
39		17	(a)	Swansea T	L	0-3		8,505
40		19	(h)	Northampton T	W	5-2	Jackson 2, Reynolds, Williams, Newman	10,281
41		20	(a)	Northampton T	L	1-3	Reynolds	19,718
42		24	(h)	Bury	D	2-2	Reynolds, Jennings	8,118

FINAL LEAGUE POSITION: 15th in Division Two

Appearances
Goals

FA Cup

3	Jan	9	(h)	Derby C	W	4-2	Jones 2, Jennings, Trebilcock	15,833
4		30	(a)	Leicester C	L	0-5		24,618

Appearances
Goals

FL Cup

2	Sep	23	(h)	Sheffield U	W	2-1	Lord 2	14,625
3	Oct	14	(a)	Bury	W	1-0	Baird	4,107
4	Nov	4	(a)	Stoke C	D	1-1	Lord	10,968
R		11	(h)	Stoke C	W	3-1	Lord 3	15,318
5		25	(h)	Northampton T	W	1-0	Newman	21,968
SF	Jan	20	(a)	Leicester C	L	2-3	Williams, Trebilcock	12,470
	Feb	10	(h)	Leicester C	L	0-1		20,780

Appearances
Goals

MacLaren	Book	Cobb	Williams	Wyatt	Newman	Sanderson	Trebilcock	Lord	Jackson	Jennings	Buckingham	Corbett	Baird	Neale	Brace	Jones	Sykes	Reeves	Leiper	Dwyer	Reynolds	Piper	Nicholas	Hore	
1	2	3	4	5	6	7	8	9	10	11															1
1	2	3	4		5		8	9	10	11	6	7													2
1	2				5	10	8	9	6	11			3	4	7										3
1	2	10			5		8	9	6	11			3	4	7										4
1	2	8			5	10	7	9	6	11			3	4											5
1	2				5	10	8	9	6	11			3	4		7									6
1	2				5		8	9	10	11			3	4		7	6								7
1	2				5	10	8	9		11			3	4		7	6								8
1	2					10	8	9	6	11			3	4		7	5								9
1	3		4		5		8	9	10	11				6		7		2							10
1	2		4		5		8	9	10	11				6		7		3							11
1	2		4		5		8	9	10				11	6		7		3							12
1	2		4		5		8	9	10	11				6		7		3							13
1	2		4		5		8	9	10	11			3	6		7									14
1	2				5	10	8	9	6	11				4		7		3							15
1	2		10		5	11	8	9	6					4		7		3							16
1	2		4		5		8	9	10	11				6		7		3							17
1	2		4		5	8		9	10	11				6		7		3							18
1	2				5	10	8	9	6	11				4		7		3							19
1	2		11		5	10	8	9	6					4		7		3							20
1	2				5	10	8	9	6	11				4		7		3							21
1	2				5	10	8	9	6	11				4		7		3							22
1	2		6		5	8		9	10	11			3	4		7									23
	2		4		5	9	8		10	11			3	6		7			1						24
	2		4		5	9	10		6	11			3		8	7			1						25
	2				5	6	10		8					4		7		3		1	9	11			26
	2		6		5	10	8			11				4		7		3		1	9				27
	2		6		5		8		10					4		7		3		1	9	11			28
	2		6		5	9	8		10	11				4		7		3		1					29
	2		6		5		8		10	11				4		7		3		1	9				30
	2		6		5	3	8		10					4		7				1	9		11		31
	2		6		5		8		10	11				4		7		3		1	9				32
	2		6		5	9	10		8	11				4		7		3		1					33
	2		6			8	9		10				5	4		7		3		1		11			34
	2		6		3	10	9	8					5	4		7				1		11			35
	2		6		7	10	9	8		11			5	4						1		3			36
	2		6		5	10	11	9	8				4			7				1		3			37
	2					4	10	9	6	11			5			7				1	8	3			38
	2		6		4	9	8		10				5	11		7				1		3			39
			6		5	4		9	8	11			2			7			1		10	3			40
			6		5	10		8		11			2	4		7				1	9			3	41
	2		6		5		9		10	11				4		7				1	8	3			42
23	40	4	29	1	39	29	38	29	37	32	1	1	20	36	3	36	3	20	3	16	10	10	1	1	
	2		3		4	2	15	11	8	3				4		4					4				

3 own-goals

	2		6		5		10		8	11				4		7		3	1		9				3
	2		6		5	10	8			11				4		7		3		1		9			4
	2		2		2	1	2		1	2				2		2		2	1	1	1	1			
							1			1						2									

1	2	10					8	9	6	11			3	4	7		5								2
1	2		4		5		8	9	10	11			3	6		7									3
1	2		10		5		8	9	6	11				4		7		3							4
1	2		4		5		8	9	10	11				6		7		3							R
1	2				5	10	8	9	6	11				4		7		3							5
	2		6		5		8					7		4				3		1	9	10	11		SF
	2		6		5		8	9	10	11				4		7		3		1					
5	7	1	5		6	1	7	6	6	6		1	2	7	1	5	1	5		2	1	1	1		
			1		1		1	6					1												

1965-66

Manager: Derek Ufton

1	Aug	21	(a)	Portsmouth	L	1-4	Baird	12,000
2		25	(h)	Charlton A	W	3-0	Williams, Trebilcock, Jackson	15,528
3		28	(h)	Bolton W	L	1-3	Lord	16,467
4		31	(a)	Charlton A	D	1-1	Trebilcock	10,481
5	Sep	4	(a)	Ipswich T	L	1-4	Trebilcock	12,783
6		8	(h)	Preston NE	L	0-1		12,651
7		11	(h)	Birmingham C	W	6-1	Trebilcock 3, Williams, Lord, Jennings	10,606
8		13	(a)	Preston NE	L	0-2		15,924
9		18	(a)	Leyton O	W	1-0	Trebilcock	6,753
10		25	(h)	Middlesbrough	D	2-2	Lord, Piper	11,772
11	Oct	2	(a)	Huddersfield T	L	1-2	Piper	16,707
12		9	(h)	Cardiff C	D	2-2	Trebilcock, Jones	10,452
13		16	(a)	Carlisle U	W	3-1	Lord, Trebilcock 2	10,321
14		23	(h)	Coventry C	L	1-2	Trebilcock	14,650
15		30	(a)	Bristol C	D	0-0		17,733
16	Nov	6	(h)	Manchester C	W	1-0	Williams	15,594
17		13	(a)	Rotherham U	L	0-2		9,147
18		20	(h)	Wolves	D	2-2	Reynolds, Wilson (og)	17,685
19		27	(a)	Norwich C	D	0-0		11,392
20	Dec	4	(h)	Bury	D	2-2	Jennings, Neale	8,787
21		11	(a)	Southampton	L	1-4	Bickle	18,179
22		27	(h)	Derby C	D	0-0		11,541
23	Jan	1	(a)	Cardiff C	L	1-5	Piper	9,028
24		8	(h)	Rotherham U	W	5-2	Piper 2, Bickle 2, Jennings	11,956
25		15	(a)	Coventry C	L	1-5	Bickle	21,315
26		29	(h)	Portsmouth	W	3-1	Book, Jackson 2	13,262
27	Feb	5	(a)	Bolton W	W	1-0	Jones	10,549
28		19	(h)	Ipswich T	W	3-0	Jackson, Bickle, Piper	11,263
29		26	(a)	Birmingham C	L	0-1		13,115
30	Mar	5	(a)	Derby C	W	2-1	Reynolds, Corbett	15,276
31		12	(h)	Leyton O	D	1-1	Bickle	11,280
32		14	(h)	Carlisle U	D	0-0		12,104
33		19	(a)	Middlesbrough	W	1-0	Bickle	12,047
34		25	(h)	Huddersfield T	D	0-0		13,902
35	Apr	2	(a)	Manchester C	D	1-1	Doyle (og)	24,087
36		8	(a)	Crystal P	L	1-3	Jackson	12,026
37		9	(h)	Bristol C	L	0-2		15,396
38		11	(h)	Crystal P	L	1-2	Bickle	11,289
39		16	(a)	Wolves	D	0-0		20,792
40		23	(h)	Norwich C	W	2-0	Jackson, Corbett	9,504
41		30	(a)	Bury	L	0-1		5,404
42	May	7	(h)	Southampton	L	2-3	Jackson, Bickle	18,922

FINAL LEAGUE POSITION: 18th in Division Two

Appearances
Sub Appearances
Goals

FA Cup

3	Jan	22	(h)	Corby T	W	6-0	Bickle 3, Piper, Jackson, Jones	16,102
4	Feb	12	(h)	Huddersfield T	L	0-2		26,335

Appearances
Goals

FL Cup

2	Sep	22	(a)	Preston NE	L	0-1		10,583

Appearances
Goals

Dwyer	Piper	Hore	Williams	Baird	Buckingham	Jones	Jackson	Lord	Tebilcock	Brace	Book	Newman	Neale	Jennings	Nicholas	Reynolds	Leiper	Reeves	Nelson	Bickle	Brimacombe	Corbett	
1	2	3	4	5	6	7	8	9	10	11													1
1	3		4			7	8	9	10		2	5	6	11									2
1	3		4			7	8	9	10		2	5	6	11									3
1	3	12	4			7	8	9*	10		2	5	6	11									4
1	3		4			7	8		10		2	5	6	11	9								5
1	3		4	5		7	8		10		2	6		11		9							6
1	8	6	4	5		7		9	10		2	3		11									7
1	8	6	4	5		7		9	10		2	3		11									8
	8	6	4	5		7		9	10		2	3		11			1						9
	8	6	4	5		7		9	10		2	3		11			1						10
1	7	6	4	5				9	10		2	8		11				3					11
1	8	6	4	3		7		9	10		2	5		11									12
	8	6	4	3		7		9	10		2	5		11			1						13
	8	6	4	3		7		9	10		2			11			1		5				14
		6	4	3		7		9	10		2	8		11			1		5				15
		6	4	3		7		9	10		2	8				11	1		5				16
		6	4	3		7		9	10		2	8		11			1		5				17
		6	4	3		7			10		2	8		11		9	1		5				18
		6		3		7			10		2	8	4	11		9	1		5				19
		6		3		7			10		2	4	8	11		9	1		5				20
	10	6		3		7					2	4	8			11	1		5	9			21
		6	4	3		7		9	10		2	8		11			1		5				22
	10	6	4	3		7		9			2	8		11			1		5				23
	10		4	3			11				2	6		7			1		5	9	8		24
	10		4	3							2	6		7			1	11	5	9	8		25
	10		4	3		7	8				2	6		11			1		5	9			26
	10	4		3		7	8				2	6		11			1		5	9			27
	8		4	3		7	10				2	6		11			1		5	9			28
	10	4	8	3		7					2	6		11			1		5	9			29
	8	4		3			11				2	6				10	1		5	9		7	30
	8	4		3		7	10				2	6		11			1		5	9			31
	8	4		3		7					2	6		11		10	1		5	9			32
	8	4		3		7	11				2	6				10	1		5	9			33
	10	4		3			11				2	6					1		5	9	8	7	34
	10	4		3			11				2	6					1		5	9	8	7	35
	4		12	3		10	11*				2	6					1		5	9	8	7	36
	10		4	3		8					2	6		11			1		5	9		7	37
	10		4	3		7					2	6	12	11		8	1		5	9*			38
	4			3		11	10				2	6				9	1		5		8	7	39
	4			3		11	8				2	6				9	1		5		10	7	40
	4			3		11	10				2	6				9	1		5		8	7	41
	10	4		3		7	11				2	6	8				1		5	9			42
10	35	27	27	38	1	36	20	17	21	1	41	40	8	30	1	13	32	2	29	17	8	8	
		1	1										1										
	6		3	1		2	7	4	11		1		1	3		2				9		2	

2 own-goals

Dwyer	Piper	Hore	Williams	Baird	Buckingham	Jones	Jackson	Lord	Tebilcock	Brace	Book	Newman	Neale	Jennings	Nicholas	Reynolds	Leiper	Reeves	Nelson	Bickle	Brimacombe	Corbett	
	10		4	3		7	8				2	6		11			1		5	9			3
	10		4	3		7	8				2	6		11			1		5	9			4
	2		2	2		2	2				2	2		2			2		2	2			
	1						1							1						3			

Dwyer	Piper	Hore	Williams	Baird	Buckingham	Jones	Jackson	Lord	Tebilcock	Brace	Book	Newman	Neale	Jennings	Nicholas	Reynolds	Leiper	Reeves	Nelson	Bickle	Brimacombe	Corbett	
	8	6		3		7	4	9	10		2	5		11			1						2
	1	1		1		1	1	1	1		1	1		1			1						

1966-67

Manager: Derek Ufton

1	Aug	20	(a)	Bury	L 0-1		4,507
2		24	(h)	Coventry C	W 4-2	Piper, Jones, Bickle 2	16,061
3		27	(h)	Preston NE	W 1-0	Reynolds	15,430
4		30	(a)	Coventry C	L 0-1		20,327
5	Sep	3	(a)	Rotherham U	L 2-4	Bickle, Neale	9,084
6		8	(h)	Birmingham C	D 1-1	Bickle	18,920
7		10	(h)	Millwall	W 3-1	Reynolds 3	12,853
8		17	(a)	Northampton T	L 1-2	Piper	9,802
9		24	(h)	Crystal P	W 1-0	Reynolds	12,865
10		27	(a)	Birmingham C	D 0-0		18,313
11	Oct	1	(h)	Hull C	W 3-1	Bickle, Reynolds 2	15,627
12		8	(a)	Huddersfield T	D 1-1	Goy (og)	11,248
13		15	(h)	Cardiff C	W 7-1	Bickle 4, Piper, Reynolds, Jennings	14,525
14		22	(a)	Wolves	L 1-2	Piper	21,199
15		29	(h)	Ipswich T	D 1-1	Piper	19,012
16	Nov	5	(a)	Bristol C	L 0-1		19,375
17		12	(h)	Carlisle U	L 1-2	Jones	13,354
18		19	(a)	Blackburn R	L 0-3		12,187
19		26	(h)	Bolton W	W 2-0	Nelson, Bickle	13,600
20	Dec	3	(a)	Charlton A	L 0-1		8,438
21		10	(h)	Derby C	L 1-2	Bloomfield	11,090
22		17	(h)	Bury	W 4-1	Sillett, Banks 2, Piper	10,445
23		26	(a)	Portsmouth	L 1-2	Jones	21,116
24		27	(h)	Portsmouth	D 0-0		20,302
25		31	(a)	Preston NE	L 0-2		14,375
26	Jan	7	(h)	Rotherham U	W 1-0	Piper	9,981
27		14	(a)	Millwall	W 2-1	Bickle, Banks	16,601
28		21	(h)	Northampton T	W 1-0	Kurila (og)	12,784
29	Feb	4	(a)	Crystal P	L 1-2	Mitten	17,695
30		11	(a)	Hull C	L 2-4	Etheridge 2	24,702
31		25	(h)	Huddersfield T	L 2-3	Bickle, Piper	12,734
32	Mar	1	(a)	Ipswich T	D 1-1	Davey	13,670
33		18	(h)	Wolves	L 0-1		18,389
34		24	(h)	Norwich C	D 2-2	Etheridge, Bickle	13,533
35		25	(a)	Cardiff C	L 1-4	Reynolds	11,857
36		27	(a)	Norwich C	L 1-3	Mitten	17,068
37	Apr	1	(h)	Bristol C	L 1-2	Davey	12,223
38		8	(a)	Carlisle U	D 0-0		11,342
39		15	(h)	Blackburn R	W 4-0	Etheridge 2, Piper 2	12,105
40		22	(a)	Bolton W	W 2-1	Banks, Hore	7,257
41		29	(h)	Charlton A	W 2-1	Piper, Davey	13,104
42	May	6	(a)	Derby C	D 1-1	Banks	11,197

FINAL LEAGUE POSITION: 16th in Division Two

Appearances
Sub Appearances
Goals

FA Cup

3	Jan	28	(a)	Nottingham F	L 1-2	Bloomfield	34,005

Appearances
Sub Appearances
Goals

FL Cup

2	Sep	14	(a)	Southampton	L 3-4	Piper, Reynolds, Neale	11,544

Appearances
Sub Appearances
Goals

Leiper	Barid	Reeves	Piper	Nelson	Newman	Etheridge	Neale	Bickle	Banks	Jackson	Rounsevell	Jones	Reynolds	Jennings	Shearing	Corbett	Bloomfield	Hore	Davey	Sillett	Mitten	Dunne	Everitt	Brimacombe	Tedasco	
1	2	3	4	5	6	7	8	9	10	11																1
1	3		4	5	6		8	9			2	7	10	11												2
1	3		4	5	6		8	9			2	7	10	11												3
1	3		4	5	6		8	9			2	7	10	11												4
1	3		4	5	6		8	9			2	7	10	11												5
1	3		4	5	6		8	9			2	7	10	11												6
1	3		4	5	6		8	9			2	7	10	11												7
	3		4	5	6		8	9			2	11	10		1	7										8
	3		4	5	6		8	9			2	7	10	11	1											9
	3		4	5	6			9			2	7	10	11	1		8									10
	3		4	5	6			9			2	7	10	11	1		8									11
	3		4	5	6			9			2	7	10	11	1		8									12
	3		4	5	6			9			2	7	10	11	1		8									13
	3		4	5	6			9			2	7	10	11	1		8									14
	3		4	5	6			9			2	7	10	11	1		8									15
	3		11	5	6			9			2	7	10		1		8	4								16
	3		4	5	6			9			2	7	10	11	1		8									17
	3		11	5	6			9			2		10		1		8	4	7							18
	3			5	4			9				7	8	11	1		10	6		2						19
	3			5	4			9				7	8	11	1		10	6		2						20
	3		8	5	4			9				7		11	1		10	6		2						21
	3		4	5					8			7	9	11	1		10	6		2						22
	3		4	5			12		8			7	9	11	1		10	6		2						23
	3		10	5			4	9	8			7		11	1			6		2						24
	3		10	5		7	4	9	8					11	1			6		2						25
	3		4	5				9	8			7		11	1		10	6		2						26
	3		4		5		12	9	8			7			1		10*	6		2	11					27
	3		4		5			9	8*			7			1		10	6	12	2	11					28
	3		4		5				8			7			1		10	6	9	2	11					29
	3		4	5	2	7			8						1		10	6	9		11					30
		3	10	5	4	7		9									8	6		2	11	1				31
	3		4	5		7		9									10	6	8	2	11	1				32
			4	5		7		9	8								10	6		2	11	1	3			33
	12		4	5		7		9					8				10	6		2	11	1	3			34
	3		4	5	7			9	10				8					6		2		1		11		35
1	3		8	5	7			9					12					6		2	11		4	10		36
			4	5	6			9					8				10		7	2	11	1	3			37
	3		10	5	6	9			8									4	7		11	1	2			38
	3		10	5	6	9			8									4	7		11	1	2			39
	3		10	5	6	9			8									4	7		11	1	2			40
	3		10	5	6	9			8									4	7		11	1	2			41
	3		10	5	6	9	12		8									4			11*	1	2		7	42
8	38	2	40	39	34	12	11	33	17	1	17	26	24	22	23	1	24	25	9	18	15	11	9	2	1	
	1						3						1						1							
			11	1		5	1	13	5			3	9	1			1	1	3	1	2					

2 own-goals

	3		4		5			9	8			7			1		10	6		2	11					3
	1		1		1			1	1			1			1		1	1		1	1					
																	1									

1	3		4	5	6		8	9			2	11	10			7										2
1	1		1	1	1		1	1			1	1	1			1										
			1				1						1													

1967-68

Manager: Derek Ufton/Billy Bingham

1	Aug	19	(a)	Cardiff C	D 1-1	Mitten	17,343
2		23	(h)	Aston Villa	W 2-1	Tedesco, Davey	20,200
3		26	(h)	Portsmouth	L 1-2	Piper	16,979
4		28	(a)	Aston Villa	W 1-0	Mitten	15,108
5	Sep	2	(a)	Norwich C	L 0-2		14,452
6		6	(a)	Crystal P	L 0-5		16,372
7		9	(h)	Rotherham U	L 0-1		9,323
8		16	(a)	Derby C	L 0-1		21,516
9		23	(h)	Preston NE	L 1-2	Piper	10,889
10		30	(a)	Charlton A	L 0-1		11,208
11	Oct	7	(h)	Huddersfield T	D 1-1	Reynolds	12,900
12		14	(a)	Middlesbrough	L 0-5		18,025
13		21	(h)	Hull C	L 2-5	Davey, Harrison	8,577
14		28	(a)	Millwall	L 0-3		11,193
15	Nov	18	(h)	Bristol C	L 0-1		11,179
16		25	(a)	Ipswich T	D 1-1	Mitten	14,919
17	Dec	2	(h)	Carlisle U	W 3-1	Peacock, Harrison, Bickle	8,791
18		9	(a)	Bolton W	W 2-1	Piper, Bickle	9,309
19		16	(h)	Cardiff C	D 0-0		10,736
20		18	(a)	Portsmouth	D 0-0		24,218
21		26	(h)	Queen's Park R	L 0-1		21,003
22		30	(a)	Queen's Park R	L 1-4	Bickle	15,889
23	Jan	10	(h)	Norwich C	D 2-2	Harrison, Bickle	7,946
24		20	(h)	Derby C	L 3-4	Mitten 2, Bickle	9,026
25	Feb	3	(a)	Preston NE	L 0-2		13,980
26		10	(h)	Charlton A	L 1-4	Mitten	9,036
27		17	(h)	Blackburn R	W 2-1	Neale, Davey	7,986
28		24	(a)	Huddersfield T	W 1-0	Reynolds	6,562
29	Mar	2	(h)	Middlesbrough	L 0-1		9,040
30		9	(h)	Blackpool	D 2-2	Reynolds, Tedesco	8,688
31		16	(a)	Hull C	W 2-0	Reynolds, Piper	11,948
32		19	(a)	Rotherham U	L 0-1		16,350
33		23	(h)	Millwall	W 2-1	Piper 2	7,728
34		30	(a)	Blackpool	L 0-2		14,586
35	Apr	13	(a)	Bristol C	L 0-2		17,076
36		15	(h)	Birmingham C	L 1-2	Bickle	13,886
37		16	(a)	Birmingham C	D 2-2	Bickle 2	29,359
38		20	(h)	Ipswich T	L 0-1		9,956
39		25	(a)	Blackburn R	D 1-1	Bickle	7,465
40		27	(a)	Carlisle U	L 0-2		5,938
41	May	4	(h)	Bolton W	L 1-2	Reynolds	5,371
42		11	(h)	Crystal P	W 2-1	Tomkins (og), Bickle	4,768

FINAL LEAGUE POSITION: 22nd in Division Two

Appearances
Sub Appearances
Goals

FA Cup

3	Jan	22	(a)	Sheffield W	L 0-3		29,283

Appearances
Sub Appearances
Goals

FL Cup

2	Sep	13	(h)	Birmingham C	L 0-2		10,038

Appearances
Sub Appearances
Goals

Dunne	Everitt	Baird	Hore	Nelson	Newman	Davey	Tedesco	Etheridge	Piper	Mitten	Reynolds	Rounsevell	Reeves	Brimacombe	Neale	Sillett	Harrison	Sealey	Peacock	Banks	Bickle	Saxton	Bloomfield	Shearing	Burnside	Sullivan	
1	2	3	4	5	6	7	8	9	10	11																	1
1	2	3	4	5	6	7	8	9	10	11																	2
1	2	3	4	5	6	7*	8	9	10	11	12																3
1	4	5	6				7	9	8	11		2	3	10													4
1	4	5	6				7	9	8	11		2	3	10													5
1	4	5	6				7	9	10	11		2	3	8													6
1	2	3	4	5	6		8	9	10	11					7												7
1	2	3	4	5	6	7	8*		10	11		12				9											8
1	2	3	4	5	6	7			10		8					9	11										9
1	3		4	5	6	8			10		9	2					11	7									10
1	2	3	6	5					10		8				4	12	11	7	9*								11
1	2	5			6				4		11		3	10				7	9	8							12
1	2	3	4	5	6	7		9	8								11			10							13
1	2	3	4	5	6	9			8						10		11	7									14
1	2	3	6	5		7			4						10		11		9		8						15
1		3	6	5		7			4	11					10	2			9		8						16
1		3	6	5		7				10					4	2	11		9		8						17
1		3	6	5					4	10					7	2	11		9		8						18
1		3	6	5					4	10	12				7	2	11		9		8*						19
1		3	6	5					4	10					7	2	11		9		8						20
1		3	6	5		9			4	10					7	2	11				8						21
1	7	3	6	5					4	10						2	11		9		8						22
1		3	6	5					4	10					7	2	11		9		8						23
1		3		5		7			6	10					4	2	11		9		8						24
1			4	5		12			7	11			3		8	2					9	6	10*				25
	2						9	7	10	6	11	12	3		4						8*	5		1			26
1			4			7	9		8	6			3		10	2					11	5					27
1	2		4			7			8	11	9		3		6						10	5					28
1	2		4			7	12		8	6	9		3*		10						11	5					29
1	3*		4			7	9	6	8	11	10			12		2						5					30
1			4			7	9		8	6	11			3		2						5			10		31
1			4			7	9		8	6	11					2						5			10	3	32
1			4				9	12	7	6*	11					2					8	5			10	3	33
1			4			12		6	8		7					2	11*				9	5			10	3	34
1			4				9	6	10		11					2					7	5			8	3	35
1			4					6	7	9	10		2								11	5			8	3	36
1			6	5				10	8		7		2								9	4			11	3	37
1			6	5				10	8		7		2								9	4			11	3	38
1			6	5				10	8		7		2								9	4			11	3	39
1			6	5				10	8		7		2								9	4			11	3	40
1			6	5				10	8		7		2								9	4			11	3	41
1			4			7			8	11	10		2								9	5			6	3	42
41	20	23	39	26	10	20	15	18	41	28	20	4	16	5	17	19	15	4	11	2	25	18	1	1	12	11	
						2	1	1			2	2		1		1											
						3	2		6	6	5				1		3		1		10						

1 own-goal

Dunne	Everitt	Baird	Hore	Nelson	Newman	Davey	Tedesco	Etheridge	Piper	Mitten	Reynolds	Rounsevell	Reeves	Brimacombe	Neale	Sillett	Harrison	Sealey	Peacock	Banks	Bickle	Saxton	Bloomfield	Shearing	Burnside	Sullivan	
1	3	6		5				12	4	10					7	2			11		8		9				3
1	1	1		1					1	1					1	1			1		1		1				
								1																			

Dunne	Everitt	Baird	Hore	Nelson	Newman	Davey	Tedesco	Etheridge	Piper	Mitten	Reynolds	Rounsevell	Reeves	Brimacombe	Neale	Sillett	Harrison	Sealey	Peacock	Banks	Bickle	Saxton	Bloomfield	Shearing	Burnside	Sullivan	
1	2	3	4	5	6	7	8		10	11						9											2
1	1	1	1	1	1	1	1		1	1						1											

1968-69

Manager: Billy Bingham

1	Aug	10	(h)	Crewe A	D	2-2	Davey, Lord	9,946
2		17	(a)	Bournemouth	W	1-0	Burnside	8,369
3		24	(h)	Reading	W	3-1	Burnside, Bickle, Meldrum (og)	8,725
4		31	(a)	Swindon T	L	0-3		12,302
5	Sep	7	(a)	Shrewsbury T	L	0-1		6,035
6		14	(h)	Bristol R	W	3-1	Bickle 2, Trainor	9,333
7		18	(h)	Walsall	W	1-0	Bickle	11,118
8		20	(a)	Stockport C	W	3-2	Trainor, Piper, Bickle	6,194
9		23	(h)	Barnsley	D	0-0		12,996
10		28	(h)	Northampton T	L	0-1		10,505
11	Oct	5	(h)	Torquay U	L	1-2	Molyneux	20,810
12		9	(h)	Hartlepool	W	3-0	Trainor, Bickle, Saxton	7,565
13		11	(a)	Southport	L	0-2		4,962
14		14	(h)	Hartlepool	D	1-1	Lord	4,738
15		18	(h)	Luton T	W	2-0	Burnside, Piper	12,659
16		26	(a)	Gillingham	L	0-1		5,170
17	Nov	2	(h)	Oldham A	D	1-1	Bickle	9,811
18		4	(h)	Mansfield T	W	1-0	Piper	6,603
19		9	(a)	Barrow	L	0-1		5,541
20		23	(a)	Barnsley	D	0-0		7,599
21		30	(h)	Orient	W	2-1	Molyneux, Piper	7,129
22	Dec	14	(h)	Southport	L	0-4		7,201
23		21	(a)	Luton T	L	0-2		10,971
24		28	(h)	Gillingham	D	1-1	Davey	7,627
25	Jan	4	(h)	Brighton & HA	D	1-1	Hore	6,774
26		11	(a)	Oldham A	W	2-0	Davey 2	5,558
27		18	(h)	Barrow	W	4-1	Davey 2, Piper, Reynolds	8,337
28	Feb	1	(a)	Rotherham U	W	1-0	Davey	9,086
29		5	(a)	Torquay U	W	1-0	Davey	15,469
30		15	(a)	Orient	W	2-1	Reynolds, Davey	4,473
31		22	(h)	Tranmere R	W	1-0	Hore	12,616
32	Mar	1	(a)	Crewe A	L	1-2	Burnside	4,034
33		5	(a)	Brighton & HA	D	0-0		13,295
34		8	(h)	Bournemouth	D	1-1	Burnside	11,961
35		11	(h)	Rotherham U	L	1-2	Burnside	6,605
36		14	(a)	Reading	W	2-1	Bickle, Burnside	4,926
37		17	(a)	Tranmere R	D	2-2	Davey, Burnside	3,035
38		22	(h)	Swindon T	W	2-1	Bickle 2	20,776
39		29	(h)	Shrewsbury T	D	1-1	Gregory (og)	11,010
40	Apr	5	(a)	Northampton T	D	1-1	Piper	6,306
41		7	(a)	Walsall	D	1-1	Burnside	5,335
42		8	(h)	Watford	L	1-2	Davey	16,203
43		12	(h)	Stockport C	D	2-2	Bickle 2	7,266
44		15	(a)	Watford	L	0-1		22,725
45		19	(a)	Bristol R	D	1-1	Tedesco	8,699
46		28	(a)	Mansfield T	L	0-1		7,174

FINAL LEAGUE POSITION: 5th in Division Three

Appearances
Sub Appearances
Goals

FA Cup

1	Nov	16	(a)	Reading	L	0-1		7,179

Appearances
Sub Appearances
Goals

FL Cup

1	Aug	14	(h)	Exeter C	D	0-0		8,862
R		21	(a)	Exeter C	D	0-0		13,432
2R		26	(n*)	Exeter C	L	0-1		10,884

*Played at the Plainmoor Ground, Torquay.

Appearances
Sub Appearances
Goals

Dunne	Reeves	Sullivan	Hore	Saxon	Neale	Davey	Piper	Lord	Burnside	Reynolds	Burgess	Trainor	Bickle	Molyneux	Tedesco	Maher	Wingate	
1	2*	3	4	5	6	7	8	9	10	11	12							1
1	2	3	4	5	6	7	8	11	10			9						2
1	2	3	4	5	6	7	8		10			11	9					3
1	2	3	4	5	6		7		10	11		9	8*		12			4
1	2	3	4	5	6	7	8		10	11		9						5
1	2	3	4	6	12		7		10	11*		9	8	5				6
1	2	3	6	4	11		7		10			9	8	5				7
1	2	3	6	4	11		7		10			9	8	5				8
1	2		6	4	3	11	7		10			9	8	5				9
1	2		6	4	3	11	7		10	12		9	8*	5				10
1	2	3*	6	4	11		7		10	12		9	8	5				11
1	2			4	3	7	6		10	11		9	8	5				12
1	2			4	3	7	6	11	10			9*	8	5	12			13
1	2			4	3	7	6	11	10			9	8	5				14
1	2			4	3	7	6		10			9	8	5		11		15
1	2		12	4	3	7	6		10*			9	8	5		11		16
1	2		12	4*	3	7	6		10			9	8	5		11		17
1	2	3	4	12	8		6	9	10*					5	7	11		18
1	2	3	4		10		6	9		12			8	5	7	11*		19
1	2	3	4		8	7	6						10	5	9	11		20
1	2	3	4		8	7*	6					12	10	5	9	11		21
1	2	3	4		8*	7	6			10			12	5	9	11		22
1	2		4		3	7	6		10	12			8	5	9*	11		23
1	2		4		3	7*	6		10	8			12	5		11	9	24
1	2		4	6	3	7*	8		9	10			12	5		11		25
1			4	6	3	7	8		9	10	2			5		11		26
1			4	6	3	7	8		9	10	2			5		11		27
1			6	4	3	7	8		9	10	2			5		11		28
1			6	4	3	7	8		9	10	2			5		11		29
1			6	4	3	7	8		9	10	2			5		11		30
1		12	6	4*	3	7	8		9	10	2			5		11		31
1	12	3	4		6	7	8		9	10	2			5		11		32
1			6	4	3	7	8		9	10	2			5		11		33
1			4	6	3	7	8		9	10	2			5		11		34
1			4*	6	3	7	8		9	11	2		10	5	12			35
1	12			4	3	7	8		9	6	2*		10	5		11		36
1	2			4	3	7	8		9	6			10	5		11		37
1	2			4	3	7	8		9	6			10*	5	12	11		38
1	2	12	4	5	3*	7	8		9	6			10			11		39
1	2		4	5	3	7	8		9	6			10			11		40
1	2		6	4	3	7	8		9				10	5		11		41
1		3	12	4	2	7	8		9	6*			10	5		11		42
1	2		12	4	3	7	8		9	6			10	5		11		43
1	2		12	4	3	7	8		9	6			10	5		11		44
1	2			4	3		7		9	6			10	5	8	11		45
1	2		4	5	3	12	7		9	6*			10		8	11		46
46	34	16	33	38	45	37	46	6	42	28	11	16	30	38	8	31	1	
	2	2	5	1	1	1				4	1	1	3		4			
			2	1		11	6	2	9	2		3	12	2	1			

2 own-goals

1	2	3	4		10		6	9		11			8	5	7			1
1	1	1	1		1		1	1		1			1	1	1			

1		3	4	5	6	7	8	9	10	11	2							1
1	2	3	4	5	6	7	8	11	10				9					R
1	2	3	4	5	6	7	8		10	11			9					2R
3	2	3	3	3	3	3	3	2	3	2	1		2					

1969-70

Manager: Billy Bingham/Ellis Stuttard

1	Aug	9	(a)	Reading	L 1-2	Shepherd	9,139
2		16	(h)	Brighton & HA	L 0-1		11,237
3		23	(a)	Torquay U	W 2-1	Bickle, Tedesco	10,946
4		26	(a)	Bristol R	L 1-3	Piper	11,562
5		30	(h)	Tranmere R	W 2-1	Piper, Molyneux	10,308
6	Sep	6	(a)	Southport	D 0-0		3,482
7		13	(h)	Halifax T	W 1-0	Sullivan	9,070
8		17	(h)	Stockport C	W 2-0	Bickle, Reynolds	9,524
9		20	(a)	Fulham	L 3-4	Horne (og), Reynolds, Bickle	12,831
10		27	(h)	Luton T	L 1-3	Nicholl (og)	14,111
11		29	(h)	Barnsley	D 0-0		9,909
12	Oct	4	(a)	Mansfield T	W 2-1	Hutchins, Shepherd	6,433
13		7	(a)	Brighton & HA	L 0-2		10,967
14		11	(h)	Rochdale	L 2-3	Davey, Shepherd	9,458
15		18	(a)	Bradford C	L 0-1		8,232
16		25	(h)	Walsall	W 1-0	Davey	7,977
17	Nov	1	(a)	Barrow	D 1-1	Davey	3,088
18		8	(h)	Orient	W 1-0	Burnside	7,951
19		21	(a)	Doncaster R	D 1-1	Bickle	8,195
20		26	(a)	Gillingham	L 0-4		4,127
21		29	(h)	Bournemouth	L 0-1		6,606
22	Dec	13	(a)	Halifax T	L 0-2		3,619
23		20	(h)	Southport	D 1-1	Davey	4,854
24		26	(h)	Torquay U	W 6-0	Bickle 4, Piper 2	17,128
25	Jan	10	(h)	Fulham	W 2-0	Piper 2	9,601
26		17	(a)	Luton T	W 2-0	Rickard, Bickle	12,358
27		24	(h)	Rotherham U	L 0-3		8,536
28		31	(h)	Mansfield T	W 1-0	Bickle	9,181
29	Feb	7	(a)	Rochdale	L 1-2	Rickard	4,853
30		9	(a)	Barnsley	W 1-0	Rickard	10,522
31		14	(h)	Reading	D 1-1	Bickle	10,095
32		25	(h)	Gillingham	D 2-2	Bickle, Rickard	8,185
33		28	(h)	Bradford C	L 0-1		7,837
34	Mar	7	(h)	Doncaster R	D 0-0		6,460
35		11	(h)	Bury	D 2-2	Rickard, Bickle	5,633
36		14	(a)	Bournemouth	W 3-2	Bickle, Maher, Shepherd	4,411
37		17	(a)	Rotherham U	L 0-1		6,984
38		21	(h)	Shrewsbury T	W 4-2	Rickard 3, Bickle	7,023
39		27	(a)	Orient	L 1-4	Maher	19,861
40		28	(a)	Bury	L 1-3	Davey	3,301
41		31	(h)	Barrow	W 1-0	Bickle	7,779
42	Apr	4	(h)	Bristol R	D 2-2	Maher, Taylor (og)	11,142
43		6	(a)	Tranmere R	L 1-3	Bickle	4,543
44		13	(a)	Stockport C	W 1-0	Rickard	2,085
45		17	(a)	Walsall	D 2-2	Bickle, Rowan	5,061
46		18	(a)	Shrewsbury T	L 0-3		3,469

FINAL LEAGUE POSITION: 16th in Division Three

Appearances
Sub Appearances
Goals

FA Cup

1	Nov	15	(a)	Brentford	D 0-0		9,950
R		19	(h)	Brentford	W 2-0	Burnside, Davey	11,554
2	Dec	6	(a)	Peterborough U	L 0-2		8,553

Appearances
Sub Appearances
Goals

FL Cup

1	Aug	13	(h)	Torquay U	D 2-2	Kitchener (og), Burnside	15,199
R		20	(a)	Torquay U	L 0-1		10,483

Appearances
Sub Appearances
Goals

Dunne	Reeves	Neale	Burgess	Molyneux	Hore	Shepherd	Piper	Burnside	Reynolds	Maher	Foster	Bickle	Sullivan	Tedesco	Hutchins	Lean	Rowan	Clamp	Rickard	Chapman	Dowling	Davey	
1	2	3	4	5	6	7	8	9	10	11													1
1	2	3		5	6	7	8	9*	10		4	11										12	2
1			2	5	6		8		10		4	11	3	9								7	3
1			2	5	6	12	8		10		4*	11	3	9								7	4
1	2			5	6	12	7		10		4*	8	3	9	11								5
1	2			5	6	8	7	9	10				3		11	4							6
1	2			5	6	7	8	9	10				3		11	4							7
1	2			5	4	9	8		6			10	3		11							7	8
1	2			5	4	9	8		6			10	3	12	11							7*	9
1	2			5	4		8	9	6			10*	3	7	11	12							10
1	2			5	4	9*	8		6			10	3	12	11		7						11
1				5	2	10	8		6				3		11	4	7					9	12
1				5	2	10	8		6				3		11	4	7					9	13
1				5	2	10	8		6				3		11	4	7					9	14
1		3		5	2	10	8		6						11	4	7					9	15
1		3		5	6		2	9	10	11	4	8										7	16
1		2			6			9	10	11	5	8	3			4						7	17
1		2					8	9	6	11	5	10	3			4						7	18
1		2			6	10	8	9		11	5	12	3			4*						7	19
1		2			6	10*	8	9		11	5	12	3			4						7	20
1					6		2	9	10		5	8	3		11	4						7	21
					6		2	9		11	5	10	3			4		1	8			7	22
					6		2	10*	8	11	5	12	3			4		1	9			7	23
					2		6		8	11	5	10	3			4		1	9			7	24
					2		8		6	11	5	10	3			4		1	9			7	25
					6		2		8	11	5	10	3			4		1	9			7	26
					6		2			11	5	8	3	10		4		1	9	12		7*	27
		10			6		2			11	5	8	3	7		4		1	9				28
					6		2		8	11	5	10	3			4		1	9			7	29
1					6		2		8		5	10	3	12	11	4			9			7*	30
1					6	7	2			11	5	8	3	10		4			9				31
1					6		2			11	5	10	3	7		4			9	8			32
1					6		2			11	5	10	3	7		4			9	8			33
1					6		2	10		11	5	8	3			4	7		9				34
1					2	12	6			11	5	10	3	7*		4			9			8	35
1	2	10		6	4	7				11	5	8	3						9				36
1	12			6	2	7	4			11	5	10	3						9*			8	37
1				6	2	7	4			11	5	10	3						9			8	38
1				6	2	7	4			11	5	10	3						9			8	39
1				6	2	7	4			11	5	10	3						9			8	40
1				6	2		7			11	5	8	3			4			9			10	41
1				3	2	7	6			11	5*	10				4			9		12	8	42
1		3			4	7		6		11		10				5	8		9		2		43
1		3			4	7	6			11		10				5	8		9		2		44
1		2			4	7	6			11		10	3			5	8		9				45
1		2			4	7	6			11	5	10	3				8		9				46
38	10	14	3	23	45	24	43	15	25	30	32	36	39	10	13	30	10	8	25	2	2	29	
	1					3						3		3		1				1	1	1	
				1		4	6	1	2	3		18	1	1	1		1		9			5	

3 own-goals

1		2					8	9	6	11	5	10	3			4						7	1
1		2			6		8	9		11	5	10	3			4						7	R
		10			6	8	2			11	5	12	3	9		4		1				7*	2
2		3			2	1	3	2	1	3	3	2	3	1		3		1				3	
												1											
								1														1	

1	2	3		5	6	7	8	9	10	11*	4	12											1
1	2	6		5	4	7*	8		10	12		11	3									9	R
2	2	2		2	2	2	2	1	2	1	1	1	1									1	
										1		1											
								1															

1970-71

Manager: Ellis Stuttard

1	Aug	15	(h)	Tranmere R	L 0-1		10,384
2		22	(a)	Aston Villa	D 1-1	Aitken (og)	29,205
3		29	(h)	Port Vale	W 2-1	Wilson (og), Bickle	7,753
4	Sep	2	(h)	Brighton & HA	D 1-1	Rickard	9,729
5		4	(a)	Mansfield T	W 5-1	Bickle 2, Hutchins, Saxton, Allen	12,500
6		12	(h)	Bristol R	D 0-0		11,268
7		19	(a)	Bradford C	W 1-0	Hutchins	7,302
8		22	(a)	Halifax T	L 1-4	Molyneux	3,112
9		26	(h)	Rotherham U	W 4-1	Hore, Rickard 2, Burnside	9,081
10	Oct	3	(a)	Fulham	D 1-1	Allen	13,334
11		10	(h)	Bury	L 3-4	Bickle, Rickard 2	9,912
12		16	(a)	Tranmere R	L 0-1		4,190
13		21	(h)	Doncaster R	D 1-1	Rickard	8,425
14		24	(h)	Preston NE	D 1-1	Molyneux	9,628
15		31	(a)	Wrexham	L 0-4		9,130
16	Nov	2	(a)	Rochdale	D 1-1	Rickard	5,033
17		7	(h)	Gillingham	W 2-1	Rickard, Burnside	7,440
18		11	(h)	Shrewsbury T	D 4-4	Moore (og), Hutchins, Wood (og), Burnside	6,966
19		14	(a)	Chesterfield	L 0-2		6,000
20		28	(a)	Barnsley	L 0-2		4,679
21	Dec	5	(h)	Walsall	W 3-1	Hutchins, Hore 2	5,947
22		19	(h)	Aston Villa	D 1-1	Allen	12,996
23		26	(a)	Torquay U	L 1-2	Rickard	12,604
24	Jan	2	(h)	Halifax T	D 1-1	Bickle	6,218
25		9	(h)	Rochdale	D 2-2	Davey, Sullivan	6,140
26		16	(a)	Doncaster R	D 0-0		2,868
27	Feb	1	(h)	Barnsley	W 2-1	Bickle, Allen	5,464
28		6	(a)	Walsall	L 0-1		3,951
29		13	(h)	Swansea C	L 2-3	Hutchins, Saxton	7,285
30		20	(a)	Shrewsbury T	D 1-1	Davey	3,326
31		27	(h)	Wrexham	D 2-2	Allen, Hinch	6,687
32	Mar	6	(a)	Preston NE	L 0-1		12,261
33		13	(h)	Chesterfield	D 1-1	Hutchins	7,450
34		17	(a)	Reading	W 2-0	Brown, Hutchins	4,145
35		20	(a)	Gillingham	W 2-0	Hutchins, Hinch	4,162
36		24	(h)	Reading	W 4-0	Hinch 2, Burnside, Allen	7,700
37		27	(h)	Mansfield T	D 0-0		8,925
38		30	(a)	Swansea C	W 2-0	Allen, Brown	7,470
39	Apr	3	(a)	Port Vale	L 1-2	Hutchins	3,518
40		10	(h)	Torquay U	L 1-2	Allen	17,175
41		12	(h)	Fulham	D 1-1	Hinch	11,712
42		13	(a)	Bristol R	W 3-1	Hinch, Hutchins, Davey	8,392
43		17	(a)	Bury	L 0-3		3,185
44		24	(h)	Bradford C	L 1-3	Hutchins	5,914
45		28	(a)	Brighton & HA	D 1-1	Allen	8,202
46	May	1	(a)	Rotherham U	D 1-1	Burnside	4,385

FINAL LEAGUE POSITION: 15th in Division Three

Appearances
Sub Appearances
Goals

FA Cup

1	Nov	21	(a)	Walsall	L 0-3	4,614

Appearances
Sub Appearances
Goals

FL Cup

1	Aug	14	(a)	Portsmouth	L 0-2	12,846

Appearances
Sub Appearances
Goals

Dunne	Wooldridge	Sullivan	Hore	Molyneux	Saxton	Davey	Allen	Bickle	Burnside	Maher	Rickard	Hutchins	Shepherd	Furnell	Harris	Lean	Dowling	Reynolds	Provan	Hinch	Brown	Wilkinson	Foster	
1	2	3	4	5	6	7	8	9	10	11														1
1	2	3	4	5	6		8	9	10		7	11												2
1	2	3	4	5	6		8	9	10		7	11												3
1	2	3	4	5	6		8	9	10		7	11												4
1	2	3	4	5	6		8	9	10		7	11												5
1	2	3	4	5	6		8	9	10		7	11												6
1	2	3	4	5	6		8	10	8		7	11												7
1	2	3	4	5	6		8	10	8		7	11												8
1	2	3	4	5	6		8	9	10		7	11												9
1	2	3	4	5	6		8		10		7	11	9											10
1	2	3	4	5	6		8	9	10		7	11												11
1	2	3	4	5	6		8	9	10	11	7													12
1	2	3	4	5	6		8	9	10		7	11												13
1	2	3	4	5	6		8	9			7	11	10											14
1	2	3	4	5	6	12	8	9*			7	11	10											15
1	2	3	4	5	6		8	11	10		9		7											16
	2	3	4	5	6		8	11*	10		9	12	7	1										17
	2	3	4	5	6		8	12	10		9*	11	7	1										18
	2	3	4		5	7	8	12	10*		9	11		1									6	19
	2	3	4		5	7	9	8*		10	12	11		1		6								20
		3	4		5	7	9	10			8	11		1		6	2							21
		3	4		5	7	9	10				11	8	1		6	2							22
		3	4		5	7	9	10			8	11		1		6	2							23
		3	4		5	7	9	10			8	11		1		6	2							24
		3	4		5	7	9	10			8*	11		1		6	2	12						25
		3	4		5	7	9	10				11		1		6	2	8						26
		3	8		5	2	7	9			10	11		1		4						6		27
		3	8		5	2	7		9		10	11		1		4	12					6*		28
		3	4		5	2	7		10			11		1		6		9		8				29
		12	4		5	2	8		10			11		1		6	3	9*		7				30
			4		5	3	9		10			11		1		6	2			8	7			31
			4		5	2	9		10			11		1	3				6	8	7			32
			4		5	2	9		10			11		1	3				6	8	7			33
		12	4		5	3	9		10			11		1		6	2*			8	7			34
			4		5	7			8			11		1	3	6			2	10	7			35
			4		5	2	9		10			11		1	3				6	8	7			36
			4		5	2	9		10			11		1	3				6	8	7			37
			4		5	2	9		10			11		1	3				6	8	7			38
			4		5	2	9		10			11		1	3				6	8	7			39
			4		5	2	9	12	10			11		1	3				6	8	7*			40
			4		5	2	9		10			11		1	3				6	8	7			41
			4		5	2	9		10			11	7	1	3				6	8				42
			4		5	2	9		10			11	7	1	3				6	8				43
			4		5	2	9		10			11	7	1	3				6	8				44
			4*		5	2	9		10		12	11	7	1	3				6	8				45
			4		5	2	9		10			11	7	1	3				6	8				46
16	20	29	46	18	46	29	45	24	36	3	24	42	12	30	14	14	9	3	14	18	11	2	1	
		2				1		3			2	1					1	1						
		1	3	2	2	3	9	6	5		9	11								6	2			

4 own-goals

1	2	3	4		6	8	7		10		9	11					12						5*	1
1	1	1	1		1	1	1		1		1	1											1	
																	1							

1	2	3	4	5	6		8	9	10	7*	12	11												1
1	1	1	1	1	1		1	1	1	1		1												
											1													

1971-72

Manager: Ellis Stuttard

1	Aug	14	(a)	Aston Villa	L 1-3	Hinch	26,327
2		21	(h)	Blackburn R	W 1-0	Hutchins	10,280
3		28	(a)	York C	W 3-2	Davey, Latcham 2	5,352
4	Sep	4	(h)	Mansfield T	W 3-1	Bickle 2, Latcham	8,343
5		11	(a)	Port Vale	D 0-0		3,707
6		13	(h)	Walsall	W 3-2	Sullivan 2, Latcham	10,393
7		18	(h)	Tranmere R	D 2-2	Hinch, Bickle	10,244
8		25	(a)	Oldham A	W 1-0	Latcham	10,149
9		27	(a)	Rochdale	L 2-3	Hinch, Hutchins	4,519
10	Oct	2	(h)	Bournemouth	D 1-1	Rickard	15,559
11		9	(a)	Notts C	L 0-1		11,828
12		12	(h)	Bolton W	W 2-0	Rimmer (og), Hutchins	13,336
13		16	(h)	Aston Villa	W 3-2	Hutchins 2, Rickard	18,570
14		23	(h)	Wrexham	L 1-2	Hutchins	14,019
15		30	(a)	Chesterfield	L 1-2	Rickard	7,475
16	Nov	6	(h)	Brighton & HA	L 1-2	Hutchins	11,429
17		13	(a)	Rotherham U	L 3-4	Reed, Saxton, Rickard	8,444
18		15	(a)	Halifax T	W 1-0	Hinch	2,832
19		27	(a)	Bristol R	D 2-2	Allen, Hutchins	9,568
20	Dec	4	(h)	Shrewsbury T	L 1-2	Hore	8,717
21		18	(a)	Mansfield T	W 3-2	Reed 2, Rickard	3,782
22		27	(h)	Torquay U	W 3-1	Rickard, Hore, Reed	20,096
23	Jan	1	(a)	Tranmere R	L 2-3	Reed, Rickard	6,711
24		8	(h)	York C	W 4-0	Rickard 3, Reed	6,943
25		15	(a)	Barnsley	D 2-2	Booth (og), Hinch	3,421
26		22	(h)	Rochdale	W 4-1	Hinch, Rickard 2, Hutchins	9,187
27		29	(a)	Bolton W	L 1-2	Rickard	5,856
28	Feb	5	(a)	Bournemouth	L 0-1		13,805
29		12	(a)	Wrexham	W 2-0	Ashcroft (og), Hutchins	3,904
30		19	(h)	Chesterfield	W 1-0	Latcham	10,208
31		26	(a)	Brighton & HA	L 0-3		15,198
32	Mar	4	(h)	Rotherham U	W 2-1	Cave 2	8,292
33		11	(h)	Notts C	D 1-1	Latcham	12,257
34		14	(h)	Barnsley	W 2-1	Hutchins, Hinch	8,660
35		18	(a)	Blackburn R	L 2-3	Hinch, Cave	7,610
36		20	(a)	Bradford C	W 1-0	Cave	5,346
37		25	(h)	Port Vale	D 0-0		8,801
38	Apr	1	(a)	Torquay U	L 1-2	Hinch	10,928
39		3	(h)	Oldham A	D 0-0		10,748
40		8	(a)	Swansea C	D 1-1	Hinch	2,974
41		11	(a)	Walsall	L 0-1		5,084
42		15	(h)	Bristol R	W 2-1	Provan, Hore	8,938
43		18	(h)	Bradford C	L 1-4	Provan	7,958
44		22	(a)	Shrewsbury T	W 2-1	Hague, Hinch	3,179
45		25	(h)	Halifax T	D 1-1	Provan	7,756
46	May	2	(h)	Swansea C	W 4-1	Provan, Rickard, Sullivan, Hinch	8,321

FINAL LEAGUE POSITION: 8th in Division Three

Appearances
Sub Appearances
Goals

FA Cup

1	Nov	20	(a)	Gillingham	L 2-3	Reed 2	7,842

Appearances
Sub Appearances
Goals

FL Cup

1	Aug	17	(h)	Bristol C	W 1-0	Hinch	11,248
2	Sep	8	(a)	Chelsea	L 0-2		23,011

Appearances
Sub Appearances
Goals

Furnell	Davey	Harris	Hore	Darke	Provan	Brown	Allen	Hinch	Latcham	Hutchins	Sullivan	Bickle	Saxton	Rickard	Reed	Hague	Balac	Cave	Dowling	
1	2	3	4	5	6	7	8	9	10	11										1
1	2	3	4		5	7	8	9	10	11	6									2
1	2	3	4	12	5	7	9*	8	11		6	10								3
1	2	3	4	12	5	7	9	8*	11		6	10								4
1	2	3	4		5	7	8	9	10		6	11								5
1	2	3	4		5	7	8	9	10		6	11								6
1	2	3	4		5	7	8*	9	10	11	6	12								7
1	2		4		6	7		8	10	11	3	9	5							8
1	2		4		6	7		9	10	11	3	8	5							9
1	2		4		6	7		9	10	11	3		5	8						10
1	2		4		6	7	12	8	10	11*	3		5	9						11
1	2	3	4		6	7	9		10	11			5	8						12
1	2	3	4		6	7	9		10	11			5	8						13
1	2	3	4		6	7	9*	12	10	11			5	8						14
1	2		4		6	7	12	9	10*	11	3		5	8						15
1	2	3	4	6		8		9*	10	11			5	12	7					16
1	2	3	4			9		8	6	11			5	10	7					17
1	2	3	4				8	9	6	11			5	10	7					18
1	2		4		6		9		10	11	3			8	7	5				19
1	2		4		6	12	9		10*	11	3			8	7	5				20
1	2		4*		6		8	12	10	11	3			9	7	5				21
1	2		4		5		9		10	11	3			8	7	6				22
1	2		4*		5		9	12	10	11	3			8	7	6				23
		2	4		5			9	10	11	3			8	7	6	1			24
		2	4		5		12	9	10	11*	3			8	7	6	1			25
		2	4		5			9	10	11	3			8	7	6	1			26
		2	4		5		12	9	10	11	3			8*	7	6	1			27
		2	4		5	12	8*	9	10	11	3				7	6	1			28
		2	4		5		8	9	10	11	3				7	6	1			29
		2	4		5		8	9	10	11	3				7	6	1			30
		2	4		5		8	9	10	11	3				7	6	1			31
		2	4		5			9	10	11	3				7	6	1	8		32
		2	4		5		12	9*	10	11	3				7	6	1	8		33
		2	4		5			9	10	11	3				7	6	1	8		34
		2	4		5			9	10	11	3				7	6	1	8		35
		2	4		5			9	10	11	3				7	6	1	8		36
		2	4		5			9	10	11	3				7	6	1	8		37
		2	4		5	7		9	10	11	3					6	1	8		38
		2			5	7	4	9	10	11*	3				12	6	1	8		39
		2	4		5		9	8	10	11	3				7	6	1			40
		2	4	12	5		8	9	10	11*	3				7	6	1			41
		2	4		5		8	9	10	11	3				7	6	1			42
	12	2	4		5		8	9	10	11*	3				7	6	1			43
	7	2	4	5*	6		8	9	10		3		12			11	1			44
	9	2	4		5	12	7	8	11*		3		10			6	1			45
		2	4		5	7	8	9	11		3			10		6	1			46
23	25	36	45	3	43	20	28	38	46	39	39	6	12	18	26	28	23	8		
	1			3		3	5	3				1	1	1	1					
	1		3		4		1	12	7	11	3	3	1	14	6	1		4		

3 own-goals

Furnell	Davey	Harris	Hore	Darke	Provan	Brown	Allen	Hinch	Latcham	Hutchins	Sullivan	Bickle	Saxton	Rickard	Reed	Hague	Balac	Cave	Dowling	
1	2	3	4			8		10	6	11			5	9*	7				12	1
1	1	1	1			1		1	1	1			1	1	1					
																			1	
															2					

Furnell	Davey	Harris	Hore	Darke	Provan	Brown	Allen	Hinch	Latcham	Hutchins	Sullivan	Bickle	Saxton	Rickard	Reed	Hague	Balac	Cave	Dowling	
1	2	3	4	5	6	7	8	9	10	11										1
1	2	3	4		5	7	8	9	10		6	11								2
2	2	2	2	1	2	2	2	2	2	1	1	1								
								1												

1972-73

Manager: Ellis Stuttard/Tony Waiters

1	Aug	12	(a)	Rotherham U	L	0-1		5,473
2		19	(h)	Southend U	W	2-0	Rickard, Hore	6,969
3		26	(a)	Chesterfield	D	2-2	Welsh, Brown	7,928
4		29	(h)	Grimsby T	W	3-1	Saxton, Welsh 2	8,472
5	Sep	2	(h)	Brentford	L	0-1		7,832
6		9	(a)	Bolton W	L	0-2		5,515
7		16	(h)	Shrewsbury T	W	3-0	Middleton, Hore, Hinch	5,958
8		20	(a)	Blackburn R	L	1-3	Hague	6,326
9		23	(a)	Bristol R	L	0-2		8,458
10		26	(h)	Oldham A	L	1-3	Davey	5,773
11		30	(h)	Walsall	L	0-2		5,257
12	Oct	7	(a)	Charlton A	L	0-3		7,340
13		10	(a)	Scunthorpe U	D	1-1	Hinch	3,650
14		14	(h)	Swansea C	W	3-1	Rickard, Hinch, Welsh	5,034
15		21	(a)	Bournemouth	W	1-0	Hague	14,024
16		24	(h)	York C	D	1-1	Provan	8,424
17		28	(h)	Halifax T	W	2-1	Hinch, Rickard	6,910
18	Nov	4	(a)	Oldham A	L	1-7	Hinch	5,618
19		11	(h)	Blackburn R	L	1-2	Provan	5,812
20		25	(a)	Port Vale	D	1-1	Saxton	3,881
21	Dec	2	(h)	Tranmere R	L	0-1		4,768
22		23	(a)	Watford	L	2-3	Saxton, Rickard	7,750
23		26	(h)	Bristol R	W	3-2	Latcham 2, Sheppard (og)	10,399
24		29	(a)	Southend U	L	1-3	Hague	4,789
25	Jan	20	(a)	Brentford	W	2-0	Provan, Latcham	7,070
26		27	(h)	Bolton W	W	1-0	Latcham	8,592
27	Feb	6	(h)	Scunthorpe U	W	3-0	Davey 2, Rickard	10,008
28		9	(a)	Shrewsbury T	D	1-1	Davey	2,600
29		17	(h)	Rotherham U	W	4-1	Davey 2, Welsh 2	8,454
30		20	(h)	Chesterfield	D	2-2	Hague, Sullivan	12,582
31		24	(a)	Rochdale	W	6-0	Rickard 2, Welsh 2, Provan, Latcham	2,622
32	Mar	3	(h)	Charlton A	W	5-0	Rickard 2, Latcham, Hore, Welsh	11,143
33		6	(h)	Wrexham	W	1-0	Hague	14,576
34		9	(a)	Swansea C	D	1-1	Hague	4,584
35		17	(h)	Bournemouth	W	1-0	Hague	20,104
36		21	(a)	Notts C	L	0-2		12,899
37		24	(a)	Halifax T	L	1-2	Lugg	1,839
38		26	(a)	York C	W	2-1	Davey 2	3,488
39		31	(h)	Port Vale	W	2-1	Hinch 2	9,416
40	Apr	6	(a)	Tranmere R	D	2-2	Hinch 2	4,513
41		14	(h)	Notts C	L	1-4	Machin	11,997
42		21	(a)	Wrexham	W	2-1	Welsh 2	3,265
43		23	(h)	Watford	D	1-1	Hague	9,722
44		25	(a)	Walsall	W	3-1	Hague, Welsh, Hinch	4,179
45		28	(a)	Grimsby T	D	1-1	Davey	7,369
46	May	1	(h)	Rochdale	W	3-2	Hague 2, Hore	9,917

FINAL LEAGUE POSITION: 8th in Division Three

Appearances
Sub Appearances
Goals

FA Cup

1	Nov	18	(h)	Hendon	W	1-0	Hague	5,697
2	Dec	9	(a)	Yeovil T	W	2-0	Dowling, Welsh	10,577
3	Jan	13	(h)	Middlesbrough	W	1-0	Hinch	15,361
4	Feb	3	(a)	Leeds U	L	1-2	Rickard	38,374

Appearances
Sub Appearances
Goals

FL Cup

1	Aug	15	(h)	Bournemouth	L	0-2		12,523

Appearances
Sub Appearances
Goals

Balac	Harris	Sullivan	Hore	Provan	Hague	Lugg	Allen	Hinch	Latcham	Welsh	Saxton	Rickard	Brown	Reed	Middleton	Davey	Jacobs	Kearns	Furnell	Dowling	Machin	Darke	
1	2	3	4	5	6	7	8	9	10*	11	12												1
1	2	3	4	5	6	8		9		11	10	7											2
1	2	3	4	5	6	8		9		11	10	7	12										3
1	2	3	4	5	6	8*		9		11	10	7											4
1	2	3	4	6	5	8		9*		11	10	7	12										5
1	2	3	4	6	5	8		9		11	10*	7		12									6
1	2	3	4	6	5	8		9		11				7	10								7
1	2	3	4	5	6*	8		9	10	11	12			7									8
1	2	3	4	5	6	8		9	10	11				7									9
1	2	3	4	5	6	7		12	10*	11				8		9							10
1		3	4	5	6	8		9	10*	12				7		11	2						11
1		3	4	5	6	7		11			10			8		9	2						12
1		3	4	5	6	7		9	10	11		8					2						13
1		3	4	5	6	8		9	10	11		7					2						14
1	2	3	4	5	6	7		9	10	11		8											15
1	2	3	4	5	6	7		9	10	11		8											16
	2	3	4	6	5	8		9	10	11		7*		12				1					17
1	2	3	4	5	6	8		9	10	11		7											18
		3	4	2	6	8		9	10	11	5	7							1				19
		3	4	2	6			9	10	11	5	7							1	8			20
		3	4	2	6			9	10	11	5	8		12					1	7*			21
		3	4	2	6			9	10*	11	5	7		12					1		8		22
		3	4	2	6			9	11	10	5	8*		12					1		7		23
		3	4*	2	6			9	11	10	5	8		12					1		7		24
		3	4	2	6			9	11	10	5	8							1		7		25
		3	4	2	6			9	11	10	5	8							1		7		26
		3	4	2	6			12	11	10	5	8*				9			1		7		27
		3	4	2	6			8	11	10	5					9			1		7		28
		3	4	2	6			9	11	10	5					8			1		7		29
		3	4	2	6				11	10	5	8				9			1	12	7*		30
		3	4	2	6			9	11	10	5	8							1		7		31
		3	4	2	6			9	10	11	5	8							1	7			32
		3	4	2	6			9	11	10	5	8							1	7			33
		3	4	2	6			9	11	10	5	8							1	7			34
		3	4	2	6			9	11	10	5	8*				12			1	7			35
		3	4	2	6	12		9	11	10	5*	8							1	7			36
		3	4	2	5	12		9	11	10		8*							1	7		6	37
		3	4	2	6			9	11	10						8			1	7		5	38
		3		2	6			9	11	10*		12				7			1	8	4	5	39
		3				2		9		11		8		6		10			1	7	4	5	40
		3	4			11		9		10	6	8				2			1		7	5	41
		3	4	2	6			9	11	10	5					8			1		7		42
		3	4	2	6			9	11	10	5					8			1		7		43
		3	4	2	6			9	11	10	5					8			1	7			44
		3	4	2	6			9	11*	10	5	12				8			1	7			45
		3	4	2	6	5		9	11*	10		12				8			1	7			46
17	14	46	44	44	44	22	1	43	37	44	29	30		7	1	16	4	1	28	14	15	5	
						2		2		1	2	3	2	6		1				1			
		1	4	4	11	1		10	6	12	3	9	1		1	9					1		

1 own-goal

Balac	Harris	Sullivan	Hore	Provan	Hague	Lugg	Allen	Hinch	Latcham	Welsh	Saxton	Rickard	Brown	Reed	Middleton	Davey	Jacobs	Kearns	Furnell	Dowling	Machin	Darke	
		3	4	2	6			9	10	11	5	8		7					1				1
		3	4	2	6			9	10	11	5	8							1	7			2
		3	4	2	6			9	11	10	5	8							1		7		3
		3	4	2	6			9	11	10	5	8							1		7		4
		4	4	4	4			4	4	4	4	4		1					4	1	2		
					1			1		1		1								1			

Balac	Harris	Sullivan	Hore	Provan	Hague	Lugg	Allen	Hinch	Latcham	Welsh	Saxton	Rickard	Brown	Reed	Middleton	Davey	Jacobs	Kearns	Furnell	Dowling	Machin	Darke	
1	2	3	4	5	6	8	7	9		10	12					11							1
1	1	1	1	1	1	1	1	1		1						1							
											1												

1973-74

Manager: Tony Waiters

1	Aug	25	(h)	Chesterfield	D 1-1	Machin	8,772
2	Sep	1	(a)	Tranmere R	L 0-2		3,304
3		8	(h)	Brighton & HA	L 0-1		7,011
4		11	(h)	Rochdale	W 5-0	Hore, Rogers, Mariner 2, Davey	7,066
5		15	(a)	Southport	D 1-1	Mariner	3,102
6		19	(a)	Aldershot	L 2-3	Davey, Joslyn (og)	4,243
7		22	(h)	Walsall	W 2-1	Bennett (og), Davey	7,268
8		29	(a)	Oldham A	L 0-1		6,292
9	Oct	2	(h)	Aldershot	W 2-1	Provan, Harley (og)	7,778
10		6	(h)	Shrewsbury T	D 2-2	Mariner, Machin	7,318
11		13	(a)	Huddersfield T	L 1-2	Mariner	4,927
12		20	(a)	Watford	W 3-0	Hague, Mariner 2	6,905
13		22	(a)	Rochdale	W 3-1	Welsh, Davey, Marsh (og)	1,432
14		27	(h)	Port Vale	W 2-0	Mariner, Davey	9,383
15	Nov	3	(a)	Blackburn R	L 0-2		7,756
16		10	(h)	Halifax T	D 1-1	Davey	8,014
17		13	(h)	Grimsby T	W 1-0	Davey	7,700
18		17	(a)	Charlton A	L 0-2		5,233
19	Dec	8	(h)	Wrexham	L 1-2	May (og)	7,638
20		26	(a)	Bristol R	L 2-4	Hore, Mariner	22,353
21		29	(a)	Brighton & HA	L 0-1		11,181
22	Jan	1	(h)	Tranmere R	W 2-0	Sullivan, Machin	13,004
23		12	(h)	Southport	W 4-1	Davey, Welsh, Mariner 2	8,484
24		19	(a)	Chesterfield	L 0-1		5,145
25	Feb	2	(h)	Southend U	D 1-1	Mariner	6,955
26		10	(a)	Walsall	W 4-0	Davey 2, Reed, Mariner	4,926
27		16	(h)	Huddersfield T	D 1-1	Machin	7,999
28		20	(a)	Hereford U	W 1-0	Reed	3,810
29		23	(a)	Shrewsbury T	D 0-0		1,993
30	Mar	2	(h)	Bristol R	W 1-0	Provan	11,374
31		10	(a)	Port Vale	L 1-2	Davey	3,108
32		16	(h)	Watford	W 2-0	Hore, Reed	7,336
33		18	(a)	Southend U	L 0-2		5,261
34		23	(a)	Halifax T	L 0-1		1,715
35		26	(h)	Hereford U	L 0-1		7,516
36		30	(h)	Blackburn R	W 2-1	Johnson, Machin	5,799
37	Apr	3	(a)	York C	D 1-1	Hague	8,257
38		6	(a)	Grimsby T	L 0-3		5,192
39		12	(a)	Bournemouth	D 0-0		7,792
40		15	(h)	Bournemouth	W 2-0	Johnson, Hore	9,431
41		16	(h)	Charlton A	W 1-0	Hague	7,154
42		20	(a)	Wrexham	L 2-5	May (og), Davey	4,104
43		27	(h)	Cambridge U	W 4-1	Burrows 2, Darke, Randell	5,078
44	May	1	(a)	Cambridge U	L 1-3	Mariner	1,722
45		3	(h)	Oldham A	D 0-0		5,497
46		6	(h)	York C	L 0-2		5,125

FINAL LEAGUE POSITION: 17th in Division Three

Appearances
Sub Appearances
Goals

FA Cup

1	Nov	24	(h)	Brentford	W 2-1	Houston (og), Mariner	11,050
2	Dec	15	(h)	Walsall	W 1-0	Mariner	7,322
3	Jan	5	(a)	Manchester U	L 0-1		31,810

Appearances
Sub Appearances
Goals

FL Cup

1	Aug	29	(a)	Torquay U	W 2-0	Davey 2	6,996
2	Oct	9	(h)	Portsmouth	W 4-0	Machin, Davey 2, Mariner	13,202
3		30	(a)	Burnley	W 2-1	Waldron (og), Hague	11,150
4	Nov	20	(a)	Queen's Park R	W 3-0	Welsh 2, Davey	19,072
5	Dec	19	(a)	Birmingham C	W 2-1	Welsh, Davey	15,273
SF	Jan	23	(h)	Manchester C	D 1-1	Davey	30,390
		30	(a)	Manchester C	L 0-2		40,117

Appearances
Sub Appearances
Goals

Furnell	Dowling	Sullivan	Hore	Provan	Hague	Welsh	Davey	Hinch	Machin	Burrows	Rogers	Saxton	Darke	Johnson	Mariner	Webb	Randell	Rickard	Foster	Rafferty	Shipperley	Aleksic	Sutton	Reed	
1	2	3	4	5	6*	7	8	9	10	11	12														1
1	2	3	4	6		7	8	9	10	11*		5												12	2
1	12	3	4	2		7	8	9	10	11		5	6*												3
1		3	4	2			8		10		11	5	6	7	9										4
1		3	4	2		12	8		10		11	5	6	7*	9										5
1		3	4	2			8		10		11	5	6	7*	9									12	6
1		3	4	2		7	8		10		11	5	6		9										7
1		3	4	2		9	8		10		11	5	6		9										8
1		3	4	2		7	8		10		11	5	6		9										9
1		3	4	2		7	8		10	12	11*	5	6		9										10
1		3	4		6	7	8				11	5	12	10*	9	2									11
1		3	4		6	7	8		10		11	5			9	2									12
1		3	4		6	7	8		10		11	5			9	2									13
1		3	4		6	7	8		10		11	5			9	2*	12								14
1		3	4		6	7	8		10		11	5			9		2								15
1		3	4		6	7	8		10		11	5			9		2								16
1			4	12	6	7	8		10	11*	3	5			9		2								17
1		3	4		6	7	8		10		11	5			9		2								18
1		3	4		6	7	8*		10		11	5			9		2							12	19
1		3	4		6	7	8		10		11	5			9		2								20
1		3	4		6		8		10	11		5			9		2	7							21
1		3	4		6	7	8		10		11	5			9		2								22
1		3	4	5	6	7	8		10		11				9		2								23
1		3	4	2	6	7*	8		10		11	5			9									12	24
1		3	4		6		8		10	11*	12	5			9		2							7	25
1		3	4		6		8		10			5	11		9		2							7	26
1		3	4	5	6		8		10*		12		11		9		2							7	27
1		3	4	6			8				10	5*	11		9		2		12					7	28
1		3	4	5			8*		10		11		6		9		2		12					7	29
1		3	4	5			8		10			6	11		9		2							7	30
1		3	4	5			8		10			6	11		9		2							7	31
1		3	4	5			8		10			6	11				2			9				7	32
1		3	4	5			8		10			6	11				2			9				7	33
1		3	4						10			6	11		9		2			8	5			7	34
1		3	4		5				10			6	11		9		2	12		8				7*	35
1		3			6				10		11	5	4	7	9		2	12		8*					36
1		3			5		8		10		12	6	2	7*	9		4	11							37
1		3			6		8		10		11	6	2		9*		4	7						12	38
1		3	11		5		12		10			6	2	7*	9		4	8							39
1		3	11		5		8		10			6	2	7	9		4								40
		3	2		5		8*		10		11	6		7	9		4	12				1			41
1		3	2		5		8		10	11		6		7	9		4								42
1		3	5				8		10	11*		6	2	7	9		4		12						43
		3	4	5			8		10		11	6		7	9		2					1			44
1		3	4				8					6	2	7	9		11		10				5		45
		3	4				8					6	2	7	9		11		10			1	5		46
43	2	45	43	20	26	20	42	3	42	8	26	42	26	14	41	4	31	4	2	5	1	3	2	11	
	1			1		1	1			1	4		1				1	3	3					5	
		1	4	2	3	2	12		5	2	1		1	2	14		1							3	

6 own-goals

1		3	4		6	7	8		10		11	5			9		2								1
1		3	4		6	7	8		10		11	5			9		2								2
1		3	4	5	6	7	8		10		11*				9		2	12							3
3		3	3	1	3	3	3		3		3	2			3		3								
																		1							
															2										

1 own-goal

1	2	3	4	6			8	9	10	11		5		7											1
1		3	4		6	7	8		10		11	5			9	2									2
1		3	4		6	7	8		10		11	5			9		2								3
1		3	4		6	7	8		10		11	5			9		2								4
1		3	4		6	7*	8		10		11	5			9		2	12							5
1		3	4		6	7	8		10		11	5			9		2								SF
1		3	4		6	7			10		11	5			9		2	8							
7	1	7	7	1	6	6	6	1	7	1	6	7		1	6	1	5	1							
																		1							
					1	3	7		1						1										

1 own-goal

1974-75

Manager: Tony Waiters

1	Aug	17	(a)	Preston NE	L 0-1		11,663
2		24	(h)	Grimsby T	W 2-1	Mariner, Rafferty	8,531
3		30	(a)	Southend U	L 1-2	Rafferty	8,600
4	Sep	4	(a)	Aldershot	L 3-4	H.Burrows, Rafferty, Green	3,756
5		7	(h)	Tranmere R	W 4-1	Mariner, Rafferty 3	5,752
6		14	(a)	Swindon T	L 0-2		5,495
7		17	(a)	Colchester U	L 0-1		5,389
8		21	(h)	Gillingham	D 1-1	Randell	5,556
9		24	(h)	Hereford U	W 1-0	Mariner	5,519
10		28	(a)	Wrexham	L 1-5	Green	3,814
11	Oct	1	(h)	Huddersfield T	W 2-0	Randell, Mariner	5,324
12		5	(h)	Walsall	W 2-1	Rafferty, Delve	5,765
13		12	(a)	Port Vale	L 0-2		3,634
14		15	(h)	Aldershot	W 1-0	Rafferty	5,175
15		19	(h)	Peterborough U	W 2-0	Green, Rafferty	6,843
16		26	(a)	Bury	W 1-0	Forrest (og)	4,697
17	Nov	2	(a)	Charlton A	W 2-0	Johnson, McAuley	8,495
18		9	(h)	Watford	D 1-1	Johnson	8,063
19		16	(a)	Crystal P	D 3-3	Rafferty, Johnson, Mariner	19,308
20		30	(a)	Chesterfield	W 2-1	Rafferty, Mariner	4,663
21	Dec	7	(h)	Bournemouth	W 1-0	Rafferty	9,897
22		21	(a)	Brighton & HA	D 2-2	Rafferty 2	9,193
23		26	(h)	Swindon T	W 4-3	Randell, Delve, Mariner, Rafferty	18,027
24		28	(a)	Halifax T	D 1-1	McAuley	2,063
25	Jan	11	(a)	Bournemouth	W 7-3	Rafferty, Mariner 2, Johnson, McAuley, Delve, Randell	7,352
26		18	(h)	Chesterfield	W 3-0	Delve, Mariner, Vassallo	13,005
27	Feb	1	(a)	Watford	W 3-1	Markham (og), Johnson, Mariner	8,563
28		4	(h)	Blackburn R	W 2-1	Rafferty, Johnson	28,744
29		8	(h)	Charlton A	D 1-1	Rafferty	22,946
30		15	(a)	Blackburn R	L 2-5	McAuley, Jones, (og)	17,734
31		22	(h)	Crystal P	L 0-1		21,002
32		28	(h)	Southend U	W 1-0	Mariner	16,321
33	Mar	8	(a)	Hereford U	W 5-1	Hardcastle, Mariner, Rafferty 2, Vassallo	9,296
34		15	(h)	Wrexham	L 0-3		14,855
35		18	(h)	Preston NE	W 2-1	Mariner 2	22,063
36		21	(a)	Tranmere R	W 3-1	Green, Johnson, Rafferty	3,040
37		28	(h)	Halifax T	W 2-0	Collings (og), McAuley	19,580
38		29	(h)	Brighton & HA	D 2-2	Green, Mariner	19,396
39		31	(a)	Gillingham	D 2-2	Green, Rafferty	11,200
40	Apr	5	(h)	Bury	W 2-1	Rafferty, Johnson	14,940
41		8	(a)	Huddersfield T	W 2-0	Mariner 2	2,947
42		12	(a)	Walsall	D 0-0		7,404
43		15	(h)	Colchester U	W 1-0	Mariner	23,551
44		19	(h)	Port Vale	D 1-1	Delve	22,447
45		22	(a)	Grimsby T	D 1-1	Mariner	9,052
46		26	(a)	Peterborough U	L 0-1		11,176

FINAL LEAGUE POSITION: 2nd in Division Three

Appearances
Sub Appearances
Goals

FA Cup

1	Nov	23	(a)	Dartford	W 3-2	Randell 2, Mariner	4,384
2	Dec	14	(h)	Crystal P	W 2-1	Green, Rafferty	17,473
3	Jan	3	(h)	Blackpool	W 2-0	Rafferty 2	23,143
4		24	(h)	Everton	L 1-3	Vassallo	38,000

Appearances
Sub Appearances
Goals

FL Cup

1	Aug	20	(a)	Bristol R	D 0-0		8,974
R		27	(h)	Bristol R	L 0-1		11,213

Appearances
Sub Appearances
Goals

Furnell	Darke	Burrows P	Hore	Griffiths	Green	Delve	Davey	Rafferty	Mariner	Burrows H	Pearson	Hardcastle	Randell	Provan	Saxton	Johnson	McAuley	Vassallo	Rogers	Sutton	
1	2	3	4	5	6	7	8	9	10*	11	12										1
1	2	3	4	5	6	7	8	10	9*	11	12										2
1	2	3	4	5	6	7	8	9	10	11											3
1	2	3	4*	5	6	7	8	9	12	11		10									4
1	2	3	12	5	6	4*	8	9	7	11		10									5
1	2	3		5	4	6	8	9	7			10	11								6
1	2		7	5	6		12	9*	8			4	11	3	10						7
1	2		7	4	6		12	10	9			8*	11	3	5						8
1	2			4	6	7		10	9	11			8	3	5						9
1	2			5	4	10		9	8	11*		12	7	3	6						10
1	2				6	4		10	9	11		8	7	3	5						11
1	2				6	4		9	8	11		10	7	3	5						12
1	2				6	4		10	9	11		8	7	3	5						13
1	2*	3		12	5	6		10	9			8	7		4	11					14
1	2	3			5	6		10	9				7		4	8	11				15
1	2	3			6	4		9	8				7		5	10	11				16
1	2	3			5	6		10	9				7		4	8	11				17
1	2	3			5	6		10	9				7		4	8	11				18
1	2	3			5	6		10	9				7		4	8	11				19
1		3	2		6	4		9*	10				7		5	8	11	12			20
1		3	2		5	6		10	9				7		4	8	11				21
1		3	2		5	4		9	8				7		6	10	11				22
1		3	2		5	6		10	9				7		4	8*	11		12		23
1		3	2		5	4		9	8			10			6	7	11				24
1		3	2		5	6		10	9				7			8	11			4	25
1		3	2		5	6*		10	9				7			8	11	12		4	26
1		3	2		5	6		10	9				7		4	8	11				27
1		3	2		5	6		10	9				7		4	8	11				28
1		3	2		5	6		10	9				7		4	8	11				29
1		3	2		5	6		10	9				7		4	8	11				30
1		3	2		6	4		10	9				7		5	8*	11	12			31
1		3	2		5			10	9			6	7		4		11	8			32
1		3	2		5			10	9			4*	7		6	8	11	12			33
1		3	2		5	4		10	9				7		6	8	11				34
1		3	2		5	6		10	9				7		4	8	11				35
1		3	2		5	6		10	9				7		4	8	11				36
1		3	2		5	6		10	9				7		4	8	11				37
1		3	2		5	6		10	9				7		4	8	11				38
1		3	2		5	6		10	9						4	8	11	7			39
1		3	2		5	4		10	9						6	8	11	7			40
1	12	3	2		5	6		10	9						4	8	11	7*			41
1		3	2		5	4		10	9						6	8	11	7			42
1		3	2		5	6		10	9				7		4	8	11				43
1		3	2		5	6		10	9				7		4	8	11				44
1		3	2		5	6		10	9				7		4	8	11				45
1		3	2		5	6		10	9				7*		4	8	11	12			46
46	19	39	33	10	46	42	6	46	45	10		12	36	7	38	32	32	5		2	
	1		1	1			2		1		2	1						5	1		
					6	5		23	20	1		1	4			8	5	2			

4 own-goals

Furnell	Darke	Burrows P	Hore	Griffiths	Green	Delve	Davey	Rafferty	Mariner	Burrows H	Pearson	Hardcastle	Randell	Provan	Saxton	Johnson	McAuley	Vassallo	Rogers	Sutton	
1		3	2		6	4		8	9				7		5	10*	11		12		1
1		3	2		5	6		10	9				7		4	8*	11		12		2
1		3	2		5	4		9	8			10*			6	7	11		12		3
1		3	2		5	6		10					7		5	8	11	9			4
4		4	4		4	4		4	3			1	3		4	4	4	1			
																			3		
					1			3	1				2					1			

Furnell	Darke	Burrows P	Hore	Griffiths	Green	Delve	Davey	Rafferty	Mariner	Burrows H	Pearson	
1	2	3	4	5	6	7	8	9	10	11		1
1	2	3	4	5	6	7	8	9*	10	11	12	R
2	2	2	2	2	2	2	2	2	2	2		
											1	

1975-76

Manager: Tony Waiters

1	Aug	16	(a)	Nottingham F	L 0-2		13,083
2		23	(h)	Charlton A	W 1-0	Johnson	14,201
3		29	(a)	Southampton	L 0-1		18,000
4	Sep	6	(h)	Sunderland	W 1-0	Rafferty	18,304
5		13	(a)	Orient	L 0-1		5,010
6		20	(h)	York C	D 1-1	Rafferty	12,818
7		24	(a)	Luton T	D 1-1	Johnson	9,226
8		27	(a)	Oldham A	L 2-3	Mariner, Horswill	8,227
9	Oct	4	(h)	Carlisle U	W 2-1	McAuley, Burrows	12,875
10		11	(h)	Bolton W	L 2-3	Johnson 2	14,595
11		18	(a)	West Brom A	L 0-1		11,149
12		21	(h)	Blackburn R	D 2-2	Delve, Rafferty	14,371
13		25	(h)	Oxford U	W 2-1	Mariner 2	12,491
14	Nov	1	(a)	Chelsea	D 2-2	Mariner 2	20,096
15		4	(a)	Notts C	L 0-1		9,234
16		8	(h)	Portsmouth	W 3-1	Johnson, Rafferty 2	13,885
17		15	(a)	Bristol R	D 0-0		14,121
18		22	(h)	West Brom A	W 2-1	Wile (og), Mariner	17,380
19		29	(a)	Hull C	L 0-4		5,098
20	Dec	6	(h)	Blackpool	L 1-2	Mariner	12,422
21		12	(a)	Charlton A	L 0-2		7,095
22		20	(h)	Nottingham F	W 1-0	Mariner	10,545
23		26	(a)	Bristol C	D 2-2	Mariner 2	21,471
24		27	(h)	Fulham	W 4-0	Randell, Rafferty 2, Johnson	24,054
25	Jan	10	(h)	Orient	W 3-0	Randell, Rafferty, Mariner	11,934
26		17	(a)	Sunderland	L 1-2	Mariner	29,737
27		24	(h)	Bristol C	D 0-0		17,887
28		31	(a)	Blackburn R	L 1-3	Foster	8,525
29	Feb	7	(h)	Notts C	L 1-3	Rafferty	11,576
30		14	(a)	Portsmouth	L 0-2		9,509
31		21	(h)	Bristol R	W 3-0	Johnson, Rafferty, Mariner	11,183
32		24	(h)	Luton T	W 3-0	Rafferty 2, Randell	13,927
33		28	(a)	Oxford U	D 2-2	Mariner, McAuley	5,778
34	Mar	6	(h)	Chelsea	L 0-3		20,638
35		13	(a)	Bolton W	D 0-0		21,147
36		20	(h)	Hull C	D 1-1	Johnson	10,631
37		27	(a)	Blackpool	D 0-0		5,497
38	Apr	3	(h)	Oldham A	W 2-1	Randell, Burrows	9,782
39		10	(a)	York C	L 1-3	Mariner	3,646
40		16	(h)	Southampton	W 1-0	Darke	25,305
41		19	(a)	Fulham	D 0-0		6,913
42		24	(a)	Carlisle U	L 0-2		7,038

FINAL LEAGUE POSITION: 16th in Division Two

Appearances
Sub Appearances
Goals

FA Cup

3	Jan	3	(a)	Hull C	D 1-1	Rafferty	6,515
R		6	(h)	Hull C	L 1-4	Green	20,208

Appearances
Sub Appearances
Goals

FL Cup

1	Aug	19	(h)	Bournemouth	W 2-0	Rafferty, Hague (og)	10,849
		26	(a)	Bournemouth	W 2-1	Burrows, Mariner	3,203
2	Sep	10	(a)	Nottingham F	L 0-1		8,978

Appearances
Sub Appearances
Goals

Aleksic	Hore	Burrows	Horswill	Green	Delve	Randell	Johnson	Rafferty	Pearson	McAuley	Saxton	Mariner	Foster	Vassallo	Darke	Rioch	Sutton	Furnell	Harrison	Hardcastle	
1	2	3	4	5	6	7*	8	9	10	11	12										1
1	2	3	7	5	6	4	10	9	12	11*		8									2
1	2	3	7	5	6	4			9*	11	12	8	10								3
1	2	3	7	5	6	4	8*	10		11		9		12							4
1	2	3	7	5	4		8	10		11	6	9									5
1	2	3	4	5	6		8	10		11			9	7							6
1	2	3	4	5	6	7	8	10		11		9*	12								7
1	2	3	4	5	6*	7	8	10		11		9	12								8
1	2	3	4	5	6	7	8	10		11		9									9
1	2	3	4*	5	6	7	8	10	12	11		9									10
1	2	3	4	5	6	7	8	10		11		9									11
1	2	3	4	5	6	7	8	10		11		9									12
1		3	4	5	6*	7	8	10		11		9	12		2						13
1		3		5	6	7	8	10		11		9			2	4					14
1		3		6	4	7	8	10		11*		9	12		2	5					15
1		3		6	4		8	10	11			9	7		2	5					16
1		3	4	5	6	7	8*	10	11			9			2	12					17
1		3	4	5	6	7	8	10		11		9			2						18
1		3	4	5	6	7	8	10		11		9			2*	12					19
1		3	4	5	6	7*	8	10		11		9		12	2						20
1		3	4		6	7	8*	10		11		9	12		2		5				21
1		3	4		6	7	8	10		11		9			2		5				22
1		3		5	6	7	8	10		11		9			2		4				23
1		3		5	6	7	8	10		11		9			2		4				24
1		3		5	6	7	8	10		11		9			2		4				25
1		3	12	5	6	7	8	10		11		9*			2		4				26
1		3	8	5	6	7*	12	10		11		9			2		4				27
1		3	7	5	6		8			11		9	10		2		4				28
1		3	8	5	6*	7		12		11		9	10		2		4				29
		3	2	5	6	7		10		11		9	8				4	1			30
		3	2	5	6	7	8	10		11		9					4	1			31
		3	2	5	6	7	8	10*		11		9	12				4	1			32
		3	6	5			8	10		11		9	7		2		4	1			33
		3	6	5			8	10	9*	11			7		2		4	1		12	34
		3	6	5		7	8	10*	9	11			12		2		4	1			35
		3	6	5		7	8	10*	12	11		9			2		4	1			36
		3		5	4	7	8	10	12	11*		9			2		6	1			37
		3		5	6	7	8	10		11		9			2		4	1			38
		3		5	6	7	8	10		11		9			2		4	1			39
		3	8	5	6	7		10		11		9			2		4	1			40
		3	8	5	6	7	12	10*		11		9			2		4	1			41
		3	8	5	6	7				11		9	10				4	1	2		42
29	12	42	32	40	38	36	35	38	6	40	1	38	9	1	26	3	22	13	1		
			1				2	1	4		2		7	2		2				1	
		2	1		1	4	8	12		2		15	1		1						

1 own-goal

1		3		5	6	7	8	10		11		9			2		4				3
1		3		5	6	7	8	10		11		9			2		4				R
2		2		2	2	2	2	2		2		2			2		2				
				1				1													

1	2	3	7	5	6	4		10	9	11			8								1
1	2	3	7*	5	6	4		10	9	11	12	8									
1	2	3	4	5	6	7	8*	10		11		9		12							2
3	3	3	3	3	3	3	1	3	2	3		2	1								
											1			1							
		1						1				1									

1 own-goal

1976-77

Manager: Tony Waiters/Mike Kelly

1	Aug	21	(a)	Oldham A	D	2-2	Mariner, Johnson	7,378
2		24	(h)	Blackburn R	W	4-0	Johnson, Collins, Hall, Mariner	13,553
3		28	(h)	Notts C	L	1-2	Mariner	14,539
4	Sep	4	(a)	Orient	D	2-2	Green, Mariner	4,808
5		11	(h)	Chelsea	L	2-3	Hall, Mariner	18,356
6		18	(a)	Millwall	L	0-3		9,883
7		25	(h)	Bolton W	D	1-1	Mariner	12,564
8	Oct	2	(h)	Luton T	W	1-0	Johnson	12,187
9		9	(a)	Blackpool	W	2-0	Collins, Horswill	12,647
10		16	(h)	Cardiff C	D	2-2	Mariner, Hall	14,198
11		23	(a)	Bristol R	D	1-1	Hall	10,258
12		30	(h)	Burnley	L	0-1		14,704
13	Nov	5	(a)	Charlton A	L	1-3	Hall	13,617
14		13	(h)	Fulham	D	2-2	Austin, Johnson	25,335
15		20	(a)	Hull C	L	1-3	Harrison	8,161
16		27	(h)	Carlisle U	L	0-1		10,204
17	Dec	4	(a)	Wolves	L	0-4		16,370
18		11	(h)	Sheffield U	D	0-0		8,827
19		18	(a)	Nottingham F	D	1-1	Austin	15,180
20		27	(h)	Southampton	D	1-1	Bannister	24,787
21	Jan	1	(h)	Charlton A	W	1-0	Austin	13,445
22		3	(a)	Burnley	W	2-0	Green, Austin	10,399
23		22	(h)	Oldham A	D	2-2	Austin, Craven	9,200
24	Feb	5	(a)	Notts C	L	0-2		9,079
25		9	(a)	Hereford U	D	1-1	Hall	5,002
26		12	(h)	Orient	L	1-2	Rogers	9,551
27		19	(a)	Chelsea	D	2-2	Austin, Bannister	22,154
28		26	(h)	Millwall	D	2-2	Hall 2	10,437
29	Mar	2	(a)	Blackburn R	L	0-2		7,755
30		5	(a)	Bolton W	L	0-3		18,496
31		12	(a)	Luton T	D	1-1	Foster	12,793
32		19	(h)	Blackpool	W	2-0	Foster, Bannister	8,893
33		26	(a)	Cardiff C	W	1-0	Austin	9,587
34	Apr	2	(h)	Bristol R	D	1-1	Peddelty	10,307
35		8	(a)	Southampton	L	1-4	Bannister	20,914
36		9	(h)	Hereford U	W	2-1	Bannister 2	9,787
37		11	(a)	Fulham	L	0-2		11,710
38		16	(h)	Hull C	L	1-2	Hall	8,694
39		23	(a)	Carlisle U	L	1-3	Hall	7,751
40		30	(h)	Wolves	D	0-0		16,795
41	May	2	(h)	Nottingham F	L	1-2	Bannister	13,542
42		7	(a)	Sheffield U	L	0-1		12,227

FINAL LEAGUE POSITION: 21st in Division Two

Appearances
Sub Appearances
Goals

FA Cup

3	Jan	8	(a)	Oldham A	L	0-3	9,889

Appearances
Sub Appearances
Goals

FL Cup

1	Aug	14	(h)	Exeter C	L	0-1	8,688
		17	(a)	Exeter C	L	0-1	8,859

Appearances
Sub Appearances
Goals

Ramsbottom	Darke	Horswill	Harrison	Sutton	Green	Hall	Johnson	Mariner	Collins	McAuley	Delve	Rogers	Randell	Hamilton	Foster	Barron	Trusson	Peddelty	Austin	Bannister	Craven	Banton	Smart	
1	2	3	4	5	6	7	8	9	10	11														1
1	2*	3	4	5	6	8	7	9	10	11	12													2
1	2*	3	4	5	6	7	8	9	10	11		12												3
1	2*	3	4	6	5	7	8	9	10	11	12													4
1		3	4*	5	6	10	8	9			7	11	2	12										5
1		3	4*	5	6	8	10	9			7	11	2		12									6
1		3	8	5	6	7	10*	9	11		4	12	2											7
1		3	8	5	6	11	7	9	10		4		2											8
1		3	11	5	6	7	8	9*	10		4		2	12										9
		3	8	5	6	7		9	10		4		2	11		1								10
1		3	10	5	6	7	12		11		4*		2	8			9							11
1		3	8	5		7	12		10		4		2	11*				6	9					12
1		3	10	5		7			11		4		2	9				6	8					13
		3	10	5		7	11		4				2	8		1		6	9					14
		3	10	5		7	4		11		12		2	8*		1		6	9					15
1		3	8	5		7	4		11	12			2		10			6*	9					16
1		3	8	5	6	7			11		4		2		10				9					17
1		3		5	6	7			10		4		2				11	8	9					18
1		3		5	6	7			11		4		2					8	9	10				19
1		3		5	8	7			11		4		2					6	9	10				20
1		3		5	6	7			11		8		2					4	9	10				21
1		3	8	5	6	7			11		4		2						9	10				22
1		3	8		6	7						11	2					5	9	10	4			23
1		3	8		6	7						11	2					5	9	10	4			24
1		3			6	7					8	11	2					5	9	10	4			25
1		3				7			8*		4	11	2					6	9	10	5	12		26
1	3	3			5	7					4	11	2					6	9	10	8			27
1	3			5		7					8	11	2					6	9	10	4			28
1	3			4		6			12		7	11*	2					5	9	10	8			29
1	3		8*	5	6	7			11		4	12						2	9	10				30
1	3	6		5								11	7		8			4	9	10			2	31
1	3	4		5								11	7		8			6	9	10			2	32
1	2	4		5								11	7		8			6	9	10			3	33
1	3	4		5								11	7		8			6	9	10			2	34
1	3			5							11*	12	8		7			6	9	10	4		2	35
1	3			5		7					12	11	2		8		9*	6		10	4			36
1	2	3		5		7					11				8			6	9	10	4			37
1	2	3		5		7	12				11				8		9	6		10	4*			38
1		3		5*		7					11		12		8			6	9	10	4		2	39
1		3				7					4		11		8			6	9	10	5		2	40
1		3				7					11		6		8			5	9	10	4		2	41
1		3				12					8	11	6*		7			5	9	10	4		2	42
39	15	37	21	34	22	36	12	10	22	4	28	15	34	6	14	3	4	29	29	24	15		9	
						1	3		1	1	4	4	1	2	1							1		
		1	1		2	10	4	7	2			1			2			1	7	7	1			

1		3	8	5	6	7	11				2							4	9	10				3
1		1	1	1	1	1	1				1							1	1	1				

	2*	3	8	5	6	7	12	9	10	11			4			1								1
1	2	3		5	6	7	8	9	10	11			4											
1	2	2	1	2	2	2	1	2	2	2			2			1								
							1																	

1977-78

Manager: Mike Kelly/Malcolm Allison

1	Aug	20	(h)	Preston NE	D 0-0		7,154
2		27	(a)	Carlisle U	D 0-0		4,853
3	Sep	3	(h)	Hereford U	W 2-0	Trusson, Rogers	5,732
4		9	(a)	Colchester U	L 1-3	Hall	5,719
5		13	(h)	Walsall	D 3-3	Hall, Austin 2	5,958
6		17	(h)	Cambridge U	L 0-1		6,022
7		24	(a)	Bradford C	W 1-0	Hall	4,031
8		27	(a)	Sheffield W	D 1-1	Austin	8,515
9	Oct	1	(h)	Gillingham	L 1-3	Hall	12,399
10		4	(h)	Shrewsbury T	D 2-2	Hall, Austin	4,661
11		8	(a)	Chester	D 1-1	Rogers	3,367
12		11	(a)	Rotherham U	W 2-1	Hall, Binney	6,286
13		15	(h)	Tranmere R	L 0-1		6,156
14		22	(a)	Oxford U	L 1-2	Austin	5,727
15		29	(h)	Portsmouth	W 3-1	Austin, Taylor, Johnson	6,594
16	Nov	5	(a)	Wrexham	L 0-2		8,548
17		12	(h)	Chesterfield	W 2-0	Austin, Johnson	5,572
18		19	(a)	Peterborough U	L 0-1		6,528
19	Dec	3	(h)	Bury	L 0-1		4,766
20		9	(a)	Port Vale	D 3-3	Austin 2, Horswill	3,650
21		26	(h)	Exeter C	D 2-2	Johnson, Craven	12,349
22		27	(a)	Swindon T	L 1-3	Binney	9,732
23		31	(h)	Wrexham	L 0-1		7,415
24	Jan	2	(a)	Lincoln C	D 2-2	Austin, Neale (og)	6,262
25		14	(a)	Preston NE	L 2-5	Foster, Johnson	6,500
26		21	(h)	Carlisle U	L 0-1		4,744
27		28	(a)	Hereford U	W 3-1	Austin, Craven, Megson	4,737
28	Feb	4	(h)	Colchester U	D 1-1	Taylor	4,639
29		11	(a)	Cambridge U	L 0-3		4,745
30		25	(a)	Gillingham	D 1-1	Megson	9,120
31	Mar	4	(h)	Chester	D 2-2	Fear, Uzzell	5,322
32		7	(a)	Walsall	L 0-1		6,722
33		10	(a)	Tranmere R	D 1-1	Perrin	3,712
34		13	(h)	Lincoln C	L 1-2	Perrin	5,208
35		18	(h)	Oxford U	W 2-1	Fear, Johnson	5,726
36		21	(a)	Portsmouth	W 5-1	Trusson, Binney 2, Taylor, Fear	11,010
37		25	(h)	Swindon T	L 0-2		9,174
38		28	(a)	Exeter C	D 0-0		8,334
39	Apr	4	(h)	Sheffield W	D 1-1	Fear	7,694
40		8	(a)	Chesterfield	L 1-4	Binney	3,996
41		11	(h)	Rotherham U	D 1-1	Foster	5,018
42		15	(h)	Peterborough U	W 1-0	Binney	5,678
43		22	(a)	Bury	D 1-1	Binney	3,177
44		25	(a)	Shrewsbury T	L 1-3	Fear	2,308
45		29	(h)	Port Vale	W 3-2	Johnson, Binney 2	9,474
46	May	1	(h)	Bradford C	W 6-0	Harrison, Taylor 2, Perrin, Foster, Fear	7,862

FINAL LEAGUE POSITION: 19th in Division Three

Appearances
Sub Appearances
Goals

FA Cup

1	Nov	26	(a)	Bath C	D 0-0		7,866
R		29	(h)	Bath C	W 2-0	Taylor 2	5,455
2	Dec	17	(h)	Cambridge U	W 1-0	Johnson	5,850
3	Jan	7	(a)	Mansfield T	L 0-1		7,402

Appearances
Sub Appearances
Goals

FL Cup

1	Aug	13	(a)	Exeter C	D 2-2	Trusson 2	6,712
		16	(h)	Exeter C	D 0-0		7,639
R		23	(h)	Exeter C	L 0-1		8,776

Appearances
Sub Appearances
Goals

Barron	Smart	Uzzell	Horswill	Foster	Craven	Johnson	Delve	Austin	Trusson	Rogers	Hall	Peddelty	Harrison	Bason	Binney	Taylor	Megson	Graves	Banton	Sutton	Fear	Perrin	James	Hodge	
1	2	3	4	5	6	7	8	9	10	11															1
1	2	3	4	5	6	8	7		9	11	10														2
1	2	3	4	5	6	8	7	9*	10	11	12														3
1	2	3	4	5	6	7*	8	9	10		11	12													4
1	2	3	4	5	6		8	9	10	11	7														5
1	2	3	4	5	6		8	9	10*	11	7	12													6
1	2	3		5	4*	10	6	9		11	7	12	8												7
1	2	3	10	5			8	9	12	11	7	6*		4											8
1	2	3		5	6		8	9	10	11	7			4											9
1	2	3	12	5	6		8	9		11*	7			4	10										10
1	2	3		5	6	12	4	9	10	11	8			7*											11
1	2	3		5	6		8	9		11*	7		12	4	10										12
1	2	3		5	6		8	9		11	7			4	10										13
1	2	3		5	6			9		11*	7		12	4	10	8									14
1	2	3		5	6	11		9			8		10			7	4								15
1	2	3		5	4	8		9		11			10			6	7								16
1	2	3	4	5		8		9		11			10			7	6								17
1	2	3		5	6	7		9		11			10			4	8								18
1	2	3	12	5	6			9		11			10			4	7	8*							19
1	2	3	10	5	6	7		9		11			4				8								20
1	2	3	10	5	6	7		9		11			8*			12	4								21
1	2	3	10	5	6	7				11			4		9		8								22
1	2*	3	4	5	6	7	12			11			10		9		8								23
1		3	10	5	6	7	4	9					2		11		8								24
1		3		5	6	10	7	9		11			2	4			8								25
1		3		5	10		7	9		11*			2	4			8		6	12					26
1		3		5	10		6	9					2	7		8	11		4						27
1		3	12	6	10		11	9					2	4*		7	8		5						28
1		3	2	6	10		11	9						4		8	7		5						29
1		3		5	4			9					2	7		10	11		6		8				30
1		3	4	5	6			9					2	7		8	11				10				31
1		3	10	5	6			9					2			4	8		7		11				32
1		3	10	5									2	4		8	11				7	9	6		33
1		3	10	5		12							2	4*		8	7				11	9	6		34
1		3		5		7			12				2	4		8	11				10*	9	6		35
1		3	6	5					12					4	9	8	11				7	10*	2		36
1		3	6	5		7			10						9	8	4				11		2		37
1		3	2	5					11	12				4	9	8*	7				10		6		38
1		3	6	5					11	7			2	4*	9	8					10		12		39
1		3	6	5						7			2		9	8					10	11	4		40
1		3	6	5						11			7		9	2					8	10	4		41
		3	6	5						11			8		9	2					7	10	4	1	42
		3	6	5		7			11				4		9	2					8	10		1	43
		2*	6	5						7			8	12	9	4					11	10	3	1	44
			6	5		7							8	2	9	4					11	10	3	1	45
			6	5		7							2	3	9	8					10	11	4	1	46
41	23	44	29	46	30	20	19	29	12	28	13	1	29	22	18	26	24	1	6		17	11	12	5	
			3			2	1		3	1	1	3	2	1		1				1			1		
		1	1	3	2	6		11	2	2	6		1		9	5	2				6	3			

1 own-goal

1	2	3	12	5	6			9	10*	11			8			4	7	1
1	2	3	12	5	6	7*		9		11			10			4	8	R
1	2	3	4	5	6	7		9		11			10				8	2
1		3	4	5	6	7	11	9		12			2		10*		8	3
4	3	4	2	4	3	3	1	4	1	3			4		1	2	4	
			2							1								
						1										2		

1	2	3	4	5	6	8	7	9	10	11		1
1	2	3	4	5	6	7	8	9	10	11		
1	2	3	4	5	6	7	8	9*	10	11	12	R
3	3	3	3	3	3	3	3	3	3	3		
											1	
									2			

1978-79

Manager: Malcolm Allison/Bobby Saxton

1	Aug	19	(a)	Chesterfield	W 3-1	Fear, Binney, Megson	3,895
2		26	(h)	Lincoln C	W 2-1	Megson, Perrin	7,806
3	Sep	1	(a)	Southend U	L 1-2	Megson	5,936
4		9	(h)	Mansfield T	L 1-4	Binney	6,052
5		12	(a)	Bury	W 2-1	Perrin, Binney	3,361
6		16	(h)	Swindon T	W 2-0	Bason, Binney	6,069
7		23	(a)	Sheffield W	W 3-2	Binney 3	12,088
8		25	(a)	Tranmere R	L 1-2	Johnson	1,907
9		30	(h)	Rotherham U	W 2-0	Binney 2	6,705
10	Oct	7	(a)	Carlisle U	D 1-1	Perrin	5,731
11		14	(h)	Shrewsbury T	D 1-1	Bason	9,901
12		18	(a)	Chester	D 0-0		3,921
13		21	(a)	Walsall	L 1-2	Binney	5,552
14		28	(h)	Blackpool	D 0-0		8,886
15	Nov	3	(a)	Colchester U	L 1-2	Binney	4,564
16		11	(h)	Southend U	D 1-1	Silkman	6,890
17		14	(h)	Peterborough U	W 3-2	Binney, Rogers, Green (og)	7,398
18		18	(a)	Lincoln C	D 3-3	Fear, Binney, Clarke	3,670
19	Dec	9	(h)	Watford	D 1-1	Silkman	11,907
20		16	(h)	Chesterfield	D 1-1	Megson	6,740
21		26	(a)	Brentford	L 1-2	Binney	7,360
22		30	(a)	Gillingham	L 0-2		5,951
23	Jan	20	(a)	Swindon T	W 3-1	Trusson, Binney 2	7,780
24		27	(h)	Sheffield W	W 2-0	Binney 2	8,596
25	Feb	3	(h)	Tranmere R	D 2-2	Trusson 2	7,418
26		10	(a)	Rotherham U	L 0-1		5,237
27		17	(h)	Carlisle U	W 2-0	Binney 2	6,294
28		20	(h)	Oxford U	L 0-1		7,094
29		24	(a)	Shrewsbury T	L 0-2		6,087
30		27	(h)	Exeter C	W 4-2	Binney, Bason, Johnson, Fear	12,637
31	Mar	3	(h)	Walsall	W 1-0	Megson	6,487
32		10	(a)	Blackpool	D 0-0		4,879
33		12	(a)	Mansfield T	L 0-5		4,325
34		17	(h)	Colchester U	D 1-1	Binney	5,342
35		24	(a)	Peterborough U	L 1-2	Johnson	4,039
36		31	(a)	Swansea C	L 1-2	Megson	11,412
37	Apr	3	(h)	Bury	W 3-0	Tucker (og), Harrison, Clarke	4,728
38		7	(h)	Hull C	L 3-4	Trusson, Binney, Clarke	5,816
39		11	(a)	Oxford U	L 2-3	Johnson 2	3,299
40		14	(h)	Brentford	W 2-1	Binney, Johnson	6,344
41		17	(a)	Exeter C	L 0-1		8,022
42		21	(h)	Gillingham	W 2-1	Johnson 2	5,868
43		24	(h)	Chester	D 2-2	Johnson, Megson	4,686
44		28	(a)	Watford	D 2-2	Trusson, Megson	14,816
45	May	1	(a)	Hull C	L 1-2	Binney	3,646
46		5	(h)	Swansea C	D 2-2	Binney, Bason	13,406

FINAL LEAGUE POSITION: 15th in Division Three

Appearances
Sub Appearances
Goals

FA Cup

1	Nov	25	(a)	Worcester C	L 0-2		8,253

Appearances
Sub Appearances
Goals

FL Cup

1	Aug	12	(h)	Torquay U	D 1-1	Parsons (og)	7,725
		16	(a)	Torquay U	W 2-1	Binney 2	6,999
2		30	(a)	Oxford U	D 1-1	Fear	4,255
R	Sep	5	(h)	Oxford U	L 1-2*	Fear	8,524

*After extra-time

Appearances
Sub Appearances
Goals

Burns	Bason	Rogers	Trusson	Foster	Perrin	Fear	Megson	Binney	Taylor	Johnson	Levy	Graves	Harrison	Brennan	Hodge	Hodges	Uzzell	Clarke	Silkman	Upton	McNeill	Chapman	Forde	James	
1	2	3	4	5	6	7	8	9	10	11															1
1	2	3	4	5	6	10	8	9	7*	11	12														2
1	2	3	4	5	6	7	10			11		8*	12	9											3
1	2	3	10	5	6	8	7	9		11		12		4*											4
		3	10	5	6		7	9	8	11				4	1	2									5
	2	3	6	5	10	12	7	9	8	11				4*	1			6							6
	2	3		5	10	8	7	9	4*	11					1		12	6							7
	2	3		5	10	8	7	9	4	11					1			6							8
	2*	3	12	5	10	8	7	9	4	11					1			6							9
	2	3*		5	10	8	7	9	4	11		12			1			6							10
	2	3		5	10	8	4	9		11					1			6	7						11
		3	2	5	10	8		9		11				7	1			6	4						12
	2	3		4	10	8		9		11				6	1			5	7						13
		3	5	2	10	8	4*	9		11			12		1			6	7						14
		3	12	5	10	7*	8	9		11					1	2		6	4						15
	2	3		5	10*	8	4	9		11		12			1			6	7						16
	2	3		5		8	7	9				10			1			6	4	11					17
1	2	3		5	10	8*	7	9				11						6	4	12					18
	2			5	10	11	7								1			6	4		3	8	9		19
1	2			5	10*	8	7	9										6	4		3	11	12		20
1	2			5		7	8	9										6	4		3	10	11		21
1	2*			5		7	8	9				10				4		6	11		3	12			22
	4	11	10	5			8	9							1		2	6	7		3				23
	4	11	10	5			8	9							1		2	6	7		3				24
	4	11	8	5		10	7	9							1		2	6			3				25
	4	11	10	5			7	9					8		1		2	6			3				26
	6	11	10*	5			8	9				12	7		1		2	4			3				27
	6	11		5*	10		7	9				12	8		1		2	4			3				28
	8	11			9					10		7*	4		1	12	2	5			3			6	29
	7	11				12	8	9*		10			4		1		2	6			3			5	30
	4	11				7	8	9		10			2		1			6			3			5	31
	7	11	10				8	9		6			4		1			2			3			5	32
	6	11	10				8	9		7			2		1			4			3			5	33
		11	10			12	7	9		6			8*		1		3	5			2			4	34
	6	11					8	9		7			10		1		2	5			3			4	35
		11	12			8	10	9		7			3		1		4*	6			2			5	36
		11	10				8	9		7			6		1		3	4			2			5	37
		11	10			12	7	9		8			4		1		3*	6			2			5	38
		11	10				8	9		7			6		1	3		4			2			5	39
	4	11	10				7	9		8			6		1	3	5				2				40
	4		10		11	12		9		7			6		1	3	2			8*				5	41
	4	11					7	9		10			8		1	3	6	5			2				42
	6	11					8	9		7			10		1	3	5	4			2				43
	6		9				8	12				7*	11		1	4	5				2		10	3	44
			6				8	9		7			10		1	3	5				2		11	4	45
	6		10				7	9		11			8		1	3	5				2			4	46
8	36	38	24	28	23	22	42	42	8	33		5	22	6	38	11	20	35	14	2	27	3	4	15	
			3			5		1			1	5	2			1	1			1		1	1		
	4	1	5		3	3	8	26		9			1					3	2						

2 own-goals

Burns	Bason	Rogers	Trusson	Foster	Perrin	Fear	Megson	Binney	Taylor	Johnson	Levy	Graves	Harrison	Brennan	Hodge	Hodges	Uzzell	Clarke	Silkman	Upton	McNeill	Chapman	Forde	James	
	2	3	12	5	10	8	7	9						11*	1			6	4						1
	1	1		1	1	1	1	1						1	1			1	1						
			1																						

Burns	Bason	Rogers	Trusson	Foster	Perrin	Fear	Megson	Binney	Taylor	Johnson	Levy	Graves	Harrison	Brennan	Hodge	Hodges	Uzzell	Clarke	Silkman	Upton	McNeill	Chapman	Forde	James	
	2	3	4	5	10	11	6	9	8	7					1										1
1	2	3	4	5	6	7	8	9	10	11															
1	2	3	10	5	6	8	7			11			9	4											2
1	2	3	10	5	6	8	7	9		11		4													R
3	4	4	4	4	4	4	4	3	2	4		1	1	1	1										
						2		2																	

1 own-goal

1979-80

Manager: Bobby Saxton

1	Aug	18	(h)	Bury	W 2-0	Binney 2	5,547
2		21	(a)	Millwall	L 1-2	Hodges	5,153
3		25	(a)	Chesterfield	L 1-3	Graves	5,510
4	Sep	1	(h)	Sheffield W	L 1-3	Hodges	6,208
5		8	(a)	Grimsby T	L 0-1		7,326
6		15	(h)	Wimbledon	W 3-0	Kemp 2, Trusson	5,744
7		18	(h)	Oxford U	D 1-1	Kemp	5,635
8		21	(a)	Southend U	L 1-4	Kemp	4,699
9		29	(h)	Blackpool	D 2-2	Binney 2	5,693
10	Oct	6	(a)	Chester	L 0-1		2,818
11		9	(h)	Millwall	D 1-1	Kemp	5,353
12		13	(a)	Blackburn R	L 0-1		6,026
13		20	(h)	Rotherham U	W 1-0	Kemp	4,850
14		23	(a)	Swindon T	L 1-2	Kemp	6,514
15		27	(h)	Brentford	L 0-1		5,206
16		31	(a)	Oxford U	D 1-1	Trusson	3,824
17	Nov	3	(a)	Bury	L 1-2	Trusson	2,641
18		6	(h)	Swindon T	W 2-0	Trusson, Sims	4,157
19		10	(a)	Carlisle U	W 4-2	Johnson, Randell, Kemp, McDonald (og)	5,216
20		16	(a)	Colchester U	L 2-5	Kemp, Cook (og)	3,520
21	Dec	1	(a)	Sheffield U	L 2-3	Hodges, Randell	14,101
22		8	(h)	Barnsley	W 2-1	Sims, Hodges	5,311
23		21	(a)	Mansfield T	D 0-0		3,000
24		26	(h)	Reading	W 2-0	Randell, Kearney (og)	6,484
25		29	(h)	Chesterfield	W 1-0	Ridley (og)	6,425
26	Jan	1	(a)	Exeter C	D 2-2	Randell 2	10,489
27		5	(h)	Hull C	W 5-1	Cook 2, Sims 2, Harrison	6,341
28		12	(a)	Sheffield W	W 1-0	Cook	13,287
29		19	(h)	Grimsby T	D 1-1	Cook	6,310
30		26	(h)	Gillingham	D 2-2	Bason, Cook	6,413
31	Feb	16	(a)	Blackpool	W 3-1	Hodges, Graves, Kemp	3,302
32		19	(a)	Wimbledon	L 1-3	Kemp	3,488
33		23	(h)	Blackburn R	L 0-1		6,918
34	Mar	1	(a)	Rotherham U	L 1-3	Kemp	3,840
35		8	(a)	Brentford	D 0-0		6,460
36		15	(h)	Chester	W 1-0	Bason	4,095
37		22	(a)	Carlisle U	L 1-2	Trusson	3,611
38		29	(h)	Colchester U	W 2-0	Trusson 2	4,330
39	Apr	1	(h)	Mansfield T	D 0-0		4,669
40		5	(a)	Reading	L 0-1		7,466
41		7	(h)	Exeter C	W 2-0	Sims, Kemp	10,214
42		12	(a)	Hull C	L 0-1		5,369
43		19	(h)	Sheffield U	W 4-1	Trusson, Sims, Kemp 2	6,322
44		22	(h)	Southend U	D 0-0		5,392
45		26	(a)	Barnsley	D 0-0		10,321
46	May	3	(a)	Gillingham	W 1-0	Sims	4,020

FINAL LEAGUE POSITION: 15th in Division Three

Appearances
Sub Appearances
Goals

FA Cup

1	Nov	24	(a)	Colchester U	D 1-1	Hodges	4,064
R		27	(h)	Colchester U	L 0-1*		6,926

*After extra-time

Appearances
Sub Appearances
Goals

FL Cup

1	Aug	1	(a)	Newport C	L 0-1		4,574
		14	(h)	Newport C	W 2-0	Binney, Bason	4,505
2		28	(h)	Chelsea	D 2-2	Trusson 2	10,802
	Sep	4	(a)	Chelsea	W 2-1	Harrison, Johnson	14,112
3		25	(h)	Wimbledon	D 0-0		6,090
R	Oct	2	(h)	Wimbledon	L 0-1		5,200

Appearances
Sub Appearance
Goals

Hards	James	Harrison	Randell	Phillipson-Masters	Foster	Bason	Megson	Binney	Hodges	Johnson	Perrin	Graves	Trusson	Uzzell	Ball	Brown	Kemp	McNeill	Crudgington	Fear	Sims	Cooper	Cook	Forde	
1	2	3	4	5	6	7	8	9	10	11*	12														1
1		3	10	4	5	6	7	9	2	11		8													2
1		3	7	5	6	4	8		2	11		9	10												3
1		3	10		5	6	7		2	11		8	9	4*	12										4
	2	3	10	5	6	12	7		4	11		8*	9			1									5
		3	10	4	5	6	7		2	11			9			1	8								6
		3	10*	4	5	6	7	12	2	11			9			1	8								7
		3		4	5	6*	7	12	10	11			9			1	8	2							8
	5	10	7		6	4		9	2	11							8	3							9
	4		10		5	6	7	9	2	11							8	3	1						10
	4	11			5	6	7	9	2								8	3	1	10					11
	4		10		5	6	7	9	2	11							8	3	1						12
	4	10	7		5	6			2	11			9				8	3	1						13
	4	10	7		5	6		12	2	11*			9				8	3	1						14
		11	10	5	6	4	7	9	2								8	3	1						15
	2	11*	4	6	5	10			7				12				8	3	1		9				16
	2	11	10	6*	5	4			7				12				9	3	1		8				17
			4	6	5	10			2	11			7				8	3	1		9				18
	12		4	6	5	10			2	11*			7				8	3	1		9				19
	12	11	4	6	5	10			2				7				8*	3	1		9				20
	2	3	4	6	5	10			7			11							1		9	8			21
	2	3	4	6	5	10			7			11							1		9	8			22
	2	3	4	6	5	10			7			11*							1		9	8	12		23
	2	3	4	6	5	10			7			11*							1		9	8	12		24
	2	3	4	6	5	10			7			11							1		9	8			25
	2	3	4	6	5	10			7			11*							1		9	8	12		26
	2	3	4	6	5	11			7										1		9	8	10		27
	2	3	4	6	5	10			7										1		9	8	11		28
	2	3	4	6	5	10			7										1		9	8	11		29
	2	3		6	5	10			7				4						1		9	8	11		30
	2	3		6	5	10			7			11*	4				12		1		9	8			31
	2	3	4	6	5	10			7								11		1		9	8			32
	2	3	4	6	5	10			7								11		1		9	8			33
		7	4	6	5	8			2	12							10	3*	1		9	11			34
	2		4	6	5	10				11		7*	8				12	3	1		9				35
	6	3	4		5	10			2	11		8	7						1		9				36
	2	3	4	6	5	10			12	11		8*	7						1		9				37
	2	3	4	6	5	10*			12	11			7				8		1		9				38
	2	3	4	6	5	10				11			7				8		1		9				39
	2	3	4	6	5	10			12	11*			7				10		1		9				40
	2	3	4	6	5	10			11				7				8		1		9				41
	2	3	4	6	5				11				7				8		1		9				42
	2	3	4	6	5				10	11			7				8		1		9				43
	2	3	4	6	5				10	11			7				8		1		9				44
	2	3	4	6	5				10	11			7				8		1		9				45
	2	3	4	6	5				10	11			7				8		1		9				46
4	35	41	42	38	46	40	12	7	41	25		14	25	1		5	27	15	37	1	31	14	4		
	2					1		3	3	1	1		2		1		2						3		
		1	5			2		4	5	1		2	8				15				7		5		

4 own-goals

	2		4	6	5	10			7			11						3	1		9	8			1
	2	12	4	6	5	10			7			11						3	1		9	8*			R
	2		2	2	2	2			2			2						2	2		2	2			
		1																							
									1																

1	2	3	7	5	6	4	8	9	12	11			10*												1
1	2	3	10	4	5	6	7	9	8	11															
1		3	10	4	5	6	7		2	11		8	9												2
	2	3	10	5	4		7		6	11		8	9			1									
	4	11	10		5	6	7*	9	2	12			8			1		3							3
	4	7	10		5	6		9	2	11*			8			1		3						12	R
3	5	6	6	4	6	5	5	4	5	5		2	5			3		2							
									1	1														1	
		1				1		1		1			2												

1980-81

Manager: Bobby Saxton

1	Aug	16	(a)	Colchester U	D 2-2	Kemp, Murphy	2,061
2		19	(h)	Chester	W 2-0	Kemp, Bason	4,823
3		23	(h)	Charlton A	D 1-1	Murphy	6,023
4		30	(a)	Oxford U	D 0-0		3,398
5	Sep	6	(h)	Carlisle U	W 4-1	Kemp 3, Murphy	4,854
6		13	(a)	Chesterfield	D 2-2	Graves, Kemp	5,561
7		17	(a)	Reading	D 1-1	Murphy	5,859
8		20	(h)	Gillingham	W 4-1	Kemp 2, Hodges, Bason	6,719
9		27	(a)	Newport C	W 2-0	Sims, Kemp	6,878
10		30	(a)	Reading	W 2-1	Bason, Kemp	11,480
11	Oct	4	(a)	Sheffield U	D 0-0		12,401
12		7	(h)	Fulham	W 2-1	Sims, Bason	11,547
13		11	(h)	Blackpool	L 0-2		10,698
14		18	(a)	Huddersfield T	L 0-2		11,655
15		21	(a)	Portsmouth	W 3-1	Kemp 2, Sims	15,635
16		25	(h)	Barnsley	L 1-3	Sims	8,911
17		28	(h)	Brentford	L 0-1		7,249
18	Nov	1	(a)	Hull C	L 0-1		3,367
19		4	(a)	Fulham	D 0-0		3,507
20		8	(h)	Walsall	W 2-0	Kemp 2	5,022
21		12	(a)	Chester	L 0-1		2,247
22		15	(h)	Colchester U	D 1-1	Kemp	4,905
23		29	(a)	Millwall	D 1-1	Hodges	3,385
24	Dec	6	(h)	Rotherham U	W 3-1	Murphy 2, Kemp	6,155
25		20	(a)	Burnley	L 1-2	Murphy	5,678
26		26	(h)	Exeter C	L 0-2		14,792
27		27	(a)	Swindon T	L 0-3		9,710
28	Jan	10	(a)	Barnsley	L 1-2	Kemp	12,355
29		17	(h)	Millwall	W 2-0	Murphy, Cooper	4,847
30		24	(h)	Oxford U	W 3-0	Cooper 2, Kemp	5,121
31		31	(a)	Charlton A	D 1-1	Kemp	8,127
32	Feb	7	(h)	Chesterfield	W 1-0	Johnson	6,305
33		14	(a)	Carlisle U	L 0-2		3,924
34		21	(h)	Newport C	W 3-2	Johnson, Hodges, Sims	4,315
35		28	(a)	Gillingham	W 1-0	Sims	4,396
36	Mar	14	(a)	Blackpool	L 0-1		3,933
37		17	(h)	Huddersfield T	D 0-0		5,433
38		21	(h)	Portsmouth	W 1-0	Murphy	6,042
39		28	(a)	Brentford	W 1-0	Kemp	5,870
40	Apr	4	(h)	Hull C	D 0-0		4,668
41		11	(a)	Walsall	W 3-1	Hodges, Kemp 2	3,556
42		14	(h)	Sheffield U	W 1-0	Hodges	4,897
43		18	(h)	Swindon T	D 0-0		6,369
44		21	(a)	Exeter C	D 1-1	Sims	8,491
45		25	(h)	Burnley	W 2-1	Kemp 2	4,331
46	May	2	(a)	Rotherham U	L 1-2	Sims	11,497

FINAL LEAGUE POSITION: 7th in Division Three

Appearances
Sub Appearances
Goals

FA Cup

1	Nov	22	(h)	Newport C	W 2-0	Kemp, Murphy	6,719
2	Dec	13	(h)	Oxford U	W 3-0	Sims, Kemp, Murphy	7,264
3	Jan	3	(h)	Charlton A	L 1-2	Kemp	9,499

Appearances
Sub Appearances
Goals

FL Cup

1	Aug	9	(h)	Portsmouth	L 0-1		7,036
		12	(a)	Portsmouth	L 1-2	Kemp	11,997

Appearances
Sub Appearances
Goals

Crudgington	Harrison	Uzzell	Cooper	Foster	Phillipson-Masters	Hodges	Kemp	Graves	Bason	Murphy	Sims	Randell	James	Johnson	McNeill	Nisbet	Collins	Peachey	
1	2	3	4	5	6	7	8*	9	10	11								12	1
1	2	3	4	5	6	7	8	9	10	11									2
1	2	3	4	5	6	7	8	9*	10	11	12								3
1	2	3		5	6	7	8		10	11	9	4							4
1	2	3		5	6	7	8	12	10	11	9*	4							5
1	2	3		5		7	8	9*	10	11		4	6					12	6
1	2	3		5	6	7	8	12	10	11	9*	4							7
1	2	3		5	6	7	8		10	11	9	4							8
1	2	3		5	6	7	8		10	11	9	4							9
1	2	3		5	6	7	8		10	11	9	4							10
1	2	3		5	6	7	8		10	11	9	4							11
1	2	3		5	6	7	8		10	11	9	4							12
1	2	3*	11	5	6	7	8		10		9	4		12					13
1	2	3*	7	5	6		8		10	11	9	4	12						14
1	2		7	5	6		8		10	11	9	4	3						15
1	2*		7	5	6	12	8		10	11	9	4	3						16
1	2*		7	5	6		8	12	10	11	9	4	3						17
1	2		7	5	6		8		10	11	9	4	3						18
1	3		7	5	6	11	8		10		9	4	2						19
1	3		7	5	6		8		10	11	9	4	2						20
1	2		7	5	6	12	8		10	11*	9	4	3						21
1	3		7	5	6	4	8		10	11	9				2				22
1	3		7	5	6	4	8		10	11	9				2				23
1		3	7	5	6	4	8		10	11	9				2				24
1	3		7	6	5	4	8		10	11	9				2				25
1	3		7	5	6	4	8		10	11	9			12	2*				26
1	3*			5	6	7	8		10	11	9	4	2	12					27
1	3		7	5	6	4	8		10	11	9					2			28
1	3		7	5	6	4	8			11	9			10		2			29
1	3		7	5	6	4	8		12	11*	9			10		2			30
1	3		7	5	6	4	8			12	9			11		2	10*		31
1	3		7	5	6	4	8			11	9			10		2			32
1	3		7	5	6	4	8			11	9			10		2			33
1	3		7	5	6	4	8				9	10		11		2			34
1	3		7	5	6	4	8				9	10		11		2			35
1	3*		7	5	6	4	8			12	9	10		11		2			36
1	3		7	5	6	4	8			10	9			11		2			37
1	3		7*	5	6	4	8	12		11	9					2		10	38
1	3			5	6	4	8			11	9	10				2	7		39
1	3			5	6	4	8			11	9	10				2	7		40
1	3			5	6	4	8			11	9	10		7		2			41
1	3			5	6	4	8			11	9	10		7		2			42
1	3			5	6	4	8			11	9	10		7		2			43
1	3			5	6	4	8			11	9	10		7		2			44
1	3	6		5		4	8			11	9	10		7		2			45
1	3			5	6	4	8			11	9	10		7		2			46
46	45	16	28	46	44	39	46	4	28	40	42	30	9	15	5	19	3	1	
						2		4	1	2	1		1	3				2	
			3			5	24	1	4	9	8			2					

Crudgington	Harrison	Uzzell	Cooper	Foster	Phillipson-Masters	Hodges	Kemp	Graves	Bason	Murphy	Sims	Randell	James	Johnson	McNeill	Nisbet	Collins	Peachey	
1	3		7	5	6	4	8		10	11	9				2				1
1	3		7	6	5	4	8		10	11	9				2				2
1	3		7	6	5	4	8		10	11	9				2				3
3	3		3	3	3	3	3		3	3	3				3				
							3			2	1								

Crudgington	Harrison	Uzzell	Cooper	Foster	Phillipson-Masters	Hodges	Kemp	Graves	Bason	Murphy	Sims	Randell	James	Johnson	McNeill	Nisbet	Collins	Peachey	
1				5	6	7	8	12	10		9	4	2	11*	3				1
1	3			5	6	7	8	12	10*	11	9	4	2						
2	1			2	2	2	2		2	1	2	2	2	1	1				
								2											
							1												

1981-82

Manager: Bobby Moncur

1	Aug	29	(h)	Oxford U	L 0-1		4,089
2	Sep	5	(a)	Burnley	L 0-1		4,022
3		12	(h)	Lincoln C	L 0-2		3,323
4		19	(a)	Brentford	D 0-0		4,890
5		22	(a)	Bristol C	L 2-3	Sims, Hodges	7,471
6		26	(h)	Chesterfield	L 0-2		3,451
7		29	(h)	Reading	D 1-1	Hodges	2,745
8	Oct	3	(a)	Southend U	L 0-3		3,470
9		10	(h)	Gillingham	L 1-2	Phillips	3,094
10		17	(a)	Carlisle U	L 1-3	Cook	3,630
11		20	(a)	Wimbledon	L 1-2	Randell	2,114
12		24	(h)	Chester	W 5-1	Cook 2, Randell 2, Sims	2,646
13		31	(a)	Walsall	W 1-0	Sims	4,549
14	Nov	3	(h)	Fulham	W 3-1	Cook 2, Sims	4,915
15		7	(h)	Portsmouth	D 0-0		6,275
16		14	(a)	Newport C	W 1-0	Sims	4,427
17		28	(h)	Doncaster R	W 4-2	Sims 2, Hodges, Cook	4,341
18	Dec	5	(a)	Huddersfield T	D 0-0		6,949
19		26	(h)	Swindon T	W 2-1	Hodges, Cook	8,185
20		28	(a)	Exeter C	D 1-1	Harrison	9,144
21	Jan	2	(h)	Bristol R	W 4-0	Cooper 2, Cook 2	7,058
22		9	(h)	Burnley	D 1-1	Hodges	5,065
23		16	(a)	Preston NE	L 0-1		4,936
24		23	(a)	Reading	D 2-2	Cooper, Hodges	2,789
25		30	(h)	Brentford	W 1-0	Hodges	5,008
26	Feb	6	(a)	Lincoln C	L 0-2		2,970
27		9	(h)	Bristol C	W 2-1	Cook, Hodges	5,260
28		13	(h)	Southend U	D 0-0		5,058
29		20	(a)	Chesterfield	D 2-2	Sims, Cook	4,381
30		27	(a)	Gillingham	L 2-3	Sims 2	4,835
31	Mar	6	(h)	Carlisle U	W 1-0	Sims	3,272
32		13	(a)	Chester	W 3-0	Uzzell, Hodges, Sims	1,988
33		16	(a)	Fulham	W 3-1	Sims, Cooper, Cook	5,165
34		20	(h)	Walsall	W 4-1	Cook 2, Nisbet, Rogers	5,134
35		27	(a)	Portsmouth	L 0-1		9,551
36	Apr	2	(h)	Newport C	L 1-2	Hodges	5,148
37		9	(h)	Exeter C	W 2-1	Nisbet, Sims	9,458
38		10	(a)	Swindon T	W 2-0	Rogers 2	4,056
39		14	(h)	Wimbledon	W 2-0	Nisbet, Sims	4,748
40		17	(h)	Huddersfield T	D 1-1	Sims	5,434
41		20	(a)	Millwall	L 1-4	Cook	2,562
42		24	(a)	Doncaster R	D 2-2	Sims, Cook	3,894
43		28	(a)	Oxford U	L 0-1		6,597
44	May	1	(h)	Preston NE	L 0-3		3,319
45		8	(a)	Bristol R	W 3-2	Uzzell, Sims, Rogers	4,025
46		15	(h)	Millwall	W 2-1	Hodges, Cooper	3,193

FINAL LEAGUE POSITION: 10th in Division Three

Appearances
Sub Appearances
Goals

FA Cup

1	Nov	21	(h)	Gillingham	D 0-0		5,471
R		24	(a)	Gillingham	L 0-1		7,370

Appearances
Sub Appearances
Goals

FL Cup

1	Sep	8	(a)	Chester	D 1-1	Storton (og)	1,690
		15	(h)	Chester	W 1-0	Dennis	2,348
2	Oct	6	(a)	Middlesbrough	L 1-2	Kemp	8,201
		27	(h)	Middlesbrough	D 0-0		6,402

Appearances
Sub Appearances
Goals

Crudgington	Nisbet	McCartney	Harrison	Phillipson-Masters	Cooper	Hodges	Kemp	Sims	Randell	Collins	Phillips	Foster	Murphy	Dennis	Uzzell	Rowe	Rogers	Cook	James	Ham	Match
1	2	3	4	5	6	7	8	9	10	11*	12										1
1	2	3	4*		6	7	8	9	10		12	5	11								2
1	2	3	4		6	7	8	9	10			5	11*	12							3
1	2		4			7	8	9	10			5		11	3	6					4
1	2		4		6	7	8	9	10			5	12	11*	3						5
1	2		4		6*	7	8	9	10			5	12	11	3						6
1	2		4			7	8	9	10			5	6		3		11				7
1	2		4			7	8	9	10			5	6		3		11				8
1	2	3			6	7	8	9			10	5			4		11				9
1	2	3		4	6	7		9	10			5					11	8			10
1	2	3		4	6	7		9	10			5					11	8			11
1	2	3	5	4	6	7		9	10								11	8			12
1	2		4	5	6	7		9	10						3		11	8			13
1	2		4	5	6	7		9	10						3		11	8			14
1	2		4	5	6	7		9	10						3		11	8			15
1	2	3	4	5	6	7		9	10								11	8			16
1	2	3	4	5	6	7		9	10								11	8			17
1	2		4	5	6	7		9			10				3		11	8			18
1	2		4	5	6	7		9			10				3		11	8			19
1	2		4	5	6	7		9	10		8*			12	3		11				20
1	2		4	5	6	7		9	10						3		11	8			21
1	2		4	5	6	7		9	10						3		11	8			22
1	2		4	5	6	7		9	10						3		11	8			23
1	2		4	5*	6	7		9			10				3	12	11	8			24
1	2		4		6	7		9	10						3		11	8	5		25
1	2		4		6	7		9	10						3		11	8	5		26
1	2		4		6	7		9	10						3		11	8	5		27
1	2		4		6	7		9	10						3		11	8	5		28
1	2		4		6	7		9	10						3		11	8	5		29
1	2		4		6	7		9	10						3		11	8	5		30
1	2		4	5	6	7		9	10						3		11	8			31
1	2		4	5	6	7		9	10						3		11	8			32
1	2		4	5	6	7		9	10						3		11	8			33
1	2		4	5	6	7		9	10						3		11	8			34
1	2		4	5	6	7		9	10						3		11	8			35
1	2		4	5	6	7		9	10						3		11	8			36
1	2	10	4	5	6	7		9							3		11	8			37
1	2	10	4	5	6	7		9							3		11	8			38
1	2	10*	4	5	6	7		9							3	12	11	8			39
1	2		4	5	6	7		9							3	10	11	8			40
1	2	3	4	5	6	7		9	10								11	8			41
1		3	4	5	6	7		9	10						12		11	8		2*	42
1	2	3	4	5	6	7		9	10								11	8			43
1	2	3	4	5	6	7		9	10								11	8			44
1	2		4	5	6	7		9	10						3		11	8			45
1	2		4		6	7		9	10		2			8	3		11				46
46	45	16	43	31	43	46	9	46	38	1	6	10	4	4	34	2	40	35	6	1	
											2		2	2	1	2					
	3		1		5	11		18	3		1				2		4	16			

Crudgington	Nisbet	McCartney	Harrison	Phillipson-Masters	Cooper	Hodges	Kemp	Sims	Randell	Collins	Phillips	Foster	Murphy	Dennis	Uzzell	Rowe	Rogers	Cook	James	Ham	Round
1	2	3	4	5	6	7		9	10*		12						11	8			1
1	2	3	4	5	6	7		9			10			12			11	8*			R
2	2	2	2	2	2	2		2	1		1						2	2			
											1			1							

Crudgington	Nisbet	McCartney	Harrison	Phillipson-Masters	Cooper	Hodges	Kemp	Sims	Randell	Collins	Phillips	Foster	Murphy	Dennis	Uzzell	Rowe	Rogers	Cook	James	Ham	Round
1	2	3	4		6	7	8	9	10			5	11								1
1	2		4			7	8	9	10			5		11	3	6					
1	2	3			6	7	8	9	10			5			4		11				2
1	2	3	4	5	6*	7		9	10				12				11	8			
4	4	3	4	1	3	4	3	4	4			3	1	1	2	1	2	1			
													1								
							1							1							

1 own-goal

1982-83

Manager: Bobby Moncur

1	Aug	26	(h)	Southend U	W	1-0	Harrison	3,850
2	Sep	4	(a)	Reading	L	2-3	Cook, Uzzell	2,102
3		7	(a)	Newport C	D	2-2	Cook, Hodges	3,741
4		11	(h)	Orient	W	2-0	Hodges 2	3,649
5		18	(a)	Sheffield U	L	1-3	Sims	13,604
6		25	(h)	Wrexham	W	2-0	Gooding, Rogers	3,628
7		28	(h)	Bristol R	L	0-4		3,542
8	Oct	2	(a)	Wigan A	L	0-3		5,011
9		9	(a)	Bradford C	L	0-4		4,690
10		16	(h)	Lincoln C	L	0-2		2,921
11		19	(h)	Bournemouth	W	2-0	Hodges, Sims	2,525
12		23	(a)	Chesterfield	W	2-1	Hodges, Nisbet	3,149
13		30	(h)	Brentford	W	2-0	Cook, Sims	4,036
14	Nov	2	(a)	Millwall	D	2-2	Cooper, Madden (og)	3,097
15		8	(a)	Doncaster R	D	2-2	McCartney, Hodges	2,942
16		13	(h)	Oxford U	W	2-1	McCartney, Sims	3,908
17		27	(a)	Preston NE	D	2-2	Cooper, Hodges	3,633
18	Dec	4	(h)	Huddersfield T	W	2-1	Cook, Hodges	4,227
19		18	(h)	Gillingham	W	2-0	Sims, Rogers	4,179
20		27	(a)	Exeter C	L	0-1		9,168
21		28	(h)	Cardiff C	W	3-2	Sims 2, Carter	8,631
22	Jan	1	(a)	Portsmouth	L	1-2	McLaughlin (og)	15,856
23		14	(a)	Southend U	L	1-3	Phillips	3,082
24		22	(h)	Newport C	L	2-4	Vaughan (og), Cook	4,287
25		29	(a)	Orient	W	2-0	McCartney, Hodges	2,699
26	Feb	1	(h)	Reading	W	3-0	Williams (og), Bremner, McCartney	3,504
27		5	(a)	Bristol R	L	0-2		6,556
28		8	(h)	Walsall	D	0-0		3,148
29		19	(h)	Bradford C	W	3-1	Cooper, McCartney, Hodges	3,644
30		26	(a)	Lincoln C	W	2-1	Hodges, Phillips	3,915
31	Mar	1	(h)	Millwall	W	3-1	Phillips 2, Sims	4,114
32		5	(h)	Chesterfield	W	2-0	Phillips, Rogers	4,466
33		11	(a)	Brentford	L	0-2		4,967
34		15	(a)	Bournemouth	L	0-1		4,258
35		19	(h)	Doncaster R	L	1-2	Phillips	3,406
36		26	(a)	Oxford U	D	1-1	Cooper	4,786
37	Apr	1	(h)	Exeter C	W	1-0	Sims	8,856
38		2	(a)	Cardiff C	D	0-0		7,226
39		9	(a)	Huddersfield T	L	0-2		9,277
40		16	(h)	Sheffield U	W	3-1	Phillips, Nisbet, Staniforth	3,665
41		19	(h)	Wigan A	L	0-2		3,097
42		23	(a)	Gillingham	L	1-2	Phillips	3,356
43		30	(h)	Preston NE	D	1-1	Smith	2,912
44	May	2	(a)	Walsall	L	0-2		3,473
45		7	(a)	Wrexham	W	3-2	Sims, Rogers 2	2,250
46		14	(h)	Portsmouth	L	0-1		14,173

FINAL LEAGUE POSITION: 8th in Division Three

Appearances
Sub Appearances
Goals

FA Cup

1	Nov	29	(h)	Exeter C	W	2-0	Hodges, Sims	10,202
2	Dec	11	(a)	Bristol R	D	2-2	Rogers, Sims	9,018
R		20	(h)	Bristol R	W	1-0	McCartney	9,130
3	Jan	8	(a)	Watford	L	0-2		17,630

Appearances
Sub Appearances
Goals

FL Cup

1	Aug	31	(h)	Bournemouth	W	2-0	Sims 2	3,103
	Sep	14	(a)	Bournemouth	L	0-3*		3,353

*After extra-time

Appearances
Sub Appearances
Goals

Crudgington	Nisbet	Uzzell	Harrison	Phillipson-Masters	Cooper	Hodges	Phillips	Sims	Gooding	Rogers	Carter	Cook	McCartney	Rowe	Dennis	Smith L	Hards	Bremner	Ham	Staniforth	
1	2	3	4	5	6	7	8	9	10	11											1
1	2	3	4	5*	6	7		9	10	11	12	8									2
1	2	3	4		6	7		10	8	11		9	5								3
1	2	3	4		6	7		9	10	11	12	8*	5								4
1	4	3			6	7	2	9	10	11	12	8*	5								5
1	2	3		4	6	7		9	10	11		8	5								6
1	2	3		4	6	7		9	10	11	12	8*	5								7
1	2	5	3	4	6	7		11		9*	10		8	12							8
1	2	3	4	5	6	7		9			8		10		11						9
1	2	3	4		6	7	12	9		11	8*		10			5					10
1	2	3	4		6	7		9		11		8	10			5					11
1	2	3	4		6	7		9		11		8	10			5					12
1	2	3	4		6	7		9		11		8	10			5					13
1	2	3	4		6	7		9		11		8	10			5					14
1	2	3	4		6	7		9		11		8	10			5					15
1	2	3	4		6	7		9		11		8	10			5					16
1	2		4		6	7		9		11		8	10	3		5					17
1	2	3	4		6	7				11	9	8	10			5					18
1	2	3	4		6	7		9		11		8	10			5					19
	2	3	4		6	7		9		11	12	8*	10			5	1				20
	2	3	4		6	7		9		11	8		10			5	1				21
1	2	3	4		6	7		9		11	8*	12	10			5					22
1	2	3			6	7	4	9		11		8	10			5					23
1	2		4		6	7	3	9		11		8	10			5					24
1	2	3	4		6	7		9		11			10			5		8			25
1	2	3	4		6	7		9		11			10			5		8			26
1	2	3	4		6	7	12	9*		11			10			5		8			27
1	2	3	4		6	7		9		11			10			5		8			28
1	2	3	4		6	7		9		11			10					8	5		29
1	2	3	4		6	7	12	9		11		8*	10						5		30
1	2	3	4			7	8	9		11			10	6		5					31
1	2	3	4		6*	7	8	9		11	12		10			5					32
1	2	3	4		6	7	8	9		11			10			5					33
1	2	3	4		6	7	8	9		11			10			5					34
1	2	3	4		6	8	11	10		9			7			5					35
1	2	3	4		6	7	8	9		11						5				10	36
1	2	3	4		6	7	8	9		11						5				10	37
1	2	3	4		6	7	8	9		11						5				10	38
1	2	3	4		6	7	8	9		11									5	10	39
1	2	3	4		6	7	8	9		11						5				10	40
1	2	3	4		6	7	8			11					9	5				10	41
1	2	3	4		6	7	8			11				12	9*	5				10	42
1	2	3*	4		6	7	8	12		11				10		5				9	43
1	2		4		6	7	8	9		11				3		5				10	44
1	2				6	7	8	9		11				3		5			4	10	45
1	2	3	4		6	7	8	9						11		5				10	46
44	46	42	41	6	45	46	20	42	7	44	6	19	33	6	3	34	2	5	4	11	
							3	1			6	1		2							
	2	1	1		4	11	8	10	1	5	1	5	5			1		1		1.	

4 own-goals

1	2		4		6	7		9		11		8	10	3		5					1
1	2	3	4		6	7		9		11		8	10			5					2
1	2	3	4		6	7		9		11		8	10			5					R
1	2	3			6	7	4	9		11		8	10			5					3
4	4	3	3		4	4	1	4		4		4	4	1		4					
						1		2		1			1								

1	2	3	4	5	6	7		9	10	11		8									1
1	2	3	4		6*	7		9	10	11	12	8	5								
2	2	2	2	1	2	2		2	2	2		2	1								
											1										
								2													

1983-84

Manager: Bobby Moncur/John Hore

1	Aug	27	(h)	Wigan A	D 0-0		3,730
2	Sep	3	(a)	Millwall	L 0-1		4,611
3		6	(a)	Rotherham U	L 0-2		4,488
4		10	(h)	Gillingham	D 1-1	Nisbet	3,192
5		17	(a)	Lincoln C	L 1-3	Tynan	3,103
6		24	(h)	Preston NE	W 1-0	Rogers	3,674
7		27	(h)	Scunthorpe U	W 4-0	Staniforth 2, Rowe, Rogers	3,821
8	Oct	1	(a)	Burnley	L 1-2	Flynn (og)	6,766
9		8	(a)	Bournemouth	L 1-2	Pearson	3,759
10		15	(h)	Oxford U	W 2-1	Nisbet, Phillips	2,990
11		18	(h)	Bristol R	D 1-1	Phillips	4,896
12		22	(a)	Hull C	W 2-1	L.Smith, Tynan	8,807
13		29	(h)	Sheffield U	L 0-1		5,458
14		31	(a)	Port Vale	W 1-0	Phillips	3,466
15	Nov	5	(a)	Brentford	D 2-2	Tynan, Hodges	4,183
16		12	(h)	Bolton W	W 2-0	Kellow, Phillips	4,624
17	Dec	3	(a)	Bradford C	L 0-2		2,955
18		17	(a)	Orient	L 2-3	Nisbet 2	2,684
19		26	(h)	Exeter C	D 2-2	Staniforth, Kellow	10,387
20		27	(a)	Newport C	L 0-2		5,154
21		31	(h)	Southend U	W 4-0	Hodges, Clark (og), Tynan, Rogers	3,978
22	Jan	2	(a)	Walsall	L 2-3	L.Smith, Tynan	4,856
23		21	(h)	Lincoln C	D 2-2	Cooper 2	3,804
24	Feb	4	(h)	Burnley	D 1-1	Staniforth	5,104
25		11	(a)	Preston NE	L 1-2	Staniforth	4,370
26		14	(h)	Port Vale	W 3-0	Staniforth, Tynan 2	3,552
27		25	(h)	Hull C	W 2-0	Tynan, Phillips	10,023
28		28	(a)	Sheffield U	L 0-2		9,541
29	Mar	3	(a)	Bristol R	L 0-2		5,619
30		6	(h)	Brentford	D 1-1	Phillips	4,332
31		17	(h)	Bournemouth	W 1-0	Staniforth	7,235
32		20	(h)	Millwall	L 0-1		4,507
33		24	(a)	Oxford U	L 0-5		7,777
34		30	(h)	Rotherham U	D 1-1	Tynan	4,736
35	Apr	3	(a)	Wigan A	D 1-1	Tynan	2,756
36		7	(a)	Scunthorpe U	L 0-3		2,780
37		10	(h)	Wimbledon	L 1-2	Tynan	6,471
38		16	(a)	Bolton W	L 1-2	Tynan	3,266
39		20	(h)	Newport C	L 0-1		7,654
40		21	(a)	Exeter C	D 1-1	Staniforth	6,870
41		28	(a)	Wimbledon	L 0-1		3,706
42	May	1	(a)	Gillingham	L 1-2	Chamberlain	3,103
43		5	(h)	Walsall	W 3-1	Rogers, Staniforth 2	5,144
44		7	(a)	Southend U	D 1-1	Chamberlain	3,540
45		9	(h)	Bradford C	W 3-0	L.Smith, Staniforth, Hodges	5,744
46		12	(h)	Orient	W 3-1	Chamberlain, L.Smith, Hodges	7,664

FINAL LEAGUE POSITION: 19th in Division Three

Appearances
Sub Appearances
Goals

FA Cup

1	Nov	19	(a)	Southend U	D 0-0		3,408
R		22	(h)	Southend U	W 2-0	Stead (og), Tynan	5,570
2	Dec	10	(h)	Barking	W 2-1	Rowe, Smith	4,754
3	Jan	7	(h)	Newport C	D 2-2	Hodges, Tynan	6,789
R		10	(a)	Newport C	W 1-0	Rogers	5,549
4		28	(h)	Darlington	W 2-1	Uzzell, Staniforth	8,918
5	Feb	18	(a)	West Brom A	W 1-0	Tynan	23,795
6	Mar	10	(h)	Derby C	D 0-0		34,365
R		14	(a)	Derby C	W 1-0	Rogers	26,906
SF	Apr	14	(n*)	Watford	L 0-1		

*Played at Villa Park, Birmingham.

Appearances
Sub Appearances
Goals

FL Cup

1	Aug	30	(a)	Swindon T	L 0-1		3,343
	Sep	13	(h)	Swindon T	W 4-1	Smith, Staniforth, Tynan, Nisbet	3,432
2	Oct	4	(a)	Arsenal	D 1-1	Nisbet	20,983
		25	(h)	Arsenal	L 0-1		22,640

Appearances
Sub Appearances
Goals

Crudgington	Nisbet	Uzzell	Harrison	Smith L	Forbes	Hodges	Phillips	Tynan	Staniforth	Rogers	Cooper	Rowe	Ham	Pearson	Kellow	Price	Cassidy	Smith M	Chamberlain	Swiggs	
1	2	3	4	5	6	7	8	9	10	11											1
1	2	3	4	5	6	7	8	9	10	11											2
1	2	3	4	5		7	8	9	10	11	6										3
1	2	3	4	5		7	8*	9	10	11	6	12									4
1		3	4	5		7	2	9	10	11	6	8									5
1	2	3		5		7		9	10	11	6*	8	4	12							6
1	2	3	4	5		7		9	10	11	6	8									7
1	2	3*	4	5		7	12	9	10	11	6	8									8
1	2	3	4	5		7	11	9			6	8		10							9
1	2	3	4	5		7	11	9			6	8		10							10
1	2	3	4	5		7	11	9	12		6	8		10*							11
1	2	3	4	5		7	11	9	10		6	8									12
1	2	3	4	5		7	11	9*	10		6	8		12							13
1	2	3	4	5		7	11	9	10		6	8									14
1	2	3	4	5		7	11	9	10*		6	8		12							15
1	2	3	4	5	6	7	11	9				8			10						16
1	2	3	4	5		7	11	9	12		6*	8			10						17
1	2	3	4	5		7	12		10	11	6	8*			9						18
1	2	3	4	5		7			10	11	6	8			9						19
1	2	3	4	5		7	12		10	11	6	8			9*						20
1	2	3	4	5		7	8	9	12	11	6				10*						21
1	2	3	4	5		7	8	9	10	11*	6				12						22
1		3	4	5		7	2	9	10	11	6			8							23
1	2	3	4	5		7	8		10	11	6			9*	12						24
1	2	3	4	5		7	8		10	11	6	12			9*						25
1	2	3	4	5		7	8	9	10	11	6										26
1	2	3	4	5		7	8	9	10	11	6										27
1	2	3	4			7*	8	9	10	11	6	12	5								28
1	2	3	4			7	8	9		11	6		5		10						29
1	2	4				7	8	9		11	6		5			3	10				30
1	2	3	4	5		7	8	9	10	11	6										31
1	2	3	4	5		7	8	9		11	6	10									32
1	2		4	5*			8	9		11	6	7	12					3	10		33
1	2		4	5		7	8	9	10	11	6							3			34
1	2		4	5*		7	8	9	10	11	6	12						3			35
1	2	3	4	5		7	8	9	10*	11	6								12		36
1	2		4	5		7	8	9	10*	11	6	3							12		37
1	2	3	4	5		7	8	9	10*	11	6								12		38
1	2	3	4	5		7	8	9	10	11	6										39
1	2	3	4	5		7	8	9*	10	11	6								12		40
1	2	3	4	5		12	8		10	11*	6	7							9		41
1	2	3	4			7			10	11	6	5							9	8	42
1	2	3	4	5			8		10	12	6	7	11*						9		43
1	2	3	4	5			8		10	11	6	7							9		44
1	2	3	4	5		12	8		10	11	6	7*							9		45
1	2	3	4	5		7	8		10*	11	6								9	12	46
46	44	42	44	42	3	41	39	35	36	36	43	24	5	5	8	1	1	3	7	1	
						2	3		3	1		4	1	3	2				4	1	
	4			4		4	6	12	11	4	2	1		1	2				3		

2 own-goals

1	2	3	4	5		7	11	9			6	8			10						1
1	2	3	4	5		7	11	9			6	8			10						R
1	2	3		5		7	6	9*	12	11		8	4		10						2
1	2	3	4	5		7	8	9	10	11	6										3
1		3	4	5	8*	7	2	9	10	11	6			12							R
1	2	3	4	5		7	8	9	10	11	6										4
1	2	3	4	5		7	8	9	10	11	6										5
1	2	3	4	5		7	8	9	10	11	6										6
1	2	3	4	5		7	8	9	10	11	6										R
1	2	3	4	5		7	8	9	10	11	6										SF
10	9	10	9	10	1	10	10	10	7	8	9	3	1		3						
									1					1							
		1		1		1		3	1	2		1									

1 own-goal

1	2	3	4	5	6	7	8	9	10	11											1
1	2	3	4	5		7		9	10	11	6	8									
1	2	3	4	5		7	12	9	10	11*	6	8									2
1	2	3	4	5		7	11*	9	10		6	8		12							
4	4	4	4	4	1	4	2	4	4	3	3	3									
							1							1							
	2			1				1	1												

1984-85

Manager: John Hore/Dave Smith

1	Aug	25	(a)	Burnley	D	1-1	Hodges	6,613
2	Sep	1	(h)	Reading	L	1-2	Staniforth	5,509
3		8	(a)	Lincoln C	D	2-2	Hodges, Tynan	2,171
4		16	(h)	Bournemouth	D	0-0		4,933
5		18	(h)	York C	D	1-1	Staniforth	4,537
6		22	(a)	Bolton W	L	2-7	Coughlin, Tynan	3,876
7		29	(h)	Preston NE	W	6-4	Coughlin, English, Hodges 2, Staniforth, Tynan	4,258
8	Oct	2	(a)	Gillingham	D	3-3	Nisbet, Rogers, Tynan	4,442
9		6	(h)	Hull C	L	0-1		5,705
10		13	(a)	Derby C	L	1-3	Tynan	11,316
11		20	(h)	Rotherham U	W	1-0	Rogers	4,067
12		23	(a)	Orient	L	0-3		2,310
13		26	(a)	Doncaster R	L	3-4	Hodges, Tynan 2	4,688
14	Nov	3	(h)	Bristol R	W	3-2	Harrison, Nisbet, Tynan	5,818
15		6	(h)	Bradford C	D	0-0		4,578
16		10	(a)	Wigan A	L	0-1		3,121
17		24	(h)	Walsall	L	1-3	Tynan	4,907
18	Dec	1	(a)	Swansea C	W	2-0	Staniforth, Tynan	3,124
19		15	(h)	Cambridge U	W	2-0	Hodges, Tynan	3,675
20		22	(h)	Millwall	W	3-1	Coughlin, Staniforth, Tynan	4,557
21		26	(a)	Bristol C	L	3-4	Tynan 3	10,339
22		29	(a)	Newport C	L	0-1		3,003
23	Jan	1	(h)	Brentford	D	1-1	Tynan	6,946
24		26	(a)	Bournemouth	L	0-1		3,695
25	Feb	2	(a)	Preston NE	W	2-1	Goodyear, Hodges	3,248
26		9	(h)	Bolton W	W	2-0	Goodyear, Tynan	4,978
27		12	(a)	York C	D	0-0		4,820
28		23	(a)	Bristol R	L	0-1		5,953
29	Mar	2	(h)	Doncaster R	W	2-1	Summerfield, Tynan	5,019
30		5	(h)	Orient	D	1-1	Uzzell	4,770
31		9	(a)	Rotherham U	W	2-0	Summerfield, Tynan	4,111
32		16	(h)	Derby C	L	0-1		6,117
33		19	(h)	Gillingham	D	1-1	Tynan	4,852
34		23	(a)	Hull C	D	2-2	Tynan 2	6,497
35		26	(h)	Burnley	D	2-2	Tynan 2	4,383
36		30	(a)	Bradford C	L	0-1		6,552
37	Apr	5	(h)	Bristol C	W	1-0	Staniforth	9,959
38		8	(a)	Brentford	L	1-3	Tynan	4,043
39		13	(h)	Wigan A	W	1-0	Tynan	4,159
40		16	(h)	Lincoln C	W	2-0	Tynan 2	4,228
41		20	(a)	Walsall	W	3-0	Hodges 2, Tynan	2,775
42		24	(a)	Reading	D	1-1	Staniforth	2,296
43		27	(h)	Swansea C	L	1-2	Tynan	4,994
44	May	4	(a)	Cambridge U	D	1-1	Tynan	1,435
45		6	(h)	Newport C	W	1-0	Hodges	5,079
46		11	(a)	Millwall	L	0-2		1,346

FINAL LEAGUE POSITION: 15th in Division Three

Appearances
Sub Appearances
Goals

FA Cup

1	Nov	17	(h)	Barnet	W	3-0	Goodyear, Tynan, Staniforth	5,568
2	Dec	8	(h)	Hereford U	D	0-0		7,882
R		12	(a)	Hereford U	L	0-2		6,956

Appearances
Sub Appearances
Goals

FL Cup

1	Aug	27	(h)	Torquay U	W	1-0	Goodyear	5,689
	Sep	4	(a)	Torquay U	W	1-0	Staniforth	3,003
2		25	(a)	Birmingham C	L	1-4	Staniforth	7,964
	Oct	9	(h)	Birmingham C	L	0-1		4,650

Appearances
Sub Appearances
Goals

Crudgington	Nisbet	Uzzell	Harrison	Goodyear	Burrows	Hodges	Cooper	Tynan	Staniforth	Coughlin	Rogers	Rowe	English	Sealey	Bannon	Ham	Summerfield	McElhinney	Philp	Obi	Rowbotham	
1	2	3	4	5	6	7	8	9	10	11												1
1	2	3	4	5	6	7	8	9	10	11*	12											2
1	2	3	4	5	6	7	8	9	10	11												3
1	2	3	4	5	6	7	8*	9	10	11		12										4
1	2	3	4	5	6	7	8*	9	10	11	12											5
1	2	3	4*	5	6	7	8	9	10	11	12											6
	2		4	5	6	7		9	10	11	8	3*	12						1			7
	2		4	5	6	7*		9	10	11	8	3	12						1			8
	2		4	5	6	7		9	10	11	8	3*	12	1								9
	2			5	6	7	4	9	10	11	8*	3	12	1								10
	2	3	4		6	7		9	10	11	8	5		1								11
	2	3*	4		6	7	12	9	10	11	8	5		1								12
	2		4	3	6	7		9	10	11	8	5		1								13
	2	3	4		6	7		9	10	11	8	5		1								14
	2	3	4	12	6	7		9	10	11*	8	5							1			15
	2	3	4	11	6	7		9	10		8	5*			12				1			16
1	2	3	4	5	6			9	10*	11	7	8			12							17
1	2	3	4		6	8	5	9	10	11	7											18
1	2		4			8	5*	9	10	11	7	3				6					12	19
1	2		4			8		9	10	11	7	3				6	5					20
1	2		4	3		7	8	11	10		6					5	9					21
1	2		12	3	6	8	11*	9	10		7					4	5					22
1	2		4	3	6	8		9	10	11	7						5*				12	23
1	2	3	12			8	6		10	11	7					4*	9	5				24
1	2	3		12		8	6	9	10		7					4	11*	5				25
1	2	3	12	11	4	8	6	9	10*		7							5				26
1	2	3	11		4	8	6	9			7						10	5				27
	2	3			4	8		9			7	6					10	5	1	11*	12	28
	2	3*		6	4	8		9		12	7						10	5	1	11		29
	2	3		6		8		9		4	7						10	5	1	11		30
1	2	3		6	12	8		9		4*	7						10	5		11		31
1	2	3		6		8		9	12	4	7						10	5		11*		32
1	2	3		6	5	8		9	11	4	7						10					33
1	2	3	12	6	5	8		9	11	4	7						10*					34
1	2	3		6	5	8		9	11	4	7						10*	12				35
1	2	3	10		6	8		9	11	4	7							5				36
1	2	3		11	6	8		9	10	4	7							5				37
1	2	3		11*	6	8		9	10	4	7							5			12	38
1	2			11	6	8		9	10	4	7							5			3	39
1	2		12	11	6	8		9	10	4	7							5			3*	40
1	2		3	11	6	8		9	10	4	7							5				41
1	2		3	11	6	8	12	9	10	4*	7							5				42
1	2		3		6	8	11	9	10	4	7							5				43
1	2			3	6	8	11	9	10	4	7							5				44
1	2		3		6	8	11	9	10*	4	7						12	5				45
1	2	4	3		6	8	11	9	10								12	5*			7	46
33	46	29	28	31	38	45	19	45	40	37	39	14		6		6	15	20	7	5	3	
			5	2	1		2		1	1	3	1	4		2		2	1			4	
	2	1	1	2		10		31	7	3	2		1				2					

Crudgington	Nisbet	Uzzell	Harrison	Goodyear	Burrows	Hodges	Cooper	Tynan	Staniforth	Coughlin	Rogers	Rowe	English	Sealey	Bannon	Ham	Summerfield	McElhinney	Philp	Obi	Rowbotham	
1	2	3	4	5	6			9	10	11	7	8										1
1	2	3	4		6	8	5	9	10	11	7											2
1	2	3	4		6	8	5	9	10	11	7											3
3	3	3	3	1	3	2	2	3	3	3	3	1										
				1				1	1													

Crudgington	Nisbet	Uzzell	Harrison	Goodyear	Burrows	Hodges	Cooper	Tynan	Staniforth	Coughlin	Rogers	Rowe	English	Sealey	Bannon	Ham	Summerfield	McElhinney	Philp	Obi	Rowbotham	
1	2	3	4	5	6	7	8	9	10	11												1
1	2	3	4	5	6	7	8	9	10	11												
	2	12	4	5*	6	7		9	10	11	8	3							1			2
	2			5	6	7		9	10	11	8	3	4						1			
2	4	2	3	4	4	4	2	4	4	4	2	2	1						2			
		1																				
				1					2													

1985-86

Manager: Dave Smith

1	Aug	17	(a)	York C	L	1-3	McElhinney	4,246
2		24	(h)	Reading	L	0-1		4,261
3		26	(a)	Swansea C	W	2-0	McElhinney, S.Cooper	3,906
4		31	(h)	Notts C	L	0-1		5,105
5	Sep	7	(a)	Brentford	D	1-1	S.Cooper	3,927
6		14	(h)	Newport C	W	2-0	Burrows, Nelson	3,686
7		17	(a)	Doncaster R	L	0-1		2,904
8		21	(h)	Wolves	W	3-1	S.Cooper, Nelson 2	5,241
9		28	(a)	Bolton W	L	1-3	Clayton	4,270
10	Oct	1	(h)	Gillingham	W	3-0	Hodges, Nelson, S.Cooper	4,135
11		5	(h)	Bristol R	W	4-2	Clayton, Coughlin, Hodges, Parkin (og)	5,662
12		12	(a)	Walsall	D	2-2	Nelson 2	4,253
13		19	(a)	Rotherham U	D	1-1	Hodges	2,942
14		22	(h)	Lincoln C	W	2-1	Hodges, Nelson	6,552
15		26	(a)	Derby C	W	2-1	Hodges, Goodyear	11,433
16	Nov	2	(h)	Chesterfield	D	0-0		7,522
17		5	(h)	Bournemouth	W	2-1	Hodges, S.Cooper	6,186
18		9	(a)	Bury	W	1-0	Clayton	2,975
19		23	(h)	Wigan A	W	2-1	Summerfield, Coughlin	6,714
20		30	(a)	Blackpool	D	1-1	Nelson	6,184
21	Dec	14	(h)	Darlington	W	4-2	Hodges 2, S.Cooper, Summerfield	6,036
22		21	(a)	Reading	L	3-4	Hodges, S.Cooper, Clayton	8,512
23		26	(a)	Bristol C	L	0-2		8,298
24		28	(h)	Swansea C	W	2-0	Clayton 2	8,622
25	Jan	1	(h)	Cardiff C	D	4-4	Nelson, Summerfield, Clayton, Hodges	8,920
26		11	(a)	Notts C	L	0-2		4,953
27		18	(h)	York C	D	2-2	Brimacombe, Coughlin	5,942
28		25	(a)	Newport C	L	1-3	Clayton	3,007
29	Feb	1	(h)	Brentford	W	2-0	Nelson 2	4,873
30		15	(h)	Doncaster R	L	0-1		4,827
31	Mar	4	(a)	Gillingham	D	1-1	Summerfield	3,490
32		8	(a)	Bristol R	W	2-1	Coughlin, Godfrey	4,667
33		11	(a)	Wolves	W	3-0	Coughlin, Summerfield, Clayton	2,367
34		15	(h)	Walsall	W	2-0	L.Cooper, Coughlin	6,097
35		18	(a)	Chesterfield	W	2-1	Summerfield, Goodyear	1,828
36		22	(h)	Derby C	W	4-1	Clayton 2, Rowbotham, Hodges	11,769
37		28	(a)	Cardiff C	W	2-1	Hodges, Matthews	3,834
38	Apr	5	(a)	Bournemouth	W	3-1	S.Cooper, Coughlin, Hodges	5,351
39		8	(h)	Rotherham U	W	4-0	Pickering (og), Tynan 2, Summerfield	13,034
40		12	(h)	Bury	W	3-0	Hodges, Tynan 2	13,625
41		16	(a)	Lincoln C	D	1-1	Tynan	2,297
42		19	(a)	Wigan A	L	0-3		9,485
43		22	(h)	Bolton W	W	4-1	Hodges, Coughlin, Tynan, Burrows	12,183
44		26	(h)	Blackpool	W	3-1	Nelson, Coughlin, Tynan	14,975
45		29	(h)	Bristol C	W	4-0	Tynan 2, Nelson, Coughlin	20,000
46	May	3	(a)	Darlington	W	2-0	Hodges, Tynan	3,306

FINAL LEAGUE POSITION: 2nd in Division Three

Appearances
Sub Appearances
Goals

FA Cup

1	Nov	16	(h)	Aldershot	W	1-0	Coughlin	7,209
2	Dec	7	(h)	Maidstone U	W	3-0	L.Cooper, Nelson, Summerfield	7,597
3	Jan	4	(a)	Hull C	D	2-2	Clayton, L.Cooper	6,776
R		7	(h)	Hull C	L	0-1		13,940

Appearances
Sub Appearances
Goals

FL Cup

1	Aug	20	(h)	Exeter C	W	2-1	Summerfield, McElhinney	4,754
	Sep	4	(a)	Exeter C	L	0-2		3,362

Appearances
Sub Appearances
Goals

Freight/Rover Trophy

G	Jan	14	(a)	Bristol C	D	0-0		2,402
G		21	(h)	Walsall	L	0-1		3,198

Appearances
Sub Appearances
Goals

Crudgington	Nisbet	Goodyear	Uzzell	McElhinney	Matthews	Hodges	Coughlin	Cooper S	Rowbotham	Nelson	Cooper L	Burrows	Clayton	Summerfield	Brimacombe	Godfrey	Tynan	Philp	
1	2	3	4	5	6	7	8	9	10	11									1
1	2	4	3	5	6	7	8	9		11	10								2
1	2	4	3	5	6	7	8	9		11	10								3
1	2			5	6	7	8	9		11	3	4	10						4
1	2	3		5		7	8	9	6	11		4	10						5
1	2	3		5	6	7	8	9		11		4	10						6
1	2	3*		5	6	7	8	9	12	11		4	10						7
1	2	3		5	6	7	8*	9	12	11		4	10						8
1	2	3		5	6	7	8	9		11		4	10						9
1	2	3		5	6	7	8	9		11	4		10						10
1	2	4		5	6	7	8	9		11	3		10						11
1	2	4		5	6*	7	8	9		11	3		10	12					12
1	2	4		5	6	7	8	9		11	3		10						13
1	2	4		5	6	7	8	9		11	3		10						14
1	2	4		5	6	7	8	9		11	3		10						15
1	2	4		5		7	8	9	12	11*	3		10	6					16
1	2	4		5	6	7	8	9		11	3		10						17
1	2	4		5*	6	7	8	9		11	3		10	12					18
1	2	4		5	12	7	8	9*		11	3		10	6					19
1	2	4		5		7	8	9		11	3		10	6					20
1	2	4		5		7	8	9	12	11	3*		10	6					21
1	2	4		5		7	8	9		11	3		10	6					22
1	2	4		5		7*	8	9	12	11	3		10	6					23
1	2	4		5		7	8	9		11	3		10	6					24
1*	2	4		5	12	7	8	9		11	3		10	6					25
1	2	4		5	6	7	12	9*		11	3		10	8					26
1	2		3*	5	6	7	8			11	12		10	9	4				27
1	2	4		5	6	7	8	9		11	3		10						28
1	2	4		5	6	7	8	9		11	3		10						29
1	2	4		5	6	7	8	9		11	3		10						30
1	2	4		5		7	8			11	3		10	6		9			31
1	2	4		5		7	8*		12	11	3		10	6		9			32
1	2	4		5		7	8		12	11*	3		10	6		9			33
1	2	4		5		7	8		11		3		10	6		9			34
1	2	4	5			7	8	12	11		3		10	6		9*			35
1	2		4	5		7	8*	12	11		3		10	6		9			36
1	2		4	5	8	7		12	11		3		10	6		9*			37
1	2		4	5	8	7	6	10	11*	12	3						9		38
1	2	4		5	6	7	8	10		11*	3			12			9		39
1	2	4		5	6	7	8	10		11	3						9		40
1	2	4		5	6	7	8	10		11*	3			12			9		41
1	2	4		5	6*	7	8	10		11	3			12			9		42
1	2	4				7	8			11	3	5	10	6			9		43
1	2	4		5		7	8			11	3		10	6			9		44
1	2	4		5	6	7	8			11	3			10			9		45
1	2	4		5*	6	7	8	12		11	3			10			9		46
46	46	41	8	44	29	46	44	34	7	41	39	7	36	21	1	7	9		
					2		1	4	7	1	1			5					
		2		2	1	16	10	8	1	13	1	2	11	7	1	1	10		

2 own-goals

1	2	4		5		7*	8	9	12	11	3		10	6					1
1	2	4		5		7	8	9		11	3		10	6					2
		4		5	8	7		9		11	3	2	10	6				1	3
		4		5	6	7		9		11	3	2	10	8				1	R
2	2	4		4	2	4	2	4		4	4	2	4	4				2	
									1										
							1			1	2		1	1					

1	2	4		5	6	7	8	9		11	3			10					1
1	2	12		5	6	7	8	9		11	3*	4	10						
2	2	1		2	2	2	2	2		2	2	1	1	1					
		1																	
				1										1					

1	2	4*	3	5	6	7	8			11		12	10	9					G
1	2	4		5	6	7	8	12		11	3		10	9*					G
2	2	2	1	2	2	2	2			2	1		2	2					
								1				1							

1986-87

Manager: Dave Smith

1	Aug	23	(a)	Bradford C	D 2-2	Coughlin, Summerfield	5,104
2		30	(h)	Reading	W 1-0	Hodges	9,659
3	Sep	6	(a)	Hull C	W 3-0	S.Cooper 2, Summerfield	6,451
4		13	(h)	Brighton & HA	D 2-2	Nelson, Matthews	9,423
5		20	(a)	Barnsley	D 1-1	Summerfield	4,163
6		30	(a)	Blackburn R	W 2-1	Summerfield, Rowbotham	5,300
7	Oct	4	(h)	Leeds U	D 1-1	S.Cooper	11,923
8		11	(a)	Grimsby T	D 1-1	S.Cooper	4,155
9		14	(h)	Sheffield U	W 1-0	Tynan	11,003
10		18	(h)	Sunderland	L 2-4	Hodges, Tynan	13,482
11		21	(h)	Ipswich T	W 2-0	Coughlin, Summerfield	12,569
12		25	(a)	Millwall	L 1-3	Walker (og)	3,558
13	Nov	1	(h)	Crystal P	W 3-1	Tynan 2, Summerfield	11,708
14		8	(a)	Shrewsbury T	D 1-1	Matthews	3,821
15		16	(h)	West Brom A	W 1-0	Nisbet	14,697
16		22	(a)	Huddersfield T	W 2-1	Clayton, Tynan	4,874
17		29	(h)	Oldham A	W 3-2	Clayton, Burrows, Tynan	17,265
18	Dec	6	(a)	Stoke C	L 0-1		10,043
19		13	(h)	Derby C	D 1-1	Tynan	15,812
20		19	(a)	Ipswich T	L 0-3		11,538
21		26	(h)	Portsmouth	L 2-3	Coughlin, Hodges	21,249
22		27	(a)	West Brom A	D 0-0		12,678
23	Jan	1	(a)	Birmingham C	L 2-3	Goodyear, Tynan	8,696
24		3	(h)	Hull C	W 4-0	Tynan 2, Hodges, Nelson	11,697
25		24	(h)	Bradford C	W 3-2	Tynan, Summerfield, Hodges	11,682
26	Feb	7	(a)	Reading	L 0-2		6,853
27		14	(h)	Blackburn R	D 1-1	Summerfield	9,884
28		21	(a)	Sheffield U	L 1-2	Coughlin	6,982
29		28	(h)	Barnsley	W 2-0	Nelson 2	9,588
30	Mar	7	(h)	Millwall	W 1-0	Tynan	9,525
31		14	(a)	Sunderland	L 1-2	Tynan	10,062
32		21	(h)	Grimsby T	W 5-0	Nisbet 2, Tynan 2, Clayton	9,671
33		28	(a)	Leeds U	L 0-4		18,618
34	Apr	4	(h)	Shrewsbury T	W 3-2	Tynan 2, Nelson	8,905
35		7	(a)	Brighton & HA	D 1-1	Tynan	6,483
36		11	(a)	Crystal P	D 0-0		10,589
37		18	(h)	Birmingham C	D 0-0		13,372
38		20	(a)	Portsmouth	W 1-0	Summerfield	17,171
39		25	(h)	Huddersfield T	D 1-1	Law	13,342
40	May	2	(a)	Oldham A	L 1-2	Law	6,542
41		4	(h)	Stoke C	L 1-3	Coughlin	13,774
42		9	(a)	Derby C	L 2-4	Nelson 2	20,798

FINAL LEAGUE POSITION: 7th in Division Two

Appearances
Sub Appearances
Goals

FA Cup

3	Jan	10	(a)	Bristol C	D 1-1	Summerfield	16,943
R		19	(h)	Bristol C	W 3-1	Summerfield, Nelson, Tynan	14,142
4		31	(a)	Arsenal	L 1-6	Rowbotham	39,029

Appearances
Sub Appearances
Goals

FL Cup

1	Aug	26	(a)	Cardiff C	L 4-5	Nisbet, Coughlin 2, Summerfield	2,503
	Sep	2	(h)	Cardiff C	L 0-1		5,829

Appearances
Sub Appearances
Goals

Crudgington	Nisbet	Cooper L	Uzzell	McElhinney	Matthews	Hodges	Coughlin	Summerfield	Clayton	Nelson	Goodyear	Cooper S	Tynan	Rowbotham	Brimacombe	Burrows	Cherry	Law	Evans	
1	2	3	4*	5	6	7	8	9	10	11	12									1
1	2	3	5		6	7	8	9	10	11	4									2
1	2	3	5		6		8	7		11	4	10	9							3
1	2	3	5		6		8	7		11	4	10*	9	12						4
1	2	3	12	5	6		8	7	10	11*	4		9							5
1	2	3		5	6		8	7	10*	11	4		9	12						6
1	2	3		5	6		8	7		11*	4	12	9	10						7
1	2	3	5		6		8	11			4	10	9	12	7*					8
1	2	3	5		6	7	8	11			4	10	9							9
1	2	3	5		6	7	8	11			4	10	9							10
1	2	3		5	6	7	8	11			4	10	9							11
1	2	3		5	6	7	8	11			4*	10	9			12				12
1	2	3		5	6	7	8	11			4	10	9							13
1	2	3			6	7	8	11	10*		4	12	9			5				14
1	2	3			6	7	8	11	10		4		9			5				15
1	2	3			6*	7	8	11	10		4		9	12		5				16
1	2	3			6	7	8*	11	10		4		9	12		5				17
	2	3*	6			7		11	10	12	4		9	8		5	1			18
	2	3			6	7	8		10	12	4		9	11*		5	1			19
	2	3			6*	7	8	12	10	11	4		9			5	1			20
	2	3*	4	5	6	7	8		10	11			9	12			1			21
1	2			5	6	7	8		10	11	3		9			4				22
1	2	10		5	6	7	8			11	3		9			4				23
1	2	3			6*	7	8			10	4		9	11	12	5				24
1	2				6	7	8	4		10	3		9	11*	12	5				25
	2	3		5	6		8*	10		11	12		9	7		4	1			26
	2	3		5	6	12	8	10		11			9	7*		4	1			27
	2	3*		5	6	7	8	10		11	12		9			4	1			28
	2		3	5	6*	7	8			11	4	10	9		12		1			29
	2		3	5		7	8		12	11	4	10*	9		6		1			30
	2		3	5		7	8		10	11	12		9		6*		1	4		31
	2	3		5	6	7	8		10	11			9				1	4		32
	2	3		5*	6	7	8			11			9	12			1	4	10	33
		3		5	6	7			10*	11			9	12	8	2	1	4		34
		3	5		6	7	8*		10	11			9	12	2		1	4		35
		3	5		6	7	8		10	11			9		2		1	4		36
		3	5		6	7	8		10	11*	12		9		2		1	4		37
		3	5		6	7	8	12	10*	11			9		2		1	4		38
		3	5		6	7	8	10		11	2*		9				1	4	12	39
		3	5		6	12	8	7*		11	2		9				1	4	10	40
	2		3	5	6*	7	8	12		11			9				1	4	10	41
	2		3		6	7*	8	12		11			9			5	1	4	10	42
21	35	35	20	20	39	33	40	24	20	30	27	10	40	7	8	16	21	12	4	
			1			2		4	1	2	5	2		9	3	1			1	
	3				2	5	5	9	3	7	1	4	18	1		1		2		

1 own-goal

1	2	3		5*	6	7	8	10		11	4		9		12					3
1	2		3	5*	6†	7	8	10		11	4		9	14		12				R
	2	3	12		6*	7	8	4	10†	11			9	14		5	1			4
2	3	2	1	2	3	3	3	3	1	3	2		3			1	1			
			1											2	1	1				
								2		1			1	1						

1	2	3	4	5*	6	7	8†	9	10	11	12	14								1
1	2	3	5		6	7*	8	9	10†	11	4	14				12				
2	2	2	2	1	2	2	2	2	2	2	1									
											1	2				1				
	1						2	1												

1987-88

Manager: Dave Smith

1	Aug	15	(a)	Manchester C	L 1-2	Law	20,046
2		18	(h)	Ipswich T	D 0-0		11,901
3		22	(h)	Huddersfield T	W 6-1	Summerfield, Tynan 2, Law, Evans, Furphy	8,811
4		29	(a)	Reading	W 1-0	Peters (og)	6,658
5		31	(h)	Sheffield U	W 1-0	Evans	14,504
6	Sep	5	(a)	Barnsley	L 1-2	Tynan	6,976
7		12	(h)	West Brom A	D 3-3	Tynan 2, Clayton	10,578
8		16	(a)	Bradford C	L 1-3	Matthews	11,009
9		19	(a)	Leicester C	L 0-4		8,872
10		26	(h)	Birmingham C	D 1-1	Tynan	8,912
11		29	(a)	Bournemouth	D 2-2	Hodges, Clayton	6,491
12	Oct	3	(h)	Aston Villa	L 1-3	Smith	10,516
13		10	(a)	Stoke C	L 0-1		8,275
14		17	(h)	Leeds U	W 6-3	Smith, Summerfield 2, Clayton 2, Tynan	9,358
15		20	(h)	Millwall	L 1-2	Evans	8,958
16		24	(a)	Blackburn R	D 1-1	Evans	6,014
17		31	(h)	Hull C	W 3-1	Smith, Tynan, Clayton	8,550
18	Nov	3	(a)	Crystal Palace	L 1-5	Brimacombe	7,424
19		14	(a)	Swindon T	D 1-1	Evans	9,616
20		21	(h)	Middlesbrough	L 0-1		9,428
21		28	(a)	Oldham A	W 1-0	Tynan	4,516
22	Dec	5	(h)	Shrewsbury T	W 2-0	Hodges, S.Cooper	7,603
23		12	(a)	Huddersfield T	L 1-2	S.Cooper	5,747
24		20	(h)	Bradford C	W 2-1	S.Cooper, Smith	11,350
25		26	(a)	Birmingham C	W 1-0	Tynan	9,166
26		28	(h)	Leicester C	W 4-0	Smith, Tynan 2, Anderson	15,581
27	Jan	1	(h)	Reading	L 1-3	Tynan	13,290
28		2	(a)	West Brom A	L 0-1		8,445
29		16	(h)	Manchester C	W 3-2	Smith, Tynan, Evans	13,291
30	Feb	13	(a)	Ipswich T	W 2-1	Law, Summerfield	10,475
31		27	(a)	Aston Villa	L 2-5	Tynan, Hodges	16,141
32	Mar	5	(a)	Leeds U	L 0-1		18,115
33		12	(h)	Stoke C	W 3-0	Tynan 2, Uzzell	8,749
34		19	(a)	Hull C	D 1-1	Evans	5,712
35		26	(h)	Blackburn R	W 3-0	Evans, Burrows, Hodges	12,359
36	Apr	4	(h)	Swindon T	W 1-0	Evans	13,299
37		9	(a)	Millwall	L 2-3	Hodges, Summerfield	11,052
38		15	(h)	Barnsley	D 0-0		8,059
39		19	(a)	Sheffield U	L 0-1		9,052
40		23	(h)	Crystal P	L 1-3	Evans	8,370
41		26	(h)	Bournemouth	L 1-2	Hodges	6,310
42		30	(a)	Middlesbrough	L 1-3	Clayton	16,615
43	May	2	(h)	Oldham A	W 1-0	Marker	6,084
44		7	(a)	Shrewsbury T	L 1-2	Clayton	4,510

FINAL LEAGUE POSITION: 16th in Division Two

Appearances
Sub Appearances
Goals

FA Cup

3	Jan	9	(h)	Colchester U	W 2-0	S.Cooper, Matthews	10,351
4		30	(h)	Shrewsbury T	W 1-0	Evans	12,749
5	Feb	20	(a)	Manchester C	L 1-3	Hodges	29,206

Appearances
Sub Appearances
Goals

FL Cup

2	Sep	23	(a)	Peterborough U	L 1-4	Tynan	3,843
'	Oct	6	(h)	Peterborough U	D 1-1	Clayton	5,524

Appearances
Sub Appearances
Goals

Cherry	Brimacombe	Cooper L	Coughlin	Law	Smith	Matthews	Summerfield	Tynan	Evans	Furphy	Uzzell	Cooper S	Clayton	Rowbotham D	Hodges	Anderson	McElhinney	Crudgington	Rowbotham J	Marker	Burrows	Morrison	
1	2	3	4*	5	6	7	8	9	10	11†	12	14											1
1	2	3		4	5	6	8	9	10	11†		7*	12	14									2
1	2	3		5	6	7	8	9	10	11				4									3
1	2	3		5	6	7	8	9	10	11		12		4*									4
1	2	3		5	6	7	8	9	10	11				4*	12								5
1	2	3	12	5†	6	7	8	9	10	11*	14				4								6
1	2	3		5	6	4	8	9	10			12	11†	14		7*							7
1	2	3		5	6	7	8*	9	10		12	14	11			4							8
1	2	3		5		4†		9	10		14		11	8*	12	7	6						9
	2	3		5	6	12	8	9	10				14		7	11†	4*	1					10
	2	3		5	6	4	8	9	10			11*	12		7			1					11
	2	3		5	6	4	8		10				9	11*	7	12		1					12
	2	3		5	6		8	4	10				9		7	11*		1	12				13
	11	3		5	6	4	8	9					10	12	7			1	2*				14
	11	3		5	6	4*	8†	9	12				10	14	7			1	2				15
1		3		5	6	4		9	8			11	10		7				2				16
1	2	3	8	5	6	4*	12	9	11				10		7								17
1	2	3	8	5	6	4	12	9	11				10*		7								18
1	2	3	8		6			9	10*			12			7	11	4			5			19
1	2†	3	8		6		12	9	10*			14			7	11	4			5			20
1	2	3	8		6			9				10			7	11				5	4		21
1	2	3	8*		6		12	9				10			7	11				5	4		22
1	2			3	6		8	9				10	12		7*	11				5	4		23
	2			3	6		8	9	12			10			7	11*		1		5	4		24
1	2	12		3	6		8*	9				10			7	11				5	4		25
1	2			3	6		8	9				10			7	11				5	4		26
1	2	12		3*	6	8		9	14			10†			7	11				5	4		27
1	2	3			6	8		9	10			12			7	11*				5	4		28
1	2	3			6	8	14	9	12			10†			7	11*				5	4		29
1		3		2		8	11	9	10						7		6			5	4		30
1	2	3				8	11	9				10			7		6*			5	4	12	31
1	2	3			6	8	11	9	12			10			7*					5	4		32
1	2				6	8	11	9	10*		3		14		7†	12				5	4		33
1	2	14			6	8	11	9	10*		3		12		7†					5	4		34
1	2	12			5	8	11	9	10		3*				7					6	4		35
1	2	3			6	8	11	9	10*				12		7					5	4		36
1	2	3			6	8	11	9	10						7					5	4		37
1	2	3			6	8	11	9	10						7					5	4		38
1	2	3			6	8	11	9	10						7					5	4		39
1	2	3			6	8	11	9	10			12				7*				5	4		40
1	2	3*		12	6	8	11	9	10						7					5	4		41
1	2				6	8	11	9	10		3		4		7					5			42
1	2				6	8	11	9*	10†		3	14	12		7					5	4		43
1	2			11	6	8†		12	14		3	9*	10		7					5	4		44
37	42	33	7	25	41	34	32	42	31	6	6	14	12	5	35	17	6	7	3	26	23		
		4	1	1		1	5	1	6		3	9	8	3	2	2			1			1	
	1			3	6	1	5	16	10	1	1	3	7		6	1	1			1	1		

1 own-goal

1	2	3			6	8		9				10			7	11				5	4		3
1		3		2	6	8	11*	9	10				12		7					5	4		4
1	12	3		2*		8	11	9				14	10†		7		6			5	4		5
3	1	3		2	2	3	2	3	1			1	1		3	1	1			3	3		
	1											1	1										
						1			1			1			1								

	2	3		5	6	8*		9	10			12	14		7	11†	4	1					2
	2	3		4	5	6*	8		10				9	11	7			1	12				
	2	2		2	2	2	1	1	2				1	1	2	1	1	2					
												1	1						1				
								1					1										

1988-89

Manager: Ken Brown

1	Aug	27	(a)	Walsall	D	2-2	Tynan, Marker	6,178
2	Sep	3	(h)	Hull C	W	2-0	Tynan, Skipper (og)	8,202
3		10	(a)	Watford	L	0-2		12,040
4		17	(h)	Stoke C	W	4-0	Tynan 3, Marker	7,823
5		21	(a)	Leicester C	L	0-1		9,117
6		24	(h)	West Brom A	D	1-1	Tynan	8,539
7	Oct	1	(a)	Crystal P	L	1-4	Brimacombe	8,047
8		4	(a)	Birmingham C	W	1-0	Tynan	4,921
9		8	(h)	Bradford C	W	3-1	Tynan 2, McCarthy	6,855
10		15	(h)	Manchester C	L	0-1		10,158
11		22	(a)	Chelsea	L	0-5		12,658
12		25	(h)	Shrewsbury T	D	0-0		6,298
13		29	(a)	Barnsley	L	1-3	Marker	5,485
14	Nov	5	(h)	Blackburn R	W	4-3	Tynan 4	7,823
15		12	(a)	Portsmouth	L	0-2		11,572
16		19	(a)	Oxford U	W	1-0	Tynan	5,429
17		26	(h)	Oldham A	W	3-0	Tynan, G.Campbell, Hodges	7,829
18	Dec	3	(a)	Ipswich T	D	2-2	G.Campbell, Stuart	9,929
19		6	(h)	Brighton & HA	W	3-0	Tynan 2, Plummer	8,133
20		10	(h)	Bournemouth	D	1-1	Summerfield	10,619
21		18	(h)	Sunderland	L	1-4	Tynan	13,478
22		26	(a)	Swindon T	L	0-1		7,883
23		31	(a)	Leeds U	L	0-2		24,043
24	Jan	2	(h)	Watford	W	1-0	Summerfield	12,142
25		14	(a)	Brighton & HA	D	2-2	Tynan, Stuart	8,504
26		21	(h)	Walsall	W	2-0	Tynan, Marker	11,505
27	Feb	4	(h)	Birmingham C	L	0-1		7,721
28		11	(a)	Bradford C	D	1-1	McCarthy	8,693
29		18	(h)	Chelsea	L	0-1		13,180
30		25	(a)	Manchester C	L	0-2		22,451
31		28	(a)	Shrewsbury T	L	0-2		2,978
32	Mar	4	(h)	Portsmouth	L	0-1		8,131
33		11	(a)	Blackburn R	W	2-1	Stuart, Tynan	7,642
34		18	(h)	Leicester C	D	1-1	Stuart	6,703
35		25	(a)	Hull C	L	0-3		5,581
36		27	(h)	Swindon T	W	4-1	Marker, Tynan, McCarthy 2	8,487
37	Apr	2	(a)	Stoke C	D	2-2	Tynan, McCarthy	8,363
38		4	(a)	Sunderland	L	1-2	Tynan	8,003
39		9	(h)	Leeds U	W	1-0	McCarthy	9,365
40		15	(a)	West Brom A	D	2-2	Brown, McCarthy	11,358
41		22	(h)	Crystal P	L	0-2		8,492
42		25	(h)	Barnsley	L	1-2	Byrne	5,468
43		29	(a)	Oldham A	D	2-2	Marker, G.Campbell	4,614
44	May	1	(h)	Ipswich T	L	0-1		6,484
45		6	(h)	Oxford U	W	3-1	Burrows, McCarthy, Stuart	4,989
46		13	(a)	Bournemouth	D	0-0		7,230

FINAL LEAGUE POSITION: 18th in Division Two

Appearances
Sub Appearances
Goals

FA Cup

3	Jan	7	(h)	Cambridge U	W	2-0	Tynan, Summerfield	8,648
4		28	(h)	Everton	D	1-1	McCarthy	27,566
R		31	(a)	Everton	L	0-4		28,543

Appearances
Sub Appearances
Goals

League Cup

1	Aug	29	(a)	Hereford U	W	3-0	Summerfield, Marker, McCarthy	2,353
	Sep	6	(h)	Hereford U	W	3-2	McCarthy 2, Marker	4,773
2		28	(a)	Manchester C	L	0-1		9,454
	Oct	12	(h)	Manchester C	L	3-6	Smith, McCarthy, Tynan	8,794

Appearances
Sub Appearances
Goals

Cherry	Brimacombe	Cooper	Burrows	Marker	Smith	Hodges	Matthews	Tynan	McCarthy	Summerfield	Evans	Uzzell	Plummer	Penhaligon	Stuart	Campbell G	Miller	Rowbotham	Wilmot	Pickard	Byrne	Barlow	Garner	Whiston	Morrison	Campbell D	Brown	
1	2	3	4	5	6	7	8	9*	10	11	12																	1
1	2	3	4	5	6		8	9	10*	11	7	12																2
1	2	3	4	5	6		8	9	10	11			7															3
1	11	3	4	5	6		8	9	10				7														2	4
1	11	3	4*	5	6		8	9	10	12			7														2	5
1	11	3	4	5	6		8	9	10				7														2	6
1	11	3	4	5	6		8	9	10				7														2	7
	11	3	4	5	6		8	9	10				7	1													2	8
1	11	3	4	5	6		8	9	10				7														2	9
1	11	3	4	5			8*	9	10	12		6	7														2	10
1	11	3	4	5	6	14	8*	9	10			12	7†														2	11
1	11	3	4	5	6	7		9	10	8																	2	12
1	11*	3	4	5	6	7		9	10	8		12															2	13
1		3	4	5				9	10	8		6	7		11												2	14
1	6	3*	4			8	12	9	10			5	7		11†	14											2	15
1	5		4			7	8	9		6		3	10		11												2	16
	5		4			8		9		6		3	7		11	10	1										2	17
	5		4	12		8		9		6		3	7*		11	10	1										2	18
	4			5		8		9		6		3	7		11	10	1										2	19
	4			5		8		9	12	6		3	7		11	10*	1										2	20
	4			5		8		9		6		3	7		11	10	1										2	21
			4	5	7	8		9	10	6		3			11		1										2	22
			4	5	7	8		9	10	6		3			11		1										2	23
			4	5	6	8		9	10	7		3			11		1										2	24
			4	5	6	8		9	10*	7		3			11	12	1	2										25
			4	5	6	8		9	10*	7		3			11	12	1	2										26
			4	5	6	10*	7	9	8			3			11	12	1										2	27
			4	5	6	10	7†	9*	8			3	14		11	12	1										2	28
			4	5	6	10	7†	9	8			3	14		11		1										2	29
			4	5	6	10	7	9	8*			3	12		11				1								2	30
			4	5	6	10	7*	9	8			3	12		11				1								2	31
			4	5	6	10	7†	9	8*				14		11			3	1	12							2	32
			4	5	6		7	9	8			3			11				1							10	2	33
			4	5	6	12	7*	9				3			11			2	1	10	8							34
			4	5	6		7	9	8			3			11			2	1		10							35
			4	5	6		7	9*	8			3			11	12			1		10						2	36
			4	5	6	12	10	9	8			3			11				1		7*						2	37
			4	5	6	12	10*	9	8			3			11				1		7						2	38
			4	5	6	12	10*	9	8			3			11				1		7						2	39
			4	5	6	11	10	9	8			3							1		7						2	40
			4	5	6	12	10*	9	8			3			11				1		7						2	41
			4	5	6		10	9	8			3			11				1		7						2	42
	8		4	5	6	12	10†	9				3*			11	14			1		7						2	43
	3		4	5	6	10		9	8						11				1		7						2	44
	3		4	5				9	8						11				1		7	14	10*	12	6		2†	45
	3		4	5		12		9					14		11	8			1		7†			10*	6		2	46
15	24	15	43	42	35	23	29	46	37	17	1	30	17	1	32	6	13	5	17	1	13		1	1	2	1	39	
				1		8	1		1	2	1	3	6			7				1		1		1				
	1		1	6		1		24	8	2			1		5	3					1						1	

1 own-goal

Cherry	Brimacombe	Cooper	Burrows	Marker	Smith	Hodges	Matthews	Tynan	McCarthy	Summerfield	Evans	Uzzell	Plummer	Penhaligon	Stuart	Campbell G	Miller	Rowbotham	Wilmot	Pickard	Byrne	Barlow	Garner	Whiston	Morrison	Campbell D	Brown	
1			4	5	6	8		9	10	7		3			11												2	3
			4	5	6	10		9	8	7		3			11		1										2	4
			4	5	6	10†	12	9	8	7*		3			11	14	1										2	R
1			3	3	3	3		3	3	3		3			3		2										3	
							1									1												
								1	1	1																		

Cherry	Brimacombe	Cooper	Burrows	Marker	Smith	Hodges	Matthews	Tynan	McCarthy	Summerfield	Evans	Uzzell	Plummer	Penhaligon	Stuart	Campbell G	Miller	Rowbotham	Wilmot	Pickard	Byrne	Barlow	Garner	Whiston	Morrison	Campbell D	Brown	
1	2	3	4	5	6	7*	8	9	10	11	12																	1
1	2	3	4	5	6		8	9	10	11		7																
1	11	3	4	5	6		8	9	10				7														2	2
1	11	3	4	5	6	12	8†	9	10	14			7*														2	
4	4	4	4	4	4	1	4	4	4	2		1	2														2	
						1				1	1																	
				2	1			1	4	1																		

Plymouth in the Football League 1920-21 to 1988-89

		HOME					*AWAY*						
	P	W	D	L	F	A	W	D	L	F	A	Pts	Pos
DIVISION THREE													
1920-21	42	10	7	4	25	13	1	14	6	10	21	43	11th
DIVISION THREE SOUTH													
1921-22	42	17	4	0	43	4	8	7	6	20	20	61	2nd
1922-23	42	18	3	0	47	6	5	4	12	14	23	53	2nd
1923-24	42	13	6	2	46	15	10	3	8	24	19	55	2nd
1924-25	42	17	3	1	55	12	6	7	8	22	26	56	2nd
1925-26	42	16	2	3	71	33	8	6	7	36	34	56	2nd
1926-27	42	17	4	0	52	14	8	6	7	43	47	60	2nd
1927-28	42	17	2	2	60	19	6	5	10	25	35	53	3rd
1928-29	42	14	6	1	51	13	6	6	9	32	38	52	4th
1929-30	42	18	3	0	63	12	12	5	4	35	26	68	1st
DIVISION TWO													
1930-31	42	10	3	8	47	33	4	5	12	29	51	36	18th
1931-32	42	14	4	3	69	29	6	5	10	31	37	49	4th
1932-33	42	13	4	4	45	22	3	5	13	18	45	41	14th
1933-34	42	12	7	2	43	20	3	6	12	26	50	43	10th
1934-35	42	13	3	5	48	26	6	5	10	27	38	46	8th
1935-36	42	15	2	4	50	20	5	6	10	21	37	48	7th
1936-37	42	11	6	4	42	22	7	7	7	29	31	49	5th
1937-38	42	10	7	4	40	30	4	5	12	17	35	40	13th
1938-39	42	9	7	5	24	13	6	1	14	25	42	38	15th
1946-47	42	11	3	7	45	34	3	2	16	34	62	33	19th
1947-48	42	8	9	4	27	22	1	11	9	13	36	38	17th
1948-49	42	11	4	6	33	25	1	8	12	16	39	36	20th
1949-50	42	6	6	9	19	24	2	10	9	25	41	32	21st
DIVISION THREE SOUTH													
1950-51	46	16	5	2	54	19	8	4	11	31	36	57	4th
1951-52	46	19	3	1	70	19	10	5	8	37	34	66	1st
DIVISION TWO													
1952-53	42	12	5	4	37	24	8	4	9	28	36	49	4th
1953-54	42	6	12	3	38	31	3	4	14	27	51	34	19th
1954-55	42	10	4	7	29	26	2	3	16	28	56	31	20th
1955-56	42	7	6	8	33	25	3	2	16	21	62	28	21st
DIVISION THREE SOUTH													
1956-57	46	10	8	5	38	31	6	3	14	30	42	43	18th
1957-58	46	17	4	2	43	17	8	4	11	24	31	58	3rd
DIVISION THREE													
1958-59	46	14	7	2	55	27	9	9	5	34	32	62	1st
DIVISION TWO													
1959-60	42	10	6	5	42	36	3	3	15	19	53	35	19th
1960-61	42	13	4	4	52	32	4	4	13	29	50	42	11th
1961-62	42	12	4	5	45	30	7	4	10	30	45	46	5th
1962-63	42	13	4	4	48	24	2	8	11	28	49	42	12th
1963-64	42	6	8	7	26	32	2	8	11	19	35	32	20th
1964-65	42	10	7	4	36	28	6	1	14	27	51	40	15th
1965-66	42	7	8	6	37	26	5	5	11	17	37	37	18th
1966-67	42	12	4	5	42	21	2	5	14	17	37	37	16th
1967-68	42	5	4	12	26	36	4	5	12	12	36	27	22nd

				DIVISION THREE									
1968-69	46	10	8	5	34	25	7	7	9	19	24	49	5th
1969-70	46	10	7	6	32	23	6	4	13	24	41	43	17th
1970-71	46	6	12	5	39	33	6	7	10	24	30	43	15th
1971-72	46	13	6	4	43	26	7	4	12	31	38	50	8th
1972-73	46	14	3	6	43	26	6	7	10	31	40	50	8th
1973-74	46	13	6	4	37	17	4	4	15	22	37	44	17th
1974-75	46	16	5	2	38	19	8	6	9	41	39	59	2nd
				DIVISION TWO									
1975-76	42	13	4	4	36	20	0	8	13	12	34	38	16th
1976-77	42	5	9	7	27	25	3	7	11	19	40	32	21st
				DIVISION THREE									
1977-78	46	7	8	8	33	28	4	9	10	28	40	39	19th
1978-79	46	11	9	3	40	27	4	5	14	27	41	44	15th
1979-80	46	13	7	3	39	17	3	5	15	20	38	44	15th
1980-81	46	14	5	4	35	18	5	9	9	21	26	52	7th
1981-82	46	12	5	6	37	24	6	6	11	27	32	65	10th
1982-83	46	15	2	6	37	23	4	6	13	24	43	65	8th
1983-84	46	11	8	4	38	17	2	4	17	18	45	51	19th
1984-85	46	11	7	5	33	23	4	7	12	29	42	59	15th
1985-86	46	17	3	3	56	20	9	6	8	32	33	87	2nd
				DIVISION TWO									
1986-87	42	12	6	3	40	23	4	7	10	22	34	61	7th
1987-88	44	12	4	6	44	26	4	4	14	21	41	56	16th
1988-89	46	10	4	8	34	22	4	8	12	21	44	54	18th

Liverpool's Alan A'Court scores one of his two goals against Plymouth Argyle at Home Park in October 1955. Liverpool won 4-1 and Argyle were relegated at the end of the season.

Plymouth Against Other League Clubs

Plymouth Argyle have played 95 clubs in the Football League since 1903. Below is Argyle's record against each club. Some clubs modified their names (eg Leicester Fosse became Leicester City) but in all cases the current name used by each club covers all games under previous names.

ABERDARE ATHLETIC

Season	*Div*	*H*	*A*
1921-22	3S	3-0	0-0
1922-23	3S	2-0	2-2
1923-24	3S	2-0	2-1
1924-25	3S	2-0	1-3
1925-26	3S	7-2	1-6
1926-27	3S	2-0	6-5

ACCRINGTON STANLEY

Season	*Div*	*H*	*A*
1958-59	3	2-4	1-1

ALDERSHOT

Season	*Div*	*H*	*A*
1950-51	3S	5-1	2-2
1951-52	3S	2-1	2-1
1956-57	3S	2-2	2-0
1957-58	3S	4-2	3-3
1973-74	3	2-1	2-3
1974-75	3	1-0	3-4

ASTON VILLA

Season	*Div*	*H*	*A*
1936-37	2	2-2	4-5
1937-38	2	0-3	0-3
1959-60	2	3-0	0-2
1967-68	2	2-1	1-0
1970-71	3	1-1	1-1
1971-72	3	3-2	1-3
1967-68	2	1-3	2-5

BARNSLEY

Season	*Div*	*H*	*A*
1930-31	2	4-0	4-0
1931-32	2	3-0	0-0
1934-35	2	3-1	4-1
1935-36	2	7-1	2-1
1936-37	2	1-2	3-1
1937-38	2	2-2	2-3
1946-47	2	3-2	3-1
1947-48	2	1-0	1-2
1948-49	2	3-1	0-0
1949-50	2	2-2	1-4
1952-53	2	4-0	3-0
1955-56	2	3-0	2-1
1968-69	3	0-0	0-0
1969-70	3	0-0	1-0
1970-71	3	2-1	0-2
1971-72	3	2-1	2-2
1979-80	3	2-1	0-0
1980-81	3	1-3	1-2
1986-87	2	2-0	1-1
1987-88	2	0-0	1-2
1988-89	2	1-2	1-3

BARROW

Season	*Div*	*H*	*A*
1968-69	3	4-1	0-1
1969-70	3	1-0	1-1

BIRMINGHAM CITY

Season	*Div*	*H*	*A*
1946-47	2	0-2	1-6
1947-48	2	0-3	1-1
1952-53	2	2-1	0-4
1953-54	2	2-2	0-3
1954-55	2	1-0	1-3
1965-66	2	6-1	0-1
1966-67	2	1-1	0-0
1967-68	2	1-2	2-2
1986-87	2	0-0	2-3
1987-88	2	1-1	1-0
1988-89	2	0-1	1-0

BLACKBURN ROVERS

Season	*Div*	*H*	*A*
1936-37	2	2-0	3-2
1937-38	2	2-2	1-2
1938-39	2	1-0	0-4
1948-49	2	3-0	1-2
1949-50	2	0-0	0-1
1952-53	2	3-1	3-1
1953-54	2	1-1	3-2
1954-55	2	0-2	2-2
1955-56	2	1-0	1-2
1966-67	2	4-0	0-3
1967-68	2	2-1	1-1
1971-72	3	1-0	2-3
1972-73	3	1-2	1-3
1973-74	3	2-1	0-2
1974-75	3	2-1	2-5
1975-76	2	2-2	1-3
1976-77	2	4-0	0-2
1979-80	3	0-1	0-1
1986-87	2	1-1	2-1
1987-88	2	3-0	1-1
1988-89	2	4-3	2-1

BLACKPOOL

Season	Div	H	A
1933-34	2	0-3	1-1
1934-35	2	1-2	1-4
1935-36	2	3-2	1-3
1936-37	2	1-3	1-1
1967-68	2	2-2	0-2
1975-76	2	1-2	0-0
1976-77	2	2-0	2-0
1978-79	3	0-0	0-0
1979-80	3	2-2	3-1
1980-81	3	0-2	0-1
1985-86	3	3-1	1-1

BOLTON WANDERERS

Season	Div	H	A
1933-34	2	3-0	0-2
1934-35	2	1-0	2-3
1964-65	2	1-3	1-6
1965-66	2	1-3	1-0
1966-67	2	2-0	2-1
1967-68	2	1-2	2-1
1971-72	3	2-0	1-2
1972-73	3	1-0	0-2
1975-76	2	2-3	0-0
1976-77	2	1-1	0-3
1983-84	3	2-0	1-2
1984-85	3	2-0	2-7
1985-86	3	4-1	1-3

BOURNEMOUTH

1923-24	3S	4-0	0-0
1924-25	3S	2-0	1-0
1925-26	3S	7-2	2-1
1926-27	3S	1-1	2-6
1927-28	3S	3-1	2-2
1928-29	3S	2-0	1-4
1929-30	3S	2-1	1-1
1950-51	3S	3-1	2-0
1951-52	3S	4-1	2-1
1956-57	3S	2-0	1-2
1957-58	3S	3-1	0-0
1958-59	3	3-1	1-1
1968-69	3	1-1	1-0
1969-70	3	0-1	3-1
1971-72	3	1-1	0-1
1972-73	3	1-0	1-0
1973-74	3	2-0	0-0
1974-75	3	1-0	7-3
1982-83	3	2-0	0-1
1983-84	3	1-0	1-2
1984-85	3	0-0	0-1
1985-86	3	2-1	3-1
1987-88	2	1-2	2-2
1988-89	2	1-1	0-0

BRADFORD

Season	Div	H	A
1930-31	2	0-0	1-7
1931-32	2	4-1	0-2
1932-33	2	3-2	0-1
1933-34	2	4-1	1-4
1934-35	2	2-2	2-2
1935-36	2	2-0	2-2
1936-37	2	2-0	0-0
1937-38	2	1-0	0-2
1938-39	2	4-1	2-2
1946-47	2	2-4	2-3
1947-48	2	2-2	0-3
1948-49	2	3-0	2-2
1949-50	2	1-1	2-3

BRADFORD CITY

Season	Div	H	A
1930-31	2	0-2	0-1
1931-32	2	3-3	3-3
1932-33	2	2-1	3-2
1933-34	2	3-0	4-3
1934-35	2	3-1	1-0
1935-36	2	0-1	2-2
1936-37	2	4-4	1-1
1958-59	3	1-1	0-0
1969-70	3	0-1	0-1
1970-71	3	1-3	1-0
1971-72	3	1-4	1-0
1977-78	3	6-0	1-0
1982-83	3	3-1	0-4
1983-84	3	3-0	0-2
1984-85	3	0-0	0-1
1986-87	2	3-2	2-2
1987-88	2	2-1	1-3
1988-89	2	3-1	1-1

BRENTFORD

Season	Div	H	A
1920-21	3	1-0	0-0
1921-22	3S	4-1	1-3
1922-23	3S	3-0	0-2
1923-24	3S	4-1	1-1
1924-25	3S	7-1	0-1
1925-26	3S	4-0	2-2
1926-27	3S	2-1	0-0
1927-28	3S	1-0	2-0
1928-29	3S	4-0	2-0
1929-30	3S	1-1	0-3
1933-34	2	1-1	0-3
1934-35	2	1-1	0-0
1947-48	2	0-0	0-0
1948-49	2	1-0	2-2
1949-50	2	2-0	0-0
1952-53	2	1-0	2-1
1953-54	2	3-2	0-1
1956-57	3S	2-0	1-4
1957-58	3S	0-0	0-2
1958-59	3	1-1	0-3
1972-73	3	0-1	2-0
1978-79	3	2-1	1-2
1979-80	3	0-1	0-0
1980-81	3	0-1	1-0
1981-82	3	1-0	0-0

1982-83	3	2-0	0-2
1983-84	3	1-1	2-2
1984-85	3	1-1	1-3
1985-86	3	2-0	1-1

BRIGHTON & HA

Season	*Div*	*H*	*A*
1920-21	3	5-0	0-1
1921-22	3S	3-1	1-1
1922-23	3S	2-2	0-1
1923-24	3S	3-0	1-4
1924-25	3S	1-0	3-2
1925-26	3S	5-3	2-1
1926-27	3S	2-0	2-1
1927-28	3S	2-0	1-4
1928-29	3S	1-0	1-2
1929-30	3S	1-1	1-0
1950-51	3S	3-3	6-0
1951-52	3S	2-2	3-2
1956-57	3S	2-0	1-3
1957-58	3S	2-1	2-3
1959-60	2	3-2	2-2
1960-61	2	1-2	0-2
1961-62	2	5-0	2-3
1968-69	3	1-1	0-0
1969-70	3	0-1	0-2
1970-71	3	1-1	1-1
1971-72	3	1-2	0-3
1973-74	3	0-1	0-1
1974-75	3	2-2	2-2
1986-87	2	2-2	1-1
1988-89	2	3-0	2-2

BRISTOL CITY

Season	*Div*	*H*	*A*
1922-23	3S	5-1	0-2
1924-25	3S	7-1	2-2
1925-26	3S	3-1	1-2
1926-27	3S	4-2	2-4
1930-31	2	5-3	1-2
1931-32	2	2-1	2-0
1950-51	3S	2-0	0-1
1951-52	3S	2-2	1-1
1955-56	2	5-0	0-6
1959-60	2	1-4	1-2
1965-66	2	0-2	0-0
1966-67	2	1-2	0-1
1967-68	2	0-1	0-2
1975-76	2	0-0	2-2
1981-82	3	2-1	2-3
1984-85	3	1-0	3-4
1985-86	3	4-0	0-2

BRISTOL ROVERS

Season	*Div*	*H*	*A*
1920-21	3	2-1	0-2
1921-22	3S	1-0	3-1
1922-23	3S	3-0	1-0
1923-24	3S	2-2	1-1
1924-25	3S	3-2	1-1
1925-26	3S	1-2	3-2
1926-27	3S	3-2	2-2
1927-28	3S	4-1	1-3
1928-29	3S	2-0	1-0
1929-30	3S	3-0	3-2
1950-51	3S	0-0	1-3
1951-52	3S	1-2	2-1
1953-54	2	3-3	1-3
1954-55	2	0-1	1-3
1955-56	2	0-1	1-2
1959-60	2	5-3	0-2
1960-61	2	5-0	5-2
1961-62	2	3-1	3-4
1968-69	3	3-1	1-1
1969-70	3	2-2	1-3
1970-71	3	0-0	3-1
1971-72	3	2-1	2-2
1972-73	3	3-2	0-2
1973-74	3	1-0	2-4
1975-76	2	3-0	0-0
1976-77	2	1-1	1-1
1981-82	3	4-0	3-2
1982-83	3	0-4	0-2
1983-84	3	1-1	0-2
1984-85	3	3-2	0-1
1985-86	3	4-2	2-1

BURNLEY

Season	*Div*	*H*	*A*
1930-31	2	1-2	2-2
1931-32	2	4-0	1-1
1932-33	2	4-0	1-1
1933-34	2	1-0	2-2
1934-35	2	2-2	2-1
1935-36	2	2-0	1-0
1936-37	2	0-1	0-2
1937-38	2	2-3	2-0
1938-39	2	1-0	0-1
1946-47	2	2-2	1-2
1976-77	2	0-1	2-0
1980-81	3	2-1	1-2
1981-82	3	1-1	0-1
1983-84	3	1-1	1-2
1984-85	3	2-2	1-1

BURY

Season	*Div*	*H*	*A*
1930-31	2	3-6	0-2
1931-32	2	5-1	2-2
1932-33	2	1-0	1-2
1933-34	2	3-3	0-4
1934-35	2	3-0	1-2
1935-36	2	3-0	0-2
1936-37	2	3-0	0-2
1937-38	2	2-1	0-2
1938-39	2	0-1	0-3
1946-47	2	3-1	3-3
1947-48	2	0-0	0-0
1948-49	2	1-0	1-1
1949-50	2	2-0	1-5
1952-53	2	0-0	2-3
1953-54	2	1-1	0-3
1954-55	2	2-4	1-3

1955-56	2	1-4	1-7
1958-59	3	3-0	1-1
1961-62	2	1-2	1-1
1962.63	2	0-0	2-1
1963-64	2	1-0	2-2
1964-65	2	2-2	2-0
1965-66	2	2-2	0-1
1966-67	2	4-1	0-1
1969-70	3	2-2	1-3
1970-71	3	3-4	0-3
1974-75	3	2-1	1-0
1977-78	3	0-1	1-1
1978-79	3	3-0	2-1
1979-80	3	2-0	1-2
1985-86	3	3-0	1-0

CAMBRIDGE UNITED

Season	*Div*	*H*	*A*
1973-74	3	4-1	1-3
1977-78	3	0-1	0-3
1984-85	3	2-0	1-1

CARDIFF CITY

Season	*Div*	*H*	*A*
1930-31	2	5-1	1-4
1947-48	2	3-0	0-3
1948-49	2	0-1	0-1
1949-50	2	0-0	0-1
1959-60	2	1-1	1-0
1962-63	2	4-2	1-2
1963-64	2	1-1	1-3
1964-65	2	3-1	0-4
1965-66	2	2-2	1-5
1966-67	2	7-1	1-4
1967-68	2	0-0	1-1
1976-77	2	2-2	1-0
1982-83	3	3-2	0-0
1985-86	3	4-4	2-1

CARLISLE UNITED

Season	*Div*	*H*	*A*
1965-66	2	0-0	3-1
1966-67	2	1-2	0-0
1967-68	2	3-1	0-2
1975-76	2	2-1	0-2
1976-77	2	0-1	1-3
1977-78	3	0-1	0-0
1978-79	3	2-0	1-1
1979-80	3	4-2	1-2
1980-81	3	4-1	0-2
1981-82	3	1-0	1-3

CHARLTON ATHLETIC

Season	*Div*	*H*	*A*
1921-22	3S	3-0	0-0
1922-23	3S	2-0	0-1
1923-24	3S	1-1	1-0
1924-25	3S	3-2	1-2
1925-26	3S	1-0	5-0
1926-27	3S	3-1	1-1
1927-28	3S	2-0	0-2
1928-29	3S	2-2	1-2
1930-31	2	1-3	3-1
1931-32	2	1-1	0-2
1932-33	2	6-1	1-4
1935-36	2	4-2	1-1
1959-60	2	6-4	2-5
1960-61	2	6-4	4-6
1961-62	2	2-1	1-3
1962-63	2	6-1	3-6
1963-64	2	1-1	0-1
1964-65	2	1-5	2-3
1965-66	2	3-0	1-1
1966-67	2	2-1	0-1
1967-68	2	1-4	0-1
1972-73	3	5-0	0-3
1973-74	3	1-0	0-2
1974-75	3	1-1	2-0
1975-76	2	1-0	0-2
1976-77	2	1-0	1-3
1980-81	3	1-1	1-1

CHELSEA

Season	*Div*	*H*	*A*
1962-63	2	2-1	1-1
1975-76	2	0-3	2-2
1976-77	2	2-3	2-2
1988-89	2	0-1	0-5

CHESTER CITY

Season	*Div*	*H*	*A*
1977-78	3	2-2	1-1
1978-79	3	2-2	0-0
1979-80	3	1-0	0-1
1980-81	3	2-0	0-1
1981-82	3	5-1	3-0

CHESTERFIELD

Season	*Div*	*H*	*A*
1931-32	2	4-0	2-1
1932-33	2	1-0	1-1
1936-37	2	1-1	1-0
1937-38	2	1-1	0-2
1938-39	2	0-0	1-3
1946-47	2	1-0	1-4
1947-48	2	1-2	1-1
1948-49	2	2-2	0-0
1949-50	2	2-1	0-2
1958-59	3	2-0	2-1
1970-71	3	1-1	0-2
1971-72	3	1-0	1-2
1972-73	3	2-2	2-2
1973-74	3	1-1	0-1
1974-75	3	3-0	2-1
1977-78	3	2-0	1-4

1978-79	3	1-1	3-1
1979-80	3	1-0	1-3
1980-81	3	1-0	2-2
1981-82	3	0-2	2-2
1982-83	3	2-0	2-1
1985-86	3	0-0	2-1

COLCHESTER UNITED

Season	*Div*	*H*	*A*
1950-51	3S	7-1	0-3
1951-52	3S	3-1	0-1
1956-57	3S	2-2	1-2
1957-58	3S	1-1	2-1
1958-59	3	1-1	0-2
1974-75	3	1-0	0-1
1977-78	3	1-1	1-3
1978-79	3	1-1	1-2
1979-80	3	2-0	2-5
1980-81	3	1-1	2-2

COVENTRY CITY

Season	*Div*	*H*	*A*
1926-27	3S	3-0	3-3
1927-28	3S	4-0	1-1
1928-29	3S	3-0	4-1
1929-30	3S	3-0	0-1
1936-37	2	1-0	0-2
1937-38	2	3-1	0-4
1938-39	2	0-2	2-1
1946-47	2	2-2	0-1
1947-48	2	1-0	0-0
1948-49	2	2-3	1-1
1949-50	2	1-2	0-3
1956-57	3S	0-0	4-1
1957-58	3S	4-0	1-1
1964-65	2	2-3	0-2
1965-66	2	1-2	1-5
1966-67	2	4-2	0-1

CREWE ALEXANDRA

Season	*Div*	*H*	*A*
1968-69	3	2-2	1-2

CRYSTAL PALACE

Season	*Div*	*H*	*A*
1920-21	3	0-1	0-0
1925-26	3S	6-2	5-5
1926-27	3S	7-1	1-1
1927-28	3S	5-1	2-0
1928-29	3S	1-1	4-1
1929-30	3S	6-1	0-3
1950-51	3S	4-0	1-0
1951-52	3S	5-0	1-0
1956-57	3S	0-1	1-2
1957-58	3S	1-0	0-3
1964-65	2	1-1	1-2
1965-66	2	1-2	1-3
1966-67	2	1-0	1-2
1967-68	2	2-1	0-5
1974-75	3	0-1	3-3
1986-87	2	3-1	0-0
1987-88	2	1-3	1-5
1988-89	2	0-2	1-4

DARLINGTON

Season	*Div*	*H*	*A*
1985-86	3	4-2	2-0

DERBY COUNTY

Season	*Div*	*H*	*A*
1953-54	2	3-2	4-1
1954-55	2	1-0	2-2
1959-60	2	0-5	0-1
1960-61	2	4-2	1-4
1961-62	2	2-3	2-2
1962-63	2	2-1	2-3
1963-64	2	0-0	1-3
1964-65	2	1-1	2-3
1965-66	2	0-0	2-1
1966-67	2	1-2	1-1
1967-68	2	3-4	0-1
1984-85	3	0-1	1-3
1985-86	3	4-1	2-1
1986-87	2	1-1	2-4

DONCASTER ROVERS

Season	*Div*	*H*	*A*
1935-36	2	1-3	2-1
1936-37	2	7-0	1-2
1947-48	2	2-2	0-2
1952-53	2	0-0	1-1
1953-54	2	0-0	3-3
1954-55	2	1-2	2-3
1955-56	2	2-2	1-3
1958-59	3	4-0	6-4
1969-70	3	0-0	1-1
1970-71	3	1-1	0-0
1981-82	3	4-2	2-2
1982-83	3	1-2	2-2
1984-85	3	2-1	3-4
1985-86	3	0-1	0-1

EVERTON

Season	*Div*	*H*	*A*
1930-31	2	2-3	1-9
1952-53	2	1-0	0-2
1953-54	2	4-0	4-8

EXETER CITY

Season	*Div*	*H*	*A*
1920-21	3	0-0	1-1
1921-22	3S	0-0	2-0
1922-23	3S	5-1	0-0
1923-24	3S	4-0	4-0

1924-25	3S	1-1	0-3
1925-26	3S	2-2	0-4
1926-27	3S	2-0	2-0
1927-28	3S	1-2	0-2
1928-29	3S	0-0	2-1
1929-30	3S	4-1	1-1
1950-51	3S	0-1	2-3
1951-52	3S	2-1	0-1
1956-57	3S	5-0	1-2
1957-58	3S	1-0	2-4
1977-78	3	2-2	0-0
1978-79	3	4-2	0-1
1979-80	3	2-0	2-2
1980-81	3	0-2	1-1
1981-82	3	2-1	1-1
1982-83	3	1-0	0-1
1983-84	3	2-2	1-1

FULHAM

Season	*Div*	*H*	*A*
1928-29	3S	4-2	2-5
1929-30	3S	3-1	3-1
1932-33	2	2-3	1-3
1933-34	2	4-0	2-3
1934-35	2	3-1	0-3
1935-36	2	2-0	2-2
1936-37	2	0-3	2-2
1937-38	2	4-0	3-2
1938-39	2	0-0	2-1
1946-47	2	2-2	1-3
1947-48	2	3-2	1-1
1948-49	2	3-1	1-6
1952-53	2	3-1	1-2
1953-54	2	2-2	1-3
1954-55	2	3-2	3-2
1955-56	2	0-0	1-2
1969-70	3	2-0	3-4
1970-71	3	1-1	1-1
1975-76	2	4-0	0-0
1976-77	2	2-2	0-2
1980-81	3	2-1	0-0
1981-82	3	3-1	3-1

GRIMSBY TOWN

Season	*Div*	*H*	*A*
1920-21	3	0-0	1-1
1932-33	2	4-0	3-2
1933-34	2	0-2	1-5
1948-49	2	0-2	2-2
1949-50	2	4-2	2-2
1962-63	2	2-0	1-1
1963-64	2	3-2	1-1
1972-73	3	3-1	1-1
1973-74	3	1-0	0-3
1974-75	3	2-1	1-1
1979-80	3	1-1	0-1
1986-87	2	5-0	1-1

GILLINGHAM

Season	*Div*	*H*	*A*
1920-21	3	3-1	1-0
1921-22	3S	3-0	2-1
1922-23	3S	2-0	0-1
1923-24	3S	3-0	0-1
1924-25	3S	2-0	3-0
1925-26	3S	2-1	0-2
1926-27	3S	0-0	1-4
1927-28	3S	2-2	1-3
1928-29	3S	3-0	0-2
1929-30	3S	3-0	0-0
1950-51	3S	2-0	2-1
1951-52	3S	4-2	2-1
1956-57	3S	2-0	3-0
1957-58	3S	2-1	0-1
1968-69	3	1-1	0-1
1969-70	3	2-2	0-4
1970-71	3	2-1	2-0
1974-75	3	1-1	2-2
1977-78	3	1-3	1-1
1978-79	3	2-1	0-2
1979-80	3	2-2	1-0
1980-81	3	4-1	1-0
1981-82	3	1-2	2-3
1982-83	3	2-0	1-2
1983-84	3	1-1	1-2
1984-85	3	1-1	3-3
1985-86	3	3-0	1-1

HALIFAX TOWN

Season	*Div*	*H*	*A*
1958-59	3	1-1	1-0
1069-70	3	1-0	0-2
1970-71	3	1-1	1-4
1971-72	3	1-1	1-0
1972-73	3	2-1	1-2
1973-74	3	1-1	0-1
1974-75	3	2-0	1-1

HEREFORD UNITED

Season	*Div*	*H*	*A*
1973-74	3	0-1	1-0
1974-75	3	1-0	5-1
1976-77	2	2-1	1-1
1977-78	3	2-0	3-1

HARTLEPOOL U

Season	*Div*	*H*	*A*
1968-69	3	3-0	1-1

HUDDERSFIELD TOWN

Season	*Div*	*H*	*A*
1952-53	2	0-2	0-4
1959-60	2	1-3	0-2
1960-61	2	2-1	5-1
1961-62	2	4-2	1-5
1962-63	2	1-1	2-4
1963-64	2	0-0	3-4

1964-65	2	0-0	2-1
1965-66	2	0-0	1-2
1966-67	2	2-3	1-1
1967-68	2	1-1	1-0
1973-74	3	1-1	1-2
1974-75	3	2-0	2-0
1980-81	3	0-0	0-2
1981-82	3	1-1	0-0
1982-83	3	2-1	0-2
1986-87	2	1-1	2-1
1987-88	2	6-1	1-2

HULL CITY

Season	*Div*	*H*	*A*
1933-34	2	1-1	4-5
1934-35	2	6-4	1-1
1935-36	2	0-1	1-2
1949-50	2	1-3	2-4
1952-53	2	1-2	1-0
1953-54	2	2-2	0-2
1954-55	2	1-2	2-0
1955-56	2	1-1	1-2
1958-59	3	1-1	1-1
1959-60	2	3-2	1-3
1966-67	2	3-1	2-4
1967-68	2	2-5	2-0
1975-76	2	1-1	0-4
1976-77	2	1-2	1-3
1978-79	3	3-4	1-2
1979-80	3	5-1	0-1
1980-81	3	0-0	0-1
1983-84	3	2-0	2-1
1984-85	3	0-1	2-2
1986-87	2	4-0	3-0
1987-88	2	3-1	1-1
1988-89	2	2-0	0-3

IPSWICH TOWN

Season	*Div*	*H*	*A*
1950-51	3S	2-1	0-2
1951-52	3S	2-0	2-2
1954-55	2	2-0	1-2
1956-57	3S	1-2	1-2
1959-60	2	3-1	3-3
1960-61	2	1-2	1-3
1964-65	2	1-1	2-2
1965-66	2	3-0	1-4
1966-67	2	1-1	1-1
1967-68	2	0-1	1-1
1986-87	2	2-0	0-3
1987-88	2	0-0	2-1
1988-89	2	0-1	2-2

LEEDS UNITED

Season	*Div*	*H*	*A*
1931-32	2	3-2	0-0
1947-48	2	1-0	0-5
1948-49	2	2-1	0-1
1949-50	2	1-2	1-1
1952-53	2	0-1	1-1
1953-54	2	1-1	1-1
1954-55	2	3-1	2-3
1955-56	2	4-3	2-4
1960-61	2	3-1	1-2
1961-62	2	1-1	3-2
1962-63	2	3-1	1-6
1963-64	2	0-1	1-1
1986-87	2	1-1	0-4
1987-88	2	6-3	0-1
1988-89	2	1-0	0-2

LEICESTER CITY

Season	*Div*	*H*	*A*
1935-36	2	2-1	0-2
1936-37	2	2-1	2-3
1946-47	2	4-0	1-4
1947-48	2	0-0	1-2
1948-49	2	1-1	1-1
1949-50	2	2-1	0-0
1952-53	2	2-1	0-2
1953-54	2	0-3	2-4
1955-56	2	0-1	1-5
1987-88	2	4-0	0-4
1988-89	2	1-1	0-1

LINCOLN CITY

Season	*Div*	*H*	*A*
1932-33	2	0-3	0-2
1933-34	2	3-0	1-1
1948-49	2	0-0	2-1
1952-53	2	0-0	0-0
1953-54	2	1-2	0-2
1954-55	2	1-0	2-3
1955-56	2	1-4	0-1
1959-60	2	0-2	1-0
1960-61	2	1-1	1-3
1977-78	3	1-2	2-2
1978-79	3	2-1	3-3
1981-82	3	0-2	0-2
1982-83	3	0-2	2-1
1983-84	3	2-2	1-3
1984-85	3	2-0	2-2
1985-86	3	2-1	1-1

LIVERPOOL

Season	*Div*	*H*	*A*
1954-55	2	1-0	3-3
1955-56	2	4-0	1-4
1959-60	2	1-1	1-4
1960-61	2	0-4	1-1
1961-62	2	2-3	1-2

LUTON TOWN

Season	*Div*	*H*	*A*
1920-21	3	1-0	1-1
1921-22	3S	2-0	0-1
1922-23	3S	4-0	1-2
1923-24	3S	0-0	2-0
1924-25	3S	4-0	1-1

1925-26	3S	4-3	1-1
1926-27	3S	1-0	3-3
1927-28	3S	4-0	1-1
1928-29	3S	2-0	2-2
1929-30	3S	6-1	2-5
1937-38	2	2-4	1-1
1938-39	2	4-1	4-3
1946-47	2	2-1	4-3
1947-48	2	1-3	0-0
1948-49	2	1-1	1-3
1949-50	2	0-0	1-1
1952-53	2	2-1	0-1
1953-54	2	2-2	1-2
1954-55	2	2-1	1-3
1960-61	2	1-1	2-3
1961-62	2	0-3	2-0
1962-63	2	3-1	0-3
1968-69	3	2-0	0-2
1969-70	3	1-3	2-0
1975-76	2	3-0	1-1
1976-77	2	1-0	1-1

MANCHESTER CITY

Season	*Div*	*H*	*A*
1938-39	2	0-0	3-1
1946-47	2	2-3	3-4
1963-64	2	2-1	1-1
1964-65	2	3-2	1-2
1965-66	2	1-0	1-1
1987-88	2	3-2	1-2
1988-89	2	0-1	0-2

MANCHESTER UNITED

Season	*Div*	*H*	*A*
1931-32	2	3-1	1-2
1932-33	2	2-3	0-4
1933-34	2	4-0	3-0
1934-35	2	0-2	1-3
1935-36	2	3-1	2-3
1937-38	2	1-1	0-0

MANSFIELD TOWN

Season	*Div*	*H*	*A*
1958-59	3	8-3	4-1
1968-69	3	1-0	0-1
1969-70	3	1-0	2-1
1970-71	3	0-0	5-1
1971-72	3	3-1	3-2
1978-79	3	1-4	0-5
1979-80	3	0-0	0-0

MERTHYR TOWN

Season	*Div*	*H*	*A*
1920-21	3	2-1	0-0
1921-22	3S	0-0	1-0
1922-23	3S	2-0	1-0
1923-24	3S	1-1	0-1
1924-25	3S	2-0	2-1
1925-26	3S	3-0	1-1
1926-27	3S	1-1	1-5
1927-28	3S	5-0	4-1
1928-29	3S	4-0	2-2
1929-30	3S	2-1	3-0

MIDDLESBROUGH

Season	*Div*	*H*	*A*
1954-55	2	2-2	1-4
1955-56	2	4-0	2-1
1959-60	2	2-2	2-6
1960-61	2	3-3	1-3
1961-62	2	1-1	1-1
1962-63	2	4-5	0-3
1963-64	2	2-0	0-5
1964-65	2	1-0	3-1
1965-66	2	2-2	1-0
1967-68	2	0-1	0-5
1987-88	2	0-1	1-3

MILLWALL

Season	*Div*	*H*	*A*
1920-21	3	0-2	0-0
1921-22	3S	2-0	1-1
1922-23	3S	1-0	0-0
1923-24	3S	1-1	0-1
1924-25	3S	1-1	0-0
1925-26	3S	2-0	0-0
1926-27	3S	1-1	3-1
1927-28	3S	3-2	0-2
1930-31	2	5-0	1-4
1931-32	2	8-1	3-1
1932-33	2	0-0	0-2
1933-34	2	1-0	0-0
1938-39	2	2-2	0-3
1939-40	2	2-0	-
1946-47	2	0-2	1-1
1947-48	2	1-1	0-2
1950-51	3S	2-2	1-1
1951-52	3S	5-0	2-0
1956-57	3S	0-0	2-2
1957-58	3S	1-0	1-0
1966-67	2	3-1	2-1
1967-68	2	2-1	0-3
1976-77	2	2-2	0-3
1979-80	3	1-1	1-2
1980-81	3	2-0	1-1
1981-82	3	2-1	1-2
1982-83	3	3-1	2-2
1983-84	3	0-1	0-1
1984-85	3	3-1	0-2
1986-87	2	1-0	1-3
1987-88	2	1-2	2-3

NEWCASTLE UNITED

Season	*Div*	*H*	*A*
1934-35	2	1-3	0-3
1935-36	2	1-0	0-5
1936-37	2	1-1	1-1
1937-38	2	2-1	1-3

1938-39	2	0-1	1-2
1946-47	2	0-1	2-3
1947-48	2	3-0	1-6
1961-62	2	1-1	2-0
1962-63	2	0-2	1-3
1963-64	2	3-4	1-1
1964-65	2	2-1	1-2

NEWPORT COUNTY

Season	*Div*	*H*	*A*
1920-21	3	5-1	0-0
1921-22	3S	1-0	0-0
1922-23	3S	1-0	0-1
1923-24	3S	3-2	2-1
1924-25	3S	0-2	0-0
1925-26	3S	3-0	3-0
1926-27	3S	4-1	1-2
1927-28	3S	2-0	1-1
1928-29	3S	5-2	0-1
1929-30	3S	3-1	2-0
1946-47	2	4-1	0-1
1950-51	3S	1-1	0-2
1951-52	3S	5-0	3-3
1956-57	3S	3-2	1-4
1957-58	3S	1-0	2-0
1958-59	3	3-2	1-0
1980-81	3	3-2	2-0
1981-82	3	1-2	1-0
1982-83	3	2-4	2-2
1983-84	3	0-1	0-2
1984-85	3	1-0	0-1
1985-86	3	2-0	1-3

NORTHAMPTON TOWN

Season	*Div*	*H*	*A*
1920-21	3	0-2	1-1
1921-22	3S	2-0	3-1
1922-23	3S	1-0	0-1
1923-24	3S	0-0	0-1
1924-25	3S	2-1	2-5
1925-26	3S	2-4	1-2
1926-27	3S	3-0	1-2
1927-28	3S	3-3	1-2
1928-29	3S	1-1	0-3
1929-30	3S	1-0	1-1
1950-51	3S	4-1	3-1
1951-52	3S	2-0	1-3
1956-57	3S	4-3	0-2
1957-58	3S	3-0	0-5
1963-64	2	0-3	0-0
1964-65	2	5-2	1-3
1966-67	2	1-0	1-2
1968-69	3	0-1	1-1

NOTTINGHAM FOREST

Season	*Div*	*H*	*A*
1930-31	2	1-0	1-1
1931-32	2	5-1	2-3
1932-33	2	1-1	1-1
1933-34	2	4-3	1-2
1934-35	2	5-2	3-1
1935-36	2	3-1	1-0
1936-37	2	4-1	3-2
1937-38	2	1-0	0-1
1938-39	2	3-0	1-2
1946-47	2	2-0	1-5
1947-48	2	1-1	1-1
1948-49	2	1-0	0-1
1950-51	3S	0-2	1-4
1952-53	2	0-3	1-3
1953-54	2	1-0	0-3
1954-55	2	1-2	0-2
1955-56	2	1-2	1-3
1975-76	2	1-0	0-2
1976-77	2	1-2	1-1

NOTTS COUNTY

Season	*Div*	*H*	*A*
1931-32	2	3-4	0-3
1932-33	2	0-2	1-4
1933-34	2	1-0	1-2
1934-35	2	4-0	3-1
1952-53	2	2-2	4-0
1953-54	2	3-3	0-2
1954-55	2	1-3	0-2
1955-56	2	1-1	0-3
1958-59	3	3-0	2-1
1971-72	3	1-1	0-1
1972-73	3	1-4	0-2
1975-76	2	1-3	0-1
1976-77	2	1-2	0-2
1985-86	3	0-1	0-2

NORWICH CITY

Season	*Div*	*H*	*A*
1920-21	3	1-1	0-0
1921-22	3S	1-1	1-1
1922-23	3S	1-1	0-1
1923-24	3S	2-0	1-0
1924-25	3S	5-0	1-1
1925-26	3S	6-3	3-0
1926-27	3S	2-1	2-0
1927-28	3S	4-2	0-2
1928-29	3S	4-0	3-0
1929-30	3S	4-1	2-1
1934-35	2	0-1	0-3
1935-36	2	5-1	0-0
1936-37	2	2-0	2-1
1937-38	2	1-1	0-4
1938-39	2	1-0	1-2
1950-51	3S	2-1	0-1
1951-52	3S	3-1	0-3
1956-57	3S	3-2	0-3
1957-58	3S	0-1	0-1
1958-59	3	0-1	1-1
1960-61	2	3-0	0-1
1961-62	2	3-1	2-0
1962-63	2	1-0	1-2
1963-64	2	1-2	1-1
1964-65	2	1-0	0-3
1965-66	2	2-0	0-0

1966-67	2	2-2	1-3
1967-68	2	2-2	0-2

OLDHAM ATHLETIC

Season	*Div*	*H*	*A*
1930-31	2	1-1	1-2
1931-32	2	5-0	3-1
1932-33	2	2-1	1-3
1933-34	2	1-0	1-1
1934-35	2	2-0	1-1
1953-54	2	5-0	1-1
1968-69	3	1-1	2-0
1971-72	3	0-0	1-0
1972-73	3	1-3	1-7
1973-74	3	0-0	0-1
1975-76	2	2-1	2-3
1976-77	2	2-2	2-2
1986-87	2	3-2	1-2
1987-88	2	1-0	1-0
1988-89	2	3-0	2-2

ORIENT

Season	*Div*	*H*	*A*
1929-30	3S	3-0	2-0
1950-51	3S	2-1	2-1
1951-52	3S	3-0	0-1
1959-60	2	1-0	3-2
1960-61	2	3-2	1-1
1961-62	2	2-1	2-1
1963-64	2	2-2	0-1
1964-65	2	1-1	0-2
1965-66	2	1-1	1-0
1968-69	3	2-1	2-1
1969-70	3	1-0	1-4
1975-76	2	3-0	0-1
1976-77	2	1-2	2-2
1982-83	3	2-0	2-0
1983-84	3	3-1	2-3
1984-85	3	1-1	0-3

OXFORD UNITED

Season	*Div*	*H*	*A*
1975-76	2	2-1	2-2
1977-78	3	2-1	1-2
1978-79	3	0-1	2-3
1979-80	3	1-1	1-1
1980-81	3	3-0	0-0
1981-82	3	0-1	0-1
1982-83	3	2-1	1-1
1983-84	3	2-1	0-5
1988-89	2	3-1	1-0

PETERBOROUGH UNITED

Season	*Div*	*H*	*A*
1974-75	3	2-0	0-1
1977-78	3	1-0	0-1
1978-79	3	3-2	1-2

PORTSMOUTH

Season	*Div*	*H*	*A*
1920-21	3	2-0	1-1
1921-22	3S	0-0	1-3
1922-23	3S	2-0	2-1
1923-24	3S	1-2	1-2
1959-60	2	1-1	0-1
1960-61	2	5-1	2-0
1962-63	2	2-0	2-1
1963-64	2	0-4	2-1
1964-65	2	2-1	1-0
1965-66	2	3-1	1-4
1966-67	2	0-0	1-2
1967-68	2	1-2	0-0
1975-76	2	3-1	0-2
1977-78	3	3-1	5-1
1980-81	3	1-0	3-1
1981-82	3	0-0	0-1
1982-83	3	0-1	1-2
1986-87	2	2-3	1-0
1988-89	2	0-1	0-2

PORT VALE

Season	*Div*	*H*	*A*
1930-31	2	2-1	1-2
1931-32	2	1-3	0-2
1932-33	2	3-1	1-4
1933-34	2	3-0	0-4
1934-35	2	2-1	2-2
1935-36	2	4-1	0-2
1950-51	3S	1-0	1-2
1951-52	3S	3-0	0-1
1954-55	2	0-0	0-1
1955-56	2	1-1	1-3
1957-58	3S	1-0	0-0
1970-71	3	2-1	1-2
1971-72	3	0-0	0-0
1972-73	3	2-1	1-1
1973-74	3	2-0	1-2
1974-75	3	1-1	0-2
1977-78	3	3-2	3-3
1983-84	3	3-0	1-0

PRESTON NORTH END

Season	*Div*	*H*	*A*
1930-31	2	1-2	1-2
1931-32	2	2-1	2-5
1932-33	2	5-0	0-3
1933-34	2	0-0	1-1
1949-50	2	1-0	0-0
1961-62	2	1-0	1-1
1962-63	2	7-1	0-0
1963-64	2	0-2	0-0
1964-65	2	0-1	3-1
1965-66	2	0-1	0-2
1966-67	2	1-0	0-2
1967-68	2	1-2	0-2
1970-71	3	1-1	0-1
1974-75	3	2-1	0-1
1977-78	3	0-0	2-5

1981-82	3	0-3	0-1
1982-83	3	1-1	2-2
1983-84	3	1-0	1-2
1984-85	3	6-4	2-1

QUEEN'S PARK RANGERS

Season	*Div*	*H*	*A*
1920-21	3	1-0	0-4
1921-22	3S	4-0	0-2
1922-23	3S	2-0	3-2
1923-24	3S	2-0	2-3
1924-25	3S	1-0	1-0
1925-26	3S	3-1	4-0
1926-27	3S	2-0	2-4
1927-28	3S	3-0	1-0
1928-29	3S	1-2	0-2
1929-30	3S	4-0	2-1
1948-49	2	3-1	1-2
1949-50	2	0-2	2-0
1956-57	3S	1-2	0-3
1957-58	3S	3-1	0-1
1958-59	3	3-2	1-2
1967-68	2	0-1	1-4

READING

Season	*Div*	*H*	*A*
1920-21	3	1-1	1-1
1921-22	3S	2-0	1-0
1922-23	3S	3-0	1-0
1923-24	3S	2-1	2-1
1924-25	3S	2-0	0-0
1925-26	3S	1-3	1-1
1930-31	2	3-1	2-1
1950-51	3S	2-0	0-4
1951-52	3S	3-2	0-2
1956-57	3S	0-6	2-3
1957-58	3S	1-0	3-1
1958-59	3	2-2	2-0
1968-69	3	3-1	2-1
1969-70	3	1-1	1-2
1970-71	3	4-0	2-0
1979-80	3	2-0	0-1
1980-81	3	2-1	1-1
1981-82	3	1-1	2-2
1982-83	3	3-0	2-3
1984-85	3	1-2	1-1
1985-86	3	0-1	3-4
1986-87	2	1-0	0-2
1987-88	2	1-3	1-0

ROCHDALE

Season	*Div*	*H*	*A*
1958-59	3	2-1	2-0
1969-70	3	2-3	1-2
1970-71	3	2-2	1-1
1971-72	3	4-1	2-3
1972-73	3	3-2	6-0
1973-74	3	5-0	3-1

ROTHERHAM UNITED

Season	*Div*	*H*	*A*
1952-53	2	4-3	3-2
1953-54	2	0-2	1-2
1954-55	2	2-1	0-2
1955-56	2	3-1	0-0
1959-60	2	1-0	1-1
1960-61	2	3-3	0-0
1961-62	2	2-5	3-1
1962-63	2	2-2	2-3
1963-64	2	0-0	1-3
1964-65	2	1-1	2-4
1965-66	2	5-2	0-2
1966-67	2	1-0	2-4
1967-68	2	0-1	0-1
1968-69	3	1-2	1-0
1969-70	3	0-3	0-1
1970-71	3	4-1	1-1
1971-72	3	2-1	3-4
1972-73	3	4-1	0-1
1977-78	3	1-1	2-1
1978-79	3	2-0	0-1
1979-80	3	1-0	1-3
1980-81	3	3-1	1-2
1983-84	3	1-1	0-2
1984-85	3	1-0	2-0
1985-86	3	4-0	1-1

SCUNTHORPE UNITED

Season	*Div*	*H*	*A*
1959-60	2	4-0	0-2
1960-61	2	3-1	0-2
1961-62	2	3-1	1-5
1962-63	2	2-3	2-2
1963-64	2	3-1	0-1
1972-73	3	3-0	1-1
1983-84	3	4-0	0-3

SHEFFIELD UNITED

Season	*Div*	*H*	*A*
1934-35	2	2-0	2-1
1935-36	2	1-1	0-0
1936-37	2	2-0	0-2
1937-38	2	2-0	0-0
1938-39	2	0-1	1-0
1949-50	2	0-1	1-1
1952-53	2	5-2	0-5
1959-60	2	1-1	0-4
1960-61	2	2-0	0-3
1976-77	2	0-0	0-1
1979-80	3	4-1	2-3
1980-81	3	1-0	0-0
1982-83	3	3-1	1-3
1983-84	3	0-1	0-2
1986-87	2	1-0	1-2
1987-88	2	1-0	0-1

SHEFFIELD WEDNESDAY

Season	*Div*	*H*	*A*
1937-38	2	2-4	1-1

1938-39	2	1-1	2-1
1939-40	2	1-0	-
1946-47	2	4-1	1-2
1947-48	2	0-2	1-1
1948-49	2	3-2	1-2
1949-50	2	0-1	4-2
1955-56	2	1-1	2-5
1977-78	3	1-1	1-1
1978-79	3	2-0	3-2
1979-80	3	1-3	1-0

SHREWSBURY TOWN

Season	*Div*	*H*	*A*
1951-52	3S	6-1	3-1
1956-57	3S	1-1	1-3
1957-58	3S	2-2	0-2
1968-69	3	1-1	0-1
1969-70	3	4-2	0-3
1970-71	3	4-4	1-1
1971-72	3	1-2	2-1
1972-73	3	3-0	1-1
1973-74	3	2-2	0-0
1977-78	3	2-2	1-3
1978-79	3	1-1	0-2
1986-87	2	3-2	1-1
1987-88	2	2-0	1-2
1988-89	2	0-0	0-2

SOUTHAMPTON

Season	*Div*	*H*	*A*
1920-21	3	0-0	0-1
1921-22	3S	1-0	0-0
1930-31	2	2-3	3-3
1931-32	2	1-2	6-0
1932-33	2	1-1	0-2
1933-34	2	0-0	1-0
1934-35	2	4-0	0-1
1935-36	2	0-0	0-2
1936-37	2	3-1	0-0
1937-38	2	4-0	0-0
1938-39	2	2-0	1-2
1946-47	2	2-3	1-5
1947-48	2	3-1	3-2
1948-49	2	1-2	0-2
1949-50	2	0-0	3-3
1952-53	2	3-1	3-2
1956-57	3S	2-1	2-2
1957-58	3S	4-0	1-0
1958-59	3	1-0	1-5
1960-61	2	1-3	1-1
1961-62	2	4-0	2-1
1962-63	2	2-1	1-1
1963-64	2	1-1	2-1
1964-65	2	4-0	0-5
1965-66	2	2-3	1-4
1975-76	2	1-0	0-1
1976-77	2	1-1	1-4

SOUTHEND UNITED

Season	*Div*	*H*	*A*
1920-21	3	0-0	1-2
1921-22	3S	4-0	0-1
1922-23	3S	1-1	1-2
1923-24	3S	7-1	2-0
1924-25	3S	6-0	3-0
1925-26	3S	6-2	0-2
1926-27	3S	2-1	2-1
1927-28	3S	3-2	0-3
1928-29	3S	1-1	1-1
1929-30	3S	1-0	1-1
1950-51	3S	2-0	0-1
1951-52	3S	2-0	1-1
1956-57	3S	0-0	1-0
1957-58	3S	2-3	1-2
1958-59	3S	3-1	0-0
1972-73	3	2-0	1-3
1973-74	3	1-1	0-2
1974-75	3	1-0	1-2
1978-79	3	1-1	1-2
1979-80	3	0-0	1-4
1981-82	3	0-0	0-3
1982-83	3	1-0	1-3
1983-84	3	4-0	1-1

SOUTHPORT

Season	*Div*	*H*	*A*
1968-69	3	0-4	0-2
1969-70	3	1-1	0-0
1973-74	3	4-1	1-1

STOCKPORT COUNTY

Season	*Div*	*H*	*A*
1937-38	2	2-1	3-1
1958-59	3	2-1	2-2
1968-69	3	2-2	3-2
1969-70	3	2-0	1-0

STOKE CITY

Season	*Div*	*H*	*A*
1930-31	2	1-2	0-0
1931-32	2	1-1	2-3
1932-33	2	1-0	0-2
1953-54	2	1-1	2-3
1954-55	2	2-0	1-3
1955-56	2	0-1	1-4
1959-60	2	2-3	0-1
1960-61	2	3-1	0-9
1961-62	2	3-1	0-2
1962-63	2	0-1	2-2
1986-87	2	1-3	0-1
1987-88	2	3-0	0-1
1988-89	2	4-0	2-2

SUNDERLAND

Season	*Div*	*H*	*A*
1959-60	2	0-0	0-4
1960-61	2	1-0	1-2
1961-62	2	3-2	0-5
1962-63	2	1-1	1-1
1963-64	2	1-1	0-1

1975-76	2	1-0	1-2
1986-87	2	2-4	1-2
1988-89	2	1-4	1-2

SWANSEA CITY

Season	*Div*	*H*	*A*
1920-21	3	1-0	0-3
1921-22	3S	3-1	0-3
1922-23	3S	2-0	1-1
1923-24	3S	2-0	0-1
1924-25	3S	1-1	0-2
1930-31	2	0-0	0-2
1931-32	2	4-2	1-4
1932-33	2	1-0	1-0
1933-34	2	2-2	1-2
1934-35	2	3-2	0-3
1935-36	2	1-2	0-2
1936-37	2	0-0	1-0
1937-38	2	2-2	0-1
1938-39	2	0-0	1-2
1946-47	2	2-1	1-3
1949-50	2	0-1	2-2
1952-53	2	3-2	2-2
1953-54	2	1-1	1-0
1954-55	2	2-2	2-4
1955-56	2	0-1	2-2
1959-60	2	3-1	1-6
1960-61	2	1-0	2-1
1961-62	2	0-0	0-5
1962-63	2	1-0	1-2
1963-64	2	3-2	1-2
1964-65	2	2-1	0-3
1970-71	3	2-3	2-0
1971-72	3	4-1	1-1
1972-73	3	3-1	1-1
1978-79	3	2-2	1-2
1984-85	3	1-2	2-0
1985-86	3	2-0	2-0

SWINDON TOWN

Season	*Div*	*H*	*A*
1920-21	3	0-0	1-1
1921-22	3S	1-0	2-1
1922-23	3S	2-0	1-2
1923-24	3S	1-3	1-0
1924-25	3S	2-0	0-1
1925-26	3S	1-1	0-2
1926-27	3S	3-1	2-1
1927-28	3S	3-0	2-2
1928-29	3S	3-0	0-0
1929-30	3S	5-0	2-1
1950-51	3S	5-1	2-1
1951-52	3S	3-0	2-2
1956-57	3S	1-0	3-0
1957-58	3S	2-2	0-1
1958-59	3	3-2	4-3
1963-64	2	2-4	1-2
1964-65	2	2-1	3-2
1968-69	3	2-1	0-3
1974-75	3	4-3	0-2
1977-78	3	0-2	1-3
1978-79	3	2-0	3-1
1979-80	3	2-0	1-2
1980-81	3	0-0	0-3
1981-82	3	2-1	2-0
1987-88	2	1-0	1-1
1988-89	2	4-1	0-1

TORQUAY UNITED

Season	*Div*	*H*	*A*
1927-28	3S	4-1	2-1
1928-29	3S	4-0	2-2
1929-30	3S	5-0	4-3
1950-51	3S	1-0	3-1
1951-52	3S	2-2	2-3
1956-57	3S	0-0	1-1
1957-58	3S	1-0	2-0
1968-69	3	1-2	1-0
1969-70	3	6-0	2-1
1970-71	3	1-2	1-2
1971-72	3	3-1	1-2

TOTTENHAM HOTSPUR

Season	*Div*	*H*	*A*
1930-31	2	2-0	1-1
1931-32	2	4-1	1-0
1932-33	2	2-2	0-0
1935-36	2	2-1	2-1
1936-37	2	2-2	3-1
1937-38	2	2-2	2-3
1938-39	2	0-1	0-1
1946-47	2	3-4	1-2
1947-48	2	1-1	0-2
1948-49	2	0-5	0-3
1949-50	2	0-2	1-4

TRANMERE ROVERS

Season	*Div*	*H*	*A*
1938-39	2	3-1	0-2
1958-59	3	4-0	0-2
1968-69	3	1-0	2-2
1969-70	3	2-1	1-3
1970-71	3	0-1	0-1
1971-72	3	2-2	2-3
1972-73	3	0-1	2-2
1973-74	3	2-0	0-2
1974-75	3	4-1	3-1
1977-78	3	0-1	1-1
1978-79	3	2-2	1-2

WALSALL

Season	*Div*	*H*	*A*
1927-28	3S	2-1	1-2
1928-29	3S	2-2	1-1
1929-30	3S	1-1	3-1
1950-51	3S	1-1	1-1
1951-52	3S	3-0	5-2
1956-57	3S	2-4	0-1
1957-58	3S	2-1	2-0

1961-62	2	2-1	0-1
1962-63	2	3-0	2-2
1968-69	3	1-0	1-1
1969-70	3	1-0	2-2
1970-71	3	3-1	0-1
1971-72	3	3-2	0-1
1972-73	3	0-2	3-1
1973-74	3	2-1	4-0
1974-75	3	2-1	0-0
1977-78	3	3-3	0-1
1978-79	3	1-0	1-2
1980-81	3	2-0	3-1
1981-82	3	4-1	1-0
1982-83	3	0-0	0-2
1983-84	3	3-1	2-3
1984-85	3	1-3	3-0
1985-86	3	2-0	2-2
1988-89	2	2-0	2-2

WATFORD

Season	*Div*	*H*	*A*
1920-21	3	0-2	1-1
1921-22	3S	3-0	1-0
1922-23	3S	1-0	0-1
1923-24	3S	1-0	1-0
1924-25	3S	1-0	0-1
1925-26	3S	2-1	1-0
1926-27	3S	4-0	4-1
1927-28	3S	0-1	2-1
1928-29	3S	2-0	3-6
1929-30	3S	2-1	2-0
1950-51	3S	3-1	1-1
951-52	3S	3-1	3-1
956-57	3S	3-3	1-0
957-58	3S	2-1	2-0
968-69	3	1-2	0-1
972-73	3	1-1	2-3
973-74	3	2-0	3-0
974-75	3	1-1	3-1
978-79	3	1-1	2-2

1988-89	2	1-0	0-2

WEST BROMWICH ALBION

Season	*Div*	*H*	*A*
1930-31	2	5-1	2-1
1938-39	2	2-1	2-4
1946-47	2	2-1	5-2
1947-48	2	2-1	1-1
1948-49	2	1-2	0-3
1975-76	2	2-1	0-1
1986-87	2	1-0	0-0
1987-88	2	3-3	0-1
1988-89	2	-	-

WEST HAM UNITED

Season	*Div*	*H*	*A*
1932-33	2	4-1	2-2
1933-34	2	4-4	1-5
1934-35	2	0-1	1-2
1935-36	2	4-1	2-4
1936-37	2	2-0	1-1
1937-38	2	2-1	1-0
1938-39	2	0-0	1-2
1939-40	2	1-3	-
1946-47	2	3-1	1-4
1947-48	2	1-1	1-1
1948-49	2	2-0	0-3
1949-50	2	0-3	2-2
1952-53	2	1-1	1-0
1953-54	2	2-1	2-2
1954-55	2	1-1	1-6
1955-56	2	0-1	0-4

WIGAN ATHLETIC

Season	*Div*	*H*	*A*
1982-83	3	0-2	0-3
1983-84	3	0-0	1-1
1984-85	3	1-0	0-1
1985-86	3	2-1	0-3

WIMBLEDON

Season	*Div*	*H*	*A*
1979-80	3	3-0	1-3
1981-82	3	2-0	1-2
1983-84	3	1-2	0-1

WOLVERHAMPTON W

Season	*Div*	*H*	*A*
1930-31	2	3-2	3-4
1931-32	2	3-3	0-2
1965-66	2	2-2	0-0
1966-67	2	0-1	1-2
1976-77	2	0-0	0-4
1985-86	3	3-1	3-0

WREXHAM

Season	*Div*	*H*	*A*
1958-59	3	2-2	1-1
1970-71	3	2-2	0-4
1971-72	3	1-2	2-0
1972-73	3	1-0	2-1
1973-74	3	1-2	2-5
1974-75	3	0-3	1-5
1977-78	3	0-1	0-2
1982-83	3	2-0	3-2

YORK CITY

Season	*Div*	*H*	*A*
1971-72	3	4-0	3-2
1972-73	3	1-1	2-1
1973-74	3	0-2	1-1
1975-76	3	1-1	1-3
1984-85	3	1-1	0-0
1985-86	3	2-2	1-3

Argyle on Tour

South America 1924

1	Jun	22	Portenos	W	1-0	Cherrett
2		29	Argentines	L	0-2	
3	Jul	4	Uruguayos	W	4-0	Smith 2, Logan, Leslie
4		6	Rosarinos	D	0-0	
4		8	Rosarinos	L	1-2	Russell
6		9	Boca Juniors	D	0-0	
7		13	Argentinos	W	1-0	Rowe
8		18	Uruguayans	D	1-1	Corcoran
9		20	Argentinos	L	0-1	

Appearances
Sub Appearances
Goals

United States 1954

1	May	7	Dortmund	L	0-4		Chicago
2		9	St Louis All Stars	W	8-4	N Langman 6, Davies, McCrory	St Louis
3		13	Colorado All Stars	W	16-2	McCrory 6, N Langman 2, Edds 2, Crawford 2, Ratcliffe, Dougall, McShane, Davies	Denver
4		16	Dortmund	L	1-3	McCrory	Los Angeles
5		20	Los Angeles All Stars	W	2-0	Davies, Edds	Los Angeles
6		23	San Francisco All Stars	W	3-2	Porteous 2, N Langman	San Francisco
7		25	Chicago All Stars	W	8-1	Ratcliffe 2, McCrory 2, Dougall 2, Crawford, N Langman	Chicago
8		29	Chicago League Champions	W	6-1	McCrory 2, Crawford 2, Edds, N Langman	Detroit
9		30	Philadelphia All Stars	W	3-2	Ratcliffe, Crawford, N Langman	Philadelphia
10	Jun	1	American All Stars	W	1-0	N Langman	New York

Appearances
Sub Appearances
Goals

Eastern Europe 1963

1	May	16	Warsaw Legia	L	1-2	Carter	100,000	Warsaw
2		18	KSC Lech	L	0-1		50,000	Poznan
3		21	BWKS Lechia	W	3-0	Carter, McAnearney, O'Neill	60,000	Gdansk
4		23	S C Turbine	L	2-3	Trebilcock, McParland	40,000	Erfurt

Appearances
Sub Appearances
Goals

Craig	Cosgrove	Russell	Logan	Preston	Rowe	Corcoran	Sloan	Cherrett	Leslie	Batten	Fishwick	Walker	Eastwood	Smith	Miller	Deacon	Wallace	
1	2	3	4	5	6	7	8	9	10	11								1
1	2	3	4	5	6	7		9	11		8	10						2
1	2	3	8	5	4	7	9		10	11			6					3
1	2	3		5	4	7		8	10	11			6	9				4
1	2*	3		5	6	7	8	9	10	11			4		12			5
1		2	8	5	6	7			10					9	3	4	11	6
1		2	8	5	6			9	10	11		7			3	4		7
1	2	3	8	5	4	7			11	10			6	9		4		8
1	2	3	8	5	6	7		9	11			10	4					9
9	7	9	7	9	9	8	3	6	9	6	1	3	5	3	2	3	1	
															1			
		1	1		1	1		1	1					2				

Shortt	Ratcliffe	Jones	Robertson	Chisholm	McShane	Davies	Crawford	Langman N	Porteous	Edds	Dougall	McCrory	Major	Morgan	
1	2	3	4	5	6	7	8	9	10	11					1
1		3	2	5	6	7	8	9	11		4	10			2
	2		5		6	7	8	9	11		4	10	1	3	3
1		3	2	5	6	7	8	9	11		4	10			4
	2		5		6	7	10	9*	11	12	4	8	1	3	5
	2		5		6	7	10	9	11		4	8	1	3	6
	2		5		6	7	10	9*	11	12	4	8	1	3	7
	2		4	5	6	7	12	9*	11	14	8*	10	1	3	8
	2		4	5		7	10	9	6	11	8		1	3	9
	2		5		6	7	10	9	11		4	8	1	3	10
3	8	3	10	5	9	10	9	10	10	2	9	8	7	7	
							1			3					
	4				1	3	6	13	2	4	3	12			

Leiper	Reeves	Davis	Williams	Newman	Buckingham	Brace	McAnearney	Carter	O'Neill	McParland	MacLaren	Robertson	Trebilcock	Roberts	
1	2	3	4	5	6	7	8	9	10	11		12			1
		3	4	5	6	12	8	9	10	11	1	2	7		2
		3		5	6	7	8	9	10		1	2	11	4	3
		3	4	5	6		8	9	10	11	1	2	7		4
1	1	4	3	4	4	2	4	4	4	3	3	3	3	1	
						1						1			
							1	2	1	1			1		

The displays of Moses Russell (pictured) in particular caught the attention of the Argentine Press and at the end of the 1924 tour The Standard *of Buenos Aires commented: 'The visit of Plymouth will be best remembered by the outstanding personality and genius of Moses Russell. His effective style, precise judgement, accurate and timely clearances, powerful kicking and no less useful work with his head . . . one of the most wonderful backs and one of the brainiest players ever seen on the football field.'*

Plymouth Internationals

Below are listed players who have won international honours whilst on Plymouth Argyle's books. Before 1925 there was only one Ireland team. Thereafter the Republic of Ireland began separate international matches and that position is reflected here.

Wales

Jones B.S. 1965 v Denmark (1).
Morris R. 1908 v Ireland (1).
Phillips D.O. 1984 v England, Northern Ireland, Norway (3).
Pullen W.J. 1926 v England (1).
Russell M.R. 1920 v England, Scotland, Ireland; 1921 v England, Scotland, Ireland; 1922 v England, Ireland; 1923 v England, Scotland, Ireland; 1924 v England, Scotland, Ireland; 1925 v England, Scotland; 1926 v England, Scotland; 1928 v Scotland; 1929 v England (20).
Shortt W.W. 1947 v Northern Ireland; 1950 v Northern Ireland, Belgium; 1952 v England, Scotland, Northern Ireland, Rest of UK; 1953 v Scotland, England, Northern Ireland, France, Yugoslavia (12).

John Pullen (second right) watches as Moses Russell heads away during the England v Wales game at Selhurst Park, London. Wales won 3-1with goals from W.Davies and Fowler (2).

'B' Internationals

England
Astall G. 1952 v France (1).

Under-23 Internationals

England
Piper N.J. 1970 v Bulgaria (1).
Sullivan C. 1974 v Poland, Denmark (2).

Wales
Baker T.G. 1958 v England; 1959 v Scotland (2).
Jones B.S. 1965 v Scotland (1).
Randell C.W. 1975 v England (1).

Under-21 Internationals

Wales
Phillips D.O. 1984 v Norway, Bulgaria, Yugoslavia (3).

Amateur Internationals

England
Raymond H.W. 1914 v Wales, Ireland, Holland (3).
Twissell C.H. 1956 v Ireland, Iceland; 1957 v Wales, Scotland, France, Bulgaria; 1957 — with Great Britain in Olympic Games at Melbourne (7).

Youth Internationals

England
Davey S. 1967
Manley K. 1967
Piper N.J. 1966
Reynolds R. 1966
Sullivan C. 1969
Chapman P. 1970
Rowbotham D. 1984

Goalkeepers Galore

The goalkeeper has usually been the least of Argyle's selection problems and in most seasons, the club has been content to rely on one or two players. 1988-9 was one of the exceptions to that rule. Four players were used, not a record, because that had happened in previous seasons but 1988-9 was unique in that two of the players concerned — Alan Miller and Rhys Wilmot — were on loan and both came from the same club, Arsenal. The full list of Argyle goalkeepers and the number of their appearances in each season since the club entered the Football League is as follows:

1920-21 • Craig 47
1921-22 • Craig 38, Cook 6
1922-23 • Craig 45, Cook 1
1923-24 • Craig 43
1924-25 • Craig 43
1925-26 • Craig 43
1926-27 • Craig 35, Thomson 7, Lee 1
1927-28 • Stanbury 27, Craig 12, Lee 3, Cann 1
1928-29 • Craig 44, Cann 2
1929-30 • Craig 34, Cann 12
1930-31 • Cann 43
1931-32 • Harper 22, Cann 16, Stanbury 6
1932-33 • Harper 37, Cann 6
1933-34 • Cann 28, Harper 16
1934-35 • Cann 39, Harper 4
1935-36 • Cann 35, Davies 9
1936-37 • Foley 19, Davies 13, Cann 12
1937-38 • Foley 22, Cann 21
1938-39 • Cann 18, Davies 14, Wright 8, Harper 3
1939-40 • Middleton 3
1946-47 • Shortt 39, Wright 4
1947-48 • Shortt 43
1948-49 • Shortt 40, Harris 3
1949-50 • Shortt 39, Major 5
1950-51 • Shortt 36, Major 14
1951-52 • Shortt 45, Major 1
1952-53 • Shortt 43, Major 1
1953-54 • Major 28, Shortt 16
1954-55 • Shortt 34, Major 9
1955-56 • Shortt 21, Major 18, Dyer 4
1956-57 • Brown 42, Dyer 4, Gee 1, Howell 1
1957-58 • Brown 26, Barnsley 23
1958-59 • Barnsley 45, Wyllie 5
1959-60 • Barnsley 43
1960-61 • Barnsley 36, MacLaren 13
1961-62 • MacLaren 43
1962-63 • MacLaren 30, Leiper 14
1963-64 • MacLaren 31, Leiper 15
1964-65 • MacLaren 28, Dwyer 19, Leiper 4
1965-66 • Leiper 35, Dwyer 10
1966-67 • Shearing 24, Dunne 11, Leiper 9
1967-68 • Dunne 43, Shearing 1
1968-69 • Dunne 50
1969-70 • Dunne 42, Clamp 9
1970-71 • Furnell 30, Dunne 18
1971-72 • Furnell 26, Balac 23
1972-73 • Furnell 32, Balac 18, Kearns 1
1973-74 • Furnell 53, Aleksic 3
1974-75 • Furnell 52
1975-76 • Aleksic 34, Furnell 13
1976-77 • Ramsbottom 41, Barron 3
1977-78 • Barron 48, Hodge 5
1978-79 • Hodge 40, Burns 11
1979-80 • Crudgington 39, Brown 8, Hards 7
1980-81 • Crudgington 51
1981-82 • Crudgington 52
1982-83 • Crudgington 50, Hards 2
1983-84 • Crudgington 60
1984-85 • Crudgington 38, Philp 9, Sealey 6
1985-86 • Crudgington 50, Philp 2
1986-87 • Crudgington 25, Cherry 22
1987-88 • Cherry 40, Crudgington 7
1988-89 • Cherry 20, Wilmot 17, Miller 15, Penhaligon 1

Individual Scoring Feats

Five goals in a game

Wilf Carter v Charlton Athletic (h), Division Two ....27 Dec 1960

Four goals in a game

Frank Richardson v Bradford (h), FA Cup (Round 2)......................3 Feb 1923
Jack Cock v Norwich City (h), Division Three South......................16 Jan 1926
Freddie Forbes v Merthyr Tydfil (h), Division Three South................27 Aug 1927
Tommy Grozier v Crystal Palace (h), Division Three South................21 Dec 1929
Jack Vidler v Norwich City (h), Division Three South.....................19 Apr 1930
Jack Leslie v Nottingham Forest (h), Division Two ....17 Oct 1931
Sammy Black v Port Vale (h), Division Two ....4 Jan 1935
Maurice Tadman v Aldershot (h), Division Three South ....14 Oct 1950
Maurice Tadman v Brighton & Hove Albion (a), Division Three South ......18 Oct 1950
Mike Bickle v Cardiff City (h), Division Two ....15 Oct 1966
Mike Bickle v Torquay United (h), Division Three.........................26 Dec 1969
Tommy Tynan v Blackburn Rovers (h), Division Two ....5 Nov 1988

Three goals in a game

Frank Richardson v Bristol Rovers (a), Division Three South..............27 Aug 1921
Frank Richardson v Swansea Town (h), Division Three South ....21 Dec 1921
Frank Richardson v Brentford (h), Division Three South ....28 Jan 1922
John Smith v Bournemouth & BA (h), Division Three South ....22 Mar 1924
Frank Sloan v Southend United (h), Division Three South ....3 May 1924
Bert Batten v Luton Town (h), Division Three South......................20 Sep 1924
Sammy Black v Norwich City (h), Division Three South ....27 Dec 1924
Jack Leslie v Bristol City (h), Division Three South......................10 Apr 1924
Jack Cock v Southend United (h), Division Three South ....29 Aug 1925
Jack Cock v Watford (h), Division Three South ....18 Sep 1926
Jack Cock v Watford (a), Division Three South ....5 Feb 1927
Jack Leslie v Crystal Palace (h), Division Three South ....12 Feb 1927
Frank Sloan v Bristol Rovers (h), Division Three South...................31 Aug 1927
Freddie Forbes v Norwich City (h), Division Three South.................29 Oct 1927
Norman Mackay v Coventry City (h), Division Three South ....28 Jan 1928
Percy Richards v Torquay United (h), Division Three South..............17 Mar 1928
Sammy Black v Blackpool (h), FA Cup (Round 3)...........................12 Jan 1929
Percy Richards v Torquay United (h), Division Three South..............29 Mar 1929
Raymond Bowden v Exeter City (h), Division Three South ....26 Oct 1929
Jack Vidler v Watford (h), FA Cup (Round 2) ....18 Dec 1929
Jack Vidler v Queen's Park Rangers (h), Division Three South ....5 April 1930
Jack Vidler v West Bromwich Albion (h), Division Two ....31 Jan 1931
Tommy Grozier v Bristol City (h), Division Two.............................2 May 1931
Jack Leslie v Bradford City (h), Division Two..............................12 Sep 1931
Raymond Bowden v Southampton (a), Division Two ....5 Dec 1931
Jack Vidler v Bury (h), Division Two ....26 Dec 1931
Jack Vidler v Millwall (h), Division Two ....16 Jan 1932
Sammy Black v Charlton Athletic (h), Division Two ....8 Oct 1932
Eugene Melaniphy v Bradford City (h), Division Two ....7 Oct 1933
Jack Vidler v Hull City (h), Division Two...................................29 Aug 1934
Sammy Black v Barnsley (h), Division Two ....12 Oct 1935
Jack Vidler v Doncaster Rovers (h), Division Two ....5 Sep 1936
Bill Hullett v Southampton (h), Division Two ....7 May 1938
Bill Hullett v Nottingham Forest (h), Division Two.........................31 Aug 1938

Bill Hullett v Luton Town (h), Division Two .... 17 Sep 1938
Fred Mitcheson v Luton Town (a), Division Two .... 21 Jan 1939
Bob Thomas v West Bromwich Albion (a), Division Two .... 19 Apr 1947
Ernie Edds v Southampton (a), Division Two .... 10 Apr 1948
Maurice Tadman v Gainsborough Trinity (a), FA Cup (Round 1) .... 25 Nov 1950
Maurice Tadman v Walsall (a), Division Three South .... 22 Dec 1951
Neil Langman v Derby County (a), Division Two .... 27 Mar 1954
Neil Langman v Liverpool (h), Division Two .... 11 Feb 1956
Neil Langman v Coventry City (h), Division Three South .... 2 Feb 1957
Neil Langman v Reading (a), Division Three South .... 4 Sep 1957
Wilf Carter v Dorchester Town (h), FA Cup (Round 2) .... 7 Dec 1957
Wilf Carter v Coventry City (h), Division Three South .... 14 Dec 1957
Wilf Carter v Queen's Park Rangers (h), Division Three South .... 15 Feb 1958
Peter Anderson v Doncaster Rovers (a), Division Three .... 2 Oct 1958
Wilf Carter v Mansfield Town (a), Division Three .... 18 Oct 1958
Barry Meyer v Gillingham (a), FA Cup (Round 1) .... 19 Nov 1958
Jimmy Gauld v Swindon Town (a), Division Three .... 28 Feb 1959
Wilf Carter v Charlton Athletic (h), Division Two .... 3 Oct 1959
George Kirby v Portsmouth (h), Division Two .... 17 Sep 1960
Wilf Carter v Leeds United (h), Division Two .... 6 Mar 1961
Wilf Carter v Charlton Athletic (h), Division Two .... 27 Oct 1962
Peter McParland v Leeds United (h), Division Two .... 6 Apr 1963
Frank Lord v Stoke City (h), FL Cup (Round 4) .... 11 Nov 1964
Mike Trebilcock v Birmingham City (h), Division Two .... 16 Oct 1965
Mike Bickle v Corby Town (h), Division Two .... 22 Jan 1966
Richard Reynolds v Millwall (h), Division Two .... 10 Sep 1966
Derek Rickard v Shrewsbury Town (h), Division Three .... 21 Mar 1970
Derek Rickard v York City (h), Division Three .... 8 Jan 1972
Billy Rafferty v Tranmere Rovers (h), Division Three .... 7 Sep 1974
Fred Binney v Sheffield Wednesday (a), Division Three .... 23 Sep 1978
David Kemp v Carlisle United (h), Division Three .... 6 Sep 1980
Tommy Tynan v Bristol City (a), Division Three .... 26 Dec 1984
Tommy Tynan v Stoke City (h), Division Two .... 17 Sep 1988

Plymouth Argyle playing staff in 1922-3. Back row (left to right): J.Devine, F.Cosgrave, J.Muir, W.Cook, P.Corcoran, W.Frost, J.Little, C.Miller. Second row: F.Haynes (trainer), I.Leathlean, J.Hill, J.Logan, R.Jack (secretary-manager), J.Jobson, C.Eastwood, S.Atterbury (assistant trainer), A.Rhodes (assistant trainer). Seated: J.Dickinson, B.Bowler, H.Batten, H.Kirk, M.Russell, W.Forbes, H.Raymond, W.Baker, A.Rowe. Front: J.Kirkpatrick, J.Fowler, J.Walker, T.Gallogley, F.Richardson, R.Jack, J.Leslie, A.Wilson.

Argyle Between The Wars

Len Woosey's Recollections

AS a member of the Argyle playing staff from 1928 to 1933, Len Woosey was a contemporary of such stalwarts as Sammy Black, Jack Leslie, Ray Bowden and Jimmy Rae. Although a regular member of the Reserve side, he never received the call to first-team duty and therefore his name does not appear in the players' list in this book. Nevertheless, his account of life at Home Park between the two World Wars, and the light it throws on such matters as players' wages and bonuses and the care of the pitch, should be of interest to the modern supporter.

‘I HAD been playing for several seasons for Torpoint Athletic in the Plymouth and District League when, in the summer of 1928, I received an official card from Argyle, inviting me to play in a pre-season practice match at Home Park. This was between the first team and the Reserves with three or four amateur players on trial playing for one half.

The score was 1-1. At half-time, the manager, Bob Jack, sent word that he would like to see me in his office with the directors, so I went round to the offices behind the stand and the doorman let me up. I went into a room where the directors were gathered and Bob Jack came across to me and said, *"Len, we thought you played very well. Would you like to sign amateur forms for us? I promise that I will give you a game in the reserve side as soon as I can."* I said, *"Will that stop me playing for Torpoint in the P and D?"* Having been reassured on that point, I signed.

The following week I had another card through the post saying that I had been selected to play for the Reserves at Home Park. After that match, Bob Jack saw me again and asked if I would consider signing as a part-time professional and I agreed. Their terms was £1 a week (not a match) with ten shillings bonus for a win. The following week I was again selected for the Reserves for an away match against Merthyr Tydfil and thereafter I was a regular reserve player for five seasons.

After I had been playing for two or three years, Mr Jack, who knew that I was a carpenter by trade, asked if I would consider joining the groundstaff and I agreed. The first job to be done was in the new stand; all the floors in the players' dressing-rooms and officials' rooms were concrete and the manager wanted them covered with oak flooring. I was allowed to order whatever materials were necessary from 'Services' and the job was completed.

I was next asked to paint the grandstand — some 300 feet long — which I did. I did further handyman jobs of this nature while Jimmy Horton, the groundsman, looked after the pitch, together with his son-in-law and Polly the pony. So I played for the Reserves and did handyman jobs round the ground.

One day, while I was working at Home Park, Jimmy Kirkpatrick (who played for Argyle between 1911 and 1924) came up to me and asked if there was any chance of a job as he was unemployed at the time. I answered, *"Well, I can do with a mate but you'll have to see the directors."* Jimmy said that he knew one of the directors, a Mr Guard, and went off to find him. Next morning, when I arrived for work, Jimmy was there waiting and told me, *"I have been to see Mr Guard. I have been told to report to you and you are my boss."* So we worked there together on the groundstaff.

I had a workshop at Home Park. *"Order whatever you want,"* said Mr Jack. Once he said, *"I want you to board up the railings behind each goal and paint them yellow."* He had seen this at some other ground and thought it would be a good idea to have a 'sightscreen'. These remained for many years. On another occasion, I noticed that one of the goalposts was some 12 inches out of upright and was asked to fix it. So I went to a blacksmith in Plymouth and got him to make some iron sockets as a priority job. As the day of the next match got close, Bob Jack came, worrying how things were going. But the sockets were in on time and thereafter Argyle's uprights were always upright!

In those days, Central Park was much more of an open area of field than it is today and Home Park was in almost a country setting. Once, when the players were in a training match, a wild rabbit ran from one end of the pitch to the other while the players tried to catch it.

Another memorable incident was when a distinguished visitor came to the ground. This was Len Harvey, originally from Devonport, who was then British heavyweight boxing champion. He was introduced to the players in the dressing-rooms before the match. I waited outside and, when he came out, reminded him that we had both once lived in the same house, 27 St Aubyn Street. We shook hands and he went to his seat in the stand to watch the game.

In 1935, Argyle were having a hard time of it financially and attendances had dropped. One day when Jimmy Kirkpatrick and I were working up in the stand, we saw Bob Jack pacing up and down below and realised that something was the matter. Eventually, he called me down and said, *"I have some bad news. The club is in a bad way financially, we don't know where the players' next week's wages are coming from. The directors have decided that you and Jimmy will have to go."*

We were not to go immediately but had to finish the jobs that we were doing and then, that was it. Bob Jack arranged for one of the directors — head of the waterworks — to offer Jimmy and me jobs. Jimmy accepted, but I said no, as my trade was a carpenter and he had no vacancies for that. So that was the end of my time on the groundstaff.

I had also finished playing for Argyle because the club wanted to alter the terms of part-timers, from £1 per week to £1 per match, although we were still expected to train, match or not. Frankie Voden (another reserve player and also a Plymothian) and I did not want this, so we both decided to quit. I was then asked by the secretary of Torpoint whether I would rejoin them and, having been reinstated as an amateur by the FA, I went back to Torpoint for a season in 1935 when we reached the Devon Senior Cup Final.

This was played at Home Park, which brought back memories for me. We played Plymouth Gasworks and lost by the odd goal. After that, I was concerned lest injuries should affect my work, so I retired and my playing career came to an end, except for one game with 'Old Argyle Favourites' against a South Hams League team with other old friends like Bill Harper, Frank Sloan, Rollo Jack and Jack Demmelweek. We won 4-1. ❜

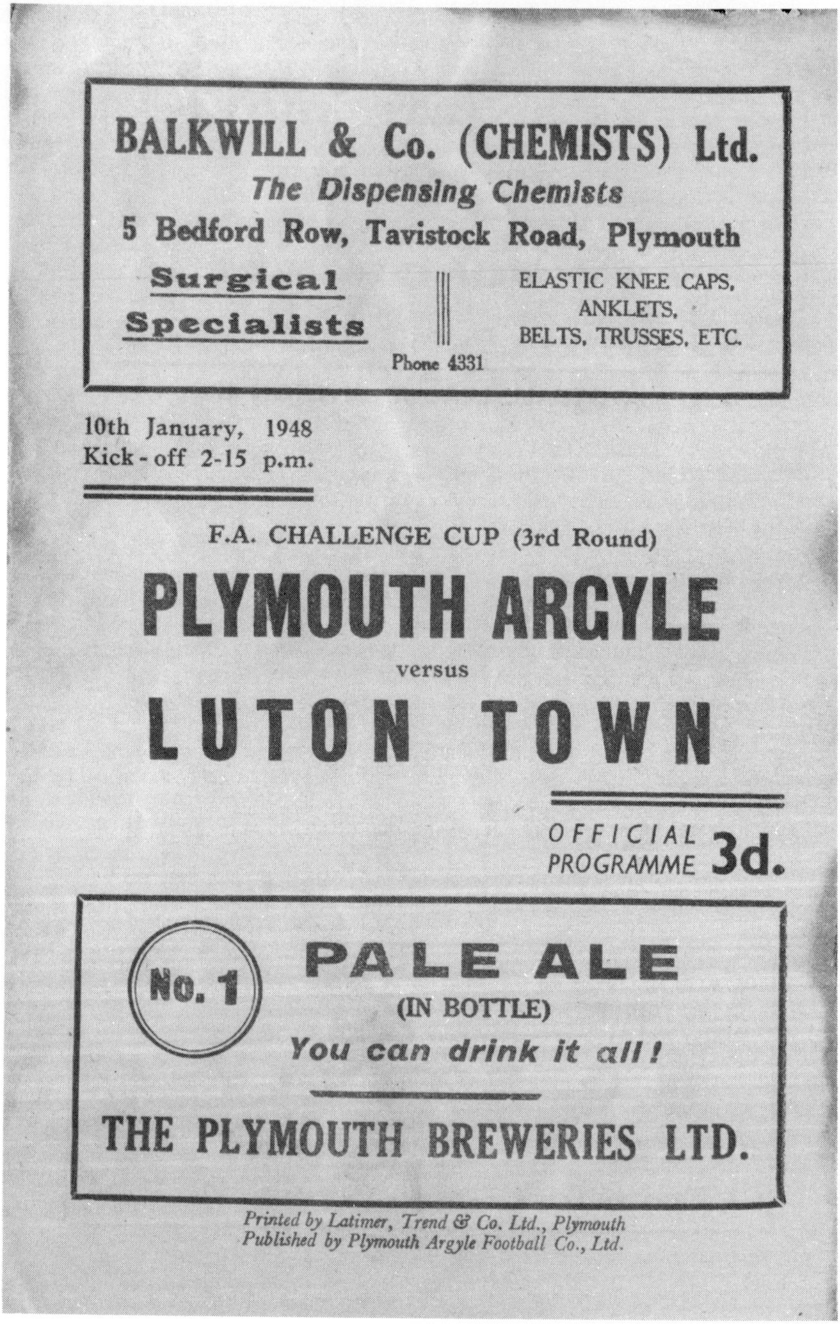

BALKWILL & Co. (CHEMISTS) Ltd.
The Dispensing Chemists
5 Bedford Row, Tavistock Road, Plymouth
Surgical Specialists
ELASTIC KNEE CAPS, ANKLETS, BELTS, TRUSSES, ETC.
Phone 4331

10th January, 1948
Kick-off 2-15 p.m.

F.A. CHALLENGE CUP (3rd Round)

PLYMOUTH ARGYLE
versus
LUTON TOWN

OFFICIAL PROGRAMME 3d.

No. 1
PALE ALE
(IN BOTTLE)
You can drink it all!
THE PLYMOUTH BREWERIES LTD.

Printed by Latimer, Trend & Co. Ltd., Plymouth
Published by Plymouth Argyle Football Co., Ltd.

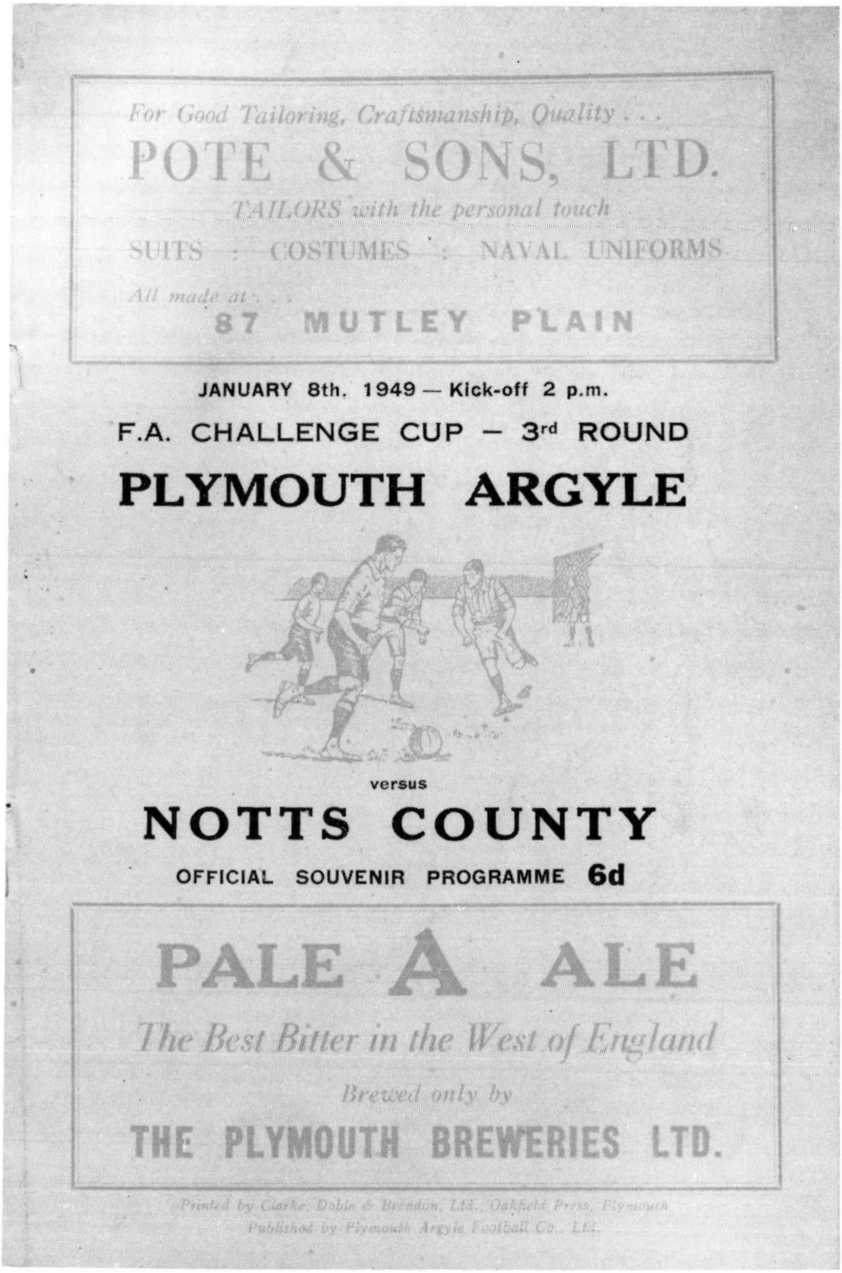
For Good Tailoring, Craftsmanship, Quality . . .

POTE & SONS, LTD.

TAILORS with the personal touch

SUITS : COSTUMES : NAVAL UNIFORMS

All made at . . .

87 MUTLEY PLAIN

JANUARY 8th, 1949 — Kick-off 2 p.m.

F.A. CHALLENGE CUP — 3rd ROUND

PLYMOUTH ARGYLE

versus

NOTTS COUNTY

OFFICIAL SOUVENIR PROGRAMME 6d

PALE A ALE

The Best Bitter in the West of England

Brewed only by

THE PLYMOUTH BREWERIES LTD.

Printed by Clarke, Doble & Brendon, Ltd., Oakfield Press, Plymouth

Published by Plymouth Argyle Football Co., Ltd.

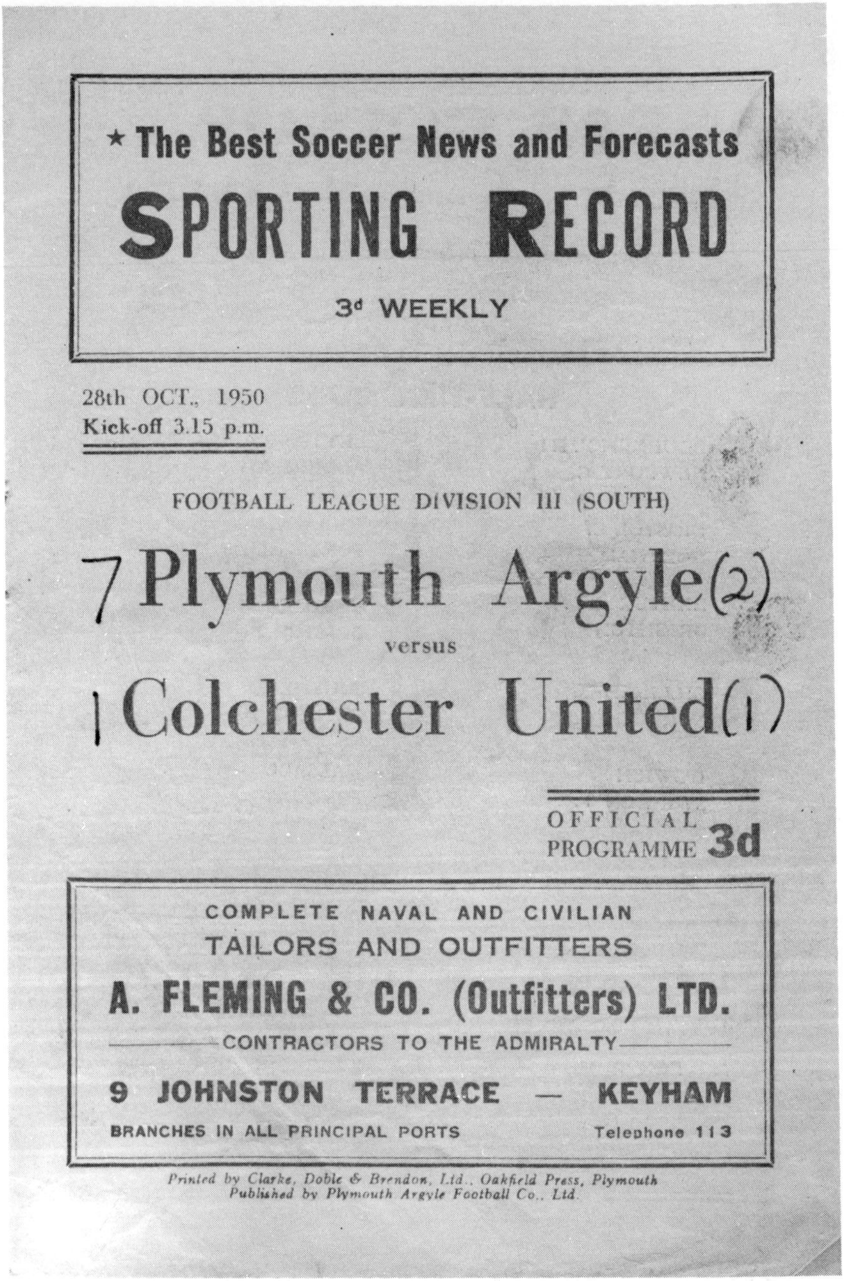

★ The Best Soccer News and Forecasts

SPORTING RECORD

3d WEEKLY

28th OCT., 1950
Kick-off 3.15 p.m.

FOOTBALL LEAGUE DIVISION III (SOUTH)

7 Plymouth Argyle (2)

versus

1 Colchester United (1)

OFFICIAL
PROGRAMME **3d**

COMPLETE NAVAL AND CIVILIAN
TAILORS AND OUTFITTERS

A. FLEMING & CO. (Outfitters) LTD.

CONTRACTORS TO THE ADMIRALTY

9 JOHNSTON TERRACE — KEYHAM

BRANCHES IN ALL PRINCIPAL PORTS Telephone 113

Printed by Clarke, Doble & Brendon, Ltd., Oakfield Press, Plymouth
Published by Plymouth Argyle Football Co., Ltd.

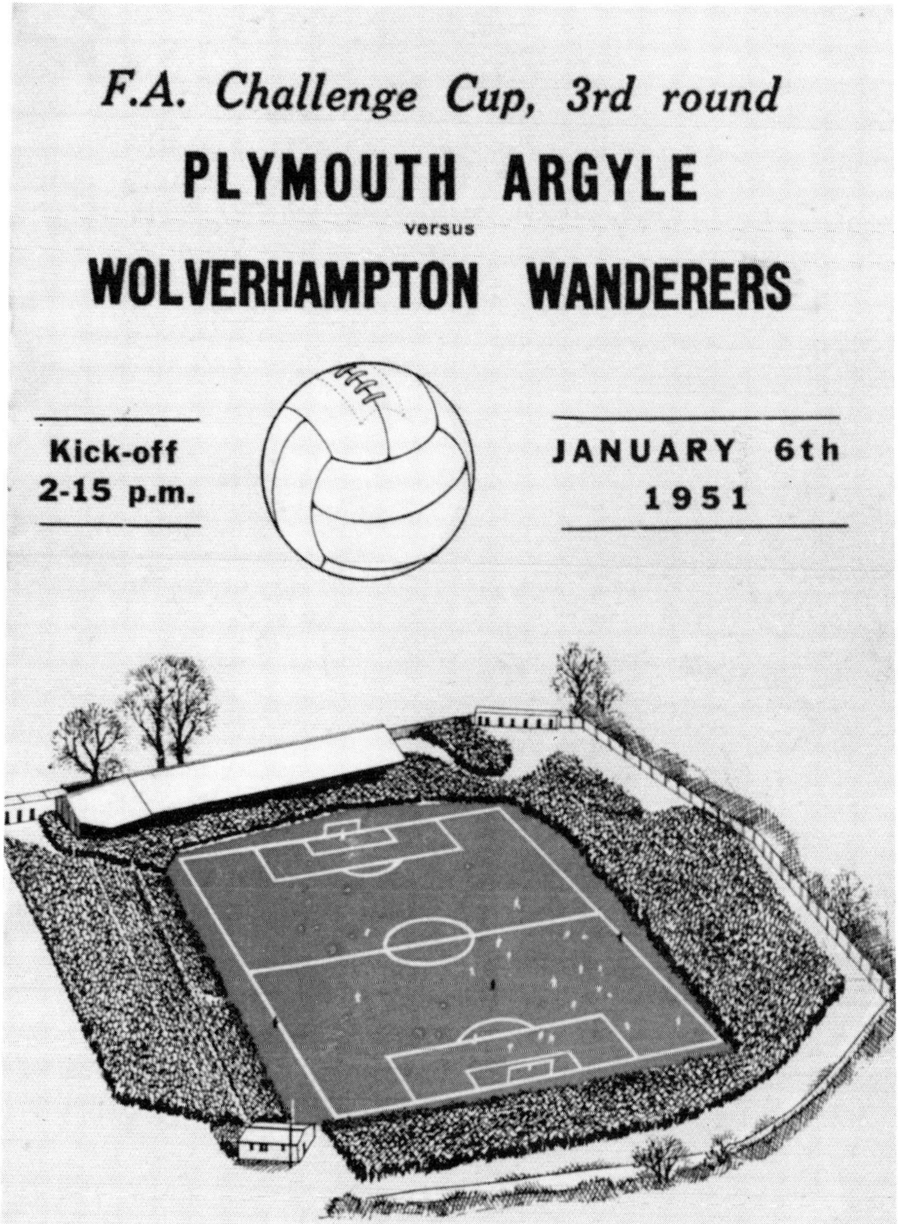
F.A. Challenge Cup, 3rd round
PLYMOUTH ARGYLE
versus
WOLVERHAMPTON WANDERERS
Kick-off
2-15 p.m.
JANUARY 6th
1951
Official Souvenir Programme 6d.

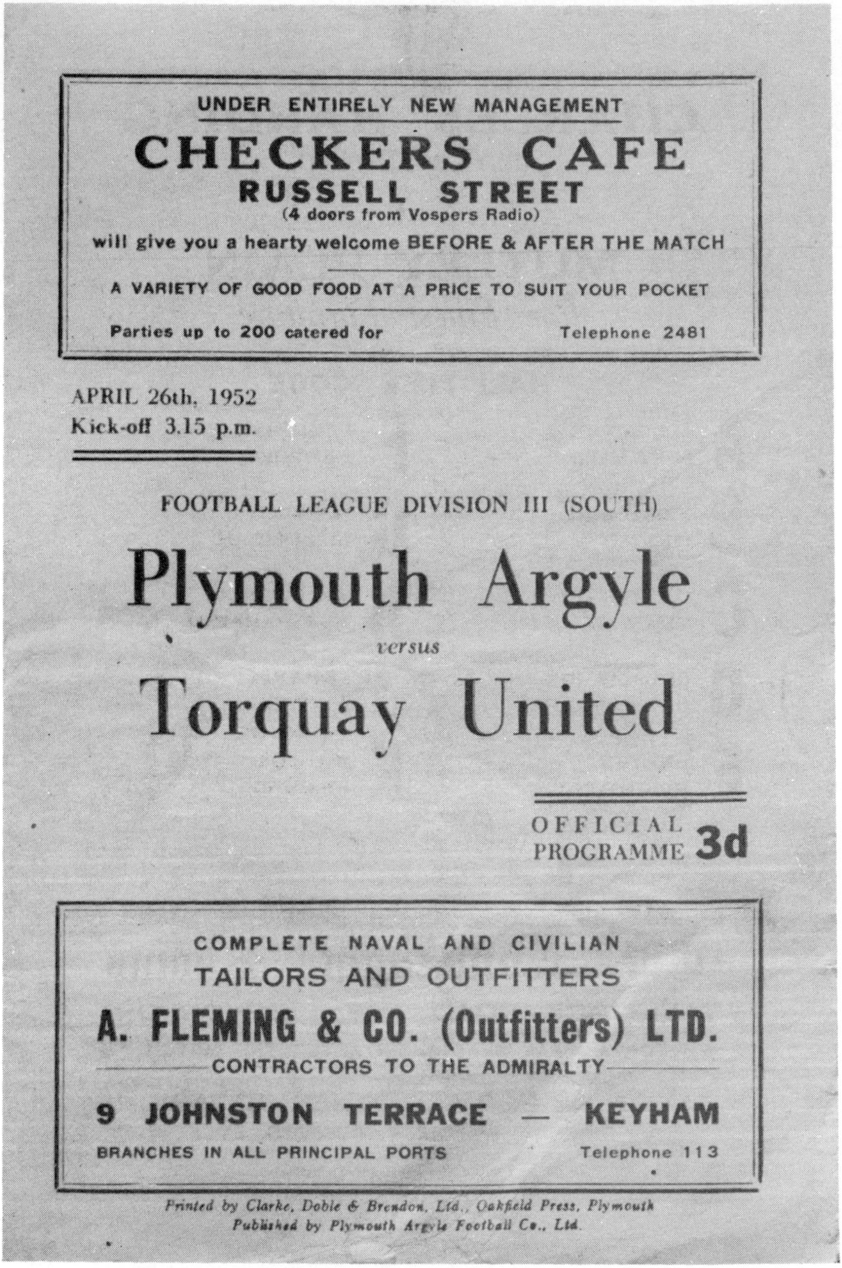

UNDER ENTIRELY NEW MANAGEMENT

CHECKERS CAFE

RUSSELL STREET

(4 doors from Vospers Radio)

will give you a hearty welcome BEFORE & AFTER THE MATCH

A VARIETY OF GOOD FOOD AT A PRICE TO SUIT YOUR POCKET

Parties up to 200 catered for — Telephone 2481

APRIL 26th, 1952
Kick-off 3.15 p.m.

FOOTBALL LEAGUE DIVISION III (SOUTH)

Plymouth Argyle

versus

Torquay United

OFFICIAL PROGRAMME **3d**

COMPLETE NAVAL AND CIVILIAN
TAILORS AND OUTFITTERS

A. FLEMING & CO. (Outfitters) LTD.

CONTRACTORS TO THE ADMIRALTY

9 JOHNSTON TERRACE — KEYHAM

BRANCHES IN ALL PRINCIPAL PORTS — Telephone 113

Printed by Clarke, Doble & Brendon, Ltd., Oakfield Press, Plymouth
Published by Plymouth Argyle Football Co., Ltd.

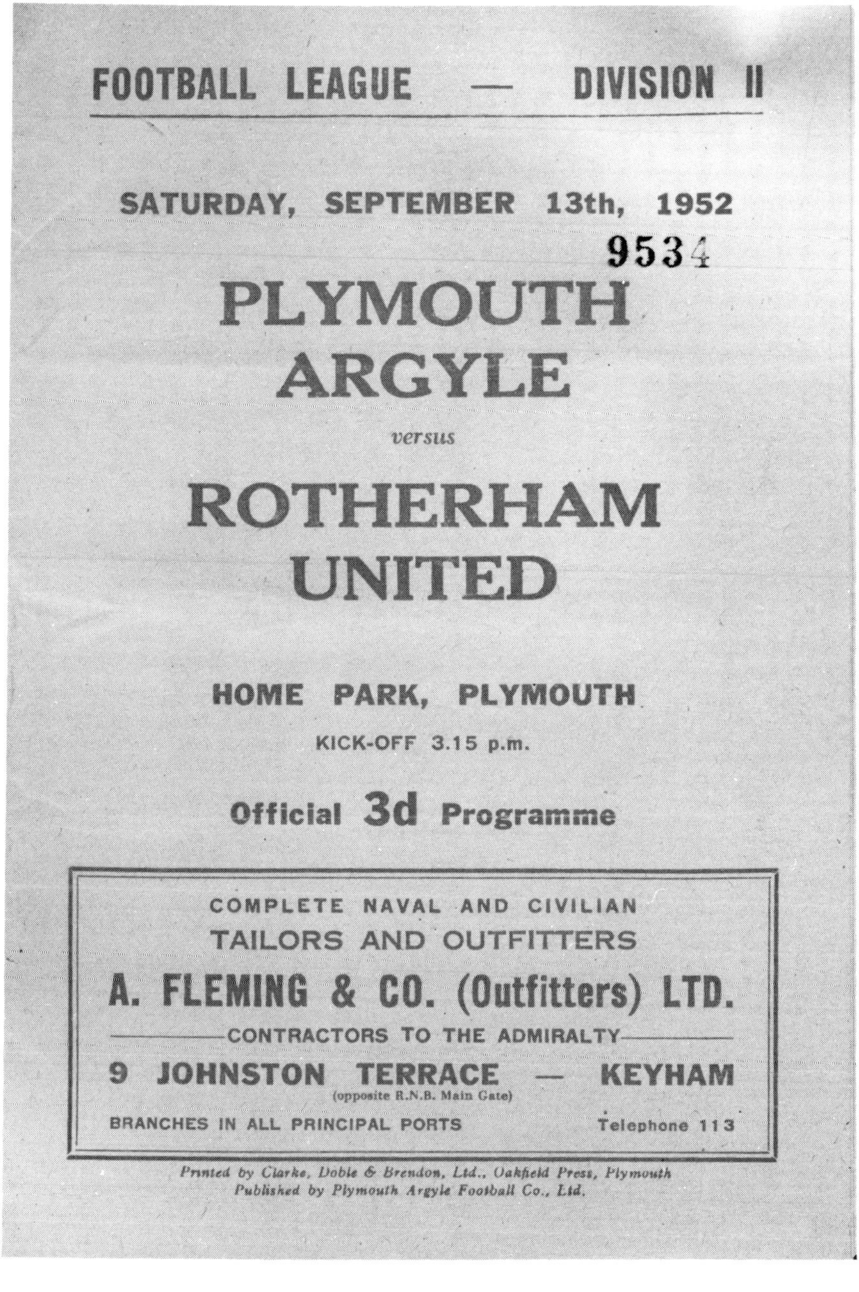

FOOTBALL LEAGUE — DIVISION II

SATURDAY, SEPTEMBER 13th, 1952

9534

PLYMOUTH ARGYLE

versus

ROTHERHAM UNITED

HOME PARK, PLYMOUTH

KICK-OFF 3.15 p.m.

Official **3d** Programme

COMPLETE NAVAL AND CIVILIAN
TAILORS AND OUTFITTERS
A. FLEMING & CO. (Outfitters) LTD.
CONTRACTORS TO THE ADMIRALTY
9 JOHNSTON TERRACE — KEYHAM
(opposite R.N.B. Main Gate)
BRANCHES IN ALL PRINCIPAL PORTS Telephone 113

Printed by Clarke, Doble & Brendon, Ltd., Oakfield Press, Plymouth
Published by Plymouth Argyle Football Co., Ltd.

5762

F.A. Challenge Cup

Fifth Round

Home Park Plymouth

Kick off 3.00 p.m.

Saturday, February 14, 1953

Plymouth Argyle

versus

Gateshead

OFFICIAL PROGRAMME **3d.**

Printed by E. J. Rickard, St. Judes, Plymouth. 'Phone : 60955
Published by Plymouth Argyle Football Co. Ltd.

Home Park : Plymouth

Football League Division 2. Kick-off 3.15 p.m.

Saturday, October 3rd, 1953

Plymouth Argyle

versus

Stoke City 3523

OFFICIAL PROGRAMME **3d.**

Printed by E. J. Rickard, St. Judes, Plymouth. 'Phone: 60955
Published by Plymouth Argyle Football Co. Ltd.

PLYMOUTH ARGYLE
Versus
WEST HAM UNITED
Home Park - Plymouth
Saturday
March 31st
1956 530
FOOTBALL LEAGUE DIVISION II
KICK OFF 3.15 p.m.
OFFICIAL PROGRAMME - 3d.
FLOODLIGHTING
of HOME PARK
—and the Emergency Lighting was executed by us — YOU can have equal service for all Electrical requirements
MADGE & SON E
ELECTRICAL CONTRACTORS

FOOTBALL LEAGUE DIVISION II
Plymouth Argyle
FOOTBALL CLUB
Saturday, January 5th, 1963
PLYMOUTH ARGYLE
versus
WEST BROMWICH A.
F.A. Cup 3rd Round — Kick-off 3.00 p.m.
Official Programme Price 4d.
SAFELY ENTRUST
ALL YOUR
ELECTRICAL
REQUIREMENTS TO
MADGE & SON E
PORTLAND SQUARE
PLYMOUTH Tel. 63315

OFFICIAL PROGRAMME 5p

The Pilgrims
P.A.F.C.

PLYMOUTH ARGYLE

ASSOCIATION FOOTBALL CLUB

SEASON 1972-73

F.A. CUP — 1st Round

SATURDAY, NOVEMBER 18th, 1972

Kick-off 3 p.m.

versus

HENDON

SOUVENIR PROGRAMME 10p.

P·A·F·C

The Pilgrims

PLYMOUTH ARGYLE

ASSOCIATION FOOTBALL CLUB

S.F.C.

S.F.C.

SEASON 1972-73

WEDNESDAY, MARCH 14, 1973

Kick-off 7.30 p.m.

versus

SANTOS of BRAZIL

ARGYLE
F.A. Cup
1st Round Replay
Tuesday 29th November
1977
Kick off 7.30 p.m.
BATH
CITY
OFFICIAL MATCH-DAY MAGAZINE OF PLYMOUTH ARGYLE
Vol.1 No.14
15p

ARGYLE
Plymouth Argyle
VERSUS CHESTER
Football League Division Three
Saturday, 15th March, 1980
Kick-off 3.00 p.m.
25p

MATCH MAGAZINE 35p
ARGYLE
Saturday, 20th November
Kick-off 3.00 p.m.
F.A. CUP FIRST ROUND
EXETER CITY

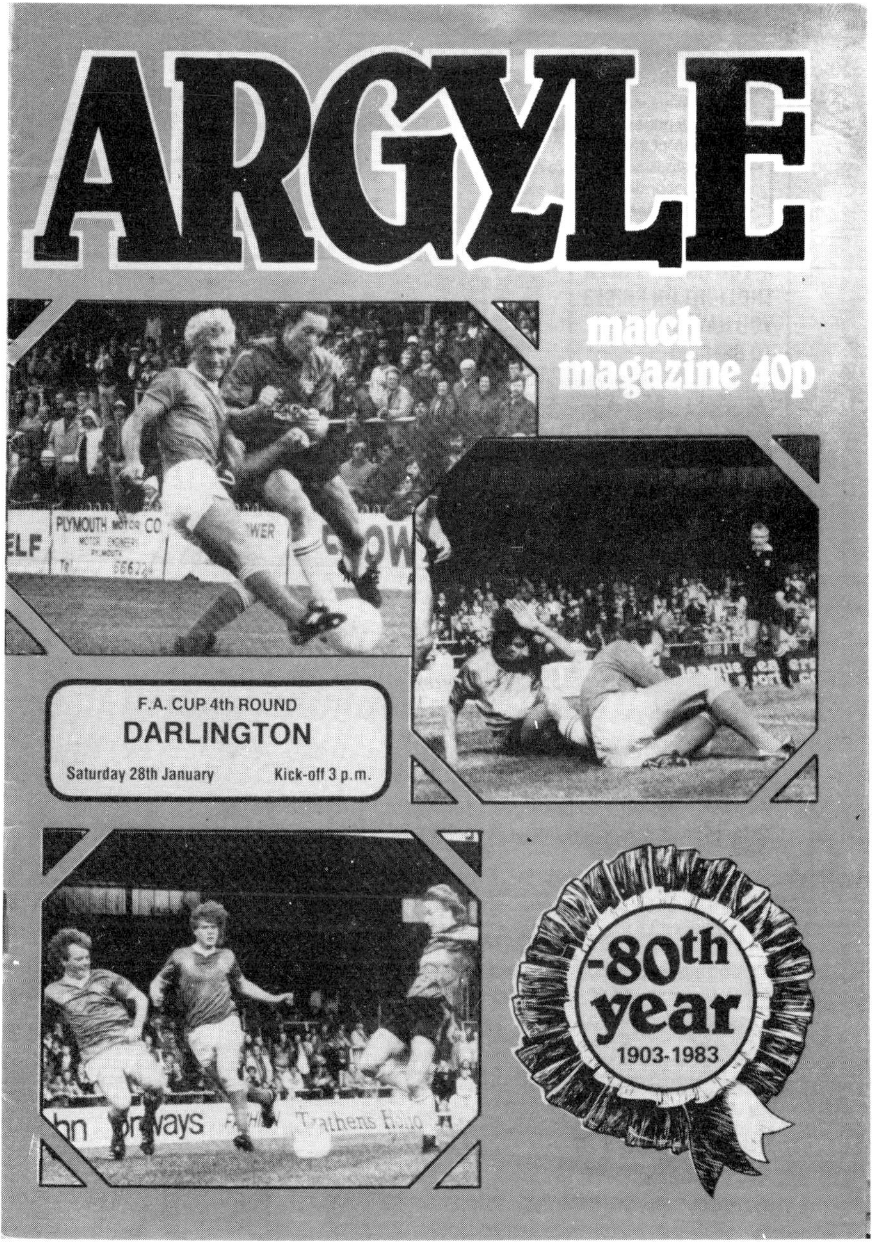
ARGYLE
match
magazine 40p
F.A. CUP 4th ROUND
DARLINGTON
Saturday 28th January
Kick-off 3 p.m.
-80th
year
1903-1983
PLYMOUTH MOTOR CO

ARGYLE
The Pilgrims
P·A·F·C
IVOR JONES
CANON LEAGUE DIVISION THREE
BURY
Saturday 12th April
Kick-off 3.00 p.m.
match magazine 50p

Sunday Independent
BARCLAY'S LEAGUE DIVISION 2
ARGYLE v SWINDON TOWN
MONDAY 27th MARCH 1989 K.O. 3.00 p.m.
Plymouth
ARGYLE
PROGRAMME 80p

Argyle in 1905-06. Back row (left to right): J.Hughes (assistant trainer), McNeil, Saul, Wilcox, Horne, R.Jack (manager), Sutcliffe, Mortimer, A.Clark, T.Cleghorn (trainer). Middle row: Bauchop, Briercliffe, Buck, Owens, F.Crouch (secretary), C.Clark, Buchanan, Wright, Corrin. Front row: Leech, Banks, Godley.

Plymouth Argyle in 1909-10. Back row (left to right): L.H.Crabb (team secretary), Fagan, Sutcliffe, Butler, Horne, Atterbury, Mr Cole (secretary & director). Third row: T.H.Haynes (assistant trainer), McCormick, Wilcox, Boyd, Evenson, Simmons, J.Upton (trainer). Second row: Leavey, Wood, Griffiths, Hindmarsh, Broom, Lamb. Front row: Evans, Burch, Raymond.

Argyle in 1910-11. Back row (left to right): Green, Baker, Wilcox, Butler, Sutcliffe, Atterbury, Horne, Crews. Middle row: Caddy, Rider, Black, Burgoyne, Couch, Worden, Peard, Rounsevill, Hosking. Front row: R.Jack (manager), Griffiths, Burch, Barton, Wood, Morrison.

Promotion celebrations at the end of 1985-6.

From left: Kevin Hodges, Russell Coughlin, John Clayton, Tommy Tynan and Gary Nelson after Argyle returned to Division Two.

Manager Dave Smith toasts his side's success.

'Golden Boot' winners John Clayton (left) and Tommy Tynan.

Plymouth Argyle in 1951. Back row (left to right): Strauss, McShane, Shortt, Taylor, Polkinghorne, Major, Chishlom, Ball, Adams, P.Langman, J.Smith. Middle row: G.Hackworthy (masseur), Silk, Dixon, Machin, Jelly, Jones, Robertson, Sim, Porteous, Rundle, John, Wyatt, Roberts, Tilley, G.Reed (trainer). Front row: Ratcliffe, Astall, Rattray, Willis, Dews, Tadman, Dougall, Govan, Dobbie, Kneebone. On ground: Short, Sweeney.

Plymouth Argyle in 1982-3. Back row (left to right): J.Edwards (reserve team coach), Nisbet, James, Ham, Crudgington, Hards, Phillipson-Masters, Sims, Uzzell, M.Harvey (first team coach). Third row: Hodges, Rogers, McCartney, Carter, Cook, R.Moncur (team manager), Harrison, Chambers, Cottrell, Phillips, Cooper. Second row: W.Pearce (commercial manager), G.Little (company secretary), R.Burroughs (director), Bloom, R.Daniel (chairman), S.Dawe (vice chairman), C.Kent (director), G.Jasper (director). Front row: Shannon, Dennis, Rowe.

Argyle Career Records

*The following is a full schedule of all players to have appeared for Plymouth Argyle in the Football League, FA Cup and League Cup, 1920-1940 and 1946-1989 only. *Denotes a player on loan.*

Player	From	To	League App	League Gls	FA Cup App	FA Cup Gls	FL Cup App	FL Cup Gls	TOTALS App	TOTALS Gls
Adams G	1958 RAF	1958 Headington U	1	0	0	0	0	0	1	0
Adams WV	1945 Plymouth U	1949 (Retired)	1	0	0	0	0	0	1	0
Aleksic M	1973 Stafford R	1976 Luton T	32	0	2	0	3	0	37	0
Allen K	1970 Luton T	1972 (Retired)	74/5	10	0	0	4	0	78/5	10
Anderson DE	1987 Tranmere R	1989 Hong Kong	17/2	1	1	0	1	0	19/2	1
Anderson PD	1950 Oak Villa	1962 Torquay U	241	41	10	4	8	1	259	46
Archer JW	1938 Coventry C	1939 RAF	21	0	1	0	0	0	22	1
Arundel FW	1957 Oak Villa	1959 Torquay U	4	0	0	0	0	0	4	0
Astall G	1947 Royal Marines	1953 Birmingham C	188	42	6	1	0	0	194	43
Atterbury S	1907 Swindon T	1921 (Trainer)	30	0	2	0	0	0	32	0
Austin T	1976 Ipswich T	1978 Walsall	58	18	5	0	3	0	66	18
Baird DM	1963 Nottingham F	1968 Tavistock T	147/1	1	5	0	5	1	157/1	2
Baker TG	1955 Mardy	1960 Shrewsbury T	78	16	5	1	0	0	83	17
Baker W	1921 Derby C	1927 (Retired)	85	11	5	1	0	0	90	12
Balac PJ	1971 (Apprentice)	1973 Cape Town	40	0	0	0	1	0	41	0
Ball SG	1977 (Apprentice)	1979 Lincoln C	0/1	0	0	0	0	0	0/1	0
Banks A	1966 Exeter C	1967 Exeter C	19	5	1	0	0	0	20	5
Bannister B	1976 Bristol R	1977 Hull C	24	7	1	0	0	0	25	7
Bannon PA*	1984 Bristol R	1984 Bristol R	0/2	0	0	0	0	0	0/2	0
Banton G	1975 Bolton W	1978 Fulham	6/1	0	0	0	0	0	6/1	0
Barnes B	1955 Bideford T	1958 Weymouth T	4	1	2	2	0	0	6	3
Barnsley GR	1957 West Brom A	1961 Norwich C	132	0	8	0	7	0	147	0
Barrett GT	1957 Manchester U	1960 Chester	26	1	1	0	0	0	27	1
Barron P	1976 Slough T	1978 Arsenal	44	0	4	0	4	0	52	0
Bason S	1977 Chelsea	1981 Crystal P	126/2	11	6	0	11	1	143/2	12
Batten HG	1921 Bristol C	1925 Everton	88	26	6	0	0	0	94	26
Bell R*	1955 Partick T	1956 Partick T	2	1	0	0	0	0	2	1
Bellett WR	1958 Chelsea	1961 Leyton O	41	1	2	0	0	0	43	1
Bickle MJ	1966 St Austell	1971 Gillingham	171/10	71	7/1	3	6/1	0	184/12	74
Binney F	1977 Brighton & HA	1980 Hereford U	67/4	39	2	0	7	3	76/4	42
Bird A	1930 Dublin Bhmns	1933 Newport C	26	7	1	0	0	0	27	7
Birks L	1930 Sheffield U	1933 (Retired)	49	0	1	0	0	0	50	0
Black S	1924 Kirkintilloch	1938 Queen's Park R	470	176	21	9	0	0	491	185
Black T	1933 Arsenal	1939 Southend U	162	0	6	0	0	0	168	0
Bland WH	1927 Royal Navy	1934 Cardiff C	130	2	6	0	0	0	136	2
Blatchford PJ	1948 Saltash U	1951 Leyton O	19	2	0	0	0	0	19	2
Bloomfield JH	1966 West Ham U	1968 Orient	25	1	2	1	0	0	27	2
Book AK	1964 Bath City	1966 Manchester C	81	3	4	0	8	0	93	3
Bourton CFT	1937 Coventry C	1938 Bristol C	8	3	1	0	0	0	9	3
Bowden ER	1927 Looe	1933 Arsenal	145	83	8	4	0	0	153	87
Bowler B	1912 Army	1923 (Retired)	53	15	7	1	0	0	62	16
Boyd LA	1946 Royal Navy	1949 Birmingham C	78	5	2	0	0	0	80	5
Brace SC	1960 Taunton T	1965 Watford	9	0	0	0	1	0	10	0
Briggs GR	1933 Birmingham	1936 (Retired)	58	11	4	3	0	0	62	14
Brimacombe A	1966 Barnet	1968 Cape Town	15/1	0	0	0	0	0	15/1	0
Brimacombe J	1985 Saltash U		75/3	3	1/2	0	6	0	82/5	3
Bremner K*	1983 Colchester U	1983 Colchester U	5	1	0	0	0	0	5	1
Brennan SA	1978 Crystal P	1979 Orient	6	0	1	0	1	0	8	0
Brown DJ*	1979 Middlesbrough	1979 Middlesbrough	5	0	0	0	3	0	8	0
Brown HS	1936 Chesterfield	1938 Reading	45	12	1	0	0	0	46	12
Brown HT	1956 Queen's Park R	1958 Exeter C	66	0	2	0	0	0	68	0
Brown J	1960 Wadebridge	1963 Bristol R	9	2	1	0	0	0	10	2
Brown K	1988 Norwich C		39	1	3	0	0	0	42	1
Brown R	1971 Blackpool	1972 Bradford C	31/5	3	1	0	2	0	34/5	3
Bryant E	1949 Yeovil T	1951 Leyton O	11	4	0	0	0	0	11	4
Buckingham CME	1961 (Apprentice)	1965 Exeter C	16	0	0	0	0	0	16	0
Buist JG	1947 New Brighton	1949 Hereford U	1	0	0	0	0	0	1	0
Bungay RH	1934 Tottenham H	1936 Bristol C	2	0	0	0	0	0	2	0
Burgess ERC	1968 Torquay U	1970 Colchester U	14/1	0	0	0	1	0	15/1	0
Burns A	1978 Crystal P	1979 Tonbridge	8	0	0	0	3	0	11	0
Burnside DG	1968 Wolves	1971 Bristol C	105	15	3	1	5	1	113	17
Burrows AM	1984 Northampton T		127/2	4	12/1	0	9/1	0	148/4	4
Burrows H	1973 Stoke C	1974 (Retired)	18/1	3	0	0	3	0	21/1	3

Player	From	To	League App	League Gls	FA Cup App	FA Cup Gls	FL Cup App	FL Cup Gls	TOTALS App	TOTALS Gls
Burrows P	1974 York C	1976 Hereford U	81	2	6	0	5	1	92	3
Byrne D	1989 Millwall		13	1	0	0	0	0	13	1
Campbell D*	1989 Charlton A	1989 Charlton A	1	0	0	0	0	0	1	0
Campbell G	1988 Sparta Rotterdam		6/7	3	0/1	0	0	0	6/8	3
Cann H	1928 Tintagel	1939 Fulham	225	0	7	0	0	0	232	0
Carless EF	1946 Cardiff C	1947 (Retired)	4	0	0	0	0	0	4	0
Carter M	1982 Bolton W	1983 Hereford U	6/6	1	0	0	0/1	0	6/7	1
Carter R	1933 Chelsea	1935 Watford	3	0	0	0	0	0	3	0
Carter W	1957 West Brom A	1964 Exeter C	253	134	11	10	10	4	274	148
Casey LJ	1958 Chelsea	1961 (Retired)	44	0	2	0	2	0	48	0
Cassidy FJA*	1984 Watford	1984 Watford	1	0	0	0	0	0	1	0
Cave ML*	1972 Bournemouth	1972 Bournemouth	8	4	0	0	0	0	8	4
Chamberlain NP*	1984 Stoke C	1984 Stoke C	7/4	3	0	0	0	0	7/4	3
Chapman LR*	1978 Stoke C	1978 Stoke C	3/1	0	0	0	0	0	3/1	0
Chapman PC	1969 (Apprentice)	1973 (Retired)	2/1	0	0	0	0	0	2/1	0
Cherrett PAM	1924 Portsmouth	1925 Crystal P	61	36	1	1	0	0	62	37
Cherry SR	1986 Walsall	1988 Notts C	73	0	5	0	4	0	82	0
Chisholm JR	1949 Sheffield U	1955 (Retired)	175	2	12	0	0	0	187	2
Chitty WS	1938 Chelsea	1939 Reading	3	1	0	0	0	0	3	1
Clamp M	1968 Coventry C	1970 Nuneaton Bor	8	0	1	0	0	0	9	0
Clark JMC	1938 Sunderland	1939 RAF	38	0	1	0	0	0	39	0
Clarke C	1978 Oxford U	1979 Kettering T	35	3	1	0	0	0	36	3
Clayton J	1985 Tranmere R	1988 Fortuna Sittard	68/9	21	6/1	1	4/1	1	78/11	23
Clelland C	1955 Aberdeen	1956 Keith (Scotland)	2	0	0	0	0	0	2	0
Cobb WW	1963 Nottingham F	1964 Brentford	31	0	1	0	1	0	33	0
Cock JG	1925 Everton	1927 Millwall	90	72	2	2	0	0	92	74
Collins D	1976 Burnley	1977 Sunderland	22/1	2	0	0	2	0	24/1	2
Collins JD	1980 (Apprentice)	1982 Falmouth T	4	0	0	0	0	0	4	0
Connor J	1936 Airdrieonians	1938 Swansea T	42	19	2	0	0	0	44	19
Cook JW*	1979 Stoke C	1979 Stoke C	4/3	5	0	0	0	0	4/3	5
	1981 Stoke C	1983 Halifax T	54/1	21	0	0	3	0	57/1	21
Cook WC	1920 Castleford T	1923 Brighton & HA	7	0	0	0	0	0	7	0
Cookson J	1933 West Brom A	1935 Swindon T	46	37	2	1	0	0	48	38
Cooper LV	1979 (Apprentice)		314/7	15	31	2	20	0	365/7	17
Cooper SB	1985 Newport C	1988 Barnsley	58/15	15	5/1	1	2/3	0	65/19	16
Corbett DF	1962 Swindon T	1968 (Retired)	84	8	1	0	4	0	89	8
Corcoran P	1920 Bathgate	1926 Torquay U	188	27	10	0	0	0	198	27
Cosgrove F	1920 Durham C	1930 (Retired)	104	0	2	0	0	0	106	0
Coughlin R	1984 Carlisle U	1987 Blackpool	128/3	18	8	1	8	2	144/3	21
Craig FG	1912 Larkhill T	1930 Barrow	361	5	23	0	0	0	384	5
Craven JR	1977 Coventry C	1978 Vancouver W	45	3	3	0	3	0	51	3
Crawford JC	1954 Leicester C	1955 Peterborough U	25	4	1	0	0	0	26	4
Crudgington G	1979 Swansea C	1988 (Retired)	326	0	28	0	20	0	374	0
Dann TE	1959 Penzance	1962 Torquay U	8	0	0	0	0	0	8	0
Darke PC	1971 (Apprentice)	1977 Torquay U	94/7	2	2	0	5	0	101/7	2
Davey SR	1966 (Apprentice)	1975 Hereford U	213/11	47	8	1	16	7	237/11	55
Davies AL	1935 Exeter C	1937 Southport	21	0	1	0	0	0	22	0
	1938 Southport	1939 (Died)	14	0	0	0	0	0	14	0
Davies JW	1947 Everton	1948 Bristol C	33	0	1	0	0	0	34	0
Davies M	1949 Aberaman	1957 Llanelly	84	15	2	0	0	0	86	15
Davis EWC	1952 Tavistock T	1957 Scunthorpe U	63	29	3	0	0	0	66	29
Davis JR	1927 Exeter C	1928 (Retired)	2	0	1	0	0	0	3	0
Davis RF	1961 (Apprentice)	1964 Southampton	23	0	0	0	1	0	24	0
Deacon LC	1921 Devon County	1929 Devon County	5	1	0	0	0	0	5	1
Delve JF	1974 Queen's Park R	1978 Exeter C	127/5	6	8	0	8	0	143/5	6
Demmelweek JW	1926 Royal Navy	1935 Southend U	32	2	2	0	0	0	34	2
Dennis A	1981 (Apprentice)	1983 Exeter C	7/2	0	0	0	1	1	8/2	1
Devine J	1921 East Stirling	1925 Charlton A	14	2	0	0	0	0	14	2
Dews G	1947 Middlesbrough	1955 Walsall	257	76	14	5	0	0	271	81
Dickinson J	1919 Royal Navy	1924 Wigan Bor	112	0	4	0	0	0	116	0
Dixon S	1939 Burnley	1951 Poole T	60	1	1	0	0	0	61	1
Dixon WA	1911 Fulham	1921 Barrow	17	2	2	0	0	0	19	2
Dobbie H	1950 Middlesbrough	1953 Torquay U	30	6	2	0	0	0	32	6
Dougall N	1949 Birmingham C	1959 (Trainer)	274	26	15	0	0	0	289	26
Dougan T	1936 Tunbridge WR	1939 Manchester U	42	6	1	0	0	0	43	6
Doughty E	1958 Arsenal	1960 Bristol C	1	0	0	0	0	0	1	0
Dowling ML	1970 (Apprentice)	1974 Bath C	27/4	0	1/2	1	1	0	29/6	1
Dugnolle JH	1938 Tunbridge WR	1946 Brighton & HA	5	0	0	0	0	0	5	0
Dunne PAJ	1967 Manchester U	1970 Shamrock R	152	0	5	0	7	0	164	0

Player	From	To	League App	League Gls	FA Cup App	FA Cup Gls	FL Cup App	FL Cup Gls	TOTALS App	TOTALS Gls
Dwyer NM	1965 Swansea T	1965 Charlton A	26	0	1	0	2	0	29	0
Dyer JA	1936 Crewe A	1947 (Retired)	53	3	1	0	0	0	54	3
Dyer PRF	1955 Oak Villa	1956 Ilfracombe T	8	0	0	0	0	0	8	0
Eastwood CM	1920 Castleford T	1925 Preston NE	105	3	11	0	0	0	116	3
Edds EF	1946 Army	1949 Blackburn R	59	18	1	0	0	0	60	18
	1953 Torquay U	1955 Swindon T	26	4	2	0	0	0	28	4
Edmunds A	1927 Royal Navy	1928 Torquay U	5	0	0	0	0	0	5	0
Eggleston A	1935 Bury	1937 Sheffield U	45	16	2	1	0	0	47	17
English TS	1984 Leicester C	1984 Leicester C	0/4	1	0	0	1	0	1/4	1
Etheridge RK	1966 St Blazey	1968 Weymouth T	40/1	5	0/1	0	0	0	40/2	5
Evans SJ	1987 West Brom A	1988 Rotherham U	36/8	10	1	1	2/1	0	39/9	11
Everitt MD	1967 Northampton T	1968 Brighton & HA	29	0	1	0	1	0	31	0
Fear K	1978 Bristol C	1980 Chester	40/5	9	1	0	4	2	45/5	11
Featherby LW	1934 Merthyr T	1935 Notts C	8	1	0	0	0	0	8	1
Fellowes WJ	1927 Tavistock	1932 Clapton O	5	0	0	0	0	0	5	0
Fincham GR	1958 Leicester C	1963 Luton T	136	4	5	0	0	0	141	4
Fishwick AE	1923 Chorley	1925 Blackpool	7	1	0	0	0	0	7	1
Fletcher CA	1937 Burnley	1938 Ipswich T	23	6	1	0	0	0	24	6
Foley J	1937 Glasgow C	1938 Cork C	39	0	1	0	0	0	40	0
Forbes FJ	1926 Everton	1929 Bristol R	158	52	7	1	0	0	165	53
Forbes RJ	1983 Exeter C	1984 Bideford T	3	0	0	0	1	0	4	0
Forbes W	1912 Denny Hibs	1924 (Retired)	133	0	7	0	0	0	140	0
Forde C	1978 Hounslow	1980 Wealdstone	4/1	0	0	0	0/1	0	4/2	0
Forrest GA	1933 Peterhead	1935 Mansfield T	3	0	0	0	0	0	3	0
Foster GW	1974 (Apprentice)	1982 Derby C	201/11	6	10	0	19	0	230/11	6
Foster WA	1969 Birmingham C	1970 Chelmsford	33	0	4	0	1	0	38	0
Fowler J	1921 Mardy	1924 Swansea T	37	25	2	0	0	0	39	25
Frost G	1920 Gillingham	1921 Chatham T	1	0	0	0	0	0	1	0
Fulton B	1957 Manchester U	1964 Exeter C	176	0	5	0	12	0	193	0
Furnell J	1968 Rotherham U	1976 (Retired)	183	0	12	0	11	0	206	0
Furphy K	1987 Atlanta Chiefs	1987 USA	6	0	0	0	0	0	6	0
Gallogley T	1913 Bedley Juns	1922 Exeter C	62	9	7	1	0	0	69	10
Garden A	1961 Aberdeen Juns	1963 Corby T	0	0	0	0	1	0	1	0
Gauld J	1957 Everton	1959 Swindon T	64	25	7	3	0	0	71	28
Gee JP	1956 Launceston T	1956 Launceston T	1	0	0	0	0	0	1	0
Gibson R	1946 Manchester U	1947 Exeter C	6	0	0	0	0	0	6	0
Glover EM	1939 Grimsby T	1939 (Retired)	3	1	0	0	0	0	3	1
Goddard R	1948 Chelsea	1949 Exeter C	43	1	1	0	0	0	44	11
Godfrey K*	1986 Orient	1986 Orient	7	1	0	0	0	0	7	1
Godfrey W	1933 Aberdeen	1936 Luton T	15	0	0	0	0	0	15	0
Gooding R	1982 Coventry C	1983 (Retired)	7	1	0	0	2	0	9	1
Goodyear C	1984 Luton T	1987 Wimbledon	99/7	5	7	1	6/2	1	112/9	7
Gooney WH	1935 Sheffield U	1936 Luton T	14	0	0	0	0	0	14	0
Gorman A	1931 Edinburgh C	1946 (Trainer)	240	2	10	0	0	0	250	2
Govan A	1946 Bridgeton BC	1953 Birmingham C	110	27	7	3	0	0	117	30
	1958 Portsmouth	1960 (Retired)	32	8	1	0	0	0	33	8
Graves M	1978 (Apprentice)	1982 Wealdstone	24/9	3	2	0	3/2	0	29/11	3
Green MC	1974 Bristol R	1977 Torquay U	108	8	7	2	7	0	122	10
Griffiths CL*	1974 Manchester U	1974 Manchester U	10/1	0	0	0	2	0	12/1	0
Grozier T	1927 Glencairn	1936 (Retired)	211	57	12	2	0	0	233	59
Hague N	1971 Rotherham U	1974 Bournemouth	98/1	15	7	1	7	1	112/1	17
Hall AE	1947 Tottenham H	1948 Chelmsford	9	0	0	0	0	0	9	0
Hall BW	1976 Liverpool	1977 Burnley	49/2	16	1	0	2/1	0	52/3	16
Ham MT	1981 (Apprentice)	1985 Saltash U	16/1	0	1	0	0	0	17/1	0
Hamilton J	1975 Sunderland	1976 Bristol R	6/1	0	0	0	0	0	6/1	0
Hancock DJ	1955 (Apprentice)	1959 Torquay U	2	0	0	0	0	0	2	0
Hardcastle P	1974 Blackpool	1976 Bradford C	12/2	1	1	0	0	0	13/2	1
Hardie A	1926 Charlton A	1933 Exeter C	232	4	9	0	0	0	241	4
Hards NA	1980 (Apprentice)	1983 Gloucester C	6	0	0	0	3	0	9	0
Harper W	1932 Arsenal	1935 (Trainer)	78	0	4	0	0	0	82	0
Harris AJ	1971 Queen's Park R	1973 Cambridge U	64	0	1	0	3	0	68	0
Harris TJG	1948 Aberaman	1948 Aberaman	3	0	0	0	0	0	3	0
Harrison CC	1974 Launceston	1985 Swansea C	315/9	7	25/1	0	21	1	361/10	8
Harrison MJ	1967 Blackburn R	1968 Luton T	15	3	0	0	0	0	15	3
Hartery J	1948 Limerick	1949 Dublin Bhmns	1	0	0	0	0	0	1	0
Healy J	1925 Glasgow C	1929 Bristol C	28	4	1	0	0	0	29	4
Heeps J	1920 Banknock Juns	1921 Airdrieonians	16	1	0	0	0	0	16	1
Hill D	1934 Hamilton A	1936 Southport	14	0	0	0	0	0	14	0
Hill JH	1920 Durham C	1923 Burnley	102	10	10	0	0	0	112	10

The Argyle team during 1928-9. Back row (left to right): Pullen, Mackay, Cosgrove, Craig, R.Jack (secretary), Titmuss, Hardie, T.Haynes (trainer). Front row: Matthews, Forbes, Richards, Leslie, Black, McKenzie.

Plymouth Argyle Football Club in 1984-5. Back row (left to right): M.Harvey (coach), Rogers, Rowe, Hodges, Harrison, Coughlin, Staniforth, J.Hore (team manager). Middle row: Tynan, Burrows, Uzzell, Philp, Crudgington, Ham, Nisbet, Cooper. Front row: W.Pearce (commercial manager), J.E.C.Kent (director), P.D.Bloom (vice chairman), S.W.Dawe (chairman), G.E.Jasper (director), B.L.Hooper (director), R.Burroughs (director), G.Little (secretary).

Player	From	To	League App	League Gls	FA Cup App	FA Cup Gls	FL Cup App	FL Cup Gls	TOTALS App	TOTALS Gls
Hinch J	1971 Tranmere R	1973 Hereford U	102/5	28	5	1	4	1	111/5	30
Hodge M	1977 (Apprentice)	1979 Everton	43	0	1	0	1	0	45	0
Hodges K	1978 (Apprentice)		406/20	74	35	3	27/1	0	468/21	77
Hore KJ	1964 (Apprentice)	1976 Exeter C	393/7	17	17	0	23	0	433/7	17
Horswill M	1975 Manchester C	1978 Hull C	98/4	3	3/2	0	8	0	109/6	3
Howell R	1956 Army	1958 Aston Villa	1	0	0	0	0	0	1	0
Hullett W	1937 Everton	1939 Manchester U	28	20	0	0	0	0	28	20
Hunter JB	1935 Mansfield T	1939 Preston NE	95	15	3	0	0	0	98	15
Hurst WR	1939 Burnley	1947 Nelson	4	0	0	0	0	0	4	0
Hutchins D	1969 Leicester C	1972 Blackburn R	94/1	23	2	0	2	0	98/1	23
Jack DBN	1919 (Juniors)	1920 Bolton W	14	3	0	0	0	0	14	3
Jack RR	1922 (Juniors)	1923 Bolton W	15	4	2	0	0	0	17	4
Jackson AJ	1960 Birmingham C	1964 Weymouth T	67	23	2	0	6	4	75	27
Jackson C	1963 Swindon T	1966 Crystal P	72	19	3	1	10	0	85	20
Jacobs TF*	1972 Bristol C	1972 Bristol C	4	0	0	0	0	0	4	0
James T	1978 Fulham	1982 Liskeard	77	0	2	0	7	0	86	0
Jasper B	1954 Astor Inst	1957 St Austell	2	0	1	0	0	0	3	0
Jelly HE	1951 Leicester C	1954 (Retired)	11	0	2	0	0	0	13	0
Jenkins R	1957 Truro C	1960 Exeter C	16	3	0	0	0	0	16	3
Jennings N	1963 Wellington T	1967 Portsmouth	98	11	4	1	7	0	109	12
Jobson JT	1922 Washington C	1924 Hartlepools U	1	0	0	0	0	0	1	0
John DC	1952 (Juniors)	1958 Swansea T	3	0	0	0	0	0	3	0
Johnson BF	1973 (Apprentice)	1981 (Retired)	186/11	40	6	1	16/2	1	208/13	42
Johnstone WK	1932 Irvine Meadow	1933 Coventry C	1	0	0	0	0	0	1	0
Jones BS	1964 Swansea T	1967 Cardiff C	98/1	9	5	3	7	0	110/1	12
Jones L	1937 Chelmsford T	1949 Southend U	40	2	1	0	0	0	41	2
Jones PJ	1947 Astor Institute	1958 St Austell	425	2	16	0	0	0	441	2
Kearns M*	1972 Oxford U	1972 Oxford U	1	0	0	0	0	0	1	0
Kearns PV	1956 Wellingborough	1962 Aldershot	65	8	2	0	0	0	67	8
Kellock W	1913 Stockport C	1920 Torquay U	6	1	0	0	0	0	6	1
Kellow T	1983 Exeter C	1984 Exeter C	8/2	2	3	0	0	0	11/2	2
Kemp DM	1978 Carlisle U	1982 San Jose E	82/2	39	3	3	5	2	90/2	44
Kirby G	1959 Sheffield W	1962 Southampton	93	38	3	0	8	1	104	39
Kirk H	1921 Bristol C	1922 Exeter C	1	0	0	0	0	0	1	0
Kirkwood SJ	1934 Arsenal	1939 (Retired)	112	1	2	0	0	0	114	1
Kirkpatrick JN	1911 Dumfries	1924 Torquay U	40	0	0	0	0	0	40	0
Knight AW	1947 Leeds U	1948 Bradford C	7	0	0	0	0	0	7	0
Lane H	1937 Southend U	1939 Southend U	50	9	1	0	0	0	51	9
Langman HN	1953 Tavistock	1957 Colchester U	97	49	3	1	0	0	100	50
Langman PJH	1951 Tavistock	1957 Weymouth T	90	0	3	0	0	0	93	0
Latcham L	1971 Burnley	1973 Bradford C	83	13	5	0	2	0	90	13
Law N	1986 Blackpool	1988 Notts C	37/1	5	2	0	2	0	41/1	5
Lawless AT	1955 Worcester C	1956 Oldham A	8	0	0	0	0	0	8	0
Lean D	1969 Embankment FC	1971 Saltash U	44/1	0	3	0	0	0	47/1	0
Lee AG	1926 Woodland V	1934 (Retired)	4	0	0	0	0	0	4	0
Leiper J	1958 Aberdeen EE	1968 Chelmsford	75	0	3	0	4	0	82	0
Leslie JF	1921 Barking T	1935 (Retired)	383	131	17	3	0	0	400	134
Levy AS	1978 (Apprentice)	1979 Torquay U	0/1	0	0	0	0	0	0/1	0
Lewis AC	1939 Grimsby T	1939 Army	1	0	0	0	0	0	1	0
Lill MJ	1962 Everton	1963 Portsmouth	21	7	1	0	0	0	22	7
Little J	1920 Castleford T	1924 Southport	7	0	0	0	0	0	7	0
Livingstone D	1926 Everton	1926 Aberdeen	22	0	0	0	0	0	22	0
Logan J	1919 Cowdenbeath	1929 Yeovil	228	14	13	0	0	0	241	14
Lord F	1963 Crewe A	1966 Stockport C	69	23	0	0	9	6	78	29
	1967 Chesterfield	1968 (Coach)	6	2	1	0	0	0	7	2
Lugg R	1972 Watford	1973 Crewe A	22/2	1	0	0	1	0	23/2	1
McAnearney J	1960 Sheffield W	1963 Watford	135	34	3	1	9	2	147	37
McArthur T	1954 Leicester C	1955 Loughboro' S	2	0	0	0	0	0	2	0
McAuley HA	1974 Tranmere R	1976 Charlton A	76/1	7	6	0	5	0	87/1	7
McCarthy S	1988 Swansea C		37/1	8	3	1	4	4	44/1	13
McCartney M	1981 Southampton	1983 Carlisle U	49	5	6	1	4	0	59	6
McColgan J	1938 St Anthony's	1939 Queen's Park R	1	0	0	0	0	0	1	0
McCrory S	1952 Ipswich T	1955 Southend U	50	11	1	0	0	0	51	11
McDonald W	1939 Coventry C	1939 RAF	2	0	0	0	0	0	2	0
McElhinney G	1984 Bolton W	1988 Peterborough U	90	2	3	0	4	1	97	3
Macey F	1925 Kingstonian	1925 Kingstonian	1	1	0	0	0	0	1	1
Machin AH	1948 Chelsea	1952 St Austell	26	1	1	0	0	0	27	1
Machin E	1973 Coventry C	1974 Brighton & HA	57	6	5	0	7	1	69	7
McJarrow H	1953 Luton T	1956 Peterborough U	30	3	3	1	0	0	33	4

Player	From	To	League App	League Gls	FA Cup App	FA Cup Gls	FL Cup App	FL Cup Gls	TOTALS App	TOTALS Gls
Mackay N	1928 Hearts	1933 Southend U	227	14	14	0	0	0	241	14
McKenna P	1952 Aberdeen	1953 Arbroath	1	0	0	0	0	0	1	0
McKenzie F	1925 Newport C	1934 Newport C	203	13	11	0	0	0	214	13
McKenzie G	1934 Arthurlie J	1935 Southend U	1	0	0	0	0	0	1	0
MacLaren D	1957 Leicester C	1965 Wolves	131	0	5	0	9	0	145	0
McNeil JL	1934 Portsmouth	1939 Clapton O	137	12	6	1	0	0	143	13
McNeill B	1978 Bristol C	1981 Hearts	47	0	5	0	3	0	55	0
McParland PJ	1963 Wolves	1964 Worcester C	38	14	1	0	1	0	40	14
McShane A	1948 Brentwood	1955 Swindon T	85	2	6	0	0	0	91	2
Maher A	1968 Everton	1971 Tranmere R	64	3	3	0	2/1	0	69/1	3
Mailey J	1938 Dundalk	1939 Swindon T	15	1	0	0	0	0	15	1
Major LD	1949 Leicester C	1956 (Retired)	75	0	3	0	0	0	78	0
Maloy KF	1959 Ilford	1964 Peterborough U	62	11	3	1	9	4	74	16
Mantle J	1931 Burnley	1932 Chester	15	7	0	0	0	0	15	7
Mariner P	1973 Chorley	1976 Ipswich T	134/1	56	8	3	12	1	154/1	60
Marker NRT	1987 Exeter C		68/1	7	6	0	4	2	78/1	9
Matthews AW	1925 Exeter C	1933 (Retired)	142	30	5	2	0	0	147	32
Matthews JM	1985 Chesterfield		131/3	4	8/1	0	10	0	149/4	4
Megson GJ	1977 (Apprentice)	1979 Everton	78	10	5	0	9	0	92	10
Melaniphy EM	1932 Finchley	1936 Cardiff C	68	33	1	0	0	0	69	33
Meyer BJ	1958 Bristol R	1959 Newport C	8	5	2	3	0	0	10	8
Middleton MY	1939 Sunderland	1946 Bradford C	3	0	0	0	0	0	3	0
Middleton PW	1972 Bradford C	1972 (Retired)	1	1	0	0	0	0	1	1
Miller A*	1988 Arsenal	1989 Arsenal	13	0	2	0	0	0	15	0
Miller AG	1939 Southport	1947 (Retired)	9	0	0	0	0	0	9	0
Miller C	1924 Bellshill A	1926 Exeter C	4	0	0	0	0	0	4	0
Milne JB	1934 Fraserburgh	1936 Southend U	3	0	0	0	0	0	3	0
Mitchell KS	1956 Whitby R	1958 North Shields	8	4	0	0	0	0	8	4
Mitcheson FJ	1935 Port Vale	1939 Ipswich T	93	25	6	0	0	0	99	25
Mitten J	1967 Coventry C	1968 Exeter C	43	8	2	0	1	0	46	8
Molyneux FG	1968 Southport	1971 Tranmere R	79	5	1	0	3	0	83	5
Morgan MM	1937 Torquay U	1938 Bristol C	11	2	0	0	0	0	11	2
Morgan AR	1953 Swansea T	1957 Barry T	36	4	0	0	0	0	36	4
Murphy DP	1980 Torquay U	1982 Blackburn R	44/4	9	3	2	2/1	0	49/5	11
Murphy MM	1946 Plymouth U	1948 Chelmsford T	15	1	0	0	0	0	15	1
Murray JBR	1937 East Stirling	1939 Rotherham U	4	0	0	0	0	0	4	0
Nail DR	1947 St Blazey	1948 St Blazey	1	0	0	0	0	0	1	0
Neale DF	1963 Newcastle U	1970 Plymouth C	141/5	8	7	0	13	1	161/5	9
Nelson AN	1964 Leyton O	1969 (Retired)	94	1	3	0	2	0	99	1
Nelson GP	1985 Swindon T	1987 Brighton & HA	71/3	20	7	2	4	0	82/3	22
Newman JHG	1960 Leicester C	1967 Exeter C	298	9	10	0	20	2	328	11
Nicholas G	1964 (Apprentice)	1966 Torquay U	2	0	0	0	1	0	3	0
Nisbet GJM	1980 Hull C	1987 Exeter C	281	14	23	0	18	3	322	17
Oakes J	1947 Charlton A	1948 Snowdon Coll	36	0	1	0	0	0	37	0
Obi AL*	1985 Aston Villa	1985 Aston Villa	5	0	0	0	0	0	5	0
Olver WE	1939 Launceston	1945 St Austell	2	0	0	0	0	0	2	0
O'Neill A	1962 Aston Villa	1964 Bournemouth	40	14	2	0	3	0	45	14
Osman HJ	1936 Poole T	1938 Southampton	5	0	0	0	0	0	5	0
Oxley B	1935 Sheffield W	1937 Stockport C	14	0	1	0	0	0	15	0
Peach GL	1956 Millwall	1958 Truro C	1	0	0	0	0	0	1	0
Peachey JM	1980 Darlington	1982 Barnstaple	1/2	0	0	0	0	0	1/2	0
Peacock A	1967 Leeds U	1968 (Retired)	11	1	1	0	0	0	12	1
Pearson IT	1974 Goole T	1977 Wycombe W	6/6	0	2/1	0	2/1	0	10/8	0
	1983 Exeter C	1983 Bideford T	5/3	1	1	0	0/1	0	6/4	1
Peddelty J	1976 Ipswich T	1977 (Retired)	30/3	1	1	0	0	0	31/3	1
Pengelly RN	1947 Looe	1951 (Retired)	9	0	0	0	0	0	9	0
Penhaligon G	1988 (Apprentice)		1	0	0	0	0	0	1	0
Penk H	1957 Portsmouth	1960 Southampton	104	14	7	2	0	0	111	16
Penny J	1955 Juniors	1959 Penzance	7	0	0	0	0	0	7	0
Perrin S	1978 Crystal P	1979 Portsmouth	34/1	6	1	0	4	0	39/1	6
Philp D	1984 Newquay	1985 Saltash U	7	0	2	0	2	0	11	0
Phillips DO	1981 (Apprentice)	1984 Manchester C	65/8	15	12/1	0	2/1	0	79/10	15
Phillipson-Masters FE	1979 Southampton	1982 Bristol C	119	0	5	0	8	0	132	0
Piper NJ	1965 (Apprentice)	1970 Portsmouth	215	35	9	1	9	1	233	37
Plummer C	1988 Nottingham F		17/6	1	0	0	2	0	19/6	1
Porteous JR	1949 Alloa A	1956 Exeter C	215	13	7	0	0	0	222	13
Powell ACH	1935 Bolton W	1936 Leeds U	2	0	0	0	0	0	2	0
Poyser GH	1946 Brentford	1947 Dover T	3	0	0	0	0	0	3	0
Preskett FM	1935 Woking T	1937 Torquay U	3	1	0	0	0	0	3	1

Player	From	To	League App	League Gls	FA Cup App	FA Cup Gls	FL Cup App	FL Cup Gls	TOTALS App	TOTALS Gls
Preston R	1923 Torquay U	1928 Torquay U	143	3	4	0	0	0	147	3
Price N*	1984 Watford	1984 Watford	1	0	0	0	0	0	1	0
Price W	1924 Aberdare	1930 Bristol R	59	0	4	0	0	0	63	0
Provan D	1971 Crystal P	1975 St Mirren	128/1	10	5	0	4	0	137/1	10
Pullen WJ	1924 Ebbw Vale	1935 (Retired)	194	17	5	1	0	0	199	18
Quinn GP	1956 Queen's Park R	1957 Tunbridge W	14	2	0	0	0	0	14	2
Rae JC	1932 Partick T	1946 (Asst manager)	249	0	10	0	0	0	259	0
Rafferty WH	1974 Blackpool	1976 Carlisle U	89/1	35	6	4	5	1	100/1	40
Ramsbottom N	1976 Sheffield W	1978 Blackburn R	39	0	1	0	1	0	41	0
Randell CW	1973 Coventry C	1977 Exeter C	137/2	5	5	2	10	0	152/2	7
	1979 Exeter C	1982 Blackburn R	110	8	3	0	12	0	125	8
Ratcliffe PC	1947 Wolves	1956 (Retired)	236	10	10	0	0	0	246	10
Rattray PK	1950 Dundee	1952 Norwich C	54	22	1	0	0	0	55	22
Rawlings JSD	1946 Everton	1948 (Retired)	56	20	1	0	0	0	57	20
Raymond HW	1908 Woodland Villa	1924 Torquay U	67	10	5	0	0	0	72	10
Reed G	1931 Leeds U	1934 Crystal P	47	1	2	0	0	0	49	1
Reed HD	1971 West Brom A	1974 Crewe A	44/12	9	2	2	0	0	46/12	11
Reeves MR	1961 Saltash U	1970 Cape Town	107/3	0	5	0	10	0	122/3	0
Reynolds RJ	1965 (Apprentice)	1971 Portsmouth	123/8	24	3	0	6	1	132/8	25
Rich LT	1935 Torpoint	1936 Luton T	3	1	0	0	0	0	3	1
Richards P	1927 Burnley	1931 Tunbridge W	29	15	1	0	0	0	30	15
Richardson F	1921 Barking T	1923 Stoke	63	37	4	4	0	0	67	41
Rickard DBP	1969 (Junior)	1974 Bournemouth	101/9	41	6/1	0	1/2	0	108/12	41
Rioch NG	1975 Aston Villa		3/2	0	0	0	0	0	3/2	0
Robbie DM	1935 Bury	1936 Manchester U	3	0	0	0	0	0	3	0
Roberts DG	1961 (Apprentice)	1964 St Austell	11	0	0	0	1	0	12	0
Roberts H	1930 Leeds U	1937 Bristol R	248	21	9	0	0	0	257	21
Robertson G	1950 Gairdoch Juns	1966 Falmouth T	359	2	18	0	5	0	382	2
Rogers A	1981 Southampton	1985 Reading	159/4	15	17	3	6	0	182/4	18
Rogers AJ	1973 (Apprentice)	1979 Portsmouth	107/10	5	7/4	0	7	0	121/14	5
Ross R	1923 Stenhousemuir	1924 Coventry C	2	0	0	0	0	0	2	0
Rounsevell A	1962 (Apprentice)	1968 Weymouth T	34	2	0	0	4	0	38	2
Rowan B	1969 Reading	1970 Exeter C	10	1	0	0	0	0	10	1
Rowbotham D	1984 (Apprentice)	1987 Exeter C	22/23	2	1/2	1	1	0	24/25	3
Rowbotham J	1987 (Apprentice)		8/1	0	0	0	0/1	0	8/2	0
Rowe AJ	1921 Barking T	1925 Queen's Park R	41	0	1	0	0	0	42	0
Rowe M	1981 (Apprentice)	1985 Saltash U	46/9	1	5	1	6	0	57/9	2
Rowley JF	1955 Manchester U‡	1957 (Manager)	56	14	2	0	0	0	58	14
Royston R	1939 Southport	1947 (Retired)	41	0	1	0	0	0	42	0
Rundle SSK	1945 St Blazey	1953 St Blazey	453	1	3	0	0	0	56	1
Russell MR	1914 Merthyr T	1929 Thames Ass	315	5	20	0	0	0	335	5
Ryan T	1935 Glasgow C	1939 Swindon T	7	0	0	0	0	0	7	0
Sanderson K	1964 Bath C	1965 Queen's Park R	29	2	1	0	1	0	31	2
Sargeant C	1939 Stockport C	1940 Army	3	2	0	0	0	0	3	2
Saxton R	1968 Derby C	1975 Exeter C	224/7	7	12	0	11/2	0	247/9	7
Sealey AW	1967 West Ham U	1967 (Retired)	4	0	0	0	0	0	4	0
Sealey LJ	1984 Luton T	1984 Luton T	6	0	0	0	0	0	6	0
Shearing PF	1966 Exeter C	1968 Exeter C	24	0	1	0	0	0	25	0
Sheffield G	1919 Loughborough	1921 Kettering T	19	4	1	1	0	0	20	5
Shepherd T	1969 Coventry C	1970 Nuneaton Bor	36/2	4	1	0	2	0	39/2	4
Shipperley D*	1974 Charlton A	1974 Charlton A	1	0	0	0	0	0	1	0
Shortt WW	1946 Chester	1056 (Retired)	342	0	14	0	0	0	356	0
Silk GH	1937 Southport	1950 Newquay	86	1	4	0	0	0	90	1
Sillett JC	1966 Coventry C	1968 Bristol C	37/1	1	2	0	1	0	40/1	1
Silkman B	1978 Crystal P	1979 Manchester C	14	2	1	0	0	0	15	2
Sims J	1979 Exeter C	1983 Torquay U	161/2	43	11	3	8	2	180/2	48
Simpson J	1932 Partick T	1934 (Retired)	5	2	0	0	0	0	5	2
Simpson P	1933 Fraserburgh	1935	6	1	0	0	0	0	6	1
Sloan F	1924 Shieldmuir C	1936 Luton T	208	49	6	1	0	0	214	50
Smart KG	1976 (Apprentice)	1978 Wigan Ath	32	0	3	0	3	0	38	0
Smith AE	1952 West Brom A	1954 Crewe A	28	9	2	1	0	0	31	10
Smith E	1938 Rotherham U	1946 (Retired)	12	5	1	0	0	0	13	5
Smith J	1921 Clydebank	1922 Clydebank	1	0	0	0	0	0	1	0
Smith J	1935 Barnsley	1946 (Retired)	82	9	3	0	0	0	85	9
Smith JR	1923 Bristol C	1924 Aberdare A	6	4	0	0	0	0	6	4
Smith JV	1951 Plymouth U	1954 Torquay U	3	0	0	0	0	0	3	0
Smith LJ	1982 Cambridge U	1984 Millwall	76	5	10	1	4	1	90	7
Smith M	1948 Preston A (Scot)	1948 Chelsea	1	0	0	0	0	0	1	0
Smith M	1983 Exmouth T		3	0	0	0	0	0	3	0

‡Player-manager

Plymouth Argyle, Third Division champions in 1958-9. Back row (left to right): J.L.Williams, Robertson, Downs, J.S.Williams, J.Rowley (manager), Barnsley, Wyatt, Barrett, Dougall, R.Blindell, Doughty, Taylor (trainer). Front row: Anderson, Gauld, Carter, Baker, Penk. Inset: Casey, Bellett, Govan.

Plymouth Argyle in 1986-7. Back row (left to right): D.Smith (manager), S.Cooper, Nelson, Nisbet, G.McElhinney, Cherry, Crudgington, Summerfield, Matthews, Law, Clayton, S.Houston, M.Musgrove (physiotherapist). Front row: E.McElhinney, L.Cooper, Hodges, Burrows, Tynan, Coughlin, Rowbotham, Uzzell, Goodyear.

Player	From	To	League App	League Gls	FA Cup App	FA Cup Gls	FL Cup App	FL Cup Gls	TOTALS App	TOTALS Gls
Smith MC	1987 Sheffield W		76	6	5	0	6	1	87	7
Smith R	1925 Manchester C	1927 Torquay U	31	1	0	0	0	0	31	1
Squires F	1947 Swansea T	1950 Grimsby T	86	13	3	0	0	0	89	13
Stacey TJ	1959 Carshalton	1962 Watford	22	0	2	0	0	0	24	0
Stanbury G	1927 Devon County	1933 Gillingham	33	0	1	0	0	0	34	0
Staniforth G	1983 Carlisle U	1985 Newport C	87/4	19	10/1	2	8	3	105/5	24
Stenner AWJ	1955 Bristol C	1956 Norwich C	9	1	0	0	0	0	9	1
Strauss WH	1946 Aberdeen	1954 (Retired)	158	40	8	2	0	0	166	42
Stuart RW	1947 Middlesbrough	1949 Whitby U	20	0	1	0	0	0	21	0
Stuttard JE	1939 Burnley	1947 Torquay U	29	1	0	0	0	0	29	1
Sullivan C	1968 (Apprentice)	1974 Norwich C	225/5	7	12	0	14	0	251/5	7
Summerfield K	1984 Cardiff C		109/18	25	12	4	6/1	3	127/19	32
Sutton D	1974 (Apprentice)	1978 Huddersfield T	60/1	0	3	0	2/1	0	65/2	0
Swiggs B	1984 Liskeard	1985 Liskeard	1/1	0	0	0	0	0	1/1	0
Swiggs R	1956 St Blazey	1957 Weymouth T	3	0	0	0	0	0	3	0
Sykes NAJ	1964 Bristol R	1965 Stockport C	3	0	0	0	1	0	4	0
Tadman MR	1947 Charlton A	1955 Belfast Dist	240	109	13	4	0	0	253	113
Taylor BJ	1977 Walsall	1978 Preston NE	34/1	5	2	2	2	0	38/1	7
Taylor GA	1948 Aberdeen	1950 (Trainer)	48	2	0	0	0	0	48	2
Tedesco JJ	1966 (Apprentice)	1970 Bristol R	34/8	4	2	0	1	0	37/8	4
Tepper G	1933 Goldthorpe U	1934 Bath C	1	0	0	0	0	0	1	0
Thomas DWJ	1938 Romford	1948 Watford	74	29	3	1	0	0	77	30
Thomas RA	1946 Brentford	1947 Fulham	41	17	1	0	0	0	42	17
Thomas WK	1953 Cardiff C	1956 Exeter C	35	8	3	0	0	0	38	8
Thomson JY	1925 Brentford	1927 Aberdare	7	0	0	0	0	0	7	0
Thorne AE	1961 Brighton & HA	1963 Exeter C	11	2	0	0	1	0	12	2
Thorpe A	1921 Loughborough		3	0	0	0	0	0	3	0
Tilley HR	1951 Chippenham T	1958 Swindon T	123	0	6	0	0	0	129	0
Timmins J	1958 Wolves	1958 Bristol R	5	0	0	0	0	0	5	0
Tinkler L	1945 Royal Navy	1948 Walsall	23	4	1	0	0	0	24	4
Titmuss FE	1926 Southampton	1932 (Retired)	166	0	7	0	0	0	173	0
Toms W	1920 Manchester U	1921 Tranmere R	24	3	4	2	0	0	28	5
Tootill GA	1937 Chorley	1938 Sheffield U	9	0	0	0	0	0	9	0
Trainor D	1968 Crusaders	1969 Waterford	16/1	3	0	0	0	0	16/1	3
Trebilcock M	1962 Tavistock	1965 Everton	71	27	2	1	8	1	81	29
Trusson MS	1977 (Apprentice)	1980 Sheffield U	65/8	15	1/1	0	12	4	78/9	19
Twissell CH	1957 Royal Navy	1958 York C	41	9	1	0	0	0	42	9
Tynan TE	1983 Newport C	1985 Rotherham U	80	43	13	4	8	1	101	48
*	1986 Rotherham U	1986 Rotherham U	9	10	0	0	0	0	9	10
	1986 Rotherham U		128/1	58	9	2	5	2	142/1	62
Upton CC	1978 (Apprentice)	1981 Basingstoke	2/1	0	0	0	0	0	2/1	0
Uzzell JE	1977 (Apprentice)		292/9	6	20/1	1	16/1	0	328/11	7
Vassallo BE	1974 Arsenal	1976 Aldershot	6/7	2	1	1	0/1	0	7/8	3
Vidler HJ	1928 Army	1939 Bristol C	243	95	13	8	0	0	257	103
Waldock R	1959 Scunthorpe U	1960 Middlesbrough	18	6	1	0	0	0	19	6
Walker JR	1922 Rutherglen W	1925 Exeter C	21	1	1	0	0	0	22	1
Wallace B	1924 Hamilton A	1925 Torquay U	1	0	0	0	0	0	1	0
Wallace R	1935 Swindon T	1937 Exeter C	9	0	1	0	0	0	10	0
Warren RE	1945 Plymouth U	1948 Chelsea	3	0	0	0	0	0	3	0
Watkins AJ	1946 Cardiff C	1948 Cardiff C	4	1	1	0	0	0	5	1
Webb J*	1973 Liverpool	1973 Liverpool	4	0	0	0	1	0	5	0
Welsh A	1972 Torquay U	1974 Bournemouth	64/2	14	7	1	7	3	78/2	18
Wetton R	1955 Tottenham H	1956 Aldershot	36	1	1	0	0	0	37	1
Wharton JE	1938 Bolton (Juns)	1939 Preston NE	11	2	0	0	0	0	11	2
Wilkinson PI*	1971 Norwich C	1971 Norwich C	2	0	0	0	0	0	2	0
Williams AS	1949 Aberdeen	1950 Dundee	35	4	2	1	0	0	37	5
Williams JL	1958 Cardiff C	1962 Torquay U	34	0	3	0	0	0	37	3
Williams JSJ	1952 EEM Dept	1966 Bristol R	411/1	48	19	1	17	6	447/1	55
Williams RAK	1961 Tranmere R	1962 Bristol R	10	4	0	0	0	0	10	4
Willis G	1949 Brighton & HA	1956 Exeter C	56	14	3	0	0	0	59	14
Wilson A	1922 Dunipace T	1923 Alloa A	3	0	0	0	0	0	3	0
Wilson JG	1931 Swindon T	1933 Cowdenbeath	2	0	0	0	0	0	2	0
Wingate J	1968 Dawlish	1969 Exeter C	1	0	0	0	0	0	1	0
Wooldridge SJ	1970 Crystal P	1972 Colchester U	20	0	1	0	1	0	22	0
Wright EV	1937 Liverpool	1939 Chelmsford C	17	7	1	0	0	0	18	7
Wright GW	1937 Kitto Inst	1947 Colchester U	12	0	0	0	0	0	12	0
Wright JW	1959 Newcastle U	1961 Millwall	42	9	1	0	3	0	46	9
Wyatt RG	1950 Astor Inst	1964 Torquay U	202	2	7	0	8	0	217	2
Wyllie RGN	1958 West Ham U	1959 Mansfield T	5	0	0	0	0	0	5	1

PLYMOUTH ARGYLE
FOOTBALL CLUB
1595
The Pilgrims
P·A·F·C

SUBSCRIBERS

Presentation Copies
1 Plymouth Argyle Football Club
2 The Football League • 3 The Football Association

4 Brian Knight
5 Dave Potham
6 J P Cheadle
7 P J Shone
8 Gordon Small
9 Les Gold
10 Jack Mills
11 Donald Noble
12 Ian Clarke
13 R J Gamble
14 P L M Lunn
15 J A Harris
16 David Woods
17 B H Standish
18 Alan Hindley
19 Stewart Fell
20 D S Ball
21 Terry Frost
22 Colin Jose
23 Dr Peter Maksimczyk
24 Trond Isaksen
25 J F Burrell
26 Jorn Brekke
27 Harold Lohr
28 R G Woolman
29 Esa Kautonen
30 Simons Martin
31 Robert Fisher
32 M Swart
33 Ake Axelsson
34 Lars-Olof Wendler
35 P W Stevenson
36 Kåre M Torgrimsen
37 G T Allman
38 Ian Griffiths
39 Mervyn R Waring
40 A Young
41 Keith Lowe
42 S P Tomlin
43 Anders Johansson
44 David Pease
45 A J P M Otten
46 Richard Stocken
47 J S Pyke
48 William Needs
49 B R Butler
50 J C Benstead
51 A F Pearson
52 Malcolm Hartley
53 Roger Hudson
54 T J Beer
55 John Treleven
56 R D N Wells
57 Domenico Polimeno
58 Helge Nordli
59 Clifford Atkins
60 W D Phillips
61 J Gardiner
62 R J Maslen
63 Ian Harraden
64 M J O'Connor
65 Keith Coburn
66 Stanley Allan Robinson
67 Moira & Frederick Furness
68 Harry Thompson
69 Stephen Berridge
70 K P Wood
71 Stephen Clark
72 Bill Clark
73 Dave Hillam
74 Derek Hyde
75 Ian Willott
76 D A R H Webster
77 Brian Tabner
78 Peter Pickup
79 Steven F Thomas
80 David Lloyd Menhennett
81 Mike Purkiss
82 Duncan Watt
83 Niall MacSweeney
84 Andrew Waterman
85 Paul Joannou
86 A Gardner
87 Graham Gardner
88 David Keats
89 Sean Jones
90 Surapot Saengchote
91 Nick House
92 J Musgrove
93 Michael Braham
94 L A Zammit
95 Douglas Bidgoud
96 Derek T Bryant
97 Brian H Hobbs
98 G E Andrews
99 John Motson
100 Alan Tooze
101 Angus W Rodger
102 Julie May
103 P Marks
104 A K Mitchell
105 Leslie King
106 Alan Davies
107 David S Wakeford
108 H P Jenkins
109 David Downs
110 Frederick J Lee
111 A M Scowcroft
112 D C Collman
113 Richard Smith
114 Andrew Anderson
115 David Wheatley
116 A Lancaster
117 Anastasios Botsis
118 David R Earnshaw
119 Harry Kay
120 Christer Svensson
121 M Golesworthy
122 Peter Baxter
123 John Clancy
124 Paul Adams
125 A B Hart
126 S P Dean
127 P A Blank
128 Paul McClellan
129 I W H Francis
130 S Rendell
131 R C Caudell
132 Irving Sweet
133 James Bilson
134 Peter Robert Easton

135 Gary O'Connell
136 Paul Dodge
137 Stuart James Weeks
138 M Bennett
139 R J Rapson
140 Jonathan Penaluna
141 David Ross
142 Stuart N Bulley
143 Mark C Glanville
144 D A Lush
145 D A Lush
146 Filippo Rossi
147 John A Pitts
148 Steven Ball
149 Richard Mark Silverwood
150 Paul Hockedy
151 Kevin Clair
152 Nicholas A Morgan
153 Neil Herring
154 Andrew Michael Sutton
155 B-J Bowden
156 P M Hollow
157 Dave Glanville
158 P Ogley
159 C R Jose
160 E J Collins
161 Jon Treharne
162 Trevor Horne
163 J L Heasman
164 Mike Pengelly
165 F A Ravenscroft
166 J C R Dean
167 F Dawe
168 A K Jones
169 David J Perry
170 Andrew Crocker
171 P C Tutten
172 James S Drew
173 G A Smith
174 A F P Wheeler
175 Barry Turner
176 Martin Clapp
177 K M Ireland
178 John McGlinchey
179 Steve McLean
180 Daniel Robinson
181 Ronald Glinn
182 J J Crocker
183 E G Clemas
184 Andrew McLoughlin
185 Glenn Martin
186 David Lenthall
187 M D Allen
188 Robert Johnson
189 Clive Sanders
190 D R Northcott
191 B A Board
192 John Stewart
193 Shaun Bennetts
194 D P Gill (Denmark)
195 Roy Varcoe
196 Paul Hobbs
197 J C Williams
198 A G Knox
199 Andrew Moore
200 Joseph Walter
201 Guthrie Lepper
202 F Dymond
203 W Hoskin
204 Garry Clark
205 Alfred M Palmer
206 Kieran Chudleigh
207 Chris Ridley
208 Gareth Hughes
209 M Ellis
210 G M Chilcott
211 Gordon Brodie
212 Harold Yelland
213 Jack Treeby
214 M Rundle
215 Philip Rees
216 John Tucker
217 R D Blackaller
218 Lester Snell
219 Les Burns
220 John Coker
221 C J Hall
222 David Richard Evans
223 Richard Brown
224 P Cannan
225 O E Swords
226 Paul E Burrows
227 Alan Oliver
228 V Walker
229 C Mills
230 Ken Purvis
231 D P Gates
232 Neal John
233 Malcolm A Townrow
234 W P Rogers
235 D P Vickers
236 Alastair Stewart
237 M C Flavell
238 Nicholas Eyre
239 Nicholas Eyre
240 Sharon Jessep
241 L D Blake
242 Brian Down
243 Richard Tucker
244 K A Marshall
245 P C Dicken
246 Alan Paul Lambourne
247 David Revell
248 Toby Jackson
249 Richard Cowdery
250 J M Moore
251 Christopher Minchin
252 Greg Wall
253 David J Godfrey
254 R J Yeomans
255 A L Tweddell
256 P H Whitehead
257 Phil Soar
258 G D Painter
259 Patricia Arthur
260 Robin Pearce
261 David Easton
262 D J Harvey
263 Andrew John Geens
264 Andrea Lavers
265 Keith Templeton
266 Andrew N Mole
267 Richard Lang
268 Gary Hurr
269 Matthew D Kemp
270 D Robjohns
271 James Chapman
272 Michael Morton
273 Steven East
274 Paul Swords
275 P E Furneaux
276 J G Ferris
277 Andrew Walmsley
278 Jeremy Wills
279 G Webster
280 Brian D Barwick
281 Colin Parsons
282 John Parsons Jnr
283 Steven P Smith
284 Miss S Wells
285 Colin Cameron
286 Kevin Bishop

287 John Qvarnberg
288 R A Kelly
289 N Doherty
290 M Joannes
291 Gordon D Henderson
292 Alec Andrew Hepburn
293 Richard S Tucker
294 Christopher R Higgins
295 Wilfred R J Higgins
296 Kerry Algar
297 John Eales
298 Andrew Hibbitt
299 Ryan Hibbitt
300 Mark Butcher
301 C G Kinver
302 James Channon
303 Ian Jolliff
304 Mike Doherty
305 David McLean
306 S A Coates
307 Robert Glanville
308 P Warren
309 David Goldsmith
310 David Fisher
311 N D Aston
312 Graham Finch
313 Mike Hughes
314 M D Mancuso
315 J A Vaughan
316 Gary Clark
317 Toby Allan Jones
318 Dominic Haughton
319 Timothy & Deborah Drew
320 Derek Vivian May
321 Harley Lawer
322 John Drew
323 R Stewart
324 M Endacott
325 Martin Timlin
326 Scott Gilbert
327 B J Palmer
328 Phillip Baker
329 Mark Jordan
330 R B Cawse
331 Ian Lawton
332 Joanne Cawse
333 J S Roose
334 Emma Brown
335 David Bailey
336 Peter J Day
337 Robert P Day
338 Colin D Reynolds
339 A Bournemouth 'Veteran'
340 C W G Greep
341 O C G Harris
342 David Pay
343 Christopher King
344 Derek J Oldham
345 A J Hindley
346 Eric Heesom
347 Ingvar Thomas
348 Ian Griffiths
349 K A Jermyn
350 Harry Thompson
351 Dave Helliwell
352 John V Guthrie
353 Warwick Franklin
354 Stephen J Hughes
355 Peter Robinson
356 John Robert Goff
357 Clive Willis
358 Chris B Coleman
359 Cyril A Coleman
360 Angus W Rodger
361 Graham E J Wilton
362 Anthony Kevin Howes
363 N Chapman
364 Jack Parsons
365 John George Parsons Snr
366 Tom Ruth
367 Paddy Ruth
368 David G Connolley
369 Colin James Hall
370 John Boulden
371 Michael J Boulden
372 David John Stephens
373 Raymond Shaw
374 David Gregg
375 Paul Eustace
376 J Hancock
377 Kevin Bowle
378 Gordon, Anji & Lauren Marks
379 J Lathan
380 J Ringrose
381 Douglas Lamming
382 Paul Cowling
383 Phillip West
384 E J & J Sherwood
385 Mark L Goodman
386 Paul Dixon
387 D Harrison
388 R Kinsman
389 David Dickens
390 Paul Jerome
391 Richard Simpson
392 Mick Pyman
393 R E Cobbledick
394 Steven Thorley
395 Kevin Helson
396 Robert Cowan
397 Sports Marketing (Australia)
398 Graham Brooks
399 M J Baggott
400 Michael Lee
401 K A Gibson
402 A G Jones
403 C J Richards
404 Roger Wash
405 Steve Lavis
406 Frank Grande
407 P D Smith
408 David W Lee
409 Stephen R Curtis
410 L J Ridge
411 Peter Batchelor
412 Dr C J Morton
413 John Northcutt
414 Miss Ann Telfer
415 Miss P Endacott
416 S J & G M Endacott
417 J A Farleigh
418 Ken Hanns
419 S L Cann
420 Gary Reed
421 Michael B Curno
422 Nigel Geens
423 Miss L Addicott
424 Simon N Veale
425 I J Ansell
426 Bernard E L Kerswill
427 Colin John Gee
428 Howard Martin Hubbard
429 Neil Prady
430 David Crawford
431 Norman Green
432 Paul Best
433 Derek & Christopher Wood
434 James Gray
435 William Grier

436 Colin Chambers
437 W P Julian
438 W H H Julian
439 Argyle Programmes Subscriber
440 N J Butland
441 Stanley R Hughes
442 John Campbell
443 C A W Harvey
444 J N R Pitts
445 David Bone
446 Denis Osborne
447 A Aburrow
448 J L Turner
449 George Newman
450 Dr Martin Wosley
451 Peter Brett
452 J A Gardener
453 Roger Hunt
454 Andrew Philip Heathman
455 Steve Nicholson
456 Andy Hutt
457 Derek Rowe
458 Terry Gill
459 Geoff Gill
460 Michael Gill
461 Ivor Creamer
462 Ray Stidwell
463 I Treloar
464 Michael Wing
465 Chris Reynolds
466 Graham Jones
467 C Bellhouse
468 R Keast
469 Fred Fielding
470 S P Lawry
471 Geoffrey Luke
472 Roy Hewitt
473 J Keane
474 Steven Carter
475 Vic Tuck
476 Andrew King
477 J Freer
478 Rob Billing
479 John Prout
480 Simon McDermott-Brown
481 Ronald Symons
482 Robin Holcombe
483 Ken Giles
484 Graham Hobbs
485 Rod Terry
486 Neil Millar
487 David Lock
488 Roger M Hutchinson
489 Graham Wright
490 D Measures
491 David Moor
492 Kevin Putt
493 David Moore
494 Albert Hall
495 Mark Warman
496 Neil McEwen
497 T M Wesley
498 Andrew Dooley
499 P M Jones
500 A Heywood